EMOTIONS IN HISTORY

General Editors

UTE FREVERT   THOMAS DIXON

German *Angst*

Fear and Democracy in the Federal Republic of Germany

FRANK BIESS

OXFORD
UNIVERSITY PRESS

OXFORD
UNIVERSITY PRESS

Great Clarendon Street, Oxford, OX2 6DP,
United Kingdom

Oxford University Press is a department of the University of Oxford.
It furthers the University's objective of excellence in research, scholarship,
and education by publishing worldwide. Oxford is a registered trade mark of
Oxford University Press in the UK and in certain other countries

© Frank Biess 2020

The moral rights of the author have been asserted

First Edition published in 2020

Impression: 1

Published in the United States of America by Oxford University Press
198 Madison Avenue, New York, NY 10016, United States of America

British Library Cataloguing in Publication Data
Data available

Library of Congress Control Number: 2020939498

ISBN 978–0–19–871418–7

Printed and bound by
CPI Group (UK) Ltd, Croydon, CR0 4YY

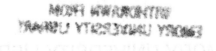

For my parents, Peter and Gudrun Bieß.

Preface

I still remember the movie that arrived in German cinemas at the end of 1983. It was entitled *The Day After*, and it described the devastations after a nuclear war in a small town in the Midwest. It was the time of the NATO double-track decision. If negotiations with the Soviet Union over the withdrawal of SS-20 missiles stationed in East Central Europe were to fail, the West would "catch up" with the stationing of US Pershing II and cruise missiles in Central Europe. At the age of 17, I saw the film in the movie theater of my Swabian hometown. Recently, I watched it again on the internet, and I sensed a hint of the state of mind that was haunting me at the time—an intense, almost apocalyptic fear. To be sure, such sensibilities may not be entirely unusual at this stage in life. The feeling of bearing the burdens of the world on hunched-over shoulders was not untypical at that age and manifested itself also in my reading of Kafka and the writing of dark—and very bad—poems. Moreover, occasional walks in the Swabian forest convinced me that it was dying, even though I was not really able to identify the catastrophic damage that commentators claimed indicated a widespread *Waldsterben* (dying of the forest). But the nearing death of the German forest fit perfectly into the imagined apocalyptic vision. What I find interesting in retrospect is that this fear did not only appear as a burden but rather as a special insight, a sensibility that one was almost proud of and liked to display in public. By casting oneself as sensitive and as emotionally as well as physically suffering from these supposed threats, one sought to cultivate the ideal of a new sensible masculinity, which, one hoped, might be appealing to female peers as well.

The planned NATO stationing of new nuclear weapons triggered by far the largest protest movement in the history of the Federal Republic: the peace movement of the early 1980s. My political coming of age took place in this movement, and through the associated fear of a "nuclear holocaust," as it was called at the time in a typical linking of a catastrophic past with an apocalyptic future. Although I was active only on the margins of the movement, I had declared my room as a nuclear weapon-free zone, a sticker with a white peace dove on a blue background adorned the door, and I had already designed in my mind my justification for becoming a conscientious objector, which was actually based on political and not personal grounds and hence theoretically unlawful. My first demonstration was the human chain, which, in October 1983, linked the NATO headquarters in Stuttgart with the Wiley Barracks in Neu-Ulm. As I learned later, my future wife was located a bit further east. So we indirectly held hands already back then before we actually met in Southern California two decades later. I was a bit embarrassed by the singing of "We Shall Overcome," but it then also moved me. Such songs made it possible to see oneself as part of a cross-border movement—"transnational," as it would be called today.

The debate over the stationing of new nuclear weapons and the peace movement became an obsession for me. I discussed the strategic benefits of land-based and sea-based nuclear weapons; I argued vehemently for the inclusion of French and British nuclear missiles; and I defended Paul Nitze's proposal for a negotiated compromise. To this day, my French proficiency still suffers because I spent most of my French classes discussing the philosophy of deterrence with a classmate whose father was a professional soldier and who later joined the *Bundeswehr* as well. I did not quite see the Soviet leader Leonid Brezhnev as an "angel of peace," as the German Communist Party (DKP) claimed, but I was convinced that the real aggressors were located in the United States, especially Ronald Reagan and his proclaimed fight against the "evil empire" as well as his, even in hindsight, stupid joke about the alleged imminent bombing of the Soviet Union during a microphone test. My picture of the US only became a bit more complex when, one year later, I came to the Midwest for a four-week exchange program and ended up with a family of committed Democrats. At that time, I recognized traveling as the best remedy against national stereotypes.

The autobiographical origin of this book lies in an attempt to understand this emotional state of mind of a 17-year-old in the late Cold War. Why was fear so important in the political socialization of young people in the 1980s? This rather autobiographical question overlapped with my academic interest in the newly emerging history of emotions. My personal experience confirmed the increasing doubts about the widespread success story of the Federal Republic, as it has been told by historians. How successful was the history of West Germany really, when millions of people experienced almost apocalyptic fears and expressed these feelings in mass demonstrations? And what did it mean that such cycles of fear pervaded the entire history of the Federal Republic? Was there not a peculiar tension between the optimistic story of the Federal Republic as told by historians and the pessimism of contemporaries?

My almost two decades in the American academic system allowed me to ask such big questions about the history of the Federal Republic. The perspective from the Southern California distance encouraged me to think about some of the larger narrative structures of the Federal Republic and to risk the attempt of writing an alternative history. It would certainly have been easier, less nerve-racking, and much less time-consuming to write a monograph on just one of the fears discussed in this book. But the broad approach turned out to be more instructive and inspiring for me, and it hopefully will be for the readers of this book as well.

The book is the product of these autobiographical and historiographic impulses. It tells the story of the Federal Republic as a history of consecutive cycles of fear. *German Angst* offers an interpretive synthesis of West German history and is thematically more comprehensive than a monograph. But it is not a complete synthesis of the history of the Federal Republic, of which there are many. I hope that the book will inspire a new, less self-evident and less self-satisfied history of the Federal Republic, which takes contemporaries' fears seriously as their often quite plausible scenarios of the future. Thinking about the fears of the past also enables us to understand better some of the fears of the present—more on this in the final chapter.

When I started working on this project much too long ago, I could have hardly imagined that some of the fears that haunted Germans in the postwar period would catch up with us again at the beginning of the twenty-first century, and in the US of all places! The presence of a right-wing populist president in the White House and the rise of a new global authoritarianism makes the survival or "success" of liberal democracy by no means certain. Paradoxically, the history of fear in the Federal Republic might also provide some hope here. It shows how and why the worst fears of the past did not come true, perhaps because they had already been imagined before. Fear is not a vaccine that confers immunity against political dangers. But the feeling can act as a warning signal. As debilitating and misleading as it may be, sometimes fear and anxiety also have a productive function. More than at any other time since the Second World War, liberal democracy has been called into question by mobilizing fears. But the parallel fear of losing democracy is perhaps also the first step toward its more than ever necessary defense.

Acknowledgments

This is a revised and updated English version of my book, *Republik der Angst: Eine andere Geschichte der Bundesrepublik*, that was published by Rowohlt in February 2019. Writing the same book in two languages—and often switching back and forth between the English and German versions—was not always fun, to put it mildly. But it allowed me to incorporate in this version some of the comments and criticism that the German version has provoked. Since both history and historiography are progressing relentlessly, I was also able to incorporate some more recent literature—as well as integrating some more recent developments—in the final chapter. Needless to say, the future looks equally, if not more, uncertain now than when I finished the German version almost a year ago.

The work on this project took too long to acknowledge all the people and institutions that have accompanied and supported me in this endeavor for more than a decade. The following list is therefore necessarily incomplete, and I apologize in advance to those individuals and institutions whom I have failed to mention here. On the other hand, the long list of debts I have accumulated over the years shows just how extremely fortunate I have been. In a world that is still characterized by too much suffering, hardship, violence, and injustice, it is a huge privilege to have the resources and the support that are necessary to complete such a project. Notwithstanding all complaints about academic life, it seems important to me to acknowledge this basic fact.

This project began with a nearly two-year scholarship from the Humboldt Foundation at the University of Göttingen. I benefited greatly from the inspiring debates at the *Lehrstuhl* of Bernd Weisbrod. Rebekka Habermas, Adalbert Hepp, Uffa Jensen, Wolfgang Knöbl, Sandra Kirchner, Miriam Rurüp, and Brigitta Schmidt-Lauber made the time in Göttingen intellectually and personally enriching. A UC President's Fellowship in the Humanities 2012–13 and a National Endowment for the Humanities (NEH) grant in 2017–18 allowed me to make progress on the English version of the book and to finish the German version. I am very grateful to both institutions for their support. I wish for the NEH that the repeated attempts to abolish this wonderful institution for political reasons will continue to fail.

The History Department at the University of California, San Diego, has served as my academic home for nearly two decades. Being part of this collective of excellent historians is an important part of the privilege mentioned above. I particularly thank our chair, Pamela Radcliff, for her support of my work, and Judith Hughes for the accurate reading of individual English-speaking chapters. The support of the Academic Senate to UC San Diego enabled several archive trips. I am also very indebted to the staff of the Interlibrary Loan Department of the Geisel Library. They made sure that even in Southern California I was only a few mouse-clicks away from even the most obscure German-language titles. I also enjoyed the exchange with our DAAD Professors, Armin Owzar, Margrit Frölich, and Jörg Neuheiser. My friends in the department—Bob Westman, Rachel Klein, Rebecca Plant, Hasan Kayali, and Michael Provence—made sure that I was always very happy in San Diego.

The same is true for my students. Many undergraduates impressed me again and again with their curiosity, their thirst for knowledge, and their ability to empathize with a culture foreign to them. One student's question in a class on Weimar as to why people voluntarily renounce their freedom preoccupies me to this day. I also learned a lot from my doctoral students. Assisting them in developing their own projects and forming their academic identities constituted one of the nicest aspects of my job. I also thank Ryan Zroka, Robert Terrell, and Teresa Walch for their work as research assistants. I miss my conversations with the late Kurt Shuler, and I am sorry that I finished the book too late for him. My friends in San Diego—Kathy Hodges and Peter Thomas, Ayse Kayali, Lor Wood, and Jens Lykke-Andersen—as well as Katrin Völkner in Berlin, made life fun and interesting outside of academia. So did my Boston Marathon training group and the beach runs with Hasan. They are probably to blame for some delays in finishing this book. But I don't regret anything.

My buddies from the graduate school, Pamela Swett and Jonathan Wiesen, again proved to be very insightful and shrewd readers of individual chapters. Arnd Bauerkämper, Norbert Frei, Ute Frevert, Cornelia Rauh, Patrick Wagner, and Ulrike Weckel gave me the opportunity to present parts of this project in their Colloquia. For helpful conversations on topics of this book, I would also like to thank Paul Betts, Alon Confino, Dagmar Herzog, Robert Moeller, Mark Roseman, Sagi Schaefer, Nick Stargardt, Uta Poiger, and Natasha Zaretsky. This project has benefited from Bernd Weisbrod's knowledge and insights from the very beginning to the end. He first served as an academic host in Göttingen, then became my neighbor across the hallway in Berlin. Urte Weisbrod's warm hospitality made us feel very welcome in Wilmersdorf. I could not have asked for better colleagues than Tanja Jung and Barbara Burger at the UCEAP Study Center in Berlin. They made my job in Berlin a real pleasure and also compensated for my absences from the office related to this book.

Bernd Pieper and Melanie von der Wiesche I thank for decades of friendship and hospitality. Bernd also labored very hard to edit the German version of the book, and I have benefited much from my conversations with him about its themes. Let's hope that at some point we will collaborate on our long-planned project on the history of soccer. Kate Epstein worked very hard to improve my English in this version.

Four anonymous reviewers for Oxford University Press provided important feedback at an earlier stage of this project. Paul Betts then read the entire final manuscript and made some very important suggestions. Cathryn Steele was a very patient editor, even though I missed more deadlines than I care to remember. Anne Abel Smith was a very conscientious copy-editor. Katie Bishop, Jane Bainbridge and Balasubramanian Shanmugasundaram got the book into production.

All the above people have contributed much to the better pages of this book. All remaining mistakes and deficiencies are my sole responsibility.

I have had many interesting discussions about the themes of this book with my brother Armin. Not only did I learn a lot from him but, as a scientist, he also always engaged with my academic interest, much more so than I was able to do with his.

My sons Noah and Moses became teenagers and young adults while I was working on this project. Being able to witness how they tackle their own challenges and become interesting and independent people has been and continues to be a great source of joy and happiness. In an increasingly uncertain world, I wish them a great deal of courage and optimism as well as the ability to be afraid of only the right things.

The story told in this book covers much of the lifetime of my parents, Peter and Gudrun Bieß. Historical circumstances denied both of them an academic education. I am therefore all the more thankful that they have made it possible for me to receive such an education and that they always supported me in my academic endeavors, first financially, then—above all—morally and emotionally. They were the first readers of the German version of this book, and their judgment helped me in my attempt to write a book for an audience beyond academia. My academic career may have led me to the other end of the world, but geographical distance has not diminished my gratitude to and affection for them. This book is dedicated to them.

No one has lived longer with this project than Ulrike Strasser. It has often strained her patience, yet she nevertheless took time off from her own busy life—her own academic projects, university service, our two sons—to listen to my stories about fear and anxiety. In the end, this book would probably not have been written without her indispensable support and encouragement. She helped me especially with her impressive analytic ability to recognize and articulate an argument behind a variety of facts. Even more importantly, her humor, intelligence, *joie de vivre*, and passion have sustained me for almost two decades now. This was—and still is—the basis for everything.

*

Earlier versions of Chapters Two, Three and Seven were previously published as the following articles: "Moral Panic in Postwar Germany: The Abduction of Young Germans into the Foreign Legion and French Colonialism in the 1950s," *Journal of Modern History* 84/4 (2012): 789–832; "'Everybody Has a Chance'." Civil Defense. Nuclear *Angst*, and the History of Emotions in Postwar Germany" *German History* 27/2 (2009): 215–43; "Die Sensibilisierung des Subjekts: Angst und "neue Subjektivität" in den 1970er Jahren," *Werkstatt Geschichte* 49 (2008): 51–72.

Berlin, November 2019

Contents

List of Figures   xvii

    Introduction   1
    Histories of Fear   2
    Fear and Democracy   4
    Fear and Trauma   8
    Emotions   9
    Scope and Themes   16

1. Postwar *Angst*   25
    Constricted Futures   28
    Jewish Revenge   31
    Violence and Displaced Persons   39
    The Shock of Occupation   46
    Postwar Angst   63

2. Moral *Angst*   66
    Germans in the Legion   70
    Scandals and the Foreign Legion   71
    Moral Panic   75
    Languages of Panic: Slavery and Homosexuality   78
    The Decline of the Abduction Narrative   84
    Voluntarism and the Fragility of Male Youth   88
    The End of an Obsession   93

3. Cold War *Angst*   95
    "Better Dead than Red": Anti-Communism and the Politics
    of Emotions in the German Cold War   97
    Re-establishing Civil Defense   107
    "Everybody Has a Chance"   116
    Emotional Change or How Germans Learned to Live with the Bomb   126

4. Modern *Angst*   130
    Modern Fears during the "Economic Miracle"   133
    Three Intellectuals on Automation: Pollock, Schelsky, Gehlen   136
    The Widening Debate: Automation in West German
    Public Discourse   141
    Shaping or Adjusting to Modernity? The Trade Union Response to
    Automation   152

5. Democratic *Angst*   158
   Democratic Fears, Fears of Democracy   159
   The Return of the Nazi Past   170
   The Emergency Laws and the Future of the Republic   184

6. Revolutionary *Angst*   195
   Utopia and Paranoia   199
   Fear and Violence   213
   Emotions and Sexuality   223
   Fears of Revolution   233

7. Proliferating *Angst*   242
   The Validation of Emotions   244
   The Rehabilitation of Fear   251
   Fear and New Subjectivity   255
      Knowledge and Feelings   255
      Self and Community   257
      Women and Men   261
      The "Hitler in Me" and Other Pathologies   265
      Holocaust and the Emotionalization of Memory   271
   Terrorism and the Escalation of Political Fears   279

8. Apocalyptic *Angst*   290
   Ecological Fear: The Environmental Movement   293
      Global Doomsday Scenarios and the Beginnings of
      Environmental Policy   293
      The Anti-Nuclear Movement   298
      "Ecological Holocaust": The Dying Forest   307
   The Peace Movement   314

9. German *Angst*   331
   German angst and Its Historical Context   332
   Deterritorialized Fears   337
   New German *Angst* 1: Germany in the World   339
   New German *Angst* 2: The World in Germany   341
   Right-Wing Fears   348
   A Democratic Politics of Emotion   362

   Conclusion   368

Primary Sources   375
Index   379

List of Figures

1.1. Demonstration of Jewish displaced persons in Frankfurt am Main, 1945.   38

Postwar Germans perceived the public presence of Holocaust survivors as a threat. They feared "Jewish revenge" based on the antisemitic notion that the Second World War was waged in the interest and on behalf of "Jewish interests."

Source: bpk-Bildagentur, No. 30050504.

1.2. Displaced persons, 1945.   39

Postwar Germans perceived the confident and optimistic demeanor of former Nazi victims as threatening and contrasted it with external pressures to downplay their own Germanness.

Source: bpk-Bildagentur, No. 30050648.

1.3. Protest march against housing requisitions in Bad Nauheim, Hesse, in the American zone of occupation, September 9, 1951.   58

Germans perceived housing requisitions as a form of retribution by the American occupation authorities. This practice lasted into the 1950s and shaped Germans' experience of the occupation period. The banner at this demonstration in Bad Nauheim, Hesse, reads: "Let us into our houses, then we want to be friends."

Source: dpa Picture-Alliance, No. 28397476.

2.1. The Young Socialists, the Social Democratic youth organization, put up this poster all over the French zone in 1952.   68

It warned "all young Germans" against "paid recruiters" and "human traffickers" whose "seductions" and "promises" would lead to "disease, agony, and death." Young Germans must not lend their "youth and their life to the service of foreign interests."

Source: Archiv der sozialen Demokratie der Friedrich-Ebert-Stiftung, 6/PLKA004301.

2.2. Image of an alleged "recruiter."   83

This image from the magazine *Stern* depicts an alleged recruiter for the Foreign Legion. The caption reads: "The handsome Fred in action. This photograph of one of the most active recruiters was taken in a dance bar in Essen. Disguised as a photographer for postcards, the *Stern* reporter took a picture of a drunken guest (in the foreground), next to whom Fred Schulze (with mustache) was sitting. Meanwhile, his victims are sending the first pictures of their existence in the Legion."

Source: Stern 5/2 (1952): 7.

3.1. Election Ad Christian Democratic Union (CDU) during the first federal election, 1949.   100

This election ad depicts a racialized Soviet soldier seeking to grab Western Europe. The image was most likely perceived as a metaphoric allusion to the mass rape of German women by Soviet soldiers during the final stages of the Second World War and in the immediate postwar period.

Source: ACDP, Plakatsammlung, 10-001-12.

3.2. Civil defense brochure, "Everybody Has a Chance" (1961).   120

This brochure was distributed to all West German households in December
1961 during a period of intense Cold War tensions. The brochure was designed
to contain fears of a nuclear war but ended up achieving the opposite.
Source: BArch, B106/50243.

3.3. Page from brochure, "Everybody Has a Chance."   122
These suggestions for personal behavior in the case of a nuclear attack
prompted a public outcry from many West Germans and determined the
largely negative reception of the first civil defense brochure.
Source: BArch, B106/50243.

4.1. Title of *Der Spiegel* 14/1964 on "Automation in Germany."   144

The 1960s were not just a period of unambiguous optimism and belief in
technological progress. This title page of *Der Spiegel* reflects the intense
debate about automation. The article predicted mass unemployment due to
the replacement of workers by machines.
Source: Copyright *Der Spiegel* 14/1964.

5.1. Defendants at the Frankfurt Auschwitz trial, 1963–5.   180

The Frankfurt Auschwitz trial (1963–5) heightened anxieties about
authoritarian undercurrents and the depths of postwar democratization.
It portrayed defendants as sadistic torturers and thus created distance from
the majority of West Germans.
Source: bpk-Bildagentur, No. 30015296.

5.2. Demonstration against the passage of the emergency laws, Frankfurt,
     May 1968.   187

Democratic fears of a possible authoritarian transformation drove protest
against the emergency laws in 1968. The banners protest against the "NS laws"
and equate them with "fascism."
Source: bpk-Bildagentur, No. 30040571.

6.1. SDS demonstration in Essen in February 1968.   212
Student activists distanced themselves from the Nazi past by projecting the
memory of the Holocaust onto the US war in Vietnam. This banner reads
"Vietnam—the Auschwitz of the Americans."
Source: bpk-Bildagentur, No. 70161670.

6.2. Use of water-cannons against student protesters during demonstrations in
     West Berlin, April 1968.   215
Revolutionary fears of student activists resulted from confrontation with police
violence yet also justified their own turn to violence as "counter-violence."
Police departments often resorted to paramilitary tactics in seeking
to "defeat" activists.
Source: bpk-Bildagentur, No. 30002158.

6.3. Counter-demonstration against the New Left in West Berlin, February 1967. 221
The New Left not only faced the opposition of state authorities but also of large
sections of the West German population. Individual attacks by enraged citizens
contributed to SDS activists' sense of fear and isolation.
Source: bpk-Bildagentur, No. 30004456.

7.1. Google Ngram graph "Angst," 1945 to the present.   243
The use of the word "*Angst*" in German publications increased steadily from
the early 1970s onward. This increased use of the term points to a proliferation
of anxieties during this period.

Source: https://books.google.com/ngrams/graph?content=Angst&year_start=1945&
year_end=2019&corpus=20&smoothing=3&share=&direct_url=t1%3B%2CAngst
%3B%2CCc0#t1%3B%2CAngst%3B%2CCc0 (last accessed March 20, 2020).

7.2. *Spiegel* Title 45/1977, "Cancer—Disease of the Soul."   249
The notion of a "cancer personality" reflected the popularization of an
expressive emotional regime. The cancer personality exhibited many
similarities to the representation of Nazi perpetrators since the 1960s.

Source: Copyright *Der Spiegel* 45/1977.

7.3. Breakfast in a *Wohngemeinschaft* (WG) in Frankfurt in 1982.   260
Communes became important sites for practicing and enacting the new culture
of emotional expressiveness. Members were expected to show their emotions
and forge emotional bonds with each other.

Source: bpk-Bildagentur, No. 30001851.

8.1. Police presence during a demonstration at Brokdorf, February 28, 1981.   302
Protests against nuclear power turned increasingly violent, as in Brokdorf
in 1981. The environmental movement cast nuclear power plants as an
absolute evil that would give rise to a fascist-like authoritarian state.

Source: bkp-Bildagentur, No. 30018694.

8.2. Poster of the Young Socialists (*Jusos*) on the occasion of the "anti-war" day,
September 1, 1983.   319
The peace movement of the 1980s combined a newly popularized memory
of the Holocaust with an apocalyptic vision of the future. This image
combines a depiction of the entrance gate of the Auschwitz extermination
camp in the foreground with a representation of a bombed city in the background.
The caption reads "Never again war, never again fascism."

Source: 6/PLKA038398. The rights for this image could not be determined.

8.3. Human chain on October 22, 1983, between Neu-Ulm and Stuttgart.   326
The peace movement was the largest protest movement in the history of the Federal
Republic—250,000 people participated in this human chain. The movement was
based on the public display of fear, which assumed the character of a higher form of
rationality. The author and his future wife were both there at different locations.

Source: dpa Picture-Alliance, No. 13694531.

9.1. Demonstration against the Gulf War in Frankfurt, January 1991.   333
The protests against the Gulf War in 1991 continued the culture of fear from
the peace movement of the 1980s. The protests fueled the notion of a "German
angst" that conservative critics used to denounce the peace movement.

Source: Bpk-Bildagentur, No. 30014147.

9.2. Google Ngram viewer "German *Angst*" and "German angst."   334
Source: https://books.google.com/ngrams/graph?content=German+Angst%2C+
German+angst&year_start=1800&year_end=2000&corpus=20&smoothing
=3&share=&direct_url=t1%3B%2CGerman%20Angst%3B%2CCc0%3B.
t1%3B%2CGerman%20angst%3B%2CCc0 (last accessed March 11, 2020).

9.3. Election ad of the "Alternative for Germany" (AfD), Berlin-Kreuzberg, September 2017.   351

The AfD increasingly became an Islamophobic and right-wing extremist party. It sought to mobilize popular fears of foreign, especially Islamic, influences. This ad demands "Stop Islamization."

Source: dpa Picture-Alliance, No. 94994278.

9.4. "Fridays-for-Future" demonstration at the Brandenburg Gate in Berlin, September 20, 2019.   362

Inspired by the Swedish schoolgirl Greta Thunberg, young people all over the world began to demonstrate for an effective policy against climate change. This movement was also based on a public display of fear. But these fears were very different than the parallel fears of migration and Islam propagated by right-wing populism.

Source: dpa Picture-Alliance, No. 124584505.

Introduction

Fear and Democracy

"One all of a sudden looks into the faces of human beings," wrote Dieter Sattler in 1947, of crossing the German–Swiss border into Switzerland, "who live without fear and who have lived like this for a long time. And one realizes how different postwar Germans look, how different their attitudes are." Writing in the prestigious journal *Frankfurter Hefte*, the Bavarian official and cultural diplomat described "relaxed, lovely people with honest and straightforward faces." He contrasted that with a distinctive form of fear among his compatriots—"German fear." "I could write pages of this fear," he added, "which everybody knows in one way or another . . . and which has become the German disease."[1]

The history of the Federal Republic is also the history of the republic's fears. Numerous other observers in postwar Germany shared Sattler's perception of a pervasive sense of uncertainty, anxiety, and fear about the country's future.[2] The self-referential discourse on a specific German *Angst* permeated the history of the "old" Federal Republic and extended beyond the fall of the Berlin Wall.[3] In the political culture of contemporary Germany, this discourse on German *Angst* is activated, transformed, sometimes denied, and often re-invented in a series of recurring fear cycles with varying and ever-shifting objects—financial crisis, immigration, terrorism.[4] The history of fear thus constitutes one of the legacies of the "old"

---

[1] Dieter Sattler, "Die deutsche Angst," *Frankfurter Hefte* 2/10 (1947): 999–1005. On Sattler, see Ulrike Stoll, *Kulturpolitik als Beruf. Dieter Sattler (1906–1968) in München, Bonn und Rom* (Paderborn: Schöningh, 2005).

[2] For an unsystematic list of examples, see Richard Tüngel, "Gespenst der Angst," *Die Zeit* 5/35 (1950), Franz Xaver von Hornstein, *Von der Angst unserer Zeit* (Frankfurt a/M: Josef Knecht, 1954), Hans Zbinden, *Der bedrohte Mensch* (Bern: Francke Verlag, 1959), Karl Schlechta, ed., *Darmstädter Gespräch 1963. Angst und Hoffnung in unserer Zeit* (Darmstadt: Neue Darmstädter Verlagsgesellschaft, 1965), Armin Mohler, *Was die Deutschen fürchten. Angst vor der Politik, Angst vor der Geschichte, Angst vor der Macht* (Stuttgart: Seewald, 1965), Heinz Wiesbrock, ed., *Die politische und gesellschaftliche Rolle der Angst* (Frankfurt a/M: Europäische Verlagsanstalt, 1967), Dietrich Langen, "Angst, das Problem unserer Zeit" *Schopenhauer-Jahrbuch* 55 (1974): 11–18, David A. Seeber, "Angst als Zivilisationskrankheit?," *Herderkorrespondenz* 31/4 (1977): 165–8, Jürgen Leinemann, *Die Angst der Deutschen. Beobachtungen zur Bewusstseinslage der Nation* (Reinbek: Rowohlt, 1982), Sabine Bode, *Die deutsche Krankheit—German Angst* (Stuttgart: Klett-Cotta, 2006).

[3] Axel Schildt, "'German Angst': Überlegungen zur Mentalitätsgeschichte der Bundesrepublik," in Daniela Münkel, Jutta Schwarzkopf, eds, *Geschichte als Experiment. Studien zu Politik, Kultur und Alltag im 19. und 20. Jahrhundert. Festschrift für Adelheid von Saldern* (Frankfurt a/M: Campus, 2004), 87–97.

[4] Heinz Bude, *Gesellschaft der Angst* (Hamburg: Hamburger Edition, 2014).

German Angst: Fear and Democracy in the Federal Republic of Germany. Frank Biess, Oxford University Press (2020).
© Frank Biess.
DOI: 10.1093/oso/9780198714187.001.0001

Federal Republic to the Berlin Republic after 1990. It constitutes an integral—and open-ended—part of contemporary history as the history of our present time.[5]

Histories of Fear

This book takes the German discourse on German *Angst* as a starting point for re-telling the history of the "old" Federal Republic. This notion of German *Angst* differed from the originally external perception of a German colletive pathology. This use of the concept did not come into being until the 1980s. To capture difference, I refer to the latter as German angst. German *Angst*, by contrast, was, as the above-cited example indicates, always part and parcel of the self-description, the self-diagnosis of West German society. From the 1940s to the 1980s, contemporary observers identified time and again a specific German fear as part of postwar political culture. These diagnoses differed widely both with respect to their interpretation as well as regarding their evaluation of this emotional predicament. Some saw these fears as indication of a collective neurosis; others perceived them as reasonable and justified. Yet the sheer existence of this self-referential discourse on German *Angst* points to widespread uncertainty and apprehension regarding the future in West Germany.

Self-descriptions are an essential part of the constitution of modern societies as political communities.[6] Arguably, fascism and genocide, total war and total defeat made postwar Germany's reflection on itself more pronounced than that of other modern political nations. Postwar Germans had good reasons to probe—and often to doubt—their potential and prospects for democracy, peace, and prosperity. As with all self-descriptions, Germany's entailed a prospective dimension. After 1945, uncertainty, anxiety, and fear often filled the inherent tension between a diagnosed present and an imagined future.

The dominant narratives of the Federal Republic's history, employing paradigms such as "Americanization," "Westernization," "liberalization," or "democratization," all suggest a positive outcome. They barely represent this self-referential discourse on German *Angst*.[7] By taking seriously the anxieties, fears, occasionally even panics that West Germans experienced and articulated between the 1940s and the 1980s, this book seeks to disrupt all too teleological and linear histories of the Federal Republic.[8] Instead, it tells the history of the Federal Republic as a

---

[5] Hans Rothfels, "Zeitgeschichte als Aufgabe," *Vierteljahreshefte für Zeitgeschichte* 1/1 (1953): 1–8.
[6] Ulrich Bielefeld, *Nation und Gesellschaft. Selbsthematisierungen in Deutschland und Frankreich* (Hamburg: Hamburger Edition, 2003).
[7] For a critical discussion of the historiography of the Federal Republic, see Frank Biess, Astrid M. Eckert, "Introduction: Why Do We Need New Narratives for the History of the Federal Republic?" *Central European History* 52/1 (2019): 1–18.
[8] For an important exception, see Christian Schletter, *Grabgesang der Demokratie. Die Debatten über das Scheitern der bundesdeutschen Demokratie von 1965 bis 1985* (Göttingen: Vandenhoeck &

series of moments of crisis, in which specific fears and anxieties emerged, served a variety of political functions, and then again abated.

Although these crises of fear featured very different protagonists and focused on a wide variety of fear objects, they nevertheless exhibited some similar features. Above all, the imagined future scenarios—of retribution by the Allies, of a new nuclear war, of an authoritarian transformation or an environmental catastrophe—did not come true. The postwar period featured a specific discrepancy between imagined futures and what actually happened, or between an anxiety-ridden fantasy and a more benign reality. This book tries to explain the origins and significance of this and other repetition structures in the history of the Federal Republic.[9] Another repetition structure was the dialectics between left- and right-wing fears with each side accusing the other of seeking to create a "different republic." A third one consisted of the recurring practice of creating consensus by ostracizing "others." As we will see, the precise nature of the "other" as a fear object varied—from displaced persons to recruiters for the Foreign Legion, to subversive Communists, to terrorist sympathizers, to Turkish guest workers, and all the way to today's asylum seekers and Muslim refugees.

The focus on repetition structures does not mean that nothing changed in postwar history. The "new" rather occurred and built on the familiar.[10] Recurring episodes of fear derived from shifting historical configurations, focused on a range of different objects, and served a variety of functions. My approach seeks to align more closely the perceptions and mentalities of contemporaries with the historical narrative of the Federal Republic. It does so by taking these fears and anxieties seriously as historical forces of their own, rather than by merely dismissing them as "hysterical," "irrational," or "neurotic."[11] Historians' frequent recourse to the language of psychopathology in the face of recurring episodes of fear and anxiety only signals their difficulties in historicizing these emotions properly. Yet, rather than merely treating them as "irrational residues" of a modernizing, liberalizing, "Westernizing" society, this book seeks to take recurring episodes of fear

---

Ruprecht, 2015). Schletter arrives at many important insights that are incorporated later in Chapters 5–7 of this book. But he limits his analysis to the period after 1965 and also only considers publications in *Der Spiegel* and *Rheinischer Merkur*.

[9] On repetition structures, see Reinhart Koselleck, "Zeitschichten," in Reinhart Koselleck, *Zeitschichten. Studien zur Historik* (Frankfurt a/M: Suhrkamp, 2008 [2003], 19–26. I would like to thank Willibald Steinmetz for this idea.

[10] Reinhart Koselleck, "Stetigkeit und Wandel aller Zeitgeschichten. Begriffsgeschichtliche Anmerkungen," in ibid. 264.

[11] Hans-Ulrich Wehler, *Deutsche Gesellschaftsgeschichte, Band Fünf: Bundesrepublik und DDR 1949–1990* (Munich: C.H.Beck, 2008), 61. Edgar Wolfrum, *Die geglückte Demokratie. Geschichte der Bundesrepublik Deutschland von ihren Anfängen bis zur Gegenwart* (Stuttgart: Klett-Cotta, 2006), 253, 391, 395. This depiction of oppositional forces as irrational and pathological also stands in a long tradition of portraying the Nazi dictatorship in similar terms. Wolfrum, for example, approvingly cites Hans-Peter Schwarz's assertion that a "completely hysterical people" of the Third Reich managed to almost immediately accomplish a "civilized peace" in the Federal Republic. Ibid. 185.

as a starting point to an alternative history of the Federal Republic.[12] It aims at a less linear and teleological history—not so much a history of success but rather one that emphasizes a pervasive sense of "negative contingency" within West German society.[13]

The book seeks to bring into view contemporary Germans' sense of uncertainty and worries about the future. Germans living through this period had no way to know that the Federal Republic would be a peaceful, prosperous, and pluralist democracy in the twenty-first century. Critics of the *Sonderweg* thesis have illuminated the sense of contingency of pre-1933 Germany, and this book extends the same perspective to the post-1945 period.[14] It seeks to give postwar Germans what we all have: an open future. Just as most Germans living in the Weimar Republic could not anticipate German society's eventual descent into the abyss and actually displayed considerable optimism about the future, Germans living in the post-1945 period were often pessimistic regarding democracy's prospects.[15] We should not view these feelings with what E.P. Thompson terms "the enormous condescension of posterity" simply because these catastrophic, even apocalyptic, visions of the future did not come true.[16] These fears in fact constitute an integral part of the history of the Federal Republic. Postwar German fears pointed to an ever-present sense of the fragility of modern democratic societies, based on Germans' experience of the catastrophic collapse of the Weimar Republic. Given the current worldwide crisis of liberal democracy and liberal political institutions, such historical fears may have become more plausible again. For West Germans in the 1950s and 1960s, the past of National Socialism and the Second World War was as close as, say, the terror attacks on 9/11 are to our present, intimately shaping their anticipation of the future. The resulting fears and anxieties, however, were not just disruptive and destabilizing. On the contrary, they contributed to the eventual stabilization of the Federal Republic: they intensified democratic alertness and created a heightened recognition that (relative) peace, increasing prosperity, and democracy are always fragile.

Fear and Democracy

This book investigates the role of fear and anxiety in a liberalizing and democratizing society. It seeks to tell anew the history of the Federal Republic from the

---

[12] On the critique for historical teleologies, see Henning Trüper, Dipesh Chakrabarty, Sanjay Subrahmanyam, eds, *Historical Teleologies in the Modern World* (London: Bloomsbury, 2015).

[13] The term comes from Arnd Bauerkämper, "The Twisted Road to Democracy as a Quest for Security: Germany in the Twentieth Century," *German History* 32/3 (2014): 431–55.

[14] The key text is David Blackbourn, Geoff Eley, *The Peculiarities of German History. Bourgeois Society and Politics in Nineteenth Century Germany* (Oxford: Oxford University Press, 1984).

[15] On optimism in Weimar, see Rüdiger Graf, *Die Zukunft der Weimarer Republik. Krisen und Zukunftsaneignungen in Deutschland 1918–1933* (Munich: Oldenbourg, 2008).

[16] E.P. Thompson, *The Making of the English Working Class* (New York: Random House, 1964), 12.

perspective of its narrativized fears and anxieties. Thus it confronts a long political and intellectual tradition dating back to the Enlightenment that has posited
fear as opposed to—even incompatible with—democracy. In his *The Spirit of the
Laws* from 1758, the French philosopher Montesquieu already defined fear as the
characteristic emotion of a tyrannical government. Fear now appeared as the
opposite of liberalism and of the rational, autonomous self.[17] In the twentieth
century, in his speech to Congress in January 1941, Franklin D. Roosevelt
famously identified the "freedom from fear" as one of the four freedoms everyone
should enjoy. The Atlantic Charter later that same year elevated the goal to enable
all "men in all the lands [to] live out their lives in freedom from fear and want" to
an Allied war aim in the Second World War.[18] In the Cold War context and
beyond, political leaders and scholars alike routinely associated fear with dictatorship and totalitarianism, liberal democracy's "other." For example, the German
émigré scholar and political scientist, Franz Neumann, identified it as one of the
main emotional motors of National Socialism and as a key impediment to postwar democratization. He called on the forces of politics and education to eradicate it lest a demagogue exploit it.[19] In the United States, the political scientist and
refugee from Stalinist Russia, Judith Shklar, described a postwar "liberalism of
fear." She considered it the liberal state's main task to keep its citizens free from
fear.[20] Shklar identified fear as a universal human condition and a liberal political
order as an universal antidote.[21] More recently, the sociologist Zygmunt Bauman
described the "story of the rise of democracy" as "eliminating, or constraining
and taming successive causes of uncertainty, anxiety, and fear."[22] And Martha
Nussbaum has recently again emphasized the detrimental effects of fear in contemporary political culture.[23] Fear, in this sense, is an emotion that exists primarily in repressive totalitarian dictatorships that deprive their citizens of basic civil
rights and terrorize them with an all-pervasive secret police.

[17] Corey Robin, *Fear. The History of a Political Idea* (New York: Oxford University Press, 2004), 51–72.
[18] Atlantic Charter, see http://www.nato.int/cps/en/natolive/official_texts_16912.htm (last accessed February 14, 2020). See also Elizabeth Borgwardt, *A New Deal for the World. America's Vision for Human Rights* (Cambridge, Mass.: Harvard University Press, 2007). Peter Stearns sees this statement as typical for the culture of emotional "anti-intensity" in the 1940s and 1950s; see Peter Stearns, *American Fear. The Causes and Consequences of High Anxiety* (London: Routledge, 2006), 14, Peter Stearns, *American Cool. Constructing a Twentieth-Century Emotional Style* (New York: New York University Press, 1994).
[19] Franz L. Neumann, *Angst und Politik. Vortrag gehalten an der Freien Universität Berlin* (Tübingen: J.C.B. Mohr, 1954), 43.
[20] Judith Shklar, "The Liberalism of Fear," in Stanley Hoffmann, ed., *Political Thought and Political Thinkers* (Chicago: University of Chicago Press, 2002 [1989]), 3–20.
[21] Max Weiss, "Introduction: Fear and Its Opposites in the History of Emotions," in Michael Laffan, Max Weiss, eds, *Facing Fear. The History of an Emotion in Global Perspective* (Princeton: Princeton University Press, 2012), 3–4.
[22] Zygmunt Bauman, *Liquid Fear* (Cambridge: Polity, 2006), 157.
[23] Martha C. Nussbaum, *The Monarchy of Fear. A Philosopher Looks at Our Political Crisis* (New York: Simon and Schuster, 2018).

Contrary to this established opposition between fear and democracy, this book investigates the relationship between the liberalization and democratization of West German society, on the one hand, and intense episodes of fear on the other. I argue that this relationship between fear and democracy turns out to be much more complex, as the thesis of fear as democracy's "other" suggests. The book offers a series of empirical investigations of the role that fear and anxiety played at various moments in Germany's postwar history. It does not seek to formulate a general theory of that relationship but rather unearths the political polyvalence of fear as an emotion that took on very different meanings and functions in different contexts. Fear did indeed have the potential to undermine civil liberties and to rally majority society against political outsiders and minorities. But it also created a heightened awareness of the threats to democracy, and it proved to be a very effective tool and emotional mechanism for political mobilization and engagement. Fear was therefore not always the antidote to postwar democracy but also an integral part of it. It undermined democracy and stabilized it as well.

By emphasizing the positive and productive functions of fear in postwar democracy, German *Angst* seeks to recuperate the complex, ambivalent, and often paradoxical role of fear within a democratizing society. This more nuanced view of fear has a long tradition and predates the pathologization of fear since the Enlightenment. In Christian thought, Augustine first distinguished between a *timor servilis* and a *timor filialis*, a servile and a filial fear. Whereas the former was the fear of God's punishment, the latter denoted the fear of sin that would be the occasion for God's punishment. Both fears did not remain neatly separated and were constantly intertwined in Christian theology. Christian theologians speculated whether and how servile fear could be transformed into filial fear. And they emphasized the potential pedagogic function of servile fear.[24] This book, too, highlights the potentially positive and productive functions of at least some fears. But, after 1945, it was not so much the fear of sin but rather the fear of a new authoritarianism that promoted postwar democracy. The emphasis on the polyvalence of fear and its myriad political functions captures better the complex historical reality of this emotion than its condemnation as the antidote to enlightenment rationalism.

The book illustrates the emotional dimension of democratization, and it points to a democratization of emotions as a central aspect of postwar history. Political theorists have begun to explore the relationships between emotions or "passions" and democracy.[25] Yet—with some notable exceptions—these insights have rarely been applied to the history of democracy and democratization in postwar West

---

[24] This paragraph follows the discussion in Andreas Bähr, *Furcht und Furchtlosigkeit. Göttliche Gewalt und Selbstkonstitution im 17. Jahrhundert* (Göttingen: V&R unipress, 2013), 79–95. On the role of fear in the Catholic tradition, see Ulrike Strasser, *Missionary Men and Pacific Journeys in the Early Modern World* (Amsterdam: Amsterdam University Press, forthcoming), Chapter 2.

[25] George E. Marcus, *The Sentimental Citizen. Emotion in Democratic Politics* (University Park: Pennsylvania State University Press, 2002), Paul Hoggett, *Politics, Identity, and Emotion* (Boulder: Paradigm Publishers, 2009).

Germany. With few exceptions, historians have invoked the role of emotions in postwar society, yet they have generally not made emotions the basis for an analysis of postwar history.[26] An ethics of "sobriety" and a "farewell to pathos" characterized the political culture of the early Federal Republic. A "pragmatic" and "realist" definition of democracy stood in contrast to the utopian and potentially catastrophic promises of fascism and Communism.[27] Yet these historians have not analyzed the implications of this finding for the political culture of the Federal Republic or its changing "emotional regime(s)." One exception is the historian Hans-Peter Schwarz's brilliant and much cited essay on the history of the Federal Republic as a "catastrophe that did not happen." He pointed to a fear of catastrophe both on the Left and on the Right as a "widespread spirit of the age" (*durchgehend weitverbreitetes Zeitgefühl*).[28] However, he then pivots to a history of "stability" and successful "stabilization" of postwar history. This book builds on his reconstruction of the Federal Republic's catastrophic consciousness, yet also seeks to show that "stability" and "security" largely remained elusive in post-National Socialist Germany. A keen sense for the potential failure of democracy pervaded the process of democratization. Contemporary German observers perceived West German democracy to be in a state of almost permanent crisis, West Germany, as it were, remained a polity constantly on alert.

Precisely because it investigates the relationship between fear and democracy, this book focuses exclusively on the Federal Republic. Although East Germans in the German Democratic Republic shared the same catastrophic past and hence developed similar fears of war or of fascism as their countrymen across the Iron Curtain, fear assumed a fundamentally different role in the context of a Communist dictatorship. West Germans did not experience the fear of a secret police or of arbitrary repressive measures of an authoritarian state. A pluralist society also produced a more complex emotional dynamics. As we will see, civil society often pushed back against official efforts at managing popular emotions, and it eventually became the site for the articulation of massive popular fears as well. While I am very much in favor of an integrated East–West German history and oppose efforts to relegate the former East Germany to a footnote in postwar history, this project remains limited to the "old" Federal Republic and to the post-unification Berlin Republic for conceptual reasons.[29]

---

[26] Anna M. Parkinson, *An Emotional State: The Politics of Emotion in Postwar West German Culture* (Ann Arbor: University of Michigan Press, 2015), Schletter, *Grabgesang der Demokratie*, Till van Rahden, "Clumsy Democrats. Moral Passions in the Federal Republic," *German History* 29/3 (2011): 485–504.

[27] See Paul Nolte, *Was ist Demokratie? Geschichte und Gegenwart* (Munich: C.H.Beck, 2012), 291.

[28] Hans-Peter Schwarz, "Die ausgebliebene Katastrophe. Eine Problemskizze zur Geschichte der Bundesrepublik," in Hermann Rudolph, ed., *Den Staat denken. Theodor Eschenburg zum Fünfundachtzigsten* (Berlin: Siedler, 1990), 156.

[29] My first book, Frank Biess, *Homecomings. Returning POWs and the Legacies of Defeat in Postwar Germany* (Princeton: Princeton University Press, 2006), tried to offer such an integrated East–West history.

Fear and Trauma

This book also seeks to distance itself from a long series of popular books that have diagnosed German *Angst* as a pathological deformation of the postwar German national character.[30] Written by journalists or psychotherapists, these books extrapolate, often in methodologically problematic ways, from an analysis of individual cases a diagnosis of an alleged German collective psychology and pathology. In so doing, this literature tends to conflate therapeutic and analytical approaches. In a somewhat tautological fashion, these books deduce the existence of German *Angst* from therapeutic analyses of individuals, which serve as evidence of a nationally specific psycho-pathology. Most recently, such books have focused on "war children" (*Kriegskinder*)—that is, individuals who experienced the Second World War as children, many of whom grew up without fathers or with fathers hobbled by the psychic and physical consequences of both world wars, and even on "war grandchildren" (*Kriegsenkel*).[31] These books generally draw on small samples of mostly well-educated and professionally successful upper-class men, who underwent psychotherapy and have made skillful use of the modern media to stylize themselves as representatives of an entire "generation."[32]

To be sure, this book participates in the broader strand of recent historiography that seeks to bring into focus the long-lasting effects of war and unprecedented violence on German and European societies.[33] The long-term effects of National Socialism, the Second World War and the Holocaust constitute the foundation of the history of fear in postwar Germany. Yet the individual and collective consequences of war and violence need to be analyzed in the context of the very well-researched history of memory in the Federal Republic. Much of the psychological literature ignores the historiography on commemorative culture.

[30] Bode, *Die deutsche Krankheit—German Angst*. Gabriele Baring, *Die geheimen Ängste der Deutschen* (Munich: Scorpio, 2011), Klaus-Uwe Adam, *Die Psyche der Deutschen. Wie wir denken, fühlen und handeln* (Düsseldorf: Patmos, 2007).

[31] Sabine Bode, *Die vergessene Generation. Die Kriegskinder brechen ihr Schweigen* (Munich: Piper, 2011) and *Kriegsenkel. Die Erben der vergessenen Generation* (Stuttgart: Klett-Cotta, 2014). For a scholarly analysis of the phenomenon of "war children," see Lu Seegers, Jürgen Reulecke, eds, *Die "Generation der Kriegskinder." Historische Hintergründe und Deutungen* (Gießen: Psychosozial-Verlag, 2009).

[32] Dorothee Wierling, "Generations as Narrative Communities: Some Private Sources of Official Cultures of Remembrance in Postwar Germany," in Frank Biess, Robert G. Moeller, eds, *Histories of the Aftermath. The Legacies of the Second World War in Europe* (New York: Berghahn Books, 2010), 102–33.

[33] Richard Bessel, Dirk Schumann, eds, *Life after Death. Approaches to a Social and Cultural History of Europe during the 1940s and 1950s* (Cambridge: Cambridge University Press, 2003), Klaus Naumann, ed., *Nachkrieg in Deutschland* (Hamburg: Hamburger Edition, 2001), Biess, *Homecomings*, Svenja Golterman, *Die Gesellschaft der Überlebenden. Deutsche Kriegsheimkehrer und ihre Gewalterfahrungen im Zweiten Weltkrieg* (Munich: DVA, 2009), Biess and Moeller, eds, *Histories of the Aftermath*, Richard Bessel, *Germany 1945. From War to Peace* (New York: Harper, 2010), Keith Lowe, *Savage Continent. Europe in the Aftermath of World War II* (New York: St. Martin's, 2012).

It thus replicates central tropes of the West German victimization discourse—for example, the notion that external prohibitions or internal censorship prevented a discussion of German suffering throughout the postwar period. This was simply not the case. German suffering as a result of war, flight, and expulsion or postwar captivity was always present in postwar German public memory.[34] It is true that the symbolic recognition of psychic suffering did not always lead to material recognition—for example in pension claims. Our current concept of "trauma" as psychic suffering induced by external events simply did not yet exist in postwar society. Trauma is a historical category, and our current conceptions of trauma cannot simply be projected onto the past, as psychological literature often does.

This literature also tends to obscure the difference between therapeutic and historical narratives. Public talk about one's own suffering is supposed to create a conscious awareness of hitherto unconscious emotions, thus allowing individual subjects to move toward the "mastering" of a difficult past. This therapeutic process would then make it possible, as Gabriele Baring argues, to "move out of the shadows of the past" and to lead a "happier, self-determined life."[35] However, this promise of a final mastering of the past is similar to the widespread desire in postwar society for a "final stroke," which would once and for all end the preoccupation with the past and, in so doing, liberate postwar Germans from the burdens of a difficult legacy. Unlike the therapeutic liberation from a difficult past that these books propagate, my book aims at an empirical reconstruction of the changing historical functions of fear and anxiety in postwar society. To do so, I analyze many of these psychological publications as historical sources, as contributions to the evolving self-descriptions and self-analysis of postwar German society. In so doing, rather than examining the existence of a German national pathology, this book treats the (self-)perception of such a pathology as an entry point into an empirically grounded history of postwar fear and anxiety.

Emotions

In analyzing the historical significance of fear and anxiety in postwar West Germany, the book draws on some key insights of a re-conceptualized history of emotions. The history of emotions dates back at least to Lucian Febvre's plea from 1941 to write the "the history of hate, the history of fear, the history of cruelty, the history of love."[36] Steeped very much in the emotional concepts of his own time,

---

[34] Robert G. Moeller, *War Stories. The Search for a Usable Past in the Federal Republic of Germany* (Berkeley: University of California Press, 2001).

[35] Baring, *Die geheimen Ängste der Deutschen*, 17.

[36] Lucien Febvre, "Sensibility and History: How to Reconstitute the Emotional Life of the Past," in Peter Burke, ed., *A New Kind of History. From the Writings of Febvre* (New York: Harper & Row, 1973), 26.

Febvre identified emotions as "primitive," "basic forces within us," and held them responsible for the rise and triumph of fascism in Europe.[37] Over the past decade or so, however, interest in emotions has grown among humanities scholars, who draw on neighboring disciplines in order to refine this understanding.[38] This renewed interest in emotions has multiple external and internal reasons. They include the search for a new material anchor in the humanities in the aftermath of post-structuralism; the ascendancy of the neurosciences and the ability to track and visualize brain regions related to emotions; and a new recognition of the political significance and efficacy of emotions, fear especially, in the aftermath of the terrorist attacks on the United States on September 11, 2001.[39]

What complicates the study of emotions is that there is no universally accepted definition of "emotion," "fear," or "anxiety." Indeed, so many emotional states fall under the category of "fear" that some researchers propose to abandon the term altogether.[40] Yet societies do have historically and culturally variable concepts of what they mean by "fear." Definitions of emotions move on a continuum between relativist social—constructivist approaches and universalist, biological approaches. This is not the place to rehearse this interdisciplinary debate.[41] But I would like to highlight four key insights from the interdisciplinary research on emotions that

---

[37] Jan Plamper, *Geschichte und Gefühl. Grundlagen der Emotionsgeschichte* (Munich: Siedler, 2012), 55.

[38] There is no shortage of recent theoretical and programmatic texts that survey the state of the field and develop a program for the history of emotions. For some of the most important texts in this genre, see Ute Frevert, "Angst vor Gefühlen? Die Geschichtsmächtigkeit von Emotionen im 20. Jahrhundert," in Paul Nolte, Manfred Hettling, Frank-Michael Kuhlemann, Hans-Walter Schmuhl, eds, *Perspektiven der Gesellschaftsgeschichte* (Munich: C.H.Beck, 2000), 95–111, William M. Reddy, *The Navigation of Feeling. A Framework for the History of Emotions* (New York: Cambridge University Press, 2001), Ingrid Kasten, Gesa Stedman, Margarete Zimmerman, "Lucien Febvre und die Folgen. Zu einer Geschichte der Gefühle und ihrer Erforschung," *Querelles. Jahrbuch für Frauenforschung* 7 (2002): 9–25, Jakob Tanner, "Das Rauschen der Gefühle. Vom Darwinschen Unversalismus zur Davidsonschen Triangulation," *Nach Feierabend. Züricher Jahrbuch für Wissensgeschichte* 2 (2006): 129–52, Barbara H. Rosenwein, "Worrying about Emotions in History," *American Historical Review* 107/3 (2002): 821–45, Daniela Saxer, "Mit Gefühl Handeln. Ansätze der Emotionsgeschichte," *Traverse. Zeitschrift für Geschichte* 2 (2007): 15–29, Bettina Hitzer, "Emotionsgeschichte. Ein Anfang mit Folgen" (2011), available from http://hsozkult.geschichte.hu-berlin.de/forum/2011-11-001 (last accessed February 14, 2020), Birgit Aschmann, "Vom Nutzen und Nachteil der Emotionen in der Geschichte. Eine Einführung," in Birgit Aschmann, ed., *Gefühl und Kalkül. Der Einfluss von Emotionen auf die Politik des 19. und 20. Jahrhunderts* (Stuttgart: Franz Steiner Verlag, 2005), 9–32. See also the discussion *fori* on the history of emotions edited by Frank Biess in *German History* 28/1 (2010): 67–80 and Jan Plamper in *History and Theory* 49/2 (2010), 237–65. See also, Nicole Eustace, Eugenia Lean, Julie Livingston, Jan Plamper, William M. Reddy, Barbara H. Rosenwein, "AHR Conversation: The Historical Study of Emotions," *American Historical Review* 117/5 (2012): 1487–531. For my own attempt to engage the history of emotions for writing the history of the postwar, see Frank Biess, "Feelings in the Aftermath: Toward a History of Postwar Emotions," in Biess and Moeller, eds, *Histories of the Aftermath*, 30–48.

[39] Plamper, *Geschichte und Gefühl*, 72–8.

[40] Ruth Leys, *The Ascent of Affect. Genealogy and Critique* (Chicago: University of Chicago Press, 2017), 300–6.

[41] For a lucid discussion, see Plamper, *Geschichte und Gefühl*, 20–34.

strike me as particularly useful for writing a history of emotions in the post-war period.

The first aspect concerns the emphasis on cognitive aspects of emotions. This insight goes back to the psychological appraisal theories of the 1960s.[42] Appraisal theories were important because they helped to overcome the Cartesian dualism between "reason" and "emotion." Theorists saw emotions as intimately linked to cognitive processes such as decision making, the formation of memory, or economies of attention, rather than as reason's "other." Martha Nussbaum, Ronald de Sousa, and others developed philosophical views of emotions that emphasize their rationality and intentionality.[43] In Nussbaum's words, emotions constitute an "appraisal or value judgment[s], which ascribe[s] to things and persons outside the person's own control great importance for that person's flourishing."[44] Similarly, historian Jakob Tanner describes emotions as part of an "affective-cognitive involvement in the world" that pre-selects themes and issues that are important to us.[45]

This view of emotions goes against the idea that emotions are universal and defined by physiological processes in the brain that do not change over time. This view has gained new currency as a result of the rise of neuroscience and the possibilities for brain imaging through magnetic resonance imaging (MRI) in recent years. Neuroscientists have sought to identify brain regions as locations of specific emotions. The neuroscientist Joseph LeDoux, for example, has located the amygdala as the site of fear and anxiety. LeDoux sees fear as a preconscious bodily response and brain state that emanates from the amygdala and circum-vents the cortex as the site of cognitive processing. "Conscious feelings" are thus only the "frills that have added icing to the emotional case,"—that is, to "brain states and bodily responses" as the "fundamental facts of an emotion."[46] Antonio Damasio's distinction between visceral and non-cognitive "emotions" and cognitive and conscious "feelings" proposes a similar dichotomy.[47] Paul Ekman's theory of six basic emotions that do not differ across space and time goes even further in

[42] On appraisal theories, see ibid. 241–4 and Nico H. Frijda, "The Psychologists' Point of View," in Michael Lewis, Jeanette M. Haviland-Jones, eds, *The Handbook of Emotions*, 2nd edn (New York: The Guilford Press, 2000), 59–75, especially 70–1.

[43] Ronald de Sousa, *The Rationality of Emotion* (Cambridge: MIT Press, 1987), Martha C. Nussbaum, *Upheavals of Thought. The Intelligence of Emotions* (Cambridge: Cambridge University Press, 2001), Robert C. Solomon, *Not Passion's Slave: Emotions and Choice* (New York: Oxford University Press, 2003), Christoph Demmerling, Hilge Landweer, *Philosophie der Gefühle. Von Achtung bis Zorn* (Stuttgart: J.B. Metzler, 2007).

[44] Nussbaum, *Upheavals of Thought*, 4.   [45] Tanner, "Das Rauschen der Gefühle," 142.

[46] Joseph LeDoux, *The Emotional Brain. The Mysterious Underpinnings of Emotional/ Life* (New York: Simon & Schuster, 1996), 302, Plamper, *Geschichte und Gefühl*, 244–96. LeDoux essentially follows the thinking of the philosopher William James, "What is an Emotion?" *Mind* 9/34 (1884): 188–205.

[47] Antonio Damasio, *Descartes' Error: Emotion, Reason, and the Human Brain* (New York: Penguin Books, 2005).

the direction of non-cognitive universalism. Yet if emotions were indeed mainly (as LeDoux and Damasio suggest) or exclusively (according to Ekman) physiological and universal, a history of emotion would be difficult and limited to a history of the body. The history of fear would thus be scarcely different from what neuroscientist Borwin Bandelow once described to me as scarcely different from the "history of the gall bladder."[48]

Significantly, the debate over the cognitive/physiological nature of emotions does not just take place between the "two cultures" of the humanities and the sciences but also within neuroscience itself.[49] Much of recent neuroscientific research challenges the theory that emotions occur within specific brain regions. It has also largely deconstructed the "myth of universal emotions" independent of time and space.[50] Instead, neuroscientific research also emphasizes the importance of prior knowledge and experience, and hence of culture, in the making of emotions.[51] Emotions are subject to cultural and historical variations: the cognitive operations underlying emotions certainly vary with changing historical and cultural contexts.[52] In the behavioral ecology of the psychologist Alan J. Fridlund, emotions appear as forms of communication that are radically dependent on specific contexts.[53] These latter approaches are highly compatible with historical approaches to the study of emotions.

Second, precisely because emotions are "constructed," changing and historically variable normative frameworks or "emotional regimes" govern their experience and articulation.[54] Such regimes constitute normative frameworks that constrain or encourage the articulation of specific emotions such as fear (and of emotions in general) at any given moment. In an age of the "scientification of the social,"

---

[48]   Interview with Borwin Bandelow, Göttingen, August 12, 2008.

[49]   On the use of neuroscience for humanistic inquiry, see William Reddy, "Humanists and the Experimental Study of Emotion," in Frank Biess, Daniel M. Gross, eds, *Science and Emotions after 1945. A Transatlantic Perspective* (Chicago: University of Chicago Press, 2014), 41–66, Daniel M. Gross, Stephanie D. Preston, "Emotion Science and the Heart of a Two-Cultures Problem," in ibid. 96–117. For critical debate of this issue, see "AHR Conversation." For a critical perspective that seeks to rescue Darwin against some of his later followers, see Daniel M. Gross, "Defending the Humanities with Charles Darwin's 'The Expression of the Emotions in Man and Animals' (1872)," *Critical Inquiry* 37/1 (2010): 34–59.

[50]   On the critique of universal emotions, see Leys, *The Ascent of Affect*; see also, Lisa Feldman Barrett, *How Emotions Are Made. The Secret Life of the Brain* (Boston: Houghton Mifflin, 2017), 42–55.

[51]   In general now, ibid.

[52]   To be sure, cognitivist approaches have also been criticized for underestimating the visceral, spontaneous, uncontrollable, and "irrational" aspect of emotions. It might therefore be important to move beyond the binary distinction between culturally variable cognitive aspects of emotions on the one hand, and universal physiological components on the other. As Monique Scheer has argued, cognitive and physiological aspects combine to form specific kinds of "practices" that are an essential part of a culturally variable historical *habitus*. See Plamper, *Geschichte und Gefühl*, 313–19 and Monique Scheer, "Are Emotions a Kind of Practice (and Is That What Makes Them Have a History)? A Bourdieuian Approach to Understanding Emotion," *History and Theory* 51/2 (2012): 193–220.

[53]   Leys, *Ascent of Affect*, 220–65.

[54]   Reddy, *Navigation of Feeling*, 129. On the long history of social constructivism in the study of emotions, see Plamper, *Geschichte und Gefühl*, 89–176.

the analysis of emotional regimes thus often harkens back to scientific discourses in fields such as psychiatry, psychology, and medicine.[55] These disciplines were especially important in defining social and cultural norms regarding the experience and expression of fear, and how these norms changed over time. This is also why this book pays particular attention to these disciplines in tracing the shifting emotional regimes during the postwar period.

Emotional regimes not only constitute abstract rules—they shape the very formation of an emotion. The third important aspect of recent emotions studies that this book draws on is the insight that the articulation of an emotion constitutes an integral part of the emotion itself. According to William Reddy, emotions form specific kinds of speech acts, what he calls "emotives." Emotives are not only descriptive ("I am afraid") or relational ("I am afraid of you") but also self-altering and self-exploring. By saying "I am afraid," a speaker gives meaning, at least provisionally and temporally, to chaotic thought material. They identify it as the emotion of fear, and hence evoke the emotion.[56] Thus the verbal and non-verbal articulation of fear actually constitutes the emotion. Articulation is therefore not only empirically but also conceptually essential for writing a history of emotions. Because the rhetoric of fear is inseparable from fear, I often quote extensively from the sources. We only have access to emotions in the past if they have been articulated in one way or another. The goal of the history of emotions is therefore not a revived psychohistory that would make visible an unarticulated individual or collective unconscious. Rather, it seeks to historicize actually articulated emotions.[57] The problem, of course, is that we cannot always know whether the external articulation of an emotion corresponds to its actual experience. People can be dishonest and insincere about their emotions. Yet, as the book will demonstrate, the relationship between the internal experience of an emotion and its external manifestation is itself subject to historical and cultural change. While emotional norms of the early postwar period, for example, encouraged subjects to contain their emotions, later periods validated precisely the accurate external performance of an inner emotional reality as a sign of healthy authenticity.

Finally and fourthly, emotions also entail a temporal element. "Fear" (and its opposite "hope") are future-oriented emotions. In logical terms, fear can be

---

[55] Uffa Jensen, Daniel Morat, eds, *Rationalisierungen des Gefühls: Zum Verhältnis von Wissenschaft und Emotionen 1880–1930* (Munich: Wilhelm Fink, 2008), Biess and Gross, eds, *Science and Emotions after 1945*,Lutz Raphael, "Die Verwissenschaftlichung des Sozialen als methodische und konzeptionelle Herausforderung für eine Sozialgeschichte des 20. Jahrhunderts," *Geschichte und Gesellschaft* 22 (1996): 165–93.

[56] Reddy, *Navigation of Feeling*, 74–130.

[57] The history of emotions does not necessarily pretend to have access to the inner reality of emotional life, contrary to the assumption in Rüdiger Schnell, *Haben Gefühle eine Geschichte? Aporien einer History of Emotions* (Göttingen: Vandenhoeck & Ruprecht, 2015).

defined as "X" does not want "Y" to occur, and "X" thinks that "Y" is likely.[58] Fear is oriented toward an uncertain future. In postwar Germany, it was intimately linked to the memory of a catastrophic past.[59] Fear thus served as an essential way to link past, present, and future. These temporal links, moreover, were contingent and subject to historical change—in other words, which pasts were invoked at what moments in order to imagine which futures varied throughout the postwar period.[60] The relatively well-researched history of memory in the Federal Republic thus forms a crucial starting point for the history of fear in postwar West Germany.[61] Yet I read this literature here not primarily retrospectively—how did West Germans make sense of the past?—but rather prospectively—how did West German memories of the past inform anticipations of the future?[62] This approach builds on recent insights of clinical psychology that have emphasized the significance of prospection for the human species more generally, even claiming a distinct *homo prospectus*. These studies also highlight the significance of emotions for predictions and prospective thinking.[63]

Episodes of fear were based on a shifting and dynamic relationship between past, present, and future. To use Reinhart Koselleck's frequently cited terms, changing "spaces of experience" produced shifting "horizons of expectations." Yet, while Koselleck highlighted the increasing separation between "space of experience" and "horizon of expectation" as a hallmark of modernity since the eighteenth century, both temporal experiences actually remained more closely related to each other in the postwar period.[64] The history of the Federal Republic

---

[58] Aaron Ben-Ze'ev, *The Subtlety of Emotions* (Cambridge, Mass.: MIT Press, 2000), 475–9. On the future-oriented dimension of fear, see also Weiss, "Introduction: Fear and Its Opposites in the History of Emotions," 1–2.

[59] For this link between past and present, see also de Sousa's notion of "paradigm scenarios" or Nussbaum's notion of a "complex narrative history" that comes with every emotion. See Sousa, *The Rationality of Emotion*, 181–90 and Nussbaum, *Upheavals of Thought*, 179.

[60] On the history of the future, see the seminal work by Lucian Hölscher, *Die Entdeckung der Zukunft* (Frankfurt a/M: Fischer, 1999). See also Joachim Radkau, *Geschichte der Zukunft. Prognosen, Visionen, Irrungen in Deutschland von 1945 bis heute* (Munich: C.H.Beck, 2017), Lucian Hölscher, ed., *Die Zukunft des 20. Jahrhunderts. Dimensionen einer historischen Zukunftsforschung* (Frankfurt a/M: Campus, 2017).

[61] For a good survey of this historiography, see Robert G. Moeller, "What Has Coming to Terms with the Past Meant in the Federal Republic of Germany?" *Central European History* 35/2 (2002): 223–56.

[62] For a similar prospective reading of memory in a different context, see Pieter Lagrou, "The Age of Total War: 1945–55," in Biess and Moeller, eds, *Histories of the Aftermath*, 287–96.

[63] Martin E.P. Seligman, Peter Railton, Roy F. Baumeister, Chandra Sripada, *Homo Prospectus* (New York: Oxford University Press, 2016); similarly, Barrett, *How Emotions Are Made*, 85–127.

[64] Reinhart Koselleck, "'Erfahrungsraum' und 'Erwartungshorizont'—zwei historische Kategorien," in *Vergangene Zukunft*, 349–75. For critical perspectives on Koselleck, see Anders Schinkel, "Imagination as a Category of History. An Essay Concerning Koselleck's Concept of *Erfahrungsraum und Erwartungshorizont*," *History and Theory* 44/1 (2005), 42–54 and the AHR forum, "Histories of the Future," in *American Historical Review* 117/5 (2012): 1402–85. Christian Geulen even identifies a reverse relationship for the twentieth century—namely, the ways in which expectations shape experiences; see Christian Geulen, "Plädoyer für eine Geschichte der Grundbegriffe des 20. Jahrhunderts," in *Zeithistorische Forschungen/Studies in Contemporary History* 7/1 (2010): 79–97.

thus exhibited a series of "feedback loops between prognoses of the future and memories of the past."[65] The history of fear in postwar Germany was the history of negative memories that were projected into the future. In experiencing and articulating fear, historical actors practiced different ways of relating to the future, which increasingly appeared in the plural—futures.[66] Postwar Germans imagined, above all, a "risk future"—that is, a future that was feared and dangerous, and that was imagined in order to be avoided.[67] Some of these impending catastrophes appeared very imminent—for example, a feared transformation into an authoritarian state or a nuclear war within a few years. Other catastrophic scenarios, by contrast, were located in a more distant future—for example, the eventual replacement of workers by robots.[68] Yet whether these futures appeared as distant or imminent, fear and anxiety resulted from an ongoing presence of a catastrophic past in postwar Germany. A dynamic and shifting commemorative culture activated different understandings of the past at different moments, and hence formed the basis for uncertain, often fearful, occasionally apocalyptic imaginations of the future.

Fear was always dynamic in the postwar period. This book will analyze the changing conditions for the experience and expression of fear. It will trace its changing objects as well as its varying political functions. It will analyze the emergence but also the disappearance of fear. Emotions are, as Reddy argues, "overlearned cognitive habits," that are "involuntary in the short run" but may be "learned and unlearned over a longer time frame."[69] It is precisely their cognitive content that makes emotions accessible to change. The question why certain fears emerged at certain moments and then disappeared again thus provides, this book contends, an original and privileged window into postwar West German culture. Time and again, fear also transmogrified into related emotions—anger, resentment, hope. The boundaries between these emotions were always fluid, which makes an isolated history of fear difficult to write. Whenever feasible, the book thus highlights fear's relationship to these other emotions and, in so doing, gestures toward a more complete history of emotions in the postwar period.

A word about terminology is in order. The philosophies of Søren Kierkegaard and Martin Heidegger point out the distinction between "fear" and "anxiety."

[65] Lucian Hölscher, "Theoretische Grundlagen," in Hölscher, ed., *Die Zukunft des 20. Jahrhunderts*, 13. Harald Welzer, "Erinnerungskultur und Zukunftsgedächtnis," *Aus Politik und Zeitgeschichte* 25–26 (2010): 16–23.

[66] Elke Seefried, *Zukünfte. Aufstieg und Krise der Zukunftsforschung, 1945–1980* (Berlin: De Gruyter, 2015).

[67] Rüdiger Graf, Benjamin Herzog, "Von der Geschichte der Zukunftsvorstellung zur Geschichte ihrer Generierung. Probleme und Herausforderungen des Zukunftsbezugs," *Geschichte und Gesellschaft* 42 (2016): 510.

[68] The temporal reach of specific futures and the relationship of these imagined futures to different policies would be a subject for future research.

[69] Reddy, *Navigation of Feeling*, 32.

Fear, according to these philosophers, is directed toward a concrete object; anxiety is a more diffuse emotion without a specific object. However, in this book, I will use both terms, "fear" and "anxiety," interchangeably in keeping with lexical studies that show that German speakers in the present use *Furcht* and *Angst* virtually interchangeably.[70] The distinction Kierkegaard and Heidegger identify is problematic because commentators in the postwar period used the distinction to dismiss certain emotions as merely neurotic and hence groundless "anxiety" while validating others as justified "fear." By adopting this distinction as part of my analytical framework, I would run the risk of making value judgments on the justified or unjustified nature of historically specific articulations of fear and anxiety. As such, my analysis would reproduce and become part of the contemporary political discourse rather than subjecting this discourse to historical analysis.[71] While I will specify in this book if certain fears are based on wrong factual historical assumptions, I have no interest in serving as retroactive judge or therapist by evaluating historical fears as justified or unjustified. Instead, I seek to demonstrate how fear and anxiety structured political debates in the Federal Republic shaped postwar Germans' expectations of the future, and defined political subjectivities.

Scope and Themes

Fear and anxiety have not only a history but also a rather extensive historiography.[72] This book thus builds on an entire series of historical studies of fear while also developing its own distinct approach to the subject. Like Jean Delumeau for early modern Europe, the book explores popular as well as elite fears. Some chapters offer an analysis of rumors and popular panics similar to the one that George Lefebvre has explored in *The Great Fear*. Other chapters analyze

---

[70] Henning Bergenholtz, *Das Wortfeld "Angst." Eine lexikographische Untersuchung mit Vorschlägen für ein grosses interdisziplinäres Wörterbuch der deutschen Sprache* (Stuttgart: Klett-Cotta, 1980), Demmerling and Landweer, *Philosophie der Gefühle*, 80–91.

[71] For a critique of this distinction, see Joanna Bourke, *Fear. A Cultural History* (Emeryville: Shoemaker & Hoard, 2005), 189–92.

[72] George Lefebvre, *The Great Fear of 1789. Rural Panic in Revolutionary France* (New York: Schocken, 1973), Jean Delumeau, *Angst im Abendland. Die Geschichte kollektiver Ängste im Europa des 14. bis 18. Jahrhunderts* (Reinbek: Rowohlt, 1989), Robin, *Fear*, Schildt, 'German Angst'; Bourke, *Fear. A Cultural History*, Stearns, *American Fear*, Bernd Greiner, Christian Th. Müller, Dierk Walter, eds, *Angst im Kalten Krieg* (Hamburg: Hamburger Edition, 2009), Patrick Bormann, Thomas Freiberger, Judith Michel, eds, *Angst in den Internationalen Beziehungen* (Göttingen: Vandenhoeck & Ruprecht, 2010), Jan Plamper, Benjamin Lazar, eds, *Fear Across the Disciplines* (Pittsburgh: University of Pittsburgh Press, 2012), Laffan and Weiss, eds, *Facing Fear*, Bude, *Gesellschaft der Angst*, Schletter, *Grabgesang der Demokratie*, Pierre-Frédéric Weber, *Timor Teutonorum. Angst vor Deutschland seit 1945: Eine europäische Emotion im Wandel* (Paderborn: Schöningh, 2015), Jacob Eder, *Holocaust Angst. The Federal Republic of Germany and Holocaust Memory since the 1970s* (New York: Cambridge University Press, 2016).

discursively constructed fears that specific events do not drive; these seek to cap-ture a more general sense of unease and anxiety. I have excluded an analysis of fear *of* Germans abroad because it has been the subject of several recent publica-tions.[73] The range of fears that I explore in this book is not as wide as those Joanna Bourke's *Fear* analyzed, and my explanations for those fears in postwar Germany do not extend as far back into German history as Peter Stearns's identification of "race fears" and "evangelical fears" as the "root causes" of fear in the United States.[74] By focusing on the historical significance of fear and anxiety in the old Federal Republic as a liberalizing and democratizing society, I seek to avoid a deficient focus on one specific fear—for example, fear of war in the Cold War—while, at the same time, seeking to prevent the topic from dissolving into a kind of "general history."[75]

I employ three distinct analytic perspectives in this book. First, the book ana-lyzes changing normative frameworks or emotional regimes that defined the discursive space for articulating fear and anxiety.[76] That is, it argues that the changing manners in which Germans expressed fear and anxiety throughout the postwar period were just as important as the shifting content of their fears. An increasingly pluralist society like West Germany produced multiple emotional regimes, or what historian Barbara Rosenwein termed "emotional communities."[77] The shift from one emotional regime to another also overlapped with generational change, especially from the 1960s onward. As historian Bernd Weisbrod has argued, "generations" are not simply age cohorts. Diverging or contrasting emo-tional styles thus constituted a central element in the self-fashioning of certain age cohorts as distinct "generations."[78]

The book's broad temporal frame also allows me to trace several of these emotional regimes covering the entire period from the 1940s to the 1980s and into our present. On the normative level, postwar history witnessed a shift from a repressive to an expressive emotional regime. The political culture of the early Federal Republic did not generally condone the public display of

---

[73] Weber, *Timor Teutonorum*, Eder, *Holocaust Angst*, Andreas Rödder, *Wer hat Angst vor Deutschland? Geschichte eines europäischen Phänomens* (Frankfurt a/M: S. Fischer, 2018).

[74] Stearns, *American Fear*, 74–5.

[75] This problem was already identified by Schildt, "German Angst."

[76] Reddy, *Navigation of Feeling*, 129, Peter N. Stearns, Coral Z. Stearns, "Emotionology: Clarifying the History of Emotions and Emotional Standards," *American Historical Review* 90/4 (1985). Reddy's framework differs from Stearns's in that he sees the articulation of an emotion ("emotives") as part of the emotional regime.

[77] On the need to discuss "emotional regime" in the plural, see Plamper, *Geschichte und Gefühl*, 310. For Rosenwein, "emotional communities" are "systems of feelings" that define "what these com-munities (and the individuals within them) define and assess as valuable or harmful to them; the evaluations that they make about others' emotions; the nature of the affective bonds between people that they recognize; and the modes of emotional expression that they expect, encourage, tolerate, and deplore." See Rosenwein, "Worrying about Emotions in History," 842.

[78] See Bernd Weisbrod, "Generation und Generationalität in der Neueren Geschichte," *Aus Politik und Zeitgeschichte* 8 (2005): 3–9.

emotions. Political emotions were widely associated with political irrationalism and totalitarianism, and the dominant emotional regime favored an ethics of sobriety and emotional anti-intensity.[79] Emotion, and fear especially, appeared as the "other" of a rational enlightenment subject (often defined as male) that West Germans sought to construct as the agent of the process of liberalization and democratization.

By the 1960s, however, a new emotional regime began to validate the public expression and performance of emotions as an indicator of political authenticity and healthy subjectivity. To explain this cultural shift constitutes one of the most important tasks of this book. These new emotional norms have shaped the political culture of the Federal Republic in decisive ways—to this day. This dramatic cultural shift enabled, for example, the successful mobilization of emotions in the peace movement of the 1980s. Emotions even advanced to a privileged epistemological position—that is, the emotional force on behalf of a political argument became an integral part of its claims. As indicated earlier, however, this more expressive emotional regime always co-existed (and remained in conflict) with an older regime that emphasized emotional restraint. This expressive emotional regime also did not only signify a gradual emancipation or liberalization. It rather signified another normative framework, a new form of governmentality that replaced external norms and constraints with an internalized disciplinary mechanism. The difficulty and, often, impossibility of living up to these cultural norms thus became a new source of fear and anxiety—for example, in the student movement and the left-alternative milieu of the 1970s.

Second, beyond changing "emotional regimes," the book also analyzes the shifting objects of fear and anxieties. It focuses on political fears in the broadest possible terms, and shows how and why the objects of postwar fears shifted from primarily external to primarily internal. From the 1940s to the early 1960s, the consequences of total war and total defeat, Allied occupation, and, eventually, the Cold War dominated West German political fears. People feared that the nascent and (for a time) provisional West German state was too weak to protect the populace against these external threats. To write the history of the Federal Republic as a history of security or "securitization" has difficulties assimilating the fact that large sections of the West German population questioned the state's promise of security.[80]

By the mid 1960s, however, the gradual internal and external stabilization of the Federal Republic and the relaxation of Cold War tensions led to a shift away from fear of external to internal threats. It is one of the important claims of this book that the history of fear in postwar Germany extends beyond the Cold War.

---

[79] For further evidence regarding this argument, see Biess, "Feelings in the Aftermath," 35–7.

[80] This strikes me as the major flaw in Eckart Conze, *Die Suche nach Sicherheit. Eine Geschichte der Bundesrepublik Deutschland von 1949 bis in die Gegenwart* (Berlin: Siedler, 2009).

The rapid modernization of West German society as well as the ever-precarious nature of the inner democratization of the Federal Republic generated its own anxieties. A more extensive and critical memory of the Nazi past, as it was reflected in the trials of Nazi perpetrators in the 1960s, played an important part in generating these inner anxieties. Fears regarding the incomplete reckoning with the legacies of Nazism increased sensitivities for the inherent fragility of democratic systems and regarding persistent authoritarian tendencies within West German society. While psychoanalytic wisdom seeks to reduce anxiety through conscious remembering, the expansion of the memory of National Socialism actually increased rather than reduced anxiety in postwar Germany. Yet these fears and anxieties also strengthened democratic alertness and thus paradoxically contributed to the stabilization of postwar democracy.

The shift to inner anxieties ultimately also affected and defined the postwar self. By the late 1960s, postwar Germans increasingly identified invisible and hitherto unknown dangers not just within postwar society but within the self. This sensitization of the self as well as the parallel internalization of anxiety marked an important moment in the history of fear in postwar Germany. In the aftermath of the student revolt in 1968, new subjectivities not only included a new awareness for much extended possibilities of the self but also a new sensitivity for virtually ubiquitous dangers threatening the self. Unlike in the early postwar period, emotions, and fear especially, became a central aspect of normative subjectivities in West Germany.[81] These subjectivities then reacted to newly emergent external dangers to form the political culture of the West German environmental and peace movements during the 1970s and 1980s, in which the experience and public performance of fear assumed center stage.

The third distinct analytic perspective that gives this book coherence is my analysis of the social and political functions of fear and anxiety in changing political contexts. I discuss the mobilization of emotions for specific social and political purposes, yet also point to the limitations and difficulties of manipulating and controlling popular emotions. The political function of fear in Germany changed significantly through the postwar decades. In the 1950s, government officials sought to balance the deployment of fear to fight the Cold War with the containment of fears that might undermine the state's promise of security. Political elites portrayed themselves as rational actors who sought to contain or at least channel the supposedly irrational and often "feminized" popular fears. Such attempts at official emotional management, however, also produced "ironic

---

[81] In this sense, the history of emotions of the postwar period also overlaps with the history of subjectivities. See Andreas Reckwitz, *Das hybride Subjekt. Eine Theorie der Subjektkulturen von der bürgerlichen Moderne zur Postmoderne* (Wellerswist: Velbrück, 2006), Moritz Föllmer, *Individual and Modernity in Berlin. Self and Society from Weimar to the Wall* (New York: Cambridge University Press, 2013), Pascal Eitler, Jens Elberfeld, eds, *Zeitgeschichte des Selbst. Therapeutisierung – Politisierung – Emotionalisierung* (Bielefeld: transcript, 2015).

effects" in that they accentuated the experience and articulation of that emotion.[82] The fears of war in the 1950s were an example of this effect. By contrast, fear served as an essential agent of mobilization for social movements of the 1970s and 1980s. Fear facilitated the creation of these movements as oppositional emotional communities. This shift points to the important function of highly gendered emotions such as fear in the construction (and transformation) of male and female subjectivities: whereas fear was clearly feminized and contrasted with a restrained and cool masculinity, its experience and performance became eventually central to the softened and gentle feminized masculinities in the alternative culture of the 1970s and 1980s. Not just the political function of fear but also its gender connotations underwent dramatic changes.

The book consists of a series of archivally based case studies covering the period from the 1940s to the 1980s. Several of these case studies analyze lesser-known aspects of postwar history while others seek to cast new light on more familiar themes. The book combines these case studies with a synthetic analysis that draws them together and will provide, I hope, a new perspective on postwar history more generally. The case study approach necessarily implies that not every postwar fear can be integrated in the analysis. However, I selected case studies to represent what appeared to me important, even paradigmatic, moments in the history of postwar Germany. I also chose episodes and conflicts in which contemporaries articulated fear and anxiety explicitly either in public or in private. The historical actors involved in the various cases include government officials, scientists, intellectuals, public commentators, political activists, labor union officials, and ordinary Germans. The analysis emphasizes the fears of (West) German majority society, also because the experience of the *Nazi Volksgemeinschaft* (racial community) formed an important starting point for the history of fear after 1945. A more complete history of postwar emotions would also have to include the feelings of former Holocaust survivors, of displaced persons, guest workers, asylum seekers and refugees, rather than treating them merely as objects of fears on the part of German majority society. In part, I simply did not have the language skills for such an analysis. But I also wanted to analyze fears that shaped postwar West German society as a whole. By focusing on fear and anxiety instead of a specific set of actors, this book seeks to provide a genuine history of emotions rather than a more traditional analysis of emotions in history. Emotions function here not merely as epiphenomenal to other social and political factors but also as historical agents and a causal force in their own right. At various moments, the book also brings into view the interrelationship of fear with other emotions such as guilt, shame, anger, trust, or hope.

---

[82] Reddy, *Navigation of Feeling*, 27.

The book consists of nine chapters. Chapters 1–3 revolve around fears caused by the very uncertain external situation of the Federal Republic from the 1940s to the early 1960s. Chapter 1, "Postwar *Angst*," focuses on popular fears of retribution in the immediate postwar period. Thus it addresses a fear more commonly analyzed with respect to the Soviet occupation zone. It focuses on ordinary Germans' fears of retribution with respect to three distinct groups: Jewish Holocaust survivors, displaced persons from Eastern Europe, and American occupation soldiers. Fears of Jewish revenge revealed ordinary Germans' knowledge of the violent persecution of the Jews and were thoroughly informed by the Nazi propaganda construct of a "Jewish war" (that is, fought on behalf of, and guided by, Jewish interests). In fact, while acts of Jewish retribution were virtually unheard of, isolated acts of violence and revenge by displaced persons, former slave workers, fed German fears of retribution. These acts and the associated feelings of helplessness and anxiety defined Germans' perception of postwar society in the 1940s. The chapter also highlights ordinary Germans' reaction to the US occupation. Rather than seeing it as the kernel of postwar democracy, the shock of occupation increased rather than alleviated postwar fears of retribution. Postwar fears of retribution, the chapter concludes, were related to and displaced feelings of guilt and shame with respect to the Nazi past.

Chapter 2, "Moral *Angst*," discusses a popular panic revolving around the alleged abduction of young German men into the French Foreign Legion during the early 1950s. Well-known at the time but little analyzed by historians, this episode revealed intense concerns over the integrity of the West German body politic and the moral fragility of male youth in the early Federal Republic. The chapter expands on the analysis of popular fears of retribution but also shows how these fears assumed a more metaphorical dimension as fears of white slavery and reverse colonization by the 1950s. Moreover, the popular imagination closely associated the recruiter for the Legion with the notion of homosexual seduction and thus revealed deep concerns about the fragility of male youth in postwar West German society.

Chapter 3, "Cold War *Angst*," documents how fears of nuclear war came to replace fears deriving from defeat and occupation by the late 1950s and early 1960s. By focusing on the issue of West German civil defense, the chapter shows how memories of German victimization in the Second World War continued to inform fearful anticipations of a new and potentially even more destructive war in the future. At the same time, the government of Konrad Adenauer (1949–63) sought to contain fears of nuclear war by invoking the fear of Communism. The politics of fear in the German Cold War thus consisted of a carefully calibrated and always fragile balance between the mobilization of fear on the one hand, and the containment of fear of nuclear war on the other. Persistent popular doubts regarding the government's promise of security at the height of the Cold War also pointed to an ongoing legitimacy deficit of the West German state. A tenuous sense of security only emerged in response to the promise of nuclear protection by the United States.

Chapters 4 and 5 trace the shift from external fears centered on postwar occupation and the Cold War to internal fears emanating from within West German society. This transition resulted from the waning of Cold War tensions and shifting memories of war and fascism. In particular, an emerging critical memory of the Nazi past contributed to an increasing public belief in underlying authoritarian tendencies beneath the veneer of liberal democracy. Moreover, in disciplines such as psychiatry, psychology, and education, fear and anxiety underwent an important re-evaluation. These emotions were no longer seen as purely negative and pathological but increasingly appeared as indications of emotional authenticity and healthy subjectivity.

Chapter 4, "Modern *Angst*," demonstrates that the economic stabilization and rapid modernization of the Federal Republic generated its own fears and anxieties. In particular, the chapter analyzes an extensive and multi-level debate over industrial modernization and "automation" in the Federal Republic. Commentators did not just project an exclusively optimistic vision of technological progress but also articulated myriad anxieties about technological unemployment and economic destabilization as a result of automation. Memories of economic collapse during the Weimar Republic informed these fears. Thus the newly gained political stability and economic modernity of the Federal Republic inspired a new set of fears and anxieties. These debates anticipated an increasingly skeptical attitude toward industrial modernity in general during the following decade.

Chapter 5, "Democratic *Angst*," discusses parallel anxieties regarding the political future of West German democracy. By the late 1950s and early 1960s, political stabilization coincided with new doubts regarding the democratic substance of the Federal Republic. A new awareness of the Nazi past (and of the fact that Nazi perpetrators continued to live in West Germany) fueled fears of a possible authoritarian transformation along the lines of de Gaulle's Fifth Republic or Franco's Spain. These new political fears instigated a democratic alertness that was to become increasingly influential within the political culture of the Federal Republic and ultimately bolstered West German democratization.

Chapter 6, "Revolutionary *Angst*," traces the increasing political polarization of the Federal Republic from the late 1960s onward. The chapter challenges common portrayals of the student movements' very optimistic visions of personal and political transformation, and highlights the student activists' catastrophic imagination of fascism at home and imperialist violence abroad. Political fears also grew beyond the political Left, increasingly affecting liberals and conservatives as well. Revolutionary fears mobilized fears of revolution and vice versa. This dialectic of fear structured political discourse and shaped political subjectivities across the political spectrum in the West German 1960s.

Chapter 7, "Proliferating *Angst*," discusses the proliferation of fear and anxiety in the wake of the student movement. It traces the emergence of new forms of subjectivity that now assigned central significance to the experience and expression of fear and anxiety. The ubiquity of fear objects in the 1970s—terrorism, immigration, economic crisis, and environmental damage—was therefore not just the result of newly emergent external threats but also of a new sensitization of the self. More than before, the self appeared as a passive seismograph for invisible threats, such as pathogens in the food or the environment. At the same time, this heightened sensitivity drew these new dangers into public discourse and made them available for political negotiations. An increased capacity for the experience and articulation of fear and anxiety thus constituted one of the essential historical preconditions for the new social movements of the 1970s and 1980s, especially the peace and environmental movements.

Chapter 8, "Apocalyptic *Angst*," demonstrates the important political consequences of this shifting emotional regime as well as of an emerging popular Holocaust memory. It highlights the centrality of the public performance of fear and anxiety for the new social movements of the 1970s and 1980s: the environmental and peace movements. The environmental movement derived from new perceptions of environmental threats that were centrally linked to newly sensitized subjectivities. With the debate about the "death of the forest" (*Waldsterben*) in the 1980s, these sentiments affected West German society as a whole. The peace demonstrations against American nuclear weapons during the early 1980s represented a culmination and a turning point within the broader history of fear and anxiety in postwar West Germany. Never before or after was fear so instrumental for the political mobilization of civil society. This chapter complements earlier studies of the movement by highlighting the significance of the movement's emotional culture and politics. A new culture of emotional expressiveness, as well as new conceptions of subjectivity that emerged in the wake of 1968, made this political mobilization possible.

Chapter 9, "German *Angst*," takes the history of fear into the post-unification period. It discusses continuities and discontinuities across the caesura of 1989 and ponders the potential impact of the history of fear and anxiety before 1989 on the political culture of the post-unification Berlin Republic. To what extent did a longer history of fear that had accompanied the Federal Republic from its inception shape fears surrounding new wars, terrorism, and immigration in the 1990s? To what extent were post-1990 fears a product of the changing national and geopolitical contexts after the end of the Cold War and hence no longer directly related to the past futures of the pre-1989 period? The chapter seeks to locate the politics of fear as propagated by an emerging and increasingly powerful right-wing populism in the longer history of postwar emotions. And it speculates about the contours of a possible democratic politics of emotions in the twenty-first century.

The book does not aim to be a comprehensive synthesis of the history of the Federal Republic of which there are many already. Instead, it seeks to offer an alternative history that seeks to complement existing narratives. It brings into view hitherto neglected aspects of postwar history, especially contemporaries' persistent and widespread sense of contingency, uncertainty, and fear. By combining a series of empirical case studies on paradigmatic fears, it offers an interpretive synthesis that provides, I hope, an alternative and original perspective on the history of the Federal Republic as a whole.

1

Postwar *Angst*

In October 1946, American occupation officials reported the following German poem from the town of Bad Tölz in Bavaria:[1]

> Betrayed by the Nazi, lied to by the Ami
> Now you stand on the street with your broom
> It would have been better to have been a real Nazi
> The Jew is a black marketeer, the Pole stabs you
> But the Ami doesn't see it
> No matter whether you were a Nazi or not
> The Ami will rob you and won't spare you
> The Ami lets the Jews come in
> Because he himself is a Jewish pig.

This blatantly antisemitic poem encapsulated the distinct fears of retribution that preoccupied many Germans in the early postwar period. It listed the alleged criminality of Holocaust survivors ("the Jew is a black marketeer") and former slave workers ("the Pole stabs you") while accusing American occupation officials of being indifferent to, or even encouraging, these offenses ("But the Ami doesn't see it"). It anticipated indiscriminate prosecution of Germans for Nazi crimes, regardless of their sympathies or actions during Nazi rule. The last two lines encapsulated the antisemitism, articulating the popular wartime notion that the US had waged the war against Nazi Germany in the service of a worldwide Jewish conspiracy.

This chapter examines German fears of retribution in the early postwar period, roughly from 1945 to 1948. The poem mentions the three main groups on which

---

[1] Periodic report for week ending October 30, 1946, National Archives, College Park, Md (NA), RG 260, Box 169.

Vom Nazi Betrogen, Vom Ami Belogen
Jetzt stehst Du auf der Straße mit dem Besen,
Wärst lieber gleich richtiger Nazi gewesen
Der Jude schiebt, der Pole sticht,
der Ami aber sieht es nicht.
Warst Du Nazi oder nicht,
Der Ami raubt und schont Dich nicht,
Der Ami holt die Juden rein,
Er ist ja selbst ein Judenschwein

German Angst: Fear and Democracy in the Federal Republic of Germany. Frank Biess, Oxford University Press (2020). © Frank Biess.
DOI: 10.1093/oso/9780198714187.001.0001

Germans trained this fear: Jewish Holocaust survivors, former slave laborers from Eastern Europe who had become displaced persons ("DPs") after 1945, and American occupation officials. By analyzing German fears of retribution, the chapter highlights massive uncertainty and fear as formative popular experiences of the early postwar period. Fear and insecurity emanated as much from Germans' imagination of the consequences of their defeat as from the threat or reality of actual acts of retribution. Violent acts of revenge do not occupy a prominent place in the historiography of the postwar period, which, however, might also have underestimated their frequency.[2] Culturally dominant perceptions of Nazi victims and survivors as passive and reticent may have rendered invisible actual acts of revenge, just as they have underestimated acts of Jewish resistance during the war.[3] By analyzing both dimensions—actual experiences of retribution as well as popular fantasies of Jewish or Allied revenge—this chapter highlights the extent to which a specific postwar fear shaped German subjectivities and anticipations of the future in the immediate postwar period.

Fear of an uncertain and possibly catastrophic future was a foundational emotion in post-1945 Germany. Commentators noted postwar fear across Europe broadly, but Germany's particular predicament in the spring of 1945 produced a specific kind of fear.[4] Rarely has a society faced such an utter moral and political collapse as Nazi Germany. Not only had "Germany" ceased to exist as a nation state and was divided into four occupation zones, the country also was about to face, for the first time in more than 130 years, a complete foreign occupation. Defeat and occupation appeared even more threatening in light of the catastrophic and unprecedented violence that had accompanied the ending of the Second World War in Europe. The tenacity of the Nazi regime in the face of certain military defeat resulted in unprecedented military and civilian casualty rates on all sides in Europe. As many German soldiers died during the last ten months of the war as during the entire preceding five-year period.[5] And while most victims of the Holocaust had already been killed by early 1945, the Nazi regime's genocidal and terrorist policies continued until the very end—for example, with notorious "death marches" of survivors from death camps in the East to

---

[2] Compare the interesting parallels to the post-Civil War American South: Steven Hahn, "Did We Miss the Greatest Slave Rebellion in Modern History?" in *The Political Worlds of Slavery and Freedom* (Cambridge, Mass.: Harvard University Press, 2009), 55–114.

[3] See Carolyn J. Dean, "Erasures. Writing History about Holocaust Trauma," in Frank Biess, Daniel M. Gross, eds, *Science and Emotions after 1945. A Transatlantic Perspective* (Chicago, University of Chicago Press, 2014), 387–413. On the difference between German fantasies of revenge and its actual reality, see Mark Roseman, "'No Herr Führer!' Jewish Revenge after the Holocaust between Fantasy and Reality," in Laura Jokusch, Andreas Kraft, Kim Wünschmann, eds, *Revenge, Retribution, Reconciliation. Justice and Emotions between Conflict and Mediation. A Cross-Disciplinary Anthology* (Jerusalem: Hebrew University Magnes Press, 2016), 69–90.

[4] A.M. Meerlo, *Aftermath of Peace. Psychological Essays* (New York: International University Press, 1946).

[5] Rüdiger Overmans, *Deutsche militärische Verluste im Zweiten Weltkrieg* (Munich: Oldenbourg, 1999).

concentration camps on German territory. These happened in full view of ordinary Germans, who confronted the Nazi victims not just with indifference but often with open hatred and violence.[6] With the gradual liberation of death and concentration camps by Allied forces between January and April 1945, moreover, the extent of Germany's moral collapse became apparent as well. The discovery and publication of images from liberated concentration camps in no small part enabled the Western Allies' acceptance of the expulsion of ethnic Germans from formerly Eastern territories, which became the largest forced population movement in modern European history.[7]

Fears of violent revenge by the Allied victors thus constituted a direct response to the extremely violent ending of the Second World War. Nazi propaganda had stoked fears of retribution already during the last years of the war. After the defeat at Stalingrad, the Nazi regime increasingly emphasized the anti-Jewish and anti-Bolshevist character of the Second World War. Popular knowledge of genocidal warfare against Soviet and Eastern European civilians, as well as of the systematic murder of European Jews, increased fears of retaliation. The extraordinary tenacity and fighting power of the German army during the last stages of the war derived from the private sphere of ordinary soldiers who believed they were defending their families against the existential threat of Jewish and Bolshevist retaliation.[8] Fears of retribution manifested themselves first and most strongly with respect to the Red Army, but eventually spread to the Western zones as well. This chapter seeks to challenge an overtly stark binary contrast between a brutal Soviet occupation in the East and a largely benign American occupation in the West. It shows that ordinary Germans experienced Allied occupation in general as a massive threat to their personal lives and imagined futures. Far from alleviating postwar

---

[6] The emphasis on these death marches was one of the insights of Daniel J. Goldhagen, *Hitler's Willing Executioners. Ordinary Germans and the Holocaust* (New York: Vintage, 1997), 327–74. See also Martin C. Winter, *Gewalt und Erinnerung im ländlichen Raum. Die deutsche Bevölkerung und die Todesmärsche* (Berlin: Metropol Verlag, 2018).

[7] Norbert Frei, "'Wir waren blind, ungläubig und langsam.' Buchenwald, Dachau und die amerikanischen Medien im Frühjahr 1945," *Vierteljahrshefte für Zeitgeschichte* 35/3 (1987): 385–401, Ray M. Douglas, *Orderly and Humane. The Expulsion of the Germans after the Second World War* (New Haven: Yale University Press, 2012). On the German collapse and the last stages of the war, see Rolf-Dieter Müller, ed., *Der Zusammenbruch des Deutschen Reiches 1945. Die militärische Niederwerfung der Wehrmacht. Das Deutsche Reich und der Zweite Weltkrieg*, vol. 10/1 (Munich: DVA, 2008), Rolf-Dieter Müller, ed., *Der Zusammenbruch des Deutschen Reiches 1945. Die Folgen des Zweiten Weltkrieges. Das Deutsche Reich und der Zweite Weltkrieg*, vol. 10/2 (Munich: DVA, 2008), Richard Bessel, *Germany 1945. From War to Peace* (New York: Harper, 2010), Ian Buruma, *Year Zero: A History of 1945* (New York: Penguin, 2013), Keith Lowe, *Savage Continent. Europe in the Aftermath of World War II* (New York: St. Martin's, 2012).

[8] Nicholas Stargardt, *The German War. A Nation under Arms, 1939–45* (New York: Basic Books, 2015), 362, 459, 564, Michael Geyer, "'There is a Land Where Everything Is Pure: Its Name Is Land of Death.' Some Observations on Catastrophic Nationalism," in Greg Eghigian, Matthew Paul Berg, eds, *Sacrifice and National Belonging in Twentieth-Century Germany* (College Station: Texas A&M University Press, 2002), Jeffrey Herf, *The Jewish Enemy: Nazi Propaganda during World War II and the Holocaust* (Cambridge, Mass.: Harvard University Press, 2006).

fear, Western, and especially American, occupation actually functioned as one of its primary sources.[9]

Constricted Futures

Individual Germans experienced a profound sense of disorientation and existential uncertainty during the last years of the war and in the immediate postwar period. It is obviously difficult to generalize about millions of individual transitions from war to postwar. Beyond social differentiation, Allied bombing, flight, expulsion, and postwar captivity created mass displacement in some areas but not in others. Still, individual testimonies clearly reveal how difficult it was for many Germans to imagine their individual and collective futures in the spring of 1945. Writing in her diary in January 1945, Edeltraut G. could "simply not imagine how it might be if the enemies take Germany by storm." She wondered, "What will be next year around this time?"[10] A few months later, in April and May 1945, Magdalena M.'s diary repeatedly invoked the future "in horrible images," and as "dark."[11] Lili H. confessed to her diary in March 1945 that "I cannot imagine any future, don't know what I should be looking forward to."[12] These statements confirm the intrusion of "history" into the personal lives of individual Germans. Momentous events such as the military defeats of the *Wehrmacht*, especially on the Eastern front, all but overwhelmed diary writers' sense of individual agency and gave rise to a sense of helplessness.[13] Total defeat in May 1945 gave no relief, and this sense of impending doom lingered in the early postwar period. The *Regierungspräsident* (high county official) of Munich reported in March 1946 that "the largest share of the population views the near and far future with utmost concern."[14]

In the spring of 1945, ordinary Germans' horizon of expectation considerably narrowed to the personal and intimate sphere. While only a minority of the most ideologically committed Germans held on to official propaganda notions of a "final victory," most Germans envisioned their immediate future in terms of their

---

[9] My focus here is on the US zone, partly because of the availability of sources, and partly because it shaped Western occupation more broadly.

[10] Diary of Edeltraud G., born 15.10.1926, entry January 1, 1945, Deutsches Tagebucharchviv (DTA) Nr. 185, I, 1.

[11] Magdalena K., Brieftagebuch, Kempowski-Archiv (KA) Berlin, Nr. 3715/2.

[12] Lilli H., Diary, March 29, 1945, in Gerhard Hirschfeld, Irina Renz, eds, "*Vormittags die ersten Amerikaner": Stimmen und Bilder vom Kriegsende 1945* (Stuttgart: Klett-Cotta, 2005), 93. For a similar view by a man, see Gerhard E. Sollbach, ed., *Aus schwerer Zeit. Tagebuch das Hagener Bürgers Bernhard Petersen, 1943–1949* (Hagen: v.d. Linnepe, 1986), 153.

[13] Susanne zur Nieden, *Alltag im Ausnahmezustand. Frauentagebücher im zerstörten Deutschland 1943 bis 1945* (Berlin: Orlanda Frauenverlag, 1993), 89.

[14] Monatsbericht des Regierungspräsidenten in München, May 1946, Bayrisches Hauptstaatsarchiv (BHStA), MSo88.

personal and family lives, especially regarding the reunion with absent family members.[15] Fear and uncertainty over absent family members serving in the military contributed to a larger sense of powerlessness. The passive voice characterizes many diary entries. Anne K.'s almost daily diary entries after her husband was reported missing south of Belgrade in December 1944 were filled with statements like "I am terribly angry about everything . . . our happy family life has been destroyed. . . . If the war ends this year, we will not see our Daddy again."[16]As individual futures narrowed to the personal sphere, family reunions had become highly uncertain by early 1945. The Nazi regime categorized 60 per cent of its casualties in 1944, 1.5 million soldiers, as "missing in action," in part in an attempt to understate German losses. Uncertainty over the fate of missing family members often lasted deep into the postwar period: the Soviet Union did not return the last of its German prisoners of war (POWs) until 1956.[17] Anne K.'s husband was not among these. In November 1945, she declared it to be "the happiest day of my life" and that "everything is bright and sunny" when she learned her husband was alive.[18]

Individual and collective futures remained inextricably intertwined.[19] In the early postwar period, Germans imagined their personal futures as subject to the nation's future. Postwar Germans did not simply abandon nationalism after 1945: instead, the radical nationalism of the Nazi period lingered into the postwar period. Defeat and occupation only perpetuated the existential significance of being part of a larger national community.[20] The close link between personal identities and national belonging continued to shape German subjectivities in the war's aftermath. Consider, for example, the diary entry of Diana-Ilse J. on June 6, 1945: "The days are passing evenly and always the same waiting. Waiting for news from the parents, waiting for you my Hein [her fiancé], waiting for the fate that Germany is to meet."[21] Diana-Ilse's worries about her fiancé were closely tied to her concerns about "Germany." Personal and intimate futures remained parallelized even at the syntactic level, to uncertainty about the national future. Along similar lines, Elisabeth L. wondered in June 1945: "Perhaps it is good if one does not have children in our times. What will the future

---

[15] On the significance of the family in this period, see Hester Vaizey, *Surviving Hitler's War. Family Life in Germany, 1939–48* (New York: Palgrave Macmillan, 2010), Stargardt, *The German War*, 449–544.

[16] Diary of Anne K., entry of November 13, 1945, DTA, Nr. 528.

[17] Frank Biess, *Homecomings. Returning POWs and the Legacies of Defeat in Postwar Germany* (Princeton: Princeton University Press, 2006).

[18] Diary of Anne K., entry of November 13, 1945, DTA, Nr. 528.

[19] See also zur Nieden, *Alltag im Ausnahmezustand*, 200.

[20] See also Ulrike Weckel, *Beschämende Bilder. Deutsche Reaktionen auf alliierte Dokumentarfilme über befreite Konzentrationslager* (Stuttgart: Franz Steiner Verlag, 2012), Jörg Echternkamp, "'Verwirrung im Vaterländischen'? Nationalismus in der deutschen Nachkriegsgesellschaft 1945–1960," in Jörg Echternkamp, Sven Oliver Müller, eds, *Die Politik der Nation. Deutscher Nationalismus in Krieg und Krisen, 1760–1960* (Munich: Oldenbourg, 2002), 219–46.

[21] Diary of Diana-Ilse J., June 6, 1945, KA, Nr. 1676.

bring? What will remain of Germany?"[22] Such anxieties reflected the flip side of the pro-natalist propaganda that asked German women to have children to serve the nation.[23] In light of traditional gender stereotypes that designated women as caretakers of the family, women's diaries especially linked personal and national futures.[24] Yet these links also appeared in men's diaries. In December 1945, for example, Hans H.C. reported a rumor that American occupation authorities would prohibit Germans from getting married for two years.[25] Thus he, too, equated defeat and occupation with a denial of private futures.

To be sure, individuals constructed the link between their personal and national futures in different ways, depending on their level of ideological commitment or religiosity. A Catholic priest from East Prussia, who was killed in April 1945, wrote in February 1945 that "one can only trust in God. He watches over us all. What plans does he have with our people?"[26] More committed Nazis such as Grete Dölker-Rehder explicitly mourned the loss of dreams of a Nazi empire—of, as she wrote, a "greater Germany with its ninety million inhabitants." Yet she also described the survival of the nation as an existential precondition for her private future. She hoped that "more than a kernel of Germany will remain" that would allow "our children and grandchildren . . . to live and work so that the German people will not totally collapse."[27] Others found it difficult to imagine a personal future that extended beyond the defeat of the Nazi regime. The 18-year-old Edeltraut G. confessed in January 1945, for example, that she "simply could not imagine what it would be like if the enemies storm across our Germany," and continued to hold on to her belief in new miracle weapons and the final victory.[28] Such a feeling of a blocked future translated into a wave of suicides among committed National Socialists in the spring of 1945.[29]

Yet most Germans did not commit suicide. They discarded their allegiance to the Nazi regime in 1945, at least outwardly. But they continued to envision themselves as members of a German national community, whose personal futures remained closely tied to the fate of the nation as a whole. And, as members of a

---

[22] Diary, Elisabeth L., June 28, 1945, Bibliothek für Zeitgeschichte (BfZ), Stuttgart.

[23] Atina Grossmann, *Jews, Germans, and Allies. Close Encounters in Occupied Germany* (Princeton: Princeton University Press, 2007), 50–89.

[24] Zur Nieden, *Alltag im Ausnahmezustand*, 124.

[25] Hanns H.C., August 5, 1945, BfZ. This rumor appears to have extended Nazi wartime propaganda according to which the victorious Americans were planning to sterilize all Germans in order to exterminate "Germanism." See Stargardt, *The German War*, 237.

[26] Otto von D., letter of February 6, 1945, KA, Nr. 3675/3. He repeated the same question on March 14, 1945.

[27] Walter Kempowski, *Das Echolot. Abgesang '45. Ein kollektives Tagebuch* (Munich: Albrecht Knaus, 2005), 106.

[28] Diary of Edeltraut G., January 1, 1945, DTA, Nr. 185, I, 1.

[29] Richard Bessel, "Hatred after War. Emotion and the Postwar History of East Germany," *History and Memory* 17/1–2 (2005): 195–216, Christian Goeschel, *Suicide in Nazi Germany* (Oxford: Oxford University Press, 2009).

national collective, they also needed to face the possibility of retribution by former Nazi victims.

Jewish Revenge

Postwar fears of retribution built on a "complex narrative history" that, according to Martha Nussbaum, comes with every emotion and extended back into the last few years of the war.[30] The intensification of the Allied air war against Germany, especially after the bombing of Hamburg in July 1943, had brought the conceptual link in the minds of many Germans between the murder of the Jews and Allied bombing as a distinct form of Jewish retribution into the open. Nazi propaganda further reinforced this link between the Holocaust and Allied bombing.[31] While the Nazi regime kept secret the precise details of the "final solution," official propaganda portrayed the intensified persecution of the Jews as legitimate wartime measures against a dangerous and potentially lethal internal enemy.[32] A series of letters to Goebbels in May and June 1944 from German civilians reflect the impact of this propaganda in that they suggested using Jews as shields or hostages against Allied air raids.[33] By this time, historian Nicholas Stargardt writes, the "Jewish" character of the war had become "axiomatic" for many Germans.[34]

The fantasy of the Second World War as a "Jewish war" even informed and mobilized Germans' critical views of the Nazi regime. According to the reports of the Security Service of the SS (SD), the population saw the Allied bombing campaign as "retribution for our actions in November 1938 against the Jews."[35] As the last public and openly violent antisemitic act in Nazi Germany in the prewar period, Germans began to see the pogrom of November 1938, the *Reichskristallnacht*, as a kind of original sin for which the Allies and the Jews now would take revenge.[36] A report from Würzburg in September 1943 speculated that "veritable Jewish cities such as Fürth and Frankfurt" had thus far been spared from bombing.[37] Another report from the vicinity of Würzburg in August 1943 surmised that the city had not yet been attacked because "no synagogue had burnt in Würzburg," yet, after the

---

[30] Martha C. Nussbaum, *Upheavals of Thought. The Intelligence of Emotions* (Cambridge: Cambridge University Press, 2001), 179.

[31] Stargardt, *The German War*, 345–81, Dietmar Süß, *Der Tod aus der Luft. Kriegsgesellschaft und Luftkrieg in Deutschland und England* (Berlin: Siedler, 2011), 110–12.

[32] Herf, *Jewish Enemy*.

[33] See Nicholas Stargardt, *Witnesses of War. Children's Lives under the Nazis.* (London: Jonathan Cape, 2005), 250–1.

[34] Stargardt, *The German War*, 417.

[35] Eberhard Jäckel, Otto Dov Kulka, eds, *Die Juden in den geheimen NS-Stimmungsberichten 1933–1945* (Düsseldorf: Droste, 2004), 706. See also 695, 706, 709, 711.

[36] Alon Confino, *A World Without Jews. The Nazi Imagination from Persecution to Genocide* (New Haven: Yale University Press, 2014), 214–41, quotation on 231, Stargardt, *The German War*, 376.

[37] Jäckel and Kulka, eds, *Die Juden in den geheimen NS-Stimmungsberichten*, 707.

last Jewish person had been deported from Würzburg, the city might now be attacked as well.[38] Catholic officials criticized the deportation of Jewish Germans to the death camps in the East on the grounds that they might "work against us" and hence also subscribed to the Nazi propaganda notion of Jews as a wartime enemy.[39] An ordinary soldier asked his wife in September 1944 to burn his Nazi Party uniform because "the Jew will take his blood revenge" if Germany were to surrender.[40] The widespread propagation of Soviet atrocities in the East Prussian village of Nemmersdorf, which had been conquered by the Red Army and then retaken by the *Wehrmacht* in October 1944, also produced unintended effects. According to the SD branch in Stuttgart, staged images of Soviet atrocities invoked memories of "how we murdered thousands of Jews" and have "shown the enemy what they can do to us if they win."[41] Defeatist and anti-Nazi attitudes were perfectly compatible with the fear of an expected Jewish revenge as well as the profoundly antisemitic concept of the Second World War as a "Jewish war." As the war drew to a close, Germans increasingly believed that Allied powers would use Nazi policy as a model in their treatment of a defeated Germany.

This was also the period when Germans began to see themselves as victims of allegedly Jewish revenge, or even as being in the same position as Jewish victims. The persecution of European Jews served as a repository of practices and images for ordinary Germans to imagine what might happen to them in the case of defeat. Germans imagined their enemies might make them wear a swastika on their clothes and parade them through streets with shaven heads.[42] Rumors spread that the US was forcing German–Americans in the US to wear the swastika, in analogy to the Jewish star.[43] Individual Germans now began to see themselves in the place of Jewish victims of Nazism. In a complete distortion of historical reality, Ernst Jünger, for example, noted in his diary in March 1945 that the "situation of the Germans now is exactly as the situation of the Jews inside Germany once had been."[44]

The "emotional community" based on fear as it emerged in 1944–5 was therefore not only directed against the Red Army. Germans also believed that a powerful

---

[38] Ibid. 699; Confino, *A World Without Jews*, 230–2, Nicholas Stargardt, "Rumors of Revenge in the Second World War," in Belinda Davis, Thomas Lindenberger, Michael Wildt, eds, *Alltag, Erfahrung, Eigensinn. Historisch-anthropologische Erkundungen* (Frankfurt a/M: Campus, 2008), 378. See also Confino, *A World Without Jews*, 230, Ian Kershaw, *The End. The Defiance and Destruction of Hitler's Germany, 1944–1945* (London, Allen Lane, 2011), 124, Stargardt, *The German War*, 375–6.

[39] Jäckel and Kulka, eds, *Die Juden in den geheimen NS-Stimmungsberichten*, 697.

[40] Ibid. 744. Also cited in Confino, *A World Without Jews*, 231, Kershaw, *The End*, 124, Stargardt, *The German War*.

[41] Jäckel and Kulka, eds, *Die Juden in den geheimen NS-Stimmungsberichten*, 749, cited in Stargardt, *The German War*, 472.

[42] Frank Bajohr, Dieter Pohl, *Der Holocaust als offenes Geheimnis. Die Deutschen, die NS-Führung und die Alliierten* (Munich: C.H.Beck, 2006), 70, Confino, *A World Without Jews*, 232.

[43] Stargardt, *The German War*, 236.

[44] Ernst Jünger, diary entry, March 28, 1945, cited in Hirschfeld and Renz, eds, *"Vormittags die ersten Amerikaner,"* 91–2.

Jewish enemy was about to take revenge for the systematic plunder, exploitation, deportation, and mass murder. Yet, precisely because the notion of a Jewish war ultimately came to exist independently or even in opposition to the Nazi regime, it survived the collapse of the Third Reich and gave rise to fears of Jewish retribution in the aftermath of defeat. In postwar interviews with researchers of the US Strategic Bombing Survey, German civilians of all ages described a causal nexus between the Allied bombing campaigns and the deportation and murder of the Jews. They justi-fied anti-Jewish policies by characterizing Jews as a wartime enemy, and expressed fears that Jewish Holocaust survivors would return to damage the postwar national community.[45] In August 1945, American intelligence in occupied Germany found that 37 per cent of Germans still believed that the extermination of the Jews had been necessary to guarantee German security.[46]

Popular expectations of violent Jewish retribution were also completely com-patible with broader European developments in the spring of 1945. Everywhere on the European continent, indigenous fascists and collaborators were subjected to spontaneous and often exceedingly violent acts of retribution.[47] Violent retri-bution was the norm rather the exception in the immediate postwar period. And even though Germany did not experience a civil war between fascist and antifas-cists, as occurred, for example, in Italy, the construction of Jews as "internal enemies"—both in official Nazi propaganda and in popular consciousness—informed postwar fears of a distinctly Jewish revenge in the aftermath of defeat.[48]

To be sure, actual acts of Jewish revenge were rare in postwar Germany. As Mark Roseman has argued, the very nature of the Holocaust as a bureaucratically organized genocide with diffused responsibility and often remote perpetrators made it difficult for victims to identify local and individual targets for possible revenge.[49] But acts of Jewish revenge did occur. The most well-known incident took place in Nuremberg in April 1946, when members of the Jewish resistance organization, *Nakam*, attempted to poison the water supply of several German cities and, when this plan failed, poisoned the bread supply of an SS internment camp in Nuremberg with arsenic. The plot ultimately failed because members of the *Hagana*, the Jewish paramilitary organization in Palestine, had thinned out the arsenic, reportedly because they did not want to jeopardize relationships with the American occupation forces who were supposed to assist with Jewish

---

[45] William I. Hitchcock, *The Bitter Road to Freedom. A New History of the Liberation of Europe* (New York, Free Press, 2008), 200.

[46] Stargardt, *The German War*, 564.

[47] Istvan Deák, Jan Gross, Tony Judt, eds, *Retribution. World War II and Its Aftermath* (Princeton: Princeton University Press, 2000).

[48] On Italy, see Claudio Pavone, *Una guerra civile. saggio storico sulla moralità nella Resistenza* (Turin: Bollati Bollinghieri, 1991).

[49] Roseman, "'No, Herr Führer!'"

emigration to Palestine. More than 200 German internees became ill but nobody died.[50] Members of the Jewish Brigade that had been formed as part of the British 8th Army in Italy also undertook unofficial excursions in Northern Italy, Austria, and Southern Germany, and arrested and executed individual Nazi perpetrators. British military command had stationed the unit in Northern Italy specifically to prevent acts of retribution. While no conclusive evidence exists, estimates put the number of victims between 100 and 300.[51] The novel *The Brigade* (1965) by the Israeli author and former brigade member, Hanoch Bartov, depicts its hero protecting the wife and daughter of an SS officer from rape by some of his comrades. Kurk, the main protagonist, remains deeply conflicted about his actions and is ultimately unable to accept the gratitude of the German women he saved. But the novel nevertheless concludes with Kurk's self-affirmation as different from Nazi perpetrators: "Thank God I did not destroy myself in Germany, thank God that was beyond me. I am what I am."[52] Aside from very few such open acts of revenge, it is possible that Jewish revenge also manifested itself in a more displaced manner for an extended period of time—for example, by boycotting German goods, refusing to accept German reparation funds, or extracting displaced revenge from Arabs in Palestine or Israel.[53] Germans fears of Jewish revenge far exceeded actual acts of retribution and were therefore primarily located in the realm of fantasy. Yet such fantasies of revenge were not less real than fears rooted in actual threats. They continued to shape German subjectivities in 1945 and strongly influenced Germans' outlook on the immediate future.

As the poem that opens this chapter suggests, ordinary Germans widely perceived American occupation forces as aligned with "Jewish interests." Because of this, according to US intelligence, Germans "hated" only the Russians more than the Americans.[54] They believed in particular that the Americans gave special privileges to Jewish DPs. The approximately eight million DPs in Germany in the spring of 1945 included only 20,000 Jewish people, all of them survivors of concentration camps. But the number grew while the overall DP population shrank through repatriation to their native countries. By early 1947, about 20 per cent of all DPs, 250,000 people, were Jewish. Most of them were Polish Jews who had fled the advancing German army and survived war and genocide behind the lines of the Red Army in the Soviet Union. They had migrated West after the war's conclu-

---

[50] Jim G. Tobias, Peter Zinke, *Nakam. Jüdische Rache an NS-Tätern* (Hamburg: Konkret Literatur Verlag, 2000), 23–56. See also *Neue Zeitung*, April 22, 1946 and ibid. April 26, 1946.

[51] Tobias and Zinke, *Nakam. Jüdische Rache an NS-Tätern*, 59–79. For isolated references to revenge acts by the members of the Jewish Brigade, see also Morris Beckman, *The Jewish Brigade. An Army with Two Masters 1944–5* (Rockville: Sarpedon, 1998), 98–9, 102.

[52] Hanoch Bartov, *The Brigade*, trans. David. S. Segal (New York: Holt, Rinehart, and Winston, 1968), 240–6. See also Roseman, "'No, Herr Führer!'"

[53] Berel Lang, "Holocaust Memory and Revenge: The Presence of the Past," *Jewish Social Studies* 2/2 (1996): 1–20.

[54] Stargardt, *The German War*, 563.

sion and fled to postwar Germany because of a wave of antisemitic pogroms in Poland.[55] By November 1946, 157,000 Jewish DPs resided in the American zone of occupation alone. Unlike other migrants from Eastern Europe, these Jewish infil-trees regularly received "refugee" status.[56] In August 1945, the report by Earl G. Harrisson, who served as envoy of the US government to investigate the situation of Holocaust survivors in Europe, requested higher caloric rations for Jewish survivors than other DPs and authorized US occupation officials to requisi-tion German homes for them.[57] Official food rations, in particular, assumed highly symbolic value, and Germans incessantly complained about allegedly preferential treatment for Jewish DPs. In reality, however, Germans had access to other food supplies besides official rations, mostly on the black market, and hence tended to consume more calories than Jewish DPs.[58] Still, historians have described the American occupation zone in postwar Germany as the most desirable place for Jewish survivors of the Holocaust in the immediate postwar period. Holocaust survivors became the "object of unprecedented philosemitism in the international area" during a "golden age" of Jewish DPs in postwar Germany.[59] Jewish survivors who experienced the period did not always concur. For example, Ruth Klüger, who had survived Auschwitz with her mother, described the first GI she met after her escape from a death march in April 1945 as indifferent, supporting her conclusion that "this war hadn't been fought for our sake."[60]

The facts of the case had little impact on Germans' perception of American officials' treatment of Jewish DPs. Germans perceived the special protection and privileges that Jewish survivors allegedly enjoyed as a clear threat to their own future. The world seemed upside down as previously reviled people enjoyed superior status under American occupation forces. Germans close to Jewish DP camps, such as in the Wolfratshausen district near the Föhrenwalde DP camp, most frequently made these accusations. A more self-confident, optimistic demeanor of former Nazi victims now appeared threatening to many Germans. "Many foreigners walk around in the city grinning. Who knows how they will behave now?" Edeltraut G. wrote in her diary in April 1945. Former Nazi victims' self-confident assertion in public stood in stark contrast to the (self-)intimidation of ordinary Germans who felt pressured to downplay their national identification.

---

[55] Grossmann, *Jews, Germans, and Allies*, 132, Wolfgang Jacobmeyer, *Vom Zwangsarbeiter zum heimatlosen Ausländer. Die Displaced Persons in Westdeutschland, 1945–51* (Göttingen: Vandenhoeck, 1985), 59–84.
[56] Gerard Daniel Cohen, *In War's Wake. Europe's Displaced Persons in the Postwar Order* (New York: Oxford University Press, 2012), 37, 126–49.
[57] Grossmann, *Jews, Germans, and Allies*, 137–42, Cohen, *In War's Wake*, 134–7.
[58] Atina Grossmann, "Grams, Calories, and Food. Languages of Victimization, Entitlement, and Human Rights in Occupied Germany, 1945–1949," *Central European History* 44/1 (2011): 118–48.
[59] Quotations from Grossmann, *Jews, Germans, and Allies*, 237, Cohen, *In War's Wake*, 137.
[60] Ruth Kluger, *Still Alive. A Holocaust Girlhood Remembered* (New York: The Feminist Press, 2001), 149.

"We are no longer Germans or at least must now show it," the same person added in her diary only one day after the previous entry.[61] Just as gestures such as the Hitler salute became an important mechanism to assert the formation of the people's community during the Nazi period, gestures and demeanor in daily life signaled to ordinary Germans a complete reversal of the social and racial order of the Third Reich.

In the German postwar imagination, this world turned upside down also contained a direct threat to personal security. American intelligence reports recorded massive German fears of Jewish acts of violent retribution. Rumors emerged especially as the seventh anniversary of the 1938 pogrom approached, which continued to assume a prominent place in the German imagination. In November 1945, American intelligence officers reported from Augsburg that "the main event of the week was the widespread rumor that 9 Nov[ember], the anniversary of the 'Beer Hall Putsch' would be marked by looting by the DPs and Jews." Intelligence in the Friedberg district further north in Hesse stated that a "strong rumor" was "going about that on Nov[ember] 8 or 9 all foreigners would have the right to loot and pillage without fear or harm." American occupation officials considered the rumors important enough that they posted notices to deny them and arrested a man in connection with them. According to another intelligence officer, this rumor was so strong that even "persons who usually pay no attention to rumor began to believe it."[62] While at least one intelligence officer believed German fears of violence centered on the failed Hitler putsch of 1923, it seems far more likely that it centered on the November 1938 pogrom. Acts of highly visible physical violence against Jews, as during the November 1938 pogrom, exerted a stronger and more lasting impact of German feelings of guilt—and hence also on fears of revenge—than the much more effective and eventually more deadly process of legal discrimination and bureaucratic persecution.

Other rumors in the US zone offered variations on the theme of an alliance between American occupation officials and Jewish DPs at the expense of ordinary Germans. In November 1945, American officials in Wertingen and elsewhere recorded the rumors that DPs will be granted a "three-day looting privilege" in response to a fake attack by DPs disguised as Germans on American soldiers.[63] Here, the stereotypical notion of Jewish DP duplicity combined with the assumption

---

[61] Diary of Edeltraut G., entries of April 13 and 14, 1945, DTA, Nr. 185, I, 1.

[62] Intelligence annex to weekly report for period November 8–15, 1945, NA, RG 260, 899 (A1), 390/47/19/1, Box 168. See also Adam R. Seipp, *Strangers in the Wild Place. Refugees, Americans, and a German Town, 1945–1952* (Bloomington: Indiana University Press, 2013), 105.

[63] L.K. Wertingen, Intelligence annex to weekly report for period November 8–15, 1945, NA, RG 260, 899 (A1), 390/47/19/1, Box 168. Similarly, 14–16 Pfarrei Griebing, Franz Ebert, Report July 31, 1945; 23–11, Pfarrei Penning, September 11, 1945 in Peter Pfister, ed., *Das Ende des Zweiten Weltkrieges im Erzbistum München und Freising. Die Kriegs- und Einmarschberichte im Archiv des Erzbistums München und Freising* (Regensburg: Schell und Steiner, 2005), 518, 785.

of an alliance between DPs and American occupation authorities in order to victimize Germans. Another report demonstrated just how fickle ordinary Germans were regarding any kind of Jewish survivors' public visibility. A parade by occupants of the DP camp Föhrenwalde on November 29, 1945, in celebration of the Jewish holiday of Tu BiShvat, which was completely orderly and created no disturbances, nevertheless became the occasion for grave concern: "The people in this neighborhood, as presumably everywhere," the report concluded, "live in some anxiety about the Displaced Persons. They are ready to believe every rumor that on such and such a time the Displaced Persons will loot."[64] In some cases, rumors also turned into actual violence between Jewish DPs and German civilians. This happened in Landsberg in April 1946. According to an American public safety officer, unfounded rumors that Germans had kidnapped two Jewish DPs led a small group of DPs to leave the camp and assault German civilians. When US soldiers sought to arrest these DPs, a riot broke out. Hundreds of DPs reportedly attacked US soldiers and several thousand "indiscriminately assaulted German civilians on the street." The report documents 18 Germans with "stab wounds, lacerations and bleeding." A curfew and deployment of more US troops restored order.[65] This incident, however, seems to be the rare exception of open violence between Jewish DPs and non-Jewish Germans.

The persistence of traditional antisemitic tropes such as ritual murder accusations fueled fears of Jewish retribution. In one 1949 case, the discovery of the body parts of a child gave rise to ritual murder speculations. Another case emerged when the two-year-old child of the servant girl Anna M. had disappeared. Rumors stated she had been sold to Jews for religious purposes—most likely ritual sacrifice.[66]

In another sign of the persistence of antisemitism, a woman who had hidden her Jewish background for the duration of the Nazi period was the victim of insults and stones were thrown at her house in Marktheidenfeld, after American occupation authorities awarded her privileged treatment as victim of racial persecution.[67] Streetcars also appeared to have been primary sites of antisemitic transgressions. In one case, a conductor forced a Jewish mother and her four-year-old child off a streetcar, denouncing them as members of a "Jewish gang, Polish gang."

---

[64] L.K. Wolfratshausen, Weekly intelligence report No. 1 for week ending December 6, 1945, Intelligence annex to weekly report for period November 8–15, 1945, NA, RG 260, 899 (A1), 390/47/19/1, Box 168.

[65] Colonel Wilson, Public Safety, April 29, 1946, NA, RG 260 (A1), 390/42/27–28/7, Box 275.

[66] Oberstaatsanwalt Kempten to Herr Generalstaatsanwalt in Munich, May 30, 1949, Anklageschrift, Amtsgericht Kaufbeuren, Oberstaatsanwalt I to Bayrische Ministerium der Justiz, November 30, 1948; BHStA, Stk 13888. Both cases were brought to the attention of the state prosecutor as potential cases of "incitement to racial hatred" (*Rassenwahn und Völkerhass*). Yet in both cases the Bavarian *Ministerpräsident*, who needed to approve all legal prosecutions under this law, decided against pressing formal charges in order not to give credence to "stupid chatter"; see Hans Erhard, Ministerpräsident to Bayrisches Staatsministerium der Justiz, January 21, 1949, BHStA, Stk 13888.

[67] Indictment, Amtsgericht Würzburg, Georg K., Konrad H., March 4, 1949, BHStA, Stk 13888.

Figure 1.1. Demonstration of Jewish displaced persons in Frankfurt am Main, 1945.
Postwar Germans perceived the public presence of Holocaust survivors as a threat.
They feared "Jewish revenge" based on the antisemitic notion that the Second World War was waged in the interest and on behalf of "Jewish interests."
Source: bpk-Bildagentur, No. 30050504.

Another streetcar conductor put a Jewish woman who had identified herself as an Auschwitz survivor off a streetcar with the remark that "it was too bad that she had not been turned into soap."[68] The number of such reported incidents was small, however, and, out of 56 investigations for the crime of "incitement to racial hatred," only two led to a conviction.[69] But they nevertheless point to antisemitic sentiments that could be activated very quickly. In postwar opinion surveys, approximately a third of the German population acknowledged subscribing to antisemitic notions. Rather than constituting a mere continuation of Nazi ideology, these attitudes amounted to "secondary antisemitism" in the wake of defeat and occupation.[70]

[68] See Oberstaatsanwalt München to Bayrisches Staatsministerium der Justiz, June 24, 1948; Oberstaatsanwalt München to Bayrisches Staatsministerium der Justiz, July 6, 1948; Oberstaatsanwalt München to Bayrisches Staatsministerium der Justiz, December 24, 1947; all in BHStA, Stk 13888. On the issue of housing requisitions, see below.

[69] Bayrisches Staatsministerium der Justiz to Bayrischen Ministerpräsidenten, Betr. Strafverfahren wegen Verbrechens gegen das Gesetz Nr. 14 gegen Rassenwahn und Völkerhass, June 17, 1949, BHStA, Stk 13888.

[70] See Werner Bergmann, Rainer Erb, *Anti-Semitism in Germany. The Post-Nazi Epoch since 1945*, trans. Belinda Cooper, Allison Brown (New Brunswick and London: Transaction Publishers, 1997), 1–24.

Figure 1.2. Displaced persons, 1945.

Postwar Germans perceived the confident and optimistic demeanor of former Nazi victims as threatening and contrasted it with external pressures to downplay their own Germanness.

Source: bpk-Bildagentur, No. 30050648.

Violence and Displaced Persons

German fears of retribution were not limited to specifically Jewish retaliation. The far larger group of eight million displaced persons who resided in the territory of postwar Germany in 1945 and who were not Jewish stoked at least as much fear. DPs were extremely heterogeneous and represented a wide variety of wartime experiences. Approximately six million civilian workers from Eastern and Western Europe and two million POWs who worked in German industry and agriculture during the war comprised the eight million in Germany just after the war. The Nazi regime had treated civilian workers from Western countries as basically equal to German workers, but workers and POWs from Eastern Europe had suffered greatly. Largely Polish, and from 1941 onward, Russian, they experienced abominable conditions. As a symbol of their racial inferiority, the regime punished these workers with death if they engaged in sexual relations with Germans.[71]

---

[71] The best treatment of foreign workers in Nazi Germany is Ulrich Herbert, *Hitler's Foreign Workers. Enforced Foreign Labor in Germany Under the Third Reich*, trans. William Templer (New York: Cambridge University Press, 1985). Figures according to table in ibid. 298. Employment of civilian workers peaked in August 1944. Figures are estimates at best. I am following here the figures in

Beyond Nazi victims, this group of DPs also entailed an unknown number of Eastern Europeans who had been conscripts or volunteers for the *Wehrmacht*. They refused to be repatriated to their country of origin because they feared retribution for their service.

Under the auspices of the United Nations' Relief and Rehabilitation Administration (UNRRA), 33,000 DPs were repatriated from Germany per day between spring and fall of 1945. The largest share were Soviet citizens, compelled to return home by the Yalta agreement and the ensuing accords between the occupation authorities.[72] By September 1945, only 1.2 million DPs remained on the territory of postwar Germany. About half these were Poles residing in the British zone of occupation, and another quarter were Poles who were in the American zone of occupation. The category of "Polish DPs" eventually declined, in part because some of them were reclassified as Ukrainians who had lived under Polish rule in 1939 or who had held Soviet citizenship at the outbreak of the war. This group accounted for 100,000–150,000 DPs in March 1946.[73] The largest group of the remaining DPs were from the Baltic states. The "other" category consisted of 41,000 who were probably disguised Soviet citizens who sought to avoid repatriation.[74]

Many DPs had been deported to Germany against their will during the war as forced workers in industry and agriculture. Fears of an uprising or violent revenge in the case of German defeat were prevalent in the final stages of the war. Extensive rumors anticipated, for example, an uprising of foreign workers that would coincide with the Allied landing in Normandy in June 1944.[75] During the last stages of the war, forced laborers—similar to the inmates of concentration camps from the East on the "death marches"—were often targeted with excessive violence, occasionally also with broad popular participation.[76] Nazi propaganda sought to instrumentalize rumors of an impending uprising by foreign workers, but no open rebellions of foreign workers occurred under the Third Reich. In fact, Allied propaganda discouraged an uprising and advised workers to disrupt German wartime production by fleeing to the countryside rather than engaging in open resistance. What Nazi officials termed "plundering" of "gangs" of escaped or bombed-out foreign workers likely referred to attempts to survive the escalating violence during the final stages of the Third Reich.[77] Still, fears of violent

Jacobmeyer, *Vom Zwangsarbeiter zum heimatlosen Ausländer*, 82–4, Anna Holian, *Between National Socialism and Soviet Communism. Displaced Persons in Postwar Germany* (Ann Arbor: University of Michigan Press, 2011), 3. On displaced persons in postwar Germany in general, see also Laura Hilton, "Prisoners of Peace: Rebuilding Community, Identity, and Nationality in Displaced Persons Camps in Germany, 1945–52" (Dissertation, Ohio State University, 2001).

[72] Jacobmeyer, *Vom Zwangsarbeiter zum heimatlosen Ausländer*, 59–84.
[73] Cohen, *In War's Wake*, 5–6.
[74] Holian, *Between National Socialism and Soviet Communism*, 3.
[75] Herbert, *Hitler's Foreign Workers*, 355–9. By referring to an "anxiety psychosis" among Germans fearing an uprising of foreign workers, Herbert reveals historians' tendency to pathologize emotions.
[76] Stargardt, *The German War*, 517–18.
[77] Herbert, *Hitler's Foreign Workers*, 364–81.

revenge by foreign workers constituted an important element in German scenarios of the future in the aftermath of defeat.[78]

Stoking fears of disorder, many former forced workers marked the moment of liberation with carnivalesque celebrations revolving around alcohol, sex, and food.[79] According to a report of the local press in Nuremberg, in May 1945, former Russian POWs and slave workers marched through the city drunken and with a "hostile and aggressive" attitude. They entered the Nuremberg zoo and killed "heartless and without mercy . . . defenseless and frightened animals." They killed deer, strangled a bear, even killed a lion and decapitated an ostrich. Some of the DPs appeared to have worked in the Nuremberg zoo during the war as forced laborers, so they may have been motivated by revenge as well as the search for food. The Nuremberg press reported that US military police did not prevent the massacre of the animals. Instead, individual soldiers witnessed the "bloody orgy" with "laughter" and a "broad grinning."[80] The symbolic significance of the incident was obvious: like the animals in the Nuremberg zoo, frightened Nuremberg citizens faced potential violence and thirst for revenge on the part of former forced laborers while not being able to count on protection by US occupation forces.[81] One Nuremberg citizen reportedly lamented the "299 creatures that had been slaughtered by these barbarians" at the zoo while a Jewish survivor commented that he should be "happy that they did not let out their hatred on him."[82]

Violence by former Eastern European workers, however, was not purely imagined or, as in the case of the Nuremberg zoo, symbolic. Constant and repeated complaints about marauding "foreigners," usually labeled as "Poles," "Russians," or "Ukrainians," sometimes also "KZlers" (concentration camp inmates), riddle reports by German officials from the American occupation zone for 1945–6 as well as individual testimonies.[83] The *Regierungspräsident* from Ansbach reported "nightly robberies" in the counties of Coburg and Hof by "gangs of Poles" who shot the unarmed and unresisting population with machine guns. "Murder, physical injuries, torture and rape of the inhabitants of the targeted farms constantly accompany these episodes of plunder," as the report from Ansbach stated.[84] In October 1945, 30 Poles broke into the

[78] For interesting parallels to the fears of Southern slaveholders of a slave rebellion at the end of the American Civil War, see Hahn, "Slave Rebellion."

[79] Lowe, *Savage Continent*, 97.

[80] Tobias and Zinke, *Nakam, Jüdische Rache an NS-Tätern*, 19. The story is based on Erhard Mossack, *Die letzten Tage von Nürnberg: Nach einem Tatsachenbericht aus einem 8-Uhr Blatt* (Nuremberg: Noris Verlag, 1952), 130–4.

[81] Compare the parallels in Robert Darnton, *The Great Cat Massacre and Other Episodes in French Cultural History* (New York: Basic Books, 2009 [1985]).

[82] Tobias and Zinke, *Nakam. Jüdische Rache an NS-Tätern*, 19. Mossack, *Die letzten Tage von Nürnberg*.

[83] Examples: Halbmonatsbericht des Regierungspräsidenten in Würzburg für die Zeit vom 16–30.9.1945, MSo73, BHStA; Halbmonatsbericht des Regierungspräsidenten in September 1945, 2. Hälfte, BHStA, MSo73. For the British zone, see Lowe, *Savage Continent*, 97–101. See also Pfister, ed., *Ende des Zweiten Weltkrieges*.

[84] Regierungspräsident Ansbach, Oktober 2, 1945, BHStA, MSo78.

home of Theodor E. in Heimbuchtal, murdered him and his war-disabled son, committed violence against his daughter and a farm laborer, and robbed the house.[85] Some Germans reported that they were relieved if incidents of theft and robbery did not include rape.[86] These occurrences did not remain limited to the immediate aftermath of the war but extended into the postwar period. In the Schongau district, "Polish gangs" committed five murders and one attempted murder within two weeks in November 1946. The gangs reportedly demanded the victims' bicycles and then executed them with a shot in the neck. The population reacted to these murders with "great embitterment" and "paralyzing fear."[87] Inhabitants of remote farms were particularly at risk of becoming a target of such attack and thus reported as being in particular fear.[88]

Ordinary Germans felt especially helpless toward these acts of violence because German police was initially prohibited from carrying any weapons. As Adam Seipp has shown, the "weaponless policemen" significantly diminished confidence in the city government among residents of Wildflecken, the site of a DP camp housing about 20,000 Polish DPs.[89] German police were also prohibited from entering DP camps, a prohibition that was reaffirmed especially for Jewish DPs after German police killed the Jewish Auschwitz survivor Szmul Dancyger, who had been reunited with his family only the night before, during a raid on a DP camp in Stuttgart in March 1946.[90] While German police gradually gained jurisdiction over DPs outside the camps, during the immediate postwar period, ordinary Germans depended on US military police for basic security. They were suspicious of the loyalties of American occupiers: a local official expressed serious doubts about the American military government's willingness to maintain law and order, and asserted that there had been "more law and order under the Nazi system."[91] Catholic priests in Bavaria alleged that Polish–American soldiers had tolerated or even participated in looting by former Polish slave workers.[92] Some

---

[85] Halbmonatsbericht des Regierungspräsidenten in Würzburg, 1–15. Oktober 1945, BHStA, MSo81.

[86] Zusammenfassung und Auszüge der Monatsberichte der Landwirtschaftsstellen und Außenstellen für den Monat Oktober 1945, BHStA, MSo70.

[87] Landrat des Kreises Schongau to Regierung von Oberbayern, November 18, 1946, BHStA, Stk 13608.

[88] Halbmonatsbericht des Regierungspräsidenten in Würzburg für die Zeit vom 16–31.10.1945 BHStA, MSo81, Halbmonatsbericht des Regierungspräsidenten in München, September 1945, 2. Hälfte, BHStA, MSo73.

[89] Halbmonatsbericht Würzburg, 1–15.10, BHStA, MSo81. On Wildflecken in general, see the local study by Seipp, *Strangers in the Wild Place*.

[90] Grossmann, *Jews, Germans, and Allies*, 176, Julia Schulze Wessel, "Zur Reformulierung des Antisemitismus in der deutschen Nachkriegsgesellschaft. Eine Analyse deutscher Polizeiakten aus der Zeit von 1945 bis 1948," in Susanne Dietrich, Julia Schulze Wessel, eds, *Zwischen Selbstorganisation und Stigmatisierung. Die Lebenswirklichkeit jüdischer Displaced Persons und die neue Gestalt des Antisemitismus in der deutschen Nachkriegsgesellschaft* (Stuttgart: Klett-Cotta, 1998), 193.

[91] Halbmonatsbericht des Regierungspräsidenten in München, Monat August 1945, 2. Hälfte, BHStA, MSo73.

[92] 17–1 Pfarrei Aufkirchen a.d. Maischach, Pfarrer Georg Graf, September 10, 1945, in Pfister, ed., *Ende des Zweiten Weltkrieges*, 594.

German citizens demanded permission to organize neighborhood watches with bells and sirens to sound the alarm in the case of danger.[93] A resident of Schongau warned that the population might begin to "stab or beat to death any Pole who is lingering at night or is otherwise suspicious."[94] German officials demanded a virtual re-establishment of the concentration camp system for DPs: "If the foreigners cannot be deported, one would have to demand at least their complete disarmament, their concentration in strictly guarded camps as well as, if the opportunity for work exists, compulsion to work."[95] Otherwise, German officials agreed that DPs would continue to terrorize ordinary Germans so long as they remained in the country. The disappearance of the DP camps increasingly appeared as a panacea for solving a multitude of problems in postwar society.[96]

A variety of factors drove DP violence against ordinary Germans. In many cases, escaped or bombed-out slave workers committed lootings and robberies simply to survive. They mostly stole food and were only violent toward those Germans who refused them.[97] Yet, in other cases, former slave laborers sought revenge. They were in a better position than Holocaust victims because they had local knowledge and often knew the identity of their tormenters. In Pullach, a former employee of the electric power station on the Isar was reportedly killed by "his slave workers" because he had "treated them badly."[98] Former superiors of DPs—"master foremen, camp commanders or plant security guards"—also frequently became targets of acts of DP violence.[99] A woman noted in November 1945 that, as part of a series of "horrific murders, attacks and robberies", "the Poles" had shot one farmer and were threatening to kill another unless he paid "back pay" for their five years of slave labor. "The fear is tremendous," she added, and "even though our policeman finally eventually [apprehended] a gang [of violent DPs]," the "gangs gain the upper hand because their numbers keep increasing."[100] In this and many other cases, former foreign workers targeted those individuals who had mistreated and tortured them during the war. DPs took less direct

---

[93] Monatsbericht des Regierungspräsidenten in München, Monat Juli 1–15, 1945, BHStA, MSo73.

[94] Landrat des Kreises Schongau to Regierung von Oberbayern, November 18, 1946, BHStA, Stk 13608.

[95] Halbmonatsbericht des Regierungspräsidenten in München, September 1945, 2. Hälfte, BHStA, MSo73.

[96] Seipp, *Strangers in the Wild Place*.

[97] 26–11, Pfarrei Priel, Georg Bachmeier, July 28, 1945; 27–13, Pfarrei Oberneukirchen, Michael Eglseer, July 25, 1945; Pfister, ed., *Ende des Zweiten Weltkrieges*, 853, 899. See also Halbmonatsbericht des Regierungspräsidenten in Würzburg, October 1–15, 1945, BHStA, MSo81.

[98] 5–14, Pfarrei Pullach, Pfarrvikar Karl Wagner, n.D. 4–11; for similar examples, see also Pfarrei München, St. Peter und Paul/Feldmoching, November 20, 1945, 38–10 Expositur Roßbach, Vikar P. August Bögle, July 29, 1945, all in Pfister, ed., *Ende des Zweiten Weltkrieges*, 285–6, 318, 1256. See also 43–5 Expositur Deggendorf, Ludwig Bettzinger, July 20, 1945, according to which a lawyer was killed by former concentration camp inmates on the instigation of a French POW who had formerly been employed by him, ibid. 1437–8.

[99] Herbert, *Hitler's Foreign Workers*, 378.

[100] Else P., Tagebuch in Briefform an Mann, Heiligenrode, November 2, 1945, DTA, 2683/1.

revenge as well. Reporting a robbery and plundering by 10 to 15 people of a farm in Mehring in the Altötttingen district, a German official cited a frequent justification, "especially by Poles," that the "German SS has done the same thing."[101] Some German observers conceded that Germans had "behaved badly in enemy land." They were therefore quite capable of making the connection between DP violence and the German war of annihilation. But they resented the fact that "innocents" now became the targets of former Nazi victims.[102] Regardless of their impression of the justification of former slave workers, violence created an individual feeling of fear and powerlessness.

Personal experiences of insecurity and violence extended far into the postwar period, at least until early 1947.[103] These were foundational experiences in that many Germans associated them with the onset of the postwar period and the transition from National Socialism to democracy. The historiography has focused on the Red Army's brutal treatment of German civilians in the Soviet zone of occupation, but experiences of uncertainty and violence affected the Western zones as well.[104] To be sure, panicked Germans clearly exaggerated the extent of actual DP violence, stoked by persistent stereotypes of Eastern Europeans as "criminals."[105] As Wolfgang Jacobmeyer has demonstrated, DP criminality remained equal or slightly below general German crime rates in the immediate postwar period and was only slightly higher than German crime rates by 1947.[106] US occupation authorities in Hesse attributed less than 3 per cent of all crimes committed between September and November 1946 to DPs.[107] Various forces would have inflated reports of DP violence in German sources. There is some evidence that German farmers occasionally also invented alleged DP robberies in order to conceal the selling of their livestock on the black market.[108] Police reports also consistently inflated DP criminality in order to lobby the occupation authorities for the expansion and re-arming of German security forces. Germans blamed DPs for their own sense of helplessness and constructed DPs as the "active

---

[101] Halbmonatsbericht des Regierungspräsidenten in München, September 1945, 2. Hälfte, MSo73, BHStA. Similar example in 38–9, Pfarrei Ranolsberg, Pfarrer Josef Jell, October 8, 1945, Pfister, ed., *Ende des Zweiten Weltkrieges*, 1253.

[102] Expositur Alling, Expositus Albert Michel, August 20, 1945, ibid. 669.

[103] According to Seipp, the apex of displaced persons' banditry occurred in the winter of 1946–7; see Seipp, *Strangers in the Wild Place*, 82.

[104] Even Richard Bessel's otherwise excellent study of the year "1945," which makes central the unprecedented experience of violence as a starting point of the postwar period, only devotes less than a page to the threat and reality of DP violence against ordinary Germans in 1945–6; see Bessel, *Germany 1945*, 165–6. See also Jacobmeyer, *Vom Zwangsarbeiter zum heimatlosen Ausländer*, 205. For another treatment of DP violence as merely episodic, see Hitchcock, *Bitter Road to Freedom*, 194.

[105] Michael Berkowitz, *The Crime of My Very Existence. Nazism and the Myth of Jewish Criminality* (Berkeley: University of California Press, 2007).

[106] Jacobmeyer, *Vom Zwangsarbeiter zum heimatlosen Ausländer*, 212–14.

[107] Hilton, "Prisoners of Peace," 259.

[108] Seipp, *Strangers in the Wild Place*, 152.

aggressive, and criminal counterpart of German society."[109] DPs themselves, such as an "action group" of DPs in Fürstenfeldbruck, protested against the press campaign that portrayed them as "criminals" and "fascists."[110] Indeed, it is important to emphasize that the overwhelming majority of DPs never resorted to violence. Some Polish Catholic priests among Polish DPs worked actively to prevent violence, sometimes working in cooperation with local German priests.[111] In fact, just as in the case of Jewish Holocaust survivors, many contemporary observers noted the absence of any desire for revenge among DPs.[112]

Still, German sources identified DPs as contributing disproportionately to *violent* crime in the postwar period.[113] According to a statistic for the year 1946 in Bavaria, "foreigners" had committed about 55 per cent of murders, 42 per cent of attempted murders, 31 per cent of "street robberies," and 61 per cent of "robberies and blackmailings," even though they comprised only about 4 per cent of the general population.[114] These figures have to be used with appropriate caution. The documentation does not reveal how officials determined that perpetrators were "foreigners." Under the chaotic conditions of the immediate postwar period, it was often difficult to ascertain the identity of the perpetrators, who often engaged in elaborate attempts at disguise and mimicry. For example, perpetrators may have disguised themselves as foreigners, aware that such disguise would intimidate their victims. In the small enclave of unoccupied territory in southeastern Germany, looting was actually committed by a gang of former SS men, who sometimes disguised themselves as DPs.[115] Those who could steal American uniforms managed to act with impunity.[116] Soviet soldiers reportedly engaged in violent transgressions such as plunder and robbery near the border in the Western zone.[117] And Germans of course also participated in many instances of looting.[118] Multiple possible perpetrators—DPs, Germans, former SS men, Russians, even US soldiers—who acted largely with impunity and could not be contained by

---

[109] Dietrich and Wessel, "Zur Reformulierung des Antisemitismus in der deutschen Nachkriegsgesellschaft," 141–224, Gerhard Fürmetz, "Betrifft: Sicherheitszustand—Kriminalitätswahrnehmung und Stimmungsanalysen in den Monatsberichten der bayrischen Landespolizei nach 1945," 1999. *Zeitschrift für Sozialgeschichte des 20. und 21. Jahrhunderts* 12/3 (1997): 39–54.

[110] *Neue Zeitung*, "Die Verschleppten," January 28, 1946.

[111] 3–5 Pfarrei Ismaning, August 2, 1945; 37–15 Pfarrei Traunstein-St. Oswald, July 20, 1945; Pfister, ed., *Ende des Zweiten Weltkrieges*, 233, 1231.

[112] Hilton, "Prisoners of Peace," 259.   [113] Seipp, *Strangers in the Wild Place*, 78–85.

[114] Zentralamt für Kriminal-Identifizierung, Polizeistatistik und Polizeinachrichtenwesen, "Die Kriminalität Bayerns im Jahre 1946," January 23, 1947, BHStA, Stk 13608.

[115] Gareth Pritchard, *Niemandsland. A History of Unoccupied Germany, 1944–45* (New York: Cambridge University Press, 2012), 116.

[116] For DPs and Germans committing crimes in American uniforms, see the report in Monatsbericht des Regierungspräsidenten in München, Monat Juli 1–15, 1945, BHStA, MSo73. Partly for this reason, American occupation authorities eventually prohibited, by spring 1946, the unauthorized wearing of American uniforms; see Jacobmeyer, *Vom Zwangsarbeiter zum heimatlosen Ausländer*, 48–50.

[117] Regierungspräsident Ansbach, October 2, 1945, BHStA, MSo78.

[118] 4–4 Kuratie München St. Christoph, Vikar Johann Baptist Wimbauer, August 17, 1945; Pfister, ed., *Ende des Zweiten Weltkrieges*, 266–7.

German police thus further aggravated the widespread sense of insecurity and confusion that marked the immediate postwar period.

Apart from any individual German's experience of DP violence in the postwar period, acts of DP violence assumed a disproportionate *symbolic* significance. Stories of DP violence tended to confirm and intensify pre-existing expectations of the consequences of defeat. And, fears of retribution from DPs were at least partly grounded in actual events. While the German imagination of DP violence exceeded by far its actual reality, these occurrences lent at least some credibility to postwar fears of retribution. Rumors of widespread DP violence were contagious and fears of retribution thus also affected those individuals who were never directly affected by it. Pre-existing and lingering racist stereotypes about "Poles" and "Russians," as well as widespread knowledge of actual Nazi atrocities, fueled popular fears of retribution. As such, the threat and imagination of DP violence intensified the general climate of uncertainty and insecurity of the immediate postwar period. Whereas hindsight might describe the period as a time of "liberation" from the repressive Nazi regime, many Germans perceived a virtual collapse of public order and felt a profound threat to their personal security. In other words, they experienced the collapse of Nazi Germany as a defeat. "We have never had such conditions in Bavaria as we are experiencing now, not even during the war," one official reported.[119] One hope, therefore, that Germans associated with the arrival of the occupation authorities, especially in the Western zones, was the restoration of order and a new sense of personal security. Yet many were shocked when they realized that, far from mitigating these anxieties, postwar occupation confronted them with new threats and challenges.

The Shock of Occupation

For the first time since the Napoleonic wars in the early nineteenth century, Germans experienced the complete occupation of their homeland by foreign powers in 1945. The fate of "Germany" as a collective, and hence of individual Germans, now rested almost completely with the Allied victors. Postwar Germans lacked the coveted "self-determination" that had served as an ideological pretext for Nazi expansionism and assumed new global significance with the onset of decolonization in 1945. Time and again, German testimonies from the spring of 1945 invoked the specter of "slavery." Lore N. from Saxony, for example, wrote to her friend Fritz E. in Silesia in March 1945 that she did not have a clear picture of the future but that she knew "one thing, that I don't want to work as slave for another

---

[119] Halbmonatsbericht des Regierungspräsidenten in München, September 1945, 2. Hälfte, BHStA, MSo73.

people, then we would have no joy in life whatsoever."[120] And in July 1945, the 16-year-old Thea D. noted in her diary that "Primitive people now want to educate and lecture to us and turn us into their slaves."[121] For many Germans, foreign occupation thus constituted an unprecedented "leap in the dark."[122]

The most intense popular apprehensions about postwar occupation centered on the Red Army. Nazi propaganda had deliberately amplified popular fears of a Soviet victory, and these fears had in large part held German society together in the last few months of the war. Panic about Soviet revenge is palpable in countless letters and diaries from the last months of the war and the early postwar period. These documents also reveal a thoroughly racist imagination mixed with these fears, many of them anticipating sexual violence.[123] Commenting on the entry of the Red Army into Leipzig, Thea D. (born in 1928), for example, described the "animal-like faces of the Asiatics" who represented to her "uncultivated humanity."[124] German soldiers and civilians alike made desperate efforts to reach British and American lines in order to escape the Red Army.[125] Thus some Germans articulated great relief, even joy and happiness, to be under American rather than Soviet occupation.[126] "They are here," one woman from Heidelberg noted in her diary in March 1945 of American troops, "now we no longer need to be afraid. Our thoughts can fly into the sky of fantasy and dreams without being bound by the greyness of daily life and the protective measure against the threat of death everywhere. We can breathe again." A few days later, she added that "the Americans are very polite and friendly."[127] Defeat and occupation also brought an end to the terroristic violence of the Nazi regime that had been increasingly directed at Germans as well. For opponents of Nazism, American occupation indeed equaled liberation. One woman whose husband had spent time in a concentration camp noted in April 1945, "I would have never thought that I would welcome foreigners as 'liberators.'"[128]

[120] Lore N. to Fritz E., March 18, 1945, cited in Hirschfeld and Renz, eds, "*Vormittags die ersten Amerikaner*," 74.

[121] Diary of Thea D., July 5, 1945, DTA, Nr. 389, 1.

[122] Michael Geyer, "Die eingebildete Heimkehr. Im Schatten der Niederlage," in Daniel Fulda, Dagmar Herzog, Stefan-Ludwig Hoffmann, Till van Rahden, eds, *Demokratie im Schatten der Gewalt. Geschichten des Privaten im deutschen Nachkrieg* (Göttingen: Wallstein Verlag, 2010), 86.

[123] For the range of popular confrontations with the issue of rape, see Norman M. Naimark, *The Russians in Germany. A History of the Soviet Zone of Occupation, 1945–1949* (Cambridge, Mass.: Harvard University Press, 1997), 69–140, Atina Grossmann, "A Question of Silence: The Rape of German Women by Occupation Soldiers," *October* 72 (1995): 43–63.

[124] Diary of Thea D., July 5, 1945, KA, Nr. 389, 1.

[125] Klaus-Dietmar Henke, *Die amerikanische Besetzung Deutschlands* (Munich: Oldenbourg, 1995), 674–95.

[126] Kershaw, *The End*, 121, 224.

[127] Evamaria K.-M., Diary 27.3.1945–29.4.1945, March 30, 1945, KA, Nr. 3237. On the absence of fear of American occupation troops, see Henke, *Die amerikanische Besetzung*, 86–7, Kershaw, *The End*, 121, 224.

[128] Diary of Margaret B. Heilers, entry of April 20, 1945, cited in Hirschfeld and Renz, eds, "*Vormittags die ersten Amerikaner*," 141.

Popular fears of the Red Army and the corresponding hopes associated with the arrival of the Americans, however, did not mean that Western occupation did not prompt any sense of apprehension or fear whatsoever. Rumors and news of Soviet atrocities in Eastern Germany enhanced existing concerns about Allied retribution in general. On May 6, 1945, the 20-year-old Renate P. noted in her diary that:

> our darkest fears have become reality over the last few days. Germany has experienced the most dishonorable and miserable defeat in centuries and has been completely defeated and thrown to the ground by the three powerful enemy powers Russia, America, and England—Germany is occupied, eradicated, it is and will be looked down upon in the whole world, the country and its people will be shunned and despised.[129]

Along similar lines, "Ferdl" from Vienna speculated in a letter to his wife in April 1945 that "neither the Russian nor the American nor the English will have mercy with us. They will conquer us and divide up the spoils."[130] Just as in the East, ordinary Germans in the West entered a zone of massive uncertainty, in which their personal futures were inextricably intertwined with the intentions and policies of the Allied victors. And most Germans expected the American occupation to last for a very long period of time. In September 1946, 37 per cent of Germans in the US zone expected the occupation to last 10 or more years, 22 per cent estimated 20 to 30 years, and 20 per cent expected an occupation of even 50 years or more. The numbers for Berlin were even higher.[131] More than three-quarters of Germans thus envisioned a future in which they depended on the Allied, especially American, victors for at least a decade.

While recent historiography has tended to portray the American occupation in a progressively more positive light as the kernel of postwar democratization, contemporary reactions to American occupiers were considerably more varied and, often, more ambivalent.[132] Ordinary Germans exhibited much grumbling, criticism, and

---

[129] Diary of Renate P., entry of May 6, 1945, DTA, Nr. 59, 4.

[130] Ferdl to his wife in Vienna, April 7, 1945, cited in Hirschfeld and Renz, eds, "*Vormittags die ersten Amerikaner*," 114. See also Stargardt, "Rumors of Revenge."

[131] Richard L. Merritt, Anna J. Merritt, *Public Opinion in Occupied Germany. The OMGUS Surveys 1945–1949* (Urbana: University of Illinois Press, 1970), 103–5. It should be noted, however, that a prolonged occupation might also have been desired by postwar Germans because of fears of a Soviet takeover. American occupation authorities also expected an occupation of ten years or longer: see *Neue Zeitung*, "Mindestens zehn Jahre Besatzung," November 30, 1945.

[132] For largely positive views of the occupation, see Konrad H. Jarausch, *After Hitler. Recivilizing Germans, 1945–1955*, trans. Brandon Hunziker (Oxford and New York: Oxford University Press, 2006), Herman-Josef Rupieper, *Die Wurzeln der westdeutschen Nachkriegsdemokratie: Der amerikanische Beitrag, 1945–1952* (Opladen: Westdeutscher Verlag, 1993).

also anxiety regarding the occupation.[133] Conversely, American soldiers did not see themselves as liberators but rather as victors and occupiers. The main directive of the Joint Chief of Staffs for General Eisenhower, JCS 1067, demanded a punitive and harsh treatment of defeated Germans. Instructions to individual American soldiers in the *Pocket Guide to Germany* stated unambiguously: "You are in enemy territory. These people are not our allies or friends." "Fraternization" with German civilians was strictly prohibited.[134] Guidelines for troop behavior warned that "the majority of Germans supported the Nazis" and that German civilians would "try to make friends with us—to get information, to get favors, to create sympathy for the 'poor down-trodden' German people, to make us disagree among ourselves, or just to get a good chance to slip a knife into Allied soldiers."[135] An opinion survey among US soldiers in April 1945 indicated that 76 per cent "hated" or had "negative feelings" toward German civilians, and that 71 per cent of soldiers felt that "all or most Germans" were responsible for the war.[136] The discovery and liberation of the camps in the following month most likely intensified these negative feelings. Whatever hopes individual Germans had associated with the arrival of American occupation troops in 1945, these positive feelings were not reciprocal.[137]

Much of the ensuing history of the relationship between German civilians and American GIs has been told as the progressive relaxation of this initially punitive and antagonistic approach. The ban on fraternization, for example, was softened early on and completely rescinded by October 1945.[138] Yet Germans did not know this would occur, and it is important not to project our knowledge of later developments onto the early postwar period. The eventual relaxation of US soldiers' negative predisposition toward ordinary Germans and Germans' anxieties did not negate their early postwar experiences. Germans were completely at the mercy of foreign occupiers who acted with virtual impunity. Occupation constituted a massive intervention into the personal and intimate lives of postwar Germans. Three areas, in particular, emerged as sources of popular fear and anxiety: violent transgressions of American occupation soldiers, the practice of housing requisitions, and the onset of denazification.

---

[133] Older studies of the American occupation tended to capture this dimension of the occupation more fully, in part because they were based on interviews with contemporaries. See John Gimbel, *A German Community under American Occupation. Marburg 1945–52* (Palo Alto: Stanford University Press, 1961). See also Hans Woller's warning against an all too positive and teleological view of the American occupation, Hans Woller, *Gesellschaft und Politik in der amerikanischen Besatzungszone. Die Region Ansbach und Fürth* (Munich: Oldenbourg, 1986), 319–20.

[134] Cited in Hitchcock, *Bitter Road to Freedom*, 173, 176–7.

[135] Headquarters, European Civil Affairs Division, "Conduct of Members of This Command in Occupied Germany," October 28, 1944, 757, NA, RG 260 (A1), 390/47/4/2, Box 1020.

[136] Johannes Kleinschmidt, *"Do not fraternize." Die schwierigen Anfänge deutsch-amerikanischer Freundschaft, 1944–49* (Trier: Wissenschaftlicher Verlag, 1997), 84.

[137] On mutual disappointment between Germans and Americans, see also Hans Habe, "Gegenseitige Enttäuschung," *Neue Zeitung*, January 25, 1946.

[138] Petra Goedde, *GIs and Germans. Culture, Gender, and Foreign Relations, 1945–49* (New Haven: Yale University Press, 2003), 42–79, Kleinschmidt, *"Do not fraternize"*.

One source of postwar fear were American acts of violence toward German civilians. Such violent transgressions were predictable in light of the ferocity of the fighting as well as the thoroughly negative image of Germans in American wartime propaganda. In Marburg, violent transgression of US soldiers was a subject of "daily conversation."[139] Such events occurred throughout the occupation period but they peaked in early 1946 and then again in 1949–50 with the renewed deployment of American soldiers to Germany in the context of the escalating Cold War.[140]

A study in the spring of 1946 came to the conclusion that soldiers stationed in Europe committed 50 per cent more disciplinary infractions than soldiers stationed domestically.[141] Serious crimes such as "homicide, rape, robbery, larceny, black market offenses, etc." reportedly increased from 3.7 per 10,000 troops in August 1945 to 11.1 per 10,000 troops in January 1946.[142] In September 1946, US occupation officials reported over 60 troop incidents during one week, which included "murder, assault, robbery and sex offences."[143] Initially, American occupation officials interpreted these disciplinary problems as a result of the "rapid demobilization" of combat troops, which had weakened the "firm ties of unit pride."[144] Later they would describe such incidents as more systemic, locating the causes in the delayed demobilization of GIs, especially after Japan's surrender in August 1945, and as a result of the replacement of combat soldiers with young and inexperienced recruits who had been insufficiently trained for service in an occupation army.[145]

The US military leadership recognized that violent transgressions by occupation soldiers against German civilians could destroy the mission of the occupation. As early as May 7, 1945, commander of the US forces in Europe, General Omar Bradley, directed army commanders' attention to widespread "looting,

---

[139] Gimbel, *A German Community under American Occupation*, 69–70. These incidents have not received much attention in the historiography. They are completely absent, for example, in the massive study by Henke, *Die amerikanische Besatzung*. For exceptions, see Jennifer V. Evans, "Protection from the Protector. Court-Martial Cases and the Lawlessness of Occupation in American-Controlled Berlin, 1945–1948," in Detlev Junker, ed., *GIs in Germany. The Social, Economic, Cultural, and Political History of the American Military Presence* (New York: Cambridge University Press, 2013), 212–33, Gerhard Fürmetz, "Insolent Occupiers, Aggressive Protectors. Policing GI Delinquency in Early 1950s West Germany," in ibid. 189–211. For the continuity into the 1950s, see also Dewey A. Browder, *Americans in Post-World War II Germany. Teachers, Tinkers, Neighbors, Nuisances* (Lewiston: Edwin Mellen Press, 1998), 155–64.

[140] Fürmetz, "Insolent Occupiers, Aggressive Protectors," 195–7.

[141] OMGUS, Office of the Director of Intelligence, "Comparative Figures on Troop Disorders," July 6, 1946, NA, RG 25 (A1), 390/40/20/2, Box 43.

[142] *Morale and Discipline in the European Command, 1945–1949*, Historical Division European Command, Karlsruhe, Germany, 1951, 1.

[143] OMGUS, Office of the Director of Intelligence, Intelligence Notes No. 8; OMGUS, Intelligence Notes, No. 26, October 12, 1946, NA, RG, 260, 108 (A1), 390/41/7/5–6, Box 330.

[144] Office of Military Government for Bavaria, Office of the Director, "Discipline," April 18, 1946, NA, RG 1476.

[145] Depredations by United States Military Personnel (Secret), NA, RG 260, 25 (A1), 390/40/20/2, Box 43; Kleinschmidt, *"Do not fraternize,"* 147–51.

pillaging, wanton destruction, rape, and other crimes" by their men.[146] All infractions were supposed to be reported to the occupation authorities and punished severely.[147] Die *Neue Zeitung*, the newspaper of the American occupation, publicized convictions of US soldiers to lifelong prison terms for the rape of German women as a deterrent.[148] Edgar Johnson, a political adviser to General Clay in Berlin, reported in June 1946 that the "number of incidents involving Germans+GIs is still alarming" even though American court martials were sending "GIs to jail for years on end because they have been guilty of assaulting Germans."[149]

GI violence against German civilians assumed a multiplicity of forms. Some transgressions, especially during the early postwar period, took place in broad daylight and hence served the purpose of publicly humiliating individual Germans for their complicity with Nazism. In July 1945, American soldiers invaded the house of ex-soldier Georg W. in Feuchtwangen, struck him in the face, and forced him to stand naked at his window in broad daylight.[150] In September 1946 in Amberg, American GIs addressed two German civilians as "Nazi pigs," knocked off one man's hat—a bourgeois symbol of respectability—and then assaulted a number of civilians.[151] Local German officials were also not safe from violent assaults by American GIs.[152]

Other cases, however, occurred at night and lacked such public dimensions. GIs approached and stopped German civilians seemingly at random, asked them for cigarettes, liquor, money, or perhaps a ride, and then beat them up, often leading to severe injuries. In several cases reported from Amberg in the fall of 1946, drunk GIs also invaded German homes, asked for liquor or girls, or asserted their superiority by brandishing their pistols. Alcoholism and rowdyism in German bars also occurred frequently.[153] Local residents in Pfaffenhofen complained

---

[146] Omar N. Bradley to Commanding General, Third US Army, "Misbehavior of Allied Troops," May 7, 1945, NA, RG 260, 757 (A1), 390/47/4/2, Box 1020.

[147] R.W. Hartman, "Discipline," April 15, 1945, NA, RG 260, 757 (A1), 390/47/4/2, Box 1020.

[148] See *Neue Zeitung* July 5, 1946; September 23, 1946; October 28, 1946.

[149] Werner Breunig, Jürgen Wetzel, eds, *Fünf Monate in Berlin. Briefe von Edgar N. Johnson aus dem Jahre 1946* (Oldenbourg: De Gruyter, 2014), Doc.56, 255. See also Doc.68, 293.

[150] Investigation of charges against Pfc. George H. Moline, July 16, 1945, NA, RG 260 (A1), 390/47/4/2, Box 1020.

[151] D-244 Mil Gov Amberg, APO 170, US Army, October 17, 1946, NA, RG 260 (A1), 390/40/20/2, Box 43.

[152] OMG for Kreis Lauf, "Ince[sic!]dent Involving American Soldier," May 2, 1946, NA, RG 260 (A1), 390/47/4/2, Box 1020. See another 1949 case in which the Bürgermeister of Weiden was kidnapped by three US soldiers, "severely mistreated," and then released outside the city; Bayrisches Staatsministerium des Innern to Bayrische Staatskanzlei, March 28, 1950, Beilage 1 "Sicherheitsstörungen durch Angehörige der Besatzungstruppen," BHStA, Stk 15008.

[153] See the examples cited in NA, RG 260 25 (A1), 390/40/20/2, Box 43. For reports of similar cases in German sources, see Halbmonatsbericht des Regierungspräsidenten in Würzburg für die Zeit vom 16–30.9.1945, BHStA, MSo81, Halbmonatsbericht des Regierungspräsidenten in München, September 1945, 2. Hälfte, BHStA, MSo73. In August 1946, German officials from Munich reported about 30 violent attacks by American soldiers against German civilians, usually robberies of watches, jewelry, and, ironically, Bavarian folk costume, yet occasionally also including violent assault; see Monatsbericht des Regierungspräsidenten München, August 1946, BHStA, MSo73.

about "reckless hunting" by American occupation soldiers, which had long been a sensitive issue in rural areas.[154] A rapid increase in automobile accidents involving American GIs—7,800 between June and November 1945 according to one source—also appeared as an indication of recklessness and lack of discipline among occupation troops.[155] A resident from Marburg spoke for many when he complained in March 1946 of random and violent assault by American occupation forces against German civilians, including several university professors. "These assaults," he added, "have become notorious among the civilian population of Marburg. Nobody risks going out in the evenings, and people feel as if they were exposed to acts of indiscriminate brutality with no means of protection."[156]

Sexual assault, including rape, constituted a permanent feature of the relationship between American GIs and German civilians as well. US court martial records documented 552 cases of rape of German women by American soldiers. This was much lower than the comparable figures in the Soviet zone, although other estimates also cite higher numbers of up to 1,500 rapes between January and December 1945.[157] German sources also reflect these incidents, as in the case of two women from Munich who reported that American soldiers raped them in July 1945.[158] Rape and sexual assault were not limited to the immediate postwar period and remained a feature of the US occupation. Among the 88 cases involving American troops that Bavarian authorities listed from October to December 1949, 13 per cent concerned sexual assault or rape.[159] There were also reports of sexual assault of boys and men.[160] A "similar script" governed rapes in both zones: they often resulted from soldiers' frustration over excessive violence and German persistence during the final stages of the war; soldiers considered German women as part of a defeated and subjugated people; sexual violence served the purpose of meting out revenge humiliating German men.[161] Internal US records from the last stages of the war and in the immediate postwar period point to a military policy of treating sexual violence with increasing laxity, in spite of official

---

[154] Zusammenfassung und Auszüge der Monatsberichte der Landwirtschaftsstellen und Außenstellen für den Monat Oktober 1945, BHStA, MSo70.

[155] Browder, *Americans in Post-World War II Germany*, 171.

[156] Otto Ropel, letter to an American official in charge of university education, March 19, 1946, NA, RG 260 25 (A1), 390/40/20/2, Box 43.

[157] Hitchcock, *Bitter Road to Freedom*, 195. For the higher figure, see Kleinschmidt, "*Do not fraternize*," 104. It is not clear, however, if this figure also includes rape on non-German territory. For another reference to rape, see the report by Edgar Johnson on a "GI who entered an apartment of a German and raped his 12-year-old daughter," Breunig and Wetzel, eds, *Fünf Monate in Berlin*, Doc.67, 285.

[158] Monatsbericht des Regierungspräsidenten in München, Monat Juli 1–15, 1945, BHStA, MSo73.

[159] See "Sicherheitsstörungen durch Angehörige der Besatzungstruppen," Beilage 1, Einzelfälle, especially No. 15, October 26, 1949, BHStA, Stk 15008.

[160] See Miriam Gebhardt, *Als die Soldaten kamen. Die Vergewaltigung deutscher Frauen am Ende des Zweiten Weltkriegs* (Munich: Deutsche Verlags-Anstalt, 2015), 39.

[161] Ibid. For evidence of individual rape, see 3–15 Pfarrei München, Lorenz Huber, July 26, 1945; 9–5 Pfarrei Haag a.d. Amper, Andreas Weingand, July 25, 1945; 10–17 Pfarrei Tuntenhausen, Innozenz Lampl, July 30, 1945, all in Pfister, ed., *Ende des Zweiten Weltkrieges*, 245, 393–4, 438.

pronouncements to the contrary.[162] Unlike sexual violence committed by Red Army soldiers in the Soviet zone of occupation, rape and sexual transgression by American occupation soldiers against German women came as largely unexpected and hence constituted a real shock for many Germans. Regardless of how extensive sexual transgressions by American solders really were, they confirmed and intensified German fears of retribution as part and parcel of occupation by the Allied victors, not just in the East but also in the West.

The involvement of African American soldiers in sexual relations (consensual or via prostitution) with German women represented a particular issue of German concern. Such relationships activated pre-existing racist dispositions among German civilians. "There are rumors that soon negroes will arrive as occupation troops," wrote Edeltraut G. in her diary in April 1945. "That will be horrible, then one will no longer be able to be in the street as a girl."[163] The experience of the occupation seemed to confirm these anxieties. "Bloody clashes" occurred near Bad Reichenhall in October 1945 as German citizens objected after African American GIs were seen with German girls.[164] German citizens petitioned the occupation authorities to intervene in what they described as the "shameless behavior of German women and girls together with colored members of the American occupation troops."[165] Undoubtedly due to their own racist dispositions in a still-segregated army, (white) American occupation officials tended to side with German officials and citizens. The alleged behavior of African American GIs became a ready scapegoat for tensions between American troops and German civilians.[166] In fact, official statistics by US occupation officials suggested a much higher rate of "serious incidents" among "colored" troops than among white troops.[167] It seems almost certain that this reflected racist selectivity, rather than disproportionately bad behavior.[168] Germans, for their part, quickly

[162] Gebhardt, *Vergewaltigung*, 115–69, quotation on 133, J. Robert Lilly, *Taken by Force. Rape and American GIs in Europe in World War II* (New York: Palgrave Macmillan, 2007).

[163] Diary of Edeltraut G., entry of April 15, 1945, DTA, Nr. 185, I, 1. It should be noted, however, that in other cases the encounter with African American GIs also led individual Germans to revise their racist stereotypes. Magdalena K. (born in 1901), for example, noted in her diary in April 1945 how after 12 years of "race education" she felt a "strong inner resistance" to African American soldiers even though "none of them has done anything to me so far" and they generally appeared to be "friendly and polite"; Diary of Magdalena K., entry of April 27, 1945, KA, Nr. 3715/2.

[164] Halbmonatsbericht des Regierungspräsidenten in München, Oktober 1945, 2. Hälfte, BHStA, MSo73.

[165] Franz Sales, Guardian of the Capuchin Monastery, to Military Government, April 30, 1946; Präsidium der Landespolizei to Military Government, July 17, 1946, NA, RG 260, 25 (A1), 390/40/20/2, Box 43.

[166] See, for example, Office of Military Government for the Kreis Weissenburg to Director, Office of Military Government for Bavaria, "Situation in Weissenburg Regarding Relations between Female Civilians and Colored Occupational Troops," June 5, 1946, NA, RG 260, 25 (A1), 390/40/20/2, Box 43. See also *Morale and Discipline in the European Command, 1945–1949*, 5–7.

[167] Serious incident rates, as reported by major commands, European Theater, 1946, NA, RG 260, 25 (A1), 390/40/20/2, Box 43.

[168] This was the case within the US army in northern France, see Mary Louise Roberts, *What Soldiers Do. Sex and the American GI in World War II France* (Chicago: University of Chicago Press,

learned that certain forms of racism were quite compatible with American military rule. Yet even the curtailed authority of African American GIs as occupiers confirmed German perceptions of the occupation period as a world turned upside down.

Fear and insecurity resulted from the fact that occupation had made Germans dependent on their occupiers for defense against violence. German police did not have any authority to arrest or prosecute US occupation soldiers until 1953.[169] As a city official from Schweinfurt described in September 1946, this created a "feeling of uncertainty and defenselessness" among the population.[170] The Office of Military Government, United States, opinion surveys also confirmed these popular apprehensions regarding the occupation. In April 1946, a survey by the military government shows that 42 per cent of Germans denied that Allied soldiers "had always acted correctly toward German civilians."[171] However one assesses the balance between positive and negative responses to American occupation forces, what mattered to postwar Germans was that they were not in control of these encounters. They were completely dependent on the intentions and, in many cases, the goodwill of individual soldiers. For postwar Germans, this situation was even more disconcerting in light of the fact that this fundamental uncertainty also concerned their personal and intimate sphere, especially their homes.

Military occupations and passing armies have requisitioned housing since at least the Napoleonic wars of the late eighteenth and the early nineteenth centuries.[172] Housing was a scarce resource in the immediate postwar period. In cities such as Würzburg, which had been subjected to heavy Allied bombing, three-quarters of the housing stock was destroyed. The average for all four occupation zones was about 30 per cent.[173] Refugees and expellees from the former German territories in the East and the gradual return of German POWs further stoked demand for housing. It is therefore not surprising that Germans perceived housing requisitions by the occupation army as a severe burden. In the spring of 1948, the American military occupied a total of 119,918 rooms while the British

2013), Maria Höhn, *GIs and Fräulein. The German-American Encounter in 1950s Germany* (Chapel Hill: University of North Carolina Press, 2002).

[169] Fürmetz, "Insolent Occupiers, Aggressive Protectors."
[170] Monatsberichte der Regierung von Unterfranken über den Monat September 1946, BHStA, MSo82; see also Bericht des Regierungspräsidenten in Würzburg über den Monat Januar 1946, February 5, 1946, BHStA, MSo82.
[171] Richard Merritt, *Democracy Imposed. US Occupation Policy and the German Public, 1945–1949* (New Haven: Yale University Press, 1995), 255–61.
[172] Ute Planert, *Der Mythos vom Befreiungskrieg. Frankreichs Kriege und der deutsche Süden. Alltag, Wahrnehmung, Deutung 1792–1841* (Paderborn: Schöningh, 2007), 245–56.
[173] Ulrich Herbert, *Geschichte Deutschlands im 20. Jahrhundert* (Munich, C.H.Beck, 2014), 554, Herbert Schott, *Die Amerikaner als Besatzungsmacht in Würzburg (1945–1949)* (Würzburg: Hart Druck GmbH, Volkach, 1985), 100.

military occupied 196,682 rooms.[174] American intelligence reported that Germans considered American troops "extremely extravagant, and wantonly careless in the requisitioning of houses for clubs, officers, and dependent quarters." In Butzbach in Hesse in December 1946, there was "no other single reason that would cause so much justified ill-feeling as the requisitioning policy of the Army."[175] In Munich, mayor Karl Scharnagl reported to the city council in December 1946 that "in every part of the city, popular concerns are growing that the same fate [of requisitioning, F.B.] could affect every street, every house."[176] Rumors and news of further requisitions caused great "concern, fear, and embitterment" among the population and Munich residents publicly proclaimed their fear of the "specter of requisitioning houses and farms."[177] Even those Germans who had initially welcomed the American occupation feared the loss of their homes. In April 1945, Evamaria Küchling-Marsden noted in her diary that the arrival of American troops had made "life in Heidelberg . . . normal again." Yet she immediately added that "we fear a confiscation of our home."[178] As a group of Catholic priests wrote to Cardinal Faulhaber, "the population, which one and a half years ago welcomed the Americans as redeemers from a horrible dictatorship, is now completely outraged that these harsh and brutal measures are taken at the onset of winter." Such "violation of human rights of the defenseless population," they argued, with an increasingly common moral equation, paralleled the "displacement and expropriation of Jews in the Third Reich."[179]

To be sure, individual Germans understood that housing requisitioning constituted a logical consequence of defeat and occupation, a "right of the victor."[180] The loss of their homes was tangible indication that, as a priest from Landshut wrote, "we are the vanquished" and that we "have much to atone for."[181] But many resented the fact that requisitions targeted ordinary Germans and former Nazis alike. They condemned "collective punishment" and demanded at least the exemption of non-Nazis. The American civilian official, Edgar Johnson, an adviser to General Clay in Berlin, criticized the fact that occupation officials "could not be bothered much about the political histories" of those whose homes

---

[174] Figures cited in Karl Christian Führer, *Mieter, Hausbesitzer, Staat und Wohnungsmarkt. Wohungsmangel und Wohnungszwangswirtschaft in Deutschland, 1914–1960* (Stuttgart: Franz Steiner Verlag, 1995), 351.

[175] Weekly intelligence report summary, November 28 – December 28, 1946, NA, RG 260, 108 (A1), 390/41/7/5–6, Box 331. See also Gimbel, *A German Community under American Occupation*, 56.

[176] Vortrag des Herrn Oberbürgermeister im Plenum des Stadtrates, December 3, 1946, Stadtarchiv München (StaMü), Bürgermeister und Rat, Nr. 1972.

[177] Verein für Wohnkultur to Oberbürgermeister der Landeshauptstadt München, January 24, 1946; Aufruf an die Bayrische Staatsregierung, November 25, 1946, StaMü, Bürgermeister und Rat, Nr. 1974.

[178] Diary of Evamaria K.-M., entry of April 13, 1945, KA, Nr. 3237.

[179] Petition to Kardinal Faulhaber, November 26, 1946, StaMü, Bürgermeister und Rat, Nr. 1974.

[180] Diary of Christa R., entry of July 5, 1945, KA, Nr. 5915.

[181] 24–4 Pfarrei Landshut St. Martin, Albert Graf von Preysing, August 1, 1945, in Pfister, ed., *Ende des Zweiten Weltkrieges*, 795.

they requisitioned.[182] Johnson cited the case of the famous cellist Max Baldner, who had suffered persecution during the Nazi period because of his Jewish wife, but whose house was nevertheless expropriated.[183] American occupation authorities insisted that they needed to requisition entire blocs and could not exempt individual houses.[184] Former Nazis allegedly also deliberately housed Nazi victims in their apartments in order to be exempted from housing requisitions.[185] Requisitions also affected evacuees or refugees who had already lost their homes and thus entailed double displacements. Anne K. wrote in her diary that when she found an apartment in Bavaria after being evacuated from Northern Germany to escape Allied bombing, Americans came to the door and demanded she leave within 15 minutes to give it to American troops.[186]

For individual Germans, the hardship of being deprived of one's dwelling was further aggravated by the real and symbolic injuries that came with requisitions. Requisitions tended to happen very quickly, in a matter of days or hours. Residents were not allowed to take any household items with them, and local communities needed to find alternative shelter for them. In some cases, residents were allowed to remain in the basements of their houses.[187] When American occupation officials requisitioned 200 houses in the Ramersdorf district in Munich, they encircled the area with barbed wire to keep former occupants out and installed checkpoints to make sure that they would not remove anything.[188] Searches of pregnant women, children, and priests at these checkpoints stoked outrage.[189] Such symbolic degradations reinforced the sense of helplessness and being at the mercy of the occupation powers.

The fact that the American military requisitioned houses for Jews, DPs, and other Nazi victims worsened German resentment. According to a statistic from Munich, the occupation authorities had requisitioned 1,413 houses and approximately 3,000 apartments by the end of 1946. Nazi victims lived in more than 40 per cent of the apartments.[190] Outrage focused on the fraction that would house Jewish survivors.[191] When the American military government ordered the requisitioning

---

[182]   Breunig and Wetzel, eds, *Fünf Monate in Berlin*, Doc.52, 238 and Doc.80, 325.

[183]   Ibid. Doc.83, 339.

[184]   Besprechung in der Militär-Regierung, München, November 7, 1946, StaMü, Bürgermeister und Rat, Nr. 1972.

[185]   Franz Fißthaler/Bertha Thaler, "Vorkommnisse anlässlich der Beschlagnahmung der 'Mustersiedlung Ramersdorf," December 5, 1946, StaMü, Bürgermeister und Rat, Nr. 1972.

[186]   Diary of Anne K., entry of May 5, 1945, KA, Nr. 528.

[187]   Führer, *Mieter, Hausbesitzer, Staat und Wohnungsmarkt*, 351.

[188]   Stadtrat der Landeshauptstadt München an Direktor der Militärregierung, November 22, 1936, StaMü, Bürgermeister und Rat, Nr. 1972.

[189]   Franz Fissthaler, Eidestattliche Erklärung, November 21, 1946; Berta John, Eidestattliche Erklärung, November 21, 1946, StaMü, Bürgermeister und Rat, Nr. 1972.

[190]   Besprechung mit Herrn Sternberg von der ICD, December 18, 1946, StaMü, Bürgermeister und Rat, Nr. 1974.

[191]   This was especially true in the aftermath of the Harrison report on the situation of Jewish DPs in September 1945, which encouraged General Eisenhower to authorize the requisitioning of German homes specifically for Jewish DPs, see Grossmann, *Jews, Germans, and Allies*, 162–4.

of 240 small houses in the Kaltherberge settlement for 2,000 Jewish Holocaust survivors in December 1945, widespread public protest ensued. Germans charged that the new inhabitants were not Nazi victims but "illegally immigrated and work-shy elements" who engaged in black market and other criminal activities.[192] Outrage about requisitions also turned into violence against Jews. A former SS leader, for example, broke into his apartment, which had been given to a Polish couple. In another case, a former Nazi and 20 friends entered his former apartment and denounced the occupants as a "Jewish gang" (*Judenbande*) and beat up one of them.[193] In September 1947, a women whose apartment had been requisitioned by US forces insulted a Jewish passenger on a streetcar and accused Jews of having "shit into the nice houses in Bogenhausen."[194] American occupation officials claimed that 95 per cent of complaints about wanton destruction and crime by new occupants following the requisitioning of houses were false. They sought to elicit Germans' empathy for Jewish Holocaust survivors, but German civilians and officials displayed little understanding for these arguments.[195] German officials argued that the housing needs of ethnic German refugees and expellees should be paramount. In a circular logic, they claimed requisitions for Jewish victims were ill-advised as they stoked antisemitism.[196] As late as March 1949, the city administrations in Munich reported that DPs in the "apartments of former Nazis" experienced increasing threats of violence.[197]

Housing requisitions also became a terrain for meting out justice and retribution among Germans. In the city of Berlin, the occupation authorities placed German housing officers in charge of securing housing for the millions of refugees and expellees who entered the country as well as for former victims of Nazism. City authorities thus ordered 386,190 requisitions of partial apartments (that is, they required the current occupants to share their housing space with refugees or Nazi victims) and 51,274 requisitions of entire apartments.[198] As a result, American occupation authorities also had to mediate inter-German acts of retribution. In a Berlin case, for example, Alexander K., a former member of the Nazi Party, appealed to the American military government to reverse a confiscation of his home. He claimed that Herr S., a concentration camp survivor who had taken

---

[192] Siedlungsleitung der Kaltherberge to Herrn Oberbürgermeister Scharnagl, November 6, 1946, StaMü, Bürgermeister und Rat, Nr. 1971.

[193] Auszug aus der 'Neuen Zeitung' vom Februar 5, 1947, Nr. 10 "SS-Führer räumt DP-Wohnung," StaMü, Bürgermeister und Rat, Nr. 1973.

[194] Oberstaatsanwalt München to Bayrisches Staatsministerium der Justiz, December 24, 1947, BHStA, Stk 13888.

[195] Referat Wohnungswesen to Herr Oberbürgermeister Scharnagl, January 16, 1946, StaMü, Bürgermeister und Rat, Nr. 1971; "Besprechung bei Captain Trott," December 14, 1945; Regierungskommissar für das Wohnungs- und Flüchtlingswesen, January 17, 1946; BHStA, Landesflüchtlingverwaltung 1276.

[196] Bayrische Arbeitsministerium to Amt der Militärregierung, Abt. Wohnungswesen, February 17, 1948, StaMü, Bürgermeister und Rat, Nr. 1971.

[197] Monatsbericht der Stadtverwaltug München, März 1–31, 1949, BHStA, MSo86.

[198] See, in general, Führer, *Mieter, Hausbesitzer, Staat und Wohnungsmarkt*, 350–70.

Figure 1.3. Protest march against housing requisitions in Bad Nauheim, Hesse, in the American zone of occupation, September 9, 1951.

Germans perceived housing requisitions as a form of retribution by the American occupation authorities. This practice lasted into the 1950s and shaped Germans' experience of the occupation period. The banner at this demonstration in Bad Nauheim, Hesse, reads: "Let us into our houses, then we want to be friends."

Source: dpa Picture-Alliance, No. 28397476.

over his home, had threatened him and told him the he would be "arrested by the Americans."[199] Several wives of former Nazis the Allies had arrested protested at the confiscation of their homes and accused other "former Nazi members" who had "denounced a Jewish woman" and sent her to Auschwitz.[200] Former Nazis protested against the requisitioning of their homes, either by highlighting that they had been only "nominal Nazis" and had never "violated the principle of human rights" or by calling into question the legality of these confiscations based on international law, sometimes with the help of a lawyer.[201] Some homeowners hired private detectives to discredit the status of DPs who were occupying their

[199] Alexander K. to "Sehr geehrter Herr Major," July 1, 1947, Hoover Institution (HI), Office of Military Government Berlin (OMGB), Box 6, folder 9.

[200] Margarete S. to OMG Berlin, Building and Housing Section, November 7, 1946; Elise D. to Liaison Officer Major M.J. Kasprzycki, October 24, 1946, HI, OMGB, Box 6, folder 1; Harry L. to Zentralwohnungsamt, August 27, 1946; HI, OMGB, Box 6, folder 9.

[201] Examples: Christian H. to OMGB, Building and Housing Section, November 24, 1946, HI, OMGB, Box 6, folder 5; Hans Frhr. von Godin to Amerikanische Militärregierung, Oktober 18, 1946, HI, OMGB, Box 6, folder 5.

homes as victims of racial or political persecutions.[202] Victims of Nazism, for their part, appealed to American occupation authorities to provide them with furniture in their new homes or to prevent the repossession of homes by the previous owners.[203] Most of the actions of individual Germans had no effect.[204] Yet these exchanges reflected the importance of housing requisitions as terrain on which Germans negotiated individual guilt and responsibility both among themselves and vis-à-vis the occupation authorities. Housing requisitions confirmed Germans' fears of retribution.

The only official program that bothered individual Germans more than housing requisition was denazification, a process designed to eliminate Nazi influence from the defeated country. Historians have long viewed American-led denazification as an abysmal failure.[205] A critical historiography describes it as a process of whitewashing former Nazis.[206] The transition of denazification to German responsibility in March 1946 worsened the problem, as did the onset of the Cold War in early 1947. At that point, the US put increasing pressure on German officials to wrap up denazification and shift attention to the Communist East as the new enemy in the Cold War. Many highly compromised former Nazis acquired the coveted label of "follower" or even "innocent." Of the 900,000 denazification proceedings in the US zone, the process only rated 1,654 persons (0.17 per cent) "major offenders," 22,122 (2.33 per cent) "offenders," and 106,422 "minor offenders."[207] Denazification, therefore, did not significantly disrupt the continuity of personnel in the civil service, the police, the educational sector, or especially the legal profession. After the founding of the Federal Republic in 1949, paragraph 131 of the West German constitution mandated the rehiring of former Nazis who were to constitute at least 20 per cent of all public administrative bodies.[208] Available evidence suggests that a similar process of a fairly easy return of former Nazis to leadership positions also occurred within the realm of commerce and private industry.

While the mid- or long-term failure of denazification to accomplish a comprehensive purge of former Nazis or significantly alter the composition of West German elites is beyond doubt, this reveals little about the subjective experience

---

[202] Max Pelzer, Privatdetektiv, May 24, 1946, HI, OMGB, Box 6, folder 11.

[203] Erna W. to OMGB, June 5, 1946; HI, OMGB, Box 6, folder 2; Bericht des Kaufmanns Gerd W. über seine Wohnungsangelegenheiten, July 2, 1946, HI, OMGB, Box 6, folder 10.

[204] Example: OMGB, Berlin Sector, Building and Housing Section to Margarete S., November 18, 1946, HI, OMGB, Box 6, folder 1.

[205] For a review of the literature, see Cornelia Rauh-Kühne, "Die Entnazifizierung und die deutschen Gesellschaft," *Archiv für Sozialgeschichte* 35 (1995): 35–70.

[206] See especially, Lutz Niethammer, *Die Mitläuferfabrik: Die Entnazifizierung am Beispiel Bayerns* (Munich: Dietz, 1982).

[207] Clemens Vollnhals, *Entnazifizierung. Politische Säuberung und Rehabilitierung in der vier Besatzungszonen 1945–1949* (Munich: dtv, 1991).

[208] Norbert Frei, *Vergangenheitspolitik. Die Anfänge der Bundesrepublik und die NS-Vergangenheit* (Munich, C.H.Beck, 1996), 66–9.

of denazification among individual postwar Germans.[209] Much like in the case of occupation policy more generally, it is important not to project retroactive knowledge of the eventual outcome of the process onto contemporaries' perception of denazification at the time. The onset of denazification confirmed some of the worst popular fears and expectations of Allied retribution. "How the Nazis are afraid now," a woman from Hamburg wrote in a letter on May 7, and quickly added "Hopefully, they will catch the right ones now."[210] While most Germans supported the idea of retribution and punishment of former Nazis, they were uncertain as to whether they could trust Allied occupation officials to punish the real culprits. Rumors speculating that 80 per cent of the assets of former Nazis would be confiscated, or that former Nazis would be excluded from any compensation for war damages, further added to popular uncertainty.[211]

Initial denazification measures in the American zone undermined popular confidence in the Allied ability to identify "real Nazis." They followed the occupation directive JCS 1067, which stipulated the dismissal of all Nazi Party members from public office as well as the "automatic arrest" of war criminals and Nazi Party functionaries down to the local level. Military Government Law No. 8 of March 1946 increased the range of affected individuals to require the dismissal of anybody who had been a member of the Nazi Party before 1937 and its affiliated organizations. Given the mass support for National Socialism, these stipulations had a significant impact on postwar German society. By the end of 1945, some 100,000 persons had been arrested and were interned in the American zone, while another 340,000 persons had lost their jobs by March 1946, more than half of them civil servants. As a result, local administrations virtually collapsed. In Munich, denazification affected a quarter of all city employees, in the city of Würzburg, up to 70 per cent, including, by August 1945, 92 per cent of all teachers.[212] Local German communities found it difficult to maintain public services as a result of denazification.[213]

Indiscriminate arrests fueled strong German popular resistance and undermined initial support for denazification. As early as August 1945, the *Regierungspräsident* from Würzburg reported that the "measures against the NSDAP [National Socialist German Worker's Party] and its members lack moral

---

[209] For an important analysis of this dimension, see now Mikkel Dack, "Questioning the Past: The Fragebogen and Everyday Denazification in Occupied Germany" (Dissertation, University of Calgary, 2015).

[210] Letter Gerda, May 7, 1945, cited in Jörg Echternkamp, *Kriegsschauplatz Deutschland 1945. Leben in der Angst—Hoffnung auf den Frieden. Feldpost aus der Heimat und von der Front* (Paderborn: Schöningh, 2006), 252.

[211] Halbmonatsbericht des Regierungspräsidenten in Würzburg, September, 1–15, 1945, BHStA, MSo81.

[212] Halbmonatsbericht des Regierungspräsidenten in Würzburg, August 16–31, 1945, BHStA, MSo81.

[213] See reports of the Regierungspräsident in Würzburg, which generally started with these complaints, BHStA, MSo82.

support among the people." The *Regierungspräsident* acknowledged that Germans "expected" punitive measures against "the leaders and other active Nazis," but that the initial denazification had been too harsh and imprecise, "depriving people of their existence and sending to concentration camps [people] who had been forced to [join] the Nazi Party, including people [who] had experienced repression (*Bedrückung*) and setbacks (*Zurücksetzung*) under Nazi rule."[214] This official thus equated Allied internment camps with Nazi concentration camps. Christian churches mobilized against denazification and church officials became the main spokespersons of popular opposition. In October 1945, for example, the South German Protestant Bishop Wurm denounced denazification as an expression of Allied "revenge and retribution," particularly objecting—in a language deliberately reflecting the Nazi persecution of Jews—to the "undifferentiated extinction of all Nazi civil servants."[215] Since the denazification of the economy proceeded on the same criteria of formal party membership, many individual Germans reportedly worried about their "possessions" and feared becoming part of "the outlaws and the dispossessed."[216] A report from Würzburg claimed in January 1946 that denazification affected 50 per cent of all people in the city and called on occupiers "to take away the fear from people."[217] Other municipal reports emphasized the "serious and depressed mood" of the population, which it attributed to "numerous arrests" and "virtual arrest waves" without declaration of the charges and in which arrestees had no contact with family members for months.[218] Individual German responses to denazification soon compared the policy to previous forms of persecution by the Nazi regime, which again shaped the ways they perceived their treatment by the Allied victors. One Fritz B., for example, noted in his diary in 1945 that:

it is always a hubris, which reminds us very much of National Socialism, if one people believes it has the historical or godly task of punishing another people, and it is this hubris which resonates from British or American broadcasts. . . . The German people has been poisoned by the injustice done to the Jews; the Anglo-Saxon peoples are about to infect themselves with the same ideas of lawlessness.[219]

Highly symbolic action such as the confrontation of the population in the Bavarian town of Neunburg vorm Wald with a mass grave of approximately 30

---

[214] Halbmonatsbericht des Regierungspräsidenten in Würzburg, August 16–31, 1945, BHStA, MSo81.
[215] Bischof Wurm to OMGUS, 3.10.1945, cited in Clemens Vollnhals, *Entnazifizierung und Selbstreinigung im Urteil der evangelischen Kirche. Dokumente und Reflexionen, 1945–49* (Munich: dtv, 1989), 57.
[216] Halbmonatsbericht des Regierungspräsidenten in Würzburg, Oktober 1–15, 1945, BHStA, MSo81.
[217] Bericht des Regierungspräsidenten in Würzburg für den Monat Januar 1946, BHStA, MSo82.
[218] Monatsbericht des Regierungspräsidenten in München, Dezember 1945, BHStA, MSo73.
[219] Diary, Fritz B. (1893–1966), 40, KA, A 68.

former concentration camp inmates from Buchenwald and Flossenbürg further aggravated popular concerns over denazification as a form of retribution. On September 30, 1946, the local military government summoned all citizens of Neunburg to view the bodies. On the following day, approximately 100 former Nazi Party members were forced to exhume and wash the bodies. The latter were then reportedly subjected to beating and kicking by "Jews and Poles," who were among the 591 foreigners residing in the city (with 2,598 residents and 1,547 refugees and evacuees). The popular reaction to this incident, however, did not only consist of fear but also of anger and outrage (*Empörung*), which entailed a greater sense of empowerment. One former Nazi with the pseudonym "Adolf Bedacht" called the incident a "crime against humanity." Citizens of Neunburg resented the implicit accusation of collective guilt and professed to be "completely innocent regarding the death of the concentration camp inmates." Germans saw the indiscriminate nature of denazification as a continuation of what they perceived to be the equally indiscriminate nature of retributive acts by Nazi victims against random Germans.[220]

German attitudes toward denazification did not significantly change with the transition of denazification into German hands in March 1946. Local denazification courts (*Spruchkammern*) comprising former anti-Nazis took charge of processing individual cases. The "Law for the Liberation from National Socialism and Militarism" required all inhabitants 18 years or older to account for their political pasts. More than 13 million Germans filled out the questionnaire on denazification, and more than one quarter—or 3,441,800 persons—needed to undergo formal denazification because they had been members of the Nazi Party or one of its organizations.[221] A completed denazification procedure was necessary to assume anything other than a manual labor position.[222] Because denazification targeted overwhelmingly middle-class men, this clause implied the temporary suspension from influential positions of a large segment of the male educated middle class. Not surprisingly, those affected by denazification reacted furiously and defiantly to these sanctions. In his novel *The Questionnaire*, the well-known right-wing activist of the interwar period, Ernst von Salomon, mocked the entire denazification procedure. The fact that this book became the most successful bestseller of the early postwar period indicates the depth of the

---

[220] For the entire incident, see Adolf Bedacht to Militärregierung des Landkreises Neunburg, October 3, 1946; Wilhelm Hoegner to Amt der Militärregierung für Bayern, October 28, 1946; Präsidium der Landpolizei von Bayern to Präsidium der Landpolizei in München, October 18, 1946, BHStA, Stk 13609.

[221] Figures based on Klaus-Dietmar Henke, "Die Trennung vom Nationalsozialismus. Selbstzerstörung, politische Säuberung, Entnazifizierung, Strafverfolgung," in Klaus-Dietmar Henke, Hans Woller, eds, *Politische Säuberung in Europa. Die Abrechnung mit Faschismus und Kollaboration nach dem Zweiten Weltkrieg* (Munich: dtv, 1991), 21–83, here 41.

[222] American occupation officials were well aware of this problem; see "Speed Up Experiment Has Encouraging Results," Weekly intelligence report No. 48, April 1947, NA, RG 260, Box 331.

resentment regarding denazification among postwar Germans.[223] The shame and embarrassment of having been called to task for one's political sins extended far into the postwar period and was still present in oral interviews more than two decades later.[224]

Feelings of resentment and anger at the occupation authorities, however, may also have concealed a quite genuine fear of being called to task for actions under the Nazi regime. Psychiatric case files demonstrate that fears of Allied retribution and prosecution assumed the clinical forms of paranoid schizophrenic disorders.[225] Clinical cases revealed an elaborate desire for self-justification that differed only in its obsessive intensity from more public protests against denazification. In November 1948, 44-year-old Hans Georg G. was sent to the Bonn psychiatric institution after he had stood naked in front of the open window for an hour. As a former civil servant, G. had voluntarily quit his job in 1945 because he knew that he had been politically compromised as a Nazi Party member and Stormtrooper (SA) bloc leader since 1932. He had withdrawn to his room and written long and elaborate tracts that sought to repudiate his denazification procedure, claiming to be a "politically persecuted person" and "reckoning with all criminal politicians all over the world." Even after his month's stay in the psychiatric institution, he continued to engage in "confused speeches" that "always concerned his past and which time and again articulated the fear of persecution."[226]

Postwar *Angst*

In her "Report from Germany" in 1950, Hannah Arendt observed that postwar Germans displayed a "genuine inability to feel" and a "general lack of emotion."[227] The intense fears of retribution during the immediate postwar period discussed in this chapter contradict this statement. Indeed, Germans exhibited intense emotions after 1945, just not the ones that Arendt would have liked to have seen. Fears of revenge and anxiety about an uncertain individual and collective future constituted a foundational experience for postwar Germans in the aftermath of the Third Reich. Germans articulated these fears both publicly and privately.

[223] Ernst von Salomon, *Der Fragebogen* (Hamburg: Rowohlt, 1951). On this book, see Anna M. Parkinson, *An Emotional State: The Politics of Emotion in Postwar West German Culture* (Ann Arbor: University of Michigan Press, 2015), 67–111.
[224] Christina von Hodenberg, *Das andere Achtundsechzig. Gesellschaftsgeschichte einer Revolte* (Munich: C.H.Beck, 2018), 91–6.
[225] Svenja Goltermann, "Angst in der Nachkriegszeit. Entnazifizierung und persönliche Desorientierung," *Zeiträume. Postdamer Almanach* 1 (2006), 29–37, Svenja Goltermann, *Die Gesellschaft der Überlebenden. Deutsche Kriegsheimkehrer und ihre Gewalterfahrungen im Zweiten Weltkrieg* (Munich: DVA, 2009), 61–75.
[226] Patient record Hans-Georg G., Archiv der Rheinischen Kliniken, Bonn.
[227] Hannah Arendt, "The Aftermath of Nazi Rule. Report from Germany," *Commentary* 10 (1950): 342.

A postwar emotional regime of sobriety and rationality, which ultimately discouraged the open expression of emotions, had not yet taken shape. The emotional function of these fears of retribution was complex and contradictory: fear served both as a veiled expression of guilt *and* as a defense mechanism against it. On the one hand, the extensive knowledge of Nazi crimes and hence a clear sense of guilt were among the causes of fear. Yet, on the other hand, private and public articulations of fear and anxiety may also have blocked a more extensive self-reflection and admission of guilt. The real and imagined consequences of this guilt might have appeared as too catastrophic to many Germans. In this way, the anticipation of a largely fictional catastrophe in an imagined future blocked a more extensive confrontation with the actual catastrophe that Germans had helped to bring about.

Fears of retribution also helped postwar Germans to imagine themselves as a community of victims. This victim identity projected, as it were, the logic of the war into the postwar period. What Germans had done to Nazi victims, especially Jews and Eastern Europeans, now formed the horizon of expectation of what would happen to Germans. The collapse of National Socialism thus by no means cured Germans from "nationalism." They rather saw their own individual futures as inextricably intertwined with the fate of the national collective. And although the self-perception as "victims" served an obviously apologetic function, victim identities also provoked fear and anxiety. They projected this perceived victimization into the immediate future, which for many postwar Germans meant, above all, to be subjected to violent retribution by real and, more frequently, imagined enemies.

By 1947, fears of Allied prosecution were increasingly relegated to the realm of psycho pathological disorders. The shift of US occupation policy from punishment to reconstruction, as well as the outbreak of the Cold War, clearly signaled that many Germans' expectations of Allied retribution were no longer justified. Still, fears and anxieties of retribution lingered on for an extended period of time, albeit in a different form. The specifically male and bourgeois experience of dislocation and disorientation in the immediate postwar period may have fueled a widespread cultural pessimism in the postwar period, which manifested in distinct public discourse on a new form of existential anxiety. Invoking intellectual figures such as Martin Heidegger and Søren Kierkegaard, many postwar commentators diagnosed a specific form of anxiety, a German *Angst*, as a distinct postwar phenomenon.[228] To be sure, this discourse also served apologetic purposes by dissolving the concrete historical and political context of the postwar period—and hence specific forms of individual guilt and responsibility—into a universal existential condition. But this intellectual discourse on postwar *Angst*

---

[228] Richard Tüngel, "'Gespenst der Angst,' 'Die gepaarten Ängste,'" *Christ und Welt* 2/45 (1949), Dieter Sattler, "Die deutsche Angst," *Frankfurter Hefte* 2/10 (1947): 999–1005.

might also have derived from a socio-historical, class- and gender-specific experience of the male educated middle class in the immediate postwar period. Members of this social group both experienced and imagined defeat and occupation, at least initially, as an existential threat to their personal and professional futures, and they therefore reacted with a great deal of apprehension, anxiety, and fear.

Fears of retribution lingered on far into the 1950s, albeit in a metaphorical, symbolic sense. The experience of defeat and occupation and the associated feelings of inferiority and helplessness informed popular German reactions to other developments in the postwar period. What had been an emotional response to a real threat intruded on Germans' fantasies and imaginations even after the aversion of the worst crisis. The next chapter discusses the alleged abduction of young German men to the French Foreign Legion during the early 1950s as one such example.

2

Moral *Angst*

In March 1952, a community near the city of Paderborn experienced a panic. Several young men had disappeared, and local journalists reported that they had been abducted into the French Foreign Legion. Journalists identified a "true Foreign Legion psychosis" and local residents saw potential "recruiters" to the Legion everywhere.[1] Similar fears spread throughout the Federal Republic in the early 1950s. In December 1952, a newspaper reported that an "elegantly dressed man" had "made drunk" 22-year-old Günter Velmer in a bar in New Ulm, who woke up in a car on its way to a French military barracks in Freiburg from where he was then deported to France.[2] In another case, a recruiter reportedly used an "opium cigarette" to render his victim unconscious, only to awaken in a military barracks in Koblenz.[3]

The West German press reverberated with such stories in the early 1950s.[4] It estimated that up to 150 recruiters were active in West Germany, primarily in North Rhine-Westphalia and in the Rhineland-Palatinate, and that they kidnapped up to 15 Germans per day to fight on behalf of French colonialism in Indochina and North Africa.[5] In the public imagination, the Foreign Legion became a major site of anxiety, a "horror of mothers."[6] Concerned parents all over Germany soon began to see the threat of abduction lingering virtually everywhere. Social and ethnic outsiders were quickly suspected as "recruiters." Citizens in Paderborn, for example, accused "Italian cloth sellers" as "potential recruiters." In another case, intoxicated witnesses gave testimony against innocent men and demanded their arrest.[7] After seeing her 16-year-old son "in a limousine at a bus

---

[1] "Menschenraub an der Senne," *Westdeutsche Allgemeine*, March 6, 1952, "Wie kam Hans Krüll zur Fremdenlegion?" *Die Welt*, March 11, 1952, "Schrecken der Mütter. Eine Psychose greift um sich," *Die Welt*, March 27, 1952, Deutscher Bundestag-Pressearchiv (DB-PA), 060–7/2.

[2] "Deutscher aus Ulm in Fremdenlegion verschleppt," *Allgemeine Zeitung*, Mainz, December 13, 1952, DB-PA, 060–7/2.

[3] "Werber bot Opium-Zigarette an," *Westfalenpost Hagen*, August 24, 1954, DB-PA, 060–7/2.

[4] "Menschenraub an der Senne," *Westdeutsche Allgemeine*, March 6, 1952, "Menschenhandel mit Jungbergleuten," *Ruhr-Nachrichten*, December 22, 1951, DB-PA, 060–7/2.

[5] "Der Bundesinnenminister wünscht es nicht," *Hamburger Echo*, June 4, 1954, "Täglich 15 Deutsche," *Industrie-Kurier*, November 25, 1952, DB-PA 060–7/2. Similar stories of abduction in Jason Verber, "The Conundrum of Colonialism in Postwar Germany" (Ph.D. Dissertation, University of Iowa, 2010), 92–5.

[6] "Schrecken der Mütter," *Die Welt*, March 27, 1952, "Kopfjäger unter uns," *Münchner Merkur*, June 25, 1954, DB-PA, 060–7/2.

[7] "Futter für die Fremdenlegion," *Die Welt*, March 14, 1952, "Schrecken der Mütter," *Die Welt*, March 27, 1952, DB-PA, 060–7/2.

German Angst: Fear and Democracy in the Federal Republic of Germany. Frank Biess, Oxford University Press (2020).
© Frank Biess.
DOI: 10.1093/oso/9780198714187.001.0001

stop," Betty E. suspected that he had been abducted and demanded that the German police take "immediate action" to protect him.[8] Local authorities in Siegen put out flyers all over town warning "parents and the youth of Siegen" against "unscrupulous seducers" who "get their victims to sign up for the Foreign Legion under the influence of alcohol." In south-western Germany, schools were instructed to alert students to the tactics of recruiters for the Foreign Legion.[9] The Young Socialists (*Jusos*), the youth organization of the Social Democratic Party (SPD) stepped up their campaign, hanging posters all over the French zone of occupation warning "all young Germans" against "paid recruiters" who "look for their victims throughout the territory of the Federal Republic."[10] By 1955, representatives of the Federal Interior Ministry complained about an increase in written petitions from parents whose sons had gone missing.[11]

Popular culture expressed similar anxieties regarding the Foreign Legion. In September 1958, the pop artist Freddy Quinn topped the German charts with "Der Legionär", a song that depicted the plight of a German soldier in the Legion. In the same year, Wolfgang Staudte, one of the most distinguished film-makers of the postwar period, directed a film, *Madeleine und der Legionär*, which featured a German member of the Legion escaping from Algeria with the help of a French woman. A serialized novel entitled *Lost Sons* and based on the movie's plot appeared from November 1957 to June 1959 in *Stern*. With a circulation of over one million, *Stern* was one of West Germany's most popular magazines. These representations of the Foreign Legion in West German popular culture echoed an intense and sustained preoccupation with the Legion throughout the first decade of the Federal Republic's existence.

The preoccupation with the Foreign Legion also did not remain limited to the tabloid press or to West German popular culture. Several state parliaments, as well as the federal parliament, debated the issue of young Germans serving in the Legion repeatedly, and the West German parliament (*Bundestag*) eventually reactivated a law that made recruitment to the Legion a criminal offense.[12] West German courts vigorously prosecuted and, in some cases, convicted alleged recruiters for the Legion, while social workers and sociologists pondered the reasons for its appeal to West German youth. In international diplomacy, the

[8] Betty E. to Bundesinnenministerium, October 30, 1952, undesarchiv Koblenz (BArch), B 106/16652.

[9] Stadt Siegen to Herr Regierungspräsident Arnsberg, February 2, 1955, "An die Siegener Eltern und unsere Siegener Jugend!" Nordrhein-Westfälisches Hauptstaatsarchiv (NRWHStA), NW061, Nr. 137, 42–3, "Aufklärungsunterricht für Fremdenlegion," *Allgemeine Zeitung*, Mainz, March 28, 1953, DB-PA 060–7/2; Kultusministerium Baden-Württemberg to Innenministerium Baden-Württemberg, August 5, 1955, Hauptstaatsarchiv Baden-Württemberg (HStA-BaWü), EA 2/302, Bü582.

[10] Archiv der Sozialen Demokratie (ASD), 6/PLKA 003958.

[11] Memo, to Herr Unterabt. Leiter ZB, June 13, 1955, BArch, B 106/16653.

[12] Major debates of the issue took place in January 1953 and December 1954, see Verhandlungen des Deutschen Bundestages (VDBT), *Stenographische Berichte*, 1. Wahlperiode, 248. Sitzung, January 29, 1953, 11856–63, and ibid. 2. Wahlperiode, 58. Sitzung, December 8, 1954, 2958–73.

Figure 2.1. The Young Socialists, the Social Democratic youth organization, put up this poster all over the French zone in 1952.

It warned "all young Germans" against "paid recruiters" and "human traffickers" whose "seductions" and "promises" would lead to "disease, agony, and death." Young Germans must not lend their "youth and their life to the service of foreign interests."

Source: Archiv der sozialen Demokratie der Friedrich-Ebert-Stiftung, 6/PLKA004301.

Foreign Legion constituted a persistent and highly sensitive obstacle to Franco–German reconciliation, which lay at the heart of the process of Western European unification.

In spite of this intense preoccupation with the Foreign Legion in the early Federal Republic, the issue does not feature very prominently in the historiography of postwar Germany.[13] The public obsession with the Foreign Legion during the 1950s highlights the legacies of total defeat and foreign occupation as persistent sources of fear and anxiety well into the 1950s. Rather than fears of direct and violent retribution as during the immediate postwar period, the panic regarding alleged abductions into the Foreign Legion resulted from lingering anxieties about the lack of sovereignty and from a strong sense of helplessness vis-à-vis the occupying powers. The Federal Republic was initially founded as a provisional state, as a "semi-sovereign non-national state" (Klaus Kiran Patel), that would become permanent only with the eventual reunification between East and West Germany. The self-perception of a "complete" and sovereign nation was therefore not self-evident in the1950s. West Germans began to perceive and accept the Federal Republic as a sovereign state only gradually.[14]

West Germany still constituted an incomplete and fragile national body in the early 1950s. The last prisoners of war (POWs) from Soviet captivity did not return until 1956. Until then, hundreds of thousands of families of missing-in-action soldiers held on to hope that their sons, husbands, or brothers were held in "silent camps" in the Soviet Union from where they were not allowed to write.[15] In addition, the influx of American popular culture—jazz, rock'n'roll, Hollywood movies—challenged West German sovereignty and national identity. Widespread concerns about the respectability and conduct of German youth assumed larger symbolic significance for the nation's future. American popular culture and its perceived erosion of gender and racial norms heightened fears of a dissolving national community, especially as normative assumptions from the Nazi period lingered.[16] In this context, the alleged endangerment of young men by the French

[13] None of the recently published syntheses, for example, even include a reference to the subject. The only monograph on the topic is Eckard Michels, *Deutsche in der Fremdenlegion 1870–1965. Mythen und Realitäten* (Paderborn: Schöningh, 1999). See also Eckard Michels, "Die Bundesrepublik und die französische Fremdenlegion, 1949–1962," in Ernst Willi Hansen, Gerhard Schreiber, Bernd Wegner, eds, *Politischer Wandel, organisierte Gewalt und nationale Sicherheit* (Munich: Oldenbourg, 1995), 447–62, Verber, "Conundrum of Colonialism", 82–123.

[14] Quotation Klaus Kiran Patel, "Ex comparatione lux: Fazit," in Sonja Levsen, Cornelius Torp, eds, *Wo liegt die Bundesrepublik? Vergleichende Perspektiven auf die westdeutsche Geschichte* (Göttingen: Vandenhoeck & Ruprecht, 2016), 296; Andreas Wirsching calls the sixth volume of his history of the Federal Republic in the 1980s "Farewell to the Provisional State": Andreas Wirsching, *Abschied vom Provisorium. Geschichte der Bundesrepublik Deutschland 1982–1990, Band 6* (Munich: DVA, 2006).

[15] Frank Biess, *Homecomings. Returning POWs and the Legacies of Defeat in Postwar Germany* (Princeton: Princeton University Press, 2006), 179–202.

[16] Uta G. Poiger, *Jazz, Rock, and Rebels. Cold War Politics and American Culture in a Divided Germany* (Berkeley: University of California Press, 2000).

Foreign Legion reflected wider anxieties over the moral foundation of postwar society.

This chapter explains how and why these stories of abduction and seduction resonated with postwar Germans in the 1950s.[17] It analyzes West German fantasies and anxieties regarding the Foreign Legion in order to reveal some of the emotional predicament of West German society during this period. Fears of the abduction of young Germans into the Legion reflected deep-seated concerns regarding the safety and integrity of male youth, which constituted the core constituency of postwar reconstruction.[18] By the late 1950s, the growing recognition that young men entered the Legion out of their own volition shifted public attention from fear of recruiters to concerns about the fragility of male youth in postwar society. West German anxieties regarding the Foreign Legion began to focus on the inner resilience and resistance of young German men rather than the external threat of seduction by French-paid recruiters. This shift from externally to internally generated fears and anxieties anticipated a general shift in the history of fear and anxiety in West Germany from the late 1950s onward, which subsequent chapters will discuss.

Germans in the Legion

The preoccupation with young Germans serving in the French Foreign Legion—as well as with the ways in which they got there—was neither new nor unique to post-1945 Germany. The Legion was founded in 1831, and the public controversy about the service of young Germans in the Legion extended back into the nineteenth century. German membership in the Foreign Legion peaked after three major wars: in the wake of the Franco–Prussian War in the 1870s, in the mid 1920s, and in the mid 1950s.[19] As historian Eckard Michels has convincingly argued, the public discourse surrounding the Foreign Legion before 1914 already "contained all the facets and arguments of the coming decades."[20] Official policies to dissuade young Germans from joining the Legion originated in the pre-1914 period and continued into the 1920s. The Nazi regime criminalized service in the Legion and arrested returnees without due process.[21] After 1945, the Allied Control Council Law No. 11 rescinded, on the initiative of French occupation authorities, paragraph 141 of the criminal code, which had prohibited the

---

[17] See Michels, *Deutsche in der Fremdenlegion*, 242–4.
[18] Kenneth Thompson, *Moral Panics* (London: Routledge, 1998), 8. Youth is also often the subject of moral panics, see ibid. 43–56.
[19] Michels, *Deutsche in der Fremdenlegion*, 11.
[20] Ibid. 71. On earlier versions of the myth, see ibid. 60, 242–4.
[21] Ibid. 103–8. Minister des Innern an den Landrat von Lörrach, December 5, 1934, Staatsarchiv Freiburg (StA Freiburg), B 719/1, Nr. 7262.

recruitment of German nationals to a foreign military, thus making renewed recruitment to the Legion in occupied Germany possible.[22] While the public preoccupation with the issue drew on and, at least partly, continued pre-1945 patterns, the continuity of rhetorical tropes in public discourse did not necessarily imply a stable historical meaning. After 1945, the service of young Germans in the French Foreign Legion was refracted through the double contexts of total defeat in the Second World War and of the decolonization of the French colonial empire.[23]

Between 1945 and the end of the war in Algeria in 1962, approximately 50,000 Germans served in the French Foreign Legion, about 70 per cent of them in the period between 1945 and the French defeat in Indochina in 1954.[24] Recruitment of Germans into the French Foreign Legion began during the last years of the Second World War in French POW camps as part of the expansion of the Legion for the planned re-conquest of the French colonies in Asia and Africa. About 5,000 German POWs, or 5 per cent of all POWs held in French captivity, joined during the immediate postwar period. Contrary to widely circulating rumors at the time, the Legion did not seek out specifically compromised former soldiers or SS men. In fact, it avoided the recruitment of prominent National Socialists, war criminals, and collaborators. Men with scars on their left upper arm, the location of characteristic tattoos in the SS, generally could not gain entrance.[25]

Scandals and the Foreign Legion

The recruitment of German POWs into the Foreign Legion did not attract much public attention throughout the 1940s. The Legion marked just one among many crisis phenomena in a society marked by destruction, displacement, and destitution. By the late 1940s, German legionnaires recruited from POW camps began to return, because the Legion generally required a five-year commitment. One indication of increased media attention to the Legion was a six-part series on "Germans in the Foreign Legion" that the magazine *Stern* ran from December 1949 to January 1950. Billed as sourced from the "authentic reports of recently released legionnaires," it documented returnees' experiences in North Africa and

---

[22] See Michels, "Die Bundesrepublik und die französische Fremdenlegion, 1949–1962," 457.

[23] While the Federal Republic was founded in 1949, an Allied High Commission comprised of representatives of France, Great Britain, and the United States needed to approve West German legislation. The Federal Republic received full sovereignty—except for matters relating to "Germany as a whole"—with its entry into NATO in May 1955. Those Allied rights also extended to matters of intelligence and surveillance, see Josef Foschepoth, *Überwachtes Deutschland. Post- und Telefonüberwachung in der alten Bundesrepublik* (Göttingen: Vandenhoeck & Ruprecht, 2012), 186–96.

[24] Michels, *Deutsche in der Fremdenlegion*, 180.

[25] For the entire paragraph, see ibid. 142–69. See also Douglas Porch, *The French Foreign Legion. A Complete History of the Legendary Fighting Force* (New York: Harper, 1991), 531–2.

Indochina.[26] The articles highlighted harsh discipline mitigated only by a sense of international comradeship and the daily ration of wine and available women. Individual contributions adopted a distinctly colonial optic that identified German legionnaires with the perspective of the French (re)colonizers. The narrative cast Indochina as a completely foreign territory where "human beings are a little bit different," where "human life" was cheap, and where "all the coloreds are our enemies."[27] It perpetuated the nightmarish myth that indigenous forces systematically beheaded and mutilated European soldiers using the *coupe-coupe*, a long knife dedicated to the purpose. As on the Western front in the Second World War, these alleged practices suggested that traditional rules of warfare did not apply, thus enabling atrocities against native soldiers and civilians on the part of the legionnaires.[28] The series did not mention the alleged abduction of young Germans into the Foreign Legion, anxieties that gripped West German society only a few months later.

Two highly publicized scandals in the early 1950s directed West Germans' attention to the practices of recruitment. Scandals are "points of social declaration and declamation, saying much about the society and/or political system wherein they occur."[29] They trigger widespread public indignation in the face of a real or alleged violation of the dominant norms of a society, largely through intensified media attention.[30] In postwar West Germany, the scandals relating to the Foreign Legion articulated nagging concerns regarding the viability and integrity of the postwar national body.

The first of these scandals concerned the fate of a group of young German legionnaires whom Viet Minh forces in French Indochina had captured and who were repatriated to East Germany through China and the Soviet Union in April 1951. When eight of these returnees crossed the border to West Berlin one month later, which was still relatively easy before the construction of the Berlin Wall in August 1961, an unwelcome surprise awaited them: on the order of British authorities, German police forces arrested four of them—Jack Holsten, Siegfried Richter, Martin Dutschke, and Heinz Müller—and handed them over to French

---

[26] "Fremdenlegionäre. Deutsche Soldaten im Sturm der Zeit," *Stern* 2/48 (1949) to 3/2 (1950). On the ways in which the Foreign Legion brought colonialism to West Germany, see also Verber, "Conundrum of Colonialism," 82–123.

[27] *Stern*, 2/50 (1949): 13–14.

[28] On stories involving the *coupe-coupe*, see *Stern*, 2/49 (1949): 15, ibid. 2/50 (1949): 15; see also "Deutsche werden nicht geköpft," *Stern* 4/29 (1951): 12; on the general context, see Raffael Scheck, *Hitler's African Victims: The German Army Massacres of Black French Soldiers in 1940* (New York: Cambridge University Press, 2006), 126–31.

[29] John Garrard, "Scandals: An Overview," in John Garrard, James L. Newell, eds, *Scandals in Past and Contemporary Politics* (Manchester: Manchester University Press, 2006), 19.

[30] My interpretation here is informed by the analyses of nineteenth-century scandals, see Frank Bösch, *Öffentliche Geheimnisse. Skandale, Politik, und Medien in Deutschland und Großbritannien 1880–1914* (Munich: Oldenbourg, 2009), Rebekka Habermas, *Skandal in Togo. Ein Kapitel deutscher Kolonialherrschaft* (Frankfurt a/M: S. Fischer, 2016).

authorities, who immediately interned them as deserters in the military prison in Landau in the French zone of occupation. While Dutschke escaped from French custody, the three others were deported back to Oran in North Africa and sentenced to prison terms of up to 10 years.[31]

As was generally the case in matters relating to the Foreign Legion, French authorities remained immune to any outside intervention. Neither petitions by Emma Richter and Rita Holsten, the mothers of two interned legionnaires, nor an official protest note by the West German Foreign Office to the Allied High Commission succeeded in freeing the former legionnaires.[32] The Holsten case gained significant media attention as a powerful reminder of the Federal Republic's ongoing status as an occupied country that could not protect its citizens against foreign powers. *Stern* described the case as suggesting that Germans were "outlaws" in their own country. Was this, one reader asked, "the widely touted freedom of the West"?[33] Letters to the editors expressed further outrage. One reader did not see any difference between the "imprisonment of our youth" in the Western and the Eastern zones and charged the police president of West Berlin, who had authorized the transfer of the returned legionnaires to British occupation authorities, with "crimes against humanity," thus invoking the charge against Nazi perpetrators in the Nuremberg trials.[34] Another reader called it simply "crazy that our youth needs to sacrifice itself for foreign peoples," bemoaning that "this shows us again how little we're still worth."[35]

These protests expressed an emotional mixture of inferiority toward the occupation authorities with considerable indignation at disrespect of German rights. Because most Germans believed that the young men had been abducted into the Legion against their will, they denied the legitimacy of returning them into the hands of the French. These reactions also point to the—real and perceived— harshness of the Western occupation of Germany that persisted well into the first half of the 1950s.[36] The Holsten case brought attention to the fact that the occupation statute trumped German law that prohibited the extradition of its citizens to foreign nations.[37] For example, French occupation authorities undertook random

---

[31] For the details of the Holsten case, see Michels, *Deutsche in der Fremdenlegion*, 222–4 and Verber, "Conundrum of Colonalism," 119–22. Both analyze this case primarily with respect to the propaganda battles of the Cold War.

[32] Emma Richter/Rita Holsten to Bundespräsident Theodor Heuss, July 21, 1951, Politisches Archiv des Auswärtigen Amtes (PAA), B 10/2/961.

[33] "Zehn Jahre Zuchthaus für deutsche Fremdenlegionäre," *Stern* 4/46 (1951): 7.

[34] W. Sonntag, "Menschenrecht," *Stern* 4/49 (1951): 34.

[35] G. Meinhardt, "Fremdenlegion," *Stern* 4/50 (1951): 31.

[36] On this point, see Richard Bessel, *Germany 1945. From War to Peace* (New York: Harper, 2009), 144, 178. Unsurpassed on the Soviet occupation is Norman Naimark, *The Russians in Germany. A History of the Soviet Zone of Occupation, 1945–1949* (Cambridge, Mass.: Harvard University Press, 1995).

[37] Heinrich H. to Innenministerium, April 13, 1953; Meyer, Bundesministerium der Justiz to Heinrich H., July 5, 1953, PAA, B10/2/960.

house searches in order to arrest potential deserters from the Foreign Legion.[38] Even more than helplessness vis-à-vis the occupation authorities, *Stern* readers were incensed by West German officials' collaboration. Writing to federal president Heuss, one citizen described Holsten's arrest by West German police forces as indication of an "evil slave spirit" that "comes from the yes-saying, the notion of following orders willingly and without thinking," thus linking the compliance of officials with Nazi crimes.[39] Public reactions to the incident revealed West Germans' fundamental distrust of the postwar state, which they felt could not guarantee their basic security.[40]

This sense of German helplessness and violated sovereignty manifested itself even more strongly in another highly publicized scandal related to the Legion. In November 1952, a French bus forced its way across the German/French border near Schweigen after German border guards had attempted to check the identity of the passengers. West German border police suspected that the passengers were German nationals in French uniforms who had signed up for the Legion. A reporter for the illustrated *Revue* witnessed the incident and subsequently published a sensationalized article claiming the bus was trafficking human beings.[41] This episode fueled the public apprehension about the abduction of young Germans into the Foreign Legion. The tabloid press and illustrated magazines took a leading role in dramatizing the Schweigen incident, but even the *Frankfurter Allgemeine Zeitung* described the event in Schweigen as an indication "that we are not yet a sovereign state." Thus the press assumed a role that many Germans felt their elected leaders had not—that of representing their national interest.[42] "A few French policemen," the *Frankfurter Allgemeine Zeitung* editorialized, "demonstrate by a very small measure that they are stronger than all German ministers and governments, simply because they represent a state that occupies us."[43]

Schweigen also placed the Foreign Legion on the agenda of regional and national politics. Oppositional Social Democrats in the state parliament of Rhineland-Palatinate charged that "the German people has been denied the right

---

[38] This happened in Bonn in November 1951, see Vermerk: Hausdurchsuchung in Bonn durch französische Gendarmerie wegen Nachforschung nach einem Fremdenlegionär, PAA, B10/2/957. In another case, a former legionnaire who had deserted from the Legion in 1929 was arrested by French authorities in 1949 and then reportedly convicted to two years in prison; Frau Frieda B. to Staatspräsident Wohleb, August 2, 1949; Badische Staatskanzlei an A.M. Guy, Docteur en Droit, Offenburg, September 8, 1949, StA Freiburg, F 30/1, Nr. 38.

[39] P. Krais to Herr Bundespräsident, August 28, 1951, PAA, B10/2/961.

[40] For a similar feeling in the context of the Cold War, see Michael Geyer, "Cold War Angst: The Case of West German Opposition to Rearmament and Nuclear Weapons," in Hanna Schissler, ed., *The Miracle Years. A Cultural History of West Germany, 1949–1968* (Princeton: Princeton University Press, 2001), 376–408. See also Chapter 3 in this book.

[41] "Schluss mit dem Menschenschmuggel," *Revue* 48 (29.11.1952), PAA B10/2/962; see also Michels, *Deutsche in der Fremdenlegion*, 237–8.

[42] On the press in the 1950s, see Christina von Hodenberg, *Konsens und Krise. Eine Geschichte der westdeutschen Medienöffentlichkeit 1945–1973* (Göttingen: Wallstein, 2006), 145–28.

[43] "An der Grenze," *Frankfurter Allgemeine Zeitung*, November 18, 1952, DB-PA, 060–a742.

to protect its own members in the same way as is common among all other civilized peoples." Minister-President Altmeier proposed a resolution to the entire state parliament to defend its citizens against recruitment to the Foreign Legion.[44] In the *Bundestag*, the Social Democrats launched a grand inquiry asking the federal government how it would prevent similar incidents involving "violent crossings of the border."[45] In response, Federal Chancellor Adenauer sent several protest notes to the Allied High Commission demanding the cessation of recruitment to the Foreign Legion in Germany as well as the full empowerment of German guards over all individuals crossing the border, including members of the occupation authorities and the armed forces.[46]

Moral Panic

The Schweigen incident reactivated a long-standing German anxiety regarding the Foreign Legion—namely, the notion that unscrupulous recruiters coerced young Germans into the Legion against their will.[47] The representation of these fears of abduction in the West German media assumed many characteristics of a "moral panic."[48] West German newspapers and magazines, for example, devoted "exaggerated media attention" and constant "over-reporting" to the issue.[49] Media reports also grossly inflated the numbers of Germans serving in the Legion and hence the alleged danger of coercion into serving. *Der Fortschritt*, for example, estimated that the French smuggled "no fewer than 40,000 Germans a year" into France.[50] A 1954 pamphlet that the Young Socialists published on the heels of the French defeat at Dien Bien Phu claimed that 232,500 Germans had served in the Legion since 1945. Further, it claimed that 46,000 Germans had died and another

---

[44] Abg, Hertle, Auszug aus der 30. Sitzung des Landtages Rheinland-Pfalz, November 18, 1952, Ministerpräsident Altmeier, ibid.; Landesarchiv Koblenz (LHAK), Best.880, Nr. 145.

[45] Große Anfrage der Fraktion der SPD betr. Grenzzwischenfall in Schweigen, Deutscher Bundestag, 1. Wahlperiode, Drucksache Nr. 3864.

[46] Adenauer to Geschäftsführenden Vorsitzenden der Alliierten Hohen Kommission, Walter J. Donnelly, PAA, B10/2/957. See also VDBT, *Stenographische Berichte*, 248. Sitzung, 29.1.1953, 11858.

[47] On earlier versions of this myth, see Michels, *Deutsche in der Fremdenlegion*, 60, 242–4.

[48] Cohen defined a moral panic as a "a condition, an episode" in which a "person or group of persons emerges to become defined as a threat to the societal values and interests; its nature is presented in a stylized and stereotypical fashion by the mass media; the moral barricades are manned by editors, bishops, politicians, and other right thinking people; socially accredited experts pronounce their diagnoses and solution; ways of coping are evolved or (more often) resorted to, the condition then disappears, submerges or deteriorates and becomes more visible." See Stanley Cohen, *Folk Devils and Moral Panics. The Creation of the Mods and Rockers* (London: MacGibbon & Kee, 1972), 1.

[49] Quotation from Erich Goode, Nachman Ben-Yehuda, *Moral Panics. The Social Construction of Deviance* (Oxford: Blackwell, 1994), 43.

[50] "Deutsche Soldaten auf dem schwarzen Markt," *Der Fortschritt*, December 1952. See also "Täglich 15 Deutsche," *Industrie-Kurier*, November 25, 1952, "Menschenräuber unter uns," *Aachener Nachrichten*, October 15, 1952, DB-PA 060–7/2.

33,000 gone missing in serving the Legion.[51] These figures amounted to about seven times the actual figures of about 35,000 Germans serving in the Legion between 1945 and 1954 with no more than 11,000 serving at a time.[52] As in other areas, West Germans grossly overestimated their alleged victimization by the Allied victors of the Second World War.[53]

To be sure, French occupation authorities maintained recruitment bureaus for the Legion all over the French zone of occupation until 1955. French officials provided young men who showed interest in serving with free train tickets from anywhere in the Federal Republic to their major recruitment sites in Landau, Kehl, Freiburg, Offenburg, Baden-Baden, or Villingen for initial screening. Health and security tests in Foreign Legion camps in Kehl or Offenburg or, after January 1952, across the border in Strasbourg followed, and those who passed would receive French uniforms. They wore these to Marseilles, where they signed five-year contracts, often facing threats of violence if they were not willing to sign. Basic training was held in Sidi-Bel-Abbès Sidi bel Abbes in Algeria, and legionnaires were deployed for at least two years to Indochina.[54]

The figure of the "recruiter"—that is, a German national who was imagined to be on the payroll of the French occupation authorities and lured Germans into the Foreign Legion against their will—played virtually no role in getting Germans into the Legion. The recruiter was a product of postwar German fantasy. He embodied the absolute opposite to dominant norms and values in postwar society and assumed the characteristics of what sociologist Stanley Cohen defined as "folk devils." Recruiters represented a "personification of evil" and "models of deviance."[55] Newspaper reports labeled them "kidnappers,"[56] "pied pipers,"[57] "sellers of souls,"[58] "dirty headhunters,"[59] and "traffickers in human beings."[60] Like

[51]   Zentralsekretariat der Jungsozialisten in der SPD, *Die Fremdenlegion ruft Dich* (Bonn, 1954). An earlier pamphlet had cited the figure of 90,000, see Zentralsekretariat der Jungsozialisten in der SPD, *Menschenschmuggel in der Fremdenlegion* (Bonn, 1952). These figures were then also adopted and spread in the contemporary press, see "Legionswerber auf Menschenjagd," *Der Mittag*, June 4, 1954, DB-PA, 060-7/2. The figure of 36,000 dead Germans in the Foreign Legion was repeated in "Fremdenlegion—ein deutsches Versagen," *Der Fortschritt*, March 3, 1954; "Der Bundesminister wünscht es nicht," *Hamburger Echo*, June 4, 1954, DB-PA, 060-7/2.

[52]   Michels, *Deutsche in der Fremdenlegion*, 180.

[53]   On the similarly inflated estimates of German prisoners of war still held in Soviet captivity from the early 1950s, see Biess, *Homecomings*, 182.

[54]   On the recruitment process, see Michels, *Deutsche in der Fremdenlegion*, 228–31. The French refrained from recruiting in the Soviet zone of occupation, largely out of concern for French citizens who had served in the German army and were still held as prisoners of war in the Soviet Union; see Michels, *Deutsche in der Fremdenlegion,* 229.

[55]   Cohen, *Folk Devils and Moral Panics*, 44, 75.

[56]   "Menschenräuber unter uns," *Aachener Nachrichten*, October 15, 1952, DB-PA, 060-7/1.

[57]   "Deutsche springen über die Klinge," *Der Fortschritt*, November 28, 1952, DB-PA, 060-7/1.

[58]   "Fremdenlegionäre," *Rheinische Post*, February 6, 1953, DB-PA, 060-7/1.

[59]   "Legionärswerber sind 'schmutzige Kopfjäger," *General-Anzeiger Bonn*, December 9, 1954, DB-PA, 060-7/2.

[60]   "Menschenhandel mit Jungbergleuten," *Ruhr Nachrichten Dortmund*, December 22, 1951, DB-PA, 060-712.

vampires, they sought out "new blood for the Foreign Legion."[61] The *Frankfurter Allgemeine* called their activities a "festering wound on Germany's body."[62] What made recruiters so dangerous was that they were difficult to identify and possessed considerable psychological skills. They employed "seduction" and "subtle violence"; they had a knack for identifying conversation topics with which to gain the confidence of their victims, such as soccer or complaints about low earnings.[63] In many cases, they were said to use alcohol and other drugs to lure their innocent victims into the Legion.

These narratives of forced abduction appeared not only in tabloid newspapers but received quasi-official confirmation when several parliamentarians denounced the activities of recruiters in a *Bundestag* debate in January 1953. Even Chancellor Adenauer declared that it was "known to the federal government that German citizens are recruited for foreign military services in the Federal Republic."[64] A deputy from the oppositional Social Democrats reported that "mercenaries" had used the "methods of the darkest Middle Ages" to recruit several young Germans.[65] The SPD deliberately inflated the threat to German youth in order to undermine Chancellor Adenauer's policy of Western integration. SPD defense expert Fritz Erler even denounced the planned West German contribution to a European Defense Community as a "Foreign Legion," claiming that it would deny equal rights to Germans.[66] Turning up the rhetoric a notch in a debate on the Foreign Legion in the Baden-Württemberg state parliament, the deputy of the Christian Democratic Union (CDU), Häußler, compared recruiters to "vermin" attacking the "well-being of our youth" while his SPD colleague Ebert denounced them as "hyenas" preying on the "stranded of the last war."[67] Despite the fiercely divisive political culture of the early Federal Republic, the characterization of alleged recruiters as the embodiment of evil folk devils enjoyed bipartisan consensus.

---

[61] First quotation "Die Legion der Verdammten," *Düsseldorfer Nachrichten*, February 16, 1954, BArch, B106/16664; similar language regarding the "dismantling" or the "export" of German blood in *Der Mittag*, Düsseldorf, November 2, 1949, NWHStA, NW22/527, 59 and *Schwarzwälder Bote*, Nr. 210, December 12, 1952, HStABaWü, EA 2/302, Bü582.

[62] Erich Dombrowski, "Deutschlands wunde Stelle," *Frankfurter Allgemeine Zeitung*, February 5, 1955, BA-PA, 060–7/2.

[63] Guido Zöller, "Nachschub für die Fremdenlegion," *Rheinischer Merkur*, May 15, 1954, "Schluss mit der Legionärswerbung," *Weser-Kurier*, Bremen, May 15, 1954, DB-PA, 060–712.

[64] "Gegen die Werbung für die Fremdenlegion. Erklärung des Bundeskanzlers im Deutschen Bundestag zum Grenzzwischenfall von Schweigen," Bulletin, January 31, 1953, DB-PA, 060–712. See VDBT, *Stenographische Berichte*, 248. Sitzung, January 29, 1953, 11858.

[65] Ibid. 11859.

[66] Fritz Erler, "Das deutsche Kontingent—eine Fremdenlegion," ASD, NL Fritz Erler, Box 40C. Otto Niebergall, the delegate from the Communist Party of Germany (KPD) also charged that Western integration would turn "our entire people into a Foreign Legion," VDBT, *Stenographische Berichte*, 1. Wahlperiode, 248. Sitzung, January 29, 1953, 11863.

[67] Abgeordnete Häußler, Abgeordnete Ebert, Auszug aus den Verhandlungen der verfassungsgebenden Landesversammlung Baden-Württemberg, 23. Sitzung, January 21, 1953, EA2/303, Bü578.

Languages of Panic: Slavery and Homosexuality

Why did media reports about the abduction of young Germans influence political discourse at the highest levels? Why did these stories fall on such fertile
ground and why did they provoke the expression of such strong emotions?
References to "mass hysteria" or "collective delusion" do not really provide
satisfying answers. As Lyndal Roper has argued, fears and fantasies need to "relate
to experience" in order to grip a population.[68] West Germans' apprehensions
regarding the Foreign Legion reflected their own memories of total war, defeat,
and occupation, which, in turn, informed the ways in which they envisioned
threats to the social and moral order in their present and future. They voiced
anxieties regarding the sovereignty and inviolability of the national body in the
aftermath of the Second World War. Their fears pointed toward culturally
significant moments of heightened popular attention.[69] The moral panic regarding the Foreign Legion thus entailed a productive function by enabling postwar
Germans to articulate emotions that otherwise remained muted.

Germans invoked two distinct languages to make sense of this alleged threat:
slavery and homosexuality. Through these distinct discourses, the obsession with
the Foreign Legion functioned as what Stuart Hall has called a "signification
spiral." It linked the recruitment of young Germans into the Foreign Legion to
larger anxieties regarding the postwar order and the integrity of male youth.[70] In
their public protests against the Foreign Legion, Germans time and again resorted
to the imagery of "slavery." One father denounced forced recruitment to the
Legion as a "slave trade in the twentieth century." Another father petitioned the
federal parliament to invoke the International Court of Justice and the United
Nations against "public kidnapping on German soil" for "slave services" in the
Foreign Legion.[71] According to West German officials, the forced recruitment to
the Foreign Legion turned postwar Germany into the "most important market for
the modern slave trade in the twentieth century," while SPD press releases compared the French "smuggling of humans" into the Foreign Legion with the "robbery of humans being" in Communist Eastern Europe.[72]

The recourse to the language of slavery in framing narratives of postwar abduction reflected intense feelings of powerlessness and inferiority. It also invoked
historically specific memories, which cast Germans as hapless victims whose fate

[68] Lyndal Roper, *Witch Craze. Terror and Fantasy in Baroque Germany* (New Haven: Yale University
Press, 2004), 8.
[69] Quotation Goode and Ben-Yehuda, *Moral Panics*, 111.
[70] On this aspect of moral panic, see Thompson, *Moral Panics*, 19–21.
[71] Wilhelm D. to Sozialministerium, Mainz, Dr. Schesmer, September 22, 1953, Konrad F. to
Petitionsausschuss des Deutschen Bundestages, May 15, 1954, both in LHAK, Best.880, Nr. 176.
[72] Abgeordnete Ebert, Auszug aus den Verhandlungen der verfassunggebenden
Landesversammlung Baden-Württemberg, 23. Sitzung, January 21, 1953, HStABaWü, EA2/303,
Bü578; SPD Pressedienst, February 4, 1953, ASD.

was completely at the mercy of foreign powers. This sense of German victimization was deeply embedded in German historical consciousness and predated the Second World War. In a debate in the state parliament of Rhineland-Palatinate in November 1952, for example, the SPD deputy Hertel invoked the Count of Hesse's practice of selling German soldiers to the English to fight in the American War of Independence in the latter half of the eighteenth century.[73] Others invoked more recent memories of France's use of colonial African soldiers in its occupation of the Rhineland from 1919 to 1930, which right-wing memories called "the black shame." The language of slavery thus echoed long-standing historical fears of being colonized by rival Western powers.[74] While, in the interwar period, Germans compared their country to a female rape victim, the abducted young male now became an allegory.[75] Stories of male abduction into the French Foreign Legion also echoed similar concerns about the "fraternization" of German women with American occupation soldiers. In both cases, a highly gendered collaboration with the Allied occupiers—either forced or voluntary—symbolized larger anxieties regarding the limited autonomy and sovereignty of the nation at large.[76]

The extreme violence during and after the Second World War further enhanced narratives of young German men's enslavement. A 1952 pamphlet by the Young Socialists, for example, equated the recruitment of young Germans into the Legion with the "brutal disregard for human beings" during and after the Second World War for which "millions of human beings needed to pay with their lives—Jews, members of other nations, and us too."[77] Two years later, another *Juso* pamphlet on the subject decried that young German men were dying next to "Moroccans" and "negroes" on behalf of a "misguided and anachronistic French colonialism."[78] Thus, it mixed statements opposing French colonialism with racist indignation

---

[73] Abg. Hertel, Auszug aus der 30. Sitzung des Landtages Rheinland-Pfalz, November 18, 1952, LHAK, Best.880, Nr. 145. I have found no references to the recruitment of German soldiers for the Napoleonic armies during the early nineteenth century. In this context, see Ute Planert, *Der Mythos vom Befreiungskrieg. Frankreichs Kriege und der deutsche Süden. Alltag-Wahrnehmung-Deutung 1792–1841* (Paderborn: Schöningh, 2007), 408–73.

[74] Before 1945, these fears served as a motivating force for German imperialism; see Shelley Baranowski, *Nazi Empire. German Colonialism and Imperialism from Bismarck to Hitler* (Cambridge: Cambridge University Press, 2011), 1–8, 155, Verber, "Conundrum of Colonialism," 26–32; Jared Poley, *Decolonization in Germany. Weimar Narratives of Colonial Loss and Foreign Occupation* (Bern: Peter Lang, 2005), 215–47.

[75] See Keith Nelson, "The 'Black Horror' on the Rhine. Race as a Factor in Post-World War I Diplomacy," *Journal of Modern History* 42/4 (1970): 602–27, Iris Wigger, "'Black Shame'—the Campaign Against 'Racial Degeneration' and Female Degradation in Interwar Europe," *Race and Class* 51/3 (2010): 33–46.

[76] Elizabeth Heineman, "The Hour of the Woman: Memories of Germany's 'Crisis Years' and West German National Identity," *American Historical Review* 101/2 (1996): 354–96, Mari Höhn, *GIs and Fräuleins. The German-American Encounter in 1950s West Germany* (Chapel Hill: University of North Carolina Press, 2002).

[77] *Juso* pamphlet, "Menschenschmuggel in der Fremdenlegion," 14. On postwar victimization, see Robert G. Moeller, *War Stories. The Search for a Usable Past in the Federal Republic of Germany* (Berkeley: University of California Press, 2001).

[78] *Juso* pamphlet, "Die Fremdenlegion ruft Dich," 7, 9.

about the equation of young Germans with non-white people. As such, these pamphlets echoed fears of Allied revenge and retribution by Jewish displaced persons or African American GIs from the immediate postwar period.[79] The postwar fantasy of German enslavement was therefore part and parcel of a lingering horizon of expectation, in which Germans feared that they would suffer treatment they had meted out to others during the war.

Germans also frequently used the language of international law and human rights to protest their alleged mistreatment by the Allied victors. For example, the leader of the Free Democratic Party, Erich Mende, argued in the federal parliament that the methods of recruitment contradicted the European Convention on Human Rights from 1950 to which France was a party.[80] A father who believed the Legion had abducted his son called on the United Nations or the "international court" to end the practice.[81] The newspaper *Westdeutsche Allgemeine* called recruiters "hunters for boys" (*Burschenjäger*), comparing their activities to the "international trafficking in girls" that the United Nations had put on its agenda to eliminate.[82] Germans also charged the Allied victors with hypocrisy. For example, a Catholic priest admonished French authorities "not to employ the same methods that they had condemned in the Nuremberg trials."[83] West German human rights activism during the 1950s centered above all on the ostensible violation of German rights by the Allied victors in the aftermath of total defeat, and it often assumed a decidedly conservative bent.[84] The alleged abduction of young Germans into the Foreign Legion served as a prime example for this conservative West German human rights discourse.

Unlike earlier historical panics around "white slavery" around the turn of the century, popular concerns in post-Second World War Germany focused on the abduction of young men, not young women.[85] This preoccupation with the moral endangerment of young men stemmed in no small part from the demographic

---

[79] See Chapter 1 in this book.

[80] Erich Mende, VDBT, *Stenographische Berichte*, 2. Wahlperiode, 58. Sitzung, December 8, 1954, 2962.

[81] Konrad F. to Petitionsausschuss des Deutschen Bundestages, May 15, 1954, LHAK, Best.880, Nr. 176, also in NRWHStA, NW 034, Nr. 007, 314.

[82] "Burschenhandel," *Westdeutsche Allgemeine*, February 20, 1953, DB-PA, 060–7/2.

[83] Walter G., Pfarrer, to Herr Bucher, Innenministerium Baden-Württemberg, February 19, 1951, HStABaWü, EA 2/303 Bü578. The whole incident turned out to be "completely fabricated," see Gottfried Leonard, Abgeordneter des Deutschen Bundestages to Innenminister Ulrich, February 27, 1951, HStABaWü, EA 2/303, Bü578.

[84] Lora Wildenthal, *The Language of Human Rights in West Germany* (Philadelphia: University of Pennsylvania Press, 2012), Samuel Moyn, *Christian Human Rights* (Philadelphia: University of Pennsylvania Press, 2015), Marco Duranti, "Conservatives and the European Convention on Human Rights," in Norbert Frei, Annette Weinke, eds, *Toward a New Moral World Order? Menschenrechtspolitik und Völkerrecht seit 1945* (Göttingen: Wallstein, 2013), 82–93.

[85] On "white slavery," see Mark Thomas Connelly, *The Response to Prostitution in the Progressive Era* (Chapel Hill: University of North Carolina Press, 1980); on the parallel German fears of trafficking in girls around the turn of the century, see Bettina Hitzer, *Im Netz der Liebe. Die protestantische Kirche und ihre Zuwanderer in der Metropole Berlin (1849–1914)* (Cologne: Böhlau, 2006), 112–19.

imbalance in postwar Germany that had resulted from predominantly male casualties in the Second World War. Young men were scarce in postwar Germany, and their alleged enslavement in the Foreign Legion threatened the very essence of postwar reconstruction. The anxiety about losing precious men for their rebuilding and reproductive capacities became, in the postwar German imagination, a distinct threat to the postwar moral order as well. Narratives of abduction cast the recruitment of young German men not just as enslavement but also as a form of sexual transgression and, especially, of homosexual seduction.[86]

West German reconstruction was crucially linked to the (re)assertion of normative heterosexuality within newly reconstructed families.[87] This definition of postwar masculinity, centering on the civilian ideals of fatherhood and family life rather than on military service, also entailed a "negative foil": the cultural stereotype of the older, corrupting homosexual who threatened to seduce young men and thus posed a severe danger to the family and to the nation at large.[88] Postwar homophobia stood in the continuity of the Nazi persecution of homosexuality, which had stoked fears of gay men's predatory seduction.[89] Fears of homosexual seduction also resulted from a keen awareness of what historian Dagmar Herzog has called the "fragility of heterosexuality," which itself derived from a conception of sexuality as fluid and as subject to a variety of external social and cultural factors. Corrupting influences, either by entrance into specific milieus or by contact with particular individuals, held the power to derail the development of a stable heterosexual identity, especially among young men.[90] Thus, Germans sought to protect their youth from sexuality in general and homo-sexuality in particular.

Stories of the abduction of young Germans into the Foreign Legion drew on the trope of homosexual seduction. Media representations located the alleged abduction into the Legion in urban spaces that were marked as sites of ill-repute and moral transgression while also being associated with homosexual seduction, such as bars, fairs, and in the vicinity of train stations. And even though service in

---

[86] On the link between moral panic and sexual transgression, see the seminal study by Judith Walkowitz, City of Dreadful Delight. Narratives of Sexual Danger in Late Victorian London (Chicago: University of Chicago Press, 1992).

[87] Robert G. Moeller, Protecting Motherhood. Women and the Family in the Politics of Postwar West Germany (Berkeley: University of California Press, 1993), Robert G. Moeller, "The Homosexual Man is a 'Man', the Homosexual Woman is a 'Woman'. Sex, Society, and the Law in Postwar West Germany," Journal of the History of Sexuality 4/3 (1994): 395–438.

[88] Moeller, War Stories, 88–122, Clayton J. Whisnant, "Styles of Masculinity in the West German Gay Scence, 1950–1965," Central European History 39/3 (2006): 359–93.

[89] Stefan Micheler, "Homophobic Propaganda and the Denunciation of Same-Sex- Desiring Men under National Socialism," in Dagmar Herzog, ed., Sexuality and German Fascism (New York: Berghahn Books, 2005), 95–130.

[90] Julia Ubbelohde, "Der Umgang mit jugendlichen Normverstößen," in Ulrich Herbert, ed., Wandlungsprozesse in Westdeutschland. Belastung, Integration, Liberalisierung 1945–1980, (Göttingen: Wallstein, 2007), 408, Dagmar Herzog, Sex after Fascism. Memory and Morality in Twentieth Century Germany (Princeton: Princeton University Press, 2005), 88–95.

the Foreign Legion often entailed the promise of "other countries, other girls," the press generally cast recruitment to the Legion in terms of the danger of homosexual transgressions.[91] Former legionnaires reported that homosexuality was common in the Legion.[92] Because recruiters were often described as veterans of the Legion, they fit an image of older homosexuals who would want to seduce innocent young German men.[93] This is also why West German officials repeatedly proposed "secret police surveillance" of veterans of the Foreign Legion.[94]

This cultural coding of alleged recruiters as corrupting homosexuals significantly contributed to their construction as "folk devils" in popular media. Recruiters were depicted as slightly effeminate yet in adherence to the demands of bourgeois respectability, which rendered them even more dangerous and difficult to identify.[95] For example, the tabloids described recruiters as the "handsome Fred" or the "handsome Willi," a "dark-haired man in his mid-thirties" who posed as harmless fabric dealers. Recruiters were described as "well dressed," "always having money," "elegant," or, in one case, "driving an American luxury limousine."[96]

Public representations also linked recruitment to prostitution and sex trade. Commentators speculated that the Foreign Legion compensated recruiters largely on the basis of the number of young men they recruited.[97] The CDU deputy Demmerle in the Rhineland-Palatinate state parliament denounced recruiters as "political and military pimps."[98] Recruiters posed a similar menace to German youth as homosexual seducers: both of these figures preyed on essentially innocent young Germans whose immaturity nevertheless rendered them susceptible to the allure of transgressive acts. The moral panic regarding the Foreign Legion

[91] "Menschenjagd auf fremde Rechnung," *Stern* 4/2 (1952): 6–7, "Werkstudent in die Fremdenlegion gelockt," *Rhein-Zeitung Koblenz*, August 10, 1954, DB-PA, 060–7/2. On train stations as sites of homosexual prostitution, see Jennifer V. Evans, "Bahnhof Boys. Policing Male Prostitution in Post-Nazi Berlin," *Journal of the History of Sexuality* 12/4 (2003): 605–36.

[92] For a former member of the Legion, see statement of Theodor S., NRWHStA, NW034, Nr. 006, 29.

[93] "So wirbt bei uns die Fremdenlegion," *Echo der Woche*, May 12, 1952, DB-PA, 060–7/2.

[94] Landeskriminalamt Baden-Württemberg, Bericht über die Sitzung des Ausschusses für Jugendfragen, January 20, 1955, HStABaWü, EA 2/303, Bü581; Innenministerium Baden-Württemberg to Regierungspräsidien, July 2, 1955, HStABaWü, EA 2/303, Bü583.

[95] The depiction of French or French-inspired men as effeminate also constituted a cultural stereotype dating back to the eighteenth century. Yet, because effeminacy is also often associated with homosexuality, the two perceptions are not mutually exclusive. See Ruth Florack,"'Weiber sind wie Franzosen geborne Weltleute.' Zur Verschränkung von Geschlechter-Klisches und nationalen Wahrnehmungsmustern," in Ruth Florack, ed., *Nation als Stereotyp. Fremdwahrnehmungen und Identität in deutscher und französischer Literatur*, (Tübingen: Niemeyer, 2000), 319–37.

[96] "Menschenhandel mit Jungbergleuten," *Ruhr Nachrichten Dortmund*, December 22, 1951, DB-PA, 060–712, "Willi lebt vom Menschenhandel," *Die Welt*, 21 March 1952, DB-PA, 060–7/2, "Bis gleich—und dann kommt die Wüstenfront," *Westdeutsche Allgemeine*, November 19, 1952, DB-PA, 060–7/2; last two quotations, Anzeige Anton R. gegen unbekannt, Polizeibehörde Köln, StA Freiburg, B728/1, Nr. 4482.

[97] "Fremdenlegionäre," *Rheinische Post*, February 6, 1953, "Menschenräuber unter uns," *Aachener Nachrichten*, October 15, 1952, DB-PA, 060–7/2.

[98] Abg. Demmerle, Auszug aus der 30. Sitzung des Landtages Rheinland-Pfalz, November 18, 1952, LHAK, Best.880, Nr. 145.

Figure 2.2. Image of an alleged "recruiter."

This image from the magazine *Stern* depicts an alleged recruiter for the Foreign Legion. The caption reads: "The handsome Fred in action. This photograph of one of the most active recruiters was taken in a dance bar in Essen. Disguised as a photographer for postcards, the *Stern* reporter took a picture of a drunken guest (in the foreground), next to whom Fred Schulze (with mustache) was sitting. Meanwhile, his victims are sending the first pictures of their existence in the Legion."

Source: Stern 5/2 (1952): 7.

both enforced and reflected the intense homophobia of the 1950s. It articulated anxieties regarding the sovereignty and moral integrity of the national body in and through narratives of deviant sexuality.

Much as fears of German enslavement derived from deeper memories of real or imagined German victimization, representations of the recruiter as corrupting homosexual drew on long-standing cultural stereotypes castigating homosexuals as a threat to normative masculine citizenship. The rhetoric of the blood-sucking parasite and the effeminate yet dangerous sexual seducer combined traditional, although now largely taboo, antisemitic ideas. Nazi antisemitism merged traditional folk beliefs in the utility of blood (as in ritual murder accusations) with more modern fears of blood pollution through miscegenation between Jewish and non-Jewish Germans.[99] Such Nazi fantasies about the Jews need to be taken seriously in order to understand the functioning of Nazi antisemitism. In light of

[99] David Biale, *Blood and Belief. The Circulation of a Symbol between Jews and Christians* (Berkeley: University of California Press, 2007), 123–61.

the persistence of antisemitism, these fantasies would have continued to exist in postwar Germany.[100] The myth of the recruiter thus replicated the structure of popular antisemitic beliefs while directing them at a new target. Similar to ritual murder fantasies, the abduction and enslavement of young Germans in the Foreign Legion implied the sacrifice of German blood for foreign interests in an alien and inhospitable context. And like the fear of race pollution, the analogy between recruitment to the Legion and homosexual seduction evoked the danger of internal decline and moral disintegration. To be sure, the ostensible threat from Jews in Nazi Germany and recruiters in postwar Germany of course triggered very different actions and policies. Still, the structural analogies between the cultural representations of Jews in Nazi Germany and of recruiters to the Legion in the 1950s might explain, at least in part, why the fantasy of the recruiter resonated so broadly in postwar society. The concept of recruiters as "folk devils" drew on a pre-existing imaginary construct in which hidden, devious, and hostile forces threatened the integrity both of the national body and of individual (male) bodies. As such, the recruiter to the Legion might have appeared to postwar Germans as a rather familiar threat in a new disguise.

The Decline of the Abduction Narrative

Widely articulated fears regarding forced abductions of young Germans to the Foreign Legion placed mounting pressure on West German officials to counter the threat through legislation. The occupation statute prevented the legal prosecution of citizens of the occupying states until 1955. In January 1946, the Allied Control Council had also declared invalid paragraph 141 of the German criminal code, which had criminalized the recruitment of Germans to a foreign military. As a result, recruitment activity was beyond the reach of West German law. Facing mounting criticism from the oppositional Social Democrats, the Adenauer government reactivated paragraph 141 in March 1953.[101] This gave West German officials a legal instrument to prosecute recruiters to the Foreign Legion who were German citizens. The law countered the sense of helplessness that West Germans experienced with respect to recruitment to the Foreign Legion. At the same time, it also led to the decline of the abduction narrative.

---

[100] See Alon Confino, "Fantasies about the Jews. Cultural Reflections on the Holocaust," *History and Memory* 17/1/2 (2005), 296–322, Werner Bergmann, Rainer Erb, *Anti-Semitism in Germany. The Post-Nazi Epoch from 1945 to 1995*, trans. Belinda Copper, Allison Brown (London: Routledge, 2017), 1.

[101] See, for example, Kleine Anfrage Nr. 279 der Fraktion der SPD—Unterbindung der Werbung für die Fremdenlegion, Deutscher Bundestag, 1. Wahlperiode, Drucksache Nr. 3468, Nr. 3558. Bundesgesetzblatt (BGbl), Teil I, Nr. 8, March 7, 1953, 42; see also Michels, "Die Bundesrepublik und die französische Fremdenlegion, 1949–1962," 456–8.

In light of the intense public discussion of this issue, West German courts were highly sensitized toward charges of recruitment to the Foreign Legion and vigorously prosecuted even the slightest suspicion of an abduction. Parents who suspected that their sons had fallen victim to a "recruiter" initiated prosecutions on the basis of paragraph 141.[102] Sometimes young men who alleged recruiters had approached them went to the police. Bystanders too reported suspicious conversations that they overheard in bars.[103] In general, it did not take much to be convicted on the basis of paragraph 141.

In February 1954, for example, the court in Wuppertal sentenced 26-year-old Joachim Hans W. to four months in prison for his role in facilitating the recruitment of a 20-year-old man to the Legion. The defendant had served in the Legion from 1947 to 1953, reportedly because he sought to escape prosecution as a member of the Waffen SS. W. had met the 20-year-old son of his accuser in the waiting room of the local unemployment office, where he had described his previous service in the Legion as "hard but nice" and shown him photographs from his time in the Legion. He had given the young man a map to the recruitment office in Landau as well as letters of introduction in French for the French authorities. Although the victim already possessed an "inner willingness" to sign up for the Legion and W. did not benefit from his actions, the court justified the verdict by citing the suffering of his accusers at their son's trying to join the Legion as well as the hope that the penalty would deter future recruitment.[104] In similar cases, the courts sentenced defendants to prison terms ranging from five to nine months because they had given positive accounts of their time in the Legion or had provided directions to recruitment bureaus.[105] According to a court in Koblenz, it did not matter whether alleged recruiters had significantly influenced the "will" of potential recruits to join the Foreign Legion—they had violated the law solely by facilitating contact between a young German and the representative of a foreign military power.[106] It also did not matter whether the alleged victim actually ended up in the Legion—in most of these cases, the French authorities turned them away. The West German Ministry of Justice interpreted paragraph 141 as distinguishing "recruitment" (anwerben) to a foreign military service by contractual agreement from the "bringing into contact" (zuführen) of a German citizen to the "sphere of activity" of a foreign military power. Both activities fell under

---

[102] Eheleute R. to Ministerium des Äusseren, March 8, 1955, BArch, B 106/16670.
[103] Regierungs- und Kriminalrat Amend to Bundesminister des Inneren, March 24, 1954, BArch, B 106/16670.
[104] Verdict, Hans Joachim W., 5 Ms75/53, February 12, 1954, NRWHStA, NW 034, Nr. 007, 269–70.
[105] See Verdict, Schöffengericht Schorndorf, October 5, 1955; Verdict, Amtsgericht Landau, April 28, 1954, both in BArch, B106/16670.
[106] Verdict, Amtsgericht Koblenz, Kurt K., March 21, 1955, BArch, B106/16670.

the provision of paragraph 141, yet most of those convicted under this law were found guilty of merely "bringing into contact" a German man with the Legion.[107]

Paragraph 141 thus exhibited parallels to the expanded version of paragraph 175 criminalizing homosexuality, because it was implemented under National Socialism in 1935 and remained in effect until 1969 in the Federal Republic.[108] Just as paragraph 141 criminalized any activity that might eventually lead to recruitment, rather than recruitment alone, paragraph 175 of the same code criminalized any kind of intimacy between same-sex people, rather than restricting its ban to sexual acts. Thus, like the public discourse, the structure of the statute suggested an analogy between recruitment to the Foreign Legion and homosexual seduction. Some prosecutors accused alleged recruiters of violating both provisions, such as a prosecutor in Düsseldorf who charged one Fritz A. with both ongoing attempts at "human kidnapping for the Legion" and intending to have homosexual sex with his victims in December 1953.[109] In another case, the court noted that an alleged recruiter had previously been arrested for exhibitionism.[110] Similar anxieties regarding the susceptibility of young Germans to the dangerous promises of older men inspired both criminal statutes.

Despite judges' and prosecutors' vigorous attempts to apply paragraph 141, the new law eventually yielded very disappointing results. Whereas the high numbers of investigations underlined prosecutors' determination to follow up on even remote suspicions, prosecution turned out to be difficult because insufficient evidence did not warrant further investigations, let alone conviction. According to a survey of the Ministry of Justice from October 1954, prosecutors had initiated 145 proceedings regarding paragraph 141, of which 115 were eventually dropped. Only nine people were convicted, six of them in the state of Rhineland-Palatinate.[111] Some commentators blamed the limited number of convictions under paragraph 141 on West German officials' cooperation with the French government.[112] But it was more common for these cases to lead observers to doubt the validity of the abduction narrative.

Police investigations of ostensible abductions often revealed that the victims had signed up for the Legion of their own volition. When Erna P.'s son

---

[107] Bundesminister der Justiz to Auswärtiges Amt und Bundesminister des Innern, September 21, 1954, BArch, B 106/16653.

[108] Geoffrey J. Giles, "The Institutionalization of Homosexual Panic in the Third Reich," in Robert Gellately, Nathan Stoltzfus, eds, *Social Outsiders in Nazi Germany* (Princeton: Princeton University Press, 2001), 233–55.

[109] Generalstaatsanwalt Dü to Justizminister NRW, March 12, 1953, NRWHStA, NW377/4936, 2–5. For a similar link between suspicions of offenses on the basis of paragraphs 141 and 175, see Oberstaatsanwalt to Justizminister, January 4, 1955, NRWHStA, NW377/4936, 28–31.

[110] Innenminister des Landes Nordrhein-Westfalen to Regierungspräsident, May 3, 1955, NRWHStA, NW034/Nr.006, 155.

[111] Ministerium der Justiz to Auswärtiges Amt, October 6, 1954, BArch, B141/4061, 64.

[112] "Fremdenlegion—ein deutsches Versagen," *Spiegel der Zeit*, March 3, 1954, BArch, B 106/16670, "Fremdenlegion—Werber unter stiller Duldung," *Der Fortschritt*, May 20, 1954, DB-PA 060-7/2.

Hans-Georg was missing shortly before he was supposed to take his final state exam at the University of Münster in November 1954, she immediately suspected that he had been abducted into the Legion. Yet a police inquiry soon exposed a different truth: Hans-Georg was no longer an active student at the university and had been involved in a relationship with an older woman who intended to divorce her husband and marry him. He had joined the Legion voluntarily in order to escape his difficult academic and personal circumstances.[113] In some cases, charges of recruitment to the Legion also backfired on the accusers. When one woman denounced a friend of her son as a potential recruiter to the Legion, the police not only quickly disproved the accusation but also charged Frau M. with slander, citing her previous history of denouncing local individuals to authorities during the Nazi period.[114] Mounting evidence began to suggest that former legionnaires, as well as individuals the Legion had turned away, invented the abduction narrative in order to obscure their own choices and failures. One alleged victim simply made up the story in order "to get a free ticket home." A man from Bonn accused a friend of having persuaded him to join the Legion to distract his family from his decision to abandon his wife and three children.[115] West German authorities increasingly began to doubt the "fairy tale of a recruitment with the help of alcohol" and suspected that rejected volunteers invented these stories.[116]

The narrative of abduction also served as a way to conceal potentially explosive and disruptive family conflicts. In one case, officials reported that a young man had joined the Legion without any recruiter's involvement in order to flee his father's "severe physical abuse."[117] Another story circulated in the author's family memory. Heinz B. was a legionnaire who died in Indochina in June 1949. His family always asserted that Heinz had been abducted into the Legion. However, it appears that Heinz sought to escape a family crisis. An aunt had sought to seduce him. When Heinz was reluctant, she threatened to inform his father of an alleged affair with him. Terrified of his authoritarian father and of a potential family scandal, Heinz volunteered for the Legion.[118]

---

[113] Erna P. to Bundesinnenministerium, November 3, 1954; Bericht, March 30, 1955; NRWHStA, NW34, Nr. 007, 292–6.

[114] Polizeiamt Mayen, LKP Nebenstelle, Ermittlungsbericht, December 30, 1953, LHAK, Best.880, Nr. 176.

[115] Vermerk, LKP Nebenstelle Frankenthal, February 4, 1954, Festnahme von Karl Heinz F.; Abt. 1-k Tgb, Nr. 169–57, Betr. Schreiben des Waffenschlossers Gustav N., December 28, 1956, both in LHAK, Best.180, Nr. 176; see also the case described in Rheinland Pfalz, Ministerium des Inneren to Bundesminister des Innern, November 24, 1954, BArch, B106/16660.

[116] To the DPA, July 9, 1954, LHAK, Best.880, Nr. 145.

[117] Memo, to Herr Unterabt. Leiter ZB, June 13, 1955, BArch, B 106/16653.

[118] Letter by Thomas to Waltraud, August 9, 1949; in my possession; oral history interview with Heinz B.'s older brother, Kurt B. (born 1928), August 18, 2010; audio-file of interview in my possession. Because a family member died in the service of the French military, the family was then provided with housing in the French zone of occupation in south-western Germany.

By the mid 1950s, evidence began to mount that young Germans entered the Legion willingly. Shortly after the reinstatement of paragraph 141, according to a March 1953 report, the heads of the West German regional police forces believed that the "overwhelming majority of young people who are recruited to the Foreign Legion come to this decision voluntarily."[119] Interviews with escaped or returned legionnaires also fostered increasing doubts regarding alleged abductions. In August 1954, only 7 of 47 German legionnaires who had been repatriated through the German embassy in Bangkok claimed anything nefarious in their recruitment. A few months later, all the 40 German legionnaires who had deserted in the Suez Canal on their transfer from Indochina to North Africa admitted that they had joined the Legion voluntarily.[120] West German officials now also criticized what they saw as the "false conception among the public regarding the procedures of the French Foreign Legion."[121] In the longest debate concerning the Foreign Legion issue in the *Bundestag* in October 1954, the Federal Minister of the Interior, Gerhard Schröder, claimed that Germans joined willingly and challenged the assumption that "recruiters are among us."[122] West German officials now increasingly denounced reports of alleged abductions. One official from the Rhineland-Palatinate criticized such reports of the tabloid press as "pure sensationalism" and as being "completely opposed to the facts."[123] Even newspaper accounts began to concede that recruiters were imaginary, and abductions and seductions the stuff of fantasy.[124]

Voluntarism and the Fragility of Male Youth

The recognition of young men's voluntarism led to a shift in West German concerns about the Legion. Rather than seeing it as an external threat, young men's decision to sign up for the Legion brought into focus the internal sources of social

---

[119] To Referent ZB 3 im Hause, Tagung der Leiter der Landeskriminalämter mit dem Bundeskriminalamt in Berlin, March 27, 1953, BArch, B 106/16652. The police chief of Mannheim held a similar view, see "Bauernfang für die Fremdenlegion," *Rhein-Neckar Zeitung*, January 13, 1953, DB-PA, 060–7/2. See also Dr. Kanter, Ministerium der Justiz to Auswärtiges Amt, August 1954, BArch, B 141/4060, 111.

[120] Bericht über die seit dem 1.4.1954 von den deutschen Vertretungen (Gesandtschaft Bangkok, Generalkonsulat Singapur) heimgeschafften ehemaligen Fremdenlegionäre deutscher Nationalität, BArch, B 141/4060, 122–4; "Keiner wurde zur Legion gezwungen," *Westdeutsche Allgemeine*, March 5, 1955, DB-PA 060–7/2.

[121] Vermerk, Herrn Unterabt. Leiter ZB, June 13, 1955, BArch, B106/16653.

[122] Schröder, VDBT, *Stenographische Berichte*, 2. Wahlperiode, 58. Sitzung, December 8, 1954, 2963 and Schneider, ibid. 2960.

[123] To the DPA, July 9, 1954, Bericht über Werbung von FL unter Alkoholeinfluss in der Tageszeitung Freiheit am 28.6.1954, LHAK, Best.880, Nr.145.

[124] "Deutsche gehen freiwillig in die Legion," *Der Mittag*, June 13, 1956, DB-PA, 060–72.

problems. By the second half of the 1950s, rearmament, West Germany's entry into the North Atlantic Treaty Organization (NATO), the concurrent granting of full sovereignty, and persistent economic growth quieted fears based on occupation, helplessness, and visions of retribution. Young Germans' voluntary entrance into the Foreign Legion now signified an internal "social and psychological problem" in West German society.[125] A changing media ethic that was increasingly willing to subject West German society and its political elites to critical scrutiny contributed to this shift of seeing the Foreign Legion primarily as an internal rather than an external threat.[126]

The recognition that most West Germans entered the Legion voluntarily was at least as disconcerting to West German officials and the general public as the fantasy of the recruiter. Rather than a clearly identifiable external threat, young Germans' attraction to the Legion now appeared as a specific symptom of much more diffuse pathologies within West German society, and within industrial modernity more generally. Social workers and youth welfare officials identified the Legion as one of the many dangers that threatened what they saw as the fragile and unstable moral well-being of West German youth.[127] West German officials thus employed various disciplinary strategies to prevent young men from signing up for the Legion. Since anybody under the age of 21 needed parental consent to get a passport, the border police tried to prevent young men from crossing the German border to Strasbourg. German police in the border town of Kehl arrested several hundred volunteers for the Legion for trying to cross the border illegally in 1954.[128] When it became legal to cross the border without a passport in 1956, efforts to combat the attraction of the Legion to West German youth through police control and arrest gave way to attempts at dissuasion.[129]

Official counter-strategies to the Foreign Legion now shifted from combating alleged recruiters to a variety of measures aimed at young Germans themselves

---

[125] Kriminalhauptkommissar Stimpfig, Ausschuss für Jugendfragen, Kurzprotokoll, 14. Sitzung, January 20, 1955, BArch, B141/4062, 33.

[126] Hodenberg, Konsens und Krise, 293–360.

[127] On West German youth, see Jaimey Fisher, Disciplining Germany. Youth, Reeducation, and Reconstruction after the Second World War (Detroit: Wayne State University Press, 2007), Mark Roseman, "The Organic Society and the 'Massenmenschen': Integrating Young Labor in the Ruhr Mines, 1945–1958," German History 8/2 (1990): 165–94, Ubbelohde, "Der Umgang mit jugendlichen Normverstößen," Edward Ross Dickinson, The Politics of German Child Welfare from the Empire to the Federal Republic (Cambridge, Mass.: Harvard University Press, 1996), 244–85.

[128] Heinrich L. Nieder, "Die französische Fremdenlegion—Légion Étrangère—und ihre Auswirkungen auf Deutsche" (Ph.D. Dissertation, Erlangen, 1962), 73. Regierungspräsidium Südbaden an das Innenministerium Baden-Württemberg, November 19, 1954, StA Freiburg, F 30/5, Nr. 26. After 1956, no passport, only a simple identification card, was necessary to cross the border to France.

[129] See Nieder, "Die französische Fremdenlegion," 79–81. On the long history of church-run "missions" at train stations, see Hitzer, Im Netz der Liebe.

that ran the gamut from establishing greater social control to developing a more effective counter-propaganda to the Legion. In keeping with their very significant role in alleviating social problems in postwar West Germany, church welfare organizations such as the Protestant Aid Society and the Catholic *Caritas* played an especially important role in these efforts. Representatives of these associations lingered in the train station in Landau and tried to identify young Germans who appeared to be willing to join the Legion, as reflected in their possession of special tickets or the French stamps in their passports.[130] Protestant and Catholic youth organizations also operated several youth homes throughout West Germany that would provide temporary shelter for potential volunteers to the Foreign Legion.[131] West German officials planned to take all volunteers under 21 into protective custody and commit them to one of these homes until they were reunited with their parents, because they could not prevent legal adults from volunteering.[132] Approximately 2,000 young men passed through these homes from mid 1953 to the end of 1955. They were either returned to their families or the homes employed them for several months until they could find a job nearby.[133]

The emphasis on young Germans' volition also promoted a renewed search for their motives to sign up for the Legion. Structural problems such as unemployment, poverty, and homelessness constituted important factors in the decision to join up. Sociological studies showed that volunteers for the Legion represented a social group that had failed to benefit from the—initially slow, yet gradually accelerating—West German economic recovery. A 1962 dissertation by Heinrich Nieder, who had worked in the unemployment office in Landau and had collected first-hand experience with volunteers, offered the most precise social profile of this group. More than half the volunteers were under 21 years of age and hence legal minors, two-thirds of them were unskilled or worked in mining and agriculture. Family difficulties accounted for about 20 per cent of volunteers for the Legion, and a similar percentage of volunteers were looking to escape prosecution for a criminal offense.[134] "The Foreign Legion appears to be one place to which young men escape if something goes wrong in their lives and if they become

[130] See the list of homes willing to take in volunteers to the Legion, Innenministerium Baden-Württemberg to Regierungspräsidium Freiburg, August 28, 1953, Staatsarchiv Freiburg, S60/1, Nr. 445.

[131] Niederschrift über die Besprechung am 8. März 1955 im Innenministerium über die Fremdenlegion, HStABaWü, EA2/303, Bü581.

[132] Hilfswerk der Evangelischen Kirche, Betreuung legionswilliger Jugendlicher und entlassener Fremdenlegionäre, NRWHStA, NW61/Nr. 029, 181.

[133] Nieder, "Die französische Fremdenlegion," 41, 53, 61.

[134] Dr. Utermann, "Kurze Stellungnahme zur Frage der aufgegriffenen Legionswilligen, die aus oder über Nordrhein-Westfalen den Weg zur Grenze in Rheinland Pfalz nehmen," NRWHStA, NW 648, Nr. 154, 3–10. Other reports, however, cited much lower figures for criminals among the volunteers, see Ausschuss für Jugendfragen, Kurzprotokoll, 14. Sitzung, January 20, 1955, Minister Zimmer, BArch, B 141/4062, 32.

desperate for some reason," as one observer put it.[135] Observers attributed young Germans' willingness to join the Legion to the social consequences of war and defeat. According to one statistic, 77 per cent of those volunteers for the Legion who were held back in the transition home in Landau grew up without a father. In this view, the lack of social and familial bonds impeded the development of a strong "sociocultural personality" and hence lessened young Germans' capacity to resist the appeal of the Legion.[136] Economic insecurity as well as social disloca-tion were believed to render young Germans' susceptible to the Legion.

As Germany reached virtually full employment by the second half of the 1950s, such structural socio-economic factors no longer sufficed to explain the lure of the Legion. West German officials frequently invoked intangible factors to explain young West Germans' decision to enter the Legion.[137] In particular, the "thirst for adventure" featured prominently in these analyses. One official study from North Rhine-Westphalia put the number who cited this motive, in combination with other factors, at 40 per cent.[138] Many volunteers, Nieder concluded, saw the Foreign Legion as an attractive alternative compared with the "uniform reality of daily life and average existence."[139] In this view, the Foreign Legion represented an escape for young men who failed to adjust to the social roles available to them in postwar West German society.[140] Many volunteers went to the Legion in search of a rugged masculinity that ran counter to the dominant emphasis on soft and civilian masculinities in the 1950s.[141]

West German officials and commentators believed modern mass culture was inciting young German men to seek adventure. According to one report by youth welfare officials, 36 young men decided to volunteer in July 1954 after having watched the movie *Frauenraub in Marokko* (*Ten Tall Men*), a Hollywood produc-tion featuring Burt Lancaster as a legionnaire.[142] Film critics warned "the young people" not to let another Hollywood production, *Desert Legion* with Alan Ladd, make them believe the Foreign Legion was "romantic," and cautioned that the

---

[135] Polizeidirektion Koblenz an die Bezirksregierung Koblenz, March 26, 1956, LHAK, Best.880, Nr. 175.

[136] Nieder, "Die französische Fremdenlegion", 59–60.

[137] Regierungsrat Schwegler, Niederschrift über die Besprechung am 8. März 1955 im Innenministerium über die Fremdenlegion, HStABaWü, EA 2/303, Bü581.

[138] Dr. Utermann, Kurze Stellungnahme zur Frage der aufgegriffenen Legionswilligen, die aus oder über Nordrhein-Westfalen den Weg zur Grenze in Rheinland-Pfalz nehmen, NRWHStA, NW 648, Nr. 154, 3–10.

[139] Nieder, "Die französische Fremdenlegion," 77–8.   [140] Ibid. 107.

[141] Ibid. 65; for similar attractions on East German youth, see Mark Fenemore, *Sex, Thugs, and Rock'n'Roll. Teenage Rebels in Cold War East Germany* (New York: Berghahn Books, 2007), 228–31. See also the brief comments in Sandra Maß, *Weiße Helden, schwarze Krieger. Zur Geschichte kolonialer Männlichkeit in Deutschland, 1918–1964* (Cologne: Böhlau, 2006), 306–11. On civilian masculinities, see Robert G. Moeller, "The 'Remasculinization' of Germany in the 1950s: Introduction," *Signs* 24/1 (1998), 101–6.

[142] Arbeitsgemeinschaft für Jugendpflege und Jugendfürsorge to BMdI, March 18, 1955, BArch, B 106/16653.

desert was not as beautiful as the "Technicolor" of the movie. Another critic expressed concern that young Germans in "desperate situation[s]" might identify with Alan Ladd or Burt Lancaster and believe that all legionnaires lived in "beautifully decorated Arab tents" and enjoyed the company of "barely dressed harem beauties."[143] Some newspapers refused to review or advertise *Desert Legion*.[144] In West German public discourse, the seductive qualities of Hollywood movies had replaced the devious activities of cunning recruiters as the primary reason for young Germans' entry into the Legion.[145]

Even critical cultural representations of the Legion might serve as an inadvertent incentive to join. West German youth welfare officials argued that "any treatment of the issue in the press, radio, or film misses its original purpose and has an opposite, stimulating and seductive effect on young Germans who generally lack the necessary experience and judgment" to understand it.[146] They included reports meant to warn young people away from the Legion. According to one report, the mere mentioning of the Foreign Legion on a school field trip to Koblenz led two students of the class to volunteer for the Legion.[147] Along similar lines, an official from North Rhine-Westphalia condemned the decision to deem a 1959 Foreign Legion movie, *Das Bataillon des Teufels*, appropriate for viewers 16 and older and proposed a rating of 18 and older. Despite its realistic portrayal of "hardship and brutality" in the Legion, he feared that the depiction of "comradeship among the legionnaires," "adventure," and the portrayal of "hardened, tough men" might exert an effect that "should not be underestimated."[148] Notwithstanding the decline of the abduction narrative, a perception of an extremely fragile male youth whose inner self-destructive tendencies could be activated by only the slightest external impulse continued to inform West German fears of the Legion.

---

[143] "Zelluloidzauber um falsche Helden," *Neue Tagespost Osnabrück*, n.d., "Ein Wüstenmärchen," *Schwäbische Tageszeitung*, December 12, 1953, Deutsches Film Museum (DFM).

[144] "Keine Inserate für Fremdenlegionär-Film," *Münchner Abendzeitung*, June 16, 1954, DFM.

[145] Poiger, *Jazz, Rock, and Rebels*, Heide Fehrenbach, *Cinema in Democratizing Germany. Reconstructing National Identity after Hitler* (Chapel Hill: University of North Carolina Press, 1995).

[146] Arbeitsgemeinschaft für Jugendfürsorge to BMdI, March 18, 1955, BArch, B 106/16653; similarly Innenminister Baden-Württemberg to Regierungspräsidien, July 2, 1955, HStABaWü, EA 2/303, Bü583.

[147] Springer-Dr.Kienle, "Fremdenlegion," December 9, 1955, HStABaWü, EA2/303, Bü584.

[148] Dr. Bommer to the Niedersächsischer Kultusminister, August 28, 1959, NRWHStA, NW 648, Nr. 155. This concern with unintended consequences of negative representations of the Legion was not new. In his autobiographical account, *Afrikanische Spiele*, Ernst Jünger, who had briefly joined the Legion in 1913, confesses how it was precisely the "reports of multiple dangers, deprivations, and cruelties" that attracted him to the Legion and that could not have been designed better by a "professional advertising chief," see Ernst Jünger, *Afrikanische Spiele* (Stuttgart: Klett-Cotta, 2013 [1936]), 8. See also Nieder, "Die französische Fremdenlegion," 77–9.

The End of an Obsession

Despite West German officials' persistent concerns, young Germans' interest in the Legion began to decline by the second half of the 1950s. French authorities closed all recruitment bureaus for the Foreign Legion on West German territory when the occupation period ended in 1954.[149] West German countermeasures may also have yielded some results, and the newly established *Bundeswehr* began to offer an alternative outlet for young men's adventurism. In addition, the Legion's focus shifted to Algeria, which had fewer attractions than Indochina. Whereas about 35,000 Germans had served in Indochina between 1945 and 1954, only 12,000 served in Algeria between 1954 and 1962. Consequently, public attention shifted from the recruitment of young West Germans—whether actually nefarious or not—to the conditions of their actual service in the Legion. Films, such as the 1958 production of *Madeleine und der Legionär*, and the serialized novel in the magazine *Stern* depicted the numerous atrocities that the French committed during their colonial wars in Indochina and Algeria. With the return of the Nazi past to public memory by the late 1950s, representations of Germans in the Legion now became a way to address the German past in and through critical engagement with French colonialism. Violent transgressions of German members of the Legion against Vietnamese or Algerian civilians became an indirect way to discuss the conduct of *Wehrmacht* soldiers in the Second World War. At the same time, the critique of Western colonialism also undermined the moral authority of the Western powers to pass judgments on German crimes during the Nazi period.[150] As a result of this changed cultural function, the Foreign Legion largely lost its role as an important site of postwar fear and anxiety by the mid to late 1950s.

Yet, for much of the 1950s, the French Foreign Legion took up a prominent part in the German postwar imagination. The Legion served as a crystallization point for a wide variety of fears and anxieties in which Germans imagined themselves as hapless victims of external forces beyond their control. The imagined threat of "white slavery" reflected the persistent terror of Germans that the extreme violence they directed to their victims in the Second World War might lead them to suffer a similar fate. The recruiter to the Foreign Legion became associated with the corrupting homosexual as a negative foil to German masculine citizenship. The belief in the fragility of male youth, whether inherent in the fantasy of forced recruitment to the Legion or the recognition of voluntarism in

---

[149] Michels, *Deutsche in der Fremdenlegion*, 262.

[150] For a more extensive discussion of these issues, see Frank Biess, "Moral Panic in Postwar Germany. The Abduction of Young Germans into the Foreign Legion and French Colonialism in the 1950s," *Journal of Modern History* 84/4 (2012): 789–832.

signing up for the Legion, pointed to a widespread uncertainty and anxiety regarding the social and moral order. The gradual stabilization of the Federal Republic occurred against a backdrop of extensive uncertainties, deep anxieties, concrete fears, and terrifying fantasies. Postwar fears of revenge and retribution did not disappear but manifested in more symbolic, indirect fashion, as in the fear of the recruiter. Yet by the second half of the 1950s, most Germans realized that they did no longer have to fear retribution from the Western Allies. Cold War fears—of Communism, of nuclear war—would take their place.

3

Cold War *Angst*

Between late October and mid November 1961, 16 million West German households received a pamphlet from the federal government entitled "Everybody Has a Chance."[1] While many citizens initially took this for an advertisement for the state lottery, their reaction changed as they identified the actual subject: how to prepare for a possible nuclear war. The brochure sought to reassure by laying out careful preparation for, and correct behavior in, the event of an attack with nuclear, biological, or chemical weapons on the territory of the Federal Republic. The publication described the potential effects of a nuclear attack and yet also outlined the possible protective measures. In particular, it advocated the construction of "adequate shelters," which—in the absence of a mandated government program—necessarily needed to be voluntary. If no actual bunker were available, a basement "with thick, strong walls and ceiling" would have to do. Furthermore, in the case of a "surprise attack" with atomic weapons, one should seek cover under a table or, if caught outside, fall to the ground. An illustration suggested a briefcase as a potential cover against the shock wave and heat of an atomic bomb. To prove the effectiveness of even simple protective measures, the publication cited the experience of a Hiroshima resident who managed to survive by putting his thumbs in his ears, covering his eyes with his fingers, and dropping to the ground, which the pamphlet termed an "automatic reaction." By contrast, an image of refugees on a cart demonstrated that "flight does not bring safety" unless an "evacuation has been ordered for specific areas." Finally, the brochure sought to make clear that the "education of citizens" regarding "civilian air defense" was part and parcel of the tasks of every responsible government: the first page of the booklet contained images of similar civil defense brochures published by the Federal Republic's Western allies, such as the United States, France, and England, and the neutral countries of Sweden, Finland, and Denmark as well as Japan. The publication of the brochure inaugurated a broader government-sponsored campaign for civil defense that also included newspaper ads, public lectures, and instructional film clips in movie theaters and on television.[2]

The distribution of the brochure came at a moment of intense international tension: only a few weeks earlier, on August 13, 1961, the East German regime had sealed the only remaining hole in the Iron Curtain by building the Berlin

---

[1] Bundesministerium des Innern, "Jeder Hat eine Chance" (Bad Godesberg, 1961).
[2] Vermerk, October 5, 1961, BArch, B 106/50243.

German Angst: *Fear and Democracy in the Federal Republic of Germany.* Frank Biess, Oxford University Press (2020).
© Frank Biess.
DOI: 10.1093/oso/9780198714187.001.0001

Wall. While morally atrocious, the Wall actually stabilized the international situation in Central Europe and paved the way to a larger Cold War settlement in Europe.[3] But, for contemporaries living at the time, the construction of the wall triggered one of the most dangerous crises of the Cold War. According to an opinion poll, the percentage of West Germans who thought that a nuclear attack was "possible" or "likely" reached an unpreceded 55 per cent in January 1962.[4] At a press conference on October 23, 1961, Walter Bargatzky from the Interior Ministry justified the publication of "Everybody Has a Chance" at that particular moment by citing "international tensions" that have "advanced to a military stage."[5] And indeed, only a few days later, Soviet and US tanks faced each other directly at the demarcation line in Berlin for the first and only time during the Cold War. On October 31, the Soviet Union broke an informal moratorium on nuclear testing between the superpowers by exploding a thermonuclear bomb of (to this day) an unprecedented 53 megatons.[6] The brochure's assurance that "Everybody Has a Chance" had therefore come at the right moment. Postwar Germans faced a particularly intense and fearful anticipation of a nuclear war in Central Europe that autumn.[7]

This chapter analyzes the politics of fear in Cold War Germany. In so doing, it does not focus on the relatively well-researched controversy over West German rearmament or, for that matter, over the debate of acquiring nuclear weapons for the West German army, the *Bundeswehr*.[8] Instead, the chapter focuses on civil defense as a civilian program that accompanied military rearmament.[9] Civil defense

---

[3] Marc Trachtenberg, *A Constructed Peace. The Making of the European Settlement 1945–1963* (Princeton: Princeton University Press, 1999).

[4] "Emnid Untersuchung vor 20 Jahren," *Emnid Informationen* 34/10 (1982): 24.

[5] Bargatzky, Pressekonferenz, October 23, 1961, BArch, B 106/50243.

[6] Soviet scientists had initially announced an explosion of up to 100 megatons, John Lewis Gaddis, *We Now Know. Rethinking Cold War History* (Oxford: Oxford University Press, 1997). 255–7, Bernd Stöver, *Der Kalte Krieg. Geschichte eines radikalen Zeitalters 1947–1991* (Munich: C.H.Beck, 2007), 129–38.

[7] Elisabeth Noelle, Erich Neumann, eds, *The Germans. Public Opinion Polls 1947–1966* (Allensbach: Verlag für Demoskopie, 1967), 604.

[8] On rearmament, see Militärgeschichtliches Forschungsamt, ed., *Anfänge westdeutscher Sicherheitspolitik, 1945–1956*, 4 vols. (Munich: Oldenbourg, 1982), David Clay Large, *Germans to the Front. West German Rearmament in the Adenauer Era* (Chapel Hill: University of North Caroline Press, 1996), Holger Nehring, *The Politics of Security. British and West German Protest Movements and the Early Cold War, 1945-1970* (Oxford: Oxford University Press, 2013).

[9] This chapter is based on my previous article, Frank Biess, "'Everybody Has a Chance.' Civil Defense. Nuclear Angst, and the History of Emotions in Postwar Germany," *German History* 27/2 (2009): 215–43. For a discussion primarily of the institutional and strategic-military aspects of West German civil defense, see the pertinent chapters in Bruno Thoß, *NATO-Strategie und nationale Verteidigungsplanung. Planung und Aufbau der Bundeswehr unter den Bedingungen einer massiven atomaren Vergeltungsstrategie, 1952–1960* (Munich: Oldenbourg, 2006), 603–721. In general, see Nicholas H. Steneck, "Everybody Has a Chance. Civil Defense and the Creation of Cold War West German Identity, 1950–1968" (Ph.D. Dissertation, Ohio State University, 2005), Martin Diebel, *Atomkrieg und andere Katastrophen. Zivil- und Katastrophenschutz in der Bundesrepublik und Großbritannien nach 1945* (Paderborn: Schöningh, 2017). On civil defense in pre-1945 Germany and in East Germany, see Bernd Lemke, *Luftschutz in Großbritannien und Deutschland 1923 bis 1939*

is particularly well suited to illustrate the functioning—and the deficits—of one aspect of the Cold War emotional regime—namely, the containment of fear. Civil defense was a critical, if always flawed, component of the quest for security in the nuclear age. It was designed to serve a crucial purpose in reducing the fear of nuclear war. The containment of these fears of war complemented the concurrent mobilization of others fears during the Cold War, those of Soviet Communism. This mobilization of fear through anti-Communism is much better known. But a deliberate politics of fear was not the only aspect of the emotional politics of the West German Cold War. Cold War fears in Germany instead entailed a carefully calibrated emotional balance, in which the mobilization of the fear of Communism served to contain popular fears of a new war. Before turning to civil defense, it is therefore important to first understand the mobilization of the fear of Communism.

"Better Dead than Red": Anti-Communism and the Politics of Emotions in the German Cold War

Anti-Communism has long been recognized as a foundational emotion and "legitimatory ideology" of the Federal Republic.[10] Yet historians have only recently begun to analyze postwar West German anti-Communism as a complex and multifaceted phenomenon that served a plethora of important functions: in domestic politics, it provided a political–ideological bond for the majority of the West German population; in international affairs, it tied the Federal Republic to the Western alliance.[11] Anti-Communism also constituted one of the central

---

(Munich: Oldenbourg, 2005), Clemens Heitmann, *Schützen und Helfen? Luftschutz und Zivilverteidigung in der DDR 1955 bis 1989/90* (Berlin: Ch. Links, 2006), Dietmar Süß, *Der Tod aus der Luft. Kriegsgesellschaft und Luftkrieg in Deutschland und England* (Berlin: Siedler, 2011). On civil defense in the US, see Elaine Tyler May, *Homeward Bound. American Families in the Cold War Era* (New York: Basic Books, 1988), Guy Oakes, *The Imaginary War: Civil Defense and American Cold War Culture* (New York: Oxford University Press, 1994), Laura McEnaney, *Civil Defense Begins at Home. Militarization Meets Everyday Life in the Fifties* (Princeton: Princeton University Press, 2000), (Chapel Hill: University of North Carolina Press, 2003), Dee Garrison, *Bracing for Armageddon. Why Civil Defense Never Worked* (Oxford: Oxford University Press, 2006).

[10] See Christoph Kleßmann, *Die dopppelte Staatsgründung. Deutsche Geschichte 1945–1955* (Bonn: Bundeszentrale für politische Bildung, 1986), 251–7.
[11] See especially Patrick Major, *The Death of the KPD. Communism and Anti-Communism in West Germany, 1945–1956* (Oxford: Oxford University Press, 1997), Eric D. Weitz, "The Ever-Present Other: Communism in the Making of West Germany," in Hanna Schissler, ed., *The Miracle Years. A Cultural History of West Germany 1949–1968* (Princeton: Princeton University Press, 2001), 219–32, Klaus Körner, *"Die rote Gefahr": Antikommunistische Propaganda in der Bundesrepublik, 1950–2000* (Hamburg: Konkret Literatur Verlag, 2003), Till Kössler, *Abschied von der Revolution. Kommunisten und Gesellschaft in Westdeutschland 1945–1968* (Düsseldorf: Droste, 2005), Bernd Faulenbach, "Erscheinungsformen des 'Antikommunismus': Zur Problematik eines vieldeutigen Begriffs," *Jahrbuch für historische Kommunismusforschung* (2011): 231–8, Stefan Creuzberger, Dierk Hoffmann, eds, *"Geistige Gefahr" und "Immunisierung der Gesellschaft." Antikommunismus und politische Kultur in der frühen Bundesrepublik* (Munich: Oldenbourg, 2014).

elements of the worldview of Chancellor Konrad Adenauer, the dominant political figure in the early Federal Republic. Adenauer's Catholic faith deeply shaped his anti-Communism. "Germany and Europe will remain Christian or become Communist," he stated in 1957.[12] Adenauer also saw the Soviet Union as an inherently expansionist force against which only the firm integration of the Federal Republic into the West could provide sufficient protection. The notion of a neutralized Germany located between East and West constituted his political nightmare, in part because he feared that a neutral Germany would not be able to withstand an aggressive and expansionist Soviet Communism. A deep skepticism regarding the political maturity and ideological reliability of the German people thus informed Adenauer's anti-Communism.[13] The flip side of his anti-Communism was a firm commitment to liberal democracy, albeit with authoritarian overtones.

Anti-Communism also provided an ideological bridge to Nazism through its ardent anti-Bolshevism. Theodor Oberländer as Minister for Expellees and Hans Globke as Adenauer's senior adviser were both former Nazi officials who occupied high positions in Adenauer's government. Beyond such ideological continuities among West German political elites, anti-Communism was rooted in the collective experience of millions of Germans who had fled from the advancing Red Army, experienced captivity in the Soviet Union, or had been subjected to violence—mass rape especially—during Soviet occupation.[14] To be sure, individual experiences of ordinary Germans with "the Russians" differed widely and often diverged from the negative perception of Soviet Communism as a political system.[15] Still, the after-effects of the Nazi propaganda of fear, as well as actual experiences of violence with the Red Army, meant that many German men and women carried visceral fears of Communism and "the Russians" that, in some cases, entered their nightmares.[16]

The electoral campaigns of Adenauer's Christian Democratic Union and Christian Social Union (CDU/CSU) sought to appeal to collective and individual fears of Communism throughout the early Federal Republic. The CDU/CSU's federal election campaign posters frequently visualized these fears of Communism,

---

[12] Thomas Brechenmacher, "Katholische Kirsche und (Anti)Kommunismus in der frühen Bundesrepublik," in ibid. This was a version of the much cited Novalis quotation that "The Occident will be Christian, or it will not be at all"; see Major, *The Death of the KPD*, 263.

[13] Lars Lüdicke, "Adenauer als Außenpolitiker und der Antikommunismus im Auswärtigen Amt," in Creuzberger and Hoffmann, eds, *"Geistige Gefahr,"* 105–22, Corinna Franz, "'Wir wählen die Freiheit.' Antikommunistisches Denken und politisches Handeln Konrad Adenauers," in ibid. 145–60.

[14] Lutz Niethammer, "Juden und Russen im Gedächtnis der Deutschen," in Walter Pehle, ed., *Der historische Ort des Nationalsozialismus. Annäherungen* (Frankfurt a/M: Fischer, 1990), 114–34. On the ways in which anti-Communism was mobilized in German memories of the Second World War, see Robert G. Moeller, *War Stories. The Search for a Usable Past in the Federal Republic of Germany* (Berkeley: University of California Press, 2001).

[15] For one example, see the autobiography of Soviet captivity by Helmut Gollwitzer, *Und führen, wohin Du nicht willst. Bericht einer Gefangenschaft* (Frankfurt a/M: Fischer, 1954).

[16] Svenja Goltermann, *Die Gesellschaft der Überlebenden. Deutsche Kriegsheimkehrer und ihre Gewalterfahrungen im Zweiten Weltkrieg* (Munich: DVA, 2009), 61–75.

often in distinctly racialized form. A CDU poster from 1949, for example, depicted a person with a racialized Asiatic face reaching for Western Europe.[17] In 1948, in the local elections in Hesse, the caption "This must not happen" ran beneath an image of death as a personified Communist breaking through the border between East and West.[18] Invoking the mass rape of German women, a 1953 poster promised "protection" against a red hand grasping a mother and child.[19] Time and again, these conservative anti-Communist campaigns also sought to tie the main opposition party, the Social Democrats, to Soviet Communism. Another poster from 1953 declared that Social Democracy constituted a version of "Marxism" that would inevitably "lead to Moscow."[20] In 1957, a CDU poster showed a German city at dawn and admonished Germans to "think of Hungary" and "to remain alert"—an invocation of the Soviet repression of the Hungarian uprising in the previous year and, therefore, the dictatorial and potentially expansive nature of Soviet Communism.[21] As a political strategy, anti-Communism served a key element in the CDU's attempts to unite non-Socialist bourgeois forces and to discredit the Socialist opposition as being tied to Moscow. In 1953, the East German uprising on June 17 fed into this political narrative and aided Adenauer's success in the federal elections in September of that year. Moreover, in 1953 and 1957, tax cuts and targeted expansions of social policy benefits, such as the adjustment of pension levels to inflation and wages, contributed to the CDU/CSU's electoral victories. In 1957, the CDU/CSU secured an absolute majority of the popular vote for the first and only time in the history of the Federal Republic.[22]

West German Social Democrats practiced their own ardent anti-Communism as well. Anti-Communism became such an important bipartisan ideological–political bond in postwar West Germany because both political forces, the Christian Democrats and the Social Democrats, subscribed to it. Conflicts between Social Democrats and Communists went back to the 1920s.[23] While there was genuine interest in overcoming the split in the labor movement in the aftermath of the Second World War, the merger between Communists and Social Democrats in the Soviet zone in April 1946, and the ensuing persecution of Social Democrats, prompted the re-emergence of Social Democratic anti-Communism in the West. The leader of the West German Social Democratic Party (SPD), Kurt Schumacher, embodied anti-Communism, and under his leadership the SPD party executive

---

[17] ACDP, Plakatsammlung, 10-001-12.   [18] ACDP, Plakatsammlung, 10-015-44.
[19] Major, *Death of the KPD*, 266. For an analysis of this image, see Elizabeth Heineman, "The Hour of the Woman: Memories of West Germany's 'Crisis Years' and West German National Identity," *American Historical Review* 101/2 (1996): 354–96. See posters in ACDP, Plakatsammlung, 10-001-414, 10-017-352.
[20] ACDP, Plakatsammlung, 10-001-411.   [21] ACDP, Plakatsammlung, 10-001-601.
[22] On the CDU's electoral strategies, see Frank Bösch, *Die Adenauer-CDU. Gründung, Aufstieg und Krise einer Erfolgspartei 1945–1969* (Stuttgart: DVA, 2001), 148–74.
[23] Weitz, "The Ever-Present Other."

Figure 3.1. Election Ad Christian Democratic Union (CDU) during the first federal election, 1949.

This election ad depicts a racialized Soviet soldier seeking to grab Western Europe. The image was most likely perceived as a metaphoric allusion to the mass rape of German women by Soviet soldiers during the final stages of the Second World War and in the immediate postwar period.

Source: ACDP, Plakatsammlung, 10-001-12.

committee outlawed any alliance with West German Communists in June 1948.[24] Echoing the emerging anti-totalitarian consensus in the West, one of the SPD's slogans in the first West German election in 1949 was "A Vote for the Communist Party Is a Vote for the Concentration Camp."[25] Social Democratic anti-Communism manifested itself especially in the city of Berlin in October 1946, where the SPD clearly defeated the East German SED (Socialist Unity Party) with 48.7 per cent versus 19.8 per cent.[26]

Semi-official organizations such as the "People's Association for Peace and Freedom" (*Volksbund für Frieden und Freiheit* VVF) and the "Fighting Group Against Inhumanity" (*Kampfgruppe gegen Unmenschlichkeit* KgU) rooted anti-Communism in civil society. These private anti-Communist groups had funding from both the West German Ministry of All German Affairs and the US Central Intelligence Agency.[27] They thus occupied a semi-official function in that they often operated with logistic and financial support of the West German government. In so doing, both organizations stood squarely in the tradition of anti-Bolshevist propaganda. The co-founder of the VVF, Eberhard Taubert, had directed anti-Bolshevist propaganda in Goebbels's propaganda ministry during the Nazi period. He embodied "the prototype of the anti-Bolshevist agitator," not least because he had also strongly emphasized the link between anti-Bolshevism and antisemitism. Because of his compromised past, Taubert used several pseudonyms in the postwar period. While his true identity was known to West German officials from the early 1950s onward, he was only forced to resign from the leadership of the VVF in 1954 when new evidence became public about his participation in death sentences of the Nazi People's Court (*Volksgerichtshof*). By contrast, the founders of the KgU, Rainer Hildebrandt and his successor Ernst Tillich, came from an anti-Nazi background, yet eventually tolerated many highly compromised former Nazis in their organization.[28] The KgU especially sought to assist the US-led "rollback" policy of destabilizing the Communist government in East

---

[24] Major, *Death of the KPD*, 40–60, Weitz, "The Ever-Present Other."

[25] Major, *Death of the KPD*, 109. Also cited in Weitz, "The Ever-Present Other," 220.

[26] Körner, "*Die rote Gefahr*," 75–120.

[27] On the *Volksbund*, see ibid. 21–30. On the *Kampfgruppe*, see Bernd Stöver, "'Politik der Befreiung?' Private Organisationen des Kalten Krieges. Das Beispiel Kampfgruppe gegen Unmenschlichkeit (KgU)," in Creuzberger and Hoffmann, eds, "*Geistige Gefahr*," 215–28, Enrico Heitzer, *Die Kampfgruppe gegen Unmenschlichkeit (KgU). Widerstand und Spionage im Kalten Krieg 1948–1959* (Cologne: Böhlau, 2015). On the link to the West German government, see Stefan Creuzberger, "Kampf gegen den inneren Feind. Das gesamtdeutsche Ministerium und der staatlich gelenkte Antikommunismus in der BRD," in Creuzberger and Hoffmann, eds, "*Geistige Gefahr*," 87–104, Stefan Creuzberger, *Kampf für die Einheit. Das gesamtdeutsche Ministerium und die politische Kultur des Kalten Krieges 1949–1969* (Düsseldorf: Droste, 2008), 141–53, 455. The VVF received 28,000 DM per month in 1955, 55,000 DM per month in 1959.

[28] Quotation in Körner, "*Die rote Gefahr*," 24; Heitzer, *Die Kampfgruppe gegen Unmenschlichkeit*, 87–157. On Täuber's Nazi past, see Mathias Friedel, *Der Volksbund für Frieden und Freiheit (VVF): Eine Teiluntersuchung über westdeutsche antikommunistische Propaganda im Kalten Krieg und deren Wurzeln im Nationalsozialismus* (Mainz: Gardez Verlag, 2001), 15–42,146–7.

Germany through subversion, sabotage, and assistance with desertion and escape.[29] But both organizations were also active in fighting Communism in West Germany. Together with the Ministry of All German Affairs, the VVF organized publicity campaigns, which invoked the fear of Communism and sought to discredit the opponents of Adenauer's policy of Western integration, such as the Protestant pastor and former leading member of the anti-Nazi "Confessing Church," Martin Niemöller. In two cases, the VVF spread posters that denounced Niemöller as fighting for the triumph of the "heroic Soviet Union" on behalf of the West German Communist Party.[30] Increasingly, these organizations also distanced themselves from left-wing anti-Communism, yet became more porous to influences from the political Right, including former Nazis and lobby groups campaigning for a general amnesty for all Nazi crimes.[31]

The anti-Communist agitation of these organizations exhibited many conceptual continuities to the Nazi past. While the *Volksbund* defined its name in positive terms as being in favor of "peace and freedom," most of its publications engaged in negative propaganda against the Soviet Union. In the face of the Communist threat that often appeared in analogy to natural disasters such as flooding, the main danger resided in Western complacency and passivity—that is, in a distinct absence of fear. Anti-Communist agitators such as Taubert thus sought to stimulate this fear of Communism as a virtually existential necessity for survival in the Cold War. Under the pseudonym Pacificus, Taubert sought to expose the East German and Soviet peace propaganda in the early 1950s as the "Trojan horse of world revolution."[32] Apart from external threats, anti-Communist agitators were especially obsessed with internal "fifth columns." A brochure from 1951, which Täubert co-authored and of which the Ministry of All German Affairs published 200,000 issues, was entitled "Open Your Eyes. Communism Through the Backdoor." According to this pamphlet, Communists were engaged in a "psychological offensive war" with "political poison." SED functionaries functioned as "hateful and destructive nuclear cores of Bolshevism" who had lost all their "Germanness" as a result of their "anti-German espionage and subversion training in Moscow." In this view, their Communist and anti-German agitation nullified German Communists' experience of antifascist resistance or internment in concentration camps. In striking continuity to the dehumanization of Slavs and Communists during the Third Reich, the brochure warned against Communists as "persistent and innovative insects" who can only be "crushed

[29] Heitzer, *Die Kampfgruppe gegen Unmenschlichkeit (KgU)*, 202–418.
[30] Creuzberger, "Kampf gegen den inneren Feind," Friedel, *Der Volksbund für Frieden und Freiheit*, 126–8.
[31] Heitzer, *Die Kampfgruppe gegen Unmenschlichkleit*, 476.
[32] Pacificus, *Die trojanische Taube. Kommunistische Friedenspropaganda ohne Maske* (Gelsenkirchen: Ruhr Verlag, 1950). See also Kurt Zentner, *Heil Stalin. Eine Fibel für die Bedrohten* (Gelsenkirchen: Ruhr Verlag, 1950), 142–4. For the flooding analogy, see Hendrik van Bergh, *Die rote Springflut* (Munich: Isar Verlag, 1958).

when you can see them."[33] A 1956 brochure, "Communism Unmasked," exposed a black ugly face behind a beautiful white mask.[34] This notion of "demasking" had been very popular in Nazi anti-Jewish propaganda—for example, in exposing a Jewish person depicted in racial stereotypes behind the mask of a fully assimilated Jewish German. In general, much like the "recruiter" to the Foreign Legion, the figure of the "Communist" as a stereotypical figure began to embody the absolute antithesis to a respectable West German citizenship—a "foreign" figure, "a person of the worst character," a "criminal, rapist, and deadly enemy."[35] Similar to the "recruiter," the "Communist" thus inherited many of the evil traits of the previous stereotypical enemy of the Nazi period, the "Jew," as well. Like the recruiter, he thus may have represented to many West Germans a new threat in a familiar guise.

The anti-Communist consensus and its anchoring in civil society explains the broad bipartisan support for an official anti-Communist policy in the early 1950s. The outbreak of the Korean War in June 1950 coincided with an ideological offensive of the Communist Party of Germany (KPD) in 1950–1 to portray itself as the main force on behalf of German unity. In response, federal and state authorities implemented a far-reaching administrative anti-Communism that increasingly limited the discursive and institutional space for Communist activity in West Germany.[36] State governments began to ban public activities by Communists or groups that were affiliated with the KPD, often at the behest of local city officials. On the federal level, the *Bundestag* passed a resolution to remove Communists from the civil service in September 1950. From July in the following year, any activities "threatening the state" (*Staatsgefährdung*) were criminalized. Initially aimed at neo-Nazis, the law was used widely to prosecute Communists, mostly for the intent to overthrow the state rather than acts of violence. About 40,000 individuals and most likely half of actual members of the KPD were subjected to legal investigation between 1953 and 1958, although only 1,905 of them were actually convicted. The goal of these investigations was to intimidate and suppress open Communist activity, not necessarily to imprison individual Communists.[37] The fear of Communism also enabled the covert surveillance of postal and telephone communication by the West German intelligence services, especially the *Verfassungsschutz*.[38] These latter measures clearly went beyond the interventions

---

[33] Friedel, *Der Volksbund für Frieden und Freiheit (VVF)*, 103–5, Bundesministerium für gesamtdeutsche Fragen, *Augen auf! Kommunismus durch die Hintertür* (Bonn: Bundesministerium für gesamtdeutsche Aufgaben, 1951), 2, 6, 53.

[34] Friedel, *Der Volksbund für Frieden und Freiheit (VVF)*,107.   [35] Ibid. 163.

[36] On the SED's campaigns for national unification from the late 1940s to the early 1950s, see Kössler, *Abschied von der Revolution*, 263–9. See also Major, *Death of the KPD*, 115–42, 253–6, Sascha Foerster, *Die Angst vor dem Koreakrieg. Konrad Adenauer und die westdeutsche Bevölkerung 1950* (Marburg: Tectum Verlag, 2013).

[37] Kössler, *Abschied von der Revolution*, 279–89, Major, *Death of the KPD*, 277–83.

[38] Josef Foschepoth, *Überwachtes Deutschland. Post- und Telefonüberwachung in der alten Bundesrepublik* (Göttingen: Vandenhoeck & Ruprecht, 2012).

that the law authorized, and significantly undermined the constitutionally guaranteed rights of privacy. This official administrative anti-Communism culminated in the petition from October 1951 to formally outlaw the KPD, similar to the earlier prohibition of the neo-Nazi Socialist Reich Party (SRP) in 1951, which the West German constitutional court eventually approved in August 1956.[39] From that point on, the Communist Party itself was illegal in the Federal Republic. This law remained in effect until the re-founding of the German Communist Party in 1968.

The local implementation of centrally mandated anti-Communist measures, however, varied significantly. While conservative southern states such as Bavaria or Baden-Württemberg exhausted the legal space to outlaw Communist activities, local and state governments in areas of traditional left-wing strength, such as the industrial Ruhr area, tended to be a lot more lenient. Local and state officials in the Ruhr area refused to implement some of the more far-reaching persecutory measures, and they continued to tolerate the activities of Communists in some labor unions and in local politics, as long as they were not openly advertised as "Communist."[40] The exclusion of Communists thus went along with a more pragmatic approach and their ongoing integration into non-Communist organizations such as labor unions. Historian Till Kössler interprets this pragmatism as evidence that the Federal Republic was not a society "gripped by fear of Communism."[41]

Still, the role of Communism as a privileged object of fear seems hardly debatable. The Federal Republic's political and administrative measures against Communism derived from its self-perception as a "militant democracy," a concept that had originated in the Weimar Republic.[42] They were supposed to counteract a widespread popular perception of the Federal Republic as a weak state that might not be capable of thwarting the ideological and political appeal of Communism. As we will see below, a similar distrust in the Federal Republic's capability to protect its citizens also informed popular fears of nuclear war. The politics of anti-Communism thus also served as a way to contain fears of a weak and defenseless state in the ideological battles of the Cold War. This function manifested itself especially in the public debate over the so-called *Rückversicherer*. These individuals were suspected to secretly collaborate with Communists in exchange for protection if Communists took over in West Germany. In the fall of 1950, newspapers reported on the confiscation of a list naming those *Rückversicherer* in a KPD office in the West German town of Recklinghausen. Small businessmen were accused of secretly funding Communist organizations as

---

[39] Major, *Death of the KPD*, 283–93.   [40] Kössler, *Abschied von der Revolution*, 357–68.
[41] Till Kössler, "Die Grenzen der Demokratie. Antikommunismus als politische und gesellschaftliche Praxis in der Bundesrepublik," in Creuzberger and Hoffmann, eds, *"Geistige Gefahr,"* 229–50.
[42] On the origins of this concept in the Weimar period, see Udi Greenberg, *The Weimar Century. German Émigrés and the Ideological Foundations of the Cold War* (Princeton: Princeton University Press, 2016), 169–210.

a kind of political contingency plan. Similar to the recruiter for the Foreign Legion discussed in Chapter 2, the *Rückversicherer* was a mythical figure that encapsulated some of the popular fears of the time—in this case, "fears regarding the loyalty of the population toward the new state."[43] While there was no evidence that these individuals actually existed, the depth of these fears manifested itself in the fact that Chancellor Adenauer himself referred to the notion of the *Rückversicherer* several years later in a cabinet meeting on October 11, 1954, equating them with "rats" who had "left the ship prematurely."[44] Political fears of Communism served a politically stabilizing function only up to a certain point. If those fears became excessive or overwhelming, public commentators and West German officials associated them with defeatist or even treasonous behavior.

West German public discourse cast Communists as a subversive force wholly in the service of Moscow, and intent on undermining and sabotaging West German democracy. The perception of a serious Communist threat went along with grave doubts as to whether West Germans would be capable of withstanding Communist propaganda. A real fear of the potential weakness of the West German anti-Communist resolve thus constituted an essential aspect of West German anti-Communism. The official outlawing of the KPD also did not alleviate these anti-Communist fears. Instead, it heightened the expectation that—with support of their masters in East Berlin and Moscow—West German Communists would resort to covert and secret subversive activities. "The citizen of the Federal Republic needs to abandon the idea that Communists are visible from the outside, that they use primitive methods," an anonymous contributor wrote. "He needs to get used to the fact that Communists appear behind every mask, and will make use of forms of public life, of all societal groups and individuals. The prohibition of the KPD alone is not sufficient to ban the danger."[45] In this view, the official outlawing of Communism only enhanced the fear of disguised, hidden, "masked" Communists.

Perhaps the most important function of anti-Communism, however, was to contain other fears, most notably the fear of war. In the emotional politics of the Cold War, the mobilization of the fear of Communism constituted an essential strategy in attracting popular support for Adenauer's policy of rearmament and Western integration. Plans for rearmament encountered significant opposition

---

[43] Kössler, *Abschied von der Revolution*, 275.

[44] Sitzung Nr. 5, October 11, 1954, Günter Buchstab, ed., *Adenauer: "Wir haben wirklich etwas geschaffen." Die Protokolle des CDU-Bundesvorstands 1953–1957* (Düsseldorf: Droste, 1990), 279.

[45] Anonymous, "Lenkung und Organisation der Methoden der kommunistischen Infiltration in der Bundesrepublik," *Aus Politik und Zeitgeschiche* B35 (1956): 560. Also cited in Rüdiger Thomas, "Zur Auseinandersetzung mit dem deutschen Kommunismus in der Bundeszentrale für Heimatdienst. Eine kritische Sondierung im Umfeld des KPD-Verbots," in Creuzberger and Hoffmann, eds, *"Geistige Gefahr,"* 134. He identifies Günter Nollau, the head of the West German *Verfassungsschutz*, as likely author of this text.

since their inception in 1948.[46] Pacifism and a general fear of war did not inspire all the popular opposition to rearmament. Some significant opposition also derived from a more nationalist orientation that rejected not rearmament per se but rather rearmament under the auspices of the Western allies. Many potential recruits feared that they would be misused as "cannon fodder" on behalf of American interests just as the Nazi regime had misused their idealism and military service. For them, the problem was that a new West German army would ultimately serve foreign rather than German national interests.[47] Yet, despite this significant opposition to rearmament and Western integration, which in some opinion polls amounted to a majority of the West German electorate, Adenauer's CDU/CSU electoral victories mounted between 1950 and 1957. Anti-Communism as a way to contain popular fears of war accounted for at least part of the electoral appeal of the CDU.

This function of anti-Communism became even more important in the context of the debate over the nuclear armament of the West German *Bundeswehr* from 1957 onward. The nuclearization of NATO strategy entailed the scenario of a possible nuclear war on German territory as part of the general Western defense strategy. Public statements by nuclear scientists such as the Göttingen Eighteen and, shortly thereafter, by the renowned medical doctor Albert Schweitzer, further fueled popular fears regarding the defenselessness of the West German population vis-à-vis a possible nuclear war at the dividing line of the Cold War.[48] At the meeting of the executive committee of the CDU in May 1957, Chancellor Adenauer professed to being deeply concerned about the emotional attitudes of the West German population. "Fear of the atomic bomb is something very emotional," he argued, which would be "very difficult to master . . . after the German people had to endure the last war." Adenauer understood that references to how "well we are doing," meaning economic growth, could not neutralize this fear. He worried that quite a few Germans professed to be "better red than dead" and were willing to accept "years of unfreedom" rather than knowing that "our children and grandchildren will be eradicated."[49] Adenauer and the CDU were especially concerned that the opposition Social Democrats would appeal to fears of nuclear war and mobilize them against Adenauer's foreign policy. According to one

[46] Hans-Erich Volkmann, "Die innenpolitische Dimension Adenauerscher Sicherheitspolitik in der EVG-Phase," in Militärgeschichtliches Forschungsamt, ed., *Anfänge westdeutscher Sicherheitspolitik, 1945–1956, vol. 2: Die EVG-Phase* (Munich: Oldenbourg, 1990), 235–604, Large, *Germans to the Front*.

[47] Michael Geyer, "Cold War Angst: The Case of West German Opposition to Rearmament and Nuclear Weapons," in Hanna Schissler, ed., *The Miracle Years. A Cultural History of West Germany, 1949–1968* (Princeton: Princeton University Press, 2001).

[48] Marc Cioc, *Pax Atomica. The Nuclear Defense Debate in West Germany during the Adenauer Era* (New York: Columbia University Press, 2014), Nehring, *Politics of Security.*

[49] Adenauer, "Bericht zur politischen Lage," Sitzung Nr. 19, May 11, 1957, in Buchstab, ed., *Adenauer: "Wir haben wirklich etwas geschaffen."* 1229.

participant in the CDU executive meeting, such excessive fear could lead to political paralysis and the inability to "make decisions that are in the national interest" because of "all this fear in our people."[50] Chancellor Adenauer thus proposed a strategy to contain what he considered to be dysfunctional fears of nuclear war. If reduced to a "justified extent," he argued, it could be fought by the fear of Communism, "an even bigger fear."[51] For Adenauer, the central operation to contain popular fears of (nuclear) war thus consisted of the mobilization of anti-Communism as a different kind of fear.

The politics of fear in the German Cold War did not simply consist of the deliberate mobilization of fear of Communism for political purposes. It rather consisted of a complex attempt to maintain a carefully calibrated emotional balance between the fear of war, on the one hand, and the fear of Communism, on the other. The containment of popular fears of nuclear war was thus supposed to work in and through the mobilization of fears of Communism. Or, to put it differently, Adenauer's political strategy in the Cold War was the transfer of fear from one object (nuclear war) to another (Communism). In the emotional economy of the German Cold War, the official promise of security against the real or perceived threat of a new war was just as important as the persistent alertness vis-à-vis a real or imagined Communist threat from the East. How exactly did West German officials seek to realize this promise of security in the nuclear age? And how successful were they in doing so? The remainder of this chapter analyzes West German civil defense as one of the central elements of containing popular fears in the Cold War.

Re-establishing Civil Defense

As part of their larger demilitarization efforts, the Allied occupation authorities had prohibited any air defense measures whatsoever and had ordered the destruction of wartime bunkers or their transformation into civilian housing.[52] West German rearmament, however, put the issue of civilian air defense back on the agenda of national politics. From November 1950 onward, the federal government petitioned the Allied High Commission to lift the restriction on civil defense and, by March 1951, Allied authorities removed all legal impediments.[53] In November 1951, the federal cabinet approved preliminary steps toward the

---

[50] Ibid. 1235.

[51] Ibid. 1236. Also cited in Holger Löttel, "Des 'Emotionalen Herr werden.' Konrad Adenauer und die 'Angst vor der Atombombe' im Jahr 1957," in Patrick Bormann, Thomas Freiberger, Judith Michel, eds, *Angst in den internationalen Beziehungen* (Bonn: V&R Unipress, 2014), 216.

[52] Minister für Wiederaufbau to Finanzminister des Landes Nordrhein-Westfalen, Betr. Entmilitarisierung der Luftschutzbunker, November 26, 1948, NRWHStA, NW 59/159, 69–70.

[53] Vermerk, Betr. Entwicklung der Luftschutzmaßnahmen bei der Bundesregierung, July 25, 1951, BArch, B 134/5444.

re-establishment of civil defense measures. In the same year, a new Federal Civilian Air Defense League (*Bundesluftschutzverband*) was founded, which primarily reactivated the former activists of the civil defense league during the Third Reich (*Reichsluftschutzbund*). Reflecting the increased significance of scientific experts in anticipating the dangers of modern warfare, a "German Committee for Protection" (*Deutsche Schutzkommission*) was established within the German Research Foundation, the central public funding agency for research in the Federal Republic.[54] In 1953, the federal government instituted a Federal Office for Civilian Air Defense and, in 1957, expanded it to a Federal Agency for Civil Defense. To emphasize their purely civilian nature, these agencies were subordinated to the Interior Ministry, not to the military leadership, as had been the case in the Third Reich. Likewise, the local official in charge of civil defense was the mayor, not the local police chief.[55]

The anticipation of negative popular reactions accompanied official efforts at re-establishing civil defense in West Germany from the very beginning. In November 1950, defense expert Theodor Blank worried that a public discussion of civil defense "might drive the population into a fear psychosis."[56] A few months later, officials warned against "making the issue [of civil defense] known among broad sections of the population"; initial preparations and discussions regarding civil defense were to be held in secret to avoid a potential "shock effect" on the population.[57] To facilitate the re-establishment of civil defense, they advocated a gradual and cautious campaign to "loosen up the population's civil defense fatigue." It was to be waged, at least initially, "from the bottom up," by at least formally private organizations such as the Federal Civilian Air Defense League, not by state agencies directly.[58]

As West German officials and civil defense activists quickly needed to realize, the issue of civil defense activated popular memories of Allied bombing in the Second World War. When the Federal Civil Defense League conducted an

---

[54] A West German official listed former civil defense activists as well as nuclear scientists as the two main groups of experts to be consulted regarding the reorganization of civil defense, Vermerk, Magistratsbaurat Schenk, January 28, 1951, BArch, B17176. A history of this commission is a gap in the historiography. On its role in the shifting definition of panic in postwar Germany, see Frank Biess, "The Concept of Panic: Military Psychiatry and Emotional Preparation for Nuclear War in Postwar West Germany," in Frank Biess, Daniel M. Gross, eds, *Science and Emotions after 1945. Transatlantic Perspectives* (Chicago, University of Chicago Press, 2014), 181–208.

[55] Bauch, "Der Aufbau des Zivilen Luftschutzes," in Bundesministerium des Innern, ed., *Grundfragen des zivilen Luftschutzes* (Koblenz, 1953). This institutional organization largely followed the Weimar model. See Lemke, *Luftschutz in Großbritannien und Deutschland*. In reality, civil defense required close cooperation between military and civilian authorities. For an extensive analysis of civil defense planning within the West German military and the Ministry of Defense, see Thoß, *NATO-Strategie und nationale Verteidigungsplanung*, 603–721. On the bureaucratic process of re-establishing civil defense up to 1957, see Steneck, "Everybody Has a Chance," Chapter 2.

[56] Sitzung über Fragen des LS im BMI, November 1950, BArch, B134/5444.

[57] Innenminister NRW, Luftschutz-Angelegenheit, Besprechung vom 17.1.1952, January 18, 1952, NRWHStA, NW112/5.

[58] Sitzung über Fragen des LS im BMI, November 1950, BArch, B134/5444.

informal survey in a Cologne city district that had suffered extensive damage during the war, the results were devastating: none of the interviewees favored civil defense while 40 per cent were indifferent and 60 per cent outright opposed.[59] To be sure, an opinion poll by the Allensbach Institute in December 1953 yielded a slight majority of 43 per cent in favor of civil defense and 37 per cent opposed.[60] Still, the perception of a strong popular resistance to civil defense based on the memory of the war ultimately also informed high politics. In March 1954, Heinrich von Brentano, head of the CDU/CSU faction in the federal parliament, warned Interior Minister Gerhard Schröder that any increased public discussion of this issue would immediately reactivate "the horrific memories of the bombing nights in the cities" of the Allied attacks, and thus create a "political shock" by "inevitably giving the impression that the policies of the federal government would lead to war." This would seriously hamper the CDU's electoral prospects in upcoming state elections.[61] West German officials doubted the emotional and hence the political reliability of ordinary Germans, whom they perceived to be still in the grip of the emotional after-effects of the war.

To counter popular apprehensions about civil defense, West German civil defense activists engaged in their own politics of memory. They highlighted the crucial role of wartime air defense in reducing casualty rates during Allied air raids. Civil defense during the Third Reich thus had preserved what former civil defense official Erich Hampe termed the "substance of the German people."[62] The moral rehabilitation of civil defense during the Third Reich was completed in 1957 when the Federal Minister of the Interior issued a "declaration of honor" for all former civil defense activists, similar to the one that had previously been issued for *Wehrmacht* soldiers.[63] What he did not mention was the fact that civil defense had been firmly integrated into the repressive features of the Nazi state. Erich Hampe, who eventually became the first president of the Federal Agency for Civilian Air Defense, had co-edited a book in 1934 that celebrated the crucial

[59] First quotation from Sitzung über Fragen des LS im BMI, November 1950, BArch, B134/5444; Geschäftsführender Vorsitzender des Bundes-Luftschutzverbandes Bundesinnenministerium, 14.6.1955, BArch, B 106/17608.

[60] Presse- und Informationsamt der Bundesregierung to Herr Bundeskanzler, March 19, 1954, BArch, B 106/50239.

[61] Von Brentano to Schröder, March 11, 1954, BArch, B106/50239. Schröder did not agree with this assessment: he argued that any effort to provide security for the population necessarily would also be politically beneficial, especially since the SPD advocated even more extensive civilian defense measures; Schröder to Brentano, March 15, 1954, BArch, B 106/50239.

[62] Erich Hampe, "Die Wandlungen des zivilen Luftschutzes während des zweiten Weltkrieges," *Ziviler Luftschutz* 23 (1959): 231–5. Hampe also published a study on civil defense in Nazi Germany that is still cited as one of the authoritative sources on this subject: Erich Hampe, *Der zivile Luftschutz im Zweiten Weltkrieg. Dokumentation und Erfahrungsberichte über Aufbau und Einsatz* (Frankfurt a/M: Bernard & Graefe Verlag, 1963). On civil defense during the Nazi period, see Steneck, "Everybody Has a Chance," 39–105, Süß, *Der Tod aus der Luft*, 501–5.

[63] Fragen an den Herrn Bundesminister des Inneren bei der Fernsehsendung des SWF Baden-Baden "Luftschutz im Atomzeitalter," February 19, 1957, BArch, B106/85509.

significance of National Socialist ideology for civil defense preparation.[64] Local Nazi Party (NSDAP) officials had also succeeded in extending their influence in and through civil defense, which then extended the Nazi regime's control and surveillance functions more generally.[65] Finally, Hitler's promise to build safe bunkers for every German remained largely unfulfilled. Despite the extensive construction of massive bunkers as what Dietmar Süß terms "potential sites of the National Socialist *Volksgemeinschaft*," only a small segment of German civilians found refuge in public bunkers. Most Germans therefore needed to resort to improvised air raid shelters or basements, which did not give effective cover against Allied bombs.[66] As a result, popular memories cast civil defense during the Second World War not as an unmitigated success story but as a failed promise that was closely tied to the repressive features of the Nazi regime. The issue of civil defense also served as a powerful reminder of the Nazi state's failure to protect ordinary Germans against the destructive impact of war. In this sense, the re-establishment of civil defense was also part and parcel of a postwar effort to re-forge a state–citizen compact that was based on the state's ability and willingness to protect its citizens against external dangers.

What ultimately made civil defense a strategic as well as a political necessity was the nuclearization of NATO military strategy in the 1950s. NATO's increasing reliance on nuclear weapons, which manifested in the stationing of US tactical nuclear weapons in the Federal Republic in 1953, created an intractable strategic dilemma for the Federal Republic: on the one hand, because of West Germany's exposed position on the frontline of the Cold War and Soviet superiority in conventional weapons, West German security depended essentially on the first and early use of nuclear weapons. At the same time, any use of nuclear weapons in response to a Soviet attack would necessarily turn Germany into a nuclear battlefield and hence into a nuclear wasteland.[67] This dilemma became

---

[64] Erich Hampe, "Luftschutz als Schicksalsfrage für das deutsche Volk," in Erich Hampe, Kurt Knipfer, eds, *Der zivile Luftschutz* (Berlin: Otto Stollberg, 1934).On Hampe, see Lemke, *Luftschutz in Großbritannien und Deutschland*, 27, Diebel, *Atomkrieg und andere Katastrophen*, 37, Steneck, "Everybody Has a Chance," 121.

[65] Detlef Schmiechen-Ackermann, "Der 'Blockwart': Die unteren Parteifunktionäre im nationalsozialistischen Terror- und Überwachungsapparat," *Vierteljahreshefte für Zeitgeschichte* 48/4 (2000): 594–6, Süß, *Der Tod aus der Luft*, 152–62, 228–37.

[66] Wilfried Beer, *Kriegsalltag an der Heimatfront. Alliierter Luftkrieg und deutsche Gegenmaßnahmen zur Abwehr und Schadensbegrenzung, dargestellt im Raum Münster* (Bremen: Hausschild, 1990), Jörn Brinkhus, "Ziviler Luftschutz im 'Dritten Reich'—Wandel seiner Spitzenorganisation," in Dietmar Süß, ed., *Deutschland im Luftkrieg. Geschichte und Erinnerung* (Munich: Oldenbourg Verlag, 2007), Ralf Blank, "Kriegsalltag und Luftkrieg an der 'Heimatfront," in Jörg Echternkamp, ed., *Das Deutsche Reich und der Zweite Weltkrieg. Vol 9/1: Die deutsche Kriegsgesellschaft 1939 bis 1945. Politisierung, Vernichtung, Überleben* (Munich: DVA, 2004), 391–416, Süß, *Der Tod aus der Luft*, 320–2, 341–57, quotation on 343.

[67] Peter Fischer, *Atomenergie und staatliches Interesse: Die Anfänge der Atompolitik in der Bundesrepublik Deutschland 1949–1955, Vol. 1* (Baden-Baden: Nomos, 1996), Christian Greiner, "Die alliierten militärstrategischen Planungen zur Verteidigung Westeuropas 1947–1950," in Militärgeschichtliches Forschungsamt, ed., *Anfänge westdeutscher Sicherheitspolitik 1945–1956,*

brutally apparent when NATO held its first air exercise over Western Europe in June 1955. The maneuver "Carte Blanche" simulated a nuclear war in which, over the course of five days, 335 atomic bombs of the size of the Hiroshima bomb were dropped in a simulated battle zone stretching from Norway to Italy. Two-thirds of those bombs (268) were dropped on the territory of the Federal Republic, resulting in an estimated 1.7 million "deaths" and 3.5 million "wounded." Although these figures clearly minimized the effect of these weapons and also did not take into consideration long-term casualties from radiation, they nevertheless shocked the West German public.[68] The exercise had demonstrated the virtually complete lack of protection for the West German civilian population in the case of nuclear war.[69] Contemporary opinion polls confirm this impression of an extensive sense of insecurity among the citizens of the Federal Republic. In July 1954, an Allensbach poll came to the conclusion that 72 per cent of West Germans (79 per cent in big cities) felt "not safe" from the threat of a nuclear attack.[70] Conversely, only 36 per cent of West Germans believed that the US and Western Europe together could withstand a Soviet attack in 1952, and this percentage actually dropped to only 20 per cent in 1958.[71]

This sense of widespread popular insecurity and, indeed, fear ultimately forced the West German government to ponder a comprehensive civil defense program, especially since the Adenauer government began to face increasing criticism from the opposition Social Democrats for focusing one-sidedly on military rearmament while "not doing enough for the protection of the civilian population."[72] Civil defense thus became the politically necessary complement to rearmament and Western integration. It served an essential function in legitimizing Chancellor Adenauer's policy of Western integration. If NATO's nuclear protective shield

---

119–323. For a discussion of the implications of NATO's strategy of "massive retaliation" for West German military and civil defense, see Thoß, *NATO-Strategie und nationale Verteidigungsplanung*.

[68] Cioc, *Pax Atomica*, Detlef Bald, *Die Atombewaffnung der Bundeswehr. Militär, Öffentlichkeit und Politik in der Ära Adenauer* (Bremen: Edition Temmen, 1994), "Über 1.7 Millionen Deutsche wären getötet worden," *Westdeutsches Tagblatt*, July 18, 1955, Presse- und Informationsamt der Bundesregierung (PIB), 925, "Folgerungen aus dem Verlauf der NATO-Luftmanöver 'Carte Blanche'," BArch, B 106/17569.

[69] "Rüstung schafft noch keine Sicherheit," *Süddeutsche Zeitung*, July 2/3, 1955, BArch, B106/17232.

[70] Institut für Demoskopie, Allensbach, "Die Stimmung im Bundesgebiet, Furcht vor dem Atomkrieg," BArch, B106/50239.

[71] Institut für Demoskopie, Allensbach, "Die Verteidigung der Bundesrepublik." These polls were based on 2,000 representative individuals. These numbers should be used cautiously because the Allensbach Institute partly functioned as a polling institute for the federal government. Some of these numbers were never made public and only served as confidential information for West German officials. In other polls, the questions were framed in a way that made a positive outcome for the government's position more likely; Bald, *Die Atombewaffnung der Bundeswehr*, 121–31. On opinion polls as a historical source, see Anja Kruke, *Demoskopie in der Bundesrepublik. Meinungsforschung, Parteien und Medien 1949–1990* (Droste: Düsseldorf, 2007).

[72] 7. Luftschutzprogramm, BMI (84. Kabinettssitzung am 2. Juni 1955), Friedrich P. Kahlenberg für das Bundesarchiv, ed., *Kabinettsprotokolle der Bundesregierung 8 (1955)*, (Munich: De Gruyter, 1997), 344–6.

provided the primary guarantee of security for West Germans, the possibility of surviving a nuclear war was essential to the credibility of Western military strategy. At the same time, West German civil defense planners confronted the same pitfalls of emotional management as their counterparts in other countries: by promoting the idea of civil defense, they gave the impression of the possibility or even likelihood of a nuclear war, thus triggering the very fears they sought to dispel. But government officials insinuated that Germany could survive a nuclear war through civil defense planning. In so doing, they indirectly undercut their own logic of deterrence, which was based on the assumption that the potential costs of a nuclear war would be too high to make it worth fighting.[73]

Designing a civil defense program that would be credible to West German citizens, however, turned out to be fraught with uncertainty. In strategic terms, the near exclusion of West German officials from NATO's nuclear planning, including the selection of possible nuclear targets on German soil after a hypothetical Soviet invasion, complicated the task.[74] Moreover, the development of even more destructive thermonuclear weapons during the early 1950s made the possibility of protection and security seem less plausible. A visit by Val Peterson, the head of the US Federal Civil Defense Administration in the Federal Republic in October 1953, alerted West German officials to US planning scenarios that also included the use of 25 megaton thermonuclear bombs.[75] During a visit to the US in the following year, a German delegation learned about the "inconceivably large destructive power of new weapons," yet nevertheless felt confirmed in its reliance on "classic measures of civil defense," which, however, needed "to be adjusted" to the new weapons.[76] West German nuclear scientists, who had been charged with assessing "more precisely the impact especially of larger nuclear bombs," also failed to provide an unambiguous answer that might serve as a scientific basis for a West German civil defense program.[77] In fact, in one of the most dramatic public interventions of scientists in postwar history, the manifesto of the "Göttingen Eighteen" in April 1957, Germany's most prominent nuclear scientists warned that, in a nuclear war, the "entire population of the Federal Republic could probably be extirpated" through the "dispersion of radioactivity from H-bombs"; the scientists said they knew of "no technical possibility of protecting large population centers

---

[73] Garrison, *Bracing for Armageddon*.

[74] Christian Tuschhoff, *Deutschland, Kernwaffen und die NATO, 1949–1967. Zum Zusammenhalt von und friedlichem Wandel in Bündnissen* (Baden-Baden: Nomos, 2002), 158–62 Fischer, *Atomenergie und staatliches Interesse*, 284.

[75] Niederschrift der am 9.1.1954 im Hotel Spiegel u. Boppard durchgeführten Tagung über "Schutzmaßnahmen gegen die Wirkungen neuzeitlicher Angriffsmittel," BArch, B 106/17161.

[76] Schröder, BMdI to Presse- und Informationsamt der Bundesregierung, January 24, 1955, BArch, B106/17156.

[77] Bemerkungen zu den Zeitungsartikeln über die Wasserstoffbombe, February 25, 1953, BArch, B106/17161; Niederschrift über die am 9.1.1954 im Hotel Spiegel zu Boppard durchgeführte Tagung über "Schutzmaßnahmen gegen die Wirkung neuzeutlicher Angriffsmittel," BArch, B106/17161.

from this danger."[78] However, the main critique of the declaration was the nuclearization of the West German armed forces and not civil defense. Several signatories found it possible to endorse the critique of nuclearization while still affirming the possibility of at least limited protection through civil defense.[79] As these public divisions illustrated, scientists no longer functioned as the sole arbiters of the conditions of security and the legitimacy of fear in the Cold War. Instead, diverging scientific testimonies gave legitimacy to competing perceptions of reality and were mobilized on behalf of antagonistic policy proposals.[80] The increasingly contested role of science anticipated the mobilization of science and scientists during future conflicts in the emerging "risk society" of the 1970s and 1980s, especially regarding the civilian use of nuclear energy. Fear scenarios no longer derived from the tangible experience of ordinary people but needed to be mediated and communicated by scientific expertise.

The first West German Civil Defense Law, as it was passed by a majority of the federal parliament in June 1957 rested on three pillars: early warnings, timely evacuations, and, especially, the construction of bunkers.[81] This mixture of protective measures resulted from a series of detailed studies by which West German civil defense planners sought to measure the likely impact of a nuclear bomb on a German city.[82] Upon closer inspection, however, all three elements of West German civil defense policy turned out to be highly problematic. These measures essentially adhered to a spatial concept of security that derived from the experience of the Second World War and defined the possibility of survival primarily in terms of distance from the point of detonation. They did not, for example, take into consideration qualitatively new aspects of nuclear war such as nuclear fall-out or the effects of radiation.[83] In light of Germany's geographical position and modern aircraft technology, moreover, timely warnings were all but impossible, because the warning time of a nuclear attack amounted to only 5 to 8 minutes.[84]

---

[78] Cited in https://www.uni-goettingen.de/de/text+des+göttinger+manifests/54320.html (last accessed February 14, 2020).

[79] Erklärung O. Haxel, P. Maier-Leibniz, W. Riezler, April 17, 1957, BArch, B106/17608.

[80] For an example, see Verhandlungen des Deutschen Bundestages, Stenografische Berichte, 2. Wahlperiode, 207. Sitzung, May 8, 1957, 11941–3.

[81] Bundesgesetzblatt (Bgbl), 1957, Teil I, 1696–1702.

[82] In the case of an attack on the area of Düsseldorf, the combination of these measures would lower casualty rates from 90 per cent deaths and 10 per cent injured to 15 per cent and 18.75 per cent respectively in Zone A (the closest to the detonation), and from 50 per cent death and 30 per cent injured to 7.5 per cent and 20 per cent respectively in Zone B; "Schadenskalkulation im Falles des Abwurfs von A bzw H-Bomben verschieder Größe auf das Gebiet von Düsseldorf," September 30, 1954, BArch, B 106/17161.

[83] The planning of civil defense based on the experience of the Second World War was not limited to West Germany but also defined civil defense in the Soviet Union; see Diebel, *Atomkrieg und andere Katastrophen*, 46. For a similar emphasis on the legacies of the Second World War, see Steneck, "Everybody Has a Chance," Chapter 2.

[84] Auszug aus der Kurzniederschrift über die vom Bundesverband der Deutschen Industrie, Abteilung Industrie Luftschutz, am 27.1.1956 durchgeführte Vortragsveranstaltung über Probleme des Industrie-Luftschutzes, BArch, B 106/51857.

Evacuations featured prominently in the massive US civil defense exercise "Operation Alert" in 1955, but they were logistically more difficult in the constrained space of West Germany. They also contradicted NATO's official and proclaimed "stay at home" policy, which was supposed to guarantee that massive civilian population movements would not obstruct military operations in Western Europe.[85] West German civil defense planners sought to circumvent this dilemma by designing scenarios for a partial evacuation (*Auflockerung*) of urban centers through a planned resettlement of 30 per cent of the population during a crisis period they believed would precede the actual outbreak of hostilities.[86] Such evacuation scenarios highlighted the absence of a comprehensive West German national emergency law that would define state authority and regulate the validity of basic constitutional rights in the case of a nuclear war.[87] Representatives of the Interior Ministry, however, were convinced that only "forced evacuations" would be possible in the case of an impending war: the basic constitutional guarantee of a "free choice of residency" would have to be suspended in this case.[88] Plans for large-scale evacuations were also extremely unpopular and produced vehement protests when they became publicly known. For example, in 1958, the press leaked a proposal by a military official to evacuate 14 million West Germans in the case of an impending war.[89] A reader of the *Frankfurter Neue Presse* found it "incomprehensible" and "unbelievable" that such plans were entertained "13 years after millions of Germans fled from the Russians" and "barely survived."[90] Private memories of flight and expulsion during and after the Second World War prompted skepticism and outrage regarding public discussions of even more extensive evacuations in a possible future war.

---

[85]   On these tensions, see Thoß, *NATO-Strategie und nationale Verteidigungsplanung*, 676–91.

[86]   On the prominence of evacuation in US civil defense planning from 1953 to 1955, McEnaney, *Civil Defense Begins at Home*, 48; on "Operation Alert", see Oakes, *The Imaginary War*, 84–104. Vermerk USA-Luftmanöver "Operation Alert," December 5, 1955, BA-K, B17232; Walter Bargatzky to Referent im Hause, "Evakuierung und Umquartierung," August 4, 1959, BArch, B106/50708; Niederschrift über die Arbeitsbesprechung der Küstenländer über Fragen des zivilen Bevölkerungsschutzes am 15.12.1960 in Hamburg, BArch, B106/50708. On internal planning for evacuations, see Steneck, "Everybody Has a Chance," 192–205.

[87]   NATO required a national emergency law, which needed a change of the constitution, with the accession of the Federal Republic in May 1955. The parliamentary requirement of a two-thirds majority to change the constitution held up the law until 1968; see Thoß, *NATO-Strategie und nationale Verteidigungsplanung*, 651–60. On the debate about the emergency law giving rise to "democratic fears," see Chapter 5 in this book.

[88]   Niederschrift über die Arbeitsbesprechung der Küstenländer über Fragen des zivilen Bevölkerungsschutzes am 15.12.1960 in Hamburg, BArch, B106/50708. This was part of broader plans within the Interior Ministry for the abrogation of basic civil liberties in the case of a national emergency; see Martin Diebel, *"Die Stunde der Exekutive." Das Bundesinnenministerium und die Notstandsgesetze* (Göttingen: Wallstein, 2019), 100–20.

[89]   "Räumungsplan. Die Nation marschiert," *Der Spiegel*, April 30, 1958, "Im Kriegsfall: 24 Millionen Deutsche evakuiert," *Der Mittag*, April 16, 1958, "Evakuierungsplan für 14 Millionen Deutsche," *Hamburger Echo*, April 16, 1958, DB-PA 911.

[90]   Ernst Roloff, *Frankfurter Neue Presse*, April 30, 1958, DB-PA 911.

The centerpiece of West German civil defense—the provision of adequate bunkers for the civilian population—also constituted a very problematic device for providing security in the nuclear age. There was considerable uncertainty as to how bunkers would have to be constructed in order to provide lasting protection against the ever-increasing destructive power of nuclear weapons.[91] But even if it were possible to devise adequate shelters, they would be prohibitively expensive, especially if they were to be financed largely by public funds. Representatives of the Federal Housing Ministry quickly pointed out the intractable contradiction between social and military security: any effort to equip new public housing with bunkers would either limit the extent of public housing—an anathema in light of the early Federal Republic's housing crisis—or drive up rents by at least 20 per cent—a serious violation of the "social" aspect of the social market economy.[92] As a result, the Federal Finance Ministry steadfastly refused to commit to an "all-consuming" state obligation for building bunkers. They defined security largely as a voluntary responsibility of individual citizens. "Whoever does not want any protection simply should let it be," a representative of the Finance Ministry declared in a 1955 meeting.[93] The 1957 law thus postponed state regulation for the constructing and financing of bunkers to a later amendment to be passed in 1959.[94] The federal government finally passed a law with guidelines for the construction of bunkers in 1965 but its financial provisions were immediately put on hold because of budgetary concerns.[95] Throughout the Cold War, the West German government never committed significant public funds to civil defense. After reaching an apex of 786 million DM or 1.47 per cent of the federal budget in 1962, expenditure for this purpose actually declined in absolute terms and amounted to only 0.36 per cent of the federal budget by 1979.[96]

The financial limitations of a publicly funded civil defense program necessarily led West German officials to emphasize again the importance of voluntary efforts by individual citizens. The mobilization of the civilian population to assume a more active role became a cornerstone of the federal government's civil defense program.[97] Invoking the concept of total war, civil defense activists like Hampe proposed a "total defense" in which every citizen was supposed to participate,

---

[91] See the discussion in Niederschrift über die Besprechung des Merkblatts für LS-Bunker, May 19, 1953, BArch, B134/2823.
[92] Bundesminister für Wohnungsbau to Bundesminister des Inneren, February 9, 1954, BArch, B134/4747.
[93] Vermerk über Ressortbesprechug zum Luftschutz, April 25, 1955, BArch, B 134/4747.
[94] Verhandlungen des Deutschen Bundestages, Stenografische Berichte, 2. Wahlperiode, 216. Sitzung, June 27, 1957, 12786–7.
[95] Bgbl, I (1965), 1232–9.
[96] Bundesministerium des Innern, *Zivilschutz heute—für den Bürger—mit dem Bürger* (Bad Godesberg, 1979). On the failure to launch an extensive bunker-building program, see Steneck, "Everybody Has a Chance," 205–23.
[97] Not surprisingly, representatives of the Ministry of Finance advanced this argument; see Vermerk, Luftschutzprogramm, Sitzung im BMI, April 22 and 25, 1955, BArch, B134/4747.

albeit largely at their own costs.[98] While West German political elites did not support this scenario of a wholesale militarization of postwar society, they endorsed the general idea of activating citizens' individual agency on behalf of civil defense. Much like in the US, security was to be privatized: it was supposed to derive not from large, government-sponsored programs but rather from the initiative of private citizens. Yet, unlike in the US, where the militarization of everyday life largely depended on mobilizing the idea of the traditional nuclear family for the purpose of national security, the main task of West German civil defense activists consisted of the containment of popular fears. These explicit efforts at managing popular emotions culminated in the planning and distribution of the brochure "Everybody Has a Chance."

"Everybody Has a Chance"

The brochure inaugurated a more direct role of the federal government in propagating the idea of civil defense. It also signaled the efforts of a newly sovereign and strengthened state to engage in official emotional management.[99] State officials now propagated an emotional regime of rationality and anti-emotionality that was often coded as distinctly male. These efforts were part of an expanding "medialization of politics" that now also entailed the use of public relations firms for developing political campaigns.[100] Officials within the Interior Ministry had developed "Everybody Has a Chance" since 1957, and several West German PR agencies had given input into its content. The PR firms had been charged with developing a sensitive and subtle advertising strategy that would also include a "short, memorable slogan." The goal of the campaign was to lead a large section of the population to a different assessment of civil defense, thus activating more volunteers for the "securing and preservation of human life."[101] "Everybody Has a Chance" thus stood at the beginning of an increasing reliance on public relations and marketing strategies for advocating government policies.[102] This development

[98] Erich Hampe, *Strategie der zivilen Verteidigung. Studie zu einer brennenden Zeitfrage* (Frankfurt a/M: Eisenschmidt Verlag, 1956), 102–5. See also Thoß, *NATO-Strategie und nationale Verteidigungsplanung*, 622–3.

[99] This is why William M. Reddy, *The Navigation of Feeling. A Framework for the History of Emotions* (Cambridge: Cambridge University Press, 2001) analyzes the construction of an emotional regime based on the example of the Napoleonic state.

[100] Bernd Weisbrod, ed., *Die Politik der Öffentlichkeit—Die Öffentlichkeit der Politik. Politische Medialisierung in der Geschichte der Bundesrepublik* (Göttingen: Wallstein, 2003).

[101] Vermerk, Betr. Merkblatt für Selbstschutzmaßnahmen der Bevölkerung, BArch, B106/50243.

[102] At about the same time, the Christian Democratic Party began to employ PR agencies for designing its electoral campaigns; see Thomas Mergel, "Verkaufen wie Zahnpasta? Politisches Marketing in den bundesdeutschen Wahlkämpfen, 1949–1990," in Hartmut Berghoff, ed., *Marketinggeschichte. Die Genese einer modernen Sozialtechnik* (Frankfurt a/M: Campus, 2007), 372–99, Matthias Weiss, "Öffentlichkeit als Therapie. Die Medien- und Informationspolitik der Regierung Adenauer zwischen Propaganda und kritischer Aufklärung," in Frank Bösch, Norbert Frei,

marked a significant departure from the Weimar period when democratic governments had been hesitant to employ modern advertising techniques on behalf of republican politics.[103] But it also reflected a two-pronged response to the memory of state-sponsored propaganda during the Nazi period that served as a foil to be both emulated and avoided. On the one hand, Goebbels's skilled use of modern advertising techniques had indicated the capacity of modern media to mold and shape public opinion. On the other hand, the outsourcing of the campaign for civil defense to private PR agencies rendered it perhaps less likely to be associated with a Goebbels-style propaganda for total war than a campaign state agencies directly orchestrated would.[104] The advertising campaign on behalf of civil defense illustrated particularly well the dominant emotional regime. In contrast to the systematic whipping-up of emotions for the purpose of warfare during the Nazi period, the aim of the PR campaign for civil defense in West Germany was the control and containment of strong emotions, and especially of popular fear.[105] The proposals of two selected PR agencies—Dorland in Düsseldorf and Westag in Cologne—were extremely cognizant of ordinary West Germans' emotional predicament. "Our proposals are based on the assumption," Dorland wrote, that "the topics 'atomic bomb,' 'war,' but also 'civil defense' are extremely sensitive . . . Many people have become very sensitive because of their memory of the last war and because of the technological developments in the area of atomic weapons. As a result, any contact with these themes might produce a shock."[106] West German PR experts subscribed to a discourse of trauma here that actually placed them in the vanguard of conventional psychiatric wisdom, which, by the late 1950s, was only beginning to recognize long-term psychic consequences of experiences of violence.[107] At the same time, West German civil defense planners clearly saw excessive fear and anxiety as leading to apathy and indifference, and hence as undermining national preparedness. And while PR experts never cast the popular fears to be overcome as specifically feminine, the popular experience that appeared

---

eds, *Medialisierung und Demokratie* (Göttingen: Wallstein, 2006), 73–120. On the history of advertising, Pamela E. Swett, S. Jonathan Wiesen, Jonathan R. Zatlin, eds, *Selling Modernity: Advertising in Twentieth Century Germany* (Durham: Duke University Press, 2007).

[103] Corey Ross, "Mass Politics and the Techniques of Leadership: The Promise and Perils of Propaganda in Weimar Germany," *German History* 24/2 (2006): 184–210.
[104] On advertising in Nazi politics, see Gerald Diesener, Rainer Gries, eds, *Propaganda in Deutschland. Zur Geschichte der politischen Massenbeeinflussung im 20. Jahrhundert* (Darmstadt: Primus Verlag, 1966), Alexander Schug, "Hitler als Designobjekt und Marke. Die Rezeption des Werbegedankens durch die NSDAP bis 1933/34," in Berghoff, ed., *Marketinggeschichte*, 325–45.
[105] Claudia Lenssen, "Unterworfene Gefühle. Nationalsozialistische Mobilisierung und emotionale Manipulation der Massen in den Parteitagsfilmen Leni Riefenstahls," in Claudia Benthien, Anne Fleig, Ingrid Kasten, eds, *Emotionalität. Zur Geschichte der Gefühle* (Cologne: Böhlau, 2000), 198–212.
[106] Dorland Werbeagentur to Bundesamt für den zivilen Bevölkerungsschutz, August 15, 1959, Anlage: Gedanken zu einem Merkblatt für den zivilen Luftschutz, BArch, B 106/50243.
[107] On these developments within the psychiatric profession, see Frank Biess, *Homecomings. Returning POWs and the Legacies of Defeat in Postwar Germany* (Princeton: Princeton University Press, 2006), 70–94 and Goltermann, *Gesellschaft der Überlebenden*.

to be underlying the emotional resistance to civil defense—the exposure to Allied bombing—had, in fact, been primarily an experience of women on the home front. At least implicitly, the PR campaign defined popular resistance to civil defense as an ultimately feminine sensibility that would indulge in passivity. The goal of the campaign was to overcome these sentiments by replacing them with an ostensibly detached, rational, activist, and masculine attitude in favor of civil defense.

The brochure was designed to exert an immediate emotional impact on citizens, and the competition between PR agencies over its visual design revealed different strategies for overcoming nuclear fear. Civil defense advertising in the US used graphic images of nuclear destructions in order to make the case for civil defense. But PR experts were well aware that a visual politics of fear would clash with a specifically German emotional disposition resulting from the experiences and memories of the Second World War. Depictions of the horrors of nuclear war would likely have the opposite effect in Germany and opponents of civil defense routinely used such images to argue for the impossibility of meaningful protection in a nuclear war.[108] The Westag agency therefore rejected an image that the Federal Civil Defense League had used in earlier campaigns for this reason. It depicted a boy and his apparent younger sister clasping hands looking at a mushroom cloud with a caption "Protection Should Be Your Concern Too" (*Schutz auch Deine Sorge*). Westag criticized this image as "depressing and hopeless" because it represented nuclear apocalypse as inevitable doom. They predicted that this image would provoke "increased fear and apathy" and a sense that any form of protection was "useless," and hence exactly the opposite feelings than the PR campaign sought to invoke.[109] Whereas depictions of impending doom might awaken and enhance popular alertness in the US, such images would seamlessly fit into existing popular perceptions in West Germany that featured individuals as the hapless victims of external forces beyond their control.

As an alternative, the Dorland agency proposed a PR strategy that drew on another aspect of US civil defense propaganda: the image of the nuclear family. The slogan, "It is about human beings," was to be coupled with an idealized image of the nuclear family: a woman (and mother) in the foreground, in the background a father playing with his two sons "either with a technical construction set or a train set" and, to the side, a little daughter playing with dolls. A garden and a "single family home" in the background were to round up this family idyll. The caption to the image was supposed to state: "This is us, a happy and content family."[110] Although this visual strategy appeared to be highly compatible with

---

[108] Vermerk, Betr. Merkblatt für Selbstschutzmaßnahmen der Bevölkerung, BArch, B106/50243.
[109] Westag Werbeagentur, Stichworte zum Luftschutzprojekt, BArch, B106/50243.
[110] Dorland Werbeagentur to Bundesamt für den zivilen Bevölkerungsschutz, August 15, 1959, Anlage: Gedanken zu einem Merkblatt für den zivilen Luftschutz, BArch, B 106/50243.

the conservative gender politics of the Adenauer government, the Interior Ministry rejected this proposal as well because it overemphasized the "emotional dimension" of civil defense and ran the risk of being ridiculed.[111] It is possible that West German officials felt that appealing to parental responsibilities would stir Germans' negative memories of the last war, when fathers had failed to protect their families against wartime destruction, and therefore rejected it as a strategy to mobilize ordinary Germans for civil defense. But the repudiation of this proposal also reflected West German officials' broader reservations regarding the injection of strong emotions into politics. They ultimately adhered to a strategy that continued to favor information and "rational" persuasion over emotional appeal. In contrast to what they perceived as emotionally driven politics under National Socialism, they embraced a culture of sobriety, an emotional style of anti-intensity, that sought to avoid the alleged emotional excesses of the Nazi regime.[112]

The ultimate title design of the brochure that West German officials approved was supposed to be more sober.[113] It depicted an image of a large and non-gendered crowd that sought to invoke the idea of solidarity while also appealing to the individual "to take charge of one's own security." Using "Everybody Has a Chance" for the title, which Westag proposed, promised an egalitarian concept of security that was not to be differentiated by class or social status yet still appealed to individual responsibility.[114] According to Westag, the neutral image from the center of a crowd of people also did not "address immediately the issue of civilian air defense," which they saw as an advantage.[115]

The content of the brochure underwent numerous revisions over a period of at least two years prior to publication. The preamble of the brochure was especially contested and the different versions reflected diverging conceptions regarding the strategic function of civil defense. Whereas the Interior Ministry emphasized the protective function of civil defense by highlighting both the dangers of nuclear war

---

[111] Bundesministerium des Innern, Betr. Merkblatt für Selbstschutzmaßnahmen der Bevölkerung, August 20, 1959, BArch, B106/50243.

[112] Thomas Mergel, "Der mediale Stil der 'Sachlichkeit.' Die gebremste Amerikanisierung des Wahlkampfs in der alten Bundesrepublik," in Weisbrod, ed., *Die Politik der Öffentlichkeit*, 29–54. In this sense, West German emotional culture converged with the emotional culture of the US, even though its historical origins of "anti-intensity" were quite different in both countries; on the US, see especially Peter Stearns, *American Cool. Constructing a Twentieth-Century Emotional Style* (New York: New York University Press, 1994).

[113] Bundesministerium des Innern, Betr. Merkblatt für Selbstschutzmaßnahmen der Bevölkerung, August 20, 1959, BArch, B106/50243. Westag also appears to have served as consultant for the Interior and Defense Ministries in designing advertising campaigns for the recruitment of volunteers for the border police and the *Bundeswehr*; ibid.

[114] Westag Werbeagentur, Stichworte zum Luftschutzprojekt, BArch, B106/50243.

[115] Ibid. While retaining this slogan, the Interior Ministry ultimately awarded the actual production and dissemination of the brochure to a third PR agency, Hartmann in Reutlingen, Bundesministerium des Innern, Vermerk: "Aufklärungsschrift 'Jeder hat eine Chance,'" August 6, 1960, BArch, B106/50243.

Figure 3.2. Civil defense brochure, "Everybody Has a Chance" (1961).

This brochure was distributed to all West German households in December 1961 during a period of intense Cold War tensions. The brochure was designed to contain fears of a nuclear war but ended up achieving the opposite.

Source: BArch, B106/50243.

and everybody's chance of survival, defense minister Franz Josef Strauß stressed more strongly the deterrent function of civil defense and portrayed it as an integral part of military preparedness.[116] By early 1961, the production and publication were again put on hold for the remainder of the year, no doubt because the governing CDU/CSU needed to prepare for the upcoming federal elections. In light of the political significance of the brochure, Chancellor Adenauer himself determined the right moment for its publication.[117] It was no accident that Adenauer's decision came a few days after the federal election in September 1961, in which Adenauer's party lost its absolute majority and was forced to enter a coalition government with the Free Democratic Party (FDP).

The contemporary press reaction to the brochure, as well as ordinary West Germans' letters to officials about it, was extremely critical. Some objected to the lack of a publicly funded bunker construction program, which the brochure pointed to by encouraging the private construction of bunkers and air raid shelters.[118] "The care for personal protection is left to the individual," one concerned citizen wrote to the Interior Minister, wondering whether "it is not the obligation of the state to step in forcefully here?"[119] Other citizens who were more positively disposed toward the general idea of civil defense inquired about possible federal subsidies for the construction of bunkers, but none was available.[120] Homeowners charged that is an "impossible demand to impose such burdens on private property owners."[121] The suggestion that individuals seek cover under a briefcase or by putting their thumbs in their ears attracted the most fury.

In letters to the editor, irate citizens criticized these guidelines as completely minimizing the destructive impact of nuclear weapons. Several readers accused the government of concealing the shortcomings of its civilian defense program by such images.[122] Other readers charged that the brochure did not provide a realistic picture of an atomic war that could only result in a "sea of blood and tears," and an "inferno of destruction," or even "extinction" against which there was no protection whatsoever.[123] In a letter to Interior Minister Höcherl, another woman

---

[116] Abteilungsleiter VII to Herr Minister, December 14, 1960, BArch, B106/50243.

[117] Abteilungsleiter VII to Herr Minister, December 14, 1960, BArch, B106/50243; To Herr Abteilungsleiter VII, January 7, 1961, BArch, B106/50243. On the production of the brochure, see also Steneck, "Everybody Has a Chance," 271–7.

[118] "Vielleicht eine Chance," *Rhein-Neckar Zeitung*, December 5, 1961; see also "So oder so kaputt," *Coburger Neue Presse*, November 25, 1961, "Konkrete Möglichkeit," *Nürnberger Nachrichten*, November 24, 1961, all in DB-PA 911–1. On the reception, see also Steneck, "Everybody Has a Chance," 277–80.

[119] Hanns G. to Bundesminister des Inneren, August 3, 1962, BArch, B106/50242.

[120] See the inquiries and official responses in BArch, B106/54684.

[121] Willy Hartmann to Bundesinnenministerium, October 24, 1961, BArch, B106/54684.

[122] "Eine Chance zu überleben?" *Süddeutsche Zeitung*, December 2, 1961, "Haben wir tatsächlich eine Chance?" *Stuttgarter Nachrichten*, 25 November 1961, all in DB-PA 911–11.

[123] Quotations in "Haben wir tatsächlich eine Chance?" *Stuttgarter Nachrichten*, November 25, 1961, "Wer hat eine Chance?" *Süddeutsche Zeitung*, November 18, 1961, "Jeder hat eine Chance," *Die Welt*, January 6, 1962, "Bei Atomangriff die Fenster vernageln," *Kölner Stadt-Anzeiger*, December 13, 1961, all in DB-PA 911–1.

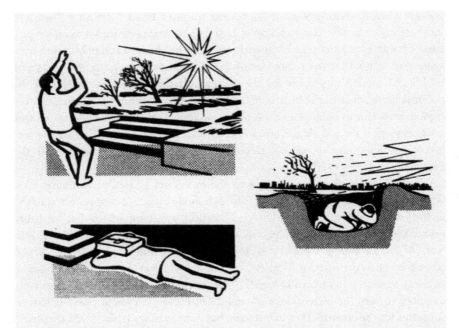

IM FREIEN:
Deckung nehmen, nicht weiterlaufen! Von der Lichterscheinung abwenden und die Augen schließen!
Wenn keine Deckung in unmittelbarer Nähe, so flach auf den Boden werfen! Augen schließen, Gesicht und Hände verbergen!

IM FAHRZEUG:
Sofort anhalten und Motor abstellen! Im Fahrzeug Deckung nehmen!
Nach der Detonation kurze Zeit liegenbleiben, bis Hitzestrahlung und Luftdruck nachlassen, dann Schutzraum, Keller oder Deckungsgraben aufsuchen! Gesicht nicht mit ungewaschenen Händen berühren!

17

Figure 3.3. Page from brochure, "Everybody Has a Chance."
These suggestions for personal behavior in the case of a nuclear attack prompted a public outcry from many West Germans and determined the largely negative reception of the first civil defense brochure.
Source: BArch, B106/50243.

spelled out this emotional link between memories of the past and catastrophic anticipations of the future: "Is this your first task to remind us again of not-yet forgotten times, and what may lie ahead in the future? I don't think that you know what it means to be reminded of…bombing war. I can only say that I am shocked."[124] The PR campaign's attempts to avoid invoking the memories of the Second World War thus obviously failed. In many cases, the campaign achieved precisely the opposite and hence backfired. This outcome suggests just how sensitively many Germans still reacted to any public discussion of war and violence in the early 1960s.

Significantly, the popular criticism of the brochure did not draw on an explicit vocabulary of fear, which the dominant emotional regime would not have condoned, but mobilized the language of mass death and genocide. West Germans' own memories of wartime violence, especially of the air war, served as a repository for enunciating their visions of a catastrophic future.[125] Contrary to the West German officials' claims, however, popular sentiments were not irrational and neurotic but rather based on a rational assessment of the nuclear threat. Popular responses to civil defense drew on well-established narratives of victimization and projected them onto the assessment of a potential future threat.[126] In this sense, these responses illustrated the *active* and *prospective* function of West German memories of the Second World War. Just as fears of retribution or, for that matter, the panic regarding the alleged abduction of young German men into the Foreign Legion, built on past "paradigm scenarios" of the victimization of Germans by an ostensible Jewish enemy, the air war transmitted negative memories of the past to an issue of pressing concern in the present.[127] An emerging memory of real and imagined German victimization as a result of Allied bombing during the war thus activated an anticipated future in which Germans feared similar victimization in the Cold War.

The emotional intensity of ordinary Germans' reactions to the brochure indicated not only their strong desire for security: it also pointed to their persistent distrust in the federal government's ability to provide this essential function of the modern state toward its citizens. Rather than enlightening the population about possible protective measures in the case of a nuclear war, "Everybody Has a Chance" mobilized a long-standing popular disposition dating back to the Second World War that suspected political elites of disregarding popular concerns for security, or even of willingly exposing the population to external threats. Nuclear fear, in this sense, also derived from a highly selective memory of the Second World War in which devilish Nazi officials freely and unnecessarily squandered

---

[124] Wilma W. to Höcherl, November 24, 1961, BArch, B106/54684.

[125] Geyer, "Cold War Angst," Holger Nehring, "Cold War, Apocalypse and Peaceful Atoms. Interpretations of Nuclear Energy in the British and West German Anti-Nuclear Weapons Movements, 1955–1964," *Historical Social Research* 29/3 (2004): 150–70. On memories of the air war, see Malte Thießen, *Eingebrannt ins Gedächtnis. Hamburgs Gedenken an Luftkrieg und Kriegsende 1943 bis 2005* (Hamburg: Dölling und Galitz Verlag, 2007) and Jörg Arnold, *The Allied Air War and Urban Memory: The Legacy of Strategic Bombing in Germany* (Cambridge: Cambridge University Press, 2011), Süß, ed., *Deutschland im Luftkrieg.*.

[126] Moeller, *War Stories.*

[127] Ronald de Sousa, *The Rationality of Emotions* (Cambridge, Mass.: Harvard University Press, 1990), 181–4, Christiane Voss, *Narrative Emotionen. Eine Untersuchung über Möglichkeiten und Grenzen philosophischer Emotionstheorien* (Berlin: De Gruyter, 2004), 213–15.

the lives of largely innocent and "good" German civilians and soldiers, which was popularized in numerous war movies of the 1950s.[128] This sense of "injured citizenship," as historian Michael Geyer has called it, not only manifested itself in popular fear and anxiety but also in a palpable anger at government officials who appeared to deceive (yet again) ordinary Germans regarding the existential conditions of their security.[129] In fact, because the emotion of anger tends to bestow a somewhat greater degree of agency to individuals than fear and anxiety, it may have helped to balance ordinary Germans' perceived sense of helplessness vis-à-vis the nuclear threat.[130] An increasingly critical press also fueled this popular distrust of, and anger at, state authorities.[131] In January 1962, the magazine *Quick* published illustrations of a highly fortified bunker near Bonn that was to serve as a refuge for the federal government's national security council in the case of a nuclear war. The government bunker under a "fifty meter high solid rock" contrasted markedly with the briefcase that the federal government had suggested as adequate cover for private citizens.[132] The federal prosecutor charged *Quick* with publication of military secrets and ordered the issue confiscated. Policemen reportedly went from newsstand to newsstand to tear out the incriminating article from issues that had already been distributed. This incident anticipated the more serious "*Spiegel* affair" only a few months later, in which several journalists of Germany's leading political magazine were imprisoned for alleged national treason.[133]

Not surprisingly, oppositional movements sought to capitalize on the popular rejection of the brochure and articulated their disagreement either with the idea of civil defense generally—like pacifist groups—or, in the case of the Social Democrats, at least with the government's version thereof.[134] Yet precisely because the popular opposition to civil defense drew on deeper resentments toward state

---

[128] See Robert G. Moeller, "Victims in Uniform: West German Combat Movies from the 1950s," in Bill Niven, ed., *Germans as Victims. Remembering the Past in Contemporary Germany* (Palgrave MacMillan Houndmills, Basingstoke, 2006), 43–61.

[129] Geyer, "Cold War Angst." Diebel also argues that the brochure "suggested a sense of security that large segments of the population no longer believed in": see Diebel, *Atomkrieg und andere Katastrophen*, 61.

[130] Christoph Demmerling, Hilge Landweer, *Philosophie der Gefühle. Von Achtung bis Zorn* (Stuttgart: J.B. Metzler, 2007), 287–9. On the history of anger, see Carol Z. Stearns, Peter Stearns, *Anger. The Struggle for Emotional Control in America's History* (Chicago: University of Chicago Press, 1986) and Barbara H. Rosenwein, ed., *Anger's Past. The Social Uses of an Emotion in the Middle Ages* (Ithaca: Cornell University Press, 1998).

[131] Christina von Hodenberg, *Konsens und Krise. Eine Geschichte der westdeutschen Medienöffentlichkeit 1945–1973* (Göttingen: Wallstein, 2006).

[132] "Landesverrat?" January 16, 1962, *General Anzeiger Bonn*. This article reproduced part of the original *Quick* article: "Landesverrat: *Quick* muss man haben," January 17, 1962, *Der Spiegel*, "Verrat und Sicherheit," *Kölnische Rundschau*, January 12, 1962, all in DB-PA 911–11.

[133] Von Hodenberg, *Konsens und Krise*, 326. On the *Spiegel* affair, see Chapter 5 in this book.

[134] Komitee gegen Atomrüstung, "Luftschutz—Wie groß ist unsere Chance?" (Munich, 1962); Bayrisches Staatsministerium des Innern to Bundesministerium des Innern, August 30, 1960, BArch, B106/5024. The Social Democrats were not generally opposed to civil defense but critical that chances of survival largely depended on income, especially since the government had not committed

authority, these movements did not necessarily benefit politically from the public criticism of the brochure. The Hartmann PR agency, which disseminated the brochure, eventually conceded that criticism of the booklet extended far beyond publications under "Communist influence."[135] Representatives of the new governing CDU/CSU and FDP coalition also began to distance themselves from the publication, which had been produced under the previous administration.[136] In response to a parliamentary inquiry by the opposition Social Democrats, the new Interior Minister Hermann Höcherl granted that future publications should take into consideration the public critique of "Everybody Has a Chance."[137]

Less than three years later the federal government distributed to all West German households a new "primer for civil defense" (*Zivilschutzfibel*) that was now consciously modeled against the previous brochure. It included, for example, a promise for protection only in the case of a limited nuclear war or a conventional war, while openly professing that there is "practically no possibility" for protection in the case of a "war of extinction."[138] PR agencies again assisted in the preparation of this new brochure, but it had also been subjected to a psychological study in which researchers interviewed 120 people to measure likely emotional reactions to the brochure's textual and visual aspects. The test warned, for example, that the phrase "substance of the people," which civil defense was supposed to protect, might invoke a "strong emotional reaction" as well as associations with "race," "race mixture," "Jewry and hatred of Jews," and "potential war," thus threatening to link the brochure to National Socialist ideology. Researchers recommended replacing "strong" and emotional arguments" with "sober" and "rational arguments" in order to avoid "negative emotional reactions."[139] In so doing, the brochure adhered to a dominant emotional regime that was highly suspicious of the injection of emotions into politics.

The careful official anticipation of possible popular reactions to the 1964 brochure seems to have paid off. Public commentators confirmed that in contrast to previous "half-truths," this publication appeared "modern, honest, informative."[140]

---

significant public funds for this purpose. See "Jeder Hat eine Chance," December 6, 1961, *Vorwärts*, DB-PA 911–11.

[135] Heinrich Hartmann Werbeagentur to Bundesminister des Innern, November 21, 1961, January 19, 1962, BArch, B106/50244.
[136] One official conceded, for example, that the brochure had been "rushed quickly, too quickly under the pressure of the Berlin Wall"; Prof. Dr. Hölzl, Staatssekretär im Bundesinnenministerium, zu Fragen des zivilen Bevölkerungsschutzes, August 19, 1963, BArch, B106/85509.
[137] Drucksache IV-191, Deutscher Bundestag, 4. Wahlperiode, 14.2.1962, Betr. Ziviler Bevölkerungsschutz, ASD, DW2-9e3.
[138] Bundesministerium des Innern, *Zivilschutzfibel* (Bonn, 1964), 5.
[139] All quotations from Forschungsgemeinschaft "Der Mensch im Verkehr" e.V. Ergebnisse einer psychologischen Untersuchung März 1963, BArch, B106/50246.
[140] "Gelernt," *Die Welt*, October 26, 1964, "'Hat wirklich jeder eine Chance?' 'Zivilschutzfibel' gibt Auskunft," *Recklinghauser Zeitung*, October 30, 1964, BArch, B106/50248. See also Steneck, "Everybody Has a Chance," 280–7.

Less negative public responses reflected a gradual shift in attitudes toward civil defense by the mid 1960s.[141] According to one opinion poll, public approval of civil defense was 44 per cent in 1952, rose to 60 per cent in 1962, and dropped again to 53 per cent in 1963.[142] Public commentators noted a "silent transformation" among West Germans who had overcome the "civil defense shock" dating back to the Second World War.[143] However, this was more of a passive acceptance rather than an active embrace of civil defense. An Allensbach study on "life in the atomic age" in 1968 revealed that only 34 per cent of the population had ever received or tried to gain information on how to prepare for a nuclear attack whereas 60 per cent had never sought such information.[144] Civil defense activists had clearly failed to mobilize the population. What declined was the strong emotional resentment toward civil defense that had been present throughout the 1950s. At least regarding matters of national security, ordinary West Germans continued to practice a thin version of citizenship that was based more on passive acquiescence to, than on active participation in, national (self-)defense.[145] By the mid 1960s, the issue of civil defense simply declined in ordinary Germans' emotional economy of attention, only to gain greater currency again during the "Second Cold War" of the 1980s.[146]

Emotional Change or How Germans Learned to Live with the Bomb

How can we explain the subtle yet important transformation in West German popular attitudes toward civil defense that took place between the mid 1950s and the mid 1960s? Had West Germans finally learned to live with the bomb, and, if so, why? Or, in other words, why did nuclear fear decline significantly during this period? This transformation most likely did not result from official propaganda efforts, which may actually have been counter-productive and have provided an

---

[141] For a similar emphasis on changing attitudes toward "the bomb" more generally, see Ilona Stölken-Fitschen, *Atombombe und Geistesgeschichte. Eine Studie der fünfziger Jahre aus deutscher Sicht* (Baden-Baden: Nomos, 1995).

[142] Presse- und Informationsamt der Bundesregierung to Bundeskanzler, September 25, 1963, BArch, B106/85502.

[143] "Stille Wandlung," *Rheinischer Merkur*, February 19, 1965, BArch, B106/85502. Diebel sees the mid 1960s and the 1964 brochure as the "high point" of a "positive attention" to civil defense in West Germany. See Diebel, *Atomkrieg und andere Katastrophen*, 55.

[144] Institut für Demoskopie, "Leben im Atomzeitalter. Eine psychologische Leitstudie," [1968], Tabelle T 13.

[145] Bryan S. Turner, "Outline of a Theory of Citizenship," *Sociology* 24/2 (1990): 189–217, Michael Walzer, *Thick and Thin. Moral Argument at Home and Abroad* (Notre Dame: University of Notre Dame Press, 1994).

[146] See, for example, Manfred Peters, Robert Pfeiffer, eds, *Zivilschutzgesetz. Friedenspolitik oder Kriegsvorbereitung?* (Cologne: Presseverlag Ralf Theurer, 1985). See also Chapter 8 in this book.

occasion for the articulation of popular fears. Long-standing emotional dispositions, it seems, were difficult to manipulate by government-sponsored efforts.
Emotional change instead resulted from at least three different causes: changing
national and international political contexts, the rise of countervailing emotions,
and shifts in West German commemorative culture.

First, by the mid 1960s, a domestic consensus between political and scientific
elites emerged regarding realistic possibilities for civil defense. This consensus
was represented in the more limited promise for protection in the 1964 publication. It also corresponded to scientific assessments that confirmed the usefulness
of civil defense in the case of a limited nuclear war or, for that matter, a conventional war. The nuclear physicist Carl Friedrich von Weizsäcker became a prominent proponent of such "pragmatic" and realistic civil defense measures.[147] The
transformation of the opposition Social Democrats' stance on military matters
was also significant in this context. The party no longer employed civil defense
primarily as a way to criticize the government's one-sided focus on *military*
defense. Instead, the SPD's emerging defense expert and future Chancellor,
Helmut Schmidt, underlined the "unity of all parties" regarding civil defense and
called on party members to become actively involved "in order not to leave the
field to others."[148] Without significant public disagreements between political,
military, and scientific elites, it became more difficult to articulate and legitimize
public resistance to the idea of civil defense. A "grand coalition" in essential matters of national security reduced popular resistance to civil defense among the
population.

Besides these domestic developments, the significance of larger international
contexts for postwar German emotional life was extremely important. Issues of
grand politics, military strategy, and international diplomacy assumed virtually
existential significance for postwar Germans and shaped into their intimate lives
and political subjectivities. The emergence of a Cold War settlement in Europe, as
well as the passing of the Berlin and Cuba crises, contributed to a gradual decline
of popular fears of nuclear war by the mid 1960s. Despite this general relaxation
of tensions, however, Central Europe remained the area with the highest concentration of nuclear weapons during the Cold War. But with the final renunciation

---

[147] See von Weizsäcker in "Diskussion über Luftschutzmaßnahmen," Hessischer Rundfunk,
November 18, 1962; on von Weizsäcker's important role, see Diebel, *Atomkrieg und andere
Katastrophen*, 60; see also "Höcherl stimmt Wissenschaftlern zu," *Frankfurter Rundschau*, October 4,
1962, ASD, DW2-9e3. A more limited civil defense program was also compatible with a changing
NATO military doctrine that gradually moved away from an emphasis on "massive retaliation" and
toward the strategy of "flexible response"; see Thoß, *NATO Strategie und nationale
Verteidigungsplanung*, 740.
[148] Niederschrift über die Sitzung des Arbeitskreises VIII (Sicherheitsfragen) am 30. November
1961, ASD, NL Erler, Box 138B. See also Helmut Schmidt, "Ziviler Bevölkerungsschutz als staat-
spolitische und wirtschaftliche Verantwortung," Vortrag vor der Handelskammer Hamburg am 11.
Juli 1962, ASD.

of West German nuclear ambitions by the early 1960s, the triggers remained firmly and exclusively under US control.[149]

This fact points to the role of the US, and to the German–American relationship specifically, as a second central factor explaining the decline of nuclear angst by the early 1960s.[150] Close attention to German–American relations reveals the relational nature of different emotions. Emotional change cannot be explained with reference to one emotion alone—in this case, fear. It also needs to consider the evolution of hope, security, trust, and love as well. Throughout the 1950s and early 1960s, West Germans' emotional relationship to America and Americans changed considerably, especially from the late 1950s to the early 1960s. According to an Allensbach poll, the percentage of West Germans who professed to "like Americans" increased from 37 per cent in 1957 to 58 per cent in 1965.[151] These figures indicate a growing emotional attachment to the US that found its iconic moment in President Kennedy's visit to Berlin in June 1963.[152] In the emotional economy of the German Cold War, increasing trust in the American nuclear umbrella reflected a kind of growing West German emotional integration in the transatlantic alliance that, at least temporarily, tempered German nuclear fear. Ordinary Germans, it seems, were ready to invest the US with the kind of trust and confidence in essential matters of national security that they did not fully bestow on their own government.

Third, because popular fears of nuclear war were so closely linked to memories of the Second World War, shifts in the West German commemorative culture also influenced anticipations of the future. Whereas West German narratives of victimization provided a central repository for articulating different kinds of fear during the 1950s, the significance of the victim trope began to decline by the early 1960s, even though it never disappeared completely. As Chapter 5 describes, the Nazi past returned to the West German public sphere from the early 1960s onward, mainly through spectacular and highly publicized trials like the Eichmann trial in 1961 and the Auschwitz trial from 1963 to 1965. Despite their serious limitations, these trials reflected a shift in the public focus away from an exclusive emphasis on German suffering and toward a greater recognition of the role of Germans as perpetrators.[153] A changing West German commemorative culture both fueled

---

[149]   Trachtenberg, *A Constructed Peace*, Christoph Hoppe, *Zwischen Teilhabe und Mitsprache: Die Nuklearfrage in der Allianzpolitik Deutschlands 1959–1966* (Baden-Baden: Nomos Verlagsgesellschaft, 1993), Bald, *Die Atombewaffnung der Bundeswehr*.

[150]   On the centrality of the German–American relationship for German conceptions of security, see Michael Geyer, "Amerika in Deutschland. Amerikanische Macht und die Sehnsucht nach Sicherheit," in Frank Trommler, Elliott Shore, eds, *Deutsch-amerikanische Begegnungen. Konflikt und Kooperation im 19. und 20. Jahrhundert* (Stuttgart: DVA, 2001), 155–87.

[151]   Noelle-Neumann and Neumann, eds, *The Germans*, 543.

[152]   Here I follow the excellent study by Andreas W. Daum, *Kennedy in Berlin. Politik, Kultur und Emotionen im Kalten Krieg* (Paderborn: Schöningh, 2003).

[153]   See Chapter 5.

and reflected new sources of fear and anxiety. With the relaxation of Cold War tensions, the *loci* of fear and anxiety increasingly shifted from external threats to perceived internal dangers regarding the viability of democracy. This shift also entailed a declining importance of anti-Communism from the early1960s onward. The construction of the Berlin Wall ended most anxieties that the Communist model could become attractive to West Germans. Instead, a growing left-liberal opposition began to see the official anti-Communist measures as disproportionate to the actual threat and increasingly castigated anti-Communism as a pretext for undermining democratic rights by an authoritarian state.[154] Declining fears of nuclear war also meant that the compensatory function of anti-Communism in the emotional balance of the German Cold War became less important. As a result, Communist front organizations like the *Kampfgruppe gegen Unmenschlichkeit* dissolved in 1959. Instruments of anti-Communism such as the Ministry of All German Affairs increasingly shifted toward supporting a policy of détente vis-à-vis the Communist East.[155]

Rather than a weak state incapable of providing security against external threats, the object of popular fears gradually shifted toward internal threats to the viability of democracy and even to the moral integrity of the democratic subject. The late 1950s and early 1960s thus witnessed an important shift from external to internal fears that was of central importance for the emotional history of the Federal Republic. The external and internal stabilization of the Federal Republic by the early 1960s thus did not bring an end to fear. Rather, the primary objects of fear moved to inner threats of economic decline or an authoritarian political transformation. Chapters 4 and 5 will explore the implications of this development with respect to both the West German economic and political systems.

---

[154] Kössler, *Abschied von der Revolution*, 357–68.
[155] Heitzer, *Die Kampfgruppe gegen Unmenschlichkeit (KgU)*, 419–69, Creuzberger, *Kampf für die Einheit*, 347–430.

4

Modern *Angst*

The future of the Federal Republic began sometime between the late 1950s and the early 1960s. As professional curators of the past, West German historians recognized this moment when they dedicated the 1962 *Historikertag*, the biannual convention of the West German Historical Association, to the theme of "the future."[1] Association president Karl Dietrich Erdmann laid out various approaches to the future in his opening address. Invoking a "teleological" and an "eschatological" future based on Christian and Enlightenment norms, Erdmann nevertheless acknowledged the essential openness and contingency of the future.[2] His diagnosis of a shift in past conceptions of the future coincided with an opening up of West German futures precisely at the same moment.[3]

This expansion of the West German horizon of expectation resulted from the external and internal stabilization of the Federal Republic. West Germany's integration into NATO and the concurrent regaining of sovereignty in May 1955 settled basic foreign policy decisions, setting the stage for the stabilization of the Federal Republic's external situation over the course of the late 1950s and early 1960s. The return of the last German prisoners of war from Soviet captivity in January 1956 marked the end of one of the most important direct consequences of the Second World War and allowed West German society to constitute itself as a complete national body.[4] The economy exhibited unprecedented growth rates. The first major recession did not occur until 1966–7. Postwar prosperity began to affect wider sections of the population who were increasingly able to participate in an emerging consumer society.[5] Economic growth also made possible the introduction of the "dynamic pension" in 1957, which significantly raised

---

[1] Rüdiger Graf, *Die Zukunft der Weimarer Republik. Krisen und Zukunftsaneignungen in Deutschland 1918–1933* (Munich: Oldenbourg, 2008), 28.
[2] Karl Dietrich Erdmann, "Die Zukunft als Kategorie der Geschichte," *Historische Zeitschrift* 198/1 (1964): 44–61.
[3] On time as a historical category, see Reinhart Koselleck, *Vergangene Zukunft. Zur Semantik geschichtlicher Zeiten* (Frankfurt a/M: Suhrkamp, 1995 [1979]), Ulrich Raulff, *Der unsichtbare Augenblick. Zeitkonzepte in der Geschichte* (Göttingen: Wallstein, 1999), Martin Sabrow, *Die Zeit der Zeitgeschichte* (Göttingen: Wallstein, 2012), Joachim Radkau, *Geschichte der Zukunft. Prognosen, Visionen, Irrungen in Deutschland von 1945 bis heute* (Munich: Carl Hanser Verlag, 2017).
[4] Frank Biess, *Homecomings. Returning POWs and the Legacies of Defeat in Postwar Germany* (Princeton: Princeton University Press, 2006), 203–26.
[5] Michael Wildt, *Vom kleinen Wohlstand. Eine Konsumgeschichte der 1950er Jahre* (Frankfurt a/M: Fischer, 1996).

German Angst: *Fear and Democracy in the Federal Republic of Germany.* Frank Biess, Oxford University Press (2020). © Frank Biess.
DOI: 10.1093/oso/9780198714187.001.0001

pensions and adjusted them to wage levels.[6] This period also constituted the culmination point of West Germany's evolution as an industrial society, with the highest percentage of workers employed in the industrial sector and a broad application of modern Fordist methods of mass production.[7] Crucial social and cultural transformations gathered steam and increasingly defined the nature of West German society and culture: older conservative traditions began to lose influence and the Federal Republic evolved into a more liberal society.[8] A depoliticized "Cold War liberalism" that defined West German citizens' cultural consumption as private and non-political increasingly replaced Christian and conservative norms.[9] Despite the founding of the *Bundeswehr* in 1957, traditional military ideals of masculinity declined and gave way to the new ideal of the "citizen in uniform."[10]

As a result of these broad socio-economic changes, the self-description of West German society began to change as well.[11] Political scientists and sociologists abandoned notions of a unitary and homogenized *Volk* and began to portray political conflict and the proliferation of interest groups as healthy indications of a vibrant liberal democracy. Amorphous concepts of the "mass" of Germans gave way to self-descriptions as industrial society. The National Socialist conception of a homogenous *Volksgemeinschaft* (that is, a national and racial community), which had survived the collapse of the Third Reich and radiated into postwar West German society, lost its currency in the minds of West Germans. As notions of a unified and homogenous German *Volk* receded from the popular imagination, West Germans began to envision individual and collective futures that no longer depended on the fate of an imagined collective *Volk*.[12]

---

[6] Hans-Ulrich Wehler, *Deutsche Gesellschaftsgeschichte. Fünfter Band: Bundesrepublik und DDR, 1949–1990* (Munich: C.H.Beck, 2008), 261–4.

[7] Gerold Ambrosius, "Wirtschaftlicher Strukturwandel und Technikentwicklung," in Axel Schildt, Arnold Sywottek, eds, *Modernisierung im Wiederaufbau. Die westdeutsche Gesellschaft der 50er Jahre* (Bonn: J.H.W. Dietz Nachf., 1993), 107–28.

[8] Ulrich Herbert, "Liberalisierung als Lernprozess: Die Bundesrepublik in der deutschen Geschichte—eine Skizze," in Ulrich Herbert, ed., *Wandlungsprozesse in Westdeutschland. Belastung, Integration, Liberalisierung 1945–1980* (Göttingen: Wallstein, 2002), 128, Uta Poiger, *Jazz, Rock, and Rebels. Cold War Politics and American Culture in a Divided Germany* (Berkeley: University of California Press, 2000), Schildt and Sywottek, eds., *Modernisierung im Wiederaufbau.*

[9] Poiger, *Jazz, Rock, and Rebels.*

[10] See Robrt G. Moeller, "The 'Remasculinization' of Germany in the 1950s: Introduction," *Signs* 24/1 (1998): 101–6.

[11] On self-description as an essential aspect of constituting the nation as a political community, see Ulrich Bielefeld, *Nation und Gesellschaft. Selbstthematisierung in Deutschland und Frankreich* (Hamburg: Hamburger Edition, 2003), 9–109.

[12] Paul Nolte, *Die Ordnung der deutschen Gesellschaft. Selbstentwurf und Selbstbeschreibung im 20. Jahrhundert* (Munich: C.H.Beck, 2000), 274–402. The arrival of non-German "guest workers" during this period undoubtedly further undermined the notion of a homogenous "*Volk*" although few observers anticipated the fundamental impact of this development on German self-perceptions and identities in subsequent decades. See Karin Hunn, *"Nächstes Jahr kehren wir zurück" Die Geschichte der türkischen "Gastarbeiter" in der Bundesrepublik* (Göttingen: Wallstein, 2005).

The period from the late 1950s to the early 1960s thus constituted a kind of West German *Sattelzeit*, a turning point in which certain memories of the past lost their claim on anticipations of the future and new futures became possible.[13] This emergence of new futures also transformed West German individual and collective fears. On the one hand, the gradual acceptance of a modern social order was one of the main reasons why, as historian Paul Nolte has written, the mid 1960s marked something like an "end to the obsessions and exaggerated fears regarding the social order in West Germany."[14] Catastrophic scenarios in which individuals feared the national decline of the German *Volk* lost their hold on the German imagination. Yet these shifting self-descriptions also entailed new uncertainties. Where would the rapid sociocultural modernization of the Federal Republic lead to? What exactly would modern futures look like? The very economic and political stabilization of the Federal Republic thus also produced its own uncertainties regarding what exactly these "modern" and "democratic" futures entailed. These uncertainties became the basis of what I would like to call "modern fears."

While West Germans left behind the existential uncertainty that had plagued them from 1945 onward, modern fears were a product of the experience of accelerated modernization. This period witnessed an increasing sensibility for the complexity and unpredictability of modern industrial societies as well as for the essential fragility of democratic regimes. The acceleration of historical time notwithstanding, memories of the German past continued to inform anxieties about the future. But these were not so much memories of catastrophic defeat but rather memories of economic dislocation and political fragility during the 1920s and 1930s. A broadening horizon of expectation drew on an expanded commemorative culture that increasingly included both the collapse of the Weimar Republic and the rise of National Socialism. The economic and political collapse of Weimar informed anxieties about the sustainability and stability of West German economic prosperity and liberal democracy.[15] How might West Germany maintain its social and economic stability during a period of accelerated structural and technological change? And how exactly could West Germans ensure that the Bonn Republic would not follow its Weimar predecessor and revert to a new authoritarianism?

---

[13] On *Sattelzeit*, see Reinhart Koselleck, "Einleitung," in Otto Brunner, Werner Conze, Reinhart Koselleck, eds, *Geschichtliche Grundbegriffe*, vol. 1 (Stuttgart: Klett-Cotta, 1979), XV. See also Edgar Wolfrum, *Die geglückte Demokratie. Geschichte der Bundesrepublik Deutschland von ihren Anfängen bis zur Gegenwart*, 14 (Stuttgart: Klett-Cotta, 2006) and Wehler, *Deutsche Gesellschaftsgeschichte. Fünfter Band*, 277.

[14] Nolte, *Die Ordnung der deutschen Gesellschaft*, 402.

[15] Sebastian Ullrich, *Der Weimar-Komplex. Das Scheitern der ersten deutschen Demokratie und die politische Kultur der frühen Bundesrepublik 1945–1959* (Göttingen: Wallstein, 2009), Christoph Gusy, ed., *Weimars lange Schatten—"Weimar" als Argument nach 1945* (Baden-Baden: Nomos, 2003).

This chapter analyzes the modern fears that the increasingly modern condition of the Federal Republic created between the late 1950s and the mid 1960s. It does so by focusing on the debate surrounding industrial "rationalization" and "automation." These issues illustrated the potentials but also the dangers of modern industrial society. To be sure, all advanced industrial societies experienced concern about technological change and its impact on economic organization and the workplace. Yet, as we will see, specifically German memories of the rationalization movement of the 1920s and its political impact on the destabilization of the Weimar Republic inflected the automation debate in West Germany.[16] A keen sensibility for the inherent instability and potential dangers of a modern economic order thus informed both optimistic and pessimistic assessments of technological change in West Germany. The perceived inevitability of technological change beyond individual human control also raised new questions regarding the ability of democratic polities to control and possibly steer key socio-economic developments. The gradual descent into an authoritarian or totalitarian society through modernization appeared as one possible future. Finally, modern fears anticipated some of the arguments and anxieties of current debates about automation and digitalization in the early twenty-first century.[17] They highlight the significance of this period as a prehistory to our own contemporary moment.

Modern Fears during the "Economic Miracle"

The self-description of West German society as an "industrial society" entailed a new sensibility for the role of technology within society. Contemporary observers assigned technological change an independent role in shaping a modern economic and social order, and they often described technology as following its own evolutionary logic independently of human will or intervention.[18] Precisely because technology appeared as an inevitable force of nature, it invoked both hopes and fears. As a *pars pro toto* for technological change in modern society more generally, the concept of "automation" functioned as a "key term" (Paul Nolte) and "dominating theme" in the larger West German discourse on technology.[19] Unlike the objects of fear during the 1940s and 1950s—political retribution, abduction and enslavement in the Foreign Legion, the threat of nuclear war—"automation"

---

[16] On rationalization in the 1920s, see Mary Nolan, *Visions of Modernity. American Business and the Modernization of Germany* (New York: Oxford University Press, 1994), Thomas von Freyberg, *Industrielle Rationalisierung in der Weimarer Republik. Untersuchungen an Beispielen aus dem Maschinenbau und der Elektroindustrie* (Frankfurt a/M: Campus, 1989).

[17] See "Mensch gegen Maschine," *Der Spiegel* 72/36 (2016): 10–18.

[18] Nolte, *Die Ordnung der deutschen Gesellschaft*, 274–9.

[19] Rüdiger Zill, "Im Wendekreis des Sputnik. Technikdiskurse in der Bundesrepublik Deutschland der 50er Jahre," in Irmela Schneider, Peter M. Spangenberg, eds, *Medienkultur der 50er Jahre. Diskursgeschichte der Medien nach 1945. Band 1* (Opladen: Westdeutscher Verlag, 2002), 41.

did not carry exclusively negative connotations. In fact, much of the existing historiography portrays this period as one of unmitigated enthusiasm regarding the promises of technological progress and a corresponding "optimism regarding the future." West Germans, it has been argued, consumed "the successes of modernization without worrying about its ambivalences."[20]

This chapter seeks to bring these ambivalences clearly into view. Upon closer inspection, more skeptical and pessimistic assessment of technological progress constituted an integral part of the automation debate. These more negative assessments were not simply the relics of a traditional cultural pessimism, even though this discursive tradition persisted as well. They also anticipated some of the later postmodern arguments regarding the negative social and economic consequences of technological change. At the very least, commentators highlighted some essential preconditions—raising educational levels and increased economic planning were among the most important—to thwarting technology's potentially negative, even catastrophic, impact. Memories of economic and political collapse dating back to the Weimar Republic continued to inform the debate about socio-economic modernization in the Federal Republic. West Germans' vision of industrial modernity remained inextricably intertwined with a keen awareness of the inherent instability of modern economies and their political consequences. This particular historical background gave the broader transnational debate about technological change its distinctly (West) German inflection.

The automation debate was central to the broader self-perception of West Germany as a modern, industrial society because it roughly coincided with other secular changes during the last third of the 1950s, as discussed earlier. To be sure, "automation" and "rationalization" did not suddenly burst onto the discursive scene in the later 1950s. The rationalization of industrial production was an economic goal already in the early Federal Republic. In 1950, a "rationalization committee of German business" (*Rationalisierungs Kuratorium der deutschen Wirtschaft*) emerged as a successor organization to the Weimar rationalization committee (*Reichskuratorium für Wirtschaftlichkeit*). It was typical for proponents of post-1945 rationalization to describe their efforts as a continuation of the Weimar rationalization movement.[21] In 1953, the rationalization committee organized a public exhibition entitled "Everybody Should Live Better," the first post-1945 effort to advocate publicly the goals of the rationalization movement. As one commentator noted at the time, the exhibition acknowledged the

---

[20] Quotations in Ulrich Herbert, *Geschichte Deutschlands im 20. Jahrhundert* (Munich: C.H.Beck, 2014), 809, and Wolfrum, *Die geglückte Demokratie*, 14. See also Gabriele Metzler, *Konzeptionen politischen Handelns von Adenauer bis Brandt. Politische Planung in der pluralistischen Gesellschaft* (Paderborn: Schöningh, 2005), 70, 145–6, Elke Seefried, *Zukünfte. Aufstieg und Krise der Zukunftsforschung, 1945–1980* (Berlin: De Gruyter, 2015). For a more balanced view analyzing both "hopes" and "fears," see Radkau, *Geschichte der Zukunft*.

[21] See, for example, Karl Matthes, "Rationalisierung eine Zeitkrankheit," Rheinisch-Westfälisches Wirtschaftsarchiv (RWWA), 3-83-2.

"mixture of emotional rejection and intellectually substantiated doubts" that the notion of rationalization invoked.[22] Rationalization here constituted an element of a broader "politics of productivity" that proponents argued would overcome the Malthusian dilemma of a steadily increasing world population as well as increasing the competitiveness of national economies.[23] The main goal of rationalization was to overcome national and international shortages and postwar scarcity. It was one way to compensate for the loss of the Eastern territories as well as for the demographic losses in the Second World War.[24]

By the mid to late 1950s, however, "rationalization" began to assume a different meaning. The Fordist or "Detroit automation"—a gradual improvement and further development of mechanized production—receded. Proponents of automation began to envision independent circuits of production that no longer required human labor.[25] As the magazine *Spiegel* reported in 1955, the "fully automated factory devoid of human beings in which a small staff of engineers and technicians controls—through an electronic brain—the entire production process is no longer utopian" and existed, "at least partially in the US, England, and the Soviet Union."[26] The new field of cybernetics, as developed by the US scientist Norbert Wiener, provided the conceptual model for this social imagination.[27] This kind of automation did not simply seek to overcome postwar scarcity but pointed to the future of an as yet unknown industrial society. It was of course no coincidence that this debate coincided with the "Sputnik shock" in the Western world. The launching of an unmanned Soviet satellite into space in October 1957 clearly heightened Western anxieties regarding a "technology gap" in the Cold War.[28] Technological progress thus appeared both indispensable and inevitable. Yet the social, economic, and cultural consequences of this kind of automation were uncertain and hence anxiety producing.[29]

It is important to emphasize that the public debate about "automation" often had little connection to actual automation processes—visions (and anxieties) of a technology-driven future often exceeded the extent of technological progress. This discrepancy between fantasy and reality had already characterized the debate

---

[22] Alexander Ross, *Wege und Ziele deutscher Rationalisierung* (Dortmund: Verkehrs- und Wirtschaftsverlag, 1955), 57. For an example, see Johannes Reinhold, "Gesellschaftliche Probleme der Automation," *Neues Beginnen: Zeitschrift der Arbeiterwohlfahrt* 9 (1958): 85–7.

[23] Charles S. Maier, "The Politics of Productivity: Foundations of American International Economic Policy after World War II," in Charles S. Maier, ed., *In Search of Stability. Explorations in Historical Political Economy* (New York: Cambridge University Press, 1988), 121–52.

[24] See the discussion in "Niederschrift über die Mitgliederversammlung des Förderkreises für Rationalisierungsfragen," December 13, 1957, RWW, GHH 400101462–16.

[25] The boundaries between these two forms of automation were fluid. See Werner Abelshauser, *Nach dem Wirtschaftswunder: Der Gewerkschafter, Politiker und Unternehmer Hans Matthöfer* (Düsseldorf: Dietz, 2009), 113–14.

[26] "Die Revolution der Roboter," *Der Spiegel* 8/31(1955): 20–30.

[27] Radkau, *Geschichte der Zukunft*, 96–7.   [28] Zill, "Im Wendekreis des Sputnik."

[29] RKW, Abt. Mensch und Arbeit, Bericht "Stand und Auswirkung der Automatisierung in Deutschland. Soziale und soziologische Auswirkungen," August 16, 1956, BArch, B149/37262.

about "Fordism" and "Taylorism" in the 1920s, to which the automation debate often referred.[30] The imagination of "automatized futures" thus also produced what historian Joachim Radkau has called an entire series of "laughable" prognoses that turned out to be wrong.[31] The inaccuracy of these predictions notwithstanding, the "automation" debate revealed modern fears that accompanied the rapid process of socio-economic modernization at every turn.[32] This chapter thus seeks to partially correct and complement existing narratives that exclusively highlight the prosperity, sense of progress, and belief in optimism during the "economic miracle," and to bring into view contemporary ambivalences, uncertainties, and, indeed, fears.

The automation debate proceeded on several discursive levels. This chapter will first analyze the discussion among some of West Germany's most prominent sociologists and philosophers. It will then trace the proliferation of the debate among a wider range of public commentators. The chapter concludes with a case study of how one of the participants in the debate—the metalworkers' union (*IG Metall*)—sought to confront the problems and pitfalls of automation processes.

Three Intellectuals on Automation: Pollock, Schelsky, Gehlen

Automation occupied a central place in West German intellectual debates of the 1950s and 1960s. Responding to the accelerated modernization of the Federal Republic during this period, intellectuals probed the likely consequences of technological change for individuals and society at large. Friedrich Pollock, Helmut Schelsky, and Arnold Gehlen represented the entire range of the political spectrum in the Federal Republic. Pollock was a founding member of the Frankfurt School who had emigrated to the United States during the Nazi period and returned to West Germany after 1945. He served as one of three directors of the Frankfurt Institute of Social Research, together with Theodor Adorno and Max Horkheimer. He thus represented a neo-Marxist critic of capitalism and automation. Schelsky was one of West Germany's most prominent sociologists. He received his academic training during the Nazi period and became, in his own

---

[30] Joachim Radkau, *Technik in Deutschland. Vom 18. Jahrhundert bis zur Gegenwart* (Frankfurt a/M: Suhrkamp, 1989), 314.

[31] Radkau, *Geschichte der Zukunft*, 126. He does concede, however, that these past prognoses were serious and based on real arguments.

[32] The main syntheses of the history of the Federal Republic do not devote any attention to this issue. For an important exception, see ibid. 95–130. See also Johannes Platz, "'Revolution der Roboter' oder 'Keine Angst vor Robotern'? Die Verwissenschaftlichung des Automationsdiskurses und die industriellen Beziehungen von den 50ern bis 1968," in Laurent Commaille, ed., *Enterprises et crises économiques au XXe siècle. Actes du colloque de Metz* (Metz: Centre régional universitaire lorrain d'histoire, 2009), 37–59. Platz characterizes the automation debate as an "exemplary crisis discourse," ibid. 39.

words, a "supporter of National Socialism." From 1953 on, he was professor of sociology in Hamburg. Schelsky was a representative of the "45ers," the leading intellectual generation of the Federal Republic. This group embraced West German liberal democracy because of their biographical experience of the collapse of National Socialism. Gehlen, who had served as Schelsky's adviser, represented the tradition of German cultural pessimism. He joined the Nazi party in 1933 and had a brilliant academic career during the Nazi Period, which earned him the Kant chair at the University in Königsberg in 1938. From 1947, he taught at the University for Public Administration (*Verwaltungswissenschaft*) in Speyer, later at the Technical University in Aachen. His compromised Nazi past prevented a return to a more prestigious position and at least partly isolated him in West German public discourse after 1945.[33]

Friedrich Pollock's 1956 study on the social and economic consequences of automation constituted one of the earliest and most comprehensive and critical assessments of the effects of automation on modern society in West Germany. The topic fit well into the Frankfurt School's larger philosophical project to expose the irrational effects of an instrumental use of reason. Pollock described the progress of automation in the US as a model for societies like West Germany, part of a second industrial revolution underway in Western societies. He predicted that its societal effects would be wide-ranging, both for industrial countries and others.[34] Pollock challenged the optimists' view, which predicted, at worst, short-term dislocations as a result of automation that market forces would eventually correct. He defined automation as an "invisible" and coming danger that could only be analyzed through theoretical reflections. He predicted both a return to the mass unemployment of the 1930s as well as a destruction of traditional jobs that would give way to a new class of "specialists." A highly qualified minority of experts would increasingly exert complete control over the work process while the "dictatorship of the machines" determined the function of the majority of workers. Such a concentration of power within a minority then might pave the way for the gradual transition to an "authoritarian social order."[35]

Pollock saw contemporary trends in 1955 as confirming his pessimistic predictions. In his view, the ideological competition of the Cold War had driven automation since the Soviet Union had portrayed itself as champion of technological progress and automation. While acknowledging that automation processes had been limited thus far, he predicted a more accelerated automation during a

---

[33] On Pollock, see Rolf Wiggershaus, *Die Frankfurter Schule. Geschichte. Theoretische Entwicklung. Politische Bedeutung* (Munich: dtv, 1988), 76–80, Volker Kempf, *Helmut Schelsky. Wider die Wirklichkeitsverweigerung. Leben, Werk, Aktualität* (Munich: Olzog, 2012), quotation on 62, Heike Delitz, *Arnold Gehlen* (Constance: UvK, 2015), 23–36; on the "45ers," see A. Dirk Moses, *German Intellectuals and the Nazi Past* (New York: Cambridge University Press, 2007).

[34] Friedrich Pollock, *Automation. Materialien zur Beurteilung der ökonomischen und sozialen Folgen* (Frankfurt a/M: Europäische Verlagsanstalt, 1956), 46.

[35] Ibid. 48, 68–9, 91, 106.

possible recession, thus producing "technological unemployment." Following Marxist political economy, Pollock believed that, because of its high fixed costs, automation would promote the concentration of capital and hence largely benefit big business. He rejected the distinction between short-term dislocations and long-term benefits of automation, and predicted "chain reactions of destructions" within all "spheres of public and private life." "Unprecedented tyranny" would ensue. The only way to avoid this horror scenario was state planning. A planned economy, he argued, would be capable of mastering the problems of automation in a rational fashion. Betraying his own hope for technological solutions, Pollock speculated that "electronic calculators" would eventually be capable of anticipating the consequences of automation and thus circumvent the market mechanism. He called for a long-term program for the integration of automation into a free societal system to turn the "second industrial revolution" into a catalyst for developing a "rational social order."[36]

In a 1957 essay, Helmut Schelsky offered perhaps the most comprehensive rejoinder to Pollock's dark view.[37] Schelsky represented a trend in West German sociology that decried normative assumptions and sought to provide an empirical description of modern industrial society.[38] He also offered a perceptive analysis of the temporal and emotional structure of the automation debate. He highlighted the essential openness of the Federal Republic's future and criticized what he saw as the widespread tendency to invoke "dangers and emergency situations of the past" in order to cope with uncertainties about the future. He argued that the fixation on past experiences often leads to the misperception of the inner logic of new situations. He therefore sought to liberate anticipations of the future from memories of the past—an argument that clearly also entailed a self-serving, apologetic dimension in light of Schelsky's own compromised past during the Nazi period. Schelsky also rejected the use of strong terms such as the "second industrial revolution" as provocative and overstated. He questioned the contemporary debate's ability to describe automation trends or their future effects. Rather, he said, the debate projected "all existing problems" West Germany experienced as a modern industrial society onto the issue of automation. Schelsky's analysis thus sought to find a middle path between the two emotional extremes of a "psychological technique of excitement and exaggeration" on the one hand, and the "counter-technique of reassurance and minimization" on the other hand. Interestingly, Schelsky was able to perceive and to critique the emotional dimension of the debate and hence offered, almost inadvertently, a reflection on changing West German emotional norms.[39]

---

[36] Ibid. 222, 284, 289.
[37] Helmut Schelsky, "Zukunftsaspekte der industriellen Gesellschaft," in Helmut Schelsky, ed., *Auf der Suche nach Wirklichkeit. Gesammelte Aufsätze* (Düsseldorf and Köln: Eugen Diedrichs Verlag, 1965 [1953]), 84–104, Schelsky, "Die sozialen Folgen der Automatisierung," in ibid. 105–31.
[38] Nolte, *Die Ordnung der deutschen Gesellschaft*, 281–2.
[39] Schelsky, "Die sozialen Folgen der Automatisierung," 125–6.

Schelsky rejected Pollock's argument that market-driven automation would inevitably produce an authoritarian social and political system. He argued that technological progress or "technologization" did not cause totalitarianism. He saw state planning, such as Pollock proposed, as a much more likely source of totalitarianism. According to Schelsky, automation would only affect 10 per cent to 20 per cent of workers. He believed automation would improve the lot of most workers by relieving them of monotonous work processes so that they could perform jobs that required more skills and attention. By reducing the length of the workday, automation might also free workers to enjoy consumption and culture. He did, however, see a risk in this greater leisure time, as his cultural pessimism led him to question individuals' ability to make meaningful use of their additional free time.[40]

Rather than offering what he called "highly speculative future scenarios," Schelsky proposed practical suggestions for workers affected by automation. He emphasized three points in particular. First, employers should keep their workforce informed regarding their planned automation. Second, workers who were laid off as a result of automation should be retrained. And, third, technical education should be reformed and expanded.[41] Schelsky sought to provide a realistic and empirical assessment of automation that acknowledged its impact yet criticized the emotional and often extreme analysis of this problem in contemporary discourse.[42] His views gained considerable attention through a series of speeches he gave to employers' organizations and trade union audiences.[43] His analysis of the discursive and emotional structure of the automation debate highlighted the significance that contemporaries assigned to this phenomenon in seeking to make sense of their uncertain future. Schelsky's attempt at a sober and rational assessment notwithstanding, "automation" remained at the center of West German apprehensions and anxieties regarding the future of industrial society.

Gehlen's *The Soul in the Age of Technology. Social Psychological Problems of Industrial Society* was a bestseller in 1957.[44] Originally published in 1949, the second edition—13 more would follow between 1957 and Gehlen's death in 1976—had significant cultural impact. The book sold more than 100,000 copies over its lifespan, which was quite impressive for a dense philosophical work. Gehlen explicitly distanced himself from the cultural skepticism of technology as it had been prevalent throughout the 1950s.[45] "Fearful conception of the ant-like

---

[40] Ibid. 123.   [41] Ibid. 129.

[42] Contemporary reviews praised this aspect of Schelsky's text. See "Neue Literatur: Wo steht die Diskussion zur Automatisierung?" *Handelsblatt*, 74, June 28, 1957.

[43] See, for example, the reference to a speech by Schelsky to the employer organization of Ruhr-Niederrhein in Duisburg in March 1956 in "Die Diskussion um Automation," *Atombrief* 2/4 (1956): 9.

[44] Arnold Gehlen, *Die Seele im technologischen Zeitalter. Sozialpsychologische Probleme in der industriellen Gesellschaft* (Frankfurt a/M: Vittorio Klostermann, 2007 [1957]).

[45] Daniel Morat, "Der lange Schatten der Kulturkritik. Arnold Gehlen über 'Die Seele im technischen Zeitalter,'" *Zeithistorische Forschungen/Studies in Contemporary History* 6/2 (2009): 320–5, Axel

state of the future, of massification, of wireless manipulation of our brains, of the loss of personality and the decline of culture are widespread in our culture," he wrote. He rejected the critique of "technology" also because technology enjoyed "tremendous popularity" in the US and in the Soviet Union.[46] Just as Schelsky had with sociology, Gehlen sought to bring philosophy close to the "phenomena of the present." He sought to offer a philosophically based, realistic assessment of the role of technology in contemporary society.

Gehlen's concept of technology derived from his philosophical anthropology of the deficient human being (*Mängelwesen*) who depended on assistance, most importantly through societal institutions and technology.[47] The scope of Gehlen's book extended far beyond the more specific topic of automation—it actually contained few references to actual automation processes. For Gehlen, "automation" constituted the endpoint of a gradual replacement of "organic" with "anorganic" matter. He predicted a circuitous and independent regulation of work process through the machine that stood in analogy to the biological circuits of human beings.[48] But Gehlen also developed a more philosophical and anthropological notion of "automation": these "automatisms" manifested themselves in routinized behaviors but also in habituated inner thought processes, which then served important functions in relieving human beings from mastering the complexity of the modern world. While this was a necessary adjustment to technological change, the process would also create an empty subjectivity that was increasingly other-directed. Here, Gehlen drew explicitly on David Riesman's sociological analysis of the lonely individual in *The Lonely Crowd*.[49] Gehlen's view of the impact of technology on the "soul" was thus pessimistic: he acknowledged a loss of direct "experience" and its replacement by "second-hand experience" mediated by mass media. The figures of the "expert" and the "functionary" as well-functioning human beings would become the most well-adjusted social types. As a counterweight to these fully adjusted individuals, he emphasized the concept of the "personality," the person who would be capable of not only accepting and adjusting to the "instrumental apparatus" of modern life but also moving beyond merely functional behavior and thinking. Gehlen's treatise concluded with the assertion that this personality would essentially function as an autonomous entity: it would represent, as he famously called it, an "institution in one case."[50]

Schildt, *Zwischen Abendland und Amerika. Studien zur Ideenlandschaft der 1950er Jahre* (Munich: Oldenbourg, 1999).

[46]   Gehlen, *Seele im technischen Zeitalter*, 5, 116, 119, 133.
[47]   Daniel Morat, "Der lange Schatten der Kulturkritik," Christoph Hubig, Alois Huning, Günter Ropohl, eds, *Nachdenken über Technik. Die Klassiker der Technikphilosophie* (Berlin: Sigma, 2000), 140–3.
[48]   Gehlen, *Seele im technischen Zeitalter*, 20–3.
[49]   David Riesman, *The Lonely Crowd. A Study of the Changing American Character* (New Haven: Yale University Press, 1950).
[50]   Gehlen, *Seele im technischen Zeitalter*, 119, 133. The notion of the "personality" as the counterweight to bureaucratization and automation in modern society constituted an important idea in

For conservatives like Gehlen, the concept of "personality" functioned as an elitist counterweight to the demands of the modern world. It also entailed the added advantage of cultivating a habitus of social distance that permitted an avoidance of a compromised past.[51]

The automation debate served as a focal point for defining the nature of West Germany as an industrial society, as well as for assessing the role of technology within a democratizing society.[52] A few years later, in 1968, the philosopher Jürgen Habermas joined the debate with a treatise on "technology and science" as ideology.[53] Unlike Schelsky and Gehlen, Habermas did not view technology as an independent force largely beyond social and political control. Contrary to what he saw as an apology for merely technocratic rule, Habermas advocated an open and equal public debate over the nature and uses of technology and science in advanced capitalist societies. Democratic institutions should enable a public discourse on "how human beings can and want to live with each other under the objective conditions of a dramatically increased disposal [over technology, F.B.]."[54] Yet such a debate had been ongoing since the late 1950s. And while the automation debate might have lacked the critical, anti-capitalist edge that Habermas promoted in 1968, it nevertheless constituted an integral aspect of the self-definition of the Federal Republic. This debate also extended far beyond individual intellectuals and took place on the pages of newspapers and magazines, in public talks, and in radio broadcasts.[55] By addressing the issue of automation, public commentators negotiated the future of the Federal Republic as an industrial society and positioned themselves vis-à-vis a new stage in the evolution of industrial modernity. It was a debate that was part of the discursive self-definition of the Federal Republic.

The Widening Debate: Automation in West German Public Discourse

Beyond the confines of intellectual discourse, contemporary observers defined "automation" as among the most pressing subjects in public discourse at the time.

conservative thought of the time. See also Hans Freyer, "Die Idee der Freiheit im technischen Zeitalter," in Hans Barion, Ernst Forsthoff, Werner Weber, eds, *Festschrift für Carl Schmitt zum 70. Geburtstag* (Berlin: Duncker & Humblot, 1959), 63–70.

[51] Dirk van Laak, *Gespräche in der Sicherheit des Schweigens. Carl Schmitt in der politischen Geistesgeschichte der frühen Bundesrepublik* (Berlin: Akademie Verlag, 1993), 115–18.
[52] See also the volume Hans Freyer, Johannes Chr. Papalekas, Georg Weippert, eds, *Technik im technischen Zeitalter. Stellungnahmen zur geschichtlichen Situation* (Düsseldorf: Joachim Schilling, 1965).
[53] Jürgen Habermas, *Technik und Wissenschaft als "Ideologie"* (Frankfurt a/M: Suhrkamp, 1968).
[54] Ibid. 107–8.
[55] Monika Boll, *Nachtprogramm. Intellektuelle Gründungsdebatten in der frühen Bundesrepublik* (Münster: Lit Verlag, 2004).

Writing in 1961, the West German economist and later Social Democratic Party (SPD) member of the *Bundestag*, Hans Georg Schachtschabel, declared that the topic had received the most public attention of any issue of public concern for seven years.[56] The Austrian economic and Socialist Party official, Karl Ausch, defined "automation" as the "great slogan of our time," saying that it invoked widely divergent reactions: while some "saw it as the harbinger of beautiful times of paradise where robots work and men party," others "passionately rejected it because they fear that automation will bring mass unemployment and misery."[57] A public conference at the Protestant Academy in Tutzing in 1959 illustrated the range of perspectives from which contemporaries addressed the issue of automation. Invited guests included economists and entrepreneurs but also theologians and philosophers, and they were charged to discuss the relationship between "growing luxury and prosperity as well as increasing scientific and technological progress," on the one hand, and a sense of "unease, anxiety, distrust, and pessimism" at the "cusp of the nuclear and automation" age, on the other hand.[58]

The debate saw automation, like nuclear energy, as a quintessentially modern technology, as "fact[s] of the 20th century."[59] Keen to portray themselves as a party of the future, the opposition Social Democrats adopted a resolution during their 1956 party congress in which they defined automation and nuclear energy as the key characteristic of a "second industrial revolution." In so doing, the SPD followed the lead of the intellectual and state official from North Rhine-Westphalia, Leo Brandt, who had popularized the notion of a "second industrial revolution" centering on these two areas.[60] Both automation and the civilian use of nuclear energy invoked hopes as well as fears. Yet in the public debate, automation appeared as an equal, if not more important, factor in shaping a modern future.[61]

The automation debate crossed national borders as well as the Atlantic. Automation appeared as part of a larger "Westernization" process which,

---

[56] Cited in Joachim Radkau, "'Wirtschaftswunder' ohne technologische Innovation? Technische Modernität in den 50er Jahren," in Schildt and Sywottek, eds, *Modernisierung im Wiederaufbau*, 142.

[57] Karl Ausch, "Probleme der Automation," *Die Zukunft. Sozialistische Monatsschrift für Politik, Wirtschaft, Kultur* 8 (1956): 214–18. For similar ambivalence, see Rolf Spaethen, "Wirtschaft-Technik-Gewerkschaft" Referat auf dem Gewerkschaftstag der DAG in München, October 9, 1957; IGMA, 5/240115.

[58] "Automation bringt kein goldenes Zeitalter," *Süddeutsche Zeitung*, 229, September 24, 1957.

[59] R. Leonardi, "Die Automation darf uns nicht überfallen," *Atombrief* 2/4 (1956): 9–10.

[60] Radkau, "'Wirtschaftswunder' ohne technologische Innovation?" Leo Brandt, *Die zweite industrielle Revolution* (Munich: Paul List Verlag, 1957), Nolte, *Die Ordnung der deutschen Gesellschaft*. Brandt served from 1954 to 1958 in a Christian Democratic and Social Democratic government in North Rhine-Westphalia. He adopted a largely positive attitude toward automation yet worried that West German society underestimated the challenges of automation. He warned against the "wheel of history" passing over the Federal Republic due to "modesty, fear of the new, and restorative thinking," Brandt, *Die zweite industrielle Revolution*, 170.

[61] On popular attitudes toward the civilian use of nuclear energy, mainly focusing on the popular press, see Dolores L. Augustine, *Taking on Technocracy. Nuclear Power in Germany, 1945 to the Present* (New York: Berghahn, 2018), 21–50.

however, was not seen as a normative goal but as deeply ambivalent. The issue was on the agenda of a meeting of the Organization for European Economic Cooperation (OEEC) in April 1957.[62] Most West German observers believed that automation was progressing on a linear modernizing continuum with Great Britain and the US leading the way. As in the interwar period, American and British developments appeared to foreshadow German futures. Precisely because some of the "basic assumptions" of automation had been accepted in the Soviet Union and in the US, Europeans felt compelled to address the issue as well.[63] In 1955, the "Reports on Social Policy" by the *Deutsche Industrieinstitut* included a report on the "The American Auto Unions and Automation."[64] As in the 1920s, West German delegations comprised of engineers, businessmen, and trade unionists traveled to the US to study the effects and implications of automation. Discussions of automation began to include the question as to what extent developments in the US applied to West Germany, given the relative size of each country's domestic market.[65] Experiences with automation in the US could also be anxiety producing: in 1964, the magazine *Spiegel* reported that there were five million unemployed people due to automation in the US.[66] With only few exceptions, most observers, optimists as well as pessimists, agreed that automation was accelerating and would continue to do so. For the journalist Louis Emrich, "automation" represented a "force with unprecedented energy, size, and forward marching character" that constituted "the future."[67]

Emotional attitudes toward automation were closely linked to socio-economic interests. Social Democrats and trade unionists feared the impact of automation on employment whereas employers celebrated increased productivity and competitiveness as a result of automation.[68] Fears and anxiety regarding automation centered on three areas: employment, deskilling of workers, and cultural consequences. In spite of the full employment of the late 1950s, the most important concern remained the specter of technological unemployment. Memories of the

---

[62] Hans Wolfgang Büttner, *Das Rationalisierungskuratorium der deutschen Wirtschaft* (Düsseldorf: Droste, 1973), 40.

[63] Leonardi, "Die Automation darf uns nicht überfallen." See also Platz, " 'Revolution der Roboter' oder 'Keine Angst vor Robotern'?" 40–2.

[64] Deutsches Industrieinstitut, Berichte zur Sozialpolitik, Nr. 2, "Die amerikanischen Automobil-Gewerkschaft und Automation," July 27, 1955, RWWA, 122-314-15.

[65] "Nachdenkliches zum Arbeitsgebiet der Rationalisierung und Betriebswirtschaft für kleine und mittlere Betriebe. Frucht einer USA Reise," Vortrag of Dr. Kurt Birk, IHK Siegen, in front of Arbeitskreis für Rationalisierungsfragen des Deutschen Industrie und Handelstages, November 23, 1959, RWWA, 181-3383-3.

[66] "Einzug der Roboter," *Der Spiegel* 18/14 (1964): 30–48.

[67] Louis Emrich, *Fabrik ohne Menschen—Unsere Zukunft im Zeitalter der Automation* (Wiesbaden: Gabler, 1957), 112–13, cited in Radkau, *Geschichte der Zukunft*, 111.

[68] On the notion that attitudes toward technological progress are fundamentally shaped by social and political interests, see Hartmut Berghoff, " 'Dem Ziele der Menschheit entgegen.' Die Verheißungen der Technik an der Wende zum 20. Jahrhundert," in Ute Frevert, ed., *Das neue Jahrhundert. Europäische Zeitdiagnosen und Zukunftsentwürfe um 1900* (Göttingen: Vandenhoeck & Ruprecht, 2000), 47–78.

Figure 4.1. Title of *Der Spiegel* 14/1964 on "Automation in Germany."

The 1960s were not just a period of unambiguous optimism and belief in technological progress. This title page of *Der Spiegel* reflects the intense debate about automation. The article predicted mass unemployment due to the replacement of workers by machines.

Source: Copyright *Der Spiegel* 14/1964.

rationalization movement of the 1920s often fueled these anxieties. Many Germans believed that "Fordism" and "Taylorism" had created technological unemployment in the 1920s, which then destabilized the Weimar Republic and ultimately facilitated the rise of Hitler. Political representatives of industrial workers such as SPD official Fritz Erler and trade union officials such as Hans Matthöfer were at the forefront of articulating these concerns.[69] Erler predicted "fatal crisis symptoms" such as "mass unemployment," which might "pave the way toward totalitarianism." Like Pollock, Erler feared the potential anti-democratic effects of the creation of a technological elite, arguing that automation might be workable in the East but would not be compatible with the Western "concept of personal and human freedom."[70] Matthöfer, who was a trade union official throughout the 1950s and 1960s and became a cabinet member under Chancellor Helmut Schmidt from 1974 to 1982, argued that market forces had never succeeded in compensating for technological unemployment. Citing Pollock, he argued that only massively expanded armament expenditure had prevented unemployment as a result of accelerated automation in the US.[71] Matthöfer actually traveled repeatedly to the US to study the effects of automation, where he most likely encountered the struggle of labor representatives such as Walter Reuther, the head of the United Auto Workers (UAW), against the negative effects of automation.[72]

Yet reformist left-wing politicians like Erler and Matthöfer did not reject automation altogether. They opposed what Erler termed "instinctive storming of machines."[73] Instead, both employed the seeming inevitability of automation as an argument in favor of a Social Democratic reform program. In particular, an increase in state planning, as it was already practiced in the Soviet Union or in Great Britain, appeared as the most important instrument to contain potentially negative aspects of automation. Because it would be "unsocial" if workers had to bear the negative consequences of automation, they advocated for a series of social policy measures that would protect individual workers against the negative effects of automation: expanded unemployment insurance, guaranteed yearly income, lowering of the retirement limit, shortening of the work hours, extensive retraining efforts, and a reform of the educational system in general. Erler's and

[69] Alfred Marchionini, Fritz Erler, Frederick Pollock, Alwin Walther, Alfred Weber, *Revolution der Roboter. Untersuchung über die Probleme der Automatisierung. Eine Vortragsreihe der Arbeitsgemeinschaft sozialdemokratischer Akademiker* (Munich: Isar Verlag, 1956).

[70] Erler, "Der Sozialismus in der Epoche der zweiten industriellen Revolution," in ibid. 162.

[71] Hans Matthöfer, "Die wirtschaftlichen und sozialen Auswirkungen der Automatisierung in der Sicht der Gewerkschaften," *Atombrief: Eine internationale Information aus Politik, Wirtschaft und Technik, der Zusammenarbeit in Europa gewidmet* 3/1 (1957), 21–4. See also E.K. Hornauer, "Automation und Arbeitslosigkeit," *Der Gewerkschafter* 10/2–3 (1962), 29–30.

[72] On Reuther, see "Automation: Die Revolution der Roboter," *Der Spiegel* 9/31 (1955).

[73] On Matthöfer, see Radkau, *Geschichte der Zukunft*, 109–10, Abelshauser, *Nach dem Wirtschaftswunder*, and Erler, "Der Sozialismus in der Epoche," 167.

Matthöfer's arguments thus represented the moderate Left's cautious embrace of automation as a vehicle to argue for an expansion of state planning and of the welfare state. In this view, socialist policies would make it possible to use the benefits of technological change to achieve what Erler termed "a higher stage of human society."[74]

Other commentators, however, sided with Schelsky, rejecting the notion of automation as a vehicle for more state planning. They condemned such alarmist views as the actual source of danger and argued that opponents of automation were seeking to revitalize concepts of economic planning that the free world had largely rejected. Rather than resorting to the "entire arsenal of Marxist critique," one commentator saw automation as a quasi-natural continuation of previous forms of technological progress. Strong and organized collective interests, unions in particular, would prevent potentially negative consequences as during the first industrial revolution.[75] Along similar lines, another observer asserted that automation had an "advantage for general welfare" and that "the compelling development of technical progress" left no alternative to automation. Pointing to a massive increase of productivity with decreasing work hours, he argued that automation would also have macro-economic benefits and thus benefit working people as well.[76]

Some voices even questioned the basic assumption of automation as ubiquitous and inevitable. They ridiculed excessive media attention to slogans such as "industrial revolution," the "age of robots," and the "specter of automation."[77] Business publications disparaged the widespread publicity of automation. A representative of Daimler-Benz in Stuttgart claimed that the extent of automation in German industry had increased only marginally from 57 per cent to 67 per cent over five years, and argued that it did not warrant the excessive public attention. He denounced the debate as a veiled attempt to increase intervention in the economy through a state agency that would have to authorize any new automation measures.[78] *Der Spiegel* criticized Germans directly for their lack of apprehension regarding automation: whereas 90 per cent of Americans professed to be afraid of automation, West German citizens adhered to an unlimited and—according to *Der Spiegel*—rather naïve, belief in progress.[79] The more critical voices cited

---

[74] Erler, "Der Sozialismus in der Epoche," 198. Matthöfer had realized at this point that the hopes he associated with automation would probably not be realized. See Abelshauser, *Nach dem Wirtschaftswunder*, 121.

[75] Josef Rainer, "Automation—Fortschritt oder Verhängnis?" *Atombrief* 3 (1957), 14–15.

[76] Harald Koch, "Automatisierung und arbeitender Mensch," *Der Volkswirt: Wirtschafts- und Finanzzeitung* 13/44 (1959), 60–1.

[77] See cartoon in *Westdeutsches Tagblatt*, 53, March 4, 1957.

[78] "Genehmigungspflicht für Automatisierung?" *Industriekurier*, 26, February 19, 1957. On business responses to automation, see Platz, "'Revolution der Roboter' oder 'Keine Angst vor Robotern'?" 44–6.

[79] "Automation. Einzug der Roboter," *Der Spiegel* 18/14 (1964), 33.

earlier, however, demonstrate that *Der Spiegel*'s perception of popular attitudes toward automation was inaccurate. Whether they saw the extensive public attention to automation as justified or not, few observers doubted that the issue constituted, for better or worse, a key element of modern industrial society.

Apart from fear of mass unemployment, critics of automation also worried about deskilling of workers. Even those who downplayed the possibility of widespread technological unemployment conceded that older workers might have difficulty in adjusting to new skill sets. Commentators demanded private and public assistance for retraining for older workers.[80] Others expected that automation would blur the distinction between blue- and white-collar workers. Such a decline in work hierarchies within the factories evoked the prospect of significant upward social mobility for individual workers, yet might also depress union membership.[81]

Observers agreed that technological change was likely to alter dramatically the profile of future jobs. An article series in *Stern* in 1964 sought to provide some guidelines and offer a scientifically based assessment of "which jobs will have chances" in the future. By bringing together German and European experts on labor and education, *Stern* published a recommendation with extensive lists of jobs and professions they expected to be in demand in the future as well as those that were in decline. In so doing, the magazine sought to mitigate what contemporaries perceived to be increased uncertainty and anxiety due to accelerated modernization. As one of the authors of the study, the sociologist Burkart Lutz argued, "life experience" was becoming increasingly less relevant for predicting future trends, which "technological and societal developments" would largely shape.[82] Parents and state officials alike lacked the knowledge to predict the future demands of the labor market and must look to scientific experts to provide guidance in the face of massive uncertainty.[83] *Stern* suggested that only professions that fit into a future scenario of accelerated automation would survive. They suggested jobs as "fitter" (*Maschinenschlosser*), "blacksmith" (*Schmied*), and metal workers would disappear. "Electro mechanics" (*Elektromechaniker*) and "technicians" (*Montage- und Wartungstechniker*), by contrast, would be in high demand in a future dominated by "electronic brains" and increasingly complicated machines.[84] *Stern* also predicted high female unemployment, as automation would especially threaten the unskilled jobs in which women were concentrated.

---

[80] E.A. Schill, "Sozialpolitische Aspekte der Automatisierung," *Arbeits- und Sozialrecht: Mitteilungsblatt des Arbeitsministeriums Baden-Württemberg* 7 (1958), 200–1.

[81] Thomas R. Brooks, "Auswirkung der Automation auf den Arbeitnehmerstatus," *Zeitschrift für Versicherungswesen* 13 (1962), 644–5, Lorenz Wolkersdorf, "Die Auswirkungen der Automatisierung auf die berufliche Fertigkeit und die Berufsstruktur," *Wirtschaftswissenschaftliche Mitteilungen* 11/2 (1958), 43–6.

[82] Burkart Lutz, *Stern* 17/51 (1964): 57.

[83] "Welcher Beruf hat Chancen?" *Stern* 17/49 (1964): 38–56.

[84] *Stern* 17/49 (1964): 42, 50.

Reflecting a beginning shift in dominant gender norms, *Stern* called for better education for girls and for more day care options to free women to work. The "modern world" of tomorrow, the magazine claimed, demanded women who would be as educated as their husbands.[85] The *Stern* series did not exclusively articulate intense fear of automation but presented a more ambivalent picture of "winners" and "losers." It left no doubt that rapid technological change would threaten traditional skills and jobs. Since these transformations were difficult to anticipate, only qualified experts could provide a well-substantiated assessment of these changes and alert policymakers to the need to prepare for a modern and "automated" future. Modern futures thus increasingly became the object of well-trained experts.[86] Non-experts, by contrast, were increasingly incapable of anticipating and forecasting the future. This fact too was one of the sources of modern fears.

The automation debate also promoted the "psychologization of social analysis" in West Germany.[87] Psychological knowledge became increasingly important for the analysis of modern society. In the context of the automation debate, this significance of psychological expertise built on the continuity of a longer tradition of industrial psychology (*Betriebspsychologie*). It brought into focus the potential impact of automation on the individual bodies and psyches of workers.[88] There was a widespread consensus that automation would shift the demands for individual workers from physical to "intellectual-psychological" (*geistig-nervige*) demands.[89] Increased division of labor might increase workers' alienation from the product of their labor. Reporting on studies from American industry, one speaker cited psychological reactions of uneasiness and even outright fear among workers in response to the introduction of automation. While work accidents decreased as a result of automation, psychosomatic and psychological difficulties increased. These symptoms were not gender-specific and occurred among both male and female workers. This diagnosis implied that hiring in an automated factory would increasingly have to consider—as military testing did—the psychological fitness of individual workers for modern jobs.[90] Thus, automation would create a new professional field for doctors and psychologists.[91] Intellectuals called

---

[85] "Neue Chancen für Frauen und Mädchen," *Stern* 17/42 (1964): 42–50.

[86] Seefried, *Zukünfte*.

[87] Paul Nolte, "Von der Gesellschaftsstruktur zur Seelenverfassung. Die Psychologisierung der Sozialdiagnose in den sechziger Jahren," in Tobias Freimüller, ed., *Psychoanalyse und Protest. Alexander Mitscherlich und die Achtundsechziger* (Göttingen: Wallstein, 2008), 70–94.

[88] On this tradition, see Anson Rabinbach, *The Human Motor. Energy, Fatigue, and the Origins of Modernity* (Berkeley: University of California Press, 1992).

[89] Koch, "Automatisierung und arbeitender Mensch."

[90] See H.J. Weber, "Werkärztliche Erfahrungen über Automation aus einem Frauenbetrieb," *Hamburger Ärzteblatt* 12 (1958): 41–2, and H. Herrmann, "Amerikanische und deutsche Erfahrungen über werkärztliche Probleme der Automation in Betrieben mit vorwiegend männlichen Beschäftigten," in ibid. 45–6.

[91] However, only 50 psychologists worked in industrial psychology in the 1950s. See Maik Tändler, *Das therapeutische Jahrzehnt. Der Psychoboom in den siebziger Jahren* (Göttingen: Wallstein, 2016), 103.

for a "psychological rationalization" that would take into consideration the psychological and physiological needs of individual workers in light of the changes automation would bring. While mere technological innovation might create unhappiness and alienation among workers, an "increase in productivity" would depend on taking "human concerns . . . into consideration," according to the psychologist Eberhard Ulich.[92] Doctors warned that automation could cause psychosomatic health problems among workers. Since automated factories would employ fewer workers, these problems might have a greater impact on overall productivity and thus should be taken seriously.[93] The journal of the West German employers' association, *Der Arbeitgeber*, articulated concerns that increasing psychological challenges—monotony, uniformity, and alienation—might replace decreasing physical demands, leading to dissatisfaction and eventual neuroses. Employers worried not just about productivity but also about keeping their employees happy during a period of full employment and labor shortages. Selecting psychologically suited employees thus became increasingly important in an automated factory.[94] Many observers believed that technological progress would lead to a virtual remaking of the body and psyche of industrial workers. Psychological conditions rather than physical skills advanced to be the most important criteria in qualifying for an automated workplace.

The tradition of cultural pessimism that extended back to the late nineteenth century informed perceptions of technological change as well. One of the main proponents of neo-liberalism in the postwar period, the economist Wihelm Röpke, for example, tempered all too optimistic hopes of expanded consumption and declining work times, not least because of the necessary high investment for automation. But, even more so, he feared the "future of man in an age of technical robots and unbound forces of nature." Following classical cultural pessimistic tropes, he worried that the "individual" and "the soul" had not kept up with the speed of technological progress. Automation thus represented a severe danger to the persistence of "freedom, human warmth, and family."[95] Other commentators shared concerns that the process of automation would ultimately exceed human control. Writing in the periodical *Neues Beginnen*, Johannes Reinhold warned against "deadly omissions" in a revolutionary process of automation whose economic and societal consequences would exceed those of the rationalization movement of the 1920s. He feared that the "stimulation to consumption" would

---

[92] Eberhard Ulich, "Psychologie und Rationalisierung," *Psychologie und Praxis: Zeitschrift für die Anwendungsgebiete der Psychologie* 1/7 (1956–7), 335–50.
[93] B.S., "Probleme der Automation," *Ärztliche Praxis* 10/14 (1958), 335.
[94] Otto Seeger, "Automatisierung und Arbeitssicherheit," *Der Arbeitgeber* 12 (1960), 244–6.
[95] Wilhelm Röpke, "Der Mensch im Zeitalter der Automation," *Das Neue Journal: Wissenswertes aus Politik, Wirtschaft und Kultur* 7/26 (1958). On the culturally conservative views of Röpke, see also Josef Mooser, "Liberalismus und Gesellschaft nach 1945. Soziale Marktwirtschaft und Neoliberalismus am Beispiel von Wilhelm Röpke," in Manfred Hettling, Bernd Ulrich, eds, *Bürgertum nach 1945* (Hamburg: Hamburger Edition, 2005), 134–63.

create "addictions" that would severely restrict individual human freedom.[96] Another observer suggested courses in drawing and arts and craft in order to compensate for the consequences of automation and to give the individual a sense of being "master of his materials" again. Yet he too expressed doubts that human beings could bear "the psychological stress that will come with these future developments."[97]

Church officials were also skeptical. Combining Hans Freyer's *Theory of Contemporary Society* as well as Horkheimer and Adorno's writings on the "culture industry," an author in the Protestant journal *Junge Kirche* worried that the self-alienation of the producer as a result of automation went along with the self-alienation of the consumer in modern mass society. Both areas followed the logic of continued expansion and thus promoted possible "massification" of society. In his view, "being human" required overcoming the functional differentiation and "distractedness" of modern society and a restoration of individuality.[98] In a less differentiated and more blunt fashion, other commentators simply criticized a modern creed that would turn "the machine into a God," which was very prevalent in Bolshevik Russia yet allegedly also found adherents in the West.[99] Automation became a synecdoche for the larger perception of a "technical world" that encompassed both work and leisure. Following David Riesman's *The Lonely Crowd* and echoing Arnold Gehlen's concerns, West German observers diagnosed a similar "loneliness of modern man in the light of the billboards and in the shadow of prosperity." Yet, unlike Riesman, West German cultural pessimists advocated a return to God and to religion as the most effective antidote to what they described as an "age of anxiety."[100] Despite their different intellectual traditions, the arguments of conservative cultural pessimists were often quite similar to those of leftist critics of automation. They both articulated a diffuse anxiety of rapid modernization that the social psychologist Peter Hofstätter also diagnosed, in a 1964 study, among students in Hamburg.[101] The automation debate thus foreshadowed an increasing convergence of leftist critique with skepticism toward modernization as it would manifest itself in the new social movements of the 1970s and ultimately the Green Party.

The most important antidote to the negative effects of automation was the public demand for improved education and professional training. Yet, here too,

---

[96] Johannes Reinhold, "Gesellschaftliche Probleme der Automation," *Neues Beginnen* 9 (1958): 85–7.

[97] Felix Schmidt, "Roboter unter uns: Von der Mechanisierung zur Automation," *Mineralöl. Eine Zeitschrift der Mineralölwirtschaft* 2/5 (1957): 6–10.

[98] Reinhold Lindner, "Mensch sein trotz Automation," *Junge Kirche: Protestantische Monatshefte* 19, 9/10 (1958): 241–6.

[99] Hermann Ullmann, "Mensch oder Maschine?" *Der Europäische Osten: Politische Monatsschrift für eine neue Ordnung* 4/4 (1958): 225–6.

[100] Bruno Pohl, "Die Vereinsamung des Menschen in der technischen Welt," *Zeitwende: Die neue Furche* 31/8 (1960): 514–23.

[101] Peter R. Hofstätter, "Das Stereotyp der Technik," in Freyer et al., eds, *Technik im technischen Zeitalter*, 209.

uncertainty regarding the precise impact of automation prevailed. Did automation require higher skill-levels and better education? Or did automation also lead to deskilling, with unskilled workers occupying the key positions in increasingly automated production processes? Most observers believed that automation would increase the demand for "skilled workers, technicians, and engineers" and thus focused on the need for higher education as a way to exert a modicum of control over the process. Even unskilled workers, as the automation proponent Peter Drucker argued, would need "intellectual capabilities, good judgments, basic mathematical skills, and quick reading and writing skills beyond the basic level."[102] Automation required a "new type of worker" who defined themselves not by their skills but rather by their "personal and intellectual" capabilities.[103] In the most optimistic scenario, automation turned out to be a "blessing for humanity": it would create more productive workers, who worked shorter hours, enjoyed higher living standards, and were better educated and hence better capable of making informed use of their additional leisure time.[104]

The widespread demand for improving educational standards as a result of increasing automation, however, also overlapped with another crisis discourse of the 1960s: the education debate. The catalyst of this debate was the publication of Georg Picht's *The German Educational Catastrophe*—a series of essays in which Picht criticized the sorry state of the West German educational system. As a reform pedagogue and specialist in ancient languages, Picht's key experience was the failure of education to prevent the rise of National Socialism. The editor of the conservative newspaper *Christ und Welt* who had also been one of the most prominent journalists in Nazi Germany, Giselher Wirsing, wrote the introduction to Picht's book. He too argued that the existing system had not kept up with technological developments and would be wholly inadequate to the demands of the future.[105] In addition to better technical training, Picht called for a general expansion of secondary education, to double the number of high school graduates and hire 300,000 new teachers. For him, the number of high school graduates defined the "intellectual potential of a people," which then determined the competitiveness of the economy, the gross national product, and the nation's political position. The Russian position as a "global superpower," Picht argued, was based on a "gigantic educational plan." The Federal Republic still suffered from the

---

[102] "Die sozialen Auswirkungen der Automation und der Atomkraft," *Atombrief* 3/5 (1957): 15–18, Peter Drucker, "Gedanken über die Automatisierung in der Industrie," *Maschine und Werkzeug* 58/20 (1957): 1061–3.

[103] Koch, "Automatisierung und arbeitender Mensch."

[104] Bernhard Herwig, "Probleme des Einsatzes menschlicher Arbeitskraft im Automationsprozeß," *Wirtschaftlichkeit. Organ des österreichischen Kuratoriums für Wirtschaftlichkeit* 3–4 (1956): 51–6.

[105] Giselher Wirsing, "Einführender Artikel aus '*Christ und Welt*'," in Georg Picht, ed., *Die deutsche Bildungskatastrophe: Analyse und Dokumentation* (Olten and Freiburg: Walter Verlag, 1964). On Wirsing's Nazi past, see Norbert Frei, Johannes Schmitz, *Journalismus im Dritten Reich* (Munich: C.H.Beck, 1999), 171–80.

consequences of the "anti-intellectualism" of the Third Reich, which had led to a decline in the number of students. The Federal Republic, he argued, was facing nothing less than a "massive national emergency in the field of education."[106]

Picht's book alarmed many. The opposition Social Democrats asked the federal government to report on the state of education in West Germany as part of an effort to portray themselves as the party of progress and modernity, leading the federal parliament to debate educational policy in March 1964.[107] Trade union representatives and moderate Social Democrats saw the seeming inevitability of automation not just as an opportunity to argue for more economic planning but also as a major reason to demand a massive "quantitative and qualitative expansion of the educational sector." This also entailed a challenge to the hierarchical structure of the "double track school system," which excluded talented students from higher education if they had a working-class or poor background.[108] Representatives of traditional crafts mounted an argument that their skills would not be superfluous in the "age of the robot." The authors argued that new apprenticeships for workers in charge of constructing and maintaining machines would make use of more traditional skills while preparing young people for work in the "age of the robot."[109] As these examples indicate, the automation debate brought into focus varying anxieties with respect to modernity more generally: whereas some commentators worried about the negative effects of technological change, others were concerned that the West German educational sector was not sufficiently prepared to meet the challenges of automation.

Shaping or Adjusting to Modernity? The Trade Union Response to Automation

Given the perceived dramatic impact of automation on employment and the workforce, it is not surprising that West German trade unions were keen observers and engaged participants in the automation debate. The titles of two "working conferences" (*Arbeitstagungen*) that the *Deutsche Gewerkschaftsbund* (DGB) organized on the subject during this period reflected the profound ambivalence with which labor unions confronted automation. The first, in 1958, was entitled "Automation—Asset or Danger?" (*Gewinn oder Gefahr*); the second, in 1965, was called "Automation—Risk and Opportunity" (*Risiko und Chance*). Speaking at the

[106] Wirsing, "Einführender Artikel."
[107] Picht was skeptical regarding the SPD's desire to expand the welfare state and argued that educational expansion should come at the expense of the welfare state; see Radkau, *Geschichte der Zukunft*, 213.
[108] Matthöfer, "Die wirtschaftlichen und sozialen Folgen der Automatisierung."
[109] Alfred Lambeck, "Nachwuchsbildung im Jahrhundert der Roboter: Auch die Automation braucht den Handwerker—Am Anfang war die Feile," *Der Lehrlingswart: Zeitschrift für die gesamte Berufserziehung im Handwerk* 6 (1958): 87–9.

1958 event, Willi Richter, the head of the DGB, took pains to emphasize that West German trade unions favored, on the whole, "economic and technological progress."[110] At the same time, speakers pointed to technological unemployment under conditions of halted or slowed-down economic expansion as well as deskilling of jobs.[111] The 1965 meeting was much larger than the 1958 meeting. It reflected the increased significance of the topic and also revealed the multiple aspects of "automation." Presenters addressed such issues as "co-determination and technological progress," "economic effects of automation in Germany and abroad," and "consequences for professional training and education."[112]

As the largest and most important labor union, the metalworkers' union, *IG Metall*, was particularly engaged in the topic. In 1958, *IG Metall* created an "automation committee" as part of its executive committee with representatives of all regional districts, thus demonstrating just how seriously it took the issue of automation. At the first meeting of the committee in June 1958 in Frankfurt, *IG Metall* chairman Otto Brenner charged the committee to "continue the work that began at the DGB automation congress" and to work through the entire problem in order to make proposals to the executive committee.[113] Günter Friedrichs led the committee from its inception and subsequently became the DGB's main expert on automation. Beginning in 1959, *IG Metall* also established courses that should allow organizers and functionaries to familiarize themselves with the problems and possibilities of automation. Between 1959 and 1965, 422 union officials participated in 19 one-week "basic" courses, and 96 officials participated in five more advanced two-week courses between 1962 and 1965.[114]

The deliberations of the automation committee reflected the hopes and fears regarding automation within the largest West German trade union. One problem in defining a union position on automation was the uncertainty about the extent, future course, and potential impact of automation. Like other commentators, union representatives sought to find evidence regarding the potential future of automation and its impact. In 1959, for example, the automation committee discussed a report about automation in US industry, which had highlighted deskilling as a result of automation. The West German unions had assumed, in accordance with Pollock's study, that automation required higher skills in individual workers. Günter Friedrich, however, described that assumption as

---

[110] Willi Richter speech, DGB Tagung "Automation—Gewinn oder Gefahr" in DGB-Nachrichtendienst, January 23, 1958, in ASD, Bonn, 5/IGMA 240184.

[111] Main speaker at 1958 event, Fritz Sternberg, cited in ibid.

[112] Program brochure, "Automation-Risiko and Chance", 2. Internationale Arbeitstagung der Industriegewerkschaft Metall, March 16–19, 1965, Oberhausen, ASD, 5/IGMA 240059. On trade union responses to automation in general, see Platz, " 'Revolution der Roboter' oder 'Keine Angst vor Robotern'?".

[113] Protokoll über die 1. Sitzung des Automationsausschusses des Vorstandes, June 26, 1958, Frankfurt a/M, Archiv der Sozialen Demokratie (ASD), 5/IGMA 240186.

[114] Teilnehmer Automationslehrgänge, June 30, 1965, ASD, 5/IGMA240185.

"somewhat dated."[115] The perceived futures changed so quickly that it was difficult for contemporaries to arrive at reliable prognoses. This was one reason why the automation committee announced plans to conduct its own studies in individual firms with questionnaires in order to keep the union leadership focused on the ongoing impact of technological change. Reports about lay-offs in several Bavarian companies due to the introduction of new technologies further increased union anxieties about automation.[116]

Technological unemployment remained labor unions' most important concern regarding automation. Developments in the US continued to be of prime significance in anticipating potential German futures. At another conference on "Automation and Technical Progress in the United States and Germany" in July 1963, Günter Friedrich argued that the pace of technological change in West Germany was higher than in the US. According to him, the "wave of automation" had reached a culmination point in West Germany in 1962–3. Yet he also argued that "modern technology" would render superfluous 1.5 million jobs per year for the foreseeable future. Only ongoing economic growth and union success in reducing working hours, he argued, had prevented an increase in the unemployment rate thus far.[117] Friedrich derived this figure from the most extensive academic study on the "social consequences of technological progress" that the Ifo-Institute for Economic Research had conducted in 30 West German firms in 1959–60.[118] The study actually never explicitly cited this figure and Friedrich was criticized for projecting the results from individual firms onto the West German labor market at large.[119] Still, officials within the West German Ministry of Economics were concerned that the "public relations" campaign of labor unions "resonates broadly with the public" whereas rival efforts by employer associations were either non-existent or not "very persuasive." The federal government thus should pay more attention to social consequences of automation and counteract the unions' "one-sided assertions" and arguments as well as the conclusions derived from them. In particular, one official wanted to mobilize industry's rationalization committee (RKW, *Rationalisierungs* kommittee *der deutschen Wirtschaft*) in order to present a different picture.[120] Along similar lines, another government official claimed that the "labor unions make too much of a fuss about automation." He asserted that during a period of full employment automation

[115] Protokoll über die 3. Sitzung des Automationsausschusses des Vorstandes, February 6, 1959, ASD, 5/IGMA 240186.

[116] Ibid.

[117] Vermerk, Internationale Arbeitstagung der IG Metall "Automation und technischer Fortschritt in Deutschland und den USA vom 3. bis 5.7.1963 in Frankfurt am Main," BArch, B149/5710; Bericht über die Internationale Arbeitstagung der IG Metall vom 3–5. Juli in Frankfurt, BArch, B102/151315. See also the interview with Günter Friedrichs, "Sind 35 Stunden genug?" *Der Spiegel* 18/14 (1964): 51–7.

[118] Ifo-Institut für Wirtschaftsforschung, *Soziale Auswirkungen des technischen Fortschrittes* (Berlin–Munich: Duncker & Humblot, 1962).

[119] Vermerk, Internationale Arbeitstagung der IG Metall "Automation und technischer Fortschritt in Deutschland und den USA vom 3. bis 5.7.1963 in Frankfurt am Main," BArch, B149/5710.

[120] Dr. Coester to MDir. Schiettinger, February 13, 1964, BArch, B102/151315.

seemed very unlikely to have significant social or economic consequences.[121] In spite of their concerns about technological unemployment, some union officials also warned against "false preachers" who sought to instill unreasonable fear of automation among workers.[122] As in the case civil defense discussed in Chapter 3, government and union officials saw themselves as emotionally restrained, rational actors who sought to quell what they perceived to be unfounded and exaggerated anxieties emanating from civil society or from rank and file workers. The "fear of fear" as a dominant element of the West German emotional regime thus continued to shape official reactions to modernization processes in West Germany.

For union officials, deskilling and internal restructuring as a result of automation were as worrisome as the prospect of mass lay-offs. According to Günter Friedrich, smaller and mid-size firms resorted to automation in order to compete with larger firms and, in the process, often relegated workers to different tasks with generally lower wages.[123] Rather than technological unemployment, which indeed appeared to be less of a problem in a period of full employment, deskilling and declining wages threatened to exclude workers from the potential benefits of automation. In addition, automation required, according to Friedrich, "entirely new perspectives for the work of trade unions." The percentage of unskilled workers, female employees, and white-collar workers was increasing while the share of skilled male workers, who had always formed the backbone of the unions, continued to decline. Technical progress, Friedrich concluded, "makes our work harder," especially since automation also tends to promote the concentration of capital.[124]

Union officials realized that they did not have any effective means to protect workers against declining wages as a result of automation. Thus, the automation committee discussed ways of influencing the wage assessment of automated workplaces and focused especially on the Volkswagen (VW) factory in Wolfsburg. They also suggested that unions might experiment with the "seniority principle," which US trade unions had implemented.[125] Ultimately, union officials concluded that the existing parameters of co-determination could not achieve protections for workers against lower wages and lay-offs as a result of automation but that collective bargaining agreements should address them. The automation committee, for example, discussed a supplement to the collective bargaining agreement with VW and a draft of a collective bargaining agreement from the textile industry that would address such effects of automation.[126] One representative even wondered whether automated and non-automated workers would need separate collective

---

[121] Schöllhorn, Betr. Öffentlichkeitsarbeit zur Automation, May 14, 1964, BArch, B136/8859.

[122] Protokoll über die 1. Sitzung des Automationsausschusses des Vorstandes, June 26, 1958, Frankfurt a/M, ASD, 5/IGMA 240186.

[123] Ibid.

[124] Günter Friedrichs, "Auswirkungen des technischen Fortschritts in der Metallindustrie, 1956–9. Anlage zum Protokoll des Automationsausschusses vom 20. Januar 1961," ASD, 5/IGMA 240085.

[125] Protokoll über die 1. Sitzung des Automationsausschusses des Vorstandes June 26, 1958, Frankfurt a/M, ASD, 5/IGMA 240186.

[126] Protokoll über die 2. Sitzung des Automationsausschusses des Vorstandes, ASD, 5/IGMA 240186.

bargaining agreements. Trade union efforts to contain the negative effects of automation converged here with considerations within the union leadership to advocate collective bargaining agreements for specific factories while also not undermining the validity of collective bargaining agreements for all members of a specific industry.[127] Employers should thus be obligated to commit not only to an "investment plan" but also to a "social plan" that would reflect the anticipated effects of automation.[128] But this attempt to expand state planning and increase union influence over investment decisions encountered firm resistance from West German employers.

IG Metall arrived at a rather differentiated position that was well aware of the potentially negative impact of automation on the skill level and wage structure of industrial workers. It also recognized the potential benefits and economic necessity of automation. The teaching materials that *IG Metall* compiled regarding this subject also reflected this ambivalence: talking points regarding automation and technical progress cautioned that full automation would affect only a limited percentage of the economy (approximately 20 per cent to 30 per cent). Yet the union also predicted that modern technology changes so rapidly that virtually every workplace might be affected. The talking points struck a balance between potential advantages of automation (economic growth, increasing profits for employers, increasing standard of living and shorter work hours for workers) and its potential dangers (overcapacities, technological unemployment, structural crises, lay-offs, decreasing wages, increasing economic concentration, and potential political misuses of economic power). Labor unions thus defined as their goal that "everybody should benefit from automation," which they hoped to accomplish mainly through economic planning, shorter work hours, and higher wages.[129]

The first economic recession in the history of the Federal Republic in 1966–7 created a new sense of urgency in the West German union's response to automation. The automation committee saw the recession not just as a result of cyclical developments but also as a product of "technical and structural problems" within the West German economy. The recession thus also appeared as the first crisis caused by automation. *IG Metall* increasingly focused on the developments of "social plans" within individual firms and also considered pushing for collective bargaining agreements that would include "protective rationalization clauses." At the same time, the union's automation section continued to develop its training program that sought to familiarize union representatives with the problem of automation.[130] While the recession of 1966–7 sensitized labor unions such as

---

[127] Protokoll über die 1. Sitzung des Automationsausschusses des Vorstandes, June 26, 1958, Frankfurt a/M, ASD, 5/IGMA 240186. On these debates, see Abelshauser, *Nach dem Wirtschaftswunder*, 108–13.

[128] Protokoll über die 3. Sitzung des Automationsausschusses des Vorstandes, 6. Februar 1959, ASD, 5/IGMA 240186.

[129] "Lehrgespräch über technischen Fortschritt und Automatisierung," ASD, 5/IGMA 240186.

[130] Protokoll über die 10. Sitzung des Automationsausschusses beim Vorstand, October 16/17, 1967, ASD, 5/IGM 240085.

IG Metall for the problematic effects of automation and also prompted a series of "wildcat strikes," the late 1960s and early 1970s did not represent a complete "turning point" in union attitudes toward automation.[131] As the example of *IG Metall*'s confrontation has shown, union officials had already adopted a deeply ambivalent attitude toward automation. They were not immune to a broader "Fordist" optimistic assessment of the potentially beneficial consequences of technological change, such as higher wages and living standards and shorter workdays through increased productivity. Yet they were also quite aware of more problematic consequences of automation. These did not just concern the fear of unemployment but also the impact of automation on skill levels, wage structures, and the gendered and generational composition of the workforce. Yearly DGB congresses in 1958 and again in 1965 reflected the intense engagement with automation and undermined criticism that unions did not develop a "broad information campaign" or "targeted defense" regarding automation during this period.[132] Rather than uncritically subscribing to an overtly optimistic belief in technological progress, union officials exhibited a deep-seated uncertainty regarding the future. Precisely because the future became increasingly unpredictable, experts assumed a more important role in seeking to anticipate future developments.[133] As such, the DGB's engagement with automation constituted an integral part of the broader self-observation of West German society that saw itself undergoing a dramatic and accelerated evolution into a new and more technology-driven stage of industrial development. This self-perception was at the heart of distinctly modern fears that derived from a new temporal perspective: no longer merely rooted in a past, modern fears were the product of an expanded horizon of expectation in the late 1950s and early 1960s, whose contours remained, however, vague and indeterminate.

The automation debate of the late 1950s and early 1960s constituted a crucial aspect of the self-commentary and self-observation of West German society. It defined West German society as a thoroughly modern society that had overcome the most direct consequences of the past and was now facing a more open, albeit more uncertain, future. This uncertainty concerned not only basic socio-economic processes such as automation but also the very nature of West German democracy. While many critics of automation feared its negative impact on democracy, the nature of West German democracy itself became the subject of an increasingly controversial debate from the late 1950s onward. Like West Germany's socio-economic development, the ongoing process of democratization had uncertain directions and hence became the object of fears and anxiety. These "democratic fears" are the subject of the next chapter.

---

[131] Rüdiger Hachtmann, "Gewerkschaften und Rationalisierung: Die 1970er Jahre—ein Wendepunkt?" in Knud Andresen, Ursula Bitzegeio, Jürgen Mittag, eds, *"Nach dem Strukturbruch": Kontinuität und Wandel von Arbeitsbeziehungen und Arbeitswelt(en) seit den 1970er Jahren* (Bonn: J.H.W. Dietz Nachf., 2011), 194.

[132] Ibid.

[133] See Platz, "'Revolution der Roboter' oder 'Keine Angst vor Robotern'?" 58–9.

5

Democratic *Angst*

"Democracy at a Turning Point,"[1] "Does Democracy Have Any Chance in Germany?"[2] "Can Our Democracy Survive?"[3] "The Dangers of an 'As-If' Democracy,"[4] "The Tired Democracy":[5] such article titles about the state of West German democracy pointed to a widespread perception of a crisis of democracy in the Federal Republic of the late 1950s and early 1960s. This sense of crisis arose alongside the automation debate, as discussed in the previous chapter, and in some ways reflected it. Some commentators even saw the socio-economic and the political crises converging. Critics described what they perceived as the marginalization of the parliament—for example, as its "cold automation." They claimed democracy functioned "like an automaton" that gets "fed the popular will and then somehow produces the right decisions" without popular participation.[6] Like the process of automation, "democracy" as a purely formal process appeared to be devoid of popular participation or control. The public debates about "automation" and "democracy" thus both illustrated how the very accomplishments and successes of the Federal Republic generated their own uncertainties and anxieties. Far from a period of unmitigated optimism and belief in progress, the 1960s constituted, in the perception of many Germans at the time, a crisis decade. The political and socio-economic fears during this period anticipated, in many ways, the broader anxieties that historians have located in the post-boom period after 1973.

This chapter analyzes the political debate about the future of West German democracy after the Federal Republic had gained sovereignty and accomplished a basic political stabilization. The fears in this period did not focus on a concrete object but on more abstract processes. They were articulated largely by intellectuals and political commentators and thus the subject of published opinion. While the voices of these participants in the public discourse on fear were not necessarily indicative, let alone representative of West German society as a whole,

---

[1] Edu Wald, "Die Demokratie in der Bundesrepublik am Kreuzweg," *Der Gewerkschafter* 8/3 (1960): 14–15.
[2] Jörg Simpfendörfer, "Hat die Demokratie in Deutschland eine Chance?" *Der Bürger im Staat* 9/3 (1959): 55–6.
[3] Weber, "Hat unsere Demokratie Bestand?" *Das Parlament* 9/21 (1959): 4–5.
[4] Hans Lampe, "Die Gefahren einer Als-Ob-Demokratie," *Wirtschaft und Erziehung* 10/4 (1958): 147–53.
[5] Werner Friedmann, "Die müde Demokratie oder Blick zurück im Zorn," *Junge Kirche: Protestantische Monatshefte* 20 (1959): 646–8.
[6] Ibid., Lampe, "Die Gefahren einer Als-Ob-Demokratie."

German Angst: Fear and Democracy in the Federal Republic of Germany. Frank Biess, Oxford University Press (2020).
© Frank Biess.
DOI: 10.1093/oso/9780198714187.001.0001

they nevertheless pointed to an insecurity and uncertainty regarding the future of West German democracy.

From the late 1950s onward, democratization prompted an intensified debate on the future development of West German democracy and thus gave rise to new kinds of "democratic fears." These fears had conservative and left-liberal versions: conservatives worried that accelerated democratization would eventually undermine the authority of the state, while leftists and liberals were primarily concerned about threats to democracy emanating from within the state. A new presence of the Nazi past during this period reinforced fear: while conservatives saw it as a threat to German national identity, liberals saw an insufficient reckoning with the Nazi past as a threat to democracy. A more critical and extensive memory of the Nazi past thus did not lead to greater confidence in West German democracy but rather fueled new anxieties at both ends of the political spectrum. A similar sense of doom or impending catastrophe afflicted conservatives and liberals alike.

The articulation of democratic fears both reflected and promoted a changed view of emotions in politics and public life. The emotional regime of the 1950s tended to portray the open expression of emotions as suspicious and closely linked to fascist irrationalism. It advocated and promoted a restrained, anti-emotional ethics of sobriety that appeared to be compatible with the reconstruction of a conservative liberal democracy.[7] By the early 1960s, however, an increasing number of liberal and leftist critics began to challenge this emotional regime both implicitly and explicitly. They increasingly highlighted the productive function of displaying emotions more publicly and openly, and they especially underlined the potentially important role of articulating democratic fears. To them, fear increasingly functioned as the equivalent of an alarm system that would identify potential threats to West German democracy and hence serve a positive role in the ongoing process of inner democratization. Notwithstanding its political and economic stabilization, the Federal Republic remained a polity on alert.

Democratic Fears, Fears of Democracy

In his 1956 book, *Bonn is not Weimar*, the Swiss journalist Fritz René Allemann highlighted the essential differences between Germany's first and second democracies. Allemann's book signaled a functional shift in the understanding of Weimar's relationship to the Federal Republic. Rather than fearing that the Bonn Republic would devolve, as its predecessor had, Allemann pointed to the "historical lessons" that postwar Germans had learned after 1945 and contrasted the

---

[7] On the larger context, see Frank Biess, "Feelings in the Aftermath: Toward a History of Postwar Emotions," in Frank Biess, Robert Moeller, eds, *Histories of the Aftermath. The Legacies of the Second World War in Europe* (New York: Berghahn Books, 2010), 30–48.

Federal Republic's success with Weimar's catastrophic failure.[8] Yet even Allemann did not paint an unambiguously positive picture of the Federal Republic in the 1950s. He criticized, for example, an only passive acceptance of democracy and parliamentarism in West Germany, and he worried that West Germans might be willing to abandon their newly gained freedom for the sake of national reunification.[9] Along similar lines, West German intellectuals and journalists increasingly emphasized that a successful "democracy" entailed more than functioning institutions and economic prosperity. Bonn's difference from Weimar thus appeared as the minimal requirement in a more extensive notion of democratization. "The future of democracy," wrote one commentator, "[does not reside in the] constitution, the structure of societal institutions, the educational system, or the solution of social and economic problems [but rather in] people's hearts."[10] Democracy thus did not just consist of an external political framework, a specific organization of the state (*Staatsform*), but also required an "inner democratization"—that is, internalized democratic values and an emotional investment in democratic processes.[11] With respect to a more extensive concept of democracy, observers such as the journalist and Jewish returned-émigré Ernst Friedländer questioned whether the preference for democracy over dictatorship was truly rooted in people's "thoughts and hearts."[12]

Both ends of the political spectrum shared these concerns about the future of democracy, even though very different conceptions of democracy informed their respective anxieties. Intensifying fears about undesirable political futures thus shaped the broader debate over the political culture of the Federal Republic. These were "democratic fears" in a double sense: the future of democracy constituted the object of these fears while the articulation of these political emotions also furthered democratization. To be sure, democratic political cultures are inherently unstable and tend to be in a constant state of crisis. But the West German political and intellectual debate assumed a truly existential dimension in which not merely diverging policy proposal but the very nature of West German democracy was at stake.[13] As the historian Jens Hacke noted, "there was hardly

---

[8] Sebastian Ullrich, *Der Weimar-Komplex. Das Scheitern der ersten deutschen Demokratie und die politische Kultur der frühen Bundesrepublik 1945–1959* (Göttingen: Wallstein, 2009), 413–20, Fritz René Allemann, *Bonn ist nicht Weimar* (Cologne: Kiepenheuer & Witsch, 1956).

[9] Ibid. 428, 438–40.

[10] Simpfendörfer, "Hat die Demokratie in Deutschland eine Chance?"; similarly, Waldemar Besson, "Bonn ist anders als Weimar," *Der Convent: Akademische Monatsschrift* 12 (1961): 243–4.

[11] Lampe, "Die Gefahren einer Als-Ob-Demokratie," 153, Simpfendörfer, "Hat die Demokratie in Deutschland eine Chance?" 56. On inner democratization, see also Konrad H. Jarausch, *After Hitler. Recivilizing Germans, 1945–1955*, trans. Brandon Hunziker (Oxford and New York: Oxford University Press, 2006).

[12] Ernst Friedländer, "Unbewältigte Vergangenheit," in Alfred Neven DuMont, ed., *Woher— Wohin? Bilanz der Bundesrepublik. Magnum Sonderheft 1961* (Cologne: DuMont, 1961), 20.

[13] On crisis and democracy, see Tim B. Müller, *Nach dem Ersten Weltkrieg. Lebensversuche moderner Demokratien* (Hamburg: Hamburger Edition, 2014), 7–21.

any observer in the first postwar decades who would have argued that democracy in West Germany was doing just fine."[14] These political emotions reflected a genuine anxiety about the future of democracy, which political commentators could articulate more easily after the Federal Republic had achieved limited sovereignty in 1955 and after the basic institutional parameters of the West German state had been determined.[15] The explicit articulation of democratic fears, moreover, constituted in itself the product of a gradually changing emotional regime that enabled a more open expression of political emotions. The political fears of the 1960s were part and parcel of the protracted self-definition and dialectical self-recognition of West German society: by articulating their deep concerns over what the Federal Republic might become, intellectuals and public commentators demonstrated their increasing emotional investment in the present and future condition of the West German political order.

What exactly were the objects of political fears during this period? For conservatives, they consisted of fears of an excess of democracy and a corresponding decline, or at least weakening, of the traditional authority of the state.[16] One expression of these sentiments came from the conservative journalist Winfried Martini. A frequent contributor to conservative periodicals and radio stations, Martini articulated his concerns in a 1960 book entitled *Freedom on Call: The Life Expectancy of the Federal Republic*. He warned that the "achievements" of the Federal Republic were "superficial." For him, the articulation of "dark images, predictions and fears" constituted "constructive pessimism" that would help guard against existential threats to the West German state. In contrast to writers like Allemann, Martini believed that decentralization and a weakening of state authority had rendered the Federal Republic less capable of confronting internal challenges, which he perceived as more dangerous than during the Weimar Republic because they were less apparent. He bemoaned the absence of a law giving emergency power to the government, like Article 48 in the Weimar Republic, which might be necessary in the face of Communist threats in the Cold War.[17] He called for a strengthening of the state similar to De Gaulle's Fifth Republic in France as well as a maintenance of the American military presence to deter against a "West German Korea"—that is, an attack from the Communist East, or,

---

[14] Jens Hacke, *Die Bundesrepublik als Idee. Zur Legitimationsbedürftigkeit politischer Ordnung* (Hamburg: Hamburger Edition, 2009), 26.

[15] West German sovereignty excluded rights pertaining to Germany "as a whole" that were reserved for the Allied victors of the Second World War.

[16] On conservativism after 1945, see Helga Grebing, *Konservative gegen die Demokratie. Konservative Kritik an der Demokratie in der Bundesrepublik nach 1945* (Frankfurt a/M: Europa Verlags-anstalt, 1971), Axel Schildt, *Konservativismus in Deutschland. Von den Anfängen im 18. Jahrhundert bis zur Gegenwart* (Munich: C.H.Beck, 1998).

[17] This was a minority position: see Karl Dietrich Bracher, "Die zweite Demokratie in Deutschland—Von Weimar nach Bonn," in Karl Dietrich Bracher, *Deutschland zwischen Demokratie und Diktatur. Beiträge zur neueren Politik und Geschichte* (Bern: Scherz, 1964), 111.

even worse, a "surrender without a fight" by the Federal Republic. His alarmist perspective culminated in the perception that "we are psychologically in the same state as 1938"—that is, at the onset of the Second World War.[18]

To be sure, even most conservative commentators distanced themselves from Martini's open endorsement of authoritarianism. They conceded that Martini rejected National Socialism and did not want a "Fourth Reich," yet also criticized his infatuation with authoritarian conservatism as it was practiced not just by De Gaulle in France but also by Franco and Salazar in Spain and Portugal.[19] But conservatives shared his broader concerns about excessive democratization. The political stabilization of the Federal Republic allowed a conservative critique of the Basic Law as an overcorrection of the perceived mistakes of the past at the expense of the empowerment of political parties and organized interests. Some of these conservative fears of too much democracy reflected the ongoing yet subterranean influence of the ideas of Carl Schmitt, the legal theorist of the Nazi regime, during the early Federal Republic.[20] Schmitt's influence was particularly apparent in the writings of one of his former doctoral students, the constitutional law professor Ernst Forsthoff.[21] Forsthoff had been an enthusiastic supporter of National Socialism and provided a legal justification of the *Führer* principle in his 1933 treatise, *The Total State*. Yet he later distanced himself from the Nazi regime as well as from his former teacher, Carl Schmitt. In the postwar period, he resumed contact with Schmitt and cited his work extensively in his own writings.[22] He saw the Basic Law as a product of an unprecedented moment of weakness in the

---

[18] Winfried Martini, *Freiheit auf Abruf. Die Lebenserwartung der Bundesrepublik* (Cologne: Kiepenheuer & Witsch, 1960), 13–14, 162–70, 221–4, 345–51, 410–12. Admiration for de Gaulle was widespread among West German conservatives. See also Armin Mohler, *Die Fünfte Republik. Was steht hinter de Gaulle?* (Munich: Piper, 1963). On Martini, see Marcus Payk, "Antikommunistische Mobilisierung und konservative Revolte. William S. Schlamm, Winfried Martini und der 'kalte Bürgerkrieg' in der westdeutschen Publizistik der späten 1950er Jahre," in Thomas Lindenberger, ed., *Massenmedien im Kalten Krieg. Akteure, Bilder, Resonanzen* (Cologne: Böhlau, 2006), 117–37. On Carl Schmitt's influence on Martini's thinking, see Dirk van Laak, *Gespräche in der Sicherheit des Schweigens. Carl Schmitt in der politischen Geistesgeschichte der frühen Bundesrepublik* (Berlin: Akademie Verlag, 1993), 172–3.

[19] Karl O. Paetel, "Das Wagnis der Demokratie: Weimar oder Bonn?" *Geist und Tat: Monatsschrift für Recht, Freiheit und Kultur* 15 (1960): 360–3. See also Ullrich, *Der Weimar Komplex*, 584.

[20] On Schmitt's ongoing influence on the critique of the Basic Law, see Laak, *Gespräche in der Sicherheit des Schweigens*, 157–70. See also A. Dirk Moses, "The 'Weimar Syndrome' in the Federal Republic of Germany. The Carl Schmitt Reception by the Forty-Five Generation of Intellectuals," in Stephan Loos, Holger Zaborowski, eds., *Leben, Tod und Entscheidung. Studien zur Geistesgeschichte der Weimarer Republik* (Berlin: Duncker & Humblot, 2003), 187–207.

[21] On Forsthoff, see Peter Caldwell, "Ernst Forsthoff and the Legacy of Radical Conservative State Theory in the Federal Republic of Germany," *History of Political Thought* 15/4 (1994): 629, Rainer Schuckart, "Kontinuitäten einer konservativen Staatsrechtslehre. Forsthoffs Positionen in der Weimarer Republik, im Dritten Reich und in der Bundesrepublik," in Stephan Alexander Glienke, Volker Paulmann, Joachim Perels, eds, *Erfolgsgeschichte Bundesrepublik. Die Nachkriegsgesellschaft im langen Schatten des Nationalsozialismus* (Göttingen: Wallstein Verlag, 2008), 85–114, Florian Meinel, *Der Jurist in der industriellen Gesellschaft. Ernst Forsthoff und seine Zeit* (Berlin: Akademie Verlag, 2012).

[22] Ibid. 36–98, 226–40.

aftermath of total defeat, which privileged individual freedoms at the expense of the authority of the state. Left-wing critics, he argued, misperceived the danger when they suspected "the state of totalitarianism at every turn." Forsthoff instead identified the danger of totalitarianism as residing "not in the state but in the people." For him, the total state exists when a "totalitarian movement captures the state and instrumentalizes it for its purpose."[23] The Nazi state thus represented to him a step in the long-term decline of state authority and hence was "too democratic."[24] In the Federal Republic, the state had disintegrated into a "state of industrial society"—that is, into a merely distributive welfare state, which "not only does not need authority but is incompatible with authority."[25] For Forsthoff, the much cited "democratization" rendered the West German state increasingly less capable of resisting its political enemy: the constitutional guarantee for a "right of resistance" represented for Forsthoff a "rare misperception and denial of the authority of the state."[26] Forsthoff's "pessimism" regarding the ability of the West German state to withstand challenges from political enemies only increased with the gradual expansion of the welfare state and the radicalization of the student movement from the mid 1960s onward.[27] His case illustrates the persistence of an authoritarian, state-oriented conservative tradition from before 1945 well into the 1960s and 1970s.

Another constitutional law professor and former Schmitt student, Werner Weber, articulated a similar critique of the Basic Law as fostering excessive federalism and the separation of powers at the expense of the authority of the state. He expressed doubts that the democratic constitution of the Federal Republic could function as a "system of rule capable of action" in an emergency, such as an attack by the Communist East or a domestic uprising. This is why he argued, in anticipation of the later debate, for a set of specific emergency laws.[28] According to the political scientist Otto Heinrich von Gablentz, the failure or refusal of West German citizens to fully support or identify with the state further compounded the weakness of the state. As a result, the future of the state was very much in doubt, especially if economic prosperity were to end or if Chancellor Konrad Adenauer were to resign.[29] These voices reflected fears of excessive democracy

---

[23] Ernst Forsthoff, *Der Staat der Industriegesellschaft. Dargestellt am Beispiel der Bundesrepublik Deutschland* (Munich: C.H.Beck, 1971), 54.

[24] Caldwell, "Ernst Forsthoff."

[25] Ernst Forsthoff, "Das politische Problem der Autorität," in Ernst Forsthoff, ed., *Rechtsstaat im Wandel. Verfassungsrechtliche Abhandlungen 1954–1973* (Munich: C.H.Beck, 1976), 22.

[26] Forsthoff, *Der Staat der Industriegesellschaft*, 64, 69.

[27] See Klaus Frey, "Vorwort zur Zweiten Auflage," in Forsthoff, *Rechtsstaat im Wandel*, xv.

[28] Werner Weber, "Die Teilung der Gewalten als Gegenwartsproblem," in Barion et al., eds, *Festschrift für Carl Schmitt*, 253–72.

[29] Otto Heinrich von Gablentz, "Autorität und Legitimität im heutigen Staat," in Otto Heinrich von Gablentz, ed., *Der Kampf um die rechte Ordnung. Beiträge zur politischen Wissenschaft* (Opladen: Westdeutscher Verlag, 1964), 79.

and a declining authority of the state as conservative reactions to the process of inner democratization in the Federal Republic.

Focusing on a different aspect of West German democracy, the Tübingen political scientist Theodor Eschenburg identified the fear of excessive pluralism, a "rule of special interests" (*Herrschaft der Verbände*) as a real danger to the democratic order in West Germany. In the preface to the second edition of his essay in 1963, Eschenburg saw these tendencies for a gradual disintegration of the state vis-à-vis "group interest" as increasing, compared with the first publication in 1955. He claimed that West German officials "unconsciously" undermined the authority of the state by privileging the interests of political parties or organized interests in making political decisions. This "deficient state" (*Unterstaat*), as he called it, was a natural consequence of the "excessive state" *(Überstaat)* of the Hitler period.[30] Eschenburg thus embraced a functionalist perspective on democracy that emphasized the governability of the democratic state as its main criterion for success. His conservative emphasis on the state over society might have also derived from his political socialization in the right-wing academic milieu of the Weimar Republic as well as from his accommodation to, perhaps even active complicity with, the Nazi dictatorship.[31]

The political scientist Rüdiger Altmann's concept of a "coordinated society" (*formierte Gesellschaft*) constituted one possible response to such fears of an excessive influence of organized interests over the state. Altmann adopted Schmitt's terminology and followed his ideas,[32] and in turn Chancellor Ludwig Erhard eventually adopted "coordinated society" as a slogan during his tenure.[33] Liberal and left-wing critics immediately saw analogies to the Nazi submission of all interest groups to the Nazi state. Yet Altmann dismissed such concerns by "left-wing and other well meaning observers" focusing too much on the "return of the old ghosts" and thus missing the real danger to the Republic: its perceived weakness vis-à-vis organized interests. Altman perceived a greater "susceptibility to crisis" in the Federal Republic than in Weimar and worried that West German democracy would not be able to withstand severe economic crisis. A weak democratic state or, as he called it, a "democracy in the wheelchair" was subservient to organized interests and thus lacked sufficient political authority. The goal of a strong executive authority, therefore, had to be rational planning, a means to

---

[30] Theodor Eschenburg, *Herrschaft der Verbände?* (Stuttgart: Deutsche Verlags-Anstalt, 1963 [1st edn 1955]), 6–7, 81–3.

[31] The extent of Eschenburg's involvement in National Socialism is controversial: see Udo Wengst, *Theodor Eschenburg. Biografie einer politischen Leitfigur 1904–1999* (Berlin: De Gruyter, 2015), Rainer Eisfeld, *Theodor Eschenburgs Beteiligung an "Arisierungen" im Nationalsozialismus* (Wiesbaden: Springer VS, 2016).

[32] Laak, *Gespräche in der Sicherheit des Schweigens*, 262–5, quotation on 264.

[33] See Herbert, *Geschichte Deutschlands*, 777–8, Edgar Wolfrum, *Die geglückte Demokratie. Geschichte der Bundesrepublik Deutschland von ihren Anfängen bis zur Gegenwart* (Stuttgart: Klett-Cotta, 2006), 218–19.

synchronize a dynamic economy and achieve an equitable distribution of the gross domestic product. Only a rational and planned fiscal policy by a strong state would prevent either gradual paralysis or a shocking collapse.[34]

A perception of the expanding welfare state as excessive as well as an interest in aligning state policies with business interests in order to ensure economic growth informed Altman's work. In this sense, it is not surprising that it was compatible with Ludwig Erhard's neo-liberal worldview. At the same time, however, Altman's emphasis on rational and long-term planning was also compatible with a more active, interventionist state and hence with a Keynesian fiscal policy such as the Grand Coalition of the Christian Democratic Union (CDU)/Christian Social Union (CSU) and the Social Democratic Party (SPD) adopted from 1966 onward. These proposals for a recalibration of the relationship between state and society emerged from an underlying conservative anxiety over the future of democracy in the Federal Republic.

Liberal and left-wing observers' anxiety over the fragility of democracy was as urgent as conservatives'. Their main concern was not a return to open fascism but rather a gradual transformation into an authoritarian system, and conservative prescriptions to strengthen the authority of the state fueled their anxiety. As early as 1955, the historian Immanuel Geiss identified the danger of attempts to create an "authoritarian regime in Christian disguise and under the auspices of an anti-Bolshevist rejuvenation of the occident similar to the clerical fascism of the Dollfuß-regime in Austria during the 1930s or Franco-Spain."[35] Adenauer's triumphant victory in the 1957 federal elections, when the CDU/CSU managed to gain—for the first and only time in the history of the Federal Republic—an absolute majority of 50.2 per cent of the popular vote, activated many of these critical sentiments among liberals and left-wing observers. Adenauer's victory intensified liberal and left-wing critics' worries regarding a "chancellor democracy" that was gradually transforming the Federal Republic into an authoritarian system. The political scientist Karl Dietrich Bracher, for example, compared Adenauer's government to the presidential cabinets of the Weimar Republic in the 1930s. He also articulated fundamental doubts regarding the stability of the Federal Republic, which he claimed was based on a "fleeting economic boom" and had not yet achieved a democratic transfer of power. Like some of the conservative critics, he was unsure whether the Federal Republic would be able to withstand a fundamental challenge.[36] Along similar lines, the SPD politician and editor of the

---

[34] Rüdiger Altman, "Die formierte Gesellschaft," in Rüdiger Altman, ed., *Abschied vom Staat: Politische Essays* (New York: Campus, 1998), 60–70. See also Moses, *German Intellectuals and the Nazi Past*, 177–8.

[35] Immanuel Geiss, "Auf dem Wege zum 'Neuen Abendland'," *Neue Gesellschaft* 2/6 (1955): 41–6, quotation 41; cited in Axel Schildt, *Zwischen Abendland und Amerika. Studien zur Ideenlandschaft der 1950er Jahre* (Munich: Oldenbourg, 1999), 68.

[36] Bracher, "Die zweite Demokratie in Deutschland—Von Weimar nach Bonn." On Bracher, see also Moses, *German Intellectuals and the Nazi Past*, 169–70.

journal *Geist und Tat*, Willi Eichler, castigated the "coordination of democratic institutions," which he saw reflected in the Adenauer government's efforts to gain increasing influence on the press, radio, and television. Liberal and leftist critiques perceived these developments as indicative of a broader transnational trend toward authoritarianism as evident in Spain, Portugal, and France. For Eichler, Adenauer's admiration for De Gaulle undermined the Western commitment to freedom and made the Western model less attractive for newly independent countries in Africa and Asia in the age of decolonization.[37]

These commentators agreed that democracy in West Germany represented merely a constitutional structure rather than a "social and intellectual way of life"[38] and that the Federal Republic was therefore susceptible to antidemocratic appeals. Writing in 1961, Jürgen Habermas argued that widespread depoliticization might initially protect against a "totalitarian party," yet also worried that a "plebiscitary coup" could "superficially politicize" such "indifferent masses" and then mobilize them "on behalf of a strong authority."[39] The political scientist Kurt Sontheimer, with whom Habermas would have intense political controversies by the end of the decade, was inclined to still agree with him at that point: he worried that the Federal Republic would lack a "continuity of freedom and a democratic way of life" until it successfully weathered a "crisis."[40]

In the run-up to the federal election in 1961, West German intellectuals articulated their grave concerns not just over the policies of the Adenauer government but over the state of democracy in the Federal Republic more generally. In a volume that the writer Martin Walser edited, all the contributors answered the book's titular question *Do We Need a New Government?* affirmatively.[41] The warning that another victory by the CDU in the 1961 elections would constitute "a severe danger to the democratic constitution of the Federal Republic" was among the more moderate statements.[42] Other contributors feared that the Federal Republic was already on a creeping and potentially irreversible path toward a new totalitarianism. "We will wake up one day and be coordinated again, not arbitrarily but through legislation," wrote Axel Eggebrecht, who saw this process as an "inconspicuous leveling" that was "preparing the ground for totalitarianism, if not already the beginning of it."[43] The government's attempt to reduce every political

---

[37] Willi Eichler, "Volksbildung oder Volkstäuschung? Zur Gleichschaltung demokratischer Einrichtungen in der Bundesrepublik," *Geist und Tat: Monatsschrift für Recht, Freiheit und Kultur* 15/1 (1960): 1–5.

[38] Bracher, "Die zweite Demokratie in Deutschland—Von Weimar nach Bonn."

[39] Jürgen Habermas, "Die Bundesrepublik. Eine Wahlmonarchie?" cited in Moses, *German Intellectuals and the Nazi Past*, 169–70. Similar diagnosis also from Walter Dirks, in DuMont, ed., *Woher—Wohin?*, 28.

[40] Kurt Sontheimer, "Die anderen zwölf Jahre," in ibid. 87.

[41] Martin Walser, ed., *Die Alternative oder, Brauchen wir eine neue Regierung?* (Reinbek: Rowohlt, 1961). For an analysis of this volume, see also Moses, *German Intellectuals and the Nazi Past*, 161–6.

[42] Fritz Schonauer, "Das schmutzige Nest," in Walser, ed., *Die Alternative*, 74.

[43] Axel Eggebrecht, "Soll die Ära der Heuchelei andauern?" in ibid. 25; also Wolfdietrich Schnurre, "Das falsche Gleis," in ibid. 71–2.

debate to the "East–West contrast" entailed, according to Gerhard Schoenberger, a "totalitarian element"; without a new government, he predicted that "inner exhaustion" would destroy the democracy because of the absence of opposition.[44] Contrary to the intentions of the volume to make an argument for a political change in the Federal Republic, some commentators feared that it might already be too late. For Wolfdietrich Schnurre, the switch had already been set wrong and the German postwar express had already passed several "stop signs warning of an impending catastrophe," thus making it difficult to change course.[45]

More than authoritarian impulses "from above," liberal and leftist critics worried about popular authoritarianism. The "people," Carl Amery wrote, were in the grip of "clericalism" and as "susceptible to authority" as during the Nazi period.[46] Paul Schallück diagnosed a "petrified" political system and expressed little confidence in "the people of a democracy," which had replaced a "twelve-year Führer state" with a "twelve-year patriarchal state."[47] In this context, the CDU's attempt to denigrate the opposition leader Willy Brandt for his emigration and anti-Nazi record reflected an attempt to mobilize the "brown resentment"—that is neo-Nazi sympathies—among the electorate and revealed the utterly problematic "foundations of this state."[48] For the leftist journalist Erich Kuby, it was only a matter of time until the "mopped up energies of the people would be discharged externally" in a new quest for German expansion.[49] Memories of the popular support for the Nazi dictatorship further underlined the sense of urgency and crisis with which intellectuals perceived the political situation of the Federal Republic of the late 1950s. "It is as late as in the early 1930s," wrote Heinz von Cramer, "only that this time there will be no Hitler but a more contemporary, more subtle dictatorship wearing a democratic mask."[50] Hans Werner Richter likewise saw "indications of a similar development as in the 1930s." For him, the "agony of democracy" had already begun and was giving way to "for the time being concealed dictatorship."[51]

These intellectuals invoked a more critical memory of the Nazi past as a vehicle to express their fear. In so doing, they presented themselves as "good Germans" who wanted to learn the lessons of the past. But their statements also indicated that a more comprehensive memory of the past did not necessarily imply democratic stabilization but rather the opposite: increased fear and anxiety. These intellectuals, moreover, were quite willing to articulate their democratic fears openly and explicitly. Wolf Dietrich Schnurre, for example, confessed his "postwar anxiety" that the Federal Republic would not draw the right consequences from the

---

[44] Gerhard Schoenberger, "Zerstörung der Demokratie," in ibid. 142, 145.
[45] Wolfdietrich Schnurre, "Das falsche Gleis," in ibid. 67–8.
[46] Carl Amery, "Eine kleine Utopie," in ibid. 16.
[47] Paul Schallück, "Versteinerungen," in ibid. 59.
[48] Gerhard Schoenberger, "Zerstörung der Demokratie," in ibid. 143.
[49] Erich Kuby, "Und ob wir eine neue Regierung brauchen," in ibid. 154.
[50] Heinz von Cramer, "Es ist so spät wie es schon einmal war," in ibid. 96.
[51] Hans Werner Richter, "Von Links in die Mitte," in ibid. 115–16, 118.

experience of the Nazi dictatorship. Hans Werner Richter articulated his "concern for the future" and his "fear of an only tactical world without ideas, whose vacuums could easily be filled again by fascist ideology." In a somewhat more concrete sense, Martin Walser professed his "goose bumps" and "fear" of the "nightmare from Bavaria"—meaning the defense minister Franz Josef Strauß, whom many intellectuals perceived as Adenauer's "less scrupulous," "power hungry" successor.[52] Such open articulations of fear were part and parcel of a gradual transformation of the emotional regime that increasingly condoned the open expression of political emotions in public discourse.

To be sure, not all West German intellectuals feared the worst. Ralf Dahrendorf, for example, saw precisely the "depoliticization" of West German society that Jürgen Habermas had identified as the potential entry point for a new authoritarian rule as an indication of a "silent revolution" toward a more liberal and pluralistic society, and hence as a protection against that very danger. "People," he argued, "who are mainly concerned about their private advantage usually don't subordinate themselves without protest to totalitarian and authoritarian claims."[53] Similarly, liberal-conservative intellectuals such as Hermann Lübbe emerged from the circles of the philosopher Joachim Ritter in Münster to express their confidence in West German liberal democracy. They did not share left-wing commentators' concern regarding a merely superficial demoralization but defended democratic institutions and endowed them with moral and ethical value. Following Carl Schmitt, they also adhered to a "pragmatic decisionism"—that is, political elites' ability to make decisions on the basis of imperfect information—as a genuinely political realm and counterweight to an overtly technocratic discourse as articulated in the automation debate. These intellectuals served an important purpose in reconciling traditionally conservative ideas with liberal democracy and hence contributed significantly to the liberal-conservative stabilization of the Federal Republic.[54]

Still, democratic fears need to be taken seriously as an important element of the West German horizon of expectation in the late 1950s and early 1960s. With the benefit of hindsight, it is easy to dismiss these political anxieties as hopelessly exaggerated or as an indication of the political marginalization of left-wing intellectuals in the Federal Republic of that period. These voices were more than just a sideshow to the ongoing political and economic stabilization of the Federal Republic. The critique of West German democracy did also not just result from extensive "campaigns against Bonn" with which the East German dictatorship sought to discredit the Federal Republic. Indeed, some of the internal and

---

[52] Martin Walser, "Das Fremdwort der Saison," in ibid. 54, 126, Gerhard Schoenberger, "Zerstörung der Demokratie," in ibid. 143.

[53] Ralf Dahrendorf, "Die stille Revolution," in DuMont, ed., *Woher—Wohin?*, 87.

[54] Jens Hacke, *Philosophie der Bürgerlichkeit. Die liberalkonservative Begründung der Bundesrepublik* (Göttingen: Vandenhoeck & Ruprecht, 2006).

external criticism of the Federal Republic overlapped. But left-wing critics aligned themselves against East Germany by arguing that conservatives were actually doing "the Ulbricht regime's bidding" by making the Federal Republic "half or completely fascist."[55] In most cases, the criticism of the Federal Republic did not go along with any sympathy for the "other Germany" across the Iron Curtain, certainly not after the building of the Berlin Wall in August 1961.[56] From the perspective of only 15 years' distance from the Third Reich and based on an often biographical experience of persecution during the Nazi regime, these fears of an authoritarian transformation were quite plausible, even though they minimized the undeniable differences between the Weimar and the Federal Republic. Still, the "paradigm scenario" of the collapse of Weimar informed anxiety-ridden anticipations of West Germany's future. Genuine democratic fears inspired left-liberals' perception of being on the verge of a new authoritarianism or, as Jürgen Habermas described it in 1958, a creeping "Hispanicization" of the Federal Republic.[57]

Such democratic fears also derived from the perception of the continuity of mental and ideological attitudes throughout 1945, especially among young people who were central to the future of the Republic. Whereas sociologist Helmut Schelsky had described German youth as a "skeptical generation" with little inclination toward authoritarianism, a study by the Frankfurt Institute of Social Research regarding the political attitudes of university students in the Federal Republic of the late 1950s found that two-thirds of the interviewed students lacked a firm commitment to the democratic order. Even more worrisome, the study concluded that, in the case of a political crisis, fewer than 10 per cent of students believed they would actively resist a gradual descent of the Federal Republic into an authoritarianism. Contrary to the intense politicization of students only a few years later, observers during the late 1950s diagnosed political passivity and anti-democratic tendencies especially among students from academic and middle-class backgrounds. While the Frankfurt study did not make any predictions regarding the future behavior of the large majority of "passive" students in a political crisis, it clearly confirmed widespread and extensive doubts regarding the depth of West German democratization ten years after the founding of the Federal Republic.[58]

---

[55] Hans Werner Richter, "Von Links in der Mitte," in Walser, ed., *Die Alternative*, 119.

[56] For a largely polemical discussion of intellectuals' reaction to the building of the wall, see Joachim Scholtyseck, "Mauerbau und Deutsche Frage. Westdeutsche Intellektuelle und der Kalte Krieg," in Dominik Geppert, Jens Hacke, eds, *Streit um den Staat Intellektuelle Debatten in der Bundesrepublik, 1960–1980* (Göttingen: Vandenhoeck & Ruprecht, 2008), 69–90.

[57] Cited in Moses, *German Intellectuals and the Nazi Past*, 184.

[58] Ludwig von Friedeburg, Jürgen Habermas, Christoph Oehler, Friedrich Welz, *Student und Politik. Eine soziologische Untersuchung zum politischen Bewußtsein Frankfurter Studenten* (Berlin: Luchterhand, 1969 [1961]), 145, 231–5, Helmut Schelsky, *Die skeptische Generation. Eine Soziologie der deutschen Jugend* (Cologne: Diederichs, 1957).

The Return of the Nazi Past

The return of the Nazi past from the late 1950s onward fueled and amplified such democratic fears. The second half of the 1950s witnessed the end of the political consensus that sought to undo the results of Allied denazification policies, especially by re-hiring former Nazis into the West German civil service. An essentially defensive politics of memory, focused on re-integrating former Nazis into postwar West German society, came to an end.[59] Debates over the continuity of West German judges complicit in Nazi crimes, the extension of the statute of limitation for Nazi crimes, the resurgence of the legal prosecution of Nazi perpetrators culminating in the Frankfurt Auschwitz trial (1963–5), and a wave of antisemitic graffiti in several German towns brought about the return of the Nazi past to the West German public sphere.

The return of the Nazi past did not result from foreign pressure but emerged from within West German society, partly as a result of generational dynamics. The arrival of the "45ers"—that is, individuals for whom the collapse of Nazism represented their key biographical experience—in leading positions in society and politics certainly played an important role. The return of the last prisoners of war in 1955–6 created a sense of a completed national body that may have made a real reckoning seem possible. The gradual relaxation of Cold War tensions from 1962–3, in the aftermath of the Berlin and Cuba crises onward, facilitated a more expansive memory as well. It is important to emphasize, however, that West German commemorative culture did not simply evolve progressively toward an inclusive and more critical memory of the Nazi past. The demand for a more extensive and more critical confrontation with the past came from a small political and cultural elite. The population at large favored a "final stroke"—that is, an end to the confrontation with the Nazi past.[60] This considerable divergence between popular and published opinion with respect to the Nazi past further enhanced liberal and leftist intellectuals' concerns regarding the West Germans' capability for democracy. The majority of the population engaged in the construction of a variety of defensive mechanisms that sought to contain the potential emotional and political impact of the Nazi past. Both fears of an apologetic popular attitude among intellectuals *and* fears of the incriminating implications of a renewed attention to the past among the population at large defined the emotional connotations of the return of the Nazi past. In both cases, more memory did not entail more security and more democracy, as psychoanalysis would have

---

[59] Norbert Frei, *Vergangenheitspolitik: Die Anfänge der Bundesrepublik und die NS-Vergangenheit* (Munich: C.H.Beck, 1997).

[60] Detlef Siegfried, "Zwischen Aufarbeitung und Schlußstrich. Der Umgang mit der NS-Vergangenheit in den beiden deutschen Staaten 1958 bis 1969," in Karl Christian Lammers, Detlef Siegfried, Axel Schildt, eds, *Dynamische Zeiten. Die 60er Jahren in den beiden deutschen Gesellschaften* (Hamburg: Hamburger Edition, 2000), 83.

it, but rather increased already existing doubts and anxieties regarding the democratic stability of the Federal Republic. While the automation debate had brought the uncertainty of the future in industrial modernity into focus, the return of the Nazi past prompted a similar insecurity with respect to West Germany's democratic future.

Vicious propaganda attacks starting in 1957 from East Germany reinforced and complicated an already existing self-critical West German discourse. They denounced West German judges who had served during the Nazi period as "blood judges" and alleged the Federal Republic was ideologically continuous with the Third Reich. While West German government officials tended to dismiss these accusations as mere Communist propaganda, individual commentators began to pay closer attention to the compromised Nazi past of West German judges, especially their service in the *Reichsjustizministerium* (Ministry of Justice) during the war or, for that matter, their role in presiding over terroristic death sentences for relatively minor infractions during the closing stages of the regime. In the fall of 1959, an exhibition on "Nazi justice" by the Socialist German Student Association (SDS) opened in Karlsruhe, the site of the West German constitutional court. Its organizers questioned the viability of the rule of law in West Germany given that former Nazi judges remained in office and had suffered no legal consequences for their actions in the Third Reich.[61] The popular West German movie, *Rosen für den Staatsanwalt* (1959), also picked up the theme of a compromised judiciary. In response to such public pressures, the West German government passed a law that would allow potentially compromised judges to retire voluntarily and with their full pension rights. By June 1962, 135 judges had done so. Still, the increased public sensitivity regarding West German judges' Nazi past led to a series of scandals in the early 1960s. The highest West German public prosecutor, *Generalbundesanwalt* Wolfgang Fränkel, had to resign in July 1962 following the release of evidence that largely originated from East Germany demonstrating that he had imposed 35 death sentences for minor infractions during the Nazi regime. West German officials had clearly been aware of Fränkel's past yet nevertheless appointed him to one of the highest offices within the West German legal system.[62] Even conservatives like *Stern* editor Henri Nannen, who had professed earlier that he did not want "to hear any more about the crimes of the Nazis," found this and other cases scandalous. He wondered in "what kind of state we live" if "highly compromised judges and prosecutors continued to practice."[63]

---

[61] "Keine unbekannten Hintermänner," *Frankfurter Allgemeine Zeitung*, November 30, 1959.

[62] Marc von Miquel, *Ahnden oder Amnestieren? Westdeutsche Justiz und Vergangenheitspolitik in den sechziger Jahren* (Göttingen: Wallstein, 2004), 97.

[63] Henri Nannen, "Liebe Sternleser," *Stern* 15/31 (1962): 5–6, 18. *Stern* published evidence that judges who had advanced to high judicial positions in the Federal Republic had sentenced a pregnant Polish worker, 21-year-old Anna Jozefowicz, to death for stealing some clothes while pregnant.

Whereas the scandals relating to West German judges called into question the democratic substance of central institutions of the West German state, antisemitic incidents of the late 1950s raised questions regarding the democratic sensibilities of the population. On the occasion of the twentieth anniversary of *Kristallnacht*, the Protestant theologian Helmut Gollwitzer called for "critical alertness" to "avoid a repetition," signaling a concern that proved reasonable when the Jewish proprietor of a café in a small town in Hesse reported what the *Frankfurter Rundschau* termed a "delayed Kristallnacht in the countryside" with attacks and broken windows a few weeks later.[64] In January 1959, the *Frankfurter Neue Presse* concluded that the "number of antisemitic incidents is increasing" after reports of a swastika on the synagogue in Düsseldorf.[65] What made these incidents even more troublesome was the perception that West German authorities—and West German courts in particular—were slow to respond. In 1959, a series of incidents reported in the West German press pointed to a lingering antisemitism: the escape to Egypt of the former concentration camp doctor from Buchenwald, Hans Eisele, his trial still pending; openly antisemitic statements by a high school teacher in Offenburg; and a businessman in Hamburg's publication of a viciously antisemitic brochure. Even rumors of Jewish ritual murder resurfaced in a small town in Franconia in January 1959.[66] These cases appeared as manifestations of latent antisemitism in the West German population of unknown depth and prevalence.[67] To be sure, as the journalist Klaus Harpprecht cautioned, the West German "alarm system" regarding antisemitism was "more sensitive" than elsewhere in Europe and Germans might be overreacting. He diagnosed a gradually declining antisemitism, especially among young people.[68] In their letters to the editor, however, several readers challenged Harpprecht's optimistic conclusions, arguing that "latent," "hidden," or "unconscious" antisemitism was more difficult to address than the open form might be, and that it remained below the radar of the well-functioning political alarm system.[69] The Social Democrat member of the *Bundestag*, Ulrich Lohmar, agreed and supported plans for a traveling exhibition on the "problem of antisemitism" that was supposed to be aimed especially

---

[64] "Noch heute lebt der Ungeist in unserer Welt. Verspätete 'Kristallnacht' auf dem Lande. Antisemitische Clique terrorisiert Cafe-Inhaber in Köppen," *Frankfurter Rundschau*, December 20, 1958.

[65] "Hakenkreuz an Synagoge: Antijüdische Aktionen häufen sich," *Frankfurter Neue Presse*, January 19, 1959.

[66] "Ungesühnter Kindesmord nach 'Stürmer' Art: Antisemitisches Kuckucksei in einer Nürnberger Abendzeitung erregt scharfe Proteste," *Frankfurter Rundschau*, January 28, 1959.

[67] Hans Gathmann, "Der latente Antisemitismus," *Die Politische Meinung: Monatshefte für Fragen der Zeiten* 4/34 (1959): 61–72.

[68] Klaus Harpprecht, "Im Keller der Gefühle," *Der Monat* (1959): 13–20.

[69] Erich Lüth, Anelene v. Caprivi, Wolfgang Stiebler in "Briefe des Monats. Deutscher Antisemitismus Heute. Stimmen zu Klaus Harpprechts Aufsatz 'Im Keller der Gefühle,'" *Der Monat*, June 1959, 78–92.

at young people.[70] As with the automation debate, those who sought to prevent the resurgence of antisemitism focused on education. These measures reveal the considerable hope among the cultural and political elites that the new generation, which had grown up under conditions of democracy, would be bearers of new democratic ideals—as well as their perception of the older generation as hopelessly infected by the anti-democratic ideals of the Third Reich.

Given these pre-existing sensibilities, it is not surprising that critics reacted with shock and anxiety to a renewed wave of antisemitic incidents in late 1959 and early 1960. On Christmas Eve in December 1959, two members of a neo-Nazi Party defaced the synagogue in Cologne with antisemitic graffiti. While press reports labeled this incident the "second crystal night of Cologne," the 470 similar attacks in the following weeks increased the fears of resurgent antisemitism. Observers abroad described the series of attacks as a signal that the Federal Republic had not succeeded in distancing itself from the Third Reich. Public officials in West Germany tended to dismiss these incidents either as deliberately engineered by the East German secret police or as the work of misguided and essentially apolitical young people.[71] Intellectuals disagreed and described these incidents as revealing the failure of the educational system in teaching about the Nazi past and in combating antisemitic stereotypes. Walter Jacobson, a psychologist working for the Federal Agency for Civic Education, argued that the:

> antidemocratic and nationalistic attitude of many Germans bears the character of something inborn, hereditary and is thus deeply rooted. It cannot be overcome quickly through rational enlightenment, pedagogy, or arguments, nor, for that matter, through silencing. Rather, it requires long and steady educational labor.[72]

Jacobson used the slogan of "Hitler within us" to articulate his thesis of a deep-seated antisemitism and authoritarianism.

Antisemitic incidents revealed a considerable gap between the increasingly self-critical discourse of cultural elites and the attitudes of a broad mass of the population. In an opinion poll, only 13 per cent of Germans saw the hundreds of antisemitic incidents as a revival of National Socialism. Forty per cent called it the work of misguided youth and 32 per cent believed the Communist East had

---

[70] Ulrich Lohmar, "Die Barbaren sind unter uns," *Berliner Stimme*, January 10, 1959.

[71] Siegfried, "Zwischen Aufarbeitung und Schlußstrich," 81–4, Annette Weinke, "'Bleiben die Mörder unter uns?' Öffentliche Reaktionen auf die Gründung und Tätigkeit der Zentralen Stelle Ludwigsburg," in Jörg Osterloh, Clemens Vollnhals, eds, *NS-Prozess und deutsche Öffentlichkeit. Besatzungszeit, frühe Bundesrepublik und DDR* (Göttingen: Vandenhoeck & Ruprecht, 2011), 265.

[72] Cited in Siegfried, "Zwischen Aufarbeitung und Schlußstrich," 84. On Jacobson, see also Maik Tändler, *Das therapeutische Jahrzehnt. Der Psychoboom in den siebziger Jahren* (Göttingen: Wallstein, 2016), 202–3.

engineered the events.[73] This complacency stoked the fears of cultural observers. In his essay "What is the Meaning of Coming to Terms with the Past?" from 1959, the philosopher Theodor Adorno described lingering "after-effects of National Socialism *within* democracy" as more dangerous than the "neo-fascism that is openly directed *against* democracy." For Adorno, "democracy" had not been sufficiently established to cause citizens to see themselves as "subjects of the political processes." He saw antisemitism as denoting the persistence of authoritarian dispositions within West German society.[74] This link between popular antisemitism and anti-democracy also became the subject of an empirical study by the Frankfurt Institute for Social Research on the popular reaction to the antisemitic incidents in 1959. Based on 232 interviews in January 1960, it confirmed the existence of a subterranean or latent antisemitism among at least 40 per cent of the respondents while only 19 per cent articulated a "decisive and clear rejection of antisemitic attitudes and opinion," an awareness of their "political significance," and "alarm."[75] These and other studies of the Frankfurt Institute thus provided empirical evidence for the fears and anxieties regarding the democratic substance of the Federal Republic.

The study was also important regarding a shifting understanding of the political function of fear: it explicitly linked fear of popular antisemitism to a pro-democratic and anti-authoritarian attitude. This finding reflected the important role of the Frankfurt School in re-evaluating fear as a purely negative emotion and in yoking the emotion of fear with a defense of West German democracy. In his essay "Education after Auschwitz" from 1966, the Adorno made the point explicitly: he argued that "education should take seriously an idea that is not foreign to philosophy: that fear should not be repressed." According to him, "if one allowed oneself to have as much fear as the reality deserves, then some of the destructive impact of unconscious and displaced fear would disappear."[76] The antisemitic incidents thus brought into focus a new political alarm system that defined, at least among an intellectual elite, fear of authoritarian tendencies as a contribution to the democratization of the Federal Republic.

A similar discrepancy between published and public opinion shaped West German reactions to a series of Nazi trials in the late 1950s and early 1960s. If the antisemitic incidents of the late 1950s and early 1960s raised questions about the persistence of fascist attitudes within West German democracy, the renewed legal prosecution of Nazi crimes from the late 1950s onward revealed that actual Nazi

[73] Siegfried, "Zwischen Aufarbeitung und Schlußstrich," 83.
[74] Theodor W. Adorno, "Was Aufarbeitung der Vergangenheit?" in Theodor W. Adorno, ed., *Erziehung zur Mündigkeit. Vorträge und Gespräche mit Hellmut Becker. Herausgegeben von Gerd Kadelbach* (Frankfurt: Suhrkamp, 1970), 10–29, here 10–11. The text was first published in November 1959 and then also became the subject of a radio broadcast in February 1960.
[75] Peter Schönbach, *Reaktionen auf die antisemitische Welle im Winter 1959/60* (Frankfurt a/M: Europäische Verlagsanstalt, 1961), 82–3.
[76] "Erziehung nach Auschwitz," in Adorno, *Erziehung zur Mündigkeit*, 92–109, here 101.

perpetrators had remained present in West German society. A series of spectacular and highly publicized trials, from the Ulm *Einsatzgruppen* trial in 1958 to the Eichmann trial in Jerusalem in 1960–1 and finally the Frankfurt Auschwitz trial in 1963–5, returned the Nazi past to the West German public sphere. These trials indicated the failure of past efforts to come to terms with the past and exposed the inaccuracy of statements such as West German Minister of Justice Fritz Schäffer's 1960 claim that all legal matters relating to National Socialism had been sufficiently resolved.[77] Commentators such as the critical journalist Ernst Müller-Meiningen instead now referenced the title of Wolfgang Staudte's 1946 movie, saying the "murderers are still among us."[78] The founding of the Central Agency for the Prosecution of Nazi Crimes in Ludwigsburg in 1958 reflected this new recognition.[79]

Public and popular reactions to Nazi trials were deeply ambivalent. On the one hand, they inflated left and liberal intellectuals' pre-existing democratic fears. On the other hand, they triggered a series of new defensive strategies that sought to manage and contain their potentially disturbing implications. Shrewd contemporary observers like the journalist Klaus Harpprecht identified this psychological mechanism as it occurred. Writing in 1965, he argued that it was the "fear of one's own implication" that produced the "defense gestures" with respect to the Nazi trials.[80] Similar to the emotional management with respect to nuclear fears in the context of civil defense, public and popular reactions to the Nazi trials displayed a series of mechanisms to create distance from the potentially unsettling implications of the return of the past. The Nazi past became an object of emotional management, which sought to limit the emotional resonance of the trials.

This emotional management manifested itself in the trial proceedings as well. Judges and prosecutors tried very hard to avoid the impression of a political show trial and sought to proceed in a distinctly detached and rational manner. The press portrayed the presiding judge in the Auschwitz trial, Hans Hofmeyer, as a "fanatic of sobriety."[81] But this attitude also meant that judges and prosecutors

---

[77] Clemens Vollnhals, "'Über Auschwitz wächst kein Gras.' Die Verjährungsdebatten im Deutschen Bundestag," in Osterloh and Vollnhals, eds, *NS-Prozesse und deutsche Öffentlichkeit*, 380.

[78] P.J. Winters, "Die Mörder sind noch unter uns," *Ansätze: Eine Semesterzeitschrift der Evangelischen Studentengemeinde in Deutschland* 28 (1962): 20–1, Ernst Müller-Meiningen, "Noch sind die Mörder unter uns," *Süddeutsche Zeitung*, July 11, 1958, cited in Claudia Fröhlich, "Der 'Ulmer Einsatzgruppen-Prozess' 1958. Wahrnehmung und Wirkung des ersten großen Holocaust Prozesses," in Osterloh and Vollnhals, eds, *NS-Prozesse und deutsche Öffentlichkeit*, 252, Fritz Bauer, "Die Mörder sind unter uns," *Stimme der Gemeinde: Zum kirchlichen Leben, zur Politik, Wirtschaft, und Kultur* 10/22 (1958): 789–92.

[79] Weinke, "'Bleiben die Mörder unter uns?'" However, the first director of the agency, Erwin Schüle, was a former National Socialist who needed to resign in 1966 because of his compromised past.

[80] Klaus Harpprecht, "Die Deutschen und die Juden," *Neue Gesellschaft* 12 (1965): 709, Habbo Knoch, *Die Tat als Bild. Fotografien des Holocaust in der deutschen Erinnerungskultur* (Hamburg: Hamburger Edition, 2001), 881.

[81] Georg Wamhof, "Gerichtskultur und NS-Vergangenheit. Performativität—Narrativität—Medialität," in Georg Wamhof, ed., *Das Gericht als Tribunal oder: Wie der NS-Vergangenheit der Prozess gemacht wurde* (Göttingen: Wallstein, 2009), 25.

deemed the accounts of Jewish eyewitnesses who expressed overwhelming emotion in testifying to Nazi crimes as unreliable precisely because of their alleged emotionality.[82] A similar ethics of sobriety defined the conduct of non-Jewish professional historians who were asked to provide expert testimony for the Auschwitz trial. All of them highlighted their emotional detachment and rationality, which supposedly reflected their ability to master the subject in a professional manner. By contrast, these historians tended to dismiss the perspective of Jewish historians as distorted and unreliable due to excessive emotions.[83] Legal and historical experts thus cultivated an ethics of emotional detachment toward the Nazi past, which they contrasted with the emotional investment and potential irrationality of Holocaust victims.

Another way to contain the emotional impact of the trials derived from the nature of German law and its application for the prosecution of Nazi perpetrators. The emphasis on individual agency and the subjective disposition of the defendants made it difficult to bring the structural and organizational element of genocide into judicial focus. The trials thus prosecuted Nazi crimes largely as a series of unrelated individual acts of atrocity.[84] Partly out of fear of conducting a politicized show trial, West German judges resisted the attempt of prosecutor Fritz Bauer to treat crimes at Auschwitz as a "unitary complex" where mere presence already constituted judicial guilt. Instead, they prosecuted Nazi perpetrators based on the statute of criminal law that required evidence of "base motives" for murder convictions. If they could not prove such motives, they convicted defendants as "accessories to murder." This also included the large majority of "desk perpetrators"—that is, individuals who were involved in the bureaucratic organization of the genocide but had not personally murdered anyone. The relatively low sentences in Nazi trials that resulted from this "accessory justice" (*Gehilfenjudikatur*)[85] suggested that only a small group of (by then mostly dead) Nazi leaders—Hitler, Himmler, Heydrich—were true perpetrators. Everybody else became an "accessory" to murder.

By turning these crimes into isolated acts of atrocity rather than systemic genocide, the trials severely limited and distorted the Nazi past and shaped the perception of Nazi perpetrators in West German popular consciousness.[86] Two

---

[82]   See Devin O. Pendas, *The Frankfurt Auschwitz Trial, 1963–65. Genocide, History, and the Limits of Law* (Cambridge: Cambridge University Press, 2006), 238.

[83]   Nicolas Berg, *Der Holocaust und die westdeutschen Historiker* (Göttingen: Wallstein, 2003).

[84]   Pendas, *The Frankfurt Auschwitz Trial*, Rebecca Wittmann, *Beyond Justice: The Auschwitz Trial* (Cambridge: Harvard University Press, 2005).

[85]   On this term, see Fröhlich, "Der 'Ulmer Einsatzgruppen-Prozess' 1958," 261.

[86]   Recent research has focused strongly on the impact of the trials on West German public opinion: see Pendas, *The Frankfurt Auschwitz Trial*, Wittmann, *Beyond Justice*, Peter Krause, *Der Eichmann-Prozeß in der deutschen Presse* (Frankfurt a/M: Campus, 2002), Marc von Miquel, "Explanation, Dissociation, Apologia: The Debate over the Criminal Prosecution of Nazi Crimes in the 1960s," in Philipp Gassert, Alan Steinweis, eds, *Coping with the Nazi Past. West German Debates on Nazism and Generational Conflict, 1955–1975* (New York: Berghahn Books, 2006), 50–63, Sabine Horn,

distinct images of Nazi perpetrators emerged from the trials in the late 1950s and early 1960s: on the one hand, perpetrators who followed orders, bureaucratic "desk perpetrators" who administrated the persecution of the Jews without ideological conviction; on the other hand, sadists and inhuman torturers with pathological personality structures who took pleasure in abusing innocent victims.[87] Both of these perpetrator representations entailed potentially disturbing implications for the state of West German democracy. Yet both of them also prompted defensive responses from the West German public and hence enabled the West German population to distance themselves emotionally from the Nazi trials.

The Eichmann trial produced the idea of "desk perpetrators." It took place in Jerusalem from April to December 1961.[88] Several German observers expressed the view of Eichmann as a mindless bureaucrat that Hannah Arendt would later popularize. For example, the psychoanalyst Horst-Eberhard Richter pointed out that Eichmann's character was far from extraordinary: he was an "ordinary, diligent, and subservient normal citizen."[89] Writing in *Die Zeit*, Robert Pendorf called Eichmann's portrayal as a "robot of terror" "much more disturbing" than the idea that he was a "sadist" or "brutal executioner."[90] It raised the question of individual responsibility in modernity. In his introduction to the autobiography of Rudolf Höß, the former commandant of Auschwitz, in 1958, which largely reproduced Höß's self-representation as merely executing orders without ideological investment, the historian Martin Broszat had anticipated this portrayal of Nazi perpetrators and articulated its disturbing implications. According to Broszat, Höß's autobiography demonstrated that "mass murder does not have to go along with personal cruelty, devilish sadism, brutality or so-called 'animal-like nature'" but only a "robot-like sense of duty." What characterized Höß's text was the "apathetic" and "penetrant sobriety," a "hygienic mass murder" which made it possible to "kill thousands of people" without having the feeling of "committing murder."[91] Here it was the absence of emotions that enabled perpetrators like Höß to carry out their horrific work.

Erinnerungsbilder: Auschwitz Prozess und Majdanek Prozess im westdeutschen Fernsehen (Essen: Klartext, 2009), Osterloh and Vollnhals, eds, *NS-Prozesse und deutsche Öffentlichkeit*; Wamhof, ed., *Das Gericht als Tribunal.*

[87] The literature on perpetrators is significant and growing. For the best survey on the evolution of perpetrator historiography, see Gerhard Paul, "Von Psychopathen, Technokraten des Terrors und 'ganz gewöhnlichen' Deutschen. Die Täter der Shoah im Spiegel der Forschung," in Gerhard Paul, ed., *Die Täter der Shoah. Fanatische Nationalsozialisten oder ganz normale Deutsche?* (Göttingen: Wallstein Verlag, 2002), 13–90.

[88] On the significance of the Eichmann trial for the emergence of witness testimony, see Annette Wieviorka, *The Era of the Witness* (Ithaca: Cornell University Press, 2006).

[89] Cited in Paul, "Von Psychopathen, Technokraten des Terrors und 'ganz gewöhnlichen' Deutschen," 21.

[90] Robert Pendorf, "Weil ich Treue geschworen hatte . . . ," *Die Zeit*, July 21, 1961, also cited in Habbo Knoch, "The Return of the Images. Photographs of Nazi Crimes and the West German Public in the 'Long 1960s,'" in Gassert and Steinweis, eds, *Coping with the Nazi Past*, 39.

[91] Martin Broszat, "Einleitung," in Martin Broszat ed., *Kommandant in Auschwitz. Autobiographische Aufzeichnungen des Rudolf Höß* (Stuttgart: Deutsche Verlags-Anstalt, 1958), 14–15, 16,

The representation of Nazi perpetrators as ordinary people without obvious pathologies clearly had disturbing implications. It not only explained why many Nazi perpetrators might still live undetected in West German society but also located complicity among Nazi crimes within the daily mechanisms of modern industrial society.[92] In his 1964 essay, "Us, Sons of Eichmann" (*Wir Eichmannsöhne*), the philosopher Günther Anders (and ex-husband of Hannah Arendt) related this perpetrator image—with rather obvious debts to his teacher Martin Heidegger—to the increasing "machinelikeness of a world" (*Maschinenhaftigkeit*). Anders depicted Eichmann as representative of a modern world devoid of individual responsibility due to the excessive division of labor. Since human beings no longer saw the end results of their actions, they could not feel a sense of moral agency. Eichmann's role in the "final solution" thus appeared as a precursor of a "machinelike totalitarianism," a possible "technical totalitarian empire" which closely resembled the "monstrosity" of the Third Reich.[93] Anders's publication highlighted the disturbing potential of the Eichmann trials for anticipating modern technocratic totalitarianism, which Anders deemed as a more dangerous and more universal threat than "political totalitarianism." His publication also illustrated the extent to which the discourse on Nazi perpetrators overlapped significantly with broader concerns about the role of the individual and the potentially negative consequences of accelerated modernization, as they had also defined the automation debate during the late 1950s and early 1960s. This confluence of anxieties contributed to the larger perception of this period as a crisis decade. The realization of the destructive, even genocidal, potential of modernity sensitized West German intellectual observers to the potentially negative consequences of technological progress and industrial modernization, probably more so than other industrially advanced societies did. Even if only indirectly or implicitly, shifting reflections on the German past shaped anticipations of West Germany's modern future at every turn.

Yet the (self-)representation of Eichmann as a small cog in a monstrous bureaucratic wheel also enabled crucial distancing mechanisms and hence constituted a new "discourse of avoidance."[94] As in the case of Höß and Eichmann, this representation often reproduced the perpetrators' own apologetic self-depictions, which sought to obscure their ideological commitment, often with the clear strategic intent to disprove the legally significant "base motives" for their actions. It also led to an overtly sanitized image of the Holocaust as a clean and "industrial"

18, 20. See also Knoch, *Die Tat als Bild*, 641–6, and Berg, *Der Holocaust und die westdeutschen Historiker*, 580–7.

[92] Knoch, *Die Tat als Bild*, 674. Knoch sees the representation of Eichmann as a Nazi perpetrator as a "turning point" in the evolution of West German perpetrator images.
[93] Günther Anders, *Wir Eichmannsöhne* (Munich: C.H.Beck, 1964), 48–56, 60.
[94] Paul, "Von Psychopathen, Technokraten des Terrors und 'ganz gewöhnlichen' Deutschen," 20.

murder that downplayed the important role of face-to-face violence in genocide. The ascendancy of the structural-functionalist approach to explaining the Holocaust during the 1960s was ultimately also part of this distancing mechanism. For all the important and undeniable insights that this approach yielded with respect to the bureaucratic organization of the genocide, it ultimately failed to explain either the motives of the perpetrators or the identity of the victims.[95] As such, this approach reflected some of the limitations of the judicial confrontation with the Nazi past in which everybody became an "accessory."

The representation of perpetrators emanating from the Frankfurt Auschwitz trial of December 1963 to October 1965 reflected a similar ambivalence. Perhaps in response to the potentially more unsettling depiction of Eichmann as an "ordinary German," perpetrator representations emanating from the Auschwitz trial reverted to a more traditional picture as brutal torturers and pathological sadists. This depiction was rooted in the parameters of West German law, which emphasized the subjective dimension and individual agency of the defendants as a precondition for conviction and in order to avoid the lesser charge of "accomplice." Much of the German press reproduced this legal emphasis on the pathology of the perpetrators as "embodiment of pure metaphysical evil"—"monsters," "demons," "devils," "beasts," "barbarians."[96] These labels reproduced the vocabulary that West Germans had previously deployed to characterize "others," such as recruiters for the Legion or Communist agitators. But now these terms were applied not to individuals in the service of foreign powers but rather to former Nazi perpetrators who had lived undetected within West German society. The threat to West German democracy now came from within.

Yet the image of the perpetrator as monster or sadist contained its own apologetic dimensions, which contemporary critics already identified. Writing in 1965, the author Martin Walser castigated the ways in which horrific examples of individual atrocities produced "our distance from Auschwitz." As a "collection of subjective brutalities," the trial encouraged ordinary Germans to think that "I am not like them" and hence made it possible to "soon forget Auschwitz again." According to Walser, the trial obscured the fact that "these perpetrators were, up to a point, similar to us between 1918 and 1945."[97] The Auschwitz trial largely confirmed this critique. Its emphasis on pathological individuals distorted the reality of systematic genocide. The trial suggested that "the Holocaust was caused by the deviant motives of a few sadistic individuals, and that torture, not genocide, was the most important characteristic of Auschwitz."[98]

The trials nevertheless also had a disruptive potential for the postwar period. For example, the realization that the alleged pathological defendants at Auschwitz

---

[95] Berg, *Der Holocaust und die westdeutschen Historiker*, 530–88.
[96] Quoted in Pendas, *The Frankfurt Auschwitz Trial*, 287.
[97] Martin Walser, "Unser Auschwitz," *Kursbuch* 1 (1965): 189–200, here 196.
[98] Pendas, *The Frankfurt Auschwitz Trial*, 287.

Figure 5.1. Defendants at the Frankfurt Auschwitz trial, 1963–5.

The Frankfurt Auschwitz trial (1963–5) heightened anxieties about authoritarian undercurrents and the depths of postwar democratization. It portrayed defendants as sadistic torturers and thus created distance from the majority of West Germans.

Source: bpk-Bildagentur, No. 30015296.

had actually succeeded in leading seemingly normal bourgeois lives after 1945 was deeply disturbing to many West Germans. One participant in the Darmstadt conversations in 1965 thus argued that the Auschwitz trial had produced a "necessary fear" in postwar Germany.[99] Just as commentators had argued that "democracy" also constituted a way of life, they now sought to find the origins of fascism in the perpetrators' private lives. Journalists went to interview the wife of one of the most incriminated defendants of the Auschwitz trial, Wilhelm Boger. Boger had been convicted to life in prison for, among other things, inventing the torture method termed "the Boger whip," one of most brutal torture methods at Auschwitz. How Boger had transformed from a sadistic perpetrator before 1945 to a well-adjusted citizen after 1945 remained puzzling. Most commentators did not question the broader social and political conditions that enabled former perpetrators to submerge within postwar society after 1945. At the same time, these stories promoted what Gerhard Paul termed the "anthropologization of the

---

[99] Kurt Ballerstedt, *Darmstädter Gespräch 1963. Angst und Hoffnung in unserer Zeit* (Darmstadt: Neue Darmstädter Verlagsgesellschaft, 1965), 133–4.

problem." They defined the perpetrators' adjustment to postwar society as a private rather than a political and societal problem.[100]

The return of the Nazi past promoted the shift from the social to the psychological sciences as primary tools for the (self-)observation and critique of West German society.[101] The potential sources of anti-democratic and authoritarian tendencies were no longer just located within externally visible social and political structures but appeared to be located within individual selves. The Nazi trials thus fueled a concern with a hidden, invisible Nazi perpetrator whose pathological self nevertheless posed a severe danger to postwar democracy. While the Frankfurt School had identified the "authoritarian personality" as a precondition for fascism already in the 1940s, the Nazi trials provided empirical evidence for its continued existence and possible negative impact on West German society.[102] The return of the Nazi past thus fueled an important cultural transformation in the diagnosis of the sources of anxiety: away from larger social and political structures toward the (interior) psychological make-up of the self.

This shift in social diagnosis also produced a critical view of the mental and ideological disposition of the majority of West Germans, who did not seem to be very much inclined to confront the Nazi past. Public opinion surveys pointed to a growing divergence between published and popular opinion. Popular support for the trials declined considerably. In 1958, 58 per cent of West Germans approved of the Ulm *Einsatzgruppen* trial, whereas only 34 per cent opposed further Nazi trials. In 1961, only 15 per cent of West Germans opposed the Eichmann trials. By contrast, in 1965, at the high point of the Auschwitz trial, 54 per cent of West Germans opposed further trials. According to another survey, 40 per cent of West Germans displayed considerable indifference and did not follow the highly publicized Auschwitz trial in any media.[103] These numbers suggest that West Germans might have realized the potentially destabilizing impact of Nazi trials and increasingly opposed them because of it. They also demonstrate a significant discrepancy between public opinion and media coverage, which was largely supportive of the trials. The Auschwitz trial, it is worth emphasizing, took place *against* the preferences and the interests of the majority of West Germans.[104] Hannah Arendt described the obvious lack of a guilty conscience among the defendants, as well as their long period of living in West German society undetected, as an indication

---

[100] Horn, *Erinnerungsbilder*, 154–61, Paul, "Von Psychopathen, Technokraten des Terrors und 'ganz gewöhnlichen' Deutschen."

[101] Nolte, "Von der Gesellschaftsstruktur zur Seelenverfassung," in Tobias Freimüller, ed., *Psychoanalyse und Protest. Alexander Mitscherlich und die Achtundsechziger* (Göttingen: Wallstein, 2008), 70–94.

[102] See the German translation of the original English version published in 1950: Theodor W. Adorno, *Studien zum autoritären Charakter* (Frankfurt a/M: Suhrkamp, 1973).

[103] Fröhlich, "Der 'Ulmer Einsatzgruppen-Prozess' 1958," 258, Pendas, *The Frankfurt Auschwitz Trial*, 252–4.

[104] Knoch, *Die Tat als Bild*, 880, Weinke, "'Bleiben die Mörder unter uns?'" 272.

that these perpetrators were in implicit agreement with the West German population.[105]

Another study by the Frankfurt Institute for Social Research highlighted defensive popular responses to the trials, which had therefore failed to ignite a more extensive confrontation with the Nazi past. A "lack of political judgment" among the population thus reduced potential resistance in West German society to "authoritarian forces threatening democracy." The study thus came to the conclusion that the "psychosocial disposition of the population" made a return to an "authoritarian regime" more likely than the further development of the Federal Republic toward a "social democracy."[106] Contrary to the assumption that the Auschwitz trial marked a crucial step in a linear history of West German democratization, it actually stimulated fears and anxieties regarding the democratic substance of West German society. As a result, West German confrontations with the Nazi past inside and outside the courtrooms engaged in significant efforts to contain and manage the emotionally destabilizing effects of the trials. The Nazi trials thus stimulated democratic fears rather than containing them.

Alexander and Margarete Mitscherlich's 1967 study, *The Inability to Mourn*, confirmed and synthesized the already existing widespread perception of a deficient confrontation with the past.[107] It also reflected the ongoing turn toward psychological analysis in explaining the threats to democracy within German society and within individual subjects. Contrary to later misunderstandings, the Mitscherlichs did not criticize West Germans' lack of mourning for Nazi victims but rather bemoaned West Germans' failure to mourn the loss of Hitler as their love object. Rather than mourning appropriately the loss of their narcissistic investments in their *Führer* and suffering the corresponding depletion of their self-worth, Germans misdirected their emotional energies into the work of economic reconstruction and postwar consumerism. Because of the absence of what they deemed to be appropriate emotional responses to the collapse of the Third Reich—guilt, shame, mourning—West Germans exhibited a "striking emotional rigidity" or a lack of "empathy."[108] They therefore failed to develop the emotions that would enable them to function as autonomous democratic citizens.

As several later critics have persuasively shown, this argument entailed a series of fundamental flaws: it projected psychoanalytic insights from the individual to the collective of West German society, and it engaged in a strong posture of moral condemnation that was at odds with the therapeutic imperative for empathy. The

---

[105] Hannah Arendt, "Der Auschwitz Prozess," in Eike Geisel, Klaus Bittermann, eds, *Hannah Arendt. Nach Auschwitz. Essays und Kommentare, Band 1* (Berlin: Klaus Bitterman, 1989), here 100–2.
[106] Regina Schmidt, Egon Becker, *Reaktionen auf politische Vorgänge. Drei Meinungsstudien aus der Bundesrepublik* (Frankfurt a/M: Europäische Verlagsanstalt, 1967), 123–6, 140.
[107] Alexander und Margaret Mitscherlich, *Die Unfähigkeit zu trauern. Grundlagen kollektiven Verhaltens* (Munich: Piper, 1967).
[108] Ibid. 79.

Mitscherlichs explained the deficits in coming to terms with the past as the result of a virtually inevitable and biologically determined psychological mechanism. At the same time, they promised a final "overcoming" of the past through successful and correct mourning. They also posited a series of normative emotions that were allegedly conducive to a democratic society while failing to acknowledge their own emotional reaction to what they deemed to be the psychological failure of their fellow citizens.[109]

Yet the book nevertheless became a bestseller and its title acquired the quality of a much cited and rarely questioned slogan. The success of the book derived not from the originality of its analysis but rather because it succeeded in synthesizing and crystallizing an already existing left-liberal critique of West German society as it had emerged from the late 1950s onward.[110] In other words, *The Inability to Mourn* constituted a culmination point of the increasing articulation of democratic fears as analyzed earlier, even though Mitscherlich himself did not want his concern for West German democracy to be seen as indication of an "anxiety-ridden pessimism."[111] The critique of a widespread "ego weakness" fitted well with the turn toward the subject as the site of societal pathologies. Like many previous critics, the Mitscherlichs identified psychological structures that they deemed to be incompatible with democracy, especially a weak subject that might be prone to authoritarian temptations or antisemitism as a specific form of psychopathology. They too increasingly located the main impediments to further democratization, not in sociological or political structures but rather in the collective mentality and individual psychology of West Germans. As one reviewer, Gerhard Sycyesny in *Der Spiegel*, noted, the book demonstrated that the "democratization of democracy is not a political but rather an individual-psychological and pedagogical problem."[112] At the same time, the Mitscherlichs promoted certain kinds of emotional expression as conducive to democracy and hence moved away from the postwar emphasis on emotional restraint. They diagnosed Germans with "deficient empathy" and a "lacking affect culture," which they blamed for the bloodlessness of West German democracy.[113] In so doing, they subverted the previous emphasis on emotional restraint as a basis of democracy. The Mitscherlichs were transitory figures between two postwar emotional regimes. They continued to hold on to a skepticism toward certain emotions as well as to the notion that

---

[109] On the reception and critique, see Parkinson, *An Emotional State*, 113–45, Tobias Freimüller, *Alexander Mitscherlich. Gesellschaftsdiagnose und Psychoanalyse nach Hitler* (Göttingen: Wallstein Verlag, 2007), 303–25, Tändler, *Das therapeutische Jahrzehnt*, 206–14.

[110] Freimüller, ed., *Alexander Mitscherlich*, 303, 314–20.

[111] Mitscherlich and Mitscherlich, *Die Unfähigkeit zu trauern*, 7.

[112] Gerhard Sycyesny, "Guter Rat für Dutschke," *Der Spiegel* 22/2 (1968): 76.

[113] Mitscherlich, in Hellmut Becker, *Hemmen Tabus die Demokratisierung der deutschen Gesellschaft? Bergedorfer Gesprächskreis zu Fragen der freien industriellen Gesellschaft* (Hamburg: R. v. Decker's Verlag, 1965), 10, 31, 36.

fascism had been a product of excessive emotions and irrationalism.[114] But they also emphasized the significance of emotions for democracy and thus pointed to a future politics of subjectivity and emotions in the student movement.

The Emergency Laws and the Future of the Republic

The broader perception of a crisis of democracy and the potentially destabilizing challenges of a return of the Nazi past coalesced in the debate about the emergency laws between 1965 and 1968. The protest against the emergency laws marked an important moment in the long-term transformation of political fears in the Federal Republic: whereas earlier fears had largely centered on a weak, even impotent state that had appeared incapable of protecting its citizens from the occupation authorities, recruiters to the Foreign Legion, or nuclear war, West German liberal and leftist critics now began to fear a too-strong and potentially authoritarian state. As one of the critics noted, "while emergency laws seek to counter dangers from below (the people, rebellions, strikes) and external dangers (military threats), the real threat emanates from above, from the misuse of power by the government."[115] In the long run, democratic fears of an authoritarian state sensitized West Germans to potential threats to democracy and hence strengthened rather than undermined democracy. Yet these fears should also not be reduced to their eventual long-term impact. At the time, contemporaries experienced them as real and plausible scenarios for the future.

The aim of the emergency laws was to replace the special emergency rights that had remained with the Western Allies after the Federal Republic had become a sovereign state in May 1955. The emergency laws were supposed to enable the West German government to restrict basic democratic rights in the case of a domestic or external emergency. Since some of these laws necessitated a change in the West German constitution, they required a two-thirds majority in the federal parliament, which was unobtainable because of the opposition of the Social Democrats. However, with the SPD's entry into a Grand Coalition in December 1966, this situation had changed. A modified version of the emergency laws, which included many, though not all, of the changes that the SPD had demanded, was eventually passed by a two-thirds majority in the federal parliament in May 1968.[116]

---

[114] Parkinson, *An Emotional State*, 144–5.

[115] Walter Schlenker, *Warum wir die Notstandsgesetze ablehnen* (Stuttgart: Kirchliche Bruderschaft, 1968), 41. See also Christian Schletter, *Grabgesang der Demokratie. Die Debatten über das Scheitern der bundesdeutschen Demokratie von 1965 bis 1985* (Göttingen: Vandenhoeck & Ruprecht, 2015), 231–41.

[116] The key text for the history of the emergency laws is Michael Schneider, *Demokratie in Gefahr? Der Konflikt um die Notstandsgesetze: Sozialdemokratie, Gewerkschaften und intellektueller Protest (1958–1968)* (Bonn: Dietz Verlag J.H.W. Nachf., 1986). See also Maren Krohn, *Die gesellschaftliche Auseinandersetzung um die Notstandsgesetze* (Cologne: Pahl-Rugenstein, 1981).

The debate over the emergency laws during the 1960s prompted a broad opposition movement of intellectuals, academics, students, and trade unionists. It functioned as one of the key incubators of the student movement and of the extra-parliamentary opposition. In retrospect, the intensity and alarmism of this debate have puzzled historians, who have called the reaction "difficult to understand," "excessive" (*hypertroph*), and even identified a "ridiculous political paranoia."[117] Such pathologizing language reflects a failure to properly historicize strong emotions. The analysis here does not seek to determine whether the anxieties of the critics of the emergency laws were justified but rather places them in the context of broader democratic fears that emerged from the late 1950s onward and then stood in constant dialectical interaction with parallel conservative fears. The emotional force of the protests against the emergency laws derived from a deeply skeptical horizon of expectation regarding the democratic future of the Federal Republic, which the Nazi trials intensified even further. For the critics, the emergency laws constituted a culmination point in what they perceived as the gradual authoritarian transformation of the Federal Republic. As one of the most outspoken critics, the constitutional law professor Helmut Ridder, described them, the laws "represented the last or the penultimate step of a decline" of West German democracy.[118]

The first organized protest against the emergency laws occurred in May 1965 at the University of Bonn, where students and intellectuals formed a *Kuratorium Notstand der Demokratie*, which henceforth organized and coordinated the protest movement.[119] The event brought together both principled opponents of the laws as well as those critics who merely opposed the version of the laws that was currently debated in the *Bundestag*.[120] The protest later fractured along those lines. What united the critics, however, was a basic lack of trust in the capacity or the willingness of West German officials to promote the process of inner democratization. They saw a "transitory generation" comprising civil servants and officials whose formative experiences had occurred in the Nazi period, who lacked a strong attachment to the democracy, and who were bent on containing or

---

[117] Axel Schildt, quoted in Boris Spernol, *Notstand der Demokratie. Der Protest gegen die Notstandsgesetze und die Frage der NS-Vergangenheit* (Essen: Klartext, 2008), 89, Schneider, *Demokratie in Gefahr?*, 279, Wolfgang Kraushaar, "Die Furcht vor einem neuen '33'. Protest gegen die Notstandsgesetzgebung," in Geppert and Hacke, eds, *Streit um den Staat*, 147. Similarly critical, Eckart Conze, *Die Suche nach Sicherheit. Eine Geschichte der Bundesrepublik Deutschland von 1949 bis in die Gegenwart* (Berlin: Siedler, 2009), 378–80, Manfred Görtemaker, *Geschichte der Bundesrepublik Deutschland. Von der Gründung bis zur Gegenwart* (Frankfurt a/M: Fischer, 2004), 453–7. Wolfram criticizes the depictions of the protesters merely as "quixotic warners against a false alarm": see Wolfrum, *Geglückte Demokratie*, 236; more balanced, also Herbert, *Geschichte Deutschlands*, 845–8.

[118] Helmut Ridder, "Rede 1," *Demokratie vor dem Notstand. Protokoll des Bonner Kongresses gegen die Notstandsgesetze am 30. Mai 1965* (Frankfurt a/M: Verlag Neue Kritik, 1965), 80.

[119] Schneider, *Demokratie in Gefahr?*, 137.

[120] See, for example, Thomas Ellwein, "Die Befristung des Ausnahmezustands," in *Demokratie vor dem Notstand*, 29–32.

reversing West Germany's democratic gains since 1945.[121] Even as proposals for the emergency laws softened between 1960 and 1968, opponents such as the historian Karl Dietrich Bracher feared a West German bureaucracy that subscribed to "authoritarian and military-technological ideas" that the emergency laws would empower.[122] At the 1965 meeting, a representative of the Interior Ministry pleaded for "trust" in the actions of the government. Yet, critics argued that distrust represented the most important requirement for democratic citizenship.

Memories of the German past, especially of the collapse of the Weimar Republic, formed an ever-present background for the critics of the emergency laws.[123] In an article in *Der Spiegel*, Bracher pointed out the "unfinished" and "uncertain" nature of West German democracy. A period of slowed-down economic growth and a sudden increase in votes for the neo-Nazi "National Democratic Party (NPD)" in several regional elections in 1966–8 appeared as signals that "Bonn" might become "Weimar" after all.[124] As the debate progressed and culminated in the protests against the laws in May 1968, the democratic fears of the critics centered on three areas: restrictions on the free press and free speech; limitations of the right of the parliament at the expense of the executive; and restrictions of the right to strike.

The limitations of the public sphere were already part of the planning of the emergency laws. According to critics such as the law professor Werner Maihofer, key agreements regarding the emergency laws were forged in secrecy and behind closed doors.[125] Critics saw this procedure as part and parcel of a larger attempt to shield the actions of the federal government from public scrutiny, especially with respect to national security. The *Spiegel* affair in 1962, in which the federal government arrested several journalists, including the editor Rudolf Augstein, and occupied the facilities of the Hamburg magazine for allegedly betraying confidential national security information, stoked these fears. While the affair ultimately ended without legal consequences for *Der Spiegel*, it resulted in the resignation of the main instigator of the affair, Defense Minister Franz Josef Strauß.[126] Historians commonly portray the *Spiegel* affair as reflecting a "push toward liberalization" and as a key indicator of the emergence of an increasingly critical public sphere.[127] Yet this focus on the long-term consequences of the affair obscures the considerable contemporary anxieties that the government's

---

[121] Werner Maihofer, "Die Demokratie vor dem Notstand," in ibid. 9, 11.

[122] Karl Dietrich Bracher, "Parlamentarische Demokratie und Staatastreich," in ibid. 23.

[123] Spernol, *Notstand der Demokratie*, Schletter, *Grabgesang der Demokratie*, 237–9.

[124] Karl Dietrich Bracher, "Wird Bonn doch Weimar?" *Der Spiegel* 21/13 (1967), Moses, *German Intellectuals and the Nazi Past*, 185. Between 1966 and 1969, the NPD gained close to 10 per cent of the vote in several regional elections: see Eckhard Jesse, "Das Auf und Ab der NPD," *Aus Politik und Zeitgeschichte* 42 (2005): 31–8.

[125] Werner Maihofer, "Die Demokratie vor dem Notstand," in *Demokratie vor dem Notstand*, 7–18.

[126] Wolfrum, *Geglückte Demokratie*, 209–11, Görtemaker, *Geschichte der Bundesrepublik*, 381–6.

[127] Conze, *Die Suche nach Sicherheit*, 275.

Figure 5.2. Demonstration against the passage of the emergency laws, Frankfurt, May 1968.

Democratic fears of a possible authoritarian transformation drove protest against the emergency laws in 1968. The banners protest against the "NS laws" and equate them with "fascism."

Source: bpk-Bildagentur, No. 30040571.

actions produced. Indeed, it brought out the "virtually apocalyptic panic with which contemporaries viewed the future of Bonn democracy." Conservatives, in turn, saw the liberal critique of the state as the real problem. They were alarmed by the clumsy actions of the government, which seemed to undermine the authority of the state.[128]

The discovery and public discussion of secret provisions for the case of a national emergency that the Interior Ministry had passed on to regional and local administrations before the actual passage of the emergency laws further increased popular suspicions regarding the government's intentions. Termed the "special laws kept in reserve" (*Schubladengesetze*), the publication of these provisions in East Germany illustrated the West German government's willingness to rely on a not fully democratized bureaucracy in order to limit basic constitutional rights. Contemporary observers interpreted these provisions as well as the secrecy with which they were disseminated as indicative of official attempts at stopping or even reversing the process of inner democratization.[129] As we know now, these

[128] Ute Daniel, *Beziehungsgeschichten. Politik und Medien im 20. Jahrhundert* (Hamburg: Hamburger Edition, 2018), 245, 255–70.

[129] Gerhard G. Gründler, "Die Bürokraten proben den Notstand," *Frankfurter Hefte* 21/9 (1966): 597–608, Krohn, *Die gesellschaftliche Auseinandersetzung*, 148–50.

concerns were not unfounded. In the absence of emergency laws, civil servants within the Interior Ministry had developed a series of emergency decrees that all but abolished the constitutional order of the Federal Republic. Based on their own experience during the Nazi period, they planned the domestic use of the West German military as well as the internment of ill-defined "enemies of the state" in special "camps." While some of these ideas encountered opposition from within the Interior Ministry, they nevertheless pointed to a persistent authoritarian tradition within the state bureaucracy.[130]

Another central issue in the debate over the emergency laws was the relationship between parliament and the executive. Critics worried that restrictions of parliamentary rights during an emergency would lead to a gradual transformation of the Federal Republic into an authoritarian state. The example of Article 48 of the Weimar constitution loomed large in these scenarios: as in Weimar, the argument went, the possibility of an emergency law with limited parliamentary rights entailed the possibility of exploitation by anti-democratic forces, even if the drafters had not intended it. Karl Dietrich Bracher argued that emergency clauses had "produce[d] the danger that they are claiming to prevent" in Weimar.[131] For critics, the possibility to limit essential democratic rights through an emergency clause was worrisome because of the still-fluid nature of West German democratization. On the one hand, they recognized an ongoing process of democratization because of the support of a younger generation and an increasingly critical press. On the other hand, they saw countervailing forces, latent and subterranean undemocratic and anti-democratic forces that could still reverse this process.[132] A left-wing critic like the law professor Helmut Ridder saw the "emergency laws" as the "final stage" of a "political development" that would signal the "end of the current Bonn system" and transform the Federal Republic into a "technologically highly functional," yet no longer democratically sanctioned, authoritarian system. Opponents of the emergency laws did not so much fear a return to a fascist dictatorship of 1933 but rather a "limited" or "coordinated" authoritarian democracy like Franco's Spain or Salazar's Portugal.[133] The military coup in Greece in April 1967 provided another example of a possible authoritarian transformation and demonstrated the possibility of reversing past democratic gains.

---

[130] Martin Diebel, *"Die Stunde der Exekutive." Das Bundesinnenministerium und die Notstandsgesetze 1949–1968* (Göttingen: Wallstein, 2019), 100–20.

[131] Bracher, "Parlamentarische Demokratie und Staatsstreich," in *Demokratie vor dem Notstand*, 7–18.

[132] Maihöfer, "Die Demokratie vor dem Notstand," in ibid. 10.

[133] Helmut Ridder, "1933 findet nicht statt. Über Inhalt und Funktion deutscher Notstandsgesetzgebung am 'Ende der Nachkriegszeit'," in *Vorbereitung auf den Notstand. 10 Antworten auf eine aktuelle Frage* (Frankfurt a/M: Fischer, 1967), 77–89. See also "Es geht so dunkel und trickreich zu. Analyse und Kritik der Notstandsgesetze," *Der Spiegel* 22/24 (1968): 30–4. On Ridder, see also Spernol, *Notstand der Demokratie*, 61–7.

Other fears concerned who could declare a "state of emergency" in West Germany and when. Here, the opposition movement resisted the long tradition in German constitutional law associated with Carl Schmitt, who had defined sovereignty as the ability to declare a state of emergency. Bracher argued that the executive should not have sole power to declare a state of emergency because it would expand its own power by doing so. Rather, it should require a two-thirds majority in parliament. Critics were not primarily concerned about a possible state of emergency in the case of an open military conflict. They worried much more about the invocation of a "state of emergency" in the case of more low-level "looming threat," "increased tensions," or to improve "military preparedness."[134] Such vague categories, critics argued, would lend themselves to abuse in order to achieve not only external security but also domestic political goals—for example, repressing a protest movement like the extra-parliamentary opposition.

Trade unions were especially concerned about the possibility of limiting the right to strike through the emergency laws, especially during an ill-defined moment of "tension."[135] Trade union critics cited the unions' general strike in response to the Kapp putsch of 1920 as historical evidence of the potential role of strikes in saving democracy. Given these historical experiences, unions claimed to know the source of threats to democracy.[136] Unlike in the debate over civil defense during the late 1950s, the focus of political fears shifted from "external" to "internal" dangers. A brochure the metal trade union *IG Metall* published, for example, criticized civil defense measures not because of their potential inadequacy, as earlier critics had done, but rather as a barely concealed vehicle for the militarization and authoritarian transformation of the Federal Republic.[137] Rather than Cold War tensions per se, which had declined anyway, political anxieties centered on the possibility that such tensions would be (mis)used to effect a domestic political transformation in an authoritarian direction. At a TV discussion one day before the final passage of the emergency laws, the psychoanalyst Alexander Mitscherlich explicitly criticized the view that "dangers emanated from external threats" and instead highlighted "dangers that emanate from our state," which for him necessitated a "permanent readiness for resistance."[138]

Nobody articulated an essentially pessimistic view of the future of the Federal Republic more comprehensively than the philosopher Karl Jaspers. The title of his 1965 essay "Where is the Federal Republic Drifting?" (*Wohin treibt die Bundesrepublik?*) suggested a quasi-natural move into a more authoritarian

---

[134] Bracher, "Parlamentarische Demokratie und Staatsstreich," 23.
[135] Otto Brenner, *Wir brauchen keine Notstandsgesetze. Rede und Materialien* (Berlin: Verlag Voltaire, n.d. [1966]).
[136] Georg Benz, "Rede 2," in *Demokratie vor dem Notstand*, 83.
[137] Fritz Opitz, *Notstandsgesetze. Notstand der Demokratie* (Frankfurt a/M: Union Druckerei, n.d.).
[138] "Es geht so dunkel und trickreich zu," *Der Spiegel* 22/24 (1968): 30; also cited in Spernol, *Notstand der Demokratie*, 86.

direction that only conscious and explicit resistance could halt.[139] Jaspers's essay synthesized many of the fears of the critics of West German democracy that eventually culminated in the opposition to the emergency laws. Writing in 1965, Jaspers identified the "awareness of approaching a catastrophe" as the "dark background" of "feeling of life" in the Federal Republic. "It is possible," he argued, "to compare the current situation with the one in the 1920s before Hitler's seizure of power."[140] For Jaspers, the presence of former Nazis in West German society constituted a severe burden for West German democracy—the first two sections of his book actually dealt with the debate over the extension of the statute of limitations for Nazi crimes, which he strongly supported. Yet Jaspers also saw many troubling symptoms in West Germany at that time. Like many critics, he saw West German democracy limited to a merely "external institutional one" not an "internal democracy" that the "thinking of its citizens" reflected.[141] Not unlike conservative critics, Jaspers worried especially about the important role of political parties who were transformed from "organs of the people" to "organs of the state."[142] Jaspers feared not a repetition of the Nazi dictatorship but a gradual and "barely noticeable" transformation into a party oligarchy and eventually an authoritarian militaristic dictatorship.[143] Like other critics, Jaspers located the main dangers facing West German democracy not in external but internal forces. Not outspoken neo-Nazis but the inherent authoritarian tendencies *within* the West German state constituted the most dangerous threat to West German democracy.[144]

This is also why Jaspers identified the emergency laws as the most important instrument in the authoritarian transformation of the Federal Republic. He saw them, not unlike the enabling law of 1933 that gave Hitler dictatorial power, as a pseudo-legal path toward the establishment of a "partly oligarchy" and a "military dictatorship" that would subordinate public life to the requirements of military preparedness for a possible nuclear catastrophe.[145] Against the background of this convergence of external and internal threats, Jaspers pleaded for the political significance of fear. Following Martin Heidegger's terminology," Jaspers pleaded for a broader "concern [*Sorge*], which does not exhaust itself in fear" that should be at the basis of public and private life. The emotion of fear allowed for a privileged epistemological position that allowed "a true recognition of realities" and was "indispensable to find paths to peace."[146] Jaspers's analysis of the political significance of fear reflected an important shift in the emotional regime of the Federal Republic: from the privileging of an ethics of sobriety and the containment of

---

[139] On Jaspers and the debate about this book, see also Moses, *German Intellectuals and the Nazi Past*, 179–82.
[140] Karl Jaspers, *Wohin treibt die Bundesrepublik?* (Munich: Piper, 1965), 171.   [141] Ibid. 128.
[142] Ibid. 133.   [143] Ibid. 172–5.   [144] Ibid. 155.
[145] Ibid. 157–70, quotations on 157, 169.
[146] Ibid. 170–1.

emotions in public to the mobilization of fear as a higher form of rationality and as enabling a privileged epistemological position.

As someone who was known to have opposed the Nazi regime, Jaspers had a receptive audience in West Germany. His critique and his negative anticipation of the Federal Republic's future resonated broadly and was highly compatible with the opposition to the emergency laws. The participation of well-known antifascists, such as Wolfang Abendroth, and of Jewish intellectuals returning from emigration during the Nazi period to the Federal Republic, such as Theodor Adorno and Ernst Bloch, lent the protest against the emergency laws antifascist credentials. A younger generation of protesters saw themselves and their activism in the continuity of the resistance against (a new) fascism. Conversely, the compromised Nazi past of proponents of the emergency laws—Interior Minister Gerhard Schröder had been a member of the National Socialist German Workers' Party (NSDAP), and the Chancellor of the Grand Coalition, Kurt Georg Kiesinger, had occupied a leading position in the Foreign Office—provided additional credibility to this belated antifascist resistance. However, the protest against the emergency laws reduced alleged continuities from the Third Reich to the Federal Republic to individual biographies and neglected the discontinuities with respect to the political system and the wider context.[147] That said, some important intellectuals took exception to the content of Jaspers's pessimistic assessment of the future of the republic as well as to his celebration of a new emotional politics. Leftist critics like Jürgen Habermas and the SPD politician Erhard Eppler, while agreeing with Jaspers's rejection of the emergency laws as well as his warning of a possible authoritarian transformation, distanced themselves from Jaspers's criticism of political parties, which they identified as a remnant of an anti-liberal, essentially conservative tradition. Liberal critics like Ralf Dahrendorf and the political scientist Kurt Sontheimer also rejected Jaspers's dire predictions regarding the future of West German democracy, which Sontheimer described as a "well functioning mass democracy . . . with all the problems that democratic institutions have elsewhere" yet "undeniable authoritarian-restorative tendencies."[148]

The debate over the emergency laws was significant for several reasons. For one, it broadened the coalition of those groups who expressed democratic fears vis-à-vis the state. The opposition to the emergency laws included liberal critics, the emerging student movement, sections of the trade unions, and even some representatives of the Christian churches.[149] It was a crystallization point for the formation of an extra-parliamentary opposition, especially after the formation of the Grand Coalition between the SPD and CDU/CSU in December 1966. While the trade unions, and especially *IG Metall* and its chairman, Otto Brenner, were

---

[147] On these points, see Kraushaar, "Die Furcht vor einem neuen '33'," 147–8.
[148] Moses, *German Intellectuals and the Nazi Past*, 180–1.
[149] For the latter, see Schlenker, *Warum wir die Notstandsgesetze ablehnen.*

among the most outspoken opponents of the emergency laws, the alliance between intellectuals and students, on the one hand, and the West German labor movement, on the other, eventually splintered. In particular, the labor unions were not willing to engage in a general political strike against the emergency laws as an increasingly radicalized student movement had demanded. Shortly before the passage of the final version of the laws in May 1968, the APO (extra-parliamentary opposition) and trade unions organized separate protest demonstrations against the laws. The coalition between students, intellectuals, and the labor movement thus fractured earlier than across the border in France where mass strikes accompanied student demonstrations in May 1968.[150] Still, the opposition to the emergency laws provided a focal point for articulating democratic fears regarding the West German state. It also constituted a delayed debate over the nature of West German democracy, in which both sides articulated competing visions of postwar democracy.[151]

Conservative fears of a non-passage of the emergency laws reflected a mirror image of left and liberal fears. Conservative proponents of the emergency laws such as the CSU politician Karl Freiherr von und zu Guttenberg arrived at a fundamentally different perception of the state of West German democratization. Whereas critics of the laws saw West German democracy as fragile and as under constant threat to revert to authoritarianism, he identified "a solidly democratic attitude of the German public and its political groups."[152] Conservatives saw the emergency laws as a necessary safeguard of democracy against a possible Communist threat, which, they feared, the critics underestimated.[153] They also began to see persistent opposition to the emergency laws, especially as the laws began to take into consideration some of the critics' concerns, as a pretext for a more fundamental opposition to the system of parliamentary democracy. Some liberal critics like Karl Dietrich Bracher later joined this view.

Significantly, proponents of the law, such as Guttenberg, began to use a distinctly different emotional style in advocating for the law. He criticized the emotional intensity of the protest movement ("euphoria" and "big demonstrations")as irrational and pleaded for "sober discussion"—that is, he defended the emotional regime of the early postwar period.[154] A growing emotional chasm thus undergirded political conflict in West Germany from the mid 1960s to the 1980s: whereas state representatives and political elites displayed a self-professed rationality and sobriety, protest movements celebrated increasing emotional intensity,

---

[150] On the gradual withdrawal of the trade unions, see Schneider, *Demokratie in Gefahr*, and Krohn, *Die gesellschaftliche Auseinandersetzung*.

[151] Herbert, *Geschichte Deutschlands*, 847.

[152] Karl Theodor Freiherr von und zu Guttenberg, in *Vorbereitung auf den Notstand. 10 Antworten auf eine aktuelle Frage*, 34, Schletter, *Grabgesang der Demokratie*, 241–7.

[153] Ibid. 245.

[154] Freiherr von und zu Guttenberg, in *Vorbereitung auf den Notstand*, 47.

and fear especially, as the basis of a new authenticity and a privileged epistemological position. In terms of content, the conflict over the emergency laws inaugurated a political dialectics in which left-wing fears of a threat to democracy became the basis of corresponding right-wing fears and vice versa. In both emotional style and content, the debate over the emergency laws prefigured the political discourse of the Federal Republic into the 1980s.

Social Democrats took a middle position in this debate. They rejected the CDU-led initiatives for "emergency laws" between 1960 and 1965 as inappropriate and threatening. They acknowledged the "deep pessimism" of many critics of the emergency laws as "honorable," a reasonable reaction to their memory of the Nazi dictatorship.[155] But in order to demonstrate the SPD's ability to govern, they also portrayed themselves as open to the emergency laws, so long as the CDU/CSU was willing to negotiate their content. The final set of laws that passed in May 1968 differed significantly from the initial CDU proposals. The definition of an "emergency situation" was gradual, from mere "tensions" to an "internal emergency" to "war." Alleviating concerns over the possible misuse of the emergency laws in domestic political conflicts, a two-thirds majority of the *Bundestag* had to declare the first step of "tensions." A "Common Committee" of members of both houses of parliament replaced the full parliament only in the case of war; otherwise the parliament was to remain in session. The right to strike and a right to resistance against threats to the democratic order became part of the emergency laws. At the same time, some aspects of the initial proposal, such as the ability to deploy the *Bundeswehr* in a domestic context as well as the lack of any temporal limitation for a declared state of emergency, remained part of the final version of the emergency laws.[156] Some strong opponents of the emergency laws, such as Karl Dietrich Bracher, nonetheless considered the concessions sufficient. And indeed, the final version differed significantly from the earlier proposals or from the secret emergency decrees circulating within the Interior Ministry during the late 1950s and early 1960s. Democratic fears, as they were articulated by the protests against the emergency laws, thus ultimately contributed to the limitation of state authority and hence to a strengthening of the idea of the rule of law. To this day, the emergency laws have never been used, in part because democratic fears created significant legal barriers to put them into practice.[157]

Still, while the opposition movement succeeded in significantly softening the emergency laws that ultimately gained the required majority in the *Bundestag*, a segment of the protest movement was no longer satisfied with piecemeal reforms and became increasingly alienated from the West German political mainstream,

---

[155] Quotation from Georg Leber, "Notstandsgesetzgebung und Gewerkschaften," in *Vorbereitung auf den Notstand*, 66.
[156] Spernol, *Notstand der Demokratie*, 87.
[157] This is also the conclusion in Diebel, "*Die Stunde der Exekutive*," 198–9.

including the trade unions. This was also reflected in the rhetorical escalation of the struggle against the emergency laws: whereas critics in 1965 warned against the "danger of a *coup d'état* from above," the "NS laws" (NS-G), as they were increasingly called, eventually became an indication for the "fascist subversion" of the Federal Republic.[158] Protest flyers against the laws invoked the Nazi past by proclaiming "One 1933 is enough," or, with reference to the military coup in Greece, "No Athens in Bonn."[159] The rhetorical escalation was a product of the perception of an increasingly authoritarian, violent, and transgressive state. While the descent into authoritarianism appeared as a worrisome future scenario for liberal critics, it increasingly assumed the status of an already existing reality for the emerging New Left in 1967–8. The fracturing of the left-liberal alliance revolved around divergent perceptions of the Federal Republic: whereas liberals continued to believe in the possibility of reform and further democratization, the New Left began to perceive the West German state exclusively as an agent of repression.[160] Their solution no longer consisted of reform but of revolution. Democratic fears increasingly gave way to revolutionary fears.

Revolutionary fears also manifested themselves in a different style of protest. In response to the passage of the emergency laws, Hans Magnus Enzensberger called for an emulation of the "Paris May"—that is, the huge demonstrations of workers and students against the de Gaule government, and the creation of "French conditions" in Germany.[161] Along similar lines, the SDS saw the "NS laws" as the "legalization of a long practiced form of repression" and called for more "offensive forms of resistance" against what increasingly appeared as a "fascistoid" or "fascist" state.[162] The New Left thus advocated a more voluntarist, subjective, and emotional form of protest against the West German state than many liberal critics were not willing to share or condone. Chapter 6 addresses the New Left's revolutionary fears as well as liberals' and conservatives' fears in response to the New Left.

---

[158] Jürgen Seiffert in *Frankfurter Rundschau*, April 26, 1965, quoted in Schneider, *Demokratie in Gefahr?*, 128, 244.

[159] Quoted in ibid. 250.   [160] Moses, *German Intellectuals and the Nazi Past*, 189–98.

[161] Spernol, *Notstand der Demokratie*, 86.   [162] Schneider, *Demokratie in Gefahr?*, 271–2.

6

Revolutionary *Angst*

The visit of the Shah of Persia and his wife Farah Diba in the early summer of 1967 became a key moment in the history of fear in the Federal Republic.[1] Ever since the Central Intelligence Agency (CIA) coup against the leftist reformer Mossadeq in 1953, the West saw Shah Reza Pahlevi as an important defender against Communism and Soviet expansionism. For the Bonn government, such visits also presented a welcome opportunity to project an image of a stable and functioning democracy to the world while West German business interests perceived Iran as a promising export market. West German officials were concerned, however, that protests by the Persian opposition might undermine the international reputation of the Federal Republic, and they feared for the foreign guests' security, especially in the aftermath of the Kennedy assassination in 1963. An extensive police presence, as well as an unprecedented control and surveillance of Persian opposition members in Germany, thus preceded and accompanied the Shah's visit.

The emerging student movement did not show much interest in the Shah initially. Some activists of the Socialist Student Association (*Sozialistischer Deutscher Studentenbund*, SDS) worried that engaging with the situation in Iran might detract from Vietnam as the focus of the New Left. Still, in the weeks leading up to the visit, students developed a greater sensitivity toward the repressive rule of the Shah, aided largely by the publication of a book by Bahman Nirumand, a Persian exile student, describing Iran as a "model of a developing country."[2] Inspired by Nirumand's book, the activist Peter Schneider designed a "wanted" poster for the Shah for "murder" while the later RAF terrorist Ulrike Meinhof published an "open letter to Farah Diba" in which she contrasted the Shah's life of luxury with the poverty of the majority of the Iranian population. Student protests accompanied the Shah's initial visits to Bonn and Munich. The night before the Shah's visit to West Berlin on June 2, some 2,000 students attended a teach-in on the situation in Iran with Nirumand and other student activists at the Free University in Berlin. Then, after the Shah's arrival in Berlin on June 2, students clashed violently with 20–30 supporters of the Shah in front of the West Berlin

---

[1] Unless otherwise indicated, my account in the next three paragraphs follows the excellent analysis in Eckard Michels, *Schahbesuch 1967. Fanal für die Studentenbewegung* (Berlin: Ch. Links, 2017).

[2] Bahman Nirumand, *Persien, Modell eines Entwicklunglandes oder, Die Diktatur der Freien Welt* (Reinbek: Rowohlt, 1967). On the significance of this book, see Quinn Slobodian, *Foreign Front. Third World Politics in Sixties West Germany* (Durham: Duke University Press, 2012), 106–11.

German Angst: Fear and Democracy in the Federal Republic of Germany. Frank Biess, Oxford University Press (2020).
© Frank Biess.
DOI: 10.1093/oso/9780198714187.001.0001

city hall in Schöneberg. Students took the appearance of the supporters as an indication that state authorities would resort to violence in suppressing their protest. In the perception of student activists, the Shah's visit emerged as a test case for the controversial emergency laws, which, as discussed in the previous chapter, had been a focal point of democratic fears from the mid 1960s onward. The Shah's visit thus became, as student activists eventually called it, a "non-declared emergency."

That same evening, some 1,000–1,500 student protestors gathered again at the West Berlin Opera to demonstrate against the Shah's attendance. They threw smoke bombs, tomatoes, and balloons filled with paint at the Shah, his entourage, and his state hosts, West Berlin mayor Heinrich Albertz and Federal President Heinrich Lübke, as they sought to enter the building. Some two dozen Shah supporters were there as well, creating an even more volatile atmosphere. The police erected a barrier and pushed demonstrators behind it, enabling the visitors to enter. Albertz charged the Berlin police chief Duensing with "clean[ing] up" the situation by the time the performance ended, and the police chief gave the order to "take out the bats" and to follow the tactics that he had described as following: "Let's take the demonstrators as a liver sausage. Then we have to stab it in the middle so that it squirts out at both ends." Frustrated by previous student provocations, police officers began to pursue and beat student demonstrators indiscriminately. One student reported that he tried to talk to a policeman but was quickly thrown to the ground and kicked in the head. When he protested, another policeman reportedly told him, "I will beat you to death if you say one more word."[3] The philosophy student Ulrike Kröger was trying to run away but was clubbed to the ground. She eventually escaped with blood all over her face and was diagnosed a day later with an injury to her kidneys.[4] Six policemen attacked another student, Hans-Rüdiger Minow, and dragged him across the street by his hair. Policemen reportedly called him "Jewish" and "Communist pig."[5] When the demonstrators tried to escape, police resorted to the plan of "fox hunting"—that is, the pursuit of fleeing demonstrators. In this context, police officer Karl-Heinz Kurras fired a shot that killed Benno Ohnesorg, a student of German literature. A photo depicting the dying Ohnesorg and the female student Friederike Dollinger holding his head became an iconic image of the student movement. While Kurras was long seen as the representative of an authoritarian state, it came to light in 2009 that he was actually an agent of the *Stasi*, the East German secret police. It is unlikely, however, that he shot Ohnesorg on East German orders.[6]

The killing of Benno Ohnesorg has been hailed as the "birth of the West German student movement."[7] In the weeks and months after Ohnesorg's death, it

---

[3] Witness 4, Knut Nevermann, *Der 2. Juni 1967. Studenten zwischen Notstand und Demokratie. Dokumente zu den Ereignissen anlässlich des Schah-Besuchs* (Cologne: Pahl Rugenstein, 1967), 14.
[4] Eyewitness report of *Die Zeit* journalist Jürgen Zimmer, ibid. 21.   [5] Ibid. 22.
[6] Norbert Frei, *1968. Jugendrevolte und globaler Protest* (Munich: dtv, 2008), 112–16.
[7] Michels, *Schahbesuch*, 236.

became clear that the student movement had found its first martyr. Student activists crafted a narrative that portrayed the Shah's visit as a test case for the planned emergency laws and as the West German state's deliberate attempt to suppress the extra-parliamentary opposition. The visit, in other words, confirmed and heightened the worst democratic fears that student activists as well as liberal critics had already articulated regarding the planned emergency laws. Students also saw the visit as a case of collusion between an authoritarian Third World dictator, who had come to power with significant American help, and domestic West German elites. The police brutality completed the picture.

To be sure, a majority of West Germans sympathized with the police, and even a majority of West German students remained indifferent or even hostile to the activists' interpretation of the events in Berlin.[8] But activists felt the killing of Benno Ohnesorg had ripped the mask off the face of West German state and society.[9] For them, it illuminated the resentment and hatred of the population at large toward the New Left, which they could only explain as the result of the right-wing Springer press's extensive manipulation. They began to describe the incident as a "pogrom" and the Federal Republic as a "democracy of anger," fearing the re-emergence of the old Nazi "racial community" (*Volksgemeinschaft*) that would aim at the "extinction" of the student movement.[10] They saw themselves as current or potential victims of a barely disguised fascist state and society. They had become, as the SDS executive committee declared on June 6, 1967, the "Jews of anti-Communism."[11]

This chapter does not attempt to provide another comprehensive analysis of "1968" because many already exist.[12] It also does not seek to analyze "1968" as

---

[8] Infas, *Student und Öffentlichkeit. Ein Bericht über die studentische Opposition im Spiegel der öffentlichen Meinung* (Bad Godesberg: Infas, 1968), 29, 37, 41.

[9] "Volkes Stimme" in "2. Juni," *Kursbuch*, April 12 (1968): 151.   [10] Ibid. 136.

[11] "Erklärung des SDS Bundesvorstandes vom 6. Juni," in Nevermann, *Der 2. Juni 1967. Studenten zwischen Notstand und Demokratie*, 97–100, quotation on 97.

[12] For some of the most important works, see Axel Schildt, Detlef Siegfried, Karl Christian Lammers, eds, *Dynamische Zeiten. Die 60er Jahre in den beiden deutschen Gesellschaften* (Hamburg, Hamburger Edition, 2000), Siegward Lönnendonker, Bernd Rabehl, Jochen Staadt, *Die antiautoritäre Revolte. Der Sozialistische Deutsche Studentenbund nach der Trennung von der SPD, Band 1: 1960–7* (Opladen: Westdeutscher Verlag, 2002), Nick Thomas, *Protest Movements in 1960s West Germany. A Social History of Dissent and Democracy* (Oxford: Berg, 2003), Christina von Hodenberg, Detlef Siegfried, eds, *Wo "1968" liegt. Reform und Revolte in der Geschichte der Bundesrepublik* (Göttingen: Vandenhoeck & Ruprecht, 2006), Frei, *1968. Jugendrevolte und globaler Protest*, Detlef Siegfried, *Time Is on My Side. Konsum und Politik in der westdeutschen Jugendkultur der 60er Jahre* (Göttingen: Wallstein, 2006), Wolfgang Kraushaar, *Achtundsechzig. Eine Bilanz* (Berlin: Ullstein, 2008), Gerd Koenen, *Das rote Jahrzehnt. Unsere kleine deutsche Kulturrevolution, 1967–77* (Cologne: Kiepenheuer & Witsch, 2001), Martin Klimke, Joachim Scharloth, eds, *1968 in Europe. A History of Protest and Activism, 1956–1977* (New York: Palgrave Macmillan, 2008), Udo Wengst, ed., *Reform und Revolte. Politischer und gesellschaftlicher Wandel in der Bundesrepublik vor und nach 1968* (Munich: Oldenbourg, 2011), Joachim Scharloth, *1968. Eine Kommunikationsgeschichte* (Munich: Wilhelm Fink, 2011), Anna von der Goltz, ed., *"Talkin' 'bout my generation." Conflict of Generation Building and Europe's "1968"* (Göttingen: Wallstein, 2011), Timothy Scott Brown, *West Germany and the Global Sixties. The Antiauthoritarian Revolt, 1962–1978* (New York: Cambridge, 2013), Ingrid Gilcher-Holtey,

part of the long sixties but focuses more precisely on student activism during the decisive period from 1967 to 1969.[13] "1968" was hardly a unitary phenomenon but rather constitutes a "cipher" that has come to stand for a variety of activists, movements, and concerns. It entailed a neo-Marxist intellectual New Left as well as a broader challenge to traditional lifestyles and values, especially pertaining to sexuality.[14] The chapter focuses on a relatively small group of activists in order to show the emergence of a new emotional regime. It thus underlines the significance of "68" as a rupture in the emotional history of the Federal Republic.[15] The student movement injected emotions into politics and advocated an emotionally more expressive way of life. The "68ers" constituted themselves as a new "emotional community," whose new culture of emotional expressiveness extended into alternative cultures in the 1970s and 1980s, and ultimately percolated into West German majority society at large.[16]

The legacies of 1968 pluralized the range of available emotional styles, celebrated the public display of emotions at least in certain subcultures, and enabled a new significance of emotions within political activism and for individual subjectivities. While student activists deliberately propagated a new emotional regime, older norms of emotional restraint and performative rationality did not disappear and were often re-affirmed as a result of confrontations with the student movement. But the explicit commitment to strong emotions as an essential force for social and emotional change ultimately transformed West German emotional cultures. Emotions and emotional change constitute an important yet often overlooked aspect of the long-term significance of "1968" for the history of the Federal Republic.[17]

This chapter brings into focus the specific role that fear and anxiety played in shaping the political outlooks and subjectivities of student activities. While historians have often emphasized the "boundless optimism" that drove the student movement, my emphasis is on the more pessimistic facets of "1968."[18] Paradoxically, activists' fears and disappointments resulted, in part, from their far-reaching, even utopian, ambitions. The realization of the massive and

---

ed., *"1968"—Eine Wahrnehmungsrevolution? Horizont-Verschiebungen des Politischen in den 1960er und 1970er Jahren* (Munich: Oldenbourg Verlag, 2013), Robert Gildea, James Mark, Anette Warring, eds, *Europe's 1968. Voices of Revolt* (Oxford: Oxford Universty Press, 2013), Christina von Hodenberg, *Das andere Achtundsechzig. Gesellschaftsgeschichte einer Revolte* (Munich: C.H.Beck, 2018).

[13] On this periodization, see Wolfgang Kraushaar, *1968 als Mythos, Chiffre und Zäsur* (Hamburg: Hamburger Edition, 2000), 31, Kraushaar, *Achtundsechzig*, 58.

[14] Kraushaar, *1968 als Mythos, Chiffre und Zäsur*. On the internal differentiation of 1968, see Scharloth, *1968. Eine Kommunikationsgeschichte*, 440–2.

[15] On the wider transatlantic context of this shift, see Frank Biess, Daniel M. Gross, eds, *Science and Emotions after 1945. Transatlantic Perspectives* (Chicago: University of Chicago Press, 2014).

[16] Barbara H. Rosenwein, "Worrying about Emotions in History," *American Historical Review* 107/3 (2002): 821–45.

[17] See also Belinda Davis, "Provokation als Emanzipation. 1968 und die Emotionen," *Vorgänge* 42/4 (2003), 41–9.

[18] Siegfried, *Time Is on My Side*, 754.

powerful forces opposing their political and social visions often produced fear and paranoia. But the attempt to transform the sociopolitical order in and through a transformation of their own selves was so ambitious that it was bound to be disappointed. For many activists, "1968" thus represented an experience of disappointment and disillusionment that is rather at odds with the historiographical emphasis on their positive role in effecting the Federal Republic's progressive liberalization.[19] Yet the life histories of a few prominent activists, such as Peter Schneider and Joschka Fischer, did not represent all of "1968." Instead, as former activist and historian Götz Aly reminds us, many 68ers "lost their bearings, became mentally ill, or committed suicide."[20]

The 68ers' visions of revolutionary transformation also triggered intense anxieties, fears, even panics among their opponents. Liberals like Karl Dietrich Bracher ultimately split with New Left activists over their embrace of emotional intensity, voluntarist direct action, and violence. They perceived the same developments from diametrically opposed perspectives from the radicals: whereas the 68ers saw the Federal Republic as engaged in a transition from a post-fascist to a pre-fascist state that was based on extensive mental, structural, and biographical continuities with the Nazi past, liberal opponents increasingly identified the student movement with the illiberal movements of the Weimar Republic that threatened to destroy the democratic accomplishments of the Federal Republic. While student activists perceived themselves as "new Jews," their opponents saw them as the opposite: a left-wing version of fascism.[21] The dialectic of fear that had already shaped the interplay between democratic fears and fears of democracy in the earlier period intensified further. Revolutionary fears and fears of revolution, the chapter argues, structured the political debate in the West German 1960s and beyond.

Utopia and Paranoia

Dark visions of their present and their future notwithstanding, student activists envisioned a future that was radically different from the West German past. Their utopianism and their paranoia were inextricably intertwined. As the previous chapters have shown, pessimistic scenarios of the future were quite prevalent in the West German 1960s. But, for the 68ers, the future was wide open and

---

[19] As Brown writes, many problems that the protagonists engaged with remain "unresolved": Brown, *West Germany and the Global Sixties*, 10.

[20] Götz Aly, *Unser Kampf 1968* (Frankfurt a/M: S. Fischer, 2008), 207.

[21] Thomas Etzemüller persuasively highlights this dialectic in the mutual perception between the 68ers and their opponents: see Thomas Etzemüller, *1968—Ein Riss in der Geschichte? Gesellschaftlicher Umbruch und 68er-Bewegungen in Westdeutschland und Schweden* (Konstanz: UVK Verlagsgesellschaft, 2005), 143–5.

expansive. Rather than seeing themselves as objects of historical forces they could not control, student activists saw the future as entirely susceptible to their own will. Whereas fears of nuclear war, economic crisis, and democratic decline had prominently shaped the horizon of expectation of liberal and leftist critics, Rudi Dutschke, the widely recognized leader of the West German student movement, publicly envisioned a "world as it has not existed to this day, a world without hunger or war."[22] Indeed, the utopianism of the New Left's future scenario knew virtually no boundaries. In the interview in *Der Spiegel* in July 1967, Dutschke stated that the possibility for "realizing the Garden of Eden, the fantastic realization of the age-old dream of humanity" had "never been closer in history."[23]

The material basis of this utopianism was the accelerated economic development in advanced industrial nations and in West Germany in particular. Student activists did not share the pessimistic or ambivalent attitudes toward technological progress of the late 1950s and early 1960s that the previous chapter described.[24] Dutschke explicitly stated that "technology in itself was not evil" and his fellow activist Christian Semler praised the role of computers in a future council democracy.[25] While the student movement constituted a product of the economic expansion of the postwar period, it also represented a reaction to and critical reflection of this unprecedented boom period.[26] Activists' utopian visions of the future coexisted with the perception that "late capitalism" in the Federal Republic had entered a severe and possibly deadly crisis. The formation of the first Grand Coalition in December 1966, the onset of the first major recession that lasted from the fall of 1966 to the summer of 1967—as well as the rise of the neo-fascist National Democratic Party (NPD), which was represented in seven state parliaments by 1968—all combined to form student activists' perception that the internal contradictions of West German capitalism had intensified and were coming to a head. To student activists, the official Keynesianism as it manifested itself in the "concerted action"—that is, the corporatist cooperation of state authorities, industrialists, and trade unions in combating the recession—represented a continuation of Chancellor Erhard's *formierte Gesellschaft* and hence a further step toward authoritarianism.[27] For Dutschke, the Grand Coalition was the "last desperate attempt to master the structural crisis" [of

---

[22] Rudi Dutschke, "Zu Protokoll," ed. Günter Gaus, https://www.youtube.com/watch?v=U6X-ZeYC54E (last accessed February 22, 2020).

[23] Rudi Dutschke, "Spiegel-Gespräch," *Der Spiegel* 19/29 (1967): 30.

[24] Etzemüller, *1968 - Ein Riss in der Geschichte?*, 81, notes how conservative critiques of mass society, bureaucracy, and alienation by West German intellectuals like Hans Freyer, Arnold Gehlen, and Helmut Schelsky were no longer present in the discourse of the New Left.

[25] "Ein Gespräch über die Zukunft mit Rudi Dutschke, Bernd Rabehl und Christian Semler," *Kursbuch* 14 (1968): 149. Similarly, Hans-Jürgen Krahl, *Konstitution und Klassenkampf. Zur historischen Dialektik von bürgerlicher Emanzipation und proletarischer Revolution. Schriften, Reden, und Entwürfe aus den Jahren 1966–1970* (Frankfurt a/M: Verlag Neue Kritik, 1971), 217–18.

[26] Etzemüller, *1968 - Ein Riss in der Geschichte?*, 15.

[27] Koenen, *Das rote Jahrzehnt*, 186; Krahl, *Konstitution und Klassenkampf.*

capitalism] and served as a "cartel of order to repress the masses."[28] Student activists no longer shared liberals' basic belief in the reformability of the West German political system.

The most pronounced statement of this diagnosis was Johannes Agnoli's text, *The Transformation of Democracy*.[29] Published in 1967 at the height of the debate about the emergency laws, the book was retrospectively labeled the "bible of the extra-parliamentary opposition."[30] Agnoli characterized liberal democracies in West Germany and elsewhere as engaged in a process of "involution," which gradually limited and withdrew democratic rights and eventually transformed them into an "authoritarian state." He argued that constitutional norms did not prevent, but rather enabled, this process. Political institutions—the rule of law, political parties, parliament—did not serve the purpose of articulating the interests of the population but systematically obscured the "inequality of political and economic power" in West Germany. Elections simply replaced one oligarchy with another; seemingly democratic rights like the freedom of the press or petitions to parliament stabilized rather than challenged the system. For Agnoli, there was therefore no inherent possibility within West German liberal democracy of stopping the gradual descent into authoritarianism. Political opposition was limited to marginal sections, especially in cultural life, and faced the threat of open fascism—"exile, prison, annihilation"—if it were to move beyond these narrow realms. This is why there had to be, according to Agnoli, a "fundamental opposition" that did not seek to reform existing institutions but rather abolish them. Violence remained a distinct option for this extra-parliamentary opposition— Agnoli characterized the "Jacobin form of terror" during the French Revolution as a "brief democratic period." While Agnoli's text remains controversial to this day, it provided the emerging student movement with the theory and the language to formulate an extremely pessimistic view of West Germany's democratic future.[31]

---

[28] Rudi Dutschke, "Vom ABC Schützen zum Agenten," in Jürgen Miermeister, ed., *Rudi Dutschke. Geschichte ist machbar. Texte über das herrschende Falsche und die Radikalität des Friedens* (Berlin: Wagenbach, 1980), 100–3, quotation on 100. See also Wolfgang Kraushaar, "Autoritärer Staat und antiautoritäre Bewegung. Zum Organisationsreferat von Rudi Dutschke und Hans-Jürgen Krahl auf der 22. Delegiertenkonferenz des SDS in Frankfurt (September 4–8, 1967)," in Wolfgang Kraushaar, ed., *Frankfurter Schule und Studentenbewegung. Von der Flaschenpost zum Molotowcocktail, 1946-1995. Vol. 3: Aufsätze und Kommentare* (Hamburg: Rogner & Bernhard, 1998), 17–18.

[29] Johannes Agnoli, Peter Brückner, *Die Transformation der Demokratie* (Frankfurt a/M: Europäische Verlagsanstalt, 1968), 10, 11, 41, 55, 85.

[30] Wolfgang Kraushaar, "Agnoli, die APO und der konstitutive Illiberalismus seiner Parlamentarismuskritik," *Zeitschrift für Parlamentsfragen* 38/1 (2007): 164.

[31] Critics see Agnoli's text in the right-wing tradition of Carl Schmitt's critique of parliamentarism. Supporters see it as an example of a critical political science that identifies actual weaknesses of liberal democracies. On the first position, see ibid.; on the second, see Wolf-Dieter Narr, Richard Stöss, "Johannes Agnolis 'Transformation der Demokratie.' Ein Beitrag zur gesellschaftskritischen Politikanalyse," *Zeitschrift für Parlamentsfragen* 38/4 (2007), 828–41. On Agnoli's biography, see Barbara Görres Agnoli, *Johannes Agnoli. Eine biographische Skizze* (Hamburg: Konkret Literatur Verlag, 2004).

The New Left drew on, but also radicalized, the fears regarding the prospects of democracy in the Federal Republic. It also assigned the Nazi past a new significance for diagnosing the alleged pathologies of a West German present. Rather than merely focusing on continuities in personnel from the Nazi to the postwar period, as in the case of compromised judges or university professors, activists increasingly emphasized broader mental and ideological continuities that defined the Federal Republic as a quasi-fascist state. Whereas liberal critics feared an authoritarian transformation in the future, student activists identified an already existing "authoritarian state capitalism" in West Germany.[32] They claimed the Federal Republic was undergoing a transformation from a post- to a pre-fascist society. Indeed, memories of the Third Reich increasingly provided the metaphors and the language to characterize the West German present. The *Kursbuch* described the Ohnesorg assassination as a signal that West German society had "not moved beyond the democracy of Goebbels's people's radio."[33] The failure to prevent the passage of the emergency laws in May 1968 increased the fearful rhetoric. For Hans-Jürgen Krahl, democracy was "finished" in Germany, predicting "open fascism" in the Federal Republic in which the state itself would become the *Führer*.[34] According to Bahman Nirumand, a "reactionary ideology" had constructed 'concentration camps' for the masses."[35] To many activists, the military coup in Greece in December 1967 provided further evidence that "fascism" could "openly come to power" with the help of NATO and the emergency laws.[36] The presence of the Nazi past in the New Left's imagination reflected a deep fear of a "re-emergence of a historical trauma" that West German society had repressed.[37]

The dialectics of utopianism and paranoia implied, however, that exactly this extremely pessimistic, even paranoid, anticipation of an essentially fascist future lay at the heart of revolutionary utopianism. According to Hans-Jürgen Krahl, another leading theorist of the West German New Left, the student movement needed to face a Manichean "world historical" and "universal" alternative of "freedom" or "barbarism." The "lethal crisis of capitalism" could only lead to

---

[32] Rudi Dutschke, "Demokratie, Universität, Gesellschaft," Mai 1967, in Miermeister, ed., *Rudi Dutschke. Geschichte ist machbar*, 73.

[33] "2. Juni," *Kursbuch* 12 (1968): 135–6. Some liberal observers shared this assessment. Sebastian Haffner characterized the assassination of Ohnesorg as an atrocity, which "had been the exception outside of the concentration camps even in the Third Reich"; see Sebastian Haffner, "Die Nacht der langen Knüppel. Der 2. Juni war ein geplanter Pogrom," in Sebastian Haffner, *Zwischen den Kriegen. Essays zur Zeitgeschichte* (Berlin: Verlag 1900, 1997), 298.

[34] "Die Demokratie in Deutschland ist am Ende," in Krahl, *Konstitution und Klassenkampf*, 149–54.

[35] Nirumand, in Sibylle Plogstedt, *Der Kampf des vietnamesischen Volkes und die Globalstrategie des Imperialismus* (Berlin: Berliner Druckgesellschaft, 1968), 62–4.

[36] Hamburger Institut für Sozialforschung (HIS), HBA 656, SDS München, Flugblatt zum 8. Mai 1968.

[37] Wolfgang Kraushaar, "Organisationsreferat," in Kraushaar, ed., *Frankfurter Schule und Studentenbewegung. Vol. 3*, 15–16. See also Wolfgang Kraushaar, "Denkmodelle der 68er Bewegung," *Aus Politik und Zeitgeschichte* B22-3 (2001): 14–27.

"revolution" or the "authoritarian state."[38] The New Left's perception of a revolutionary situation in the Federal Republic and the West more generally went along with a renewed emphasis on voluntarism. The movement rediscovered and appropriated subjectivist and voluntarist Marxist traditions. As Rudi Dutschke argued in the famous television interview with Günter Gaus in December 1967, "we" are not simply "hopeless idiots of history who are incapable of taking charge of our own fate."[39] The expansion of means of communication, television especially, endowed student activists with a perception that they were part of a truly global wave of protest. This affirmed their sense of surfing on the crest of history. Indeed, they felt there was virtually no limit to their ability as activists to bring about social and political change. At the SDS conference in Hanover in June 1967, Dutschke argued that everything depended on "the conscious will of human beings to become conscious of the history that they have always made, to control and to subjugate that history."[40] A few months later, at the perhaps most hopeful moment of the New Left, the Vietnam Congress in Berlin in February 1968 when 5,000 participants from 14 countries gathered at the Technical University in West Berlin to protest the war in Southeast Asia, he went even further and assigned student activists a truly historical and transformative authority. Now "it primarily depends on *our* will," he argued, "how this period of history will end."[41]

Like many self-stylized revolutionaries, Karl Marx included, student activists outlined this revolutionary future rather vaguely. In June 1967, Dutschke would only describe "a process of the liberation of all human beings from war, exploitation, and fear" as "a complicated and very long path."[42] In a conversation on the future in October 1967, *Kursbuch* editor Hans Magnus Enzensberger encouraged activists to outline their vision more specifically. Their idea was to turn all West Berlin into a "great university, a huge learning society, a big school" to achieve the main task: the conscious raising of the masses. Activists sought to lower or erase the boundaries between the universities and society at large: they strove to introduce larger social and political problems into the university and they

---

[38] "Zur Geschichtsphilosophie des autoritären Staates, Mai 1968–August 1968," in Krahl, *Konstitution und Klassenkampf*, 204–11, here 209, 212, and "Antwort auf Jürgen Habermas," in ibid. 242–5.

[39] Rudi Dutschke, "Zu Protokoll." Interview mit Günter Gaus, December 3, 1967, https://www.rbb-online.de/zurperson/interview_archiv/dutschke_rudi.html (last accessed February 22, 2020).

[40] Rudi Dutschke, Professor Habermas, "Ihr begriffsloser Objektivismus erschlägt das zu emanzipierende Subjekt," in Kraushaar, ed., *Frankfurter Schule und Studentenbewegung. Vol. 2: Dokumente*, 251–3; similarly, in Rudi Dutschke, "Demokratie, Universität, Gesellschaft," in Miermeister, ed., *Rudi Dutschke. Geschichte ist machbar*, 73.

[41] Rudi Dutschke, in Plogstedt, *Der Kampf des vietnamesischen Volkes*, 123.

[42] Rudi Dutschke, Interview mit *Konkret*, Juni 1967, in Miermeister, ed., *Rudi Dutschke. Geschichte ist machbar*, 19.

conceived of the university as a model for society.[43] A council republic organized in collectives of 3,000 to 5,000 people would then enable everybody to rotate to different spheres of production, and to acquire the skills even for highly specialized jobs. Work would serve the purpose of the "self-fashioning [*Selbsterzeugung*]" of the individual rather than contribute to "alienation." Such a council republic in West Berlin, Dutschke and Rabehl claimed, would serve an important function in the Cold War by provoking both East and West Germany, and thus help to explode the "repressive institutions of both Stalinism and bureaucracy."[44] As far-fetched as this utopian perspective might appear in retrospect, activists seemed to genuinely believe in the feasibility of this revolutionary utopia as well as in their own ability to bring it about. In June 1967, in light of the increased popular mobilization in the aftermath of Benno Ohnesorg's assassination, Dutschke noted in his diary that "it is no longer crazy to raise the question of the the seizure of power in this city and to answer it positively."[45]

This vision of a small activist minority in charge of raising the consciousness of the masses and instigating a world historical transformation reflected a very heroic self-understanding as politically conscious revolutionary avant-garde. It was also a very male vision, which celebrated the activism of the individual male revolutionaries.[46] Yet this self-perception of a revolutionary vanguard in charge of changing the course of history also imposed an awesome responsibility on the small group of student activists. What if they failed to seize the historically unique moment? At the Vietnam Congress in Berlin, Rudi Dutschke explicitly worried that "we do not have much time."[47] This intense fear of missing the revolutionary moment also spurred the New Left's rejection of more long-term reformist projects in favor of immediate revolutionary change. Another activist, Klaus Hartung, remembered "the fear of missing the unique chance to shake up the *status quo*" by being "too tentative."[48] The utopian future that many 68ers activated thus always

[43] For the role of the "68ers" in debates about academic reform, see Anne Rohstock, *Von der "Ordinarienuniversität" zur "Revolutionszentrale." Hochschulreform und Hochschulrevolte in Bayern und Hessen, 1957–1976* (Munich: R. Oldenbourg, 2010), 155–67.

[44] All quotations are from "Ein Gespräch über die Zukunft mit Rudi Dutschke, Bernd Rabehl und Christian Semler." Dutschke's comrade, Bernd Rabehl, later characterized this idea as a quest for "national liberation," which then also explains Rabehl's later move into neo-fascism; see Lönnendonker et al., *Die antiautoritäre Revolte*, 472–8.

[45] Quoted in Koenen, *Das rote Jahrzehnt*, 40.

[46] Aribert Reimann, "Zwischen Machismo und Coolness. Männlichkeit und Emotion in der westdeutschen 'Kulturrevolution' der 1960er und 1970er Jahre," in Manuel Borutta, Nina Verheyen, eds, *Die Präsenz der Gefühle. Männlichkeit und Emotion in der Moderne* (Bielefeld: transcript, 2010), 237–41. Koenen, *Das rote Jahrzehnt*, 15. On the self-confidence and heroic self-stylization of male revolutionaries, see also Stefanie Pilzweger, *Männlichkeit zwischen Gefühl und Revolution. Eine Emotionsgeschichte der bundesdeutschen 68er-Bewegung* (Bielefeld: transcript, 2015), 109–12.

[47] Rudi Dutschke, in Plogstedt, *Der Kampf des vietnamesischen Volkes*, 123.

[48] Klaus Hartung, "Selbstkritische Überlegungen und Überlegungen zur Selbstkritik nach 40 Jahren," in *Ästhetik und Kommunikation* 39/140–1(2008): 101.

went along and was inextricably intertwined with "dark and threatening scenarios" that invoked the virtually apocalyptic consequences of possible failure.[49]

Despite such self-doubts, this notion of a predominantly male revolutionary elite in charge of raising the consciousness of the masses and bringing about a world historical transformation also constituted a way to assert authority within the anti-authoritarian movement. A small number of activists, who were capable of articulating the concerns of the student movement in an appropriate revolutionary rhetoric, stood at the helm of the New Left. One of them, Wolfgang Lefèvre, later reported that, while he and other leaders had already mastered the Marxist literature, others "knew nothing" and joined the movement only because of a "psychic emotion" against their parents and against the university.[50] The flip side of the self-confidence and revolutionary utopia of leading New Left activists was the fear of intellectual and rhetorical inadequacy. Given the male dominance of the New Left, women articulated this anxiety most explicitly. Elke Regehr, for example, remembered her suffering because "I did not dare to speak." Dagmar Pryztulla confirmed this impression: "The dominant attitude among left-wingers was for women to sit there and listen." Christel Kalisch recalled in 2002 her "anxiety" when she remembered the "pretentious language" of her male comrades. "I could not have imagined speaking among all these theoreticians," she reflected.[51] For Inga Buhmann, the sociology jargon in the seminar of Jürgen Habermas was, above all, an "arrogant instrument of power that was especially used against women."[52] Occasionally, such inhibitions also went along with being intimidated by famous New Left activists. Annette Schwarzenau recalled how she saw Rudi Dutschke as a "hero" and "almost could not breathe" when she met him for the first time after her arrival in Berlin.[53] To be sure, at least some men experienced similar anxieties. Bahman Nirumand, too, remembered how he "was afraid of losing the red thread or to say something stupid" after he had been asked to speak right after Rudi Dutschke.[54] Still, the culture of the New Left was highly gendered: with only few exceptions, speaking and revolutionary activism were associated with men, whereas women tended to adopt the passive behavior of listening in silence.[55]

---

[49] See Axel Schildt, "Überbewertet? Zur Macht objektiver Entwicklungen und zur Wirkungslosigkeit der '68er,'" in Wengst, ed., *Reform und Revolte*, 89–102, here 100.

[50] Cited in Lönnendonker et al., *Die antiautoritäre Revolte*, 307.

[51] Elke Regehr, Dagmar Pryztulla, Christel Kalisch, in Ute Kätzel, *Die 68erinnen. Porträt einer rebellischen Frauengeneration* (Berlin: Rowohlt, 2002), 85, 205, 266.

[52] Inga Buhmann, *Ich habe mir eine Geschichte geschrieben*, 3rd edn (Munich: Trikont, 1979), 62.

[53] Annette Schwarzenau, in Kätzel, *Die 68erinnen*, 45. Interestingly, female activists tended to exempt Dutschke from these critiques. Inga Buhmann described him as "not arrogant" and "always friendly": see Buhmann, *Ich habe mir eine Geschichte geschrieben*, 199.

[54] Bahman Nirumand, *Weit entfernt von dem Ort an dem ich sein müsste. Autobiographie* (Reinbek: Rowohlt, 2011), 144.

[55] See also von Hodenberg, *Das andere Achtundsechzig*, 114–15. Women's role in the revolt was also underestimated, including by themselves, as von Hodenberg shows. Several female activists cite

The New Left's revolutionary utopia always stood in marked contrast to its actual popular strength. Dutschke himself estimated a membership of around 4,000 to 5,000 in the SDS with approximately 150 to 200 activists. Thus the New Left comprised only a very small segment of the West German student population. In fact, an Allensbach opinion poll commissioned by *Der Spiegel* in July 1967 revealed that the support for the emergency laws was greater among West German students than in the general population (55 per cent versus 37 per cent). Similarly, only 42 per cent of West German students said that there should be an ongoing discussion of German war crimes. The second most-cited role model among West German students was the conservative former Chancellor, Konrad Adenauer, and the most-cited was the philosopher and scientist Carl Friedrich von Weizsäcker. To be sure, a reformist political agenda enjoyed broad support among West German students. Another poll in 1968 revealed, for example, that two-thirds of West German students supported the demonstration in large cities, which explains some of the revolutionary optimism of the New Left at that time. Yet only about a quarter of young people in West Germany openly supported Rudi Dutschke and his revolutionary vision.[56]

Student activists explained their relative isolation as the result of direct state repression as well as, more importantly, the more subtle mechanism of manipulation. Their perception of the "masses" that they sought to "liberate" was thus often rather condescending. In September 1967, for example, Rudi Dutschke wrote that "through years of functional manipulation, the system has succeeded in turning human beings to the equivalent of amphibians, who like Pavlovian dogs, only react to the signals of the powerful; with their vote every four years, they are allowed to prove their intellectual limitations and immaturity."[57] When construction workers interfered with Dutschke's speech at a demonstration in Berlin, he encouraged his comrades to "let them be" because they "did not know any better."[58] Only a "few privileged students," he later explained, had the capacity to "see through the subtle mechanisms of domination" and "to work against them."[59] Contemporary critics like the philosopher Jürgen Habermas underlined the paternalistic nature of this outlook and charged activists with "presumptively seeking to identify with a

especially Sigrid Fronius, the chairperson of the Berlin General Students' Committee (ASTA) as equal to male revolutionary leaders. See Christel Kalisch in Kätzel, *Die 68erinnen*, 281.

[56] "Was denken die Studenten?" *Der Spiegel* 21/26 (1967): 28–39, "Zwei Drittel zum Protest bereit," *Der Spiegel* 22/8 (1968): 40–1; also cited in Anna von der Goltz, "A polarised generation? Conservative Students and West Germany's '1968'," in Goltz, ed., *"Talkin' 'bout my generation,"* 195–215, quotation on 201. Lönnendonker et al., *Die antiautoritäre Revolte*, 398, interprets these numbers as indicating a significant shift in favor of the New Left.

[57] Rudi Dutschke, "Besetzt Bonn," in Miermeister, ed., *Rudi Dutschke. Geschichte ist machbar*, 96–9. With almost similar language, see Krahl, *Konstitution und Klassenkampf*, 25.

[58] Cited in Thomas, *Protest Movements in 1960s West Germany*, 159.

[59] Dutschke, "Besetzt Bonn."

yet-to-be produced future consciousness of enlightened masses" while trying to "already act today on behalf of this as of yet non-existent consciousness."[60]

Activists saw the level of consciousness among West Germans as the main obstacle to a revolutionary transformation, rather than in the development of productive forces, as classical Marxism would have it. Large sections of the population and the working class were not capable of recognizing the repressive conditions under which they lived and thus of "find[ing] a meaningful place in the world."[61] For the activist, the conservative Springer press, in particular, appeared as the greatest impediment to the awakening of the population's political consciousness. Television had not yet superseded print media in its influence. In 1964, about 70 per cent of West Germans read a daily newspaper and 17.3 million newspapers were sold daily. The publishing house of Axel Springer dominated the media landscape, controlling 39.2 per cent of the newspaper market and 18.2 per cent of the magazine market. The most important Springer publication was *Bild*, a tabloid paper that had been founded in 1952 and sold 4.2 million copies in 1967. Approximately 30 per cent of adult males read it on a daily basis.[62] *Bild* was also therefore, a main target of a student-organized "Springer tribunal" in West Berlin in February 1968.[63] Ironically, student activists' analysis of *Bild* drew on a published study of the popular appeal of *Bild* that the Springer company itself had commissioned.[64] Students cited the study's findings that analyzed the emotional relationship between *Bild* and its readers, showing that the tabloid functioned as a quasi "super ego" that compensated for the fears and uncertainties of a complicated world. The study also claimed that *Bild* appealed to readers' subconscious by stimulating wishes and sexual desires, often through soft pornographic images, yet also communicated the impossibility of actually fulfilling those wishes. It then directed the resulting aggression to alleged internal and external enemies, such as the student movement.[65] These keen and rather sophisticated analyses exposed the considerable forces and power that student activists faced. They not only needed to confront the authority of the state but also the workings of a powerful means of mass persuasion that was formally independent yet nevertheless

---

[60] "Die Scheinrevolution entlässt ihre Kinder. Sechs Thesen über Taktik, Ziele, und Situationsanalysen der oppositionellen Jugend," in *Die Linke antwortet Jürgen Habermas* (Frankfurt a/M: Europäische Verlagsanstalt, 1968), 15.

[61] Rudi Dutschke, "Vom Antisemitismus zum Antikommunismus," in Uwe Bergmann, *Rebellion der Studenten oder, Die neue Opposition* (Reinbek: Rowohlt, 1968), 75.

[62] Figures according to Hans-Ulrich Wehler, *Deutsche Gesellschaftsgeschichte. Fünfter Band: Bundesrepublik und DDR, 1949–1990* (Munich: C.H. Beck, 2008), 391–2.

[63] See the recollections in Peter Schneider, *Rebellion und Wahn. Mein "68"* (Munich: Kiepenheuer & Witsch, 2008), 243–50.

[64] Axel Springer AG, *Qualitative Analyse der Bild-Zeitung* (Berlin: Axel Springer, 1996).

[65] SDS Autorenkollektiv-Springer Arbeitskreis der KU, *Der Untergang der Bild-Zeitung* ([1968]), 48–52, 96–100, 103, and Heiner Schäfer, "Die Bild -Zeitung: Eine Ordnungsmacht im Spätkapitalismus," in Heinz Grossmann, Oskar Negt, eds, *Die Auferstehung der Gewalt. Springerblockade und politische Reaktion in der Bundesrepublik* (Frankfurt a/M: Europäische Verlagsanstalt, 1968), 19–29.

functioned, as the sociologist Oskar Negt wrote, as a "violent instrument of the existing dominant system of rule."[66]

The dangers of *Bild* were manifest on April 11, 1968, when the young worker and *Bild* reader Josef Bachmann tried to assassinate Rudi Dutschke. Student activists immediately blamed the Springer press. The "Easter riots" broke out in response, with student demonstrators attacking the production and distribution network of the Springer press, and seeking to blockade the delivery of the newspapers. Fifty policemen and 400 demonstrators were injured. Rüdiger Schreck, a student, and Klaus Frings, a news photographer, were killed. During the most violent demonstrations in the history of the Federal Republic up to this point, police arrested 827 people, among them not just students but also several hundred workers and public employees.[67] The fact that workers had demonstrated with them led activists to see these events as the beginning of a range of violent actions that might bring about the revolution; in their minds, no longer would enlightenment and consciousness raising be sufficient. The problem of *Bild* readers was not their "stupidity" but their "helplessness" (*Ohnmacht*). They felt that they had demonstrated to workers that mass resistance could lead to "solidarity" and empowerment, making political transformation possible. The events of May 1968 in Paris, when students and workers demonstrated together, fueled these hopes.[68]

Although the Nazi past provided the repository for students' analysis of the West German presence, a paradox marked the New Left's actual confrontation with the Nazi past. Many activists recalled their profound emotional shock on hearing for the first time about Nazi crimes, including the Holocaust.[69] Yet, the Marxist concept of "fascism" conceptualized the Nazi past as wholly external to themselves and thus distanced students from "the human side of this human drama," as Tilman Fichter noted retrospectively.[70] By highlighting the structural and mental preconditions for fascism and their continuities in the Federal Republic, student activists detached themselves from their parents' culpability and its implications for themselves. Thus, in the words of Reinhard Kühnl, one of the most important popularizers of the New Left's theory of fascism, National Socialism became simply another form of "bourgeois rule."[71] The 68ers thus

---

[66] Oskar Negt, "Rechtsordnung, Öffentlichkeit, Gewalt," in Oskar Negt, ed., *Die Auferstehung der Gewalt*, 184.

[67] Thomas, *Protest Movements in 1960s West Germany*, 170–6; Koenen, *Das rote Jahrzehnt*, 128.

[68] SDS-Autorenkollektiv, *Der Untergang der Bild-Zeitung*, 66, 77, 124. See also Peter Schneider's reflections on the turn to violence: Schneider, *Rebellion und Wahn*, 269–78.

[69] Christel Kalisch, in Kätzel, *Die 68erinnen*, 260–61. See also Gildea et al., eds, *Europe's 1968*. 21–45, and Wilfried Mausbach, "Wende um 360 Grad? Nationalsozialismus und Judenvernichtung in der 'zweiten Gründungsphase' der Bundesrepublik," in von Hodenberg and Siegfried, eds, *Wo "1968" liegt*, 26–8.

[70] Cited in ibid. 37.

[71] Reinhard Kühnl, *Formen bürgerlicher Herrschaft. Liberalismus-Faschismus* (Reinbek: Rowohlt, 1971) and Reinhard Kühnl, *Der Staat der Gegenwart. Formen bürgerlicher Herrschaft II* (Reinbek: Rowohlt, 1978).

contributed relatively little to West German confrontation with the Nazi past.[72] As indicated earlier, the renewed presence of the Nazi past in West German public discourse preceded the New Left. Also, student activists had little interest in the distinctive historical features of the Nazi regime, including its racism and antisemitism.[73] Beyond their theoretical concept of "fascism," remembering Nazi crimes did not lend itself to legitimizing activists' vision of personal and political transformation. Rudi Dutschke reportedly rejected proposals for a Holocaust exhibition in 1966 because it would have been "too demoralizing" in favor of "future-oriented actions" and "solidarity with the Third World."[74]

Did antisemitism inform the dialectics of utopia and paranoia in the New Left's political and ideological vision? Historians have well documented the shift of the New Left from a pro-Israel to a predominantly anti-Zionist position in the context of the Six-Day War in June 1967.[75] Issues of local and domestic politics played an important part in this shift. West German conservatives and the Springer press enthusiastically celebrated the Israeli military triumph. For New Left activists, conservative support for Israel derived from admiration of the Israeli military abilities, and, as Ulrike Meinhof described it, "solidarity with brutality, expulsion and conquest."[76] In the imagination of the New Left, West German solidarity with Israel now appeared as yet another facet of a threatening transnational alliance of authoritarianism and militarism. In a similar way, anti-Zionism now became part and parcel of the New Left's anti-imperialism. Conversely, the New Left's growing sympathy for Arab, and especially Palestinian, nationalism appeared as a quite logical result of the New Left's general support for national liberation movements in the Third World. Extensive indifference regarding the specific historical and political condition of these conflicts now made it possible for the New Left to equate the Palestinian struggle against Israel with the struggle of the Vietcong against the US military. Or, as Dieter Kunzelmann put it: "Palestine is for the

---

[72] With similar findings on the basis of an analysis of student newspapers in 1968, see Rohstock, *Von der "Ordinarienuniversität" zur "Revolutionszentrale,"* 180.

[73] Siegfried, "Zwischen Aufarbeitung und Schlußstrich," Mausbach, "Wende um 360 Grad?" 15–47, Volker Paulmann, "Die Studentenbewegung und die NS-Vergangenheit in der Bundesrepublik," in Stephan Alexander Glienke, Volker Paulmann, Joachim Perels, eds, *Erfolgsgeschichte Bundesrepublik? Die Nachkriegsgesellschaft im langen Schatten des Nationalsozialismus* (Göttingen: Wallstein, 2008). This critique did not just apply to the "68ers": see Nicolas Berg, *Der Holocaust und die westdeutschen Historiker. Erforschung und Erinnerung* (Göttingen: Wallstein, 2003).

[74] Tilman Fichter, Ute Schmidt, "SDS und NS Vergangenheit," *Ästhetik und Kommunikation* 39/140–1 (2008): 155–7; see also Rolf Stolz, "Innenansichten des SDS in den Achtundsechziger Jahren," in Gerrit Dworok, Christoph Weißmann, eds, *1968 und die "68er." Ereignisse, Wirkungen und Kontroversen in der Bundesrepublik* (Cologne: Böhlau, 2013), 27.

[75] Martin W. Kloke, *Israel und die deutsche Linke. Zur Geschichte eines schwierigen Verhältnisses,* 2nd edn (Frankfurt a/M: Haag & Herrchen, 1994), 111–32, Jeffrey Herf, *Undeclared Wars with Israel. East Germany and the West German Far Left, 1967–1989* (New York: Cambridge University Press, 2016), 75–88, 96–108.

[76] Cited in Kloke, *Israel und die deutsche Linke,* 113.

Federal Republic and Europe what Vietnam is for the Amis."[77] For much of the New Left, anti-Zionism thus became part of a rather Manichean and essentially paranoid imagination in which fascists and anti fascists, imperialists and anti-imperialists, were lined up very neatly in opposing camps. It is quite possible that the emotional identification with Palestinian national liberation also entailed some unconscious longing for a utopian nationalist self-determination, a surrogate national identity that West German leftists could not develop within Germany. The eventual shift of at least some former members of the New Left to the radical Right—Bernd Rabehl and Horst Mahler are the most prominent examples—makes this hypothesis at least somewhat plausible.

In some cases, the New Left's anti-Zionism transmogrified into open antisemitism. The most infamous example was the failed bombing attack on the Berlin Jewish Community Center on November 9, 1969, the thirty-first anniversary of *Reichskristallnacht*, by Dieter Kunzelmann and his followers. According to historian Wolfgang Kraushaar, the terrorism that emanated from the New Left emerged in a foundational "anti-Semitic act."[78] Kunzelmann's antisemitic convictions became apparent when he blamed a "Jewish neurosis" (*Judenknax*) for the shocked reaction of the West German public to the attack. Yet Kunzelmann and his followers were largely ostracized from the Berlin underground scene as New Left activists struggled to maintain a distinction between "anti-Zionism" and "antisemitism."[79] To some extent, the New Left just reflected the general public's employing of distancing mechanisms that, as Chapter 5 described, characterized West German reactions to the Nazi trials in the early 1960s. The New Left's anti-Zionism enabled activists to avoid a confrontation with a specific German past and fostered an emotional identification with rather abstract principles of international anti-imperialism. As such, activists were able to avoid a confrontation not only with specific possible culpability of their parent generation but also with the extent to which mental and ideological continuities from the Nazi past might have affected them as well.[80] Many activists struggled with the problem of reconciling their individual emotional attachment to their parents with a rejection of the parental generation, hence the turn against the abstract fathers at the university or in politics.[81] Revolutionary fear thus also entailed a potentially unconscious fear of being implicated in the national past,

[77] Cited in Wolfgang Kraushaar, *Die Bombe im Jüdischen Gemeindehaus* (Hamburg: Hamburger Edition, 2005), 283.

[78] Ibid. 289–94. For a similar emphasis on the New Left's antisemitism, see Herf, *Undeclared Wars*, 75–118.

[79] Aribert Reimann, *Dieter Kunzelmann. Avantgardist, Protestler, Radikaler* (Göttingen: Vandenhoeck & Ruprecht, 2009), 241–6. Kunzelmann was arrested in June 1970, sentenced to nine years in prison, and then released in 1975.

[80] Kloke, *Israel und die deutsche Linke*, 296–8.

[81] See von Hodenberg, *Das andere Achtundsechzig*, 67. On the biographic burdens, see also Heinz Bude, *Adorno für Ruinenkinder. Eine Geschichte von 1968* (Munich: Hanser, 2018).

which the New Left sought to displace by developing an abstract concept of fascism and by identifying with revolutionary struggles in faraway places, especially in Vietnam. Their own biographical implications in the Nazi past only became an issue with the left-alternative turn toward subjectivity in the 1970s.

Rather than addressing the German past directly, the New Left provided the language and the metaphors for the German 68ers to make sense of the war in Vietnam. As Tilman Fichter noted, "Vietnam was the Spain of our generation."[82] Resistance to the US war in Vietnam thus appeared to echo antifascist resistance in the 1930s, and the war in Vietnam became an important "projective screen" for criticizing West German society as well as "the West" more generally.[83] While the anti-colonial movements in Vietnam and elsewhere provided the revolutionary force that student activists missed in Western industrial societies, the "concrete interaction [*Vermittlung*] between the metropolis and the Third World" that Rudi Dutschke demanded required the virtual convergence of diverse movements in the West and the non-West.[84] "Do you think anything will change in Vietnam if you protest here?" a judge reportedly asked a student? "No," he is said to have replied, "but here."[85] While their US counterparts had the concrete impetus of possibly being drafted into military service in Vietnam, student activists in Germany had less of a personal stake. The personal significance of the war in Vietnam was harder to see for them. Dutschke acknowledged that communicating to activists that the "struggle of the Vietcong" is "our struggle" was a "huge, almost unsolvable task."[86] Rainer Langhans, another prominent activist, acknowledged that "our suffering is not the suffering of the Vietnamese."[87] His comrade, Dieter Kunzelmann, put it more drastically: "Why should I be concerned with Vietnam—I have orgasm problems!"[88] According to Dutschke, it was only through direct action—as, for example, in the protests against the visits of Moïse Tshombe, the Prime Minister of the Congo in December 1964 or then the Shah visit in June 1967—that the problems of the Third World became "alive" in West Berlin.[89] Another way in which student activists made the war in Vietnam personally relevant was through equating Vietnamese civilians with Jewish victims of

[82] Fichter, "Meine Uni war der SDS," 23.

[83] Kraushaar, "Denkmodelle der 68er Bewegung," 24. For an important critique of this notion of "projection," see Slobodian, *Foreign Front*.

[84] Rudi Dutschke, in Plogstedt, *Der Kampf des vietnamesischen Volkes*, 86.

[85] Cited in Infas report, *Student und Öffentlichkeit*, 1.

[86] Dutschke, "Vom Antisemitismus zum Antikommunismus," in Bergmann, *Rebellion der Studenten*, 69.

[87] Quoted in Lönnendonker et al., *Die antiautoritäre Revolte*, 313.

[88] Quoted in Rainer Langhans, *Ich bin's. Die ersten 68 Jahre* (Munich: Blumenbar, 2008), 64, and in Kätzel, *Die 68erinnen*, 210.

[89] Dutschke, "Vom Antisemitismus zum Antikommunismus," in Bergmann, *Rebellion der Studenten*, 63–4, 79. On the larger significance of these protests for the New Left's attitude toward the Third World, see Slobodian, *Foreign Front*, 61–77.

Figure 6.1. SDS demonstration in Essen in February 1968.

Student activists distanced themselves from the Nazi past by projecting the memory of the Holocaust onto the US war in Vietnam. This banner reads "Vietnam—the Auschwitz of the Americans."

Source: bpk-Bildagentur, No. 70161670.

the Holocaust and the war in Vietnam as "genocide."[90] Oskar Negt, for example, stated that bemoaning the Nazi past was hypocritical if it was not turned into "actions against any form of present mass killing," including the war in Vietnam.[91] Such rhetorical equations often went along with a visual strategy in which images of US napalm bombings evoked images of Holocaust victims. None other than New Left theoretician Herbert Marcuse emphasized the similarity of images of victims of the Vietnam War with images from Buchenwald and Auschwitz.[92] While such rhetorical equations promoted an emotional identification with the anti-war movement, they also distanced activists from the negative consequences of the Holocaust by projecting it onto a geographically and mentally distant

---

[90] Wilfried Mausbach, "Wende um 360 Grad?" 15–47, quotation on 29. Günther Anders, in Plogstedt, *Der Kampf des vietnamesischen Volkes*, 97–101.

[91] Nr. 158, Oskar Negt, "Politik und Protest" Referat auf einer sozialistischen Arbeitskonferenz, 28. 10. 1967 in Kraushaar, ed., *Frankfurter Schule und Studentenbewegung. Vol. 2*, 297–303.

[92] Winfried Mausbach, "Auschwitz and Vietnam," in Andreas Daum, Lloyd C. Gardner, Wilfried Mausbach, eds, *America, the Vietnam War, and the World* (New York: Cambridge University Press, 2003), 279–98, Slobodian, *Foreign Front*, 149–51.

conflict.[93] The equation between Vietnam and the Holocaust thus also perpetuated the distancing mechanisms that West German society had developed vis-à-vis the return of the Nazi past beginning in the late 1950s.

The war in Vietnam not only served as a positive model for revolutionary movements at home, it also constituted a horror scenario—a virtual realization of the worst atrocities in the present. Susanne Schunter-Kleemann, for example, remembered reports of GIs torturing Vietnamese women in an extremely brutal and sexualized fashion when she was part of the Berlin SDS.[94] Vietnam not only represented a positive revolutionary perspective but also signified a dark and pessimistic vision of the future. If Vietnam stood for global fascism, the victory of antifascism and anti-imperialism was by no means certain. For Rudi Dutschke, the "tactical situation" even appeared "miserable." How much was at stake in the struggles of student agitators became apparent in envisaging the consequences of potential failure. As Dutschke declared at the Vietnam Congress: "If US imperialism can show in Vietnam that it can defeat the people's war, a long period of authoritarian world rule would begin from Vladivostok to Washington."[95] At every turn, the New Left's vision of a utopian future was deeply intertwined with a dark, even catastrophic, imagination if the desired revolution were to fail.

Fear and Violence

The confrontation with state violence further enhanced these revolutionary fears. This was the case even though New Left activists attributed a positive, consciousness-raising dimension to the direct experience of state violence. According to Rudi Dutschke's and Hans-Jürgen Krahl's lecture on "organization" at the SDS conference in Frankfurt in September 1967, the "sensual experience of the organized individual fighters in the confrontation with the executive power of the state" would allow the "spread of the radical opposition" and initiate a "consciousness-raising process" among "passive and suffering masses." This theory of consciousness raising through activism derived from the model of the guerrilla fighter in Latin America, and especially Che Guevara, as revolutionary idols. Dutschke and Krahl advocated the introduction of the "urban guerilla" as the embodiment of the "great refusal" and as the antithesis to "cynicism" and "integration into the system."[96] Direct action was necessary because it entailed the

[93] This is Wolfgang Kraushaar's point: see Kraushaar, *1968 als Mythos, Chiffre und Zäsur*, 127.
[94] Susanne Schunter-Kleeman in Kätzel, *Die 68erinnen*, 107.
[95] Rudi Dutschke, in Plogstedt, *Der Kampf des vietnamesischen Volkes*, 123. Also cited in Rudi Dutschke, "Die geschichtlichen Bedingungen für den internationalen Emanzipationskampf," in Bergmann, *Rebellion der Studenten*, 92.
[96] See Rudi Dutschke, Hans-Jürgen Krahl, "Organisationsreferat, auf der 22. Delegiertenkonferenz des SDS, 5.9.1967," in Kraushaar, ed., *Frankfurter Schule und Studentenbewegung. Vol. 2*, 287–90, Kraushaar, "Autoritärer Staat und antiautoritäre Bewegung."

sensual and emotional experience of the violence that was inherent in the system. A "dialectic of sentiment and emotions" and of "theory" was supposed to forge a holistic revolutionary subjectivity against an authoritarian state and society.[97] "Action" and "enlightenment" were supposed to mutually inform each other.[98] With this emphasis on direct action, the group around Dutschke distanced itself from the traditionalists within the SDS, which continued to place its hopes in the working class. To be sure, Dutschke and others explicitly rejected the open use of violence in industrial Western countries, and castigated targeted assassinations of state representatives as "inhumane" and "counter-revolutionary."[99] Yet they nevertheless invoked the potentially mobilizing force of violence, especially if it was directed against "objects" instead of "persons."[100]

It was this emphasis on voluntarism, direct action, and revolutionary catharsis in the confrontation with the state that provoked the philosopher Jürgen Habermas's earlier accusation of "left-wing fascism" at the Congress that took place in Hanover on June 9, 1967, in the aftermath of the memorial for Benno Ohnesorg.[101] Habermas had already left the event late in the evening when he decided to return and ask Rudi Dutschke to clarify whether his "voluntarist ideology" had been designed to provoke state violence, alluding to the consequent "risk of injury to human beings."[102] This intervention, which occurred after Dutschke had already left the room, followed Habermas's earlier contribution, in which he highlighted the important and constructive function of the student opposition, yet also warned against "theoretical simplifications," "fetishized beliefs," and an "irrational glorification of immediacy."[103] Habermas's criticism reflected the "affective discomfort" of left-wing and liberal sympathizers with the New Left's open and explicit propagation of direct action and emotional catharsis.[104] He did not share the broad suspicion of all emotions that had characterized the West German emotional regime, and he clearly recognized the potential political function of fear and of a new sensibility within the student movement. Yet what one of

---

[97] Rudi Dutschke, "Die geschichtlichen Bedingungen für den internationalen Emanzipationskampf," in Bergmann, *Rebellion der Studenten*, 91.

[98] Nr. 129 Rudi Dutschke, "Professor Habermas, Ihr begriffsloser Objektivismus erschlägt das zu emanzipierende Subjekt," in Kraushaar, ed., *Frankfurter Schule und Studentenbewegung. Vol. 2*, 251–3; see also Davis, "Provokation als Emanzipation."

[99] Nr. 132, Rudi Dutschke, "Zum Verhältnis von Organisations- und Emanzipationsbewegung— Zum Besuch Herbert Marcuse, unter dem Pseudonym R.S., 12. Juni 1967" in Kraushaar, ed., *Frankfurter Schule und Studentenbewegung. Vol. 2*, 255–60.

[100] Rudi Dutschke, interview with *Konkret*, Juni 1967, in Miermeister, ed., *Rudi Dutschke. Geschichte ist machbar*, 21.

[101] Stefan Müller-Doohm, *Jürgen Habermas. Eine Biographie* (Berlin: Suhrkamp, 2014), 191–3. Habermas later regretted the term.

[102] Jürgen Habermas, "Meine Damen und Herren, ich hoffe, dass Herr Dutschke noch hier ist . . . ," in Kraushaar, ed., *Frankfurter Schule und Studentenbewegung. Vol. 2*, 254–6.

[103] Jürgen Habermas, "Rede über die politische Rolle der Studentenschaft in der Bundesrepublik," in ibid. 246–9, quotation 249.

[104] "Antwort auf Jürgen Habermas," in Krahl, *Konstitution und Klassenkampf*, 245.

Figure 6.2. Use of water-cannons against student protesters during demonstrations in West Berlin, April 1968.

Revolutionary fears of student activists resulted from confrontation with police violence yet also justified their own turn to violence as "counter-violence." Police departments often resorted to paramilitary tactics in seeking to "defeat" activists.

Source: bpk-Bildagentur, No. 30002158.

Dutschke's followers called his "unprecedented pathos" nevertheless took Habermas aback.[105] He therefore castigated the notion of a possible "seizure of power by students" as equivalent to a "clinical diagnosis of delusion." He criticized the students' "ridiculous fantasies of power," and warned against provoking the violent reaction of a powerful state.[106] Dutschke, for his part, described the accusation of voluntarism as a "compliment" and highlighted the preventive and pre-emptive function of what he called "organized counter-violence."[107]

Increasingly violent confrontations between student protesters and the police throughout 1968 in major West German urban centers put to the test the theory that violent confrontation would lead to consciousness raising. Violence escalated

---

[105] See Jürgen Habermas, "Die Scheinrevolution entlässt ihre Kinder. Sechs Thesen über Taktik, Ziele, und Situationsanalysen der oppositionellen Jugend," in *Die Linke antwortet Jürgen Habermas*, 5–15, quotation on 8, Hartung, "Selbstkritische Überlegungen," 95–112, quotation on 101.

[106] Habermas, "Die Scheinrevolution entlässt ihre Kinder," 13–14.

[107] Rudi Dutschke, "Tagebuch Notiz zum Habermas-Vorwurf, 10 June 1967," in Kraushaar, ed., *Frankfurter Schule und Studentenbewegung. Vol. 2*, 255.

especially in the aftermath of the assassination attempt on Rudi Dutschke in April 1968. More than 300,000 people participated in the Easter marches in more than 20 cities, and 400 students and 54 policemen were injured.[108]

The escalation of violence culminated in the "Battle of Tegeler Weg" in November 1968, which *Der Spiegel* would call the "most violent street battle in Berlin's postwar history."[109] The occasion for the demonstration was a hearing to consider rescinding the lawyer's license of activist (and later neo-Nazi) Horst Mahler because of his participation in violent anti-Springer demonstrations earlier that year. It is not clear to this day whether student violence was planned or developed spontaneously. Approximately 1,000 demonstrators used stones and eggs to attack the police, who responded with tear gas and water. Demonstrators reportedly also included a violent "rocker gang" as surrogate for the "proletariat" that the students had not been able to mobilize. Some 100 policemen as well as 22 demonstrators were injured and 48 demonstrators were arrested.[110] Mahler kept his license, but some 3,000 supporters of the Extraparliamentary Opposition (APO) were subjected to criminal prosecutions and the APO frequently responded with violent demonstrations.[111]

Another example of the escalating violence were the demonstrations on the occasion of the awarding of the peace prize of the German Book Trade to the Senegalese president, Léopold Senghor, at the Frankfurt Book Fair in October 1968. Senghor had inflamed student activists because he had distanced himself from Marxism and favored Senegal's ongoing ties with France, its former colonizer, and because of the Senegalese government's violent repression of striking students and workers at the University of Dakar in May 1968.[112] Student activists therefore denounced him as a "marionette of French imperialism" and a "Quisling."[113] The anti-Senghor demonstration quickly escalated into violence. An SDS report collected individual students' experiences of police violence that included being "beaten almost unconscious as a result of beatings against legs, body, and head," being "thrown on the ground and beaten," and "being beaten from behind in the kidneys and on the back so that my upper body was completely exposed"—the last being a female demonstrator.[114] Recollections described the police as "hysterical," out of control, and eager to cause injury. "Get

---

[108] Thomas, *Protest Movements in 1960s West Germany*, 171–3, Rohstock, *Von der "Ordinarienuniversität" zur "Revolutionszentrale,"* 189.

[109] *Der Spiegel* 22/46 (1968): 67.

[110] Thomas, *Protest Movements in 1960s West Germany*, 152, Pilzweger, *Männlichkeit zwischen Gefühl und Revolution*, 315.

[111] Koenen, *Das rote Jahrzehnt*, 172, Brown, *West Germany and the Global Sixties*, 116–20.

[112] On Senghor, see Frederick Cooper, *Citizenship between Empire and Nation. Remaking France and French Africa, 1945–1960* (Princeton: Princeton University Press, 2014).

[113] "Wer ist Senghor?" in Dokumentation des SDS, 10–15, Anti-Senghor Demonstration, HIS, HHE 642.

[114] Ibid. 1–10.

her," one female protester reported a policeman had yelled before other nearby policemen "swoop[ed] down on" her and "beat away" a group of demonstrators who tried to protect her.[115] Individual reports, especially of female protestors, seemed to confirm the notion that police forces were willing to transgress traditional gender boundaries. The SDS painted a portrait of policemen driven by sadistic sexual impulse against women. Indeed, New Left publications followed the theories of Wilhelm Reich in sexualizing the violence that agents of the state, such as policemen, meted out.[116] Other reports of policemen labeling student protesters as "Jews" or "Communists" further confirmed this perception and underlined student activists' perception of the increasingly fascist nature of the West German state.

The tactics and strategy that at least some West German police departments still embraced during the 1960s significantly contributed to this gradual escalation of violence. Many police departments confronted student demonstrations with the ideals and practices of the 1920s. Student activists appeared as the equivalent of left-wing paramilitary formations in the Weimar Republic that were engaged in a Communist attack on the state. As a result, police forces aimed at defeating rather than defusing student protest. They believed in the notion that a small group of "ringleaders" drove and organized protests, and therefore needed to be arrested and isolated. Because these alleged agitators were difficult to identify, police forces often took external characteristics—long hair especially—as sufficient basis for violence and arrest.[117] West German police forces also struggled to cope with the students' deliberate strategy of provocation that remained below the level of actual violence, such as, for example, during the Christmas demonstrations in December 1966. Several activist followers of Rudi Dutschke and Dieter Kunzelmann, the founder of *Kommune 1*, mingled among Christmas shoppers on Kurfürstendamm, engaging them in political debates and forming spontaneous demonstrations only to disperse quickly when police arrived. The entire action culminated in the singing of Christmas carols while burning paper figures of US President Lyndon Johnson and East German leader Walter Ulbricht. Police officers arrested 86 individuals, which included many innocent passersby.[118] Police officers perceived these protest methods as deliberate humiliation and often simply did not know how to react to such unknown and unconventional protest forms other than resorting to violence. Class resentments of often

---

[115] Ibid.
[116] Massimo Perinelli, "Lust, Gewalt, Befreiung. Sexualitätsdiskurse," Rotaprint 25, ed., *agit 883. Bewegung, Revolte, Underground in Westberlin 1969–1972* (Berlin: Assoziation A Verlag, 2006), 85–98, quotation on 87.
[117] In general, see Klaus Weinhauer, *Schutzpolizei in der Bundesrepublik: Zwischen Bürgerkrieg und innerer Sicherheit—die turbulenten sechziger Jahre* (Paderborn: Schöningh, 2003).
[118] Reimann, *Dieter Kunzelmann*, 135–36, Lönnendonker et al., *Die antiautoritäre Revolte*, 310–12.

lower-class male police officers toward what they perceived as spoiled and privileged youth further fueled police violence against student demonstrators.[119]

To be sure, West German police forces also underwent a learning process in confronting student protesters. Some police departments, such as the one in Munich, had adopted a different strategy during the Shah's visit that aimed at defusing confrontation and avoiding violence. After the disastrous confrontations in Berlin on June 2, 1967, police forces in other parts of the Federal Republic began to adopt these practices. They aimed at avoiding rather than winning battles with student demonstrators. Police forces were demilitarized and officers were trained in the psychology of protest and in not responding disproportionately to provocations, even in using humor to defuse tense situations. Interestingly, the use of the Federal Border Police (BGS) in confronting student demonstrations, which the passage of the emergency laws made possible, aided rather than hindered this process of modernizing West German police forces.[120]

How did student activists react to the escalation of violence? What emotional history accompanied this experience of an increasingly violent confrontation with the state? At least for some activists, the experience of state violence led to ever more elaborate justification of legitimate "counter-violence." The distinction between violence against "objects" and violence against "persons" began to dissolve gradually. APO activist Christian Semler, for example, justified violence on Tegeler Weg in November 1968 as liberation from being merely "passive victims."[121] Student activists did not hesitate to associate passivity with Holocaust imagery. "We will not play the Jews; we will not go to prison," one activist declared.[122] The notion of non-violence now appeared as an "ideology" that served to legitimize violence and hence raised the need to discuss "under which historical forms of repression that use of violence would be legitimate."[123] Following the theories of Herbert Marcuse and Frantz Fanon, Oskar Negt insisted on a right to "counter-violence."[124] The notion of the "latent violence" of the West German state thus became one of the main arguments to legitimize counter-violence. Former activist Peter Schneider later characterized this theory as a "linguistic sleight of hand" that would deem "any sort of rule in late capitalist society" as "structural violence" and hence as legitimizing counter-violence.[125]

---

[119] Etzemüller, *1968 - Ein Riss in der Geschichte?*, 138–40, Michels, *Schahbesuch*, 179, 194–5.

[120] Etzemüller, *1968 - Ein Riss in der Geschichte?*, 140. On the process of the modernization of the BGS in the 1960s, see David Livingstone, "The Bundesgrenzschutz: Re-civilizing Security in Postwar West Germany, 1950" (Ph.D. Dissertation, University of California, San Diego, 2018), Chapter 7.

[121] Semler cited in "Apo. Nach vorn geträumt," *Der Spiegel* 22/46 (1968): 67–72, Thomas, *Protest Movements in 1960s West Germany*, 152.

[122] Cited in Hanno Balz, "Militanz, Blues und Stadtguerilla. Konzepte politischer Gegengewalt," Rotaprint 25, ed., *agit 883*, 127–39,, here 135.

[123] C. Rainer Roth, "Zum Ritual der Gewaltlosigkeit," in Grossmann and Negt, eds, *Die Auferstehung der Gewalt*, 148–67.

[124] Oskar Negt, "Rechtsordnung, Öffentlichkeit und Gewalt," in ibid.

[125] Schneider, *Rebellion und Wahn*, 272.

At least in some cases, violent confrontation with the authority of the state yielded activists the desired effect of forming and intensifying communal bonds. Protest activities or demonstrations offered an alternative to endless discussions of Marxist theories. Marion, a member of *Kommune 2*, who did not have a high school diploma (*Abitur*) and was not well versed in Marxist revolutionary rhetoric, described her silence in discussions as pathological and sought to compensate for her perceived rhetorical deficits with "courage and aggression in illegal action."[126] Breaking through a police cordon thus became an important aspect in overcoming a "fear of authority."[127] Another activist reported that big demonstrations at the Free University or in the Berlin city center produced "euphoria" in activists, and that "everybody secretly hoped to be arrested or imprisoned in order to play the political martyr." Conversely, Marion acknowledged "some disappointment" when they could not provoke the police to violence. One tended to be "distinctly sad that everything remained lame and quiet," an activist reported.[128] At the same time, the SDS was aware of the necessity to control and channel the students' volatile emotions. As Inga Buhmann reported, it was important not to "frustrate the inflamed emotions" and to guide them "into politically useful and sustainable channels." Otherwise, one might run the risk of "running into police traps."[129]

The direct experience of state authority and police violence thus not only fostered common emotional bonds, it also produced fear and helplessness. Student activists recognized the considerable power of the West German state in violent incidents. "Our resources for enlightenment and instruments of power are simply ridiculous compared to the tremendous media institutions as well as the powerful state and party administrations," Hans-Jürgen Krahl noted in May 1968. "Flyers" or "ongoing discussions" hardly offered an adequate counterweight to the forces of the modern state.[130] Many activists began to experience intense fear of police violence. In the aftermath of the demonstrations on Kurfürstendamm in December 1966, students agonized over "how not to panic" in the street when the police arrived.[131] After the escalation on June 2, 1967, Rudi Dutschke discerned a "passive" and "resigned" attitude among fellow activists. He warned against

---

[126] Christl Bookhagen, Eike Hemmer, Jan Raspe, Eberhard Schultz, Marion Stergar, *Kommune 2: Versuch der Revolutionierung des bürgerlichen Individuums. Kollektives Leben mit politischer Arbeit verbinden!* (Berlin: Oberbaumverlag, 1969), 290–1. On silence as pathological, see Nina Verheyen, *Diskussionslust. Eine Kulturgeschichte des "besseren Arguments" in Westdeutschland* (Göttingen: Vandenhoeck & Ruprecht, 2010), 283.

[127] Ibid. 32, 47.

[128] Charlotte Rieden, *Ich lebte in einer Kommune. Eine Stundentin berichtet über ein Experiment junger Menschen und ihre Erfahrungen* (Berlin: Morus Verlag, 1970), 13.

[129] Buhmann, *Ich habe mir eine Geschichte geschrieben*, 200.

[130] Hans-Jürgen Krahl, "Römerbergrede," in Krahl, *Konstitution und Klassenkampf*, 153.

[131] Cited in Lönnendonker et al., *Die antiautoritäre Revolte*, 310.

rationalizing "one's own helplessness" and—again referencing the contemporary stereotype of the passive Jewish victim—thus turning themselves into "Jew[s]."[132]

Such sentiments reflected real feelings of isolation among student activists. Rather than raising the consciousness of the "masses" by exposing the repressive features of the West German state, violence mobilized the population against the student activists.[133] In the aftermath of the Ohnesorg assassination, 41 per cent of West Germans blamed the students, while only 12 per cent held the police responsible for the escalation. In West Berlin, the support for the police was even stronger and amounted to 78 per cent, and 94 per cent of the working class supported the police.[134] In the aftermath of the anti-Vietnam War demonstrations in Berlin, some 80,000 Berliners demonstrated in support of the United States in February 1968. The New Left's attack on the American involvement in Vietnam, in particular, challenged West Germans' trust in US protection in the Cold War, which, as we have seen in Chapter 3, had been crucial in reducing popular Cold War fears by the early 1960s. This popular backlash against the New Left generated significant emotional force in the counter-demonstrations, which employed hostile and ugly slogans that branded Dutschke as "Public Enemy No. 1" or professed "Better Dead than Red." At the same demonstration, the incensed crowd falsely identified the 25-year-old passerby Lutz Dieter Mende as Dutschke and threatened to "beat him to death" or to "lynch him." A policeman saved him.[135] A few months earlier, on Christmas Eve 1967, Friedrich Wilhelm Reinhard Wachau, a war veteran, actually beat Dutschke bloody at a demonstration at the Berlin Gedächtniskirche. He later bragged publicly about his Nazi past and suggested that all Berliners should follow his example.[136] After the Easter riots in the wake of the Dutschke assassination attempt in May 1968, *Stern* published a letter by a writer identifying himself as an "ordinary worker" who argued that the state should "[g]ive the police the authority to use flame throwers rather than water cannons," such that the "entire affair would be over."[137] For most West Germans, increasingly violent demonstrations did not expose the fascist nature of the state but rather led to increasing solidarity with the state and increasing aggression toward the students. The activist Inga Buhmann remembered that when she was in Berlin she was constantly afraid of "spontaneous attacks."[138] Similarly, Wolfgang Lefèvre

---

[132] Rudi Dutschke, "Vom Antisemitismus zum Antikommunismus," in Bergmann, *Rebellion der Studenten*, 80. Krahl described similar attitudes after an eviction of students from the Free University: see Hans-Jürgen Krahl, "Zur Geschichtsphilosophie des autoritären Staates, Mai 1968–August 1968," in Krahl, *Konstitution und Klassenkampf*, 206.

[133] Infas report, *Student und Öffentlichkeit*, 33.   [134] Ibid. 29, 37, 41.

[135] Thomas, *Protest Movements in 1960s West Germany*, 160, Brown, *West Germany and the Global Sixties*, 236, "Hängt ihn auf," *Stern* 21/9 (1968): 188.

[136] Nirumand, *Weit entfernt*, 154–5, "Der Mann, der Dutschke schlug," *Stern* 21/4 (1968): 177–9. For critical responses to this article by readers, see Martin Meierkord, Pastor, in *Stern* 21/20 (1968): 5, Otto Alfred Bouda, *Stern* 21/7 (1968): 5.

[137] *Stern* 21/19 (1968): 5, also cited in Etzemüller, *1968—Ein Riss in der Geschichte?*, 131.

[138] Buhmann, *Ich habe mir eine Geschichte geschrieben*, 195.

Figure 6.3. Counter-demonstration against the New Left in West Berlin, February 1967.

The New Left not only faced the opposition of state authorities but also of large sections of the West German population. Individual attacks by enraged citizens contributed to SDS activists' sense of fear and isolation.

Source: bpk-Bildagentur, No. 30004456.

actually got a haircut after the Berlin Vietnam Congress because he "was afraid of the inflamed population."[139]

How to confront their fears of police violence as well as violence emanating from the population thus became an increasingly important topic within the student movement.[140] Rainer Langhans reported that conquering fear had made the later terrorist Andreas Baader popular among student activists. He compared Baader favorably to "the little sons of the bourgeoisie," including himself as well as Baader's eventual accomplice, Ulrike Meinhof, whom he saw as "very torn, bourgeois, and anxiety-ridden."[141] Bernd Rabehl also stressed the limitations of middle-class people, including himself, saying that "only workers are capable of" more extreme forms of protest.[142] Hours before the attempted assassination on April 11, 1968, Rudi Dutschke said he was not afraid because "friends watch[ed]

---

[139] "Dutschke lässt seine Revoluzzer allein," *Stern* 21/8 (1968): 22.

[140] Pilzweger, *Männlichkeit zwischen Gefühl und Revolution*, 307.

[141] Langhans, *Ich bin's*, 91–2, also cited in Pilzweger, *Männlichkeit zwischen Gefühl und Revolution*, 187.

[142] Bernd Rabehl, in *Die Linke antwortet Jürgen Habermas*, 156.

over him" and he was careful not to "drive around by himself."[143] Student activists thus propagated an explicit denial of fear as an essential element of male revolutionary subjectivity.

Humor and parody were other ways of containing fear of state violence. Student activists consciously displayed humor and a relaxed habitus in order to contain their own fear. "Our strength is our disorder, which makes us flexible," a flyer the Berlin SDS published in 1968 read. "Insecurity makes us inflexible. If we are afraid, tense, and cannot laugh anymore, we are finished."[144] Activists considered humor an essential element of revolutionary masculinity.[145] Inspired by the "provo" group in Amsterdam, the members of *Kommune 1* planned a "pudding" attack on US Vice-President Hubert Humphrey during his visit to West Berlin on April 6, 1967. However, the Berlin police, acting on US intelligence, arrested Fritz Teufel, Dieter Kunzelmann, and other activists before they could carry out the plan. Their goal was to elicit an excessive and hysterical reaction of state authorities, which they could then readily ridicule.[146] *Kommune 1* eschewed the theoretical discussions of the SDS and adopted a more activist stance.[147] Undeterred, *Kommune 1* published a series of flyers in response to a fire in a department store in Brussels in which 250 had been killed. They characterized the fire as an "unusual performance" in which a "burning department store with burning people conveyed for the first time in a European metropolis the crackling feeling of Vietnam that we have thus far missed in Berlin." They asked, "When will the Berlin department stores burn?"[148] These actions led to the arrest of Teufel and Langhans for "incitement to arson" on June 2, 1967. The ensuing trial, in which an entire series of literary critics analyzed the meaning of the flyers, then became another occasion to ridicule state authorities.[149] The answer to the question as to when Berlin department stores would burn was answered in April 1968, when Andreas Baader and Gudrun Ensslin set fire to two Frankfurt department stores. This marked the foundational moment of West German terrorism.[150] In retrospect, the satirical use of violent rhetoric thus does not seem so funny anymore.

---

[143] Rudi Dutschke, interview with *Stern*, April 11, 1968, Rudi Dutschke, *Mein langer Marsch. Reden, Schriften, Tagebücher aus zwanzig Jahren* (Reinbek: Rowohlt, 1980), 128; see Reimann, "Zwischen Machismo und Coolness," 236.

[144] Cited in Pilzweger, *Männlichkeit zwischen Gefühl und Revolution*, 188.   [145] Ibid. 187.

[146] On the entire episode, see Reimann, *Dieter Kunzelmann*, 143–47, and Koenen, *Das rote Jahrzehnt*, 154.

[147] This distinction is emphasized in Scharloth, *1968. Eine Kommunikationsgeschichte*.

[148] Cited in Reimann, *Dieter Kunzelmann*, 150–1. The fire most likely did not result from arson.

[149] Ibid. Koenen, *Das rote Jahrzehnt*, 155–7.

[150] Koenen, *Das rote Jahrzehnt*, 156; see also Gerd Koenen, *Vesper, Ensslin, Baader. Urszenen des deutschen Terrorismus* (Frankfurt a/M: S. Fischer, 2005), 133–49.

Emotions and Sexuality

On May 5, 1967, the student Peter Schneider gave a speech to the full assembly of all faculties at the Free University in Berlin. Schneider, who had become one of the spokespersons of the West German New Left, began by conceding that "we have made mistakes." Roughly a month before the murder of Benno Ohnesorg, Schneider criticized a too-compromising attitude among his fellow student activists, which, he argued, was morally problematic in the face of injustices and hypocrisies on a global scale. "We have accepted congratulations for passing our Gothic exam while our Federal President congratulated the South African government on its racist policies. We believed in the freedom of academia just as others believed in the freedom of South Vietnam." While peaceful protests and playing by the rules had been ineffective, Schneider now advocated a strategy of deliberately breaking the rules, of direct action:

> We realized that we first need to destroy the grass before we can destroy the lies about Vietnam, that we first need to change the direction of our marching before we can change the emergency laws, that we first need to break the rules of the house before we can change the rules of the university.

Schneider closely tied this strategy of direct action to a new emotional intensity. He castigated a "rationality, which only indicates fatigue; a condemnation of emotions that allows the ruling class to talk about torture in Vietnam as calmly as about the weather; an allegedly democratic behavior that seeks to prevent democracy; and law and order that only allow the oppressors to relax." For him, the best strategy against a "hypocritical rationality and the dearth of emotions" was to stop making arguments and embrace direct action—that is, "to sit down right here in the hallway."[151]

Schneider's speech encapsulated not just the content of the student protest but also its emotional dimension. He linked his and his peers' dissatisfaction with life at the university with national debates (the emergency laws) as well as global injustices (South Africa, Vietnam). Yet the emotional style of his speech was as important as its content. While Schneider distanced himself from many aspects of the student movement in the autobiography he published 40 years later, he espoused continuing commitment to a new emotional intensity, saying that ordinary Berliners' and his own family's "blocked emotions" (*Gefühlsstau*) had

---

[151] Peter Schneider, "Wir haben Fehler gemacht," in Peter Schneider, *Ansprachen. Reden-Notizen-Gedichte* (Berlin: Wagenbach, 1970), 7–14. On this speech, see Kraushaar, *Achtundsechzig*, 82–4, and Pilzweger, *Männlichkeit zwischen Gefühl und Revolution*, 183.

been a major impetus for the movement.[152] To be sure, fear and anxiety, as well as other strong emotions, were being de-pathologized and could be expressed more openly from the late 1950s onward. And "emotional dearth" did not always shape the relationship between generations: many activists appeared to have had an emotional and warm relationship with their parents.[153] Still, the emphasis of the 68ers on a new emotionality, as well as the long-term effects of this "new sensibility" for West German emotional culture, was profound.[154] To use Marxian terms, the 68ers transformed an already existing quantitative change within West German emotional culture into qualitative change with far-reaching implications for the ensuing history of the Federal Republic.[155]

Student activists' new sensibility derived from a variety of factors. The emotional shock of the encounter with Nazi crimes and the projection of the suffering of Nazi victims onto the suffering of people in the Third World played an important role. While activists' self-description as the "new Jews" echoed postwar narratives of German victimization, they also propagated an identification with the suffering of faraway people. The growing concern for the suffering of others, constituted one of the central, if not very well understood, cultural transformations of the Federal Republic in the 1960s. It was a key factor that distinguished the first postwar generation, who had experienced the losses, suffering, and hardships of war and postwar, from the ensuing generation. This increasing sensitization to the suffering of others in the Third World provided the emotional basis for the development of the West German human rights movement.[156]

Student activists also felt that they suffered more intensely than others from the "political and psychological barbarism" in the Federal Republic. According to Reimut Reiche, who later became a psychoanalyst, student activists' perception of reality reflected a new "awareness of reality" that was more sensitive to existing injustices and hence became the basis of political activism.[157] The discrepancy between students' own sensitivity and the callousness and emotional dullness of the majority in society gave the 68ers their sense of a political and revolutionary mission.[158] According to Reiche, the only option for thus sensitized activists was

---

[152] Schneider, *Rebellion und Wahn*, 35, 55.

[153] Von Hodenberg, *Das andere Achtundsechzig*, 53–65.

[154] Reimut Reiche, "Verteidigung der neuen Sensibilität," in *Die Linke antwortet Jürgen Habermas*, 90–103.

[155] On the significance of the student movement in transforming emotional culture, see also Maik Tändler, *Das therapeutische Jahrzehnt. Der Psychoboom in den siebziger Jahren* (Göttingen: Wallstein, 2016), 103.

[156] Lora Wildenthal, *The Language of Human Rights in West Germany* (Philadelphia: University of Pennsylvania Press, 2013), Jan Eckel, Samuel Moyn, eds, *The Breakthrough: Human Rights in the 1970s* (Philadelphia: University of Pennsylvania Press, 2013), Lasse Heerten, *The Biafran War and Postcolonial Humanitarianism. Spectacles of Suffering* (Cambridge: Cambridge University Press, 2017).

[157] Reimut Reiche, "Verteidung der 'neuen Sensibilität," in *Die Linke antwortet Jürgen Habermas*, 90–103.

[158] Pilzweger, *Männlichkeit zwischen Gefühl und Revolution*, 114; see also 100–6.

either an emotional collapse in light of the intolerable political and societal conditions or a "psychic stabilization" through political activism and engagement in organizations like the SDS. Rebellion thus became a psychological and emotional necessity. The "Easter riots" in the aftermath of the attempted Dutschke assassination in April 1968 enabled, for example, a "temporary overcoming of individual psychological deformations."[159]

Activists advanced a dialectical understanding of the relationship between feelings and action: emotions inspired and motivated action, while political action entailed important sensual and emotional aspects. Thus emotions heightened activists' political consciousness and forged a path to personal liberation.[160] This understanding formed the theoretical basis of revolutionary subjectivity. Yet, in practice, this mutually constitutive relationship did not always function as leaders might have expected. Indeed, the failure of alignment between inner psychological states and external political action became one of the central and ultimately unresolved problems of the New Left. Political action often remained removed from the subjective concerns of activists, and their personal lives were often difficult to coordinate with their political ideas.

The sexual lives of activists proved particularly difficult to mold to their ideals. For student activists, emotions were virtually identical with sexuality. They believed they should articulate and perform the new emotional expressiveness through sexuality. Sexuality also distinguished the New Left from the generation that came of age in the 1950s. Student activists conceived of the sexuality of the postwar period as repressive, inhibited, and anxiety-producing. Following the theories of Wilhelm Reich, they associated repressive sexuality with authoritarian political inclinations and eventually with fascism. However, as historian Dagmar Herzog has shown, the New Left reacted against the conservative and Christian postwar reaction to the fascist transgressions of sexual norms, not against fascist sexuality. Their sexual politics was therefore not anti fascist but anti-*post*fascist.[161]

Many student activists believed Reich's theories and saw heterosexual intercourse as the path to personal and political liberation, the way to overcome anxiety and repression. The personal ads in the New Left publication *agit 883* almost all expressed the desire for political liberation in and through sex. Almost all were men seeking women. One B. Schibrowski, for example, asked:

Who knows a psychoanalyst who adheres to the analytical theory of Wilhelm Reich? Which patient, politically aware woman (17–20 years) is prepared to help

---

[159] Reimut Reiche, "Verteidigung der 'neuen Sensibilität,'" 95, 100.

[160] See Reimut Reiche, "Sexuelle Revolution—Erinnerungen an einen Mythos," in Kraushaar, ed., *Frankfurter Schule und Studentenbewegung. Vol. 3*, 150–66.

[161] Dagmar Herzog, *Sex after Fascism. Memory and Morality in 20th Century Germany* (Princeton: Princeton University Press), 154–62. See also Brown, *West Germany and the Global Sixties*, 304–9.

me out of my sexual distress and thereby help me to overcome the repressive bourgeois fetters of my bourgeois environment? The attempt to do so will not be entirely easy.[162]

The link between theoretical enlightenment and practical sexual liberation was especially apparent here. While activists thought to overcome the allegedly repressive and anxiety-ridden sexuality of the previous generation, their parents often had a more sympathetic attitude toward sexual liberalization.[163] It is also hard to tell whether activists experienced sexual suffering or whether, as Reimut Reiche suggested, the New Left engaged in a "sexualization of political problems"—that is, in the idea that difficult political and social problems could be solved sexually.[164] In either case, the theoretical link between sexuality and politics, and the added significance that sexual behavior assumed for political activism, constituted a central innovation of the New Left as well as a major source of revolutionary anxiety. Sexuality now assumed a huge significance for antifascist politics, and this theoretical ideal rarely lived up to the reality of lived experiences. "The sexual revolution overwhelmed us all. We slept with each other rather quickly, but not much exciting happened there," the former activist Sigrid Fronius remembered.[165] The New Left overburdened sexuality with political significance and overestimated its role for political emancipation.[166]

The link between sexual and political liberation was also difficult to maintain because student activists' demand for sexual liberation aimed at a moving target that no longer fit contemporary West German society. Contemporaries described a veritable "sex wave" and an increasing public visibility of sexuality.[167] The introduction of the pill in 1961 further accelerated this trend.[168] Debate over sexuality and sexual practices was increasingly mainstream years before student protests erupted. For theorists like Reimut Reiche, this liberalization of sexuality in West German society constituted a particularly cunning strategy of capitalist rule. Sexuality had become a commodity whose increasing consumption stabilized the social and political order. There was only a "seeming sexualization" (*Scheinsexualisierung*) of

---

[162] Cited in Massimo Perinelli, "Longing, Lust, Violence, Liberation. Discourses on Sexuality on the Radical Left in West Germany, 1969–1972," in Scott Spector, Helmut Puff, Dagmar Herzog, eds, *After the History of Sexuality. German Genealogies with and beyond Foucault* (New York: Berghahn, 2012), 258. Also cited in Pilzweger, *Männlichkeit zwischen Gefühl und Revolution*, 262.

[163] Von Hodenberg, *Das andere Achtundsechzig*, 171–5.

[164] Reiche, "Sexuelle Revolution—Erinnerungen an einen Mythos," 160.

[165] Sigrid Fronius in Kätzel, *Die 68erinnen*, 29.

[166] See also Sven Reichardt, *Authentizität und Gemeinschaft. Linksalternatives Leben in den siebziger und frühen achtziger Jahren* (Berlin: Suhrkamp, 2014), 675, 720.

[167] Elizabeth Heineman, *Before Porn Was Legal. The Erotica Empire of Beate Uhse* (Chicago: University of Chicago Press, 2011), Sybille Steinbacher, *Wie der Sex nach Deutschland kam. Der Kampf um Sittlichkeit und Anstand in der frühen Bundesrepublik* (Munich: Siedler, 2011), von Hodenberg, *Das andere Achtundsechzig*, 151–86.

[168] Eva-Maria Silies, *Liebe, Lust und Last. Die Pille als weibliche Generationserfahrung in der Bundesrepublik, 1960–1980* (Göttingen: Wallstein, 2010).

mainstream public life: sexual desires were manipulated, artificially stimulated, and commodified. Traditional bourgeois society, Reiche argued, had been based on the sublimation of sexual drives—that is, the channeling of sexual desire into social or culturally useful and productive activities. Following Herbert Marcuse, Reiche argued that contemporary society had advanced the "repressive de-sublimation" of sexual drives—that is, the acting out of sexual desire in ways that either stabilized the social order or converted them into aggression against groups that might destabilize the social order, such as the student movement. In either case, a "naïve confidence" in the "liberation of genital sexuality," as Reich had displayed it, was misleading. He called for more than a "quantitative increase in sexual freedom" to advance "radical systemic opposition and class struggle." Ultimately, sexual emancipation could only be had in conjunction with "political" and "individual" emancipation.[169]

Communes were figured as a place to translate such theoretical insights about sexuality into lived reality. These living arrangements were supposed to free the individual from bourgeois and repressive education to forge the new human being. The most prominent example was *Kommune 1*, which centered around Dieter Kunzelmann, Fritz Teufel, and Rainer Langhans.[170] When the commune formed in early 1967, internal discussions focused on its role in political activism, not on sexual liberation.[171] Yet, sex ultimately shaped the public reception of *Kommune 1*, aided in no small part by frequent media reporting on the commune. A commune member, Ulrich Enzensberger, in a letter to Andreas Baader in prison, described "group sex" as a "selling point" for the commune, meaning that members promoted a vision of sexual freedom in the press in order to attract media attention.[172] The commune received extensive fan mail from throughout West Germany. "Your last letter (that is your first to us) of 6 January 1968 made us very happy," two girls wrote to Fritz Teufel. "The fact that the famous enfant terrible (*Bürgerschreck*) descends to our level and writes to us personally is just great."[173] Others, especially young women, sent pictures and announced that they would "stop by," offering themselves as groupies might to rock stars.[174] The members of the commune thus appeared as glamorous practitioners of an enlightened sexuality and politics, and as highly advertised role models for young people throughout West Germany.

[169] Reimut Reiche, *Sexualität und Klassenkampf. Zur Abwehr repressiver Entsublimierung* (Frankfurt a/M: Neue Kritik, 1968), 8, 11, 138.

[170] The other members were Ulrich Enzensberger, Hans-Joachim Hameister, Dorothea Ridder, Dagmar Seehuber, Dagrun Enzensberger, and, later, Antje Krüger; see Brown, *West Germany and the Global Sixties*, 52–3.

[171] Koenen, *Das rote Jahrzehnt*, 154.

[172] Letter, Ulrich Enzensberger to Andreas Baader, May 10, 1968, HIS, SAK 130,01.

[173] Maris and Michaela P., letter to Fritz Teufel, HIS, STK, 130,02.

[174] Letter, Edelgard to Fritz Teufel, December 4, 1967, HIS, SAK 13.0,01.

The fantasies and desires that outside observers projected onto *Kommune 1*, however, stood in sharp contrast to its conflict-ridden inner reality. Members were hesitant to abandon the safety of their own apartments and to join the commune. They also felt fear and distrust for each other.[175] Indeed, members saw Dieter Kunzelmann as a "tyrant."[176] According to a female activist, Inga Buhmann, "a few guys who believed they had the right, because they possessed the truth about the world" ruled the commune in a "brutal authoritarian manner," and "were allowed to destroy everyone who still had scruples or even just enormous difficulties."[177] Another woman, Dagmar Pryztulla, said that *Kommune 1* reflected the "patriarchal structure of society" in spite of its supposedly revolutionary nature. "A sadism ruled there, especially against women," she added, "that was unbelievable."[178] Some imitations of *Kommune 1* also replicated its problematic gender dynamics. "Sven," for example, wrote to "Dieter, Rainer, Fritz etc." about his own experiment with communal living and how they "fired a frigid girl" who harbored a "dream of a traditional relationship in bourgeois style."[179] Such statements exposed the male camaraderie and sheer misogyny of some of these conceptions of sexual liberation.

The clownish performance of *Kommune 1*, however, should not detract from young activists' real agony and anxiety in seeking to align their personal lives with their political commitments. The report about the internal dynamics of another experiment at communal living, *Kommune 2*, reflected this difficulty. It documented the "attempt to revolutionize the bourgeois individual" by "combining collective living" with "political work" and "overcome[ing] fear and isolation." The book became a bestseller in the left-wing milieu, but it brutally exposed the difficulties and internal contradictions as well as the eventual failure of the project.[180] *Kommune 2* did not exclude traditional couples, as *Kommune 1* had, but it demanded the free articulation of feelings in frequent group discussions. "We were fascinated by the possibility to finally reveal our sexual and authority-fixated problems," the report stated of such discussions. The open expression of emotions, especially regarding sexuality, was to create new forms of emotional bonds, an alternative community with its own emotional culture and sociability that was different from majority society.[181]

---

[175] Reimann, *Dieter Kunzelmann*, 137.

[176] See letter of Reinhold (not sent), June 29, 1967, HIS, SAK 130,01.

[177] Cited in Brown, *West Germany and the Global Sixties*, 54.

[178] Dagmar Pryztulla in Kätzel, *Die 68erinnen*, 218. Dagmar actually became pregnant by Dieter Kunzelmann but then decided to have an abortion after the issue was discussed and decided by the entire commune.

[179] Letter by Sven to Dieter, Rainer, Fritz usw., December 4, 1967, HIS, SAK 130,01.

[180] Bookhagen et al, *Kommune 2*, Koenen, *Das rote Jahrzehnt*, 162–4, Reichardt, *Authentizität und Gemeinschaft*, 382–3.

[181] Bookhagen, *Kommune 2*, 34, 41. On "emotional community," see Rosenwein, "Worrying about Emotions in History." See also the excellent analysis in Scharloth, *1968. Eine Kommunikationsgeschichte*, 195–210.

Yet the utopian expectations that members of the communes invested in new forms of conversing and interacting were ultimately disappointed. Members of *Kommune 2* realized, for example, that the open articulation of inner psychological problems tended to produce only "banalities," rather than political liberation. Conversely, Marxist theory was "too abstract" to capture "subjective experiences and emotions (suffering, fear, aggression, loneliness)."[182] Christel Kalisch perceived house discussions as "heroic" and "very intense," but criticized that commune members used psychic confessions against each other in daily conflicts.[183] The failure of reality to live up to their ideals became a source of anxiety for student activists. The experience of the communes thus pointed to the work on the self as an important precondition of political transformation.[184]

Activists' attempt to forge new forms of communal living pertained not only to interpersonal relations but also to the question of education. In light of student activists' self-perception of the damaging effects of bourgeois socialization on the individual's psyche, it was only logical that the 68ers would begin to focus on child-rearing as well. Like many of their more reformist predecessors, student activists believed in the power of education to remedy the ills of bourgeois society. "The problem of today's fascism," Dutschke argued, "resides in the daily transformation of people into authoritarian personalities; it resides in education."[185] Activists began to organize alternative day care sites, so-called *Kinderläden*, at which they would practice "anti-authoritarian" child-rearing and hence raise children who would be free of the submissiveness and authoritarianism they attributed to the nuclear family. The first *Kinderladen* was *founded* in Frankfurt by Monika Seifert, the daughter of Alexander Mitscherlich, in the fall of 1967.[186] In Berlin, the idea for *Kinderläden* emerged during the Vietnam Congress in February 1968 when "otherwise fearful" children of participants put together flags from rags and sticks and played "demonstrator."[187] Observing this behavior led to the foundation of a "Central Council of Socialist *Kinderläden*" (*Zentralrat sozialistischer Kinderläden*) in West Berlin, which existed from

[182] Christl Bookhagen, *Kommune 2*, 23, 33, 34, 41.
[183] Christel Kalisch in Kätzel, *Die 68erinnen*, 265.
[184] Heide Berndt, "Kommune und Familie," *Kursbuch* 17 (1969): 140.
[185] Cited in Paulmann, "Die Studentenbewegung und die NS-Vergangenheit in der Bundesrepublik," 208.
[186] Monika Seifert, "Diese Wiederholung zu durchbrechen, individuell und politisch, dazu muss eine Veränderung in der Situation von Kindern kommen," in Karl-Heinz Heinemann, Thomas Jaitner, eds, *Ein langer Marsch. 1968 und die Folgen* (Cologne: PapyRossa Verlag, 1993). See also Reichardt, *Authentizität und Gemeinschaft*, 721–81, Till van Rahden, "Eine Welt ohne Familie. Über Kinderläden und andere demokratische Heilsversprechen," *WestEnd. Neue Zeitschrift für Sozialforschung* 14/2 (2017): 3–26.
[187] Katia Sadoun, Valeria Schmidt, Eberhard Schultz, *Berliner Kinderläden. Antiautoritäre Erziehung und sozialistischer Kampf* (Cologne: Kiepenhäuer & Witsch, 1970), 33–4, Hille Jan Breiteneicher, Rolf Mauff, Manfred Triebe, Autorenkollektiv Lankwitz, *Kinderläden. Revolution der Erziehung oder Erziehung zur Revolution?* (Reinbek: Rowohlt, 1971), 28.

summer 1968 to summer 1969.[188] By 1970, some 176 *Kinderläden* reportedly existed in West Germany.[189]

Interestingly, the *Kinderläden* highlighted the containment of fear as their primary goal. Irrational fears and guilt among small children pertaining mainly to childhood sexuality or bodily function, as the argument went, ultimately led to a conservative need for security. If the channeling or sublimation of drives was not possible, outright aggression and, eventually, a psychic disposition for fascism might ensue. The normative demand to abandon desire among children, they argued, caused massive damage to children's psyches.[190] Prohibitions often served, according to Monika Seifert, as "surrogates for hostility toward sexuality."[191] Authoritarianism, even sadism, and a penchant for persecuting minorities might be the result. Rejecting traditional means of socialization such as "fear and punishments," in the nuclear family, *Kinderläden* activists advocated for a possibly unlimited expression of childhood emotions, including aggression, because "acting out" those emotions was considered better than "repression." Group dynamic processes or children's own insights, rather than threats of punishments, would resolve possible conflicts.[192]

This approach entailed not just passive tolerance but active encouragement of childhood sexuality. In the Charlottenburg *Kinderladen*, for example, a huge bathtub was supposed to allow children to engage in sex games.[193] Sometimes, this also entailed sexual encounters between children and adults, which today would be seen as clear cases of pedophilia. Yet it reflected activists' genuine belief in the liberating force of early childhood sexuality.[194] The absence of fear and punishment related to sexuality and also to defecation, the theory went, would eventually produce ego-strong individuals capable of resistance.[195] The *Kinderladen* movement thus exemplified the emergence of a culture of emotional expressiveness that propagated the acting out and public performance of emotions as essential for the healthy development of democratic subjectivity.

---

[188] According to Helke Sander, this institution also served to establish the control of male activists over the *Kinderläden*: see Helke Sander in Kätzel, *Die 68erinnen*, 167. See also Brown, *West Germany and the Global Sixties*, 297, and Reichardt, *Authentizität und Gemeinschaft*, 731.

[189] Sadoun, *Berliner Kinderläden*, 15, 205, Reichardt, *Authentizität und Gemeinschaft*, 732–3.

[190] Breiteneicher, *Kinderläden*, 115.

[191] Breiteneicher, *Kinderläden*, 115, Monika Seifert, "Kinderschule Frankfurt, Eschenheimer Landstrasse," *Vorgänge* 9/5 (1970): 160. See also the memories of repressed childhood sexuality in Buhmann, *Ich habe mir eine Geschichte geschrieben*, 14.

[192] Breiteneicher, *Kinderläden*, 59, Reichardt, *Authentizität und Gemeinschaft*, 744–6, 750–1, Andreas Oswald, Sibylle Raue, *Über aggressives Verhalten in einem Kinderladen. Eine Beobachtungsstudie* (Münster: Deutsches Institut für wissenschaftliche Pädagogik, 1971).

[193] Sadoun, *Berliner Kinderläden*, 98.

[194] *Kommune 2*, "Kindererziehung in der Kommune," *Kursbuch* 17 (1969): 168–69, Koenen, *Das rote Jahrzehnt*, 166; on pedophilia, see Reichardt, *Authentizität und Gemeinschaft*, 762–77. Monika Seifert emphasized already in 1970 that children should not be overburdened by abstract theories of adults: Seifert, "Kinderschule Frankfurt, Eschenheimer Landstrasse," 162.

[195] Bookhagen, *Kommune 2*, 107.

Given the significant shortcomings of pre-school education at the time, the public reception of *Kinderläden* was surprisingly positive. As historian Till van Rahden has shown, liberal and even conservative commentators were quite receptive to the search for new approaches to education and family life.[196] The West Berlin city government was similarly sympathetic and made an initial funding commitment of 80,000 DM for the *Kinderläden*. It was a reflection of the (self-)isolation and paranoia of *Kinderläden* activists that they tended to ignore these positive responses and instead focus on negative reports in *Bild* as well as in an article in *Stern* in March 1969, which ridiculed the *Kinderläden* as chaotic, dirty, permissive, and neglectful of children.[197] More importantly, activists soon realized the difficulty and even impossibility of living up to the ideal of anti-authoritarian child-rearing. Notwithstanding the rejection of bourgeois criticism, they found that the anti-authoritarian approach often descended into chaos and rendered any political work impossible. Even though the *Kinderladen* approach did not imply simply *laissez-faire*, but was supposed to encourage the self-regulation of children, practical difficulties abounded. In the *Kinderladen* S., for example, all the toys were spread out on the floor, making it impossible for the children to play with any of them.[198]

Ultimately, it was not the hostility of the bourgeois press or, for that matter, the practical problems of anti-authoritarian education that doomed the *Kinderläden* as a political project in the eyes of the activists. The "effectiveness of the *Kinderläden*," as one report concluded self-critically, had been exaggerated both "within the liberal and the conservative press" but also within the "student movement."[199] It was impossible, another report concluded, to achieve a "politicization of the parents" in and through "work with children."[200] Instead, *Kinderladen* activists increasingly became aware of their own emotional and psychic limitations. The extremely high pedagogical ambition left educators in constant fear that they would "make a mistake."[201] Activists thus eventually deemed their own failure to "totally and radically eradicate" their own "internalized bourgeois self" responsible for the failure of the project.[202] As a member of *Kommune 2* put it, the precondition of "child raising without fear" was the sensitization of the teacher to their own "authoritarian behavior towards the children." To affirm children's sexuality, educators had to become aware of their own "repressions."[203]

---

[196] Van Rahden, "Eine Welt ohne Familie," 16–17, Reichardt, *Authentizität und Gemeinschaft*, 757–62.

[197] "Deutschlands unartigste Kinder," in *Stern* 9 (March 1969), reprinted in Sadoun, *Berliner Kinderläden*, 153–6. See also Reichardt, *Authentizität und Gemeinschaft*, 755.

[198] Breiteneicher, *Kinderläden*, 44.   [199] Ibid. 147.

[200] Sadoun, *Berliner Kinderläden*, 228.

[201] Tändler, *Das therapeutische Jahrzehnt*, 276–8. This also meant an exploration of one's own unconscious: see Anthony D. Kauders, *Der Freud-Komplex. Eine Geschichte der Psychoanalyse in Deutschland* (Berlin: Berlin Verlag, 2014), 220–1.

[202] Breiteneicher, *Kinderläden*, 122, Herzog, *Sex after Fascism*, 170.

[203] Bookhagen, *Kommune 2*, 104–5.

The logical conclusion was that they had to fix themselves first. The former activist Karl Heinz Heinemann recalled, for example, his "anxiety to overcome his own authoritarian character and his habitual repression of sexuality."[204] The "education of the educators" thus necessarily needed to precede anti-authoritarian education.[205] This was an important and consequential insight because it located authoritarianism and a fascist disposition not just in external structures, as had been common within the New Left up to this point, but also within antifascist selves. It introduced a new anxiety about and within the self, which became important for West German emotional culture in the aftermath of 1968.

Activists saw at least two solutions to this perceived failure to reconcile the "anti-capitalist struggle" with "non-bourgeois life." Given their own inability to put aside "bourgeois ideology" and their attachment to an "individualistic psychic structure," they decided to embrace proletarian consciousness more explicitly. They put aside work with children in favor of working among the proletariat in West Germany's factories.[206] Communist splinter groups formed in the 1970s. They resolved the tension between personal liberation and political activism by solely embracing the latter, often also adopting and accepting a new rigid and authoritarian discipline that all but abandoned their earlier emphasis on sexual or emotional liberation.

Other activists retained their commitment to changed lifestyles and new cultural norms, and became part of the "hedonistic left."[207] They did not completely abandon their political aspirations but felt they were rooted in practices of daily life. For example, Frank Böckelmann, the author of a volume called *Liberation in Daily Life*, faulted the early commune activists for their "completely irrational hopes" and their exaggerated expectations of "quick successes, a comforting collective, and the strengthening of their own selves."[208] Yet they did not abandon entirely the search for ongoing forms of communal solidarity that would allow a certain degree of self-determination and "exterritoriality" in capitalist society. The lessons of "68" paved the way for a broadly left-wing alternative milieu that sought to retain a commitment to social and political change yet anchored it more strongly in a wide variety of private arrangements. The goal was to achieve a form of togetherness free of "the pressure to perform, of frustration, and of fear," as the title of Böckelmann's book advocated. Yet activists now recognized and respected a multitude of paths to this goal that did not always follow neo-Marxist

---

[204] Seifert, "Diese Wiederholung," 73.

[205] Reichardt, *Authentizität und Gemeinschaft*, 742.

[206] Breiteneicher, *Kinderläden*, 149, Bookhagen, *Kommune 2*, 304.

[207] Diethart Kerbs, ed., *Die hedonistische Linke. Beiträge zur Subkultur Debatte* (Berlin and Neuwied: Luchterhand, 1970).

[208] Frank Böckelmann, *Befreiung des Alltags. Modelle eines Zusammenlebens ohne Leistungsdruck, Frustration und Angst* (Munich: Roger & Bernhard, 1970), 30–1. See also Peter Brückner, "Nachruf auf die Kommunebewegung," in Kerbs, ed., *Die hedonistische Linke*, 124–42.

concepts.[209] The understanding of the liberating force of sexuality and of a non-repressive sexual education, for example, gave way to a broader embrace of emotional expressiveness. The 68ers' emphasis on sexuality shifted to a more general emphasis on emotions and emotionality as a central aspect of non-conformist, alternative subjectivity that would continue to affect West German society.[210]

Fears of Revolution

"1968" constituted an important turning point not just for the Left but also for West German conservatism.[211] A new kind of liberal-conservatism emerged as a result of liberals' confrontation with the ideology and activism of the New Left. Intellectuals who had initially shared many of the concerns of the student movement ultimately turned against the New Left. They did not abandon their earlier commitment to social and political reform (which made them "liberals") but now also engaged in a fierce defense of the West German democratic order against what they perceived to be an existential threat by the New Left (hence their "conservatism"). This group included several Social Democrats such as the philosopher Hermann Lübbe, who actually served as undersecretary of education in the Social Democratic Party (SPD)/Free Democratic Party (FDP) state government of North Rhine-Westphalia from 1966 to 1969; the political scientist Richard Löwenthal; the historian Thomas Nipperdey; and the sociologist Erwin Scheuch. The increasing radicalization of the student movement ultimately led these liberal critics to turn to the right and side with conservatives, who had rejected the demands of the student movement all along.[212]

While recent historiography has analyzed the formation of West German liberal-conservatism well, it has not sufficiently analyzed its emotional aspects.[213] The emergence of liberal-conservatism implied a shift of fear objects. Whereas

[209] On the long-term effects of the communes on lifestyles, see Scharloth, *1968. Eine Kommunikationsgeschichte*, and Reichardt, *Authentizität und Gemeinschaft*, 351–571.

[210] See also Tändler, *Das therapeutische Jahrzehnt*, 345. In general, Reichardt, *Authentizität und Gemeinschaft* and Chapter 7 in this book.

[211] Anna von der Goltz, Britta Waldschmidt-Nelson, eds, *Inventing the Silent Majority in Western Europe and the United States. Conservativism in the 1960s and 1970s* (Cambridge: Cambridge University Press, 2017).

[212] For an example of a conservative rejection of the Left, see Alfred Dregger, *Systemveränderung. Brauchen wir eine andere Republik?* (Stuttgart: Seewald, 1972). A similar shift occurred among center-right students, who organized the Association of Christian Democratic Students (RCDS), the youth organization of the Christian Democratic Union (CDU); see Anna von der Goltz, "A Vocal Minority: Student Activism of the Center-Right and West Germany's 1968," in von der Goltz and Waldschmidt-Nelson, eds, *Inventing the Silent Majority*, 82–104.

[213] Jens Hacke, *Philosophie der Bürgerlichkeit. Die liberalkonservative Begründung der Bundesrepublik* (Göttingen: Vandenhoeck & Ruprecht, 2006), A. Dirk Moses, *German Intellectuals and the Nazi Past* (New York: Cambridge University Press, 2007), Nikolai Wehrs, *Protest der Professoren. Der "Bund Freiheit der Wissenschaft" in den 1970er Jahren* (Göttingen: Wallstein Verlag, 2014). Moses and Wehrs cite this emotional dimension but do not really analyze it.

intellectuals like Erwin Scheuch and Karl Dietrich Bracher had shared many of the democratic fears of the early 1960s, they now harbored an increasingly intense fear of revolution as envisioned by the New Left.[214] They strongly objected to what they saw as the New Left's "irrationalism" and "emotionality." They used this foil to present themselves as defenders of a more traditional West German regime of emotional anti-intensity and engaged in a performative display of rationality, even though their own actions against the New Left reflected strong emotions, especially the fear of revolution. Liberal-conservatives' fears of revolution in turn inflamed fears among leftist activists that the Federal Republic was evolving into an authoritarian or fascist state. A dialectic of fear thus fueled the intense political and ideological polarization that defined the political culture of the Federal Republic after 1968.[215]

Liberal-conservatives did not react to student movement per se but rather to the splintering of the New Left in the aftermath of the dissolution of the SDS in 1969–70. The post-1968 period witnessed a proliferation of activism. Political concerns about the emergency laws and the war in Vietnam gave way to a stronger focus on activism at the universities. Direct action against academic authorities replaced theoretical reflection. Activists had decided that communication with authorities was no longer possible, in part because of the assassination attempt on Rudi Dutschke and the state response to the ensuing Easter riots.[216] Activism at the universities now often descended into obscenities or the use of firecrackers to disrupt lectures. Wilhelm Hennis, a liberal-conservative political scientist at the University of Freiburg, described observing graffiti that read "Hit Hennis on the penis" in the summer of 1969.[217] Even Theodor W. Adorno, who had inspired many of the student activists early on, also became the target of such disruptions. On April 22, 1969, three female students approached Adorno and displayed their bare breasts. He left in shock, and died three weeks later of a heart attack.[218] In the first six months of 1969, university officials called the police more than twice as often in response to student protests than during the previous six months.[219]

Liberal-conservatives saw student protests not just as infringing upon academic freedom but also as an attack on the West German state. The Munich political scientist Kurt Sontheimer, who had exhibited considerable sympathies for the student movement until 1967–8, now denounced these actions as a

---

[214] Riccardo Bavaj, "Deutscher Staat und westliche Demokratie: Karl Dietrich Bracher und Erwin K. Scheuch zur Zeit der Studentenrevolte von 1967/68," *Geschichte im Westen* 23 (2008): 149–71.
[215] Here I follow the assessment of Götz Aly, who cites a mutual "weakness" as the main factor of this dynamic; see Aly, *Unser Kampf 1968*, 200.
[216] On this shift, see Scharloth, *1968. Eine Kommunikationsgeschichte.*
[217] Wehrs, *Protest der Professoren*, 124.
[218] See Wolfgang Kraushaar, "Streit um 'Busenattentat' auf Theodor W. Adorno," *Die Welt*, August 14, 2009.
[219] Rohstock, *Von der "Ordinarienuniversität" zur "Revolutionszentrale*," 224–32.

"barbarization of political morals that extends into terrorism."[220] Liberal-conservatives worried especially about the forms and the style of the New Left protest. Whereas student activists had identified emotional expressiveness as an important element of a new revolutionary subjectivity, liberal-conservatives castigated the same phenomenon as "bubbles of irrationality" emerging from universities.[221] The authors of a volume critical of the New Left described it as a "chiliastic movement" that appealed primarily to "emotions." Its "emphasis on subjective action in the revolutionary process" led into "irrationalism." The charge of irrationalism and emotionalism thus not only helped liberal-conservatives to distance their own ostensible rationalism from the New Left but also to associate the New Left with fascism as an earlier manifestation of irrationalism. The student movement consisted, as the editor of the volume, the sociologist Erwin Scheuch, wrote, of "left-wing people from the Right."[222]

This association of the New Left with fascism was particularly powerful when it came from returned Jewish emigrants such as the Berlin political science professor Ernst Fraenkel or, from his colleague at the Otto Suhr Institute for Political Science, the Social Democrat Richard Löwenthal. Fraenkel had emigrated in 1938 and returned to Berlin in 1951. He was widely seen as one of the founding figures of West German political science and initially quite sympathetic to the concerns of the student movement—for example, by joining leftist activists' critique of right-wing fraternities. Yet, in 1967, Fraenkel came into conflict with students when he claimed an anonymous review of one of his seminars in the student newspaper *FU Spiegel* in April 1967 had infringed on his "freedom of research and teaching." While Fraenkel objected to the presence of what he called "spies" in his courses, he offered to engage in a public discussion regarding the legitimacy of anonymous reviews with students.[223] But he compared the methods of student activists with Nazi stormtroopers in an interview with the *Berliner Morgenpost* in September 1967. He repeated the statement in another interview with *Die Welt am Sonntag* in February 1968. The fact that these interviews appeared in publications of the Springer press further incensed students.[224] Richard Löwenthal engaged in the same rhetorical escalation two years later in the controversy over Walter Pabst, a professor in the Romance Language Department whom students

---

[220] Kurt Sontheimer, "Gefahr von Rechts—Gefahr von Links," in Kurt Sontheimer ed., *Der Überdruß an der Demokratie. Neue Linke und alte Rechte—Unterschiede und Gemeinsamkeiten* (Cologne: Markus Verlag, 1970), 30.

[221] Hermann Lübbe, *Endstation Terror. Rückblick auf lange Märsche* (Stuttgart: Seewald, 1978), 35.

[222] Erwin K. Scheuch, ed., *Die Wiedertäufer der Wohlstandsgesellschaft. Eine kritische Untersuchung der "Neuen Linken" und ihrer Dogmen* (Cologne: Markus Verlag, 1968), 11, 31, 34–5, 147, 184.

[223] See the materials on this controversy in BArch, NL Fraenkel, 274/74, 274/90. See also Wehrs, *Protest der Professoren*, 73, and James F. Tent, *The Free University of Berlin. A Political History* (Bloomington: Indiana University Press, 1988), 311–12.

[224] Wehrs, *Protest der Professoren*, 73. See also interview with Hans Erich Bilges, February 2, 1968, in BArch, NL Frankel, 274–92. On Fraenkel, see also Aly, *Unser Kampf 1968*, 131–5.

accused of having a compromising Nazi past. Because student protesters would not let anybody speak in defense of Pabst, including a Jewish Holocaust survivor, at a student-organized "tribunal" in December 1969, Löwenthal compared their actions to those of National Socialist students of the early 1930s.[225] Both Fraenkel and Löwenthal also feared an excess of popular sovereignty that threatened the principle of representative democracy and might lead to another popular dictatorship such as the Third Reich. Such comparisons of student protesters with fascists highlighted the importance of the Nazi past in articulating and invoking fears of revolution. Thus, both the 68ers' and their opponents' fears invoked the ghosts of the past in order to legitimize their divergent fears of revolution and denigrate their respective opponents. These parallel rhetorical strategies highlighted the presence and significance of the Nazi past in articulating political fears in the 1960s. They also constituted a strategy of rhetorical escalation that completely eliminated any residual opportunity for meaningful dialogue. Precisely because each side labeled the other as "fascist," they had no chance for meaningful dialogue or reform. After all, nobody wanted to talk to "fascists."

For liberal-conservatives, the New Left's totalitarian inclination manifested itself especially in its rejection of liberal values such as the separation between public and private and the division of powers. Whereas the expansion of the "political" into the "personal" had constituted one of the central innovations of the New Left—as well as the source of tremendous agony and anxiety—liberal-conservatives defined the existence of a non-political private sphere as an important safeguard against totalitarian intrusion. In fact, the mostly bourgeois middle- and upper-middle-class men might have perceived the New Left's attack on their private and presumably thoroughly patriarchal family life as fundamental and threatening as the New Left's ideological challenges.[226] Liberal critics like Gerhard A. Ritter were especially worried about the Left's "anti-parliamentarism" and "anti-pluralism," which, they argued, resembled the right-wing theories of Carl Schmitt. Like Schmitt, the New Left aspired to an identity of the rulers and the governed through its embrace of a council democracy and, like Schmitt, it conceived of politics primarily as the relationship between "friend" and "foe."[227] Critics also highlighted the New Left's tendency to ignore and belittle the established rules and procedures of parliamentary democracy in favor of direct action.

---

[225] Wehrs, *Protest der Professoren*, 116, Tent, *The Free University of Berlin*, 364–8.

[226] On the bourgeois liberal-conservative milieu, see Hacke, *Philosophie der Bürgerlichkeit*, and Michael Wildt, "Furcht vor dem Volk. Ernst Fraenkel in der deutschen Nachkriegsgesellschaft," in Michael Wildt, *Die Ambivalenz des Volkes. Der Nationalsozialismus als Gesellschaftsgeschichte* (Berlin: Suhrkamp, 2019), 365–86.

[227] Ritter, "Direkte Demokratie und Rätewesen," 188–216, quotations on 205–7, and "Der Antiparlamentarismus und Antipluralismus der Rechts- und Linksradikalen," in Sontheimer, ed., *Der Überdruß an der Demokratie*, 41–91. See also Erwin Scheuch's public attacks on the political scientist Peter von Oertzen in 1972. Von Oertzen had argued that councils were, in principle, compatible with the basic law: see Wehrs, *Protest der Professoren*, 247.

Even if the New Left's prospect of actually seizing power seemed remote, Löwenthal worried that it would eventually destroy the "climate of tolerance and rational discourse" that he saw as underlying liberal democracy.[228] Helmut Schelsky worried that the "excessive claim of basic rights" was underlying the strategy of the New Left to "overcome the system."[229] The critics of the New Left did not have a shared ideology but were united by a negative consensus—namely, their opposition to the New Left. Their fear of revolution thus also served as an attempt at "demarcation" from the New Left and their sympathizers at the universities.[230]

The institutional expression of the increasing distance between the most vocal portion of the student body and most professors at West German universities in the wake of "1968" was the formation of the "League for the Freedom of Science" (*Bund Freiheit der Wissenschaft*, BFW) by some of the liberal-conservative academics mentioned earlier. The founding congress in Bonn in November 1970 had 1,700 participants, and the organizers received an additional 2,000 affirmative letters. At its height in 1973, the BFW claimed a membership of 5,200. According to its first president, the Frankfurt University rector Walter Rüegg, 50 per cent were non-university members, 35 per cent were professors, 9 per cent were assistants (that is, non-tenured faculty members), and 6 per cent were students.[231] From its inception, the BFW needed to confront the accusation that it merely represented a "right-wing cartel" of conservative professors. It thus emphasized prominent Social Democrat academics like Richard Löwenthal, Hermann Lübbe, and Thomas Nipperdey within its leadership. According to one of the founding members, the political scientist and later CSU Minister of Education in Bavaria, Hans Maier, the League was supposed to counteract the massive "climate of indoctrination and fear" at the university and to encourage "intimidated and fearful professors" to resist left-wing agitators' subversion of the universities.[232] Interestingly, the League thus served a similar function as the SDS for left-wing activists: the psychic and emotional stabilization of its members. The League followed the protest model of the student movement in other ways as well: it engaged in a massive production of flyers that were supposed to counteract the flyers of left-wing student organizations; it produced posters to be displayed within the universities; it even sought to send representatives to factory gates, department stores, and into the streets to agitate on behalf of the League.[233]

---

[228] Richard Löwenthal, *Unreason and Revolution. Reflections on the Dissociation of Revolutionary Practice from Marxist Theory* (Palo Alto: Stanford University Press, 1969), 28.

[229] Helmut Schelsky, *Systemüberwindung, Demokratisierung und Gewaltenteilung. Grundsatzkonflike der Bundesrepublik* (Munich: C.H.Beck, 1973), 19–37.

[230] Wehrs, *Protest der Professoren*, 487.   [231] Ibid. 221.

[232] "Professoren sind nicht mutiger als andere," *Der Spiegel*, November 23, 1970.

[233] Bund Freiheit der Wissenschaft (BFW) Geschäftsstelle an die Sektionen und Ortskomitees, an die örtlichen Vertrauensleute, February 21, 1973, HI, BFW Box 2.

The League saw itself as a primarily defensive organization against at least three threats: first, radical students who undermined academic freedom at the university; second, professorial colleagues who, either out of conviction or because of fear and intimidation, sought to accommodate the demands of radical students; and third, university reform, especially the attempt to give equal representation to professors, non-tenured faculty members, and students within university committees.[234] The League's founding document in 1970 painted these threats in vivid colors. Left-wing forces used the legitimate demand for university reform as a cover for achieving much broader political and ideological goals. They sought to use conflicts at the university as a way to wage a "struggle of annihilation" against the so-called "late capitalist society." Another founding member, the historian Ernst Nolte, who warned against a growing "Neo-Marxism" that would turn the universities into the equivalent of "academies for political parties" (*Parteihochschulen*) designed to instruct students in "agitation and propaganda."[235] The BFW expected that New Left activism would not remain limited to the universities and would eventually expand into an attack on the West German state. Their fears of revolution thus eventually led liberal-conservatives to abandon their democratic fears of an overtly authoritarian and excessive state. Instead they called on the state to intervene and to limit the autonomy of the universities in order to circumscribe the activities of the New Left.

This perception of a threat was not purely imagined but also the product of frequent disruptions in lectures and seminars. At the University of Cologne, a "Hillgruber Committee" of student activists challenged the conservative historian Andreas Hillgruber and his approach to diplomatic and military history, and disrupted his lectures. Much of the conflict revolved around the question of how to assess student demands for critical discussion of Hillgruber's lectures: what student representatives claimed as a democratic right, Hillgruber saw as a deliberate effort to subvert his lecture. He cancelled the class, as did some other professors, rather than permit activists to take over the room.[236] The Heidelberg historian Werner Conze ended his lectures when he experienced even a minor disruption.[237] Others were more likely to engage, especially those who were used to a more active role of students from previous teaching experience in the US.[238] Still, the overall feeling was that communication was no longer possible.[239] A few incidents of physical violence on campus fed the BFW's sense of threat. In June 1971, for

---

[234] On this subject in general, see Rohstock, *"Ordinarienuniversität" zur "Revolutionszentrale."*

[235] Studentische Information, "Bund Freiheit der Wissenschaft gegründet," December 3, 1970, HI, BFW Box 22.

[236] See the extensive description of the controversy in Bund Freiheit der Wissenschaft, Sektion Köln e.V., Hillgruber und das "Hillgruber-Komitee"—ein historisches Seminar als politische Kampfstätte. Eine Dokumentation, Juni 1973, HI, BFW Box 2. See also Wehrs, *Protest der Professoren*, 306.

[237] Ibid. 302.   [238] Rohstock, *Von der "Ordinarienuniversität" zur "Revolutionszentrale,"* 207.

[239] Scharloth, *1968. Eine Kommunikationsgeschichte*, 82–94.

example, students in the Political Science Department of the Free University engaged in an exercise of "pig hunting" in which they targeted liberal professors. They threatened to throw the political scientist Alexander Schwan out of the ground-floor window and then carried him out of the room.[240] Similar incidents led the Social Science faculty at the University of Cologne to cancel all courses for the remainder of the semester in January 1973.[241]

The BFW put together several reports about such incidents. With the aid of photos, it sought to convey the impression of a reign of political extremism, chaos, and lawlessness at the universities. It claimed the Free University had become a "madhouse."[242] The BFW thus needed to engage in constant alarmist agitation to justify its continued existence. Any indication that university reform or "democratization" might actually succeed in alleviating student discontent at the university threatened to undermine the legitimacy of its existence. The permanent propagation of fears of revolution was central to the BFW's existence.[243] It countered the suggestion that 90 per cent of university courses proceeded without disruption with a reference to persecution of minorities in the Third Reich. Terrorizing even one professor would ultimately compromise the freedom of all, and left-wing radicals, like Nazis before them, would use the university as an entry point into a free society only to destroy it. Ultimately, the League's dramatization of the situation of West German academia also became problematic for state officials. In a 1972 letter, the West German Minister of Education, the SPD politician Klaus von Dohnanyi, admonished the League not to lose "a sense of proportion and sobriety" in characterizing the situation at the universities.[244] In this case, state authorities criticized the emotional intensity, not of the New Left but of their liberal-conservative opponents. Time and again, however, BFW representatives were frustrated that West German media accurately conveyed the political dangers emanating from student radicalism at the universities. Replicating the New Left's concern with the Springer press, the BFW claimed that the New Left had co-opted the press.[245] The perception of biased public media dominated by left-wing sympathizers eventually became one reason for conservatives' advocacy to privatize television in the 1980s.[246]

---

[240] Wehrs, *Protest der Professoren*, 314–15. Götz Aly, one of the student participants in this action, later characterized it as having been of a "particularly disgusting" nature: Aly, *Unser Kampf 1968*, 131. For other examples of physical attacks on professors, see Rohstock, *Von der "Ordinarienuniversität" zur "Revolutionszentrale,"* 372.

[241] Wehrs, *Protest der Professoren*, 307.

[242] For example, "Dokumentation Bilder aus deutschen Universitäten," BFW, Materialien zur Schul- und Hochschulpolitik, 4.74, HI, BFW Box 24.

[243] Wehrs, *Protest der Professoren*, 267.

[244] Bund Freiheit der Wissenschaft, "Radikalismus nicht verharmlosen," March 24, 1972, HI, BFW Box 19; Klaus von Dohnanyi to Prof. Dr. Richard Löwenthal, Prof. Dr. Walter Rüegg, Prof. Dr. Erwin K. Scheuch, Herrn Michael Zöllner, March 29, 1972, HI, BFW, Box 19.

[245] Bund Freiheit der Wissenschaft, Bundesausschusssitzung, May 31, 1975, HI, BFW Box 2.

[246] See Frank Bösch, "Campaigning against 'Red Public Television': Conservative Mobilization and the Invention of Private Television in West Germany," in von der Goltz and Waldschmidt-Nelson, eds, *Inventing the Silent Majority*, 275–94.

Calls to empower students and non-tenured lecturers in the running of the country's universities fed the BFW's anxieties, as did the fact that left-wing groups dominated the student parliaments of 46 out of 52 universities in 1973. They worried especially about the activities of the *MSB Spartacus*, the youth organization of the German Communist Party (DKP), which gained significant strength in the early 1970s and counted approximately 2,000 members at 40 universities.[247] Erwin Scheuch, for example, detected a shift in leftist strategies from their earlier "explosive excitement" to a "cold fanaticism" that aimed at systematically demoralizing individual professors. Seeking to build on anti-Communist Cold War fears that had somewhat declined over the course of the 1960s, Scheuch identified a "power struggle" between "late Marxists" and more moderate forces underway at German universities. Marxist forces especially targeted fields that trained high school teachers, which meant that, in some fields, the training of teachers turned into an "ideological indoctrination" against the free and democratic order. Some departments, he feared, would soon fall completely under the "control of late Marxists." If the current trend continued, he wrote in April 1972, moderate forces would collapse "within three semesters."[248]

Liberal-conservative academics lobbied against the ostensible "democratization" of the university that left-liberal reformers like Jürgen Habermas and Ludwig von Friedeburg, who served as Minister of Education in the state of Hesse from 1969 to 1974, still supported, even if Habermas and Friedeburg generally did not endorse demands for equal one-third representation of professors, staff, and students.[249] BFW professors demanded a system that would give them a majority role in key decisions such as the hiring of new faculty members. Only such continued dominance of professors, they claimed, would ensure the principle of performance (*Leistung*)—another key term of liberal-conservatives—rather than ideological conformity as key criteria for academic advancement. While the BFW clearly exaggerated the left-wing threat at the universities, its agitation nevertheless succeeded in delegitimizing university reform even before the West German constitutional court asserted the dominance of professors within the universities in May 1973.[250] The public agitation of the BFW also rendered it more difficult to appoint and give tenure to outspoken Marxists, especially after the SPD/FDP government had passed a law that prohibited the appointment of political extremists to positions in the civil service (*Radikalenerlass*) in February 1972.

[247] The "Sozialistische Hochschulbund" (SHB) even listed 3,000: see Rohstock, *Von der "Ordinarienuniversität" zur "Revolutionszentrale,"* 365.

[248] Erwin K. Scheuch to Klaus von Dohnanyi, April 17, 1972, HI, BFW, Box 19.

[249] Wehrs, *Protest der Professoren*, 53. On Friedeburg's tenure in Hesse, see Rohstock, *Von der "Ordinarienuniversität" zur "Revolutionszentrale,"* 315–31.

[250] Wehrs, *Protest der Professoren*, 362–70, Rohstock, *Von der "Ordinarienuniversität" zur "Revolutionszentrale,"* 364–404.

It is not surprising that the BFW and liberal-conservative academics blamed the left-wing influences at universities, and what they saw as accommodation and appeasement of leftist professors and administrators for the descent of a small segment of the New Left into violent terrorism in the 1970s. Liberal-conservative fears of revolution had transmogrified into fears of violent left-wing terrorism that had ostensibly emanated from a broader leftist milieu of "sympathizers" within the universities. Such escalating liberal-conservative fears of the Left were part and parcel of a more general proliferation of fear objects during the 1970s. This is the subject of the next chapter.

7

Proliferating *Angst*

> Wherever you look and wherever you move, whether you are involved
> in political debates or if you are following the public debate in the pre-
> political sphere, whether you engage in private conversations or follow
> what is being discussed in the media: you encounter a phenomenon that
> one does not suspect to exist in opulent societies with strong security
> guarantees, but which seems to be typical for our time, also and espe-
> cially for our immediate present: people are afraid.—David A. Seeber[1]

This diagnosis of an anxious society opened an article entitled "Fear as a Disease
of Civilization" in the *Herder Correspondence*, a Catholic monthly, in April 1977.
The author, David A. Seeber, cited a long list of fears he saw as prevalent in
German society ranging from physical and psychic illness to fears of the future
among young people, fears of social decline, of pollution, and of being dominated
by a technical and administrative apparatus. In his view, omnipresent anxiety was
a response to the naïve optimism and utopia of the previous decade. He
denounced the leftist vision of student movement and advocated a return to God.
His article was part and parcel of what contemporary intellectuals diagnosed as a
conservative shift in the public discourse at the time.[2]

Seeber's article captured a social and emotional reality in the 1970s. While it is
impossible to quantify collective emotions precisely, evidence points to a massive
increase in publicly articulated individual and collective fears in the 1970s. The
Google Ngram graph, which measures the appearance of the term "fear" (*Angst*)
in German-language literature, for example, points steadily upward from 1973
onward.[3]

According to an opinion poll in *Der Spiegel* in April 1974, West Germans were
afraid "that everything is getting worse" and expressed "growing distrust of the
ability of the government to avert such misfortune."[4] The historiography attributes
these fears to the end of an unprecedented economic boom period and the onset

---

[1] David A. Seeber, "Angst als Zivilisationskrankheit?" *Herder-Korrespondenz* 31/4 (1977): 165.
[2] Axel Schildt, "'Die Kräfte der Gegenreform sind auf breiter Front angetreten.' Zur konservativen
Tendenzwende in den Siebzigerjahren," *Archiv für Sozialgeschichte* 44 (2004): 449–78.
[3] https://books.google.com/ngrams/graph?content=Angst&year_start=1945&year_end=2018
&corpus=20&smoothing=3&share=&direct_url=t1%3B%2CAngst%3B%2Cc0 (last accessed February
29, 2020).
[4] "Umfrage: Angst und Sorge wählen CDU/CSU," *Der Spiegel* 28/16 (1974): 38.

German Angst: *Fear and Democracy in the Federal Republic of Germany.* Frank Biess, Oxford University Press (2020).
© Frank Biess.
DOI: 10.1093/oso/9780198714187.001.0001

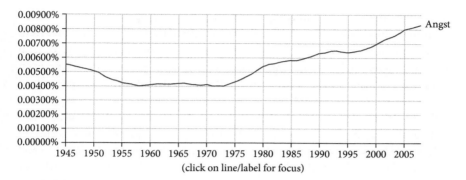

Figure 7.1. Google Ngram graph "*Angst*," 1945 to the present.

The use of the word *Angst* in German publications increased steadily from the early 1970s onward. This increased use of the term points to a proliferation of anxieties during this period.

Source: https://books.google.com/ngrams/graph?content=Angst&year_start=1945&year_end=2019&corpus=20&smoothing=3&share=&direct_url=t1%3B%2CAngst%3B%2Cc0#t1%3B%2CAngst%3B%2Cc0 (last accessed March 20, 2020).

of an economic crisis that featured increased inflation, reduced growth, and, above all, permanent structural unemployment.[5] Without belittling the influence of economic factors, this chapter situates the proliferating fears of the 1970s somewhat differently. The expansion of fear and anxiety was more of a continuity than a sharp rupture from the previous decade. As we have seen in the previous chapter, modern, democratic, and revolutionary fears always co-existed and counteracted with the reputed "optimism" of the 1960s. Nor can economics alone explain the proliferating fears of the 1970s. They were not simply an automatic reaction to a material crisis. Many contemporaries did not immediately recognize a long-term structural economic transformation and perceived the economic crisis, like previous ones, as merely cyclical.[6] The proliferation of fear thus resulted from broad, multi-causal shifts that cannot be reduced to economic factors alone. It also needs to be explained from within the history of emotions. Four factors were especially important.

First, the 1970s saw the establishment and broad cultural acceptance of a new regime of emotional expressiveness, whose origins extended back to the late 1950s. This emotional regime co-existed and, at times, competed with an older, repressive emotional regime, which sought to suppress the public articulation of emotions. Second, this new emotional regime also entailed a de-pathologization and validation of fear as a positive and useful emotion. The proliferation of fear in the 1970s reflected a new willingness to experience and express emotions, especially

---

[5] Konrad H. Jarausch, ed., *Das Ende der Zuversicht? Die siebziger Jahre als Geschichte* (Göttingen: Vandenhoeck & Ruprecht, 2008), Anselm Doering-Manteuffel, Lutz Raphael, *Nach dem Boom. Perspektiven auf die Zeitgeschichte seit 1970* (Göttingen: Vandenhoeck & Ruprecht, 2012).

[6] Ulrich Herbert, *Geschichte Deutschlands im 20. Jahrhundert* (Munich: C.H.Beck, 2014), 902.

fear and anxiety. A massive expansion of psychotherapeutic services fueled both the cultural appreciation of emotional expressivity as well as the concurrent rehabilitation of anxiety. The emergence of a therapeutic society in the Federal Republic increasingly brought into focus the self as a source and site of fear. Even as external dangers such as war receded in the age of détente, inner threats moved to the center of public attention. An emotionally expressive and anxiety-ridden self arose as part of the cultivation of a new subjectivity in the left-alternative milieu of the post-1968 period. While this milieu pioneered new forms of anxiety-ridden subjectivity, the new cultural norm of an emotionally sensitive and often fragile self also radiated into mainstream society. It manifested itself, for example, in new body fears regarding cancer or toxic substances in the food chain.

A third factor in the proliferation of anxiety was rooted in the transformation of commemorative culture. As it had in the preceding decades, the memory of a catastrophic past remained closely intertwined with the anticipation of a fearful future in the 1970s and 1980s. Yet both the substance and the manner in which the future was imagined changed. The highly emotional public reaction to the broadcast of the American television series *Holocaust* in January 1979 both indicated and promoted the new cultural norm of emotional expressivity. and promoted it as well. It led to a genuinely popular Holocaust memory. *Holocaust* also challenged the psychic mechanisms that had allowed many Germans to keep the Nazi past at an emotional distance. The discrepancy between published and public opinion regarding the Nazi past decreased at last. The popular memory of the mass murder of the Jews also changed West Germans' anticipation of the future. In particular, it shaped increasingly apocalyptic visions in the environmental and peace movements of the 1970s and 1980s.

Fourth, the fight against the leftist terrorism of the Red Army Faction (RAF) radicalized and intensified the already existing dialectics of democratic and revolutionary fears. Both the fear *of* the state and the fear *for* the state reached a climax in the "German Autumn" of 1977. This crisis situation also revealed the polyvalent political function of fear: on the one hand, fear of terrorism supported restrictions of fundamental political rights, not only through state policy "from above" but also in reaction to a populist mobilization of fear "from below." On the other hand, the fear of an overly powerful and transgressive state, as well as of a radicalized population, exercised an inhibiting function and supported the preservation of the rule of law and democratic procedures even in a pronounced crisis situation.

The Validation of Emotions

"The psychologization of society cannot be stopped," the psychotherapist Helmut Enke stated in the journal *Psychologie Heute* in November 1976. He was referring to the gradual expansion and growing cultural significance of psychotherapeutic approaches in West German society from the late 1960s onward. The Federal Republic experienced a veritable "psychoboom" in the 1970s.[7] This psychoboom continued the shift in the diagnosis of social and political problems toward "inner" and psychological factors that had already begun during the 1960s. It promoted the broader psychologization of sociological and political analysis. In this context, books such as Alexander and Margarete Mitscherlich's *The Inability to Mourn* became bestsellers. The offshoots of the student movement also increasingly placed the transformation and therapy of the self at the center of their vision of social and political change. Psychotherapy became part of the universal healthcare system. Although coverage would require a referral until 1999, this guaranteed a level of outpatient psychotherapeutic care that was unique in the world at that time.[8]

One hallmark of the psychoboom was the gradual dissolution of the boundaries between the mentally ill and supposedly healthy people. A commission of the German parliament wrote in a 1975 report that "every third person" suffers from a mental disorder at least once in a lifetime.[9] Psychologists now claimed to be able to help patients, even without obvious symptoms of mental illness, to increase their quality of life and develop greater "ego strength." Mental illnesses, conversely, no longer appeared as pathological but rather as an "extreme expression" of a "common mode of experiencing and reacting," as the popular psychoanalyst Horst-Eberhard Richter put it.[10] Richter saw apparent psychic normality potentially as indicative of a "well-functioning repression" and hence of hidden pathologies. In this view, symptoms of mental illnesses, such as an anxiety neurosis, appeared as a more honest and authentic expression of a problem that the allegedly normal people simply tended to repress.

A general revalidation of emotions accompanied this broader psychologization. The psychoboom of the 1970s sanctioned and popularized the new expressive emotional regime that had already come into being from the late 1950s onward. Psychotherapeutic experts now emphasized the crucial significance of the open articulation of emotions for the development of an authentic and healthy self. An entire series of new therapeutic offerings arose—from primal scream therapy to the Orientalism of the disciples of Bhagwan and anxiety-free pottery with herbal tea. All these approaches aimed to promote the open expression of feelings.[11] Conversely, the inability or unwillingness to express one's emotions was cast increasingly as pathological. A March 1977 article in *Psychologie Heute* (*Psychology Today*), the "official magazine of the psychoboom," described

---

[7] Georg R. Bach, Haja Molter, *Psychoboom. Wege und Abwege moderner Therapie* (Düsseldorf: Eugen Diederichs Verlag, 1976).
[8] Tändler, *Das therapeutische Jahrzehnt*, 18.   [9] Ibid. 91.
[10] Horst-Eberhard Richter, *Flüchten oder Standhalten* (Reinbek: Rowohlt, 1976), 51.
[11] On the variety of therapeutic approaches, see Molter, *Psychoboom*, Tändler, *Das therapeutische Jahrzehnt*, 322–60.

"alexithymia," the inability to have or express emotions as a pathological condition.[12] In an interview on the subject, the psychoanalyst Johannes Cremerius explained that lower-class people had higher incidence of alexithymia than the higher classes. He described the expression of feelings as closely intertwined with political emancipation, arguing that if blue-collar workers cultivated their own emotionality, they would be able to fight better for their interests. This reflected a continuity with the New Left, which also saw the expression of feelings as closely intertwined with political emancipation.[13]

The increasing popularity of psychosomatic medicine also played an important role in the general revalidation of emotions. The origins of psychosomatic medicine extended back to the late nineteenth century when a variety of approaches sought to understand the relationship between psychic conditions and somatic disease.[14] In the Federal Republic, psychosomatic approaches built on several traditions. Some segments of internal medicine increasingly focused on the relationship between "extreme experiences" and disease—for example, among returning prisoners of war from the Soviet Union. Another source was the anthropological approach to medicine that Viktor von Weizsäcker had developed during the interwar period, which assumed close links between biographical life history and disease.[15] Von Weizsäcker's former assistant and then partner, Alexander Mitscherlich, created and led a clinic for psychosomatic medicine in 1950, where he analyzed psychosomatic development through Freudian psychoanalysis and thus turned away from the medical anthropology of his mentor, von Weizsäcker.[16] Psychosomatic medicine assigned emotional life a central role in the etiology of organic diseases. For example, Mitscherlich argued in 1957 that,

[12] H. Ernst, C. Koch, "Warum Menschen gefühlsleer sind," *Psychologie Heute* 4/3 (1977): 14–17, quotation in Tändler, *Das therapeutische Jahrzehnt*, 171.

[13] "Am Fließband kann man sich keine feindifferenzierte Seele leisten. Interview mit Johannes Cremerius," *Psychologie Heute* 4/3 (1977): 15–19. On the history of this diagnosis, see Cornelius Borck, "Alexithymie oder wie der Mangel an Gefühl zur Krankheit wurde," in Alexa Geisthövel, Bettina Hitzer, eds, *Auf der Suche nach einer anderen Medizin. Psychosomatik im 20. Jahrhundert* (Frankfurt a/M: Suhrkamp, 2019), 415–33.

[14] Anne Harrington, *The Cure Within. A History of Mind-Body Medicine* (New York: W.W. Norton, 2008). On the history of psychosomatic medicine, see Geisthövel and Hitzer, eds, *Auf der Suche nach einer anderen Medizin*, especially the three introductory chapters by the editors in ibid. 23–44, 179–200, 325–48.

[15] Martin Dehli, *Leben als Konflikt. Zur Biographie Alexander Mitscherlichs* (Göttingen: Wallstein, 2007), 87–123. Von Weizsäcker's approach was compatible with some aspects of National Socialist health politics. He supervised compulsory sterilizations of patients with epilepsy and he may have been involved in medical experiments with the brains of murdered children in the so-called "euthanasia" program; see Alexa Geisthövel, "Viktor von Weizsäcker oder die 'monumentale Unruhe' einer subjektiven Medizin," in Geisthövel and Hitzer, eds, *Auf der Suche nach einer anderen Medizin*, 144–54, especially 145.

[16] Mitscherlich's conversion to Freudian analysis occurred during a four-month stay in the United States in 1951 paid for by a grant from the Rockefeller Foundation. See ibid. 176–216; Bettina Hitzer, "Oncomotions: Experiences and Debates in West Germany and the United States after 1945," in Frank Biess, Daniel M. Gross, eds, *Science and Emotions after 1945. Transatlantic Perspectives* (Chicago: University of Chicago Press, 2014), 157–78.

among 30 per cent to 50 per cent of patients, emotional relations—that is, "tensions," "arousals," and "fears"—caused their symptoms.[17] Mitscherlich identified a "two-phase repression": the first repression resulting in a classical neurosis, the second in a somatic disease.[18] The expression and articulation of (possibly unconscious) emotions that took place in a psychoanalytic conversation with a therapist thus appeared as a central means of preventing and curing organic diseases. Conversely, psychosomatic medicine identified "emotional disturbances" as etiologically relevant for the emergence of physical diseases. Although psychosomatic literature found it difficult to correlate specific psychic states or emotions with specific diseases, the general assumption of a close relationship between psyche and body reflected a new cultural validation of the emotions.

Psychosomatic theories promoted a dissolution of the boundaries between the external "social" world and the "inner" emotional and psychological reality of the self. The self became a kind of passive sounding board for pathological influences from the outside, but it also reflected those influences to the outside world through illness. This emphasis on the subjective experience of diseases could also engender social and political critique. For example, medical activists now portrayed "alienation from one's spontaneous emotionality" as a precondition of the functioning of the individual in capitalist society. The medical doctor Knut Sroka wrote in 1980 that the "dialectics of heart attack" was rooted less in "individual wrongdoing" than in "psycho-social factors" that pointed to a broader "societal crisis."[19]

Psychosomatic approaches also influenced the etiology of cancer.[20] Following studies from the United States, West German cancer experts debated whether a certain emotional condition caused, or at least contributed to, the development of cancer. An article from 1969 cited a study of over 3,200 cancer patients claiming that "cancer patients" exhibited a "stronger tendency to deny or suppress emotional conflicts" and led an impoverished emotional life—"alienated, depersonalized, with low emotionality and libido"—even before they developed the

---

[17] Alexander Mitscherlich, "Die Krankheiten der Gesellschaft und die psychosomatische Medizin," in Alexander Mitscherlich, ed., *Krankheit als Konflikt. Studien zur psychosomatischen Medizin 1* (Frankfurt a/M: Suhrkamp, 1967), 13.

[18] Mitscherlich had developed this theory already in the 1950s, see Alexander Mitscherlich, "Zur psychoanalytischen Auffassung psychosomatischer Krankheitsentstehung," *Psyche* 7/10 (1953): 561–78, and Dehli, *Leben als Konflikt*, 182–6. See also Tobias Freimüller, "Alexander Mitscherlich oder wie ein Grenzgänger zum Makler der psychosomatischen Medizin wurde," in Geishövel and Hitzer, eds, *Auf der Suche nach einer anderen Medizin*, 201–10.

[19] See "Der Preis der Entfremdung," *Psychologie Heute* 7/12 (1980): 28, Knut Sroka, *Zur Dialektik des Herzinfarkts* (Frankfurt a/M: Syndikat, 1980), 8–9, and now in general Bettina Hitzer, *Krebs fühlen. Eine Emotionsgeschichte des 20. Jahrhunderts* (Stuttgart: Klett-Cotta, 2020). This study appeared too late to be fully integrated into this book.

[20] Hitzer, "Oncomotions," 168, Bettina Hitzer, "Krebs oder wie weit reicht die psychosomatische Medizin?" in Geishövel and Hitzer, eds, *Auf der Suche nach einer anderen Medizin*, 258–72.

disease.[21] Cancer patients also showed an increased "tendency towards denial and repression." Their appearance as outwardly "well-adjusted citizens" resulted from a "blocked emotionality," from an "inability to express their feelings and affects," which then contributed to the disease.[22] Another author described the same condition as a "façade of normalcy," "a degree of mental disorder" that made it seem like a miracle that these patients succeeded in "adjusting to reality."[23] A cover story of the magazine *Der Spiegel* in 1977 thus described cancer as a "disease of the soul." According to this view, people seemingly free of anxiety and resistant to stress, who did not display hostile feelings or aggression and had adjusted well to dominant authorities and norms, might have already signed their own death certificate.[24] The related repression of emotions ran the risk of turning inward and of triggering a cancerous tumor. Breast cancer especially was often portrayed as the consequence of deficient and unfulfilled sexuality. This is why, according to *Der Spiegel*, nuns who practiced celibacy were particularly likely to suffer from cancer.[25] Even after the onset of the disease, the article stated, breast cancer patients rarely showed "open anxiety or open despair" and instead resorted to a compensatory focus on performance, repression, denial, and fantasies of self-punishment.[26] Many of these studies focused on female patients criticizing either their independence or their emotional and sexual repression, thus also negotiating changing notions of femininity and the place of women in society.[27] Psychosomatic theories of the etiology and therapy of cancer reflected the changing emotional regimes. They described a deviation from the increasingly hegemonic culture of emotional and sexual expressivity as pathological and illness-inducing. The ability to experience emotions and express them openly thus became existentially important for a healthy and viable self.

The thesis of a specific "cancer personality" formed the pathological counterpart to the culture of emotional expressiveness. While medical and popular opinion in the nineteenth century often saw cancer as a product of mental overload, the

[21] Hans-Joachim F. Baltrusch, "Einige psychosomatische Aspekte der Krebserkrankung unter Berücksichtigung psychotherapeutischer Gesichtspunkte," *Zeitschrift für Psychosomatische Medizin und Psychoanalyse* 15/1 (1969): 31–6. On Baltrusch's career, see Hitzer, *Krebs fühlen*, 78–9.

[22] Quotations in Christoph Hürny, Rolf Adler, "Psycho-onkologische Forschung," in Fritz Meerwein, ed., *Einführung in die Psycho-Onkologie*, 3rd edn (Hans Huber: Bern, Stuttgart, and Toronto, 1985), 35, Maria Blohmke, Irmgard Cramer, H. Scherg, "Krebs auch ein psychosoziales Problem?," *Fortschritte der Medizin* 95/27 (1977): 1709, Christof Jenner, "Zur Frage einer persönlichkeitsspezifischen Disposition zum Magen-Carcinom," *Zeitschrift für Psychosomatische Medizin und Psychoanalyse* 27/1 (1981): 74.

[23] Stephan Lermer, *Krebs und Psyche* (Munich: Causa, 1982), 36–7.

[24] "Krebs durch Seelenschmerz und soziale Qual?" *Der Spiegel* 31/45 (1977): 102–16.

[25] Ibid. See also Hürny and Adler, "Psycho-Onkologische Forschung," 41.

[26] D. Beck, U. König, P. Blaser, R. Meyer, J. Styk, O. Ryhiner, "Zur Psychosomatik des Mamma Carcinoms," *Zeitschrift für Psychosomatische Medizin und Psychoanalyse* 21/2 (1975): 107, 11, Michael Wirsching, "Zur Psychosomatik des Brustkrebs—Stand der Forschung und neuere Entwicklungen," *Zeitschrift für Psychosomatische Medizin und Psychoanalyse* 25/3 (1979): 240–50.

[27] For the first example, see Hitzer, "Krebs," 266.

Figure 7.2. *Spiegel* Title 45/1977, "Cancer–Disease of the Soul."

The notion of a "cancer personality" reflected the popularization of an expressive emotional regime. The cancer personality exhibited many similarities to the representation of Nazi perpetrators since the 1960s.

Source: Copyright *Der Spiegel* 45/1977.

modern cancer personality was imagined as "inhibited in [their] affective utterances."[28] The idea of a cancer personality emerged from psychoanalytically inspired research in the United States since the 1940s, which tended to attribute psychological problems to problematic relationships to one's mother. The result was an inability to experience and articulate healthy and authentic feelings. The cancer personality was emotionally stunted, and such repressed emotions, the theory went, caused through unknown mechanisms the growth of malignant tumors.[29] In the Federal Republic, the "cancer personality" exhibited obvious similarities to the representation of Nazi perpetrators as discussed in the previous chapter. Both were imagined as emotionally and sexually deficit, whereas an antifascist and "healthy" individual was believed to be sexually liberated and emotionally expressive. The representation of Nazi perpetrators in the trials of the 1960s and 1970s also often portrayed them as having outwardly normal personalities that masked invisible and destructive internal pathologies. The interpretation of breast cancer as a "failure to mourn," which invoked Alexander Mitscherlich's thesis of the "inability to mourn," further illustrates this rhetorical link between the cancer debate and the memories of the Nazi past.[30] Just as the democratic and revolutionary fears of the 1960s produced a fascist fear scenario for the future of the Federal Republic, the thesis of the cancer personality implied a similarly catastrophic future for the emotionally and sexually inhibited subject in the ensuing therapeutic decade.

The thesis of the cancer personality was also heavily contested. Critics pointed to the lack of scientific evidence for the psychological origins of cancer and pointed out that cancer diagnosis was the cause, not the result of such symptoms. Many studies in support of the cancer personality lacked a control group with non-cancer patients.[31] In her 1978 treatise, *Illness as Metaphor*, the US literary critic Susan Sontag formulated one of the most potent critiques of the "cancer personality," which she described as a particularly insidious form of stigma that blamed the disease on the patient.[32] Sontag's book was widely received in the Federal Republic. Feminists especially criticized the inherent misogynist

[28] Reinhold Schwarz, "Melancholie und Krebs. Wandel der psychosomatischen Deutung von Krebserkrankungen aus medizinisch-historischer Sicht," *Zeitschrift für Psychosomatische Medizin und Psychoanalyse* 33/2 (1987): 101–10.

[29] Hitzer, *Krebs fühlen*, 68–77. On the broader context of blaming mothers for social ills or "momism" in the United States, see Rebecca Jo Plant, *Mom: The Transformation of Motherhood in Modern America* (Chicago: University of Chicago Press, 2010).

[30] Beck et al., "Zur Psychosomatik des Mamma Carcinoms," 107, 113. On this notion of the cancer personality as a "critique of the pathology of postwar society," see Hitzer, "Krebs," 267–8.

[31] Wirsching, "Zur Psychosomatik des Brustkrebs," Schwarz, "Wandel der psychosomatischen Deutung von Krebserkrankungen aus medizinisch-historischer Sicht," 108. On this problem, see also Ronald Grossarth-Maticek, "Psychosoziale Faktoren der Krebserkrankung: Wer sich exponiert, ist gefährdet," *Psychologie Heute* 5/6 (1978): 32–9. The critique of the notion of the cancer personality did not imply a rejection of psychic or emotional etiologies: see, for example, Rolf Verres, *Die Kunst zu leben. Krebs und Psyche* (Munich: Piper, 1991).

[32] Susan Sontag, *Illness as Metaphor* (New York: Farrar, Strauss, Giroux, 1978).

assumptions of the theory of the cancer personality.[33] But this did not entail a wholesale rejection of psychosomatic approaches. These theories also empowered the subject by suggesting that biological and medical processes were quite susceptible to human will or human intervention. Psychosomatic approaches to cancer thus enabled a more holistically oriented medicine and made possible new forms of subject-centered therapies.

The demand for emotional expressivity in medical and psychiatric literature was not linked to a far-reaching political utopia, as in the preceding student movement. It resulted from a more defensive attitude that sought to protect the individual against invisible and internal dangers, which nevertheless threatened the physical and psychic integrity of the self. Fear and anxiety became particularly important emotions for this sensitization of the self to new and proliferating threats. The new cultural norm of emotional expressivity thus also included a rehabilitation of fear.

The Rehabilitation of Fear

In a 1969 article in the journal *Psychologische Beiträge*, the physician Immo von Hattingberg declared that the number of publications on the subject suggested that practitioners and scientists in a variety of fields were paying increased attention to fear. He argued that this was giving "rise to the impression that our time is particularly affected by fear."[34] In public discourse from the late 1960s onward, a wide variety of disciplines offered a reassessment of fear. Fear increasingly appeared not only as a negative but also as a quite positive emotion. In 1967, contributors to a book "on the political and societal role of fear" thus assessed the role of fear quite positively. The historian August Nitschke stated that fear—contrary to the view articulated by the Enlightenment philosopher Montesquieu—did not remain limited to tyrannical systems of government but was also present in democracies. Fear was not "unequivocally negative" and its complete elimination was not "desirable."[35] The political scientist Heiner Flohr agreed and argued that a "negative evaluation of fear was not self-evident."[36] Other authors described a "social adaptive function" from the perspective of developmental psychology or

---

[33] On the reception of this text, see Hitzer, *Krebs fühlen*, 90–3.

[34] Immo von Hattingberg, "Grundfragen und Methoden der Angstforschung," *Psychologische Beiträge* 11/3 (1969): 305–6.

[35] August Nitschke, "Wandlungen der Angst," in Heinz Wiesbrock, ed., *Die politische und gesellschaftliche Rolle der Angst* (Frankfurt a/M: Europäische Verlagsanstalt, 1967), 22–35, quotations on 31, 33–4.

[36] Heiner Flohr, "Angst und Politik in der modernen parlamentarischen Demokratie," in ibid. 43–53, quotation on 43.

highlighted the positive "signal effect of fear" in analogy to pain.[37] Psychologically, fear often served as a motivating factor and could enhance an individual's ability to perform.[38] As the education scholar Günther Bittner argued, fear also served a positive function in the education of children. He pleaded for its narrativization rather than its repression, because "one must let oneself be told about it."[39] Even though "objective fears" of external dangers were declining in modern society, the sociologist Gerhard Kleining identified an increase in internal fears and a "re-evaluation of fear" as a "new cultural norm."[40]

These intensified reassessments of fear from scholars across several disciplines received their academic sanctioning in synthesis on the subject of "fear" published by the psychiatrist couple Walter von Baeyer and Wanda von Baeyer-Katte in 1971. Both psychiatrists were highly influential in their field in the Federal Republic; as the director of the psychiatric-neurological clinic in Heidelberg and co-editor of the magazine *Der Nervenarzt*, Walter von Baeyer was particularly so. Von Baeyer had served as a consulting psychiatrist to the *Wehrmacht* on the Eastern Front during the Second World War, then moved into the direction of an anthropological psychiatry. He moved away from psychiatric diagnoses that tended to attribute diseases to constitutional or hereditary weakness of the individual patient and instead took into consideration external circumstances of human existence as well.[41] Von Baeyer also drew on the findings of the American psychologist Richard S. Lazarus, who did not see emotions as purely physiological processes or as reactions to an external stimulus but identified an important cognitive component in emotions as well.[42] Accordingly, von Baeyer and von Baeyer-Katte characterized fear as a "complex, multi-layered structure" that reflected a complicated and nuanced relationship to the social world and resulted from complex psychological processes of the "social, religious, and individual conscience." Fear was "not by definition pathological, abnormal and always in need of therapy."[43] The study thus reaffirmed the cultural reassessment of fear, celebrating

---

[37] Günther Mühle, "Furcht und Angst unter entwicklungspsychologischem Aspekt," in ibid. 217–30, quotation on 223. von Hattingberg, "Grundfragen und Methoden der Angstforschung.".

[38] Franz Thurner, "Ängstlichkeit: Eine Persönlichkeitsvariable und ihre Auswirkungen," *Psychologische Rundschau* 21/3 (1970): 193.

[39] G. Bittner, "Die Erziehung und die Angst," in Wiesbrock, ed., *Die politische und gesellschaftliche Rolle der Angst*, 246–57.

[40] Gerhard Kleining, "Angst und Ideologie," in ibid. 194–216, quotation on 214–15.

[41] On von Baeyer's academic biography, see his self-representation in Ludwig J. Pongratz, ed., *Psychiatrie in Selbstdarstellungen* (Bern: Hans Huber, 1977), 25, and Svenja Golterman, *Die Gesellschaft der Überlebenden. Deutsche Kriegsheimkehrer und ihre Gewalterfahrungen im Zweiten Weltkrieg* (Munich: DVA, 2009), 310–19.

[42] On this development, see Ruth Leys, *The Ascent of Affect. Genealogy and Critique* (Chicago: University of Chicago Press, 2017), especially 129–219.

[43] Walter von Baeyer, Wanda von Baeyer-Katte, *Angst* (Frankfurt a/M: Suhrkamp, 1971), 205, 227. On the reception of Lazarus's theory of emotions in Germany, see Gerda Lazarus-Mainka, *Psychologische Aspekte der Angst* (Stuttgart: W. Kohlhammer, 1976), Heinz W. Krohne, ed.,*Theorien zur Angst*, 2nd edn (Stuttgart: W. Kohlhammer, 1981), 85–97.

the fact that people could now "admit to being afraid" without the worry of being seen as "coward[s]."[44]

Von Baeyer and von Baeyer-Katte criticized three aspects of the prevalent view of fear. The first was the traditional distinction of an object-related fear from an objectless anxiety that had always served to pathologize anxiety as neurotic and unfounded. They argued that neither spoken language nor literature supported such a strict distinction of "fear" from "anxiety." Rather, both forms of fear were closely intertwined. Just as anxiety had at least a vague object, fear of a genuine existing threat usually pointed beyond its immediate object.[45] Second, von Baeyer and von Baeyer-Katte rejected a sharp distinction between pathological and non-pathological, normal and abnormal anxiety. Although they acknowledged the existence of a pathological anxiety that required therapy, they saw most fears as a natural element of human existence.[46] Their psychoanalytic viewpoints allowed them to see fear as a symptom of other feelings, with a "hidden and unacknow-ledged guilt" being the most prominent.[47] Third, von Baeyer and von Baeyer-Katte revised the traditional notion in German psychiatry that long-lasting anxiety could not be the result of external experiences of violence but derived from endogenous causes rooted in the individual. Rather, violence, including war, could cause psychological trauma. Von Baeyer and von Baeyer-Katte attributed to both victims of Nazism and the German prisoners of war who had spent more than a decade in Soviet captivity the idea of an "experience-induced personality change" and therefore lasting psychological symptoms, which entitled them to a pension from the state. Fear appeared less as a neurotic or pathological weakness, or as a hereditary personality deficit, but rather as a reasonable and quite adaptive symptom of extreme "psycho-physical" stress.[48]

This cultural reassessment of fear and anxiety and emotions had a tangible impact on approaches to fear in different institutional settings. One of them was the officer training in the West German military, the *Bundeswehr*. Instructors at the School for Psychological Defense began to criticize traditional notions of fear and panic as indications of cowardice and individual psychological failure as they were propagated by those psychiatrists who had served in the Second World War. For example, a 1977 leaflet regarding behavior in catastrophic situations such as a nuclear conflict explained that "fear and anxiety... are normal reactions to an external danger" and that having feelings was the right of "every human being." While the military still had an interest in containing fear among soldiers and avoiding panic, military experts were ready to acknowledge that these emotions were appropriate responses to external stress.[49]

---

[44] Von Baeyer and von Baeyer-Katte, *Angst*, 7.   [45] Ibid. 23, 25–6.   [46] Ibid. 133.
[47] Ibid. 156.   [48] Ibid. 178–92.
[49] Merkblatt zum Verhalten in Katastrophensituationen, BArch, B106/73388. See also Frank Biess, "The Concept of Panic: Military Psychiatry and Emotional Preparation for Nuclear War in Postwar West Germany," in Biess and Gross, eds, *Science and Emotions after 1945*, 181–208, and Hitzer, *Krebs fühlen*, 85–88.

The shift in thinking also had an impact in West German schools in the 1970s. The period witnessed an intensified discussion on fear in schools. One reason was the introduction of the *numerus clausus* in 1968, which restricted admission to certain majors like medicine based on grade point average. It increased the pressure to perform in secondary school and therefore students' anxiety.[50] According to a 1977 study, 70 per cent of West German students suffered from a variety of fear.[51] Students also suffered anxiety in social behavior, with girls being more anxious than boys, and lower-class children being more anxious than middle-class children. Another study showed that authoritarian parents caused school anxiety.[52] The debate on the role of anxiety in schools also addressed the fear of the teachers, such as, for example, fear of unruly students or the inability to live up to one's own pedagogical expectations. Much like in military psychology, teachers' fears no longer appeared as merely an individual failure but as a natural response to difficult external circumstances, as a product of the "objective (and often contradictory) demands of the job."[53] The debate not only stressed the legitimacy of fear but also the necessity of its articulation. A group of teachers, for example, realized their fears only in the context of increasingly popular group discussions in which they articulated their feelings.[54] Fear thus appeared as an important subjective gauge for external objective problems, which needed to be articulated and communicated in order to address these difficulties. As such, fear also served a productive function.

Another publication that illustrated the new significance of fear was Dieter Duhm's 1972 study, *Fear in Capitalism*. The book was a bestseller among left-wing activists and appeared in a fourteenth edition in 1977.[55] Duhm's study addressed "young, non-academic readers" to encourage them to reflect on their own

[50] See the title story of *Der Spiegel* on school anxiety in 1976: "Schule: Es gibt keine fröhliche Jugend mehr," *Der Spiegel* 30/23 (1976): 38–52.

[51] Rainer Winkel, "Angst in der Schule," in Klaus E. Grossmann, Rainer Winkel, eds, *Angst und Lernen. Angstfreie Erziehung in Schule und Elternhaus. Mit einem Vorwort von Reinhart Lempp* (Munich: Kindler, 1977), 85–165, 97, 109, quoted in Dirk Schumann, "From Emotionality to Objectivity and Back? Emotions in German Pedagogy after 1945," unpublished manuscript. See also Dieter Lüttge, "Angst und Schulleistung," *Westermanns Pädagogische Beiträge* 25/5 (1973): 291–3.

[52] See Heinz W. Krohne, "Schulangst—empirische Befunde, Erklärungsansätze, therapeutische Möglichkeiten," in Heinz W. Krohne, *Fortschritte der pädagogischen Psychologie* (Munich: Ernst Reinhardt Verlag, 1975). See also Jens-Jörg Koch, Dietmar Wienke, "Angst und Schulangst in der Berufsschule," *Psychologie in Erziehung und Unterricht* 25 (1978): 149.

[53] Herbert Gudjons, "Umgang mit Angst: Erfahrungen einer Lehrergruppe," *Westermanns Pädagogische Beiträge* 32/1 (1980): 28, Wolfgang Hofsommer, "Lehrerängste in Anforderungssituationen," *Westermanns Pädagogische Beiträge* 32/1 (1980): 14–19.

[54] Gudjons, "Umgang mit Angst." For a similar example, see. Norbert Klein-Alstedde, "Schulangst," *Psychologie Heute* 2/16 (1974): 54–62. On group therapy in the 1970s, see Tändler, *Das therapeutische Jahrzehnt*, 363–400.

[55] Dieter Duhm, *Angst im Kapitalismus* (Hagen: Kübler KG, 1972). The book was based on Duhm's thesis from 1968 with the same title. On Duhm, see Sven Reichardt, *Authentizität und Gemeinschaft. Linksalternatives Leben in den siebziger und frühen achtziger Jahren* (Frankfurt a/M: Suhrkamp, 2014), 493–4, and Tändler, *Das therapeutische Jahrzehnt*, 298–301, Joachim C. Häberlen, *The Emotional Politics of the Alternative Left. West Germany, 1968–1984* (Cambridge: Cambridge University Press, 2018), 127–31.

problems and to find an "engaged and political answer" to them.[56] Duhm described the "human psyche" as the missing link of Marxist analysis. While he did not share the positive view of fear cited earlier, he nevertheless assigned fear a very important status as the central psychic mechanism in capitalist domination, as a "building block" without which "everything would collapse." The crux of the study was a list of the various mechanisms by which capitalism generated fear. According to Duhm, popular culture, consumption, and even the widely diagnosed sex-wave, were all attempts to counter an all-pervasive fear. Although Duhm described the fear capitalism generated as pathological, his argument nonetheless highlighted its central role in the workings of capitalism and hence also contributed to the broader rehabilitation of fear.

Duhm's book both fueled and reflected an increasing interest in the emotional and psychic dimension of the subject. He identified the empowerment of the self as an indispensable precondition for progressive social change. Fear revealed the psychically destructive effect of capitalism and thus provided the link between the individual and society. Recognizing the centrality of fear would provide the impetus transforming "paralysis and resignation" to a "moment of activity." As the most important psychic sensor for the mechanisms of capitalist rule, fear therefore also included what Duhm called a "progressive element" and thus pointed to a "residual freedom." While Duhm's study on fear also provoked fierce criticism from the Left, its popularity underlined the growing significance of fear within the self-conception of the left-alternative milieu during the 1970s.[57]

Fear and New Subjectivity

Knowledge and Feelings

The new cultural norm of emotional expressivity and the validation of fear as an important, even positive emotion shaped new conceptions of subjectivity. Both increasingly popular psychological science and heightened individual introspection subjected the self to increasing scrutiny during the post-1968 period. The thrust of the revolutionary subjectivity of the student movement was thus reversed: the emotionality of the "68ers" was directed from the inside to the outside: the experience and articulation of emotions became a precondition of social change. In the transition to the 1970s, the cultural emphasis shifted to the impact of external forces on subjects. Body and psyche increasingly became a passive and often suffering sounding board for a pathological environment.

---

[56] Duhm, *Angst im Kapitalismus*, 10.
[57] Reichardt sees Duhm's study as part of the debate over the identity of the left-wing milieu; see Reichardt, *Authentizität und Gemeinschaft*, 493–6.

At the same time, increasing introspection identified the self as a source of new dangers, which needed to be contained or managed—often also with the help of psychotherapy. Members of the left-alternative milieu increasingly understood psycho-knowledge of the self as a prerequisite for individual and political liberation. While the "new subjectivity" of the 1970s arose out of the student movement, this understanding differentiated it from the revolutionary subjectivity of the 68ers.[58] In contrast to the emotional dearth that had shaped the culture of the New Left, the writer Michael Schneider described the emerging "therapeutic left" as focused on "anxiety-free communication" and "personal sensitivity." But this transition from "old radicalism" to "new sensibility" also ran the risk of "elevating any personal toothache to the level of [a] world event."[59]

The diary of a female student from the left-wing milieu in Frankfurt illustrates the functioning of this new emotional regime very well.[60] Bärbel H. was born in 1953, experienced a difficult childhood growing up with relatives, and eventually joined the squatter movement in Frankfurt. Already at the age of 16, she had read British author A.S. Neill's book on "repression-free" child-rearing at the Summerhill school, which inspired her to reflect on the ways in which her own childhood experiences had given her a "negative attitude toward sexuality" and produced the "unconscious feeling of not being loved."[61] This self-diagnosis linking emancipation with liberated sexuality replicated the concern of the 68ers. Yet she focused her energies not primarily on political activism but rather on her own and her friends' and romantic partners' work on the self. The main goal was to gain more insight into her own psychological mechanism, and to be able to experience and articulate her emotions as freely as possible, especially in relationships. Torn between two possible partners, she focused on their emotional and psychological self-understanding. She stated:

> I like U. very much, his way of being, his openness...But I don't know if it's possible to change him regarding important issues such as his self-conception, his sexuality. It would not be too difficult to start with politics, but it would be tedious, and I would have to act as an analyst and therapist.

It was "very different with B." Even though he was "not yet ready to see through his own psychic processes, he thinks about them and works on them." Therapy

[58] Here I disagree with the emphasis on continuity in both Reichardt, *Authentizität und Gemeinschaft* and Tändler, *Das therapeutische Jahrzehnt*.

[59] Michael Schneider, "Von der alten Radikalität zur neuen Sensibilität. Tendenziöses zur Tendenzwende," in Michael Schneider, *Den Kopf verkehrt aufgesetzt, oder, Die melancholische Linke. Aspekte des Kulturzerfalls in den siebziger Jahren* (Darmstadt: Luchterhand, 1981), 142–65, quotations on 150, 152, 157.

[60] Bärbel H., Diaries, DTA 1495, I, 1–I,4. On this diary, see also Tändler, *Das therapeutische Jahrzehnt*, 9, 266–7, and Frank Biess, "Die Sensibilisierung des Subjekts. Angst und 'neue Subjektivität' in den 1970er Jahren," *Werkstatt Geschichte* 49 (2008): 68.

[61] Bärbel H., Diaries, DTA 1495, I, 1–I,4, June 8, 1970.

would be "very necessary" for him although he did not realize it. On the other hand, "with B., my attitude is much more rational," which made her "wary" precisely because she trusted her emotions more than her thoughts. "I really need to talk to P. about it," she concluded with a quite typical wish for further communication about her feelings.[62]

Bärbel H. had internalized the new cultural norm of emotional expressiveness that required the open articulation of one's emotions. She criticized her friend E. for her "great anxiety to show her emotions" and stated that she herself would "prefer to show her emotions to everybody."[63] She saw psychotherapy, which she received for years, as intended to help her in this endeavor, and recorded on multiple occasions that a successful session had helped her feelings "come out."[64] Yet the articulation of feelings was also threatening, in part because it brought out vague and unclear anxieties. "I am afraid to show my emotions. If only I knew what I am afraid of, my mother, of course, but what specifically?" she noted in her diary in May 1975.[65] Then she wrote that she began to be sexually attracted to her therapist, which made things even worse and intensified her "fear to expose myself."[66]

The permanent work on the self also caused its own problems. In January 1975, it dawned on Bärbel H. that "I revel too much in this psycho-shit."[67] She made a similar statement in December 1977, almost two years after terminating treatment.[68] She struggled to link her reflections on her psychic state with larger political and societal factors, and saw her "feelings of anxiety" as an expression of her inability to reconcile the external world with her inner state.[69] Her desire for theoretical frameworks to understand the world notwithstanding, she was searching for an ever-elusive synthesis of her personal and political life, an alignment of the external social world with her inner psychic states.[70] Like the activists of the student movement, Bärbel H. sought to link political transformation with the transformation of the self. But her emphasis was clearly on the work on the self, on her inner life, and that also made her different from the 68ers.

Self and Community

Within the left-alternative milieu, a yearning for community and "warmth" always accompanied the quest for self-knowledge and self-realization.[71] Yet this relationship between the self and community always remained tense and eventually became a source of anxiety as well. For example, Bärbel H.'s attempt to create

---

[62] Ibid. June 27, 1973.   [63] Ibid. December 20, 1973.
[64] Ibid. April 28, 1975; May 14, 1975; January 26, 1976.   [65] Ibid. May 14, 1975.
[66] Ibid. May 5, 1975.   [67] Ibid. January 6, 1975.   [68] Ibid. January 26, 1977.
[69] Ibid. October 18, 1977.   [70] Ibid. March 25, 1978.
[71] Reichardt, *Authentizität und Gemeinschaft*, 186–94, 195–203.

an anxiety-free relationship with a partner entailed a constant reflection on the right mixture of attachment, security, and warmth on the one hand, and individual freedom and autonomy, on the other. Early on, she worried about a "too close relationship," which would mean not being independent, hence "alone" and "isolated." [72] Her "emotional blockages," as she stated repeatedly, made her "incapable of having real relationships either with women or with men."[73] But she immediately countered this fear of isolation with the contrasting anxiety that her above-mentioned partner B. was becoming "too fixated on her."[74] More than before, such relationship concerns were articulated openly and thus became a constant subject of (self-)conversations.

A similar tension manifested itself in alternative forms of living, in particular the communes (*Wohngemeinschaften*, WGs), which increased rapidly after the mid 1970s. By 1980, there were 30,000 to 40,000 WGs with 400,000 to 600,000 residents.[75] As the sociologist Gudrun Cyprian stated in her 1978 study on communes, the main problem the WGs faced was how to calibrate the "tension between the 'I' and the 'We.'"[76] Because the communes no longer followed a predetermined ideological script as the pioneering *Kommune 1* and *Kommune 2* did, communal life within them needed to be constantly (re)negotiated in an often quarrelsome process.[77] A commune resident described as his source of "frustration and joy" a search for the "optimal balance between privacy and the collective."[78] Communes were an ideal space for satisfying the need for intense group communication about emotions. For outsiders, such arrangements undermined the supposedly natural forms of living together in a family and subjected them to a new need for reflection. Who should live together with whom and how was no longer a quasi-natural given, as in the traditional nuclear family. Instead, everyday activities became the object of increasing reflection and discussion, and hence also a new source of uncertainty and anxiety.[79]

Communes nurtured the new expressive emotional culture. A resident highlighted his need for "a strong emotional affection and a climate of trust and warmth" within the commune, which was based on the ability and willingness of all members to communicate about their emotions.[80] The vague and often elliptical language that was typical within the left-alternative milieu thus often also

---

[72] Bärbel H., Diaries, DTA 1495, I, 1–I,4, October 14, 1973.   [73] Ibid. April 21, 1975.
[74] Ibid. June 18, 1975.   [75] Figures cited in Reichardt, *Authentizität und Gemeinschaft*, 361.
[76] Gudrun Cyprian, *Sozialisation in Wohngemeinschaften: Eine empirische Untersuchung ihrer strukturellen Bedingungen* (Stuttgart: Enke, 1978), 33. On the dynamic within communes, see Reichardt, *Authentizität und Gemeinschaft*, 351–93.
[77] Cyprian, *Sozialisation in Wohngemeinschaften*, 179.
[78] Johann A. Schülein, *Vor uns die Mühen der Ebenen. Alltagsprobleme und Perspektiven von Wohngemeinschaften* (Gießen: Focus Verlag, 1980), 62.
[79] Reichardt, *Authentizität und Gemeinschaft*, 427–32.
[80] Schülein, *Vor uns die Mühen der Ebenen*, 153.

reflected persistent difficulties in verbalizing emotions.[81] One commune resident, Herbert, for example, noted in his diary on July 27, 1976:

> The moments, when I think and feel and also show it are too rare, but because it is like this right now, I have the joyful urge to write them down. Am I euphoric? Yes, that too, but I do not know. Yeah, you can call me crazy, but sometimes there are moments when I'm fine—rarely enough, dammit.[82]

This statement illustrates William Reddy's theory of the "emotive" as a speech act, according to which the articulation of emotions is an integral part of the emotion. The search for an appropriate language that names and verbalizes these emotions thus constituted an important aspect of the ongoing work on the self, precisely because the subject increasingly defined him- or herself through the expression of his or her emotions.[83]

This creation of emotional communities within the communes proceeded not only through verbal but also through physical communication, although mostly below the threshold of sexuality. One resident stated after a morning of shared cuddling with other members of his commune: "Your warmth gives me a feeling of great security." In another case, it was a disco night where "we discovered our affection (as opposed to our minds) and experienced tender and sympathetic feeling for each other."[84] Communes hoped that the verbal—or non—verbal articulation of individual emotions would become the basis for the emotional cohesion of the group. Yet some members also complained that the permanent work on the self and on the group also produced the frustration "that one only stewed in one's own juice" and became incapable of acting at all because of an ubiquitous control atmosphere and the sheer complexity of self-actualization.[85]

The high rate of turnover in the communes also indicated that the emotional equilibrium, even if it were achieved, was seldom long-lasting.[86] The practice of emotional expressivity promised no permanent stabilization of the self. In addition, emotional needs changed with individual members' new life situations—graduating from university, the start of a new job, a new relationship, or parenting a child. The frequent turnover in communes thus also resulted from the attempt to optimize external conditions for individual self-realization. Moving out and/or recruiting new members thus ended up as an anxiety-ridden process for all involved parties. In some cases, moving out of communes was often synonymous with an admission of individual and collective failure. "I moved out of the old

---

[81] Reichardt, *Authentizität und Gemeinschaft*, 307.
[82] Quoted in Schülein, *Vor uns die Mühen der Ebenen*, 38.
[83] Reddy, *Navigation of Feeling*, 63–111.
[84] Schülein, *Vor uns die Mühen der Ebenen*, 46, 50, 60. [85] Ibid. 167.
[86] Reichardt, *Authentizität und Gemeinschaft*, 427–8.

Figure 7.3. Breakfast in a *Wohngemeinschaft* (WG) in Frankfurt in 1982.

Communes became important sites for practicing and enacting the new culture of emotional expressiveness. Members were expected to show their emotions and forge emotional bonds with each other.

Source: bpk-Bildagentur, No. 30001851.

apartment because my relationship went south, another guy moved in and fell in love with my girlfriend or vice versa, the pig!" one frustrated commune member reported.[87] Given the ongoing housing shortage in university towns, however, existing commune residents tended to be in a stronger position than individuals seeking to move into a commune. Looking for a spot in a commune often ended up being an embarrassing and hurtful process that, according to one participant, did not always entail a considerate and humane treatment of applicants.[88] Existing communes were well aware of these problems. "Please come by in the evening; maybe we can get it over with without having you be on a catwalk," one commune wrote in the ad; another one assured potential applicants that we too "would be scared to move in with people we don't know" and promised "not to be mean" to people who feel "insecure."[89] Still, the selection often proceeded on the basis of "vague psychic...sympathies, which will not be explained [to the applicant] in detail."[90] The general vagueness of communication within the left-alternative

---

[87] Schülein, *Vor uns die Mühen der Ebenen*, 223.   [88] Ibid. 207.

[89] Franz-Maria Sonner, ed., *Werktätiger sucht üppige Partnerin: Die Szene der 70er Jahre in ihren Kleinanzeigen* (Munich: Antje Kunstmann, 2005), 24–5, 52.

[90] Schülein, *Vor uns die Mühen der Ebenen*, 223.

milieu could also be anxiety-producing, in part because the acceptance into a new commune was usually not based on objective criteria but rather derived from a vague overall evaluation of the personality of the applicant.

Women and Men

One of the most important consequences of the New Left was the emergence of the women's movement.[91] West German feminism arose as part of, and in confrontation with, the male-dominated New Left. The link between the "private" and the "political" assumed a new meaning within feminism because it called into question gender roles in everyday life formerly considered natural. Feminism was part of the transformation of West German emotional culture because it elevated an allegedly female capacity to experience and articulate emotions to a new cultural norm. Bestselling autobiographic literary works such as Karin Struck's *Klassenliebe* (1973) and especially Verena Stefan's *Häutungen* (1975) designed a specifically female subjectivity, often defining it in explicit demarcation from New Left positions.[92] Stefan's book recorded her gradual shift away from male-dominated heterosexuality to a homosexual relationship with "Fenna" as a form of female self-discovery, which she repeatedly described, as in the title, with its nature metaphor.[93] Much like Alice Schwarzer in her more famous feminist manifesto from 1975, *Der kleine Unterschied*, Stefan conceived of female self-discovery as a fight against ubiquitous patriarchal oppression, which manifested itself in coital sexuality and fixation on orgasm. Stefan distanced herself both from newly fashioned Marxism ("Sexism goes deeper than class struggle and racism") and from Reich's demand for political liberation through liberated (hetero) sexuality. Emphasizing female difference, she postulated a female sensibility unlike the "truncated," "repressed," or "misguided" emotional life of "male atrophy." She emphasized "female, not male anxieties," but she also acknowledged the "uncontrollable longings, pains, and catastrophes" that came with an unbound emotional life.

The left-alternative milieu received Stefan's book enthusiastically. Bärbel H. read *Häutungen* in September 1976 and was "deeply impressed."[94] Almost simultaneously, she criticized the men of the Frankfurt left-wing magazine,

---

[91] Gisela Notz, "Die autonome Frauenbewegung der Siebzigerjahre. Entstehungsgeschichte, Organisationsformen, politische Konzepte," *Archiv für Sozialgeschichte* 44 (2004): 123–48.

[92] Karin Struck, *Klassenliebe* (Frankfurt a/M: Suhrkamp, 1973), Verena Stefan, *Häutungen. Autobiografische Aufzeichnungen. Gedichte. Träume. Analysen* (Munich: Verlag Frauenoffensive, 1975). *Häutungen* appeared in 10 editions until 1977 and sold 125,000 copies, see Reichardt, *Authentizität und Gemeinschaft*, 618.

[93] On the significance of the symbolism of nature, see Andrew Plowmann, *Social Change and the Self in Recent German Autobiography* (Frankfurt a/M: Peter Lang, 1998), 149.

[94] Bärbel H., Diary, DTA 1495, I, 1-I,4, September 13, 1976.

Pflasterstrand, for their chauvinism.[95] A few months earlier, she had already noted her turn toward feminism as well her desire to "go to the women's café" because she "definitely needed women."[96] Her emerging feminist consciousness also increasingly shaped her attitude toward her own sexuality. She now realized that she had idealized her boyfriend's non-repressive sex education as "liberated sexuality." Now she increasingly felt herself to be his "object, tool" and even remembered having been raped by him. These feminist insights marked a clear turning point for her: "As a woman, I cannot do this, or not anymore. Above all, I do not want to do it anymore."[97]

Female subjectivity and the establishment of a supposedly feminine emotionality as a new cultural norm in the left-alternative milieu also promoted changed ideas of masculinity. As a result, the 68ers' emphasis on sexuality as a means of political transformation receded into the background. Instead, as former activist Peter Schneider stated in a 1974 article, the challenge for men now resided in the long-term goal of "harmonizing emotional and sexual life."[98] The new cultural norm of emotional expressivity now also became an important aspect of male subjectivity, first in the left-wing milieu and ultimately in society at large. Reports from communes acknowledged that men often found it difficult to live up to this ideal. They often repressed "bad and unclear feelings" and needed to learn "in small steps how to articulate their disappointments, fears, desires" while "women were more open with their feelings."[99]

Men's groups, a counterpart to feminist women's groups, emerged in the 1970s and became sites for learning and enacting the new culture of emotional expressiveness.[100] Members of these groups articulated their difficulties with one-sided rationality and deficient emotionality within the New Left. One man reported that he "felt deficient" ever since he became politicized because he could not "integrate" his "personality...emotions and...anxieties." He cited Verena Stefan's book as a model and aspired "to write something similar."[101] Another participant criticized the distance between leftist theory and personal experience.[102] While the New Left had one-sidedly emphasized rationality, the men's group provided a

[95] Ibid., mid December 1976.
[96] Ibid., June 23, 1976. On the newly emerging female spaces, see Reichardt, *Authentizität und Gemeinschaft*, 608–24.
[97] Bärbel H., Diary, DTA 1495, I, 1-I,4, October 18, 1977, and November 25, 1977.
[98] Peter Schneider, "Die Sache mit der 'Männlichkeit.' Gibt es eine Emanzipation der Männer?" *Kursbuch* 35 (1974): 103–32, quotations on 107, 116, 126, 131. See also Reichardt, *Authentizität und Gemeinschaft*, 699. For a similar point, see Frank Böckelmann, "Aspekte der Männlichkeit," in Frank Böckelmann, Anita Albus, Bazon Brock, Peter Gosen, Hazel E. Hazel, Rita Mühlbauer, eds, *Maskulin-Feminin. Die Sexualität ist das Unnatürlichste der Welt* (Munich: Rogner & Bernhard, 1975).
[99] Schülein, *Vor uns die Mühen der Ebenen*, 41.
[100] On men's groups, see Reichardt, *Authentizität und Gemeinschaft*, 703–18.
[101] Wolfang Müller, Volker Elis Pilgrim, Herbert Pross, Karlheinz Roesch, Walter Schörling, Wieland Speck, Bodo Teising, *Männerbilder. Geschichte und Protokolle von Männern* (Munich: C. Trikont Verlag, 1976), 28–9. See also ibid. 21.
[102] Ibid. 42.

place for cultivating one's emotional life. "I had learned through the men's group to approach my feelings more directly," one participant reported. Crying was not uncommon in these settings.[103] Participants also bemoaned the difficulty of opening up. "Manfred" reported, for example, that his group focused on the difficulty of "communicating emotionally with each other at all.... For example, to embrace one another." Suggesting the importance of physical contact in these gatherings, according to the minutes of the first German men's group meeting on February 22, 1975, "Hans" said at one point that everything was "typically male, too overblown" and suggested "that we take a half hour break, a bit of music will do it, touch each other or not touch each other, at least do something other than with our heads."[104]

Fear was the central emotion in many men's groups, and it provided a space for men to articulate their fears of failure.[105] Some participants criticized the New Left for internalizing the norms of academic performance. Others felt oppressed by the prevailing norms of masculinity. Participants knew that the men's group might not last forever and they feared to lose—in the words of one participant— the "warmth, security, understanding" it offered.[106] To be sure, not all members liked the format; "Peter" described his men's group as "constant stress. We can't ever catch our breath," while "Karl-Heinz" felt "constantly unsettled" because of the "constant reflection about what I do."[107] Participants' ambivalence in the assessment of their men's group seems to reflect an uncertainty and an ongoing search for a stable self that remained elusive. A similar uncertainty and ambivalence shaped the attitude toward homosexuality. On the one hand, men's groups rejected homophobia and celebrated the importance of physical contact between men. On the other hand, however, they did not want to be perceived automatically as "gay." "Schippy" declared that most men's groups feared to be "exclusively gay or not be gay at all" whereas he yearned for flexibility and wanted "to figure out his bisexuality."[108]

Unlike the theories of sexual liberation during the student movement, the internal discourse in the left-wing alternative scene prioritized feelings over sexuality. Sexuality was less a vehicle for personal and political liberation than a secondary aspect of one's emotional sensibility. Bärbel H. expressed similar sentiments in her diary when she repeatedly attributed her difficulties of having an "orgasm" to her inability to express her feelings.[109] Rather than liberation, she experienced sexuality as a substitute for a more authentic communication with others. According to her self-perception, she had fallen victim to Herbert Marcuse's notion of "repressive de-sublimation"—that is, the practice of a free

---

[103]   Ibid. 28–9. See also ibid. 21.   [104]   Ibid. 67, 36.
[105]   Reichardt, *Authentizität und Gemeinschaft*, 709, Müller et al., *Männerbilder*, 76.
[106]   Ibid. 79.   [107]   Ibid. 147–8.   [108]   Ibid. 76.
[109]   Bärbel H., Diary, DTA 1495, I, 1-I,4, March 24, 1976. Then again January 23, 1977.

sexuality that nevertheless assumed the status of a commodity.[110] She subscribed to the subordination of sexuality to emotions, because it was typical in the left-alternative scene. She consequently described as her main problem how "to show my own feelings and to not be fixated on the equation of fucking = relationship."[111]

Similar self-reflections also took place among men. The privileging of emotions over sexuality complicated heterosexual relationships for men and prompted complex discussions. Not everybody agreed with the prioritizing of feelings over sexuality. "Peter," for example, explained that he left his men's group because it gave him the idea of "penetration as oppression," saying that it had made it impossible to have an orgasm in sex even though he ejaculated.[112] Peter's criticism sparked a controversial discussion in which individual members also expressed their feelings toward him. Wolfgang, for example, said that he found Peter threatening and anxiety-producing. Others, in turn, defended Peter against the accusation of seeking to brag about "ejaculation," until Karl-Heinz desperately proclaimed that "ejaculation was not in itself bad, God forbid!"[113] These discussions reflected that male sexuality too had become increasingly more complicated. On the one hand, some men propagated an extension of male sexuality that was no longer limited to sexual intercourse but embraced an erotic directed toward the entire body.[114] But other men were also part of a male backlash that, in response to increased uncertainty about masculinity, propagated harder masculinities that might also include fantasies of rape.[115]

One thing that participants in the group could generally agree on, however, was that sexuality was worth talking about. Sexuality—male and female, homosexual and heterosexual—thus became another site for the ongoing emotionalization, psychologizing, and, at times, pathologization of individual subjects during the 1970s. The intensified talk about sexuality produced new expectations and norms that were increasingly difficult to navigate. In this context, Michel Foucault's work became increasingly popular. In the first volume of *The History of Sexuality* (*The Will to Knowledge*), published in Germany in 1977, he unmasked this discourse of sexuality as a new configuration of power and knowledge, which constituted subjects but also subjugated them to new norms and constraints. The above-cited self-reports from the left-alternative milieu illustrate, as it were, Foucault's notion of a "decentered subject," its ongoing "liquefaction and

---

[110] Ibid. October 18, 1977.   [111] Ibid. March 24, 1976.
[112] Müller et al., *Männerbilder*, 146–7.
[113] Ibid. 154.
[114] Joachim C. Häberlen, "Feeling Like a Child. Visions and Practices of Sexuality in the West-German Alternative Left during the Long 1970s," *Journal for the History of Sexuality* 25 (2016): 219–45, quotation on 230.
[115] See Reichardt, *Authentizität und Gemeinschaft*, 711–18.

individualization." They also explain the enthusiastic reception of Foucault's work in the left-alternative milieu from the 1970s onward.[116]

The "Hitler in Me" and Other Pathologies

Increasing introspection also meant that the sensitized subjects of the 1970s identified a myriad of pathologies that either affected the subject from the outside or were already enshrined in it. This led, among other things, to a renewed discussion of the psychological and emotional sources of fascism. While the 68ers had distanced themselves from the Nazi past by locating fascism almost exclusively in the external structures of capitalist and bourgeois society, the left-alternative milieu placed new significance on the individual psyche. Fear of a new authoritarianism was directed to destructive and authoritarian impulses anchored within the self. Klaus Theweleit's book, *Male Fantasies*, which was published in 1977 and became a bestseller, analyzed the inner life of the paramilitary Free Corps members from the Weimar Republic as an example of a fascist personality. Theweleit's book echoed the condemnation of emotional coldness and identified it as a precondition of fascist violence. His book exemplified the transition from Marxist to psychoanalytic and postmodern theories of fascism.[117] Bärbel H. read the book and it led her to reflect in her diary on the "psychological origins of the Nazi era" and how it resulted in the ongoing "oppression of the woman" in the Federal Republic.[118]

Theweleit's book echoed some of the themes of another left-wing cult book published the same year: Bernward Vesper's autobiographical report, *Die Reise*.[119] On more than 600 pages, Vesper reflected on the emotional and psychological legacy of his father, the Nazi poet Will Vesper, from which he distanced himself only in a slow and gradual process. As late as 1964, Vesper had moved within the right-wing national milieu, where he had tried repeatedly (together with his fiancée, the later RAF terrorist Gudrun Ensslin) to publish the writings of his deceased father.[120] After he had converted to the New Left, Vesper increasingly

---

[116] Philipp Felsch, *Der lange Sommer der Theorie. Geschichte einer Revolte 1960–1990* (Munich: C.H.Beck, 2015), 102–48, Ulrich Raulff, *Wiedersehen mit den Siebzigern. Die wilden Jahre des Lesens* (Stuttgart: Klett-Cotta, 2015), Martin Kindtner, "Strategien der Verflüssigung. Poststrukturalistischer Theoriediskurs und politische Praktiken der 1968er Jahre," in Anselm Doering-Manteuffel, Lutz Raphael, Thomas Schlemmer, eds, *Vorgeschichte der Gegenwart. Dimensionen des Strukturbruchs nach dem Boom* (Göttingen: Vandenhoeck & Ruprecht, 2016), 373–92, quotation on 392.

[117] My interpretation of the popularity of male fantasies follows. Sven Reichardt, "Klaus Theweleits 'Männerphantasien'—ein Erfolgsbuch der 1970er-Jahre," *Zeithistorische Forschungen/Studies in Contemporary History* 3/3 (2006): 401–21.

[118] Bärbel H., Diary, DTA 1495, I, 1-I,4, July 6, 1978, August 23,1978.

[119] Michael Schneider, "Über die Außen- und Innenansicht eines Selbstmörders. Notwendige Ergänzungen zu Bernward Vespers 'Die Reise'," in Schneider, ed., *Den Kopf verkehrt aufgesetzt*, 65–79.

[120] This is well documented in Koenen, *Vesper, Ensslin, Baader*, 57–102.

explained his political and personal difficulties as a result of biographically induced pathologies, which he called the "Hitler in me."[121] Under the influence of an LSD trip, Vesper described this predicament to his Jewish friend Burton as follows: "Yes, I knew exactly that I was Hitler, all the way down to the belt, that I could not come out of it, that it is a struggle for life and death that contaminates my life, his God-damned existence stuck to mine like napalm."[122] Vesper committed suicide in 1971 before the publication of *Die Reise*. The apparent inevitability of his fate, in combination with his parentage, gave his particular take on the authoritarian origins of one's own character extra authenticity, reflecting as it did the destructive and ultimately lethal effects of internal pathologies.[123] While Vesper became a martyr of the left-alternative scene, contemporary critics noted elements of Nazi ideology in his writings—for example, in the dehumanizing characterization of ordinary citizens as "vegetables."[124] In seeking to distance himself from his own upbringing, he adopted an aggression toward majority society that illustrated one possible path into the terrorist camp of the RAF.[125]

Vesper and others articulated not only their suffering from the after-effects of fascism but also from the capitalist society of the present.[126] They displayed a "preventive basic anxiety" (*vorbeugende Grundangsthaltung*) toward what they perceived as a dehumanizing capitalism.[127] Left-alternative publications blamed the soullessness and anonymity of West German cities for their alienation from majority society. These anxieties did not just represent individual psychological difficulties but were seen as a result of hostile external capitalist structures.[128] The Decree on Radicals in Public Service (*Radikalenerlass*), which banned members of radical political groups from employment in the West German civil service, as well as the rising academic unemployment, constituted the structural contexts for these anxieties.[129] Unlike in the student movement, however, this suffering in and from society did not produce a revolutionary utopia. Rather, the counter-movement to the fear-inducing effect of capitalist modernism manifested itself in a more

---

[121] Ibid. 197.

[122] Bernward Vesper, *Die Reise. Romanessay. Ausgabe letzter Hand* (Berlin: März Verlag, 1977). See also Plowmann, *Social Change*, 57–8.

[123] This biographical implication was an important theme of the literature on fatherhood in the 1970s and 1980s: see Claudia Mauelshagen, *Der Schatten des Vaters. Deutschsprachige Väterliteratur der siebziger und achtziger Jahre* (Frankfurt a/M: Peter Lang, 1995).

[124] Schneider, "Über die Außen- und Innenansicht eines Selbstmörders," 71–2.

[125] Klaus-Michael Bogdal, "Verändern oder Sterben. Imperative der Revolte," in Nicole Colin, Beatrice de Graaf, Jacco Pekelder, Joachim Umlauf, eds, *Der "Deutsche Herbst" und die RAF in Politik, Medien und Kunst. Nationale und internationale Perspektiven* (Bielefeld: transcript, 2008), 124–30.

[126] Joachim Häberlen, Jake Smith, "Struggling for Feelings: The Politics of Emotions in the Radical New Left in West Germany, c.1968–84," *Contemporary European History* 23/4 (2014): 615–37, Joachim C. Häberlen, Maik Tändler, "Spaces for Feeling Differently. Emotional Experiments in the Alternative Left in West Germany During the 1970s," *Emotion, Space and Society* 25 (2017): 103–10.

[127] Quoted in Häberlen and Smith, "Struggling for Feelings," 620.

[128] See also Häberlen, *Emotional Politics of the Alternative Left*, 123–66.

[129] On this law, see Reichardt, *Authentizität und Gemeinschaft*, 207–16.

small-scale fashion, in the search for warmth and empathy in shared flats, discussion groups, alternative projects, or neighborhood initiatives.

The members of the leftist alternative scene experienced the destructive effects of capitalist society not only intellectually but also physically and emotionally. This then also led to frequent self-representation as a "broken type." Again, Vesper's *Die Reise* was paradigmatic here. He wrote: "I'll auction myself off: On offer: totally fucked up guy, 31, completely incapable of love, etc. The low bid should be: enough money to travel wherever one wants."[130] Indeed the first personal ad in *Pflasterstrand*, the main journal for the Frankurt left-alternative scene, which appeared in 1977, read as follows: "Depressive, sensitive, almost totally screwed up guy seeks understanding female in order to build up a long-term and understanding relationship."[131] Other examples offer "a student with neurotic deficits," "nonconformist with fear neurosis," a "difficult case," an "orally, phallically, and socially damaged asshole," and individuals "psychologically damaged," with "severe traumas" and "high-grade solipsism," and "mentally and socially isolated paranoi[a]."[132] According to the statistical data of the research group of the historian Sven Reichardt, up to 20 per cent of the contact ads in left-wing media adopted such open admissions of emotional weaknesses. This is how individuals sought to distance themselves from the commercial advertising of capitalist markets and to present themselves as open and authentic selves.[133] This negative self-representation illustrated the positive significance of fear and suffering in the left-alternative milieu. Many ads characterized fear and anxiety as positive emotions. One advertiser described how fear was circulating like "a hot lava" through his system; a woman confessed she was afraid because "politics intruded more and more" into her "personal life" while she only wanted "just a little bit of love in this world."[134] Self-descriptions as "frustrated" also appeared frequently. They implied that one's own sensibilities and emotional qualities repeatedly failed when confronted with a hostile outside world.[135] Such self-portrayals as weak, frustrated, or anxious were by no means negative but served as indicators of a particularly sensitized self. Whoever did not present him or herself as "isolated," "problem-ridden," or "psychopathic" appeared as emotionally mute, as not possessing the finely tuned emotional register to "suffer the consequences of our alienated society."[136] In this view, the sensitized self served as a passive register of a multitude of external grievances.

This heightened sensibility for dangers that penetrated the subject from the outside and destroyed it from the inside did not remain limited to the

---

[130] Vesper, *Die Reise*, 41.
[131] Quoted in Reichardt, *Authentizität und Gemeinschaft*, 662. On the personal ads, see also 659–74.
[132] Sonner, ed., *Werktätiger sucht üppige Partnerin*, 8, 9, 24, 91.
[133] Reichardt, *Authentizität und Gemeinschaft*, 667–8.   [134] Ibid. 63.
[135] Sonner, ed., *Werktätiger sucht üppige Partnerin*, 132.   [136] Ibid. 38.

left-alternative milieu. The anxiety-ridden subject emerged within this milieu but then also radiated into mainstream society. Between 1953 and 1969, the "fear of disease" was never the greatest fear of more than 12 per cent of respondents in the nationally representative polls conducted by the Emnid Institute but, in 1978, it was 26 per cent.[137] By contrast, the "fear of war" stayed roughly the same at 12 per cent. This development resulted not from external conditions (such as the appearance of new illnesses) but rather from changing sensibilities, reflecting a shift in views on health and illness that accompanied inwardly oriented fears. A study from 1976 observed a new understanding of health that was no longer based on "nature," "randomness," not subject to "individual will" but rather derived from "socio-psychic conditions" and based on the "actions of individual human beings."[138] A new awareness of inner vulnerability accompanied the new emphasis on individuality, self-realization, and autonomy. These fears for the inner integrity of the self were expressed, for example, through new concerns for invisible toxins in the air and in the food, which penetrated the self from the outside and destroyed it from the inside out. *Der Spiegel* published its first cover story on the issue in October 1970.[139]

The subjective appropriation of the above-cited psychosomatic etiologies of cancer were likewise a manifestation of the new sensibility. In an almost paradigmatic form, cancer appeared as the inner enemy, who entered the subject—driven by external pathologies—first unnoticed, and then destroyed it from the inside. A whole series of literary cancer autobiographies, which often adopted the psychosomatic interpretation of cancer, described this process. These narratives evoked both pathological external circumstances as well as an inner "emotional rigidity" (*Gefühlsstarre*) as the cause of the often fatal disease. Fritz Zorn's autobiography, *Mars*, another bestseller of the 1970s, articulated this view most radically. The author described his illness as the product of an emotionally and culturally hostile bourgeois environment, as a symptom of "swallowed tears."[140] Other authors likewise interpreted cancer as the consequence of unsatisfactory living conditions, especially in East Germany (Christa Wolf, *Nachdenken über Christa T.*) as a product of stress, the pressure to perform, and environmental toxins (Lydia Stephans, *Du hättest gerne noch ein bisschen gelebt*) or as a result of the destruction of the environment (Ingeborg Bruns, *Das wiedergeschenkte Leben. Tagebuch*

---

[137] *Emnid Informationen* 21/6 (June 1969): 11. The exception was the year 1961 at the high point of the Cold War when the fear of war was at 24 per cent and the fear of disease at 3 per cent. See Chapter 3, *Emnid Informationen* 30/9 (1978): 8.

[138] Peter Kmieciak, *Wertstrukturen und Wertewandel in der Bundesrepublik Deutschland. Grundlagen einer interdisziplinären empirischen Wertforschung mit einer Sekundäranalyse von Umfragedaten* (Göttingen: Otto Schwarz, 1976), 291.

[139] "Morgen kam gestern," *Der Spiegel* 34/41 (1970): 74–96.

[140] Fritz Zorn, *Mars. Roman* (Frankfurt a/M: Fischer, 1979), 132.

einer Leukämieerkrankung eines Kindes).[141] Similar psychosomatic explanations also existed in popular understandings of the causes of cancer. According to a study on the lay etiology of cancer, many patients cited "psychic factors" as an important cause of their disease, together with purely biological factors such as "heredity" and external influences like "air pollution" or "toxins in the food."[142] Precisely because many of these causes of cancer remained beyond the control of the individual, they needed to be politicized through a broader societal discourse. This emphasis on the sociopolitical causes of deadly diseases bestowed a newly existential significance on political criticism that the New Left had often lacked.

How did newly sensitized subjects cope with these anxieties? What consequences did they draw from this identification of multiple internal and external dangers? To some extent, attempts to stabilize the self remained on the level of the individual. This included a new turn to an ever-increasing variety of psychotherapies as well as a growing popularity of drugs in the left-alternative scene.[143] Attempts at self-stabilization also led to the emergence of a new spirituality, especially a fascination with Far Eastern mysticism and the resulting travel to India.[144] People increasingly saw global travel or the spatial dislocation as an important means in the search for one's identity, and falling air travel costs made it possible. Bärbel H. visited Persia, the US, and Israel, and her diary contains many reflections on her travel's impact on her self-conception and self-understanding.[145]

The sensitization of the self also implied an increased responsibility of the self for its own well-being. For example, cancer etiologies stressed individual behavior, such as smoking. But the most important interface between the external world and the interior psychological make-up of the self in the 1970s was food.[146] In her autobiographical novel, *Klassenliebe*, Karin Struck wondered, for example, "Why I haven't had cancer yet" in light of her constant over-eating.[147] The growing popularity of individual health strategies—jogging, for example, and the related construction of fitness paths all over the Federal Republic—pointed to

---

[141] Zur Krebsliteratur der 1970er Jahre, see Claudia Boldt, "Die ihren Mörder kennen. Zur deutschsprachigen literarischen Krebsdarstellung der Gegenwart" (Phil. Dissertation, University of Freiburg, 1989), Marion Moamai, *Krebs schreiben. Deutschsprachige Literatur der siebziger und achtziger Jahre* (St. Ingbert: Röhrig, 1997), and Thomas Anz, *Gesund oder krank? Medizin, Moral und Ästhetik in der deutschen Gegenwartsliteratur* (Stuttgart: J.B. Metzler, 1989).

[142] Jutta Dornheim, *Kranksein im dörflichen Alltag. Soziokulturelle Aspekte des Umgangs mit Krebs* (Tübingen: Tübinger Verein für Volkskunde, 1983), 198–249, especially 201, 221, 225.

[143] Reichardt, *Authentizität und Gemeinschaft*, 831–69, Robert P. Stephens, *Germans on Drugs. The Complications of Modernization in Hamburg* (Ann Arbor: University of Michigan Press, 2007).

[144] Reichardt, *Authentizität und Gemeinschaft*, 807–31, and Tändler, *Das therapeutische Jahrzehnt*, 349–58.

[145] Bärbel H., Diaries, DTA 1495, I, 1-I,4, October 14, 1973, November 21, 1977, May 29, 1983.

[146] See, for example,Ernst L. Wynder, "Ernährung und Krebs," *Münchener Medizinische Wochenschrift* 177/31 (1975): 1265–72, who argued that a third of all cancers among men and half of them among women were caused by nutrition.

[147] Struck, *Klassenliebe*, 228.

the emerging neoliberal subjectivity of the 1980s.[148] If the leftist alternative discourse had called for solidarity in individual suffering, the turn toward the self now fueled a self-optimization and seamless integration into the demands of a capitalist society. The sensitization of the subject to the experience and articulation of emotions was thus perfectly compatible with the turn toward an increasingly individualistic, neoliberal, and market-driven order in the 1980s.[149]

Yet this sensitization of the self also led to its renewed politicization. The transition from fear and suffering to a new activism manifested itself in the *Tunix* (Do Nothing) Congress in West Berlin in February 1978, which at least 20,000 activists attended.[150] The squatters of the early 1980s in Hamburg and West Berlin also represented an activist response to the preceding sense of insecurity and anxiety.[151] The most consequential effect of the sensitization of subjects, however, was its renewed politicization in the environmental and peace movements from the late 1970s onward. Ecology and peace advanced to new external fear objects, which made proliferating anxieties more concrete and tangible again. Bärbel H.'s diary reflects this transition as well. Having cultivated her ability to understand and express her feelings for years, she became increasingly involved in an "ecological group" (*Ökogruppe*) and also articulated her fears of a "Third World War."[152] This also entailed a gradual distancing from the Frankfurt alternative scene, which, as she stated in May 1983, she could "no longer stand." At the same time, she articulated new fears: "I'm afraid. I am afraid of Germany. Of what is happening here."[153] The social movements of the 1970s and 1980s were not simply an extension of "1968" but also constituted a genuinely new "politics of the first person." The emotionalization and sensitization of individual subjects in the wake of the student movement were an essential precondition for the ascendancy of these movements.[154] The continuities and transformations of fear from the 1970s to the 1980s will be taken up in Chapter 8. Before doing so, it is important

---

[148] Tobias Dietrich, "Laufen als Heilsuche? Körperliche Selbstfindung von den 1970er bis zu den 1990er Jahren in transatlantischer Perspektive," in Eitler, Elberfeld, eds, *Zeitgeschichte des Selbst*, 147–61.

[149] On these continuities, see Ulrich Bröckling, *Das unternehmerische Selbst. Soziologie einer Subjektivierungsform* (Frankfurt a/M: Suhrkamp, 2007). See also Maik Tändler, Uffa Jensen, "Psychowissen, Politik und das Selbst. Eine neue Forschungsperspektive auf die Geschichte des Politischen im 20. Jahrhundert," in Maik Tändler, Uffa Jensen, eds, *Das Selbst zwischen Anpassung und Befreiung. Psychowissen und Politik im 20. Jahrhundert* (Göttingen: Wallstein, 2012), 9–35, Tändler, *Das therapeutische Jahrzehnt*, 447.

[150] Timothy Scott Brown, *West Germany and the Global Sixties. The Antiauthoritarian Revolt, 1962–1978* (New York: Cambridge, 2013), 356–62, Reichardt, *Authentizität und Gemeinschaft*, 123–4.

[151] Häberlen and Smith, "Struggling for Feelings," 628–36, Häberlen, *Emotional Politics of the Alternative Left*, 222–64, and Lukas J. Hezel, "'Was gibt es zu verlieren, wo es kein Morgen gibt?' Chronopolitik und Radikalisierung in der Jugendrevolte 1980/81 und bei den Autonomen," in Fernando Esposito, ed., *Zeitenwandel. Transformation geschichtlicher Zeitlichkeit nach dem Boom* (Göttingen: Vandenhoeck & Ruprecht, 2017), 119–52.

[152] Bärbel H., Diaries, DTA 1495, I, 1-I,412.2.1980; April 14, 1980, July 15, 1980.

[153] Ibid. May 29, 1983.   [154] See also Häberlen and Tändler, "Spaces for feeling differently."

to analyze another important context for the history of fear and emotions in the Federal Republic: the popularization and emotionalization of West German commemorative culture in the 1970s.

Holocaust and the Emotionalization of Memory

It was a surprise because it was a spontaneous outburst of emotion from Willy Brandt when he stood before this monument, which commemorated the victims of the Jewish ghetto in Warsaw. That a chancellor, a head of government, went to his knees at a political meeting has never been seen before.

This is how the *Frankfurter Allgemeine* reporter Hansjakob Stehle described Chancellor Willy Brandt's emotional gesture during his state visit to Poland in December 1970.[155] The occasion for Brandt's visit was the signing of the Warsaw Treaty in which Federal Republic de facto recognized the Oder–Neisse line as Poland's western border and thus renounced any claims to formerly Eastern German territories that were now part of Poland and the Soviet Union. The photo quickly assumed iconic stature, and it significantly contributed to Brandt's receipt of the Nobel Peace Prize in 1971. Brandt described the gesture in his 1989 memoir thus: "On the abyss of German history and burdened by millions of murdered victims, I did what one does when language fails."[156] It was one of many descriptions that emphasized the spontaneity of the gesture, suggesting the changed emotional regime. Unlike in the early Federal Republic, it was now quite possible even for the Federal Chancellor to show emotions in public. Still, this new expressive emotional regime remained controversial. CDU general secretary Bruno Heck, for example, framed his critique of Brandt's *Ostpolitik* explicitly as a critique of this emotionalization. It was "devastating," he argued, that the federal government sought to cover up the "uncertainties of [the Warsaw Treaty] with emotions." He accused Brandt of defying "political reason" by appealing only to "the heart and to emotions."[157] Many West Germans agreed. According to a survey in *Der Spiegel*, 41 per cent of the population approved of the gesture while 48 per cent criticized it as "exaggerated."[158]

---

[155] Interview with Stehle, https://www.youtube.com/watch?v=QTHft_6HjpA (last accessed March 1, 2020).

[156] Willy Brandt, *Erinnerungen* (Frankfurt a/M: Propyläen, 1989), 214.

[157] Quoted in Friedrich Kießling, "Täter repräsentieren: Willy Brandts Kniefall in Warschau. Überlegungen zum Zusammenhang von bundesdeutscher Außenrepräsentation und der Erinnerung an den Nationalsozialismus," in Johannes Paulmann, ed., *Auswärtige Repräsentationen. Deutsche Kulturdiplomatie nach 1945* (Cologne: Böhlau, 2005), 217. See also Eckart Conze, *Die Suche nach Sicherheit. Eine Geschichte der Bundesrepublik Deutschland von 1949 bis in die Gegenwart* (Berlin: Siedler, 2009), 439.

[158] Ibid. "Kniefall angemessen oder übertrieben?" *Der Spiegel* 51/24 (1970): 27.

It was no coincidence that this debate over the adequacy of displaying emotions in public occurred on the field of commemorative culture. The increased presence and significance of emotions in West German culture also entailed a gradual collapse of the mechanisms of emotional distancing, which, as we have seen in the previous chapters, had shaped confrontations with the Nazi past up to this point. The New Left also constructed its own attempts at emotional distancing from the past. For activists, the fascist "other" resided either in anonymous capitalist structures or was anchored in specific social types: the industrialist, the media mogul, the university teacher, or the policeman.

Yet this sharp demarcation of a fascist "other" became increasingly porous by the end of the 1960s. Because it was increasingly difficult to determine the sources of fascism, many leftist activists began to localize the fascist impulse within their own self, which then also served as an explanation for the political failure of the 1968 revolt.[159] Such uncertainty about the exact location of the fascist "other" not only plagued left-wing or radical subjectivities: it also existed in the broader public discourse. Here, the general reduction of external pressure during the period of détente enabled a wider recognition and diffusion of guilt and responsibility within West German society. One example of this process was the West German reception of the psychological Milgram experiment, which demonstrated the potential of individuals for authoritarian, cruel, and violent behavior if an authority figure indicated that they must follow orders. While professional historians of National Socialism largely ignored the experiment, the public generally considered it a significant illuminator of Nazism.[160] Even before the publication of the German edition of the study, the psychiatrist David Mantell duplicated the experiment in Germany and arrived at similar results as Milgram: 85 per cent of his test subjects administered the maximum and potentially lethal penalty of electric shocks with 450 volts to the test persons.[161] The affirmation of an inherently aggressive potential among humans reversed the distancing mechanisms of the previous decade. The public discussion of the Milgram experiment illustrated a subjectivity that could never be quite certain of its own moral integrity and hence required increased introspection for reassurance.

A greater recognition of the willingness to succumb to authority and the potential for violence among individuals constituted one aspect of the gradual decline of efforts at dissociation from the Nazi past. The other aspect was a

---

[159]   See Chapter 6 in this book.

[160]   Holocaust research largely ignored the Milgram experiment: see Thomas Sandkühler, Hans-Walter Schmuhl, "Milgram für Historiker. Reichweite und Grenzen einer Übertragung des Milgram-Experiments auf den Nationalsozialismus," in Thomas Sandkühler, Hans-Walter Schmuhl, *Analyse und Kritik. Zeitschrift für Sozialtheorie* 20 (1998): 3–26, "Gehorsam: Genügend Kretins," *Der Spiegel* 40/24 (1970): 247–8, Hans Krieger, "Ist Gehorsam eine Tugend? Quälen auf Befehl. Milgrams Experimente über das Verhalten gegenüber Autorität," *Die Zeit* 43 (1974): 31.

[161]   David Mantell, "Das Potential zur Gewalt in Deutschland: Eine Replikation unter Erwachsenen des Milgram-Experiments," *Der Nervenarzt* 42 (1971): 252–7.

growing empathy with the victims. The Eichmann trial in Jerusalem had already signaled the onset of what historians would dub an "era of the witness," which bestowed a larger space to victim testimony in legal proceedings.[162] The Frankfurt Auschwitz trial (1963–5) displayed an at least limited sensitivity to the interests of the victims. It provided, for example, non-Jewish assistants and guides to Jewish victims who testified during the trial.[163] This development continued in the 1970s. Unlike in the trials of the 1960s, the figure of the Jewish survivor became central to the television coverage of later Nationalist Socialist trials, such as the Düsseldorf Majdanek trial from 1975 to 1981. Likewise, the fortieth anniversary of the so-called *Reichskristallnacht* marked a quantitative and qualitative turning point in the commemoration of this 1938 event and increasingly brought into view a "specifically Jewish history of persecution."[164] While the number of television programs on the Nazi period declined slightly during the first half of the 1970s, these programs adopted a more critical perspective and often focused on the persecution of the Jews and on the complicity of ordinary Germans during the Nazi period.[165]

New forms of medialization in film and television promoted a more subjective and more emotional discussion of the Nazi past. By the mid 1970s, 18 million West German households possessed a TV and, for the first time, a majority of West Germans had not directly experienced the Nazi period.[166] In this context, the journalist Peter Märthesheimer of the West German Broadcasting Station (WDR) initiated the purchase of the US TV series *Holocaust* for German TV. Against significant resistance both from West German politicians and from TV journalists, the four episodes of *Holocaust* were broadcast on all regional channels, not on the national Channel One, in January 1979. More than any other media event, the reception of *Holocaust* signaled the new emotionalization of the

---

[162] Annette Wieviorka, *The Era of the Witness* (Ithaca: Cornell University Press, 2006), Henri Lustiger Thaler, Habbo Knoch, eds, *Witnessing Unbound: Holocaust Representation and the Origins of Memory* (Detroit: Wayne State University Press, 2017), Martin Sabrow, Norbert Frei, eds, *Die Geburt des Zeitzeugen nach 1945* (Göttingen: Wallstein, 2012).

[163] Susanne Hillman, "Auschwitz All Over Again? Victim-Witnesses at the Frankfurt Trial, 1963–5," unpublished paper, 2018.

[164] Frank Bösch, "Film, NS-Vergangenheit und Geschichtswissenschaft. Von 'Holocaust' zu 'Der Untergang'," *Vierteljahreshefte für Zeitgeschichte* 55/1 (2007): 1–32, Frank Bösch, *Zeitenwende 1979. Als die Welt von heute begann* (Munich: C.H.Beck, 2019), 368.

[165] Sabine Horn, "'Jetzt aber zu einem Thema, das uns diese Woche alle beschäftigt.' Die westdeutsche Fernsehberichterstattung über den Frankfurter Auschwitz-Prozess (1963–65) und den Düsseldorfer Majdanek-Prozess (1975–81)—ein Vergleich," *1999. Zeitschrift für Sozialgeschichte des 21. Jahrhunderts* 17 (2002): 13–43, Bösch, "Film, NS-Vergangenheit und Geschichtswissenschaft," Harald Schmid, *Erinnern an den "Tag der Schuld." Das Novemberpogrom von 1938 in der deutschen Geschichtspolitik* (Hamburg: Ergebnisse Verlag, 2001), 325–93.

[166] Wulf Kantsteiner, "Nazis, Viewers and Statistic: Television History, Television Audience Research and Collective Memory in West Germany," *Journal of Contemporary History* 39/4 (2004): 575–98.

West German commemorative culture.[167] After each instalment, the WDR held a discussion with experts on the subject, which also gave viewers the opportunity to ask questions over the telephone.

Holocaust achieved unprecedented ratings for a TV broadcast on historical fiction: no less than 41 per cent of the West German households saw the last episode of the *Holocaust* series. Estimates suggest that about one in two German adults (approximately 20 million) saw at least part of the series, and about a third of all adults saw all four episodes. According to a study commissioned by WDR by the Media Research Institute Marplan, the mini-series was slightly more popular among men than women, and young Germans between 14 and 29 were especially well represented among *Holocaust* viewers.[168] More than 10,000 viewers called WDR to ask questions during the broadcast discussions, and the WDR received 5,494 letters, postcards, telegrams and postcards during the first week of the broadcast.[169]

The emotional reaction to the TV series was profound: 67 per cent of viewers stated that the TV show had "deeply shaken" them, and 22.2 per cent confessed to "almost having cried" during some scenes. Indeed, many viewers reported "uninhibited crying" while viewing the mini-series.[170] Three-quarters of all viewers stated that they had discussed the topic during or immediately after the broadcast of *Holocaust*, and a third said they were still having such discussions two and more months later.[171] Months after the broadcast, German daily newspapers were still receiving letters to the editor about it.[172] The series promoted an increasing identification with the victims of the Nazi regime. According to the WDR, 72.5 per cent of viewers had a positive reaction to the series, only 7.3 per cent rejected it, and 19.6 per cent were "indecisive."[173] The popular identification with the fate of the fictional Weiss family portrayed in the series enabled a kind of emotional

---

[167] In November 1982, the series was shown again on Channel 1: see Jürgen Wilke, "Die Fernsehserie 'Holocaust' als Medienereignis," *Historical Social Research/Historische Sozialforschung* 30/4 (2005): 9–17. On the context and reception of *Holocaust*, see Martina Thiele, *Publizistische Kontroversen über den Holocaust im Film* (Münster: LitVerlag, 2001), 298–338. On *Holocaust* and as a turning point in West German commemorative culture in general, see Bösch, *Zeitenwende 1979*, 363–95.

[168] Fifty-nine per cent of the adult population saw at least two half hours of *Holocaust*, Holocaust-Begleituntersuchung, Zusammenfassende Darstellung der Wellen 1–3, Historisches Archiv, WDR, Nr. 5403.

[169] Julius H. Schoeps, "Angst vor der Vergangenheit. Notizen zu den Reaktionen auf 'Holocaust'," in Peter Märtesheimer, Ivo Frenzel, eds, *Im Kreuzfeuer: Der Fernsehfilm Holocaust. Eine Nation ist betroffen* (Frankfurt a/M: Fischer, 1979), 225–30, here 230. Numbers according to WDR-Information. Fernsehen. Reaktionen auf Holocaust, May 3, 1979, Historisches Archiv WDR, D 1797.

[170] Examples in Heiner Lichtenstein, Michael Schmid-Ospach, eds, *Holocaust. Briefe an den WDR* (Wuppertal: Peter Hammer, 1982), 32, 42, 46. On reports about crying, see also Bösch, *Zeitenwende 1979*, 383.

[171] Holocaust-Begleituntersuchung, Zusammenfassende Darstellung der Wellen 1–3, Historisches Archiv, WDR, Nr. 5403. All the following figures are based on this document.

[172] Andrei S. Markovits, Rebecca S. Hayden, "'Holocaust' before and after the Event: Reactions in West Germany and Austria," *New German Critique* 19 (1980): 53–80.

[173] WDR Information, January 30, 1979, Historisches Archiv WDR, D 1797.

"catharsis," which stirred up the "most basic feelings" and hence allowed the ushering of "redemptive tears."[174]

The emotional reaction to *Holocaust* also included a reduction of fear, which had prevented, as we saw in Chapter 1, a broader recognition of guilt and responsibility during the immediate postwar period. Now emotions like shame and guilt became more prominent in popular reactions to *Holocaust*. Up to 42 per cent of viewers felt "shame that we committed and tolerated such things." Almost half of all conversations (48.1 per cent) about the mini-series revolved around the "causes" of the Holocaust and the associated "guilt question."[175] The gradual decline of fears of retribution now enabled a broader discussion of guilt and responsibility. This emotional shift to guilt and shame also entailed gender- and generation-specific dimensions. Women, for example, began to articulate their mistrust regarding their husbands' narratives from the Eastern Front.[176] And, according to the Marplan survey, children initiated close to 60 per cent of family conversations about *Holocaust*, whereas parents only started a third of them. These discussions thus often assumed the character of children interrogating their parents about the Nazi past. Among younger viewers aged between 14 and 44 years, only one-third exhibited a tendency to affirm German innocence compared with 61 per cent of older viewers.[177]

The emotional identification *Holocaust* engendered stood in stark contrast to the sober analysis of the mini-series by experts such as the professional historians Karl Dietrich Bracher, Golo Mann, Hans Jacobsen, and, after the last broadcast, the director of the Munich Institute for Contemporary History, Martin Broszat, who had joined the Nazi Party in 1944 but then went on to become one of the most important historians of National Socialism in the Federal Republic. In an article published after the *Holocaust* broadcast, Broszat conceded that historians, filmmakers, and journalists had thus far approached "the delicate subject of Jewish destiny only in a very cautious and emotionally distant manner." The rather cursory treatment of the Holocaust even in historical works on the Nazi period, Broszat argued, was due to historians' "stylistic embarrassment." The "historicist language used to describe noble historical ideas" in scholarship was simply not suitable to capture "gas chambers and mass executions."[178] Broszat acknowledged a need for the increased integration of Jewish sources in the historiography but criticized the mini-series' "emotionalization" of the subject, which, he cautioned, might stir up legitimate parallel "emotional national

---

[174] Sendemanuskript Kulturmagazin, February 21, 1979, Historisches Archiv WDR, Nr. 11375.

[175] Holocaust-Begleituntersuchung, Zusammenfassende Darstellung der Wellen 1–3, Historisches Archiv, WDR, Nr. 5403, S.77.

[176] Schoeps, "Angst vor der Vergangenheit," 228.

[177] Holocaust-Begleituntersuchung, Zusammenfassende Darstellung der Wellen 1–3, Historisches Archiv, WDR, Nr. 5403, S.77.

[178] Martin Broszat, "'Holocaust' und die Geschichtswissenschaft," *Vierteljahreshefte für Zeitgeschichte* 27/2 (1979): 285–98.

resentments" among ordinary Germans. He had previously also questioned the objectivity of the Jewish historian and Holocaust survivor Joseph Wulf because of his excessive emotional concerns, but did not question his own possible biases.[179]

Broszat's skepticism regarding political emotions and his plea for emotional restraint seemed increasingly unconvincing. In line with the new cultural norm of emotional expressivity, it was the open and public expression of emotions that appeared to be positive and innovative. The Swiss psychoanalyst Alice Miller praised the TV journalist Peter Märthesheimer, who had been instrumental in bringing the *Holocaust* series to German TV, for expressing his feelings openly in the TV discussion, which she felt the other members of the panel had failed to do. "[C]oping with the past without emotions" was ineffective, she wrote, because there would be no real confrontation with the past without "outrage and mourning." According to Miller, feelings were a protection against dehumanization and brutalization. As she wrote:

A feeling person has a moral basis and will not let himself be used as a mass murderer. Mass murderers did not have this grounding; they only learned to obey and were proud to have no "weaknesses." They despised tears and similar emotions, which they sought to gas with the Jews in the closed chambers. And they became more and more callous, empty, obedient automatons. Their fears, their helplessness, their grief, everything that makes one an individual, was repeatedly gassed and burned there with the Jews, while their thinking worked perfectly.[180]

Miller's perspective expressed the emotional culture of new subjectivity, which identified emotional catharsis as the true significance of the *Holocaust* mini-series. In a similar way, the influential philosopher Günther Anders characterized "emotional blindness" as a precondition for mass murder. By contrast, the "collective shock" of the mini-series triggered a healing effect and hence represented, according to Anders, the "psychologically most significant event of the post-Hitler history of Germany."[181] The validation of strong and expressive feelings with regard to *Holocaust* also prevailed in response to a leftist critique that categorized

---

[179] Ibid. On Broszat's essay, see also Frank Bösch, "Versagen der Zeitgeschichtsforschung? Martin Broszat, die westdeutschen Geschichtswissenschaft und die Fernsehserie 'Holocaust'," *Zeithistorische Forschungen/Studies in Contemporary History* 6/3 (2009): 477–82. On sobriety and anti-emotionality in the historiography, see Sybille Steinbacher, "Zeitzeugenschaft und die Etablierung der Zeitgeschichte in der Bundesrepublik Deutschland," in Frei and Sabrow, eds, *Die Geburt des Zeitzeugen nach 1945*, 145–56, especially 154–5.

[180] Alice Miller to Peter Märtesheimer, January 31, 1979, and "Betr.TV, Redaktion der Reihe Holocaust," Historisches Archiv WDR, Nr. 07943. Similarly, Margarete Mitscherlich-Nielsen, "Die Notwendigkeit zu trauern," in Märtesheimer and Frenzel, eds, *Im Kreuzfeuer: Der Fernsehfilm Holocaust*, 207–16.

[181] Günther Anders, *Besuch im Hades. Auschwitz und Breslau, 1966. Nach "Holocaust" 1979* (Munich: C.H.Beck, 1979), 189, 199.

the series as a typical Hollywood product with "lots of emotion, cheap effects, atrocities, etc.," which "failed to stimulate a rational discussion" on the subject.[182] In a very perceptive essay from 1980, the literary critic Andreas Huyssen disparaged this "fear of emotion and subjectivity" on the Left as "partly...a legacy of the Third Reich." Precisely because Hitler succeeded in exploiting "emotions, instincts and the '*irrational*,'" this entire sphere had become suspicious to postwar generations. According to Huyssen, the *Holocaust*-induced "emotional explosion" enabled an identification with the victims and had succeeded in overcoming the "mechanisms of repression and denial."[183]

In fact, the *Holocaust* series marked a turning point in both the popular and the academic representation of the Nazi past. Several television broadcasts on the Nazi past in the 1980s portrayed the experiences of Jewish victims or Jewish families, humanizing the victims for viewers. However, unlike *Holocaust*, these accounts tended to eschew the portrayal of violence, and they usually portrayed Germans as passive followers rather than perpetrators.[184] Historical studies also adopted a stronger focus on the perspective of ordinary people, especially in the new "history of everyday life." Here too, the local history of Jewish communities and Jewish individual fates came into focus.[185] Such approaches tended to emphasize the emotional and subjective dimension of the Nazi past, which, in turn, provoked strong objections from established historians. Writing in 1985, the doyen of a social science-oriented history of society, the Bielefeld historian Hans-Ulrich Wehler attributed the significance of "feelings, emotions, affects" to "generation-specific experiences." In a footnote, he provided a fairly accurate description of shifting emotional regimes in the history of the Federal Republic:

For those generations who have consciously witnessed the Second World War, flight, and the postwar period, the control of affects constituted an essential precondition for psychic and physical survival. Feelings were revealed openly only within the family or among close friends and girlfriends; in a more mediated form, they of course also entered into political and academic work. For younger people, the expression and defense of emotions appears to have a different significance; they are no longer considered strictly private; control mechanisms do not snap in almost automatically.[186]

---

[182] Brigitte Weinberger to Peter Märtesheimer, o.D., Historisches Archiv WDR, Nr. 07943.

[183] Andreas Huyssen, "The Politics of Identification: 'Holocaust' and West German Drama," *New German Critique* 19/1 (1980):117–36.

[184] Bösch, "Film, NS-Vergangenheit und Geschichtswissenschaft." On the after-effects in West German commemorative culture, see also Bösch, *Zeitenwende 1979*, 387–95.

[185] This often also meant the local experiences of Jewish Germans: see, for example, Dietrich Heither, Wolfgang Matthäus, Bernd Pieper, *Als jüdische Schülerin entlassen. Erinnerungen und Dokumente zur Geschichte der Heinrich-Schütz-Schule in Kassel* (Kassel: Gesamthochschulbibliothek,1984).

[186] Hans-Ulrich Wehler, "Alltagsgeschichte: Königsweg zu neuen Ufern oder Irrgarten der Illusionen?" in Hans-Ulrich Wehler, ed., *Aus der Geschichte lernen? Essays* (Munich: C.H.Beck, 1988), 309, footnote 13.

The impact of the *Holocaust* series also fueled a distinctly West German Holocaust research beginning in the early 1980s.[187] For example, historians of the Munich Institute for Contemporary History had blocked the translation of the classic 1961 work of the American historian Raul Hilberg, *The Destruction of European Jews*. *Holocaust* made it difficult for the Institute to maintain its opposition and the small left-wing publisher, Olle & Wolter, published a translation in 1982.[188] This period also saw the broad anchoring of a popular Holocaust memory in West German society, which then also became the subject of repeated commemorative controversies, especially in the "Historians' Debate" regarding the historical "singularity" of the Holocaust.

The shifts in West German commemorative culture related to the *Holocaust* series had a twofold significance for the history of fear in West Germany in the 1980s. First, the public response to *Holocaust* reflected and promoted emotional expressivity as a new cultural norm. For young Germans especially, the public display of emotions regarding the Nazi past constituted one way to demonstrate their empathy with the victims and to confront German guilt and responsibility. It signaled the collapse of the mechanisms of emotional distancing and disavowal that had characterized West German confrontations with the Nazi past up to that point. Second, the integration of the Holocaust into West German memory enhanced the significance of the event for contemporaries' understanding of their present and anticipation of their future. The outrage of some viewers of *Holocaust*, for example, was directed at contemporary genocides in Cambodia or torture in Latin America. *Stern* editor Henri Nannen went as far as to declare that "Holocaust is Everywhere."[189] The event also increasingly shaped younger Germans' horizon of expectation and anticipation of future catastrophe, which then became important in the environmental and peace movements of the 1970s and 1980s. Holocaust memory served as a foil for the imagination of a "nuclear holocaust" in the context of the Second Cold War. The memory of "Auschwitz" and "Hiroshima" merged and formed the basis of a catastrophic anticipation of the future, which formed a central element of the apocalyptic fears of the 1980s.[190] But before turning to this culmination of the history of fear and anxiety in West Germany, it is necessary to analyze another form of intensified political fears during the 1970s, those triggered by the terrorism of the RAF.

---

[187] Bösch, "Film, NS-Vergangenheit und Geschichtswissenschaft," 5, Bösch, *Zeitenwende 1979*, 393.
[188] Ibid. Götz Aly, "Wie deutsche Historiker und Verlage die Übersetzung von Raul Hilbers Buch 'The Destruction of European Jews' behinderten. Ein Sittenbild," lecture manuscript, https://www.perlentaucher.de/essay/goetz-aly-das-institut-fuer-zeitgeschichte-und-die-verzoegerte-deutsche-ausgabe-von-raul-hilberg.html (last accessed March 1, 2020).
[189] Henri Nannen, "Ja, ich war zu feige," in Märthesheimer and Frenzel, eds, *Im Kreuzfeuer*, 277–80, here 280.
[190] Anders, *Besuch im Hades*, 203–7.

Terrorism and the Escalation of Political Fears

The dialectics of political fears that had shaped the political discourse of the Federal Republic since the 1950s culminated in the debate over the left-wing terrorism of the RAF in the 1970s. Left-wing terrorism originated from the student movement, even though there was no direct causal link between the New Left and the RAF.[191] While many of the members of the RAF had been active in the student movement, most left-wing activists did not embrace terrorism and distanced themselves in an often gradual and painful process from the violent acts of the RAF.[192] Left-wing terrorism killed 34 people in West Germany between 1972 and 1998, and many others were severely injured.

The founding act of the RAF was the violent prison liberation of Andreas Baader by Ulrike Meinhof, Gudrun Ensslin, and others in October 1970, during which the 62-year-old prison guard Georg Linke was seriously injured. After several attacks during the "May Offensive" in 1972, which killed 4 people and injured over 70, the West German police arrested the entire RAF leadership, including Andreas Baader, Jan-Carl Raspe, Gudrun Ensslin, Ulrike Meinhof, Irmgard Möller, and Brigitte Mohnhaupt, in early July 1972. From that point on, the strategy of the remaining RAF members centered on the liberation of these "political prisoners." The public criticism of the conditions of detention was the central tool for the politicization and recruitment of new members for the RAF. From January 1973 onward, RAF prisoners started several hunger strikes to demand to be held together and to be treated as "prisoners of war." They described their separation from each other as "solitary confinement." In November 1974, one former RAF member, Holger Meins, died as a result of his third hunger strike. A picture of his completely emaciated body in *Der Spiegel* evoked images of concentration camp victims, yet also appealed to Christian notions of sacrifice.[193] Ulrike Meinhof's suicide in May 1976 had a similar effect and contributed significantly to RAF recruitment.

Despite the rapid arrest of the RAF's founding members, terrorist violence continued. Members of the terrorist group *Bewegung 2. Juni* assassinated the West Berlin judge Günter von Drenkmann in November 1974. The same organization achieved the release of several detained terrorists in February 1975 through the kidnapping and subsequent release of the West Berlin CDU politician Peter

[191] On this debate, see Wolfgang Kraushaar, ed., *Die RAF und der linke Terrorismus. Vol. 2* (Hamburg: Hamburger Edition, 2006). On the term "terrorism," see Petra Terhoeven, *Die Rote Armee Fraktion. Eine Geschichte terroristischer Gewalt* (Munich: C.H.Beck, 2017), 16.

[192] Belinda Davis, "Jenseits von Terror und Rückzug. Die Suche nach politischem Spielraum und Strategien im Westdeutschland der siebziger Jahre," in Klaus Weinhauer, Jörg Requate, Heinz-Gerhard Haupt, eds, *Terrorismus in der Bundesrepublik: Medien, Staat und Subkulturen in den 1970er Jahren* (Frankfurt a/M: Campus, 2006), 154–86.

[193] Petra Terhoeven, *Deutscher Herbst in Europa. Der Linksterrorismus der siebziger Jahre als transnationales Phänomen* (Munich: Oldenbourg, 2014), 267–74.

Lorenz. Two months later, in April 1975, a "Commando Holger Meins" occupied the West German embassy in Stockholm and murdered the diplomats Andreas von Mirbach and Heinz Hillegaart. An accidental detonation of explosives killed two RAF members, Ulrich Wessel and Siegfried Hauser. The terrorism of the RAF climaxed in the year 1977 with the assassination of the West German main prosecutor Siegfried Buback, his assistant Georg Wurster, and his driver Wolfgang Göbel in April, as well as the banker Jürgen Ponto in July. On September 5, 1977, the RAF commando "Siegfried Hauser" abducted the president of the West German employer association, Hanns Martin Schleyer, and killed his driver Heinz Marcisz as well as three police officers, Reinhold Brändle, Helmut Ulmer, and Roland Pieler.

Terror was increasingly internationalized. German terrorist groups joined forces with Palestinian terrorist groups to attack the Munich Olympics in September 1972, taking 11 Israeli athletes hostage, all of whom were killed in a failed liberation attempt.[194] The fear and controversy surrounding the group peaked in 1977 with the hijacking of a Lufthansa airplane. The terrorist group, "Popular Front for the Liberation of Palestine," murdered the pilot, Jürgen Schumann, and took the passengers hostage on October 13, 1977, in an attempt to achieve the release of the detained RAF members. Chancellor Helmut Schmidt refused and ordered an ultimately successful liberation operation. This prompted the interned RAF members Andreas Baader, Gudrun Ensslin, and Jan-Carl Raspe to commit suicide in the Stammheim prison; a fourth prisoner, RAF member Irmgard Möller, survived badly injured.[195] The RAF remained in existence until 1998, yet it did not provoke the same fears or controversial debates as in the 1970s.

This short chronicle of terrorism does not explain its significance for the history of political fears in the Federal Republic. Historians have often invoked categories of psychopathology such as "hysteria" in their analysis of societal reactions to the RAF.[196] Yet, much as they had in earlier eras, such labels are hardly adequate for explaining and historicizing political fears. The RAF's significance resulted from its symbolic meaning for West German society. Terrorist violence represents a performative act, which aims—then and now—at producing fear by demonstrating the possibility of terrorist violence everywhere and at any time.[197]

---

[194] Ulrike Meinhof had declared her solidarity with a Palestinian terror group that had killed 11 Israeli athletes during the Olympic Games in Munich in 1972; see "Die Aktion des 'Schwarzen September' in München. Zur Strategie des antiimperialistischen Kampfes, November 1972," in *Rote Armee Fraktion. Texte und Materialien zur Geschichte der RAF* (Berlin: ID-Verlag, 1997), 151–77. See also Koenen, *Vesper, Ensslin, Baader*, 333–4.

[195] Stefan Aust, *Der Baader-Meinhof Komplex* (Hamburg: Hoffmann und Campe, 2008), 573–80. While the suicides of the inmates are rarely questioned, it is not clear whether these acts happened with or without knowledge of the security forces.

[196] Koenen, *Vesper, Ensslin, Baader*, 322, Hanno Balz, *Von Terroristen, Sympathisanten und dem starken Staat. Die öffentliche Debatte über die RAF in den 70er Jahren* (Frankfurt a/M: Campus, 2008), 179.

[197] Bernd Weisbrod, "Terrorism as Performance. The Assassination of Walter Rathenau and Hanns-Martin Schleyer," in Heinz-Gerhard Haupt, Wilhelm Heitmeyer, Stefan Malthaner, Andrea

The media representation of terrorist acts and of the detained RAF members were therefore central to its significance. The protest against the conditions of internment for RAF members, the fight against "solitary confinement" and "torture" became central to the public communication strategy of the RAF and advanced to be the most important tool of recruiting new members.[198]

Like the moral panic of the 1950s regarding the alleged abduction of young men to the Foreign Legion, the public response to terrorism contained a symbolic excess. The RAF was able to produce fear because it was able to build on and inflate already existing fears within West German society. The emotional intensity of the confrontation with the RAF thus derived from dialectically reinforcing political fears from the late 1950s onward. The terror of the RAF mobilized and inflated the worst political fears on the Left and on the Right. Both sides saw the terrorism of the RAF and the state's reaction as confirmation of their long-held suspicion that the other side was seeking to construct a "different" republic. While conservatives saw the RAF as the logical extension of the student revolt, the Left interpreted the state's response to terror as an attempt to activate already existing authoritarian tendencies in West German society. The open expression of those political fears both perpetuated and enhanced the culture of emotional expressiveness. For a small minority on the Left, the RAF represented one option for the expression of political emotions that the student movement had instigated.[199] But the Right too moved away from its previous emphasis on anti-emotionality and rationality in its reaction to terrorism, and pushed rhetorical and emotional boundaries. More than in the debate over "democratic" and "revolutionary" fears in the 1950s and 1960s, this dialectic of fear regarding terrorism involved wide sections of West German society. The significance of the RAF for the history of political fears resided in its broad emotional resonance within West German society.

Among conservatives, the mobilization of fear entailed the delimitation of its object. Anger, outrage, and anxiety no longer just focused on the perpetrators of the RAF terror, but rather on a more diffuse and increasingly invisible group of supporters or "sympathizers." The persons belonging to that category also expanded gradually over the course of the 1970s. Whereas in 1972, the term still referred to clearly identifiable left-wing intellectuals such as Heinrich Böll or the Hanoverian psychology professor Peter Brückner, it tended to encompass the entire left-wing scene by the mid 1970s. The distinction between "terrorists,"

Kirschner, eds, *Control of Violence. Historical and International Perspectives on Violence in Modern Societies* (New York: Springer, 2011), 365–94.

[198] Martin Jander, "Isolation oder Isolationsfolter. Die Auseinandersetzung um die Haftbedingungen der RAF-Häftlinge," in Colin et al., eds, *Der "Deutsche Herbst" und die RAF*, 124–30.
[199] On the question of "political passions," see Heinz Bude, "Erbschaft dieser Zeit: Die RAF und die Geschichte der Bundesrepublik," in Kraushaar, ed., *Die RAF und der linke Terrorismus. Vol. 2*, 1343–52.

"supporters," and "sympathizers" became increasingly blurred. Even *Der Spiegel* now described, in biologizing language, a "scene...in which the metastases of 'Baader/Meinhof'...grow: remnants of the old BM-circle, former followers of the Socialist Patient Collective, radical squatters, and militant demonstrators."[200] The expansion of the "sympathizer" culminated in the spring of 1977, when a self-named "Mescalero," who later turned out to be the German teacher Klaus Hülbrock, admitted in a student newspaper in Göttingen to his "secret joy" about the murder of state prosecutor Buback. While the writer distanced himself from RAF violence in the remainder of the text, public discourse paid little attention to this part. Conservatives like *Die Welt* journalist Werner Kahl painted the mysterious "Mescalero," and other "sympathizers" as the "silent reserve army of the terrorists."[201] The terrorist threat suddenly no longer consisted of a dozen perpetrators of violence but emanated from within West German society, especially from the universities. Conservative intellectuals and the activists of the *Bund Freiheit der Wissenschaft* (BFW) also blamed left-wing groups at universities for terrorism. For the BFW, the origins of terrorism resided in the "systematic defamation of the Federal Republic" and the "daily practice of breaking the law" at German universities. Student criticism and attacks of conservative professors now appeared as a precursor to the murders of the RAF. These accusations now also targeted professors who allegedly had tolerated left-wing extremism.[202] Even more liberal observers, such as the Munich political science professor Kurt Sontheimer, now argued that terrorism had emerged from left-wing political critique, from, as he characterized it, an "ad nauseum stirred aversion toward our political system, especially among students."[203]

The extension of the sympathizer concept also had legal consequences. In August 1976, the federal government passed anti-terror legislation that identified the "Advertising for a Terrorist Group" (paragraph 129a), the "Instigation to a Criminal Offense" (paragraph 130a), and the "Advocacy of Anti-Constitutional Acts" (paragraph 88) as criminal offenses.[204] Based on these laws, not only active terror acts but also the discursive support of the RAF became criminalized. In

---

[200] Quoted in Balz, *Von Terroristen, Sympathisanten und dem starken Staat*, 97. For the Böll debate, see Angelika Ibrügger, "Die unfreiwillige Selbstbespiegelung einer lernenden Demokratie. Heinrich Böll als Intellektueller zu Beginn der Terrorismusdiskussion," in Colin et al., eds, *Der "Deutsche Herbst" und die RAF*, 156–69.

[201] Quoted in Balz, *Von Terroristen, Sympathisanten und dem starken Staat*, 109, and Hanno Balz, "Der 'Sympathisanten'-Diskurs im Deutschen Herbst," in Requate et al., eds, *Terrorismus in der Bundesrepublik*, 320–50. On "the Mescalero," see also Stefan Spiller, "Der Sympathisant als Staatsfeind. Die Mescalero-Affäre," in Kraushaar, ed., *Die RAF und der linke Terrorismus, Vol. 2*, 1227–59, Weisbrod, "Terrorism as Performance."

[202] "Terrorismus und Hochschule, Pressekonferenz des Bundes Freiheit der Wissenschaft, September 29, 1977, HI, BFW, Box 24, Nikolai Wehrs, *Protest der Professoren. Der "Bund Freiheit der Wissenschaft" in den 1970er Jahren* (Göttingen: Wallstein Verlag, 2014), 403–5.

[203] "Die Terrorismusdebatte," in Kurt Sontheimer, *Die verunsicherte Republik. Die Bundesrepublik nach 30 Jahren* (Munich: Piper, 1979), 110–26, quotation on 110.

[204] Bundesamt für Verfassungsschutz to the Bundesminister des Innern, June 13, 1977, BArch, B141/48332.

May 1977, the Federal Bureau for the Protection of the Constitution sought to determine whether the public reporting in the media would embolden sympathizers of terrorism. The state thus demarcated positions that could remain part of the debate in an open society and other positions that now became illegal.[205]

Those measures also responded to numerous petitions from ordinary citizens, which articulated a multitude of threats. A city official, for example, asked in a letter to Attorney General Hans-Jochen Vogel why the "names of sympathizers" would not be published so that "colleagues and neighbors" could put pressure on them.[206] Another letter writer denounced the "sympathizers of a gang of criminals" as "accomplices of murder" and wondered what could be done against those "masters of education"—that is, professors at West German universities who presumably harbored sympathies for terrorists.[207] In the fear cycle of the terror of the 1970s, the terrorist or the "sympathizer" took over the place of the absolute "other," the "folk devil," and instigator of "moral panic," analogous to the role of the "recruiter" for the Foreign Legion or the "Communist" in the Cold War. In fact, one letter writer characterized the terrorists as "devil like" and as completely isolated from mainstream society.[208] Unlike in the 1950s, however, the terrorist or the sympathizer represented an exclusively internal threat and was not, unlike the "recruiter" or the "Communist," a stooge of an external power. But here too, the "signification spiral" was operative and associated ever-expanding threat scenarios with terrorists. In autumn 1977, the historian Golo Mann cast the confrontation with terrorism as a "kind of new civil war" against a "lethal enemy."[209] The Federal Republic entered a "political-communicative state of war" that entertained ever-escalating fantasies of violence, including the terrorist use of poison gas or nuclear weapons.[210] In some cases, these fantasies even included the revival of genuinely neo-Nazi fantasies that cast Germans as victims of a Jewish conspiracy. A letter writer "M.S." thus asked Vogel "how many Jews" were "part of the Baader Meinhof team" and propagated a conspiracy theory blaming Jews for all internal and external conflicts in West Germany.[211]

Political elites contributed to this escalation of political fears from above. State officials no longer sought to contain fear, as in the 1950s, but further fueled the fear and uncertainty that came from within German society. Conservative politicians

---

[205] Balz, *Von Terroristen, Sympathisanten und dem starken Staat*, 92–3, Stephan Scheiper, *Innere Sicherheit. Politische Anti-Terror-Konzepte in der Bundesrepublik Deutschland während der 1970er Jahre* (Paderborn: Schöningh, 2010), 375–8. The latter two paragraphs were deleted in 1981.

[206] A.V. Kreisrat to Vogel, August 5, 1977, BArch, B141/48429.

[207] H.S. to Vogel, July 1977, BArch, B141/48429.   [208] Ibid.

[209] *Die Welt*, September 7, 1977, quoted in Andreas Musolff, "Terrorismus im öffentlichen Diskurs der BRD: Seine Deutung als Kriegsgeschehen und die Folgen," in Haupt et al., eds, *Terrorismus in der Bundesrepublik*, 302–19, quotation on 304.

[210] Quoted in Musolff, "Terrorismus im öffentlichen Diskurs der BRD," 315, Balz, *Von Terroristen, Sympathisanten und dem starken Staat*, 189–97.

[211] M.S. to H.J. Vogel, December 4, 1974, BArch, B141/48421. An official from the Ministry of Justice replied that Vogel had "diligently read this petition" but could not "follow, agree or use it [in] any fashion," Jürgen Jekewitz to M.S., December 18, 1974, BArch, B 141/48421.

contributed to the rhetorical delimitation of the "sympathizer." For example, the CDU politician Bernhard Vogel explained that the use of the word "group" instead of "gang" to refer to the "Baader–Meinhof Gang" might signal a "sympathizer;" while CSU chairman Franz Josef Strauß wrote that "as many crimes have been committed with ink and from the lectern as have been committed on the street."[212] Similarly, in the autumn of 1977, the recently appointed CDU party secretary Heiner Geißler put together a collection of quotations running the gamut from Federal Chancellor Helmut Schmidt to members of the RAF, which were supposed to demonstrate a "a shared responsibility" for terrorism extending into the moderate Social Democratic camp.[213] Conservative commentators used women's prominence within the RAF as a way to criticize the women's movement and other social movements associated with it. The later president of the Federal Bureau for the Protection of the Constitution, Günther Nollau, who, in the 1950s, had warned against the danger of Communist subversion, warned against an "excess of women's liberation."[214]

Many West German citizens shared this perception of terrorism as a product of misguided societal development or as an effect of the social and political reforms of the center-left government. In January 1975, in the aftermath of the murder of the Berlin judge Günter von Drenkmann, "R.M." asked in a letter to Attorney General Vogel whether "it would not be time to put an end to the so-called 'democratization' in all areas of our society and return to a harsher reality."[215] Similar to the fear of a weak state vis-à-vis the danger of nuclear war, these petitions revealed concerns over a similarly weak state that would not be capable of protecting its citizens against an internal threat. Letter writers criticized the prison where RAF members were held as a "health spa for convicted murderers" or a "vacation-like imprisonment at the expense of the taxpayer."[216] Official care for RAF prisoners on hunger strike also provoked popular consternation. An SPD

[212] Quoted in Balz, *Von Terroristen, Sympathisanten und dem starken Staat,* 110–11. See also Andreas Musolff, *Krieg gegen die Öffentlichkeit. Terrorismus und politischer Sprachgebrauch* (Opladen: Westdeutscher Verlag, 1996), 165–6.

[213] CDU-Bundesgeschäftsstelle, *Terrorismus in der Bundesrepublik Deutschland—eine Auswahl von Zitaten* (Bonn: CDU-Bundesgeschäftsstelle, 1957), quoted in Karrin Hanshew, *Terror and Democracy in West Germany* (New York: Cambridge, 2012), 212, and Jörg Requate, "Gefährliche Intellektuelle? Staat und Gewalt in der Debatte um die RAF," in Dominik Geppert and Jens Hacke, eds, *Streit um den Staat. Intellektuelle Debatten in der Bundesrepublik, 1960–1980* (Göttingen: Vandenhoeck & Ruprecht, 2008).

[214] "Meinhof/Baader: Löwe Los," *Der Spiegel* 25/9 (1971): 27, quoted in Hanshew, *Terror and Democracy in West Germany,* 187. See also Alan Rosenfeld, "'Anarchist Amazons.' The Gendering of Radicalism in 1970s West Germany," *Contemporary European History* 19/4 (2010): 351–74.

[215] R.M. to B.J.M. Vogel, January 15, 1974, BArch, B141/48416. See also Christian Schletter, *Grabgesang der Demokratie. Die Debatten über das Scheitern der bundesdeutschen Demokratie von 1965 bis 1985* (Göttingen: Vandenhoeck & Ruprecht, 2015), 259–68. On petitions in general, see Michaela Fenske, *Demokratie Erschreiben. Bürgerbriefe und Petitionen als Medien politischer Kultur 1950–1974* (Frankfurt a/M: Campus, 2013).

[216] Dr. W.L. to Bundesjustizministerium, March 4, 1975, BArch, B141/48423. Einer der für Recht und Ordnung ist, March 14, 1973, BArch, B141/48413; Frau M.R. to Vogel, May 1977, BArch, B141/48429; R.T. to Bundesjustizministerium, October 20, 1974, BArch, B141/48416.

voter was "stunned" that "one made such a big deal out of the death of Holger Meins."[217] After the Drenkmann assassination and the Lorenz kidnapping in 1974–5, petitioners demanded the death penalty or even threatened to take matters into their own hands and resort to mob-justice, although they conceded that they spoke from "emotional outrage" rather than "clear thinking."[218] But such attitudes became more popular during the Schleyer kidnapping when, according to an Emnid poll, two-thirds of West Germans supported the death penalty. These positions were also not limited to the Right. A "Social Democrat from birth," for example, proposed the "successive liquidation of all interned RAF member[s] until Schleyer gets released."[219] Other citizens referenced the practice of "hostage taking" during the Second World War as a model for how to fight "inner enemies."[220] Leading CDU politicians like Alfred Dregger joined this popular sentiment and openly called for the reintroduction of the death penalty. Within the small "crisis cabinet," a bipartisan executive committee of the federal government, some members suggested the deliberate shooting of detained RAF members during the Schleyer kidnapping.[221] In an Allensbach survey of February 1978, three-quarters of all respondents demanded more severe punishment for terrorists, including quicker trials, the exclusion of defense lawyers, and higher penalties.[222] These petitions revealed an explicit "fear of terrorism," or even a more general fear of an "increase in violent crimes" against which the state was not able to offer effective protection.[223] In October 1977, one letter writer expected more "kidnappings and blackmail" and despaired over his impression that the "apocalypse was possible" and might even be "close."[224]

The official responses of the center-left federal government to societal anxiety adopted a deliberate stance of emotional restraint based on "sobriety and calmness" as well as "firmness," and the use only of "methods that the constitution and the rule of law" permitted. As "escalation of outrage" would not be compatible with the nature of the rule of law, not "emotional excitement" but the "firm application of existing laws" was the most promising approach to fighting terrorism.[225] Attorney General Vogel, for example, characterized the demand for the

---

[217] P.M. to Bundesministerium der Justiz, n.d, BArch, B141/48416.

[218] R.M. to B.J.M. Vogel, January 15, 1974, BArch, B141/48417.

[219] R.K., September 10, 1977, BArch, B141/48434.

[220] Dr. W.L. to Bundesjustizministerium, March 4, 1975, BArch, B141/48423, S.R. to Schmidt, September 6, 1977, BArch, B141/48432; W.S., "Heimatvertriebener, der zwei Weltkriege miterlebt hat," September 17, 1977, BArch, B141/48434; Todesstrafe, Notstandsgesetz, R.K., September 10, 1977, BArch, B141/48434. Letter, Dr. H.J., September 20, 1977, BArch, B141/48432.

[221] Hanshew, *Terror and Democracy in West Germany*, 212.

[222] Institut für Demoskopie Allensbach, Allensbacher Berichte, No. 9, 1978, Zentralarchiv für empirische Sozialforschung, Köln (ZAK).

[223] Letter to H.J. Vogel, November 16, 1974, BArch, B141/48419; W.D. Studiendirektor a.D., August 2, 1977, BArch, B141/48429.

[224] O.K. Gerichtsvollzieher, October 14, 1977, BArch, B141/48436.

[225] Bundesregierung to Herr H., 1.13.1975, BArch, B141/48419.

death penalty as "emotionally understandable" but ultimately not persuasive.[226] The federal government thus presented itself as a sober and rational actor that sought to reduce "anxiety and insecurity within the population."[227] Chancellor Helmut Schmidt personified this anti-emotional, sober attitude when, in a TV address on the evening of the Schleyer kidnapping, he called for a "cool head."[228] Some of the petitioners quickly realized that their demands could be dismissed as "emotional over-reaction." One petitioner thus took issue with the practice of political elites of "belittl[ing] the outrage as a purely emotional attitude of a few individuals."[229] The debate over RAF terrorism was therefore also a self-reflective debate over the status of political emotions in public. Many petitioners as well as opposition politicians practiced a new emotional style, which sanctioned and even encouraged the public articulation of outrage and fear. By contrast, the representatives of the federal government continued to practice a more traditional emotional management, which sought to contain public emotions.

Notwithstanding the emphasis on political restraint, the center-left government responded to RAF terror with successive restrictions of the rule of law. However, these always fell short of what conservative CDU politicians had demanded. Horst Herold, the president of the Federal Criminal Police, introduced computerized methods in the search for terrorists. This modern approach to law enforcement was supposed to prevent arbitrary police violence as in the case of the shooting of Benno Ohnesorg in June 1967. The SPD also resisted demands to limit the RAF prisoners' constitutional rights, ultimately ceded to the RAF demand to be detained together, and eased some other conditions. It was only in the context of the Schleyer kidnapping that the social-liberal coalition agreed to a law barring RAF members from contact with their lawyers. The government now also pushed for restrictions of the freedom of the press and asked journalists to practice a form of self-censorship in reporting on the RAF.[230]

These anti-terror policies also triggered feelings of anxiety and indignation on the Left. Left-wing fears centered on the fear of an excessively authoritarian response by the state. These fears thus expanded on the "democratic fears" as they had been articulated in the 1960s. In a letter to Attorney General Vogel, for example, "Dr. B.T." from Tübingen articulated a fear, for example, that the political polarization in the Federal Republic reflected the "spirit of Weimar," which pitted a "leftist anarchism" against the "attitude of the masses."[231] In November 1974, a professed Social Democrat expressed concern that the "Baader–Meinhof

---

[226] Hans-Jochen Vogel, "Forderung nach Todesstrafe nicht überzeugend," *Recht* 52 (1977).
[227] "Konzeption der Öffentlichkeitsarbeit zur Terrorismusbekämpfung," BArch, B106/70995.
[228] Helmut Schmidt, TV speech, September 5, 1977, https://www.zdf.de/nachrichten/heute-sendungen/videos/schmidt-ansprache-in-voller-laenge-100.html (last accessed March 10, 2020).
[229] H.J. to Vogel, September 13, 1977, BArch, B141/48436.
[230] Hanshew, *Terror and Democracy in West Germany*, 217–24.
[231] Dr. B.T. Tübingen to Bundesminister der Justiz, August 4, 1972, BArch, B141/48413.

Gang" would produce an "anti-Baader–Meinhof Gang" in order to destroy the rule of law.[232] Distrust of the state among the left-alternative milieu intensified in the spring of 1977 when the surveillance of interned RAF members became known, with the knowledge of the state parliament in Baden-Württemberg. The Federal Criminal Police's massive data collection and the dragnet also raised, for the first time, fears of an Orwellian surveillance state.[233] The publicity campaign regarding the conditions of imprisonment of RAF members also resonated within the left-alternative milieu, at least before 1977. A "committee for the abolition of isolation torture" affiliated with the Protestant church in Bad Canstatt, for example, called for relief for what they called "political prisoners."[234] Another pastor described being questioned by the Criminal Police because his name had appeared on a list of supposedly sympathetic clergy as reminiscent of "interrogation by the Gestapo."[235] Such uses of the Nazi past to assess the present were not unusual. Similarly, a local official articulated his concerns in a letter to Chancellor Schmidt in February 1974 about the "physical and mental health" of the terrorist Astrid Proll, saying that the West German judiciary denied her the "minimum of humanity" that it had previously granted to "former concentration camp thugs" in the Nazi trials.[236] Some citizens did not shy away from explicitly supporting the RAF. In January 1973, "K.N." declared that even a show trial would not be able to destroy his solidarity with RAF prisoners, and he anticipated that there would be "new Ensslins and Baaders" to follow them. Although he loathed the terrorist attack during the Munich Olympics, he did not see it as significantly different from "what the Americans do in Vietnam."[237]

In light of the ensuing series of murders by the RAF, such expressions of sympathy for, or at least apologetic responses to, terrorism became very rare, even in the left-wing milieu. Yet, the events of the autumn of 1977 again activated fears of an authoritarian state. Bärbel H. noted in her diary her "fear" that "the fate of the RAF could also hit others." Many of her friends "felt the same way."[238] Likewise, prominent intellectuals such as Jürgen Habermas continued to resist the causal nexus of leftist theory and terrorism as conservative intellectuals and politicians asserted it. According to Habermas, this argument constituted only a "pretext" to do away with "200 years of critical bourgeois thinking." The government's

---

[232] R.O. to BM der Justiz, November 29, 1974, BArch, B141/48419.

[233] Schletter, *Grabgesang der Demokratie*, 315–16. On Stammheim, see Aust, *Der Baader–Meinhof Komplex*, 421–30. On surveillance, see Klaus Weinhauer, "Zwischen 'Partisanenkampf' und 'Kommissar Computer.' Polizei und Linksterrorismus in der Bundesrepublik bis Anfang der 1980er Jahre," in Haupt et al., eds, *Terrorismus in der Bundesrepublik*, 244–70.

[234] Ev. Dekanat Stuttgart Bad Canstatt to Bundesjustizministerium, June 7, 1973, BArch, B141/48415.

[235] Dr. theol. O.K. to Bundesjustizminister Jahn, February 5, 1972, BArch, B141/48413.

[236] W.H. Regierungsrat to Herr Bundeskanzler, February 2, 1974, BArch, B141/48415.

[237] K.N. to Minister Jahn, 8.1.1973, BArch, B141/48414.

[238] Bärbel H., Diaries, DTA 1495, I, 1-I,4, October 18, 1977.

response to terrorism reactivated Habermas's democratic fear, which he had expressed from the 1950s onward, that CSU chairman Franz Josef Strauß wanted to turn the Federal Republic into an authoritarian state. Even in retrospect, Habermas noted that "at no time was there a stronger pogrom mood" as in the autumn of 1977, as all the known "resentments and stereotypes" were again mobilized.[239] Still, the escalation of terrorist violence pushed leftist intellectuals toward the defensive. Contrary to the 1960s, the claim to moral superiority had now been reversed: while conservative intellectuals claimed to defend democracy, leftist intellectuals were under pressure to distance themselves from attacks on democracy. Leftist intellectuals now mobilized a series of arguments that included rejection of any violence (by the Americans in Vietnam and by the RAF) as well as the reference to the long tradition of internal leftist criticism of terrorist violence. Jürgen Habermas, for example, placed the RAF more in the right-wing tradition of glorifying violence, which ranged from Sorel to Mussolini.[240] The association with the violence of the RAF also threatened to discredit the simultaneously emerging environmental and anti-nuclear movement. For this reason, too, activists of the early environmental movement, like Walter Mossmann, distanced themselves from the violence of the RAF.[241] The RAF method of targeted assassinations of people was completely isolated in the left milieu since 1977 at the latest, even though the much touted "new sensibility" on the Left rarely extended to the victims of terrorism.[242] Nonetheless, the principle of non-violence clearly dominated in social movements of the 1980s, also in response to the RAF terror.[243]

Did the challenge of terrorism and the governmental response to it lead to a new consensus that contained both right- and left-wing fears and therefore entailed a new "emotional acceptance" of the Federal Republic? Contemporary observers such as Kurt Sontheimer were skeptical. The debate over terrorism, he wrote, "did not really strengthen the consensus on the foundations of the republic, which has weakened considerably since the student revolt."[244] Here again, a consistent pattern of the history of fear in the Federal Republic became

---

[239] First quotation: Jürgen Habermas, "Probe für die Volksjustiz," *Der Spiegel* 28/42 (1974): 32; second quotation in a letter to the historian Ulrich Herbert, July 31, 1999, quoted in Stefan Müller-Doohm, *Jürgen Habermas. Eine Biographie* (Berlin: Suhrkamp, 2014), 341.

[240] See Requate, "Gefährliche Intellektuelle?"

[241] See Hanshew, *Terror and Democracy in West Germany*, 167–82.

[242] This deficit is emphasized in Terhoeven, *Die Rote Armee Fraktion*.

[243] Walter Mossmann, "Der lange Marsch von Wyhl nach Anderswo," *Kursbuch* 50 (1977): 1–22. On the re-orientation of the Left after 1977, see also Jake Smith, "Strangers in a Dead Land. Redemption and Regeneration in the European Counterculture," (Ph.D. Dissertation, University of Chicago, 2017).

[244] Quotation in Conze, *Die Suche nach Sicherheit*, 485; similarly, Edgar Wolfrum, *Die Geglückte Demokratie. Geschichte der Bundesreublik Deutschland von ihren Anfängen bis zur Gegenwart* (Stuttgart: Klett-Cotta, 2006), 346; somewhat more skeptically, Herbert, *Geschichte Deutschlands*, 929, Sontheimer, *Die verunsicherte Republik*, 117.

apparent—namely, that the perception of the contemporaries was often much more pessimistic than the retroactive historical interpretation. Paradoxically, it was precisely the increasingly articulated democratic fears that might have prevented the Federal Republic from sliding into a new authoritarianism. The public fear scenario of an authoritarian state thus helped to avoid it.[245] More than ever before in the history of the Federal Republic, the confrontation with the terrorist threat revealed the political polyvalence of political fears: they were the emotional driving force of the demand for a restriction of the rule of law as well as its defense. Thus, the mobilization of fears on both sides resulted at least in a procedural consensus—namely, the normative ideal of the "rule of law," even though its specific meanings remained controversial.[246]

Political fears did not come to an end in the 1970s but continued on another terrain in undiminished or even intensified form. Yet, political fears no longer primarily centered on the structure of West German democracy but rather focused on existential threats—on no less than life and death. The environmental and peace movements of the late 1970s and 1980s cultivated apocalyptic fears, as they had not yet been articulated in the Federal Republic. Only at that point arose the external perception of a specifically German and proverbial German angst. The new social movements combined the emergence of an expressive emotional culture and a new subjectivity with a perception of a renewed external threat in the context of renewed Cold War tensions. In the 1980s, the history of fear in the Federal Republic reached its culmination and climax.

---

[245] On this argument, see Hanshew, *Terror and Democracy in West Germany*, 261.
[246] On the consensus about the "rule of law," see Jörg Requate, "Demokratisierung der Justiz? Rechtsstaatlichkeit im Zeichen der Provokation," in Habbo Knoch, ed., *Bürgersinn mit Weltgefühl. Politische Kultur und solidarischer Protest in den sechziger und siebziger Jahren* (Göttingen: Wallstein, 2007), 181–202.

8

Apocalyptic *Angst*

We drove on the Kassel autobahn to Alsfeld, then we turned off into the Vogelsberg. It was a beautiful July day. My father started singing and we sang along. My mother took the second voice. When we drove through Lanthen, everything was still as usual. But in the forest between Lanthen and Wietig, just when we entered the curve at the Kaldener Feld, it suddenly flashed so brightly that we had to close our eyes. My mother screamed and my father hit the brake so hard that the tires creaked. The car skidded and stopped across the road. We were knocked around in the seat belts. As soon as the car stopped, we saw a blinding light in the sky between the treetops, white and terrible, like the light of a huge torch or a bolt of lightning that does not go away. I just looked at it for a moment. Nevertheless, I was like blind for a while afterwards. Heat came in through the open window.[1]

This is how 12-year-old Roland describes the sudden dropping of a nuclear bomb over North Hesse in Gudrun Pausewang's 1983 novel for young adults, *The Last Children of Schewenborn*. In this scene, he is on the way to visit his grandparents in Schewenborn with his two sisters and their parents. They will soon learn that the grandparents were in Fulda, the center of the bombing, and did not survive. Roland's mother gives birth to a child without eyes after the bombing. She and Roland's two sisters die in the course of the book from radiation sickness or, in his younger sister's case, typhoid. Another boy who survives denounces Roland's father as a "murderer" because "he and almost all people of his generation idly and calmly watched in the years before the day of the bomb how the destruction of mankind had been prepared." His experience prompts Roland to commit himself to creating a "peaceful world" for himself and his contemporaries, even if they will be "the last children of Schewenborn" because of the long-lasting radiation damage.[2]

Pausewang's novel, which was widely read and taught in schools, was a typical example of contemporary notions of the apocalypse. Other books also imagined

[1] Gudrun Pausewang, *Die letzten Kinder von Schewenborn: Oder—sieht so unsere Zukunft aus?* (Ravensburg: Otto Meier Verlag, 1983), 13.
[2] Ibid. 124–5.

German Angst: *Fear and Democracy in the Federal Republic of Germany.* Frank Biess, Oxford University Press (2020).
© Frank Biess.
DOI: 10.1093/oso/9780198714187.001.0001

an impending nuclear war.[3] The journalist Anton Andreas Guha published a novel for adults—*ENDE: Diary from the Third World War*—in 1983.[4] And, in November 1983, the American movie *The Day After* came to German cinemas, showing the experience of nuclear war in a small town in Kansas. In Germany alone, 3.6 million viewers watched the movie.[5] Thus, many Germans consumed these depictions of a "long death," of hopelessness and post-nuclear war. While past visions of the end always also entailed hopes of redemption—such as the revolutionary future of the New Left—these future scenarios revealed a "curtailed apocalypse."[6] Nuclear war would be the end of history. Such apocalyptic visions were the culmination of the history of fear in the Federal Republic.

Contemporary commentaries and opinion polls confirm this diagnosis of the 1980s as a period of apocalyptic fear. The number of West Germans who considered a world war "possible" or "probable" within the next three years amounted to 49 per cent in January 1980—the highest value ever since 1962—and reached 44 per cent again in June 1982.[7] These figures likely resulted from increased international tensions such as the Soviet invasion of Afghanistan in December 1979; the election of Ronald Reagan in November 1980; and the imposition of martial law in Poland in December 1981. Because it was generally understood that a third world war would mean the end of history, seeing it as imminent constituted a very dark view indeed. Fear of war more broadly also increased. In 1975, West Germans showed equal fear of "illness" and "war, nuclear warfare," with 17 per cent indicating that each was the most frequent object of their fears. By 1981, this ratio had shifted drastically: 19 per cent said "illness" and 35 per cent said "war."[8] In October 1980, in response to the question as to what constituted the greatest threat for the future of mankind, 70 per cent named a "war between the major powers," 46 per cent "atomic annihilation" and "energy scarcity," and 45 per cent "radioactive contamination."[9] The escalation of fear was accompanied by declining trust. Polls by the Institute for Demoscopy in Allensbach found that the number of West Germans saying they were "able to trust most people" fell from 83 per cent in 1953 to 39 per cent in 1976 and to only 28 per cent in 1981.[10] The Institute's

---

[3] This depiction reflected a general theme of youth literature at the time. See Bettina Hitzer, "Jim Button's Fear," in Ute Frevert et al., eds, *Learning How to Feel. Children's Literature and Emotional Socialization 1870–1970* (Oxford: Oxford University Press, 2014), 173–90.

[4] Anton-Andreas Guha, *Ende: Tagebuch aus dem Dritten Weltkrieg* (Bodenheim: Athenaeum, 1983).

[5] Eckart Conze, Martin Klimke, "Introduction: Between Accidental Armageddons and Winnable Wars: Nuclear Threats and Nuclear Fears in the 1980s," in Eckart Conze, Martin Klimke, Jeremy Varon, eds, *Nuclear Threats, Nuclear Fear and the Cold War of the 1980s* (New York: Cambridge University Press, 2017), 2–3.

[6] Klaus Vondung, *Die Apokalypse in Deutschland* (Munich: dtv, 1988), 11–13, 315–18, 422.

[7] *Emnid-Informationen* 33/1 (1981): 8, *Emnid Informationen* 34/6–7 (1985): 10.

[8] *Emnid-Informationen* 33/8 (1981): 12.

[9] Emind Institute, "Zukunftserwartungen und Zukunftsverhalten," October 1980, Zentralarchiv für Empirische Sozialforschung-Köln (ZAK).

[10] Edgar Piel, "Angst: Eine neue Ideologie?" *Allensbacher Berichte* 18 (1981): 1–9.

report described this as the complement to a "wave of fear" that gripped Germans at that time. In 1982, *Spiegel* reporter Jürgen Leinemann described this intense anxiety as a national characteristic, as a "German fear," saying it had "shaped the image of the Federal Republic abroad."[11] Together with the notion of the dying forest as a specifically German phenomenon, "le *Waldsterben*" in France, the title page of *Time Magazine* identified in August 1981 a "moment of Angst" in West Germany. The culture of fear in the 1980s thus began to shape an emerging *external* perception of Germans as being especially prone to anxiety.[12]

Fear particularly gripped younger Germans. A study by German Shell's youth department in 1981 came to the conclusion that 58 per cent of young people saw the future as gloomy, while only 42 per cent were confident.[13] According to another study published by the Sinus Institute in 1983, young Germans between the ages of 15 and 30 showed "a high level of personal concern for the major problems of our time," especially environmental destruction (two-thirds) and nuclear armament (half). The study described fear as the "psychological motivation for the perception and processing of political problems among a majority of the younger generation."[14] This fear was especially strong among supporters of the newly founded Green Party (*Die Grünen*). In an opinion poll commissioned by the magazine *Spiegel*, 54 per cent of Germans stated that they were "sometimes afraid," yet 70 per cent of the supporters of the Green Party confessed to their anxieties. Even more, 89 per cent of them, considered a new world war to be "possible or likely" within the next three years.[15] The general mood of anxiety amounted to an "apocalyptic fear" in the left-alternative milieu.[16]

This escalation of fear and anxiety ran counter to a historiography that has described the 1980s mostly as a period of a renewed stabilization. According to historian Andreas Wirsching, the Federal Republic was no longer "provisional" and had accomplished a new form of self-recognition.[17] The dialectics of fear that had peaked in the late 1970s, when both the Left and the Right suspected each other of trying to create a different kind of republic, came to an end. While Chancellor Helmut Kohl had promised "spiritual and moral turnaround," his liberal-conservative government actually continued many policies of its Social Democratic predecessor. The philosopher Jürgen Habermas, for example, described how the conservative Kohl government had reconciled him with the

---

[11] Jürgen Leinemann, *Die Angst der Deutschen. Beobachtungen zur Bewusstseinslage der Nation* (Reinbek: Rowohlt, 1982), 7.

[12] "West Germany—Moment of Angst," *Time Magazine. International Edition*, August 24, 1981, "Le Waldsterben," *Der Spiegel* 38/42 (1984): 186–90.

[13] SINUS-Institut, *Die verunsicherte Generation. Jugend und Wertewandel* (Opladen: Leske & Budrich, 1983), 37.

[14] Ibid. 38, 41–2. See also Sven Reichardt, *Authentizität und Gemeinschaft. Linksalternatives Leben in den siebziger und frühen achtziger Jahren* (Frankfurt a/M: Suhrkamp, 2014), 163.

[15] Leinemann, *Die Angst der Deutschen*, 148–9, 153.

[16] Reichardt, *Authentizität und Gemeinschaft*, 164.

[17] Andreas Wirsching, *Abschied vom Provisorium. Geschichte der Bundesrepublik 1982–1990* (Munich: DVA, 2006).

(old) Federal Republic, precisely because an authoritarian transformation did not occur.[18] Yet the new apocalyptic fears of the 1980s extended beyond the future of West German democracy. They now concerned the sheer existence of humanity.

Fear served as the emotional driving force of the two most important social movements of the 1970s and 1980s: the environmental and the peace movements. These movements decisively shape the political culture of the Federal Republic to this day. Germany is still home to what is probably the most powerful environmental movement in the Western world. The peace movement was by far the largest protest movement in the history of the pre-unification "old" Federal Republic, and some of its consequences shape the political culture of the Berlin Republic to this day, such as a policy of restraint when it comes to military interventions.

Ecological Fear: The Environmental Movement

Global Doomsday Scenarios and the Beginnings of Environmental Policy

The modern environmental movement in Germany began around 1970. To be sure, there had been individuals and organizations committed to preserving nature since the period of high industrialization in the late nineteenth century. However, such conservation initiatives remained limited to the local level even during the time of the "economic miracle" in the 1950s.[19] A new awareness of a global environmental crisis, which then launched the environmental movement in the Federal Republic, emerged only toward the end of the 1960s. The environmental movement was not just a response to external problems or specific environmental disasters. Rather, it was the product of new "mental and social structures" that enabled a new perception of environmental issues at the local, national, and global levels.[20]

A new view of the earth as a result of the American Apollo program and the moon landing on July 20, 1969, made the perception of a planetary crisis possible. In December 1968, the astronauts of Apollo 8 described the image of the earth "with her brownish colored continents and glittering oceans, the fields of clouds and the blue shimmering thin shell of air."[21] The notion of the earth as a vulnerable entity received its iconic representation in the image of "Blue Marble" taken by Apollo 17 in December 1972. The new perspective also made possible the

---

[18] Jürgen Habermas, "Meine Jahre mit Helmut Kohl," *Die Zeit*, March 11, 1994. https://www.zeit.de/1994/11/meine-jahre-mit-helmut-kohl (last accessed March 4, 2020).

[19] Sandra Chaney, *Nature of the Miracle Years. Conservation in West Germany, 1945–1975* (New York: Berghahn, 2008).

[20] Kai F. Hünemörder, *Die Frühgeschichte der globalen Umweltkrise und die Formierung der deutschen Umweltpolitik (1950–1973)* (Stuttgart: Franz Steiner Verlag, 2004), 182.

[21] Cited in ibid. 205.

metaphor of earth as a "spaceship" with limited supplies of air and other resources, while also obscuring the massive inequalities between the southern and northern hemispheres.[22] As historian Kai Hünemörder has shown, the view from space engendered, for the first time, the idea of a global environmental crisis, and a number of English-language books that were then also published in German explored this idea. Such books included British historian of science Gordon Rattray Taylor's *The Biological Time Bomb* (1968), American biologist Paul R. Ehrlich's *The Population Bomb* (English 1968, German 1971), futurologist Alvin Toffler's *Future Shock* (1970), and microbiologist René Dubos's *The Unencumbered Progress* (1970).[23] These books warned of uncontrolled population growth such that the earth could not sustain it. Insecticides or toxins in food also became the object of growing environmental concern. Don Widener prophesied in his bestseller, *No Place for Human Beings*, a "programmed suicide" as a result of the slow accumulation of lead in human organs.[24] Rachel Carson's environmental classic, *Silent Spring* (1962), about the negative effects of pesticides such as DDT for animals and humans, gained popularity in Germany in the 1970s as well.[25] Another book by Gordon Rattray Taylor, *Das Selbstmordprogramm* (*The Suicide Program*) (1970) topped the bestseller list for months and sold over 100,000 copies in Germany. It developed, on the basis of several scientific disciplines, an environmental doomsday scenario.[26] One year later, the British magazine *The Ecologist* predicted, in light of a confluence of destructive tendencies, a "collapse of society and the irretrievable destruction of the life-support systems of our planet, possibly until the end of the century, but certainly within the lifetime of our children."[27]

The already existing perception of a global environmental crisis explains the broad reception of the report of the Club of Rome in 1972, *The Limits of Growth*. Unlike previous prophets of the apocalypse, the authors of the study based their prediction on computerized models that criticized the logic of exponential growth as leading to ecological collapse. The book thus provided a scientific confirmation of ecological alarms. Its success derived from the fact that it resonated

---

[22] This view obscured the injustice of the massive inequality of human living conditions between the northern and southern hemispheres, but it furthered a sense of shared stake in the survival of the planet. See Thomas Lekan, "Fractal Eaarth: Visualizing the Global Environment in the Anthropocene," *Environmental Humanities* 5/1 (2014): 171–201.

[23] For a critique of the discourse of population explosion, see Matthew Connelly, *Fatal Misconception. The Struggle to Control World Population* (Cambridge, Mass.: Harvard University Press, 2008).

[24] Kai F. Hünemörder, "Kassandra im modernen Gewand. Die umweltapokalyptischen Mahnrufe der frühen 1970er Jahre," in Frank Uekötter, Jens Hohensee, eds, *Wird Kassandra heiser? Die Geschichte falscher Ökoalarme* (Stuttgart: Franz Steiner, 2004), 79.

[25] Hünemörder, *Die Frühgeschichte der globalen Umweltkrise*, 121.

[26] On these titles and their significance, see ibid. 209–21 and Hünemörder, "Kassandra im modernen Gewand," 78–97.

[27] Cited in Hünemörder, *Die Frühgeschichte der globalen Umweltkrise*, 217.

with already existing concerns.[28] By October 1973, it achieved a global circulation of 2.5 million in 25 languages. The book's explosive argument was that the newly perceived environmental problems could not be solved within the logic of the existing system, but rather required a departure from the ideology of growth.[29]

In a relatively short period between the late sixties and early seventies, the transnational discourse on a global environmental crisis reached the Federal Republic.[30] In January 1970, *Der Spiegel* identified a "sort of negative list, a series of catastrophic developments," for the future, which included the problem of "world hunger," the "energy gap," and the "problem of the ecological balance."[31] In October 1970, the *Spiegel* title story on the "poisoned environment" depicted a variety of environmental hazards, ranging from air and water pollution to growing mountains of garbage to increasing car exhaust fumes.[32] Environmental historians explained this recognition of a global environmental crisis in the Federal Republic of Germany as a "sensitization of the public to new threats."[33] However, the historical genesis of this sensitization itself needs to be explained from within the history of emotions. It was a result of the already analyzed shifts in West German emotional culture from the late 1960s onward.[34] The new expressive emotional regime, as well as the re-evaluation of fear, facilitated the articulation of environmental fears. Fear and the scientific publications cited above were not mutually exclusive but rather reinforced each other.[35] Environmental hazards came into focus for a West German economy of attention as part of a new "affective-cognitive" way of perceiving the world.[36] A newly emotionalized subjectivity became more receptive to dangers to the self emanating from the environment.

This sensitivity also manifested itself in new anxieties about health hazards from food and airborne toxins. Air pollution was seen as direct cause of cancer

---

[28] Hünemörder, "Kassandra im modernen Gewand," 89.

[29] Hünemörder, *Die Frühgeschichte der globalen Umweltkrise*, 222–7. On the significance of the Club of Rome report, see also Frank Uekötter, "Simulierter Untergang. 40 Jahre nach dem Bericht 'Grenzen des Wachstums'—was haben wir für den Umgang mit Prognosen gelernt?" *Die Zeit* 48 (2012).

[30] On this period as a turning point, see also Patrick Kupper, "Die '1970er Diagnose.' Grundsätzliche Überlegungen zu einem Wendepunkt der Umweltgeschichte," *Archiv für Sozialgeschichte* 43 (2003): 325–48.

[31] "Ritt auf dem Tiger," *Der Spiegel* 34/1 (1970): 42.

[32] "Morgen kam gestern," *Der Spiegel* 35/41 (1970): 74–96, Joachim Radkau, *Die Ära der Ökologie. Eine Weltgeschichte* (Munich: C.H.Beck, 2011), 149.

[33] Hünemörder, *Die Frühgeschichte der globalen Umweltkrise*, 184.

[34] On the necessity of connecting environmental and cultural history, yet without reference to emotions, see Frank Uekötter, *The Greenest Nation? A New History of German Environmentalism* (Cambridge: Cambridge University Press, 2014), 8–10.

[35] This contrast is emphasized in Radkau, *Die Ära der Ökologie*, 151, Joachim Radkau, "Mythos German Angst. Zum neuesten Aufguss einer alten Denunziation der Umweltbewegung," *Blätter für deutsche und internationale Politik* 56/5 (2011): 73.

[36] Jakob Tanner, "Das Rauschen der Gefühle. Vom Darwinischen Unversalismus zur Davidsonschen Triangulation," *Nach Feierabend. Züricher Jahrbuch für Wissensgeschichte* 2 (2006): 142.

and heart disease.[37] Similarly, consumers feared that the increased use of antibiotics and other medicines in factory farming would make the food dangerous. *Der Spiegel* identified the novel and frightening elements of these dangers: they were "invisible, imperceptible, insidious" and their contribution to heart disease and cancer could not be clearly proven, which further increased popular uncertainty.[38] The toxins were the external counterpart to the "internal pathologies" as potential causes of cancer: here it was not emotional or mental blockages that caused deadly diseases, as in the "cancer personality," but no less dangerous substances that entered the subject largely uncontrolled and unnoticed from the outside and then destroyed it from the inside. According to *Der Spiegel*, in a blood test of 5,000 German citizens, one in four had an accumulation of heavy metals in their blood and one in nine patients with unexplained symptoms turned out to have lead poisoning.[39] Body fears had already spread in the 1970s; now they also mobilized the early environmental movement.[40]

A growing awareness of the threat to wild animals was closely linked to these body fears. Widely watched animal films by Heinz Sielmann, Bernhard Grzimek, and Horst Stern popularized the notion that animals were victim to the human-caused destruction of nature. Occasionally, the directors of these films resorted to cultural pessimism or even to neo-colonialist ideas. Bernhard Grzimek, for example, portrayed the indigenous Masai in the Serengeti as a threat to an allegedly "untouched" natural space.[41] The dramatization of the human–animal relationship also took place in the language of mass destruction. In criticizing industrial farming, Grzimek, for example, employed the concept of "concentration camp eggs" or criticized overland power lines as causing the "mass execution of birds."[42] A growing presence of the memory of National Socialism and the Holocaust shaped the discourse on current and future environmental damage. Viewers writing to the investigative journalist and animal filmmaker Horst Stern also engaged questions of individual and collective guilt for the suffering of the animals. "Why should not we humans, who are guilty of gluttony, smoking, and air pollution not also die as a result?"[43] These films thus sensitized West German society to environmental hazards and increased empathy for animal and human suffering.[44]

---

[37] "Morgen kam gestern," "Wenn sie nicht fressen, spritze ich sie selbst," *Der Spiegel* 36/26 (1971): 46–62.

[38] "Morgen kam gestern," 80.   [39] Ibid. 82.

[40] This is the argument in Radkau, "Mythos German Angst," 74–5, and Uekötter, *The Greenest Nation?* Uekötter also emphasizes the long-term effects of the scandal over the medical drug Thalidomide/Contergan, which caused severe birth defects among 2,000 newborn babies. This causal link was discovered only in 1961, even though the drug had been available since October 1, 1957.

[41] Thomas Lekan, "Serengeti Shall Not Die": Bernhard Grzimek, Wildlife Film, and the Making of a Tourist Landscape in East Africa," *German History* 29/2 (June 2011): 224–64.

[42] Jens Ivo Engels, *Naturpolitik in der Bundesrepublik. Ideenwelt und politische Verhaltensstile in Naturschutz und Umweltbewegung 1950–1980* (Paderborn: Schöningh, 2006), 249.

[43] Cited in ibid. 260.

[44] Contemporaries also criticized that empathy with animals can replace empathy with other human beings, see ibid. 265.

These threats of environmental damage required a different security regime from the inner fears discussed in Chapter 7: not introspection and psychotherapy, but rather the containment and reduction of pollutants through government intervention. Environmental fears acted as an impetus for a renewed politicization of emotional concerns. National and international environmental policy strove to satisfy a new desire for security that now focused on the protection of natural resources. The term "environmental protection" (*Umweltschutz*) was coined in November 1969 and became a separate department within the Interior Ministry under Hans-Dietrich Genscher (Free Democratic Party). On this institutional basis and reinforced by dedicated civil servants such as Peter Menke-Glückert, the Brandt government adopted the Federal Republic's first environmental action program in September 1970. This defined the three future guidelines for environmental policy: the polluter principle, which made polluters liable for environmental damage; the precautionary principle, which sought to prevent environmental damage; and the principle of cooperation, which sought to ensure the cooperation of state authorities with citizens in environmental policy. From the summer of 1971 onward, several environmental laws followed, with provisions such as mandating reduced levels of lead in gasoline and prohibiting the use of DDT as insect repellent. After a change in the Basic Law increased the authority of the federal government in environmental protection in 1974, the West German parliament passed a federal law limiting emissions. By 1976, the center-left government had enacted more than 50 environmental laws and regulations. The budget for environmental protection rose from 117 million DM in 1969 to 243 million DM in 1971.[45]

The balance sheet of the early federal environmental policy was quite impressive. The number of West Germans who recognized the term "environmental protection" (*Umweltschutz*) increased from 59 per cent in 1970 to 90 per cent a year later.[46] A belief in technocratic measures to curb environmental pollution characterized early environmental policy, and a majority of the population agreed. However, environmental policy also raised high expectations among citizens, who complained in letters to the Interior Ministry about the slow progress of environmental protection. Growing public awareness of environmental protection resulted from a new sensitivity to the permeability of the self to external environmental hazards. The right to a healthy environment now appeared as a constitutionally guaranteed individual right, as the equivalent of the inviolability of the dignity of the individual or of the right to physical integrity.[47]

---

[45] On early environmental policy in the Federal Republic, see Hünemörder, *Die Frühgeschichte der globalen Umweltkrise*, 155–6, Chaney, *Nature of the Miracle Years*, 186–7, Franz Brüggemeier, *Tschernobyl, 26. April 1986. Die ökologische Herausforderung* (Munich: dtv, 1998), 208–9, Uekötter, *The Greenest Nation?*, 87–9, Hans-Peter Vierhaus, *Umweltbewusstsein von oben. Zum Verfassungsgebot demokratischer Willensbildung* (Berlin: Duncker & Humblot, 1994).

[46] Chaney, *Nature of the Miracle Years*, 190.

[47] Ibid. 188–91. Cited in Hünemörder, *Die Frühgeschichte der globalen Umweltkrise*, 185.

With the onset of the oil crisis of 1973, the environmental demand for more forceful state regulation increasingly conflicted with a diminished regulatory capacity of the nation state during a time of global economic crisis.[48] An ecological perspective also called for a paradigm shift away from a purely quantitative to qualitative growth, as the American economist E.F. Schumacher in his 1974 publication *Small Is Beautiful* exemplified.[49] The rapid growth of citizens' initiatives, which formed the National Association for Citizens' Initiatives for Environmental Protection (*Bürgerinitiative Unweltschutz*, [BBU]) in 1972, reflected a new mobilization from below that increasingly questioned the state's technological environmental policy.[50] Environmental activists began to see the West German state as a threat rather than a force for preserving nature. This perception of a hostile state became especially evident in one area: nuclear energy.

The Anti-Nuclear Movement

In the 1950s and 1960s, nuclear power appeared as the great technology of the future, as a potentially unlimited source of energy for a still-expanding industrial age, as the epitome of modernity. Even those scientists who, like the "Göttingen Eighteen," publicly opposed the equipment of the *Bundeswehr* with nuclear weapons in April 1957, fully supported the civilian use of nuclear power. The strict separation of "bad" nuclear weapons and "good" nuclear energy became one of the most important arguments in favor of the civilian use of nuclear power. The first experimental nuclear reactor in the Federal Republic went into operation in 1960 in Kahl in Franconia, and the first commercial nuclear power plant was built in Gundremmingen in 1966. The third nuclear program of the federal government for the period from 1968 to 1972 planned to expand nuclear power in order to cover 40 per cent of West Germany's energy needs. The oil crisis in 1973 gave even greater importance to the further expansion of nuclear energy as envisioned in the fourth nuclear program.[51]

The expansion of nuclear energy, however, did not proceed without opposition. By the mid fifties, the public was well aware of the harmful effects of radioactive radiation from nuclear testing. In 1956, the physician Bodo Manstein founded the Fighting League Against Nuclear Damage (*Kampfbund gegen Atomschäden*), which warned against the dangers of radioactive radiation as a

---

[48] This problem is emphasized in Uekötter, *The Greenest Nation?*, 11.

[49] Hünemörder, *Die Frühgeschichte der globalen Umweltkrise*, 276–91.

[50] Ibid. 286. By 1975, 100 organizations were part of the BBU, see Chaney, *Nature of the Miracle Years*, 195–6.

[51] Dieter Rucht, *Von Wyhl nach Gorleben. Bürger gegen Atomprogramm und nukleare Entsorgung* (Munich: C.H.Beck, 1980), 26–7, Joachim Radkau, *Geschichte der Zukunft. Prognosen, Visionen, Irrungen in Deutschland von 1945 bis heute* (Munich: Carl Hanser Verlag, 2017). Lothar Hahn, Joachim Radkau, *Aufstieg und Fall der deutschen Atomwirtschaft* (Munich: Oekom, 2013).

result of nuclear tests. His 1961 book, *In the Chokehold of Progress* (*Im Würgegriff des Fortschritts*), discussed "the potentials and dangers of nuclear energy at a high level of knowledge."[52] At the end of the 1960s, less specific fears related to radioactive emissions in general increased as well. In a letter to the Max Planck Institute for Biophysics in September 1969, one Helene K. reported her "great sensitivity to radioactive radiation," which she described as the "whipping of her entire organism" and which she blamed for the condition "from which I have suffered from my 42nd birthday to the age of 56." Further, she said, she knew of "60 other people, many of whom are just as unhappy and hopeless as I am."[53] Opposition to nuclear power also emerged locally. The resistance of the city of Nuremberg meant, for example, that a planned nuclear power plant was not built in nearby Bertoldsheim but rather in Gundremmingen, where protests emerged as well. Contrary to official announcements, uncertainty and fear regarding nuclear power were quite widespread.[54]

The nationwide anti-nuclear movement originated in Wyhl in south-western Germany. In the summer of 1973, the Baden-Württemberg state government decided to build one of 14 planned nuclear power plants in Wyhl. In February 1975, members of 30 citizens' initiatives occupied the construction site. After 650 police officers had evicted them from the site, 28,000 people demonstrated against the nuclear power plant and reoccupied the construction site on February 23. In March 1975, a court in Freiburg withdrew the partial permission for building the nuclear power plant in Wyhl. After negotiations with the state government, the occupiers largely vacated the site in October 1975 and only left a "monitoring service" in place. In March 1977, the Freiburg court withdrew the entire permission for the plant due to security concerns. After a revision of this verdict in 1982, the state government issued a moratorium. It took until 1994 for the state to officially abandon the project, but the nuclear power plant in Wyhl was never built.[55]

---

[52] Brüggemeier, *Tschernobyl, 26. April 1986*, 207, also for the citation.

[53] Helene K. to Max-Planck-Institut für Biophysik, September 30, 1969, B142/1749, 103, BAK, cited in Caitlin Murdock, "Public Health in a Radioactive Age: Environmental Pollution, Popular Therapies, and Narratives of Danger in the Federal Republic of Germany, 1949–1970," *Central European History* 52/1 (2019): 45–64, quotation on 45.

[54] Brüggemeier, *Tschernobyl, 26. April 1986*, 207, Dieter Rucht, "Anti-Atomkraftbewegung," in Dieter Rucht, Roland Roth, eds, *Die sozialen Bewegungen in Deutschland seit 1945. Ein Handbuch* (Frankfurt a/M: Campus, 2008), 249, and Dolores L. Augustine, *Taking on Technocracy. Nuclear Power in Germany, 1945 to the Present* (New York: Berghahn, 2018), 21–50.

[55] On the history of Wyhl, see Rucht, *Von Wyhl nach Gorleben*, 81–7, Brüggemeier, *Tschernobyl, 26. April 1986*, 249–50, Engels, *Naturpolitik in der Bundesrepublik*, 350–76, Andreas Pettenkofer, *Die Entstehung der grünen Politik. Kultursoziologie der westdeutschen Umweltbewegung* (Frankfurt a/M: Campus, 2014), 141–65, Stephen Milder, *Greening Democracy. The Anti-Nuclear Movement and Political Environmentalism in West Germany and Beyond, 1968–1983* (New York: Cambridge University Press, 2017), 1–128, Augustine, *Taking on Technocracy*, 93–125. On the transnational dimension, see Andrew S. Tompkins, *Better Active than Radioactive. Anti-Nuclear Protest in 1970s France and West Germany* (Oxford: Oxford University Press, 2016).

For the first time, the anti-nuclear movement succeeded in preventing the construction of a nuclear power plant; this was Wyhl's historical significance.

Fear was an ambiguous and multi-faceted motive in these early protests against nuclear power. Many activists explicitly rejected fear as their motivation in order to avoid the charge of irrationalism. Others emphasized it when they thought it served their cause.[56] The objects of fear also changed throughout the process. At first, the protestors in Wyhl did not articulate fear of radioactive radiation. Instead, winegrowers worried about a change in the local climate as a result of the moisture released by the cooling towers. Fog and increased rainfall would affect the quality of the wine. Residents also strongly opposed relocations because of their memories of displacement during and after the Second World War. Conservative values informed the local protest against the Wyhl nuclear plant. The hypermodern nuclear power technology appeared as a threat to a rural and traditional notion of *Heimat* (homeland).[57]

Unlike earlier protests, the protests in Wyhl were not against a nuclear power plant at a particular location but rather against nuclear energy in general. The participation of left-wing activists from Freiburg and French Alsace gave the protest a national and transnational dimension. The New Left, however, approached ecological issues quite hesitantly. As late as 1973, the writer and New Left activist Hans Magnus Enzensberger categorized the ecology movement as a pure middle-class movement that was based on a hypothetical prediction of an impending ecological catastrophe.[58] Yet the protests of local peasants also offered a solution to the nagging problem of the New Left since 1968—namely, the search for a revolutionary subject. Maoist groups especially identified the protesting peasants as the kind of popular movement that they had missed for so long in the Federal Republic. The participation of external activists helped to open up local milieus but occasionally also encountered skepticism and resentment.[59] What united the activists across these divisions was not just the common opposition to nuclear power but also the shared experience of protest, especially the occupation of the site and the violent reaction of the state. The first clearing of the site in Wyhl in February 1975, in particular, conveyed images of an excessively authoritarian and potentially violent state acting with undue force against peaceful demonstrators and ordinary citizens. This official reaction of the state was the main reason why the anti-nuclear movement adopted a strong anti-state attitude in the subsequent period.

---

[56] The French sociologist Alain Touraine argued that "fear was denied by some activists, emphasized by others and accentuated or rejected by the same activists, depending on the state of the debate," quoted in Tompkins, *Better Active than Radioactive*, 34.

[57] Hans-Helmut Wüstenhagen, *Bürger gegen Kernkraftwerke: Wyhl, der Anfang?* (Reinbek: Rowohlt, 1975), Milder, *Greening Democracy*, 36–50.

[58] Hans Magnus Enzensberger, "Zur Kritik der politischen Ökologie," *Kursbuch* 33 (1973): 1–42.

[59] On this opening, see Tompkins, *Better Active than Radioactive*, 228.

The conflict also took place on the terrain of competing emotional styles. Defenders of nuclear power criticized the media reporting on Wyhl as overtly emotional. They cast themselves as rational and following scientific evidence. But they also sought to mobilize the population's fear if the anti-nuclear movement were to be successful. The Minister-President of Baden-Württemberg, Hans Filbinger, thus predicted in 1975 that the lights would go out in 10 years' time in Germany if the country did not build the Wyhl nuclear power plant.[60] At the same time, protestors now openly embraced an emotionally expressive culture. They deployed the new sensibilities as they had emerged in the post-1968 period for the purpose of political activism. The TV journalist Hans-Gerd Wiegand expressed this new emotional norm when he declared with respect to the protests in Wyhl: "It is completely legitimate to show emotions."[61]

The following anti-nuclear protests brought out this emotional conflict and the confrontation with state authority even more clearly, especially the conflict over the nuclear power plant in the northern German town of Brokdorf. Violent demonstrations took place in October and November 1976, and again in February 1977. To prevent a similar occupation of the construction site as in Wyhl, the state government had the Brokdorf site fenced with barbed wire. When some demonstrators tried to cross the barbed wire fence, the police resorted to the use of water cannons, tear gas, and helicopters. Activists perceived this use of state violence as a shock and compared their situation to the Vietnam War. "Because we had the images of Vietnam with us," one participant recalled, "we were scared enough to run for our lives." "The state really succeeded in spreading fear at that time in Brokdorf," the same demonstrator recalled.[62] This fear also resulted from the experience of a too-strong, possibly authoritarian state in the context of state reactions to the student movement and to left-wing terrorism in the 1970s. For the anti-nuclear movement, the nuclear power plant now became the epitome of an authoritarian and potentially totalitarian state.

Analogies with the Nazi state also fueled this fear scenario. The fence in Wyhl appeared like a concentration camp symbol, and this was also true for the nuclear power plant with barbed wire and watchtowers. Such associations of nuclear power with National Socialism continued to spread. Activists feared that a reactor accident would trap them in a "nuclear ghetto." A steel plate with the words "New Auschwitz" was attached to the gate of the construction site of the planned nuclear power plant in Grohnde.[63] According to the sociologist Andreas

---

[60] Cited in Rucht, *Von Wyhl nach Gorleben*, 36, and Augustine, *Taking on Technocracy*, 108. On ways in which the articulation of fear not only prevents but also fuels technological development, see Anna Åberg, Karena Kalmbach, Andreas Marklund, "Crises and Technological Futures. Experiences, Emotion, and Action," *Technology and Culture* 61/1 (2020): 272–81.

[61] Cited in Augustine, *Taking on Technocracy*, 108.

[62] Cited in https://www.ndr.de/fernsehen/Hamburg-damals,hamj51720.html (last accessed March 4, 2018). See also the analysis of media reporting in Augustine, *Taking on Technocracy*, 131–9.

[63] Pettenkofer, *Die Entstehung der grünen Politik*, 209–10, 216.

Figure 8.1. Police presence during a demonstration at Brokdorf, February 28, 1981.

Protests against nuclear power turned increasingly violent, as in Brokdorf in 1981. The environmental movement cast nuclear power plants as an absolute evil that would give rise to a fascist-like authoritarian state.

Source: bkp-Bildagentur, No. 30018694.

Pettenkofer, the nuclear power plant became a "negative sacrilege," the symbol of the "impure saint, an absolute evil that threatens to emerge from the inside of one's own political unity, here the feared fascist potential of the German state."[64] Similar to the notion of a "Hitler in me" with respect to individual subjects, the nuclear power plant became, in the view of the critics, the internal fear object of the West German state, which crystallized all its negative features: greed for profit, police violence, the ideology of unlimited growth, and environmental pollution.[65]

Political fears increasingly also focused on the danger of radiation. As a result of the escalating battle over nuclear energy, the anti-nuclear movement developed a scientific counter-expertise, which challenged the scientific legitimacy of nuclear power as well as propagating alternative forms of energy generation. This scientific counter-expertise was closely intertwined with the fundamental

---

[64] Ibid. 208.

[65] Thomas Dannenbaum, "'Atom-Staat' oder 'Unregierbarkeit.' Warnehmungsmuster im westdeutschen Atomkonflikt der siebziger Jahre," in Franz-Josef Brüggemeier, Jens Ivo Engels, eds, *Natur- und Umweltschutz nach 1945. Konzepte, Konflikte, Kompetenzen* (Frankfurt a/M: Campus, 2005), 268–86.

skepticism regarding a potentially authoritarian state, as the scandal revolving around the nuclear expert Klaus Traube demonstrated.[66] Traube was an engineer involved in the development of the breeder reactor, a nuclear power plant that produces nuclear energy as well as new fissile material. In the early 1970s, he began to distance himself from the idea of nuclear power. *Der Spiegel* reported in 1977 that the Federal Bureau for the Protection of the Constitution (*Bundesverfassungsschutz*) had been surveilling him for two years because of alleged connections to the left-wing "sympathizer" scene. Opponents of nuclear power frequently referenced this affair as evidence of an authoritarian "nuclear state" in which the nuclear industry was intimately intertwined with and connected to the state. Much like critics of automation in the 1960s, opponents of nuclear power like Robert Jungk saw the danger of an authoritarian state as inherent to nuclear technology. More than other technologies, it would require permanent protection by the police and state authorities, and it manipulated citizens with the promise of material well-being. Beyond the Traube affair, opponents evoked the state's response to terrorism as evidence of a latent, transgressive, authoritarian state.[67] The environmental movement developed a comprehensive counter-vision to the feared "nuclear state"—namely, an "ecological society." Memories of the Nazi past always remained part of this fear scenario, and nuclear power extended these fears into the future. "Gas chambers yesterday, the nuclear state tomorrow," ran an article headline in an environmental magazine in 1979.[68]

These fear perceptions fueled the mobilization of the anti-nuclear movement since 1976–7: the total number of demonstrators against nuclear energy increased from 300,000 in 1977 to 400,000 in 1979. More and more violent demonstrations with up to 100,000 participants took place, as in Gorleben in 1979 and Brokdorf in 1981. The anti-nuclear movement thus mobilized significantly more people than the student movement of the 1960s. The nuclear accident at the Three Mile Island reactor in Harrisburg, USA, with a partial meltdown and release of radioactive gases in March 1979 further fueled skepticism regarding nuclear power.[69] At the same time, the state deployed police forces with up to 10,000 men, as in Kalkar in September 1977, during the high point of the Red Army Faction terrorism. This escalation of conflict brought both sides to new insights: nuclear oppon-

---

[66] Dannenbaum, "'Atom-Staat' oder 'Unregierbarkeit,'" 410.

[67] Robert Jungk, *Der Atom Staat. Vom Fortschritt in die Unmenschlichkeit* (Munich: Heyne, 1981). On Jungk, see Engels, *Naturpolitik in der Bundesrepublik*, 349–50, and Augustine, *Taking on Technocracy*, 128.

[68] Annekatrin Gebauer, "Apokalyptik und Eschatologie. Zum Politikverständnis der Grünen in ihrer Gründungsphase," *Archiv für Sozialgeschichte* 43 (2003): 405–20, quotation on 413, Reichardt, *Authentizität und Gemeinschaft*, 204.

[69] On Harrisburg, see Natasha Zaretsky, *Radiation Nation. Three Mile Island and the Political Transformation of the 1970s* (New York: Columbia University Press, 2018); on the significance in West Germany, see Augustine, *Taking on Technocracy*, 143–6.

ents recognized that a paramilitary attack on the construction fences as in Brokdorf was not a sound strategy to oppose the peaceful use of nuclear energy, especially after a first protester was killed in an anti-nuclear protest in the French town of Malville in the summer of 1977. From the late 1970s to the early 1980s, support for non-violent forms of protest increased within the anti-nuclear movement.[70] State authorities, by contrast, needed to realize that some nuclear projects might be "politically untenable," as the Minister-President of Lower Saxony, Ernst Albrecht, stated with respect to the planned depot for nuclear waste in Gorleben.[71] The solution to this predicament was the transformation of the anti-nuclear movement into a parliamentary force with the founding of *Die Grünen* in January 1980. *Die Grünen* were soon represented in several state legislatures and overcame the 5 per cent electoral threshold to the *Bundestag* for the first time in the federal elections in 1983. With the emergence of the Green Party, subjective sensibilities, including the open expression of fear, as they had been formed in the environment and the anti-nuclear movements, entered the official political culture of the Federal Republic.[72]

The development of an ecological counter-expertise focusing on the risks of nuclear power, such as radioactive emissions, nuclear accidents, and nuclear waste, became an essential element of the anti-nuclear movement. This emphasis on knowledge and "enlightenment" did not stand in contrast to the fear of nuclear power.[73] Instead, the new discourse on the considerable risks of nuclear power served as scientific confirmation of fear, and hence was part and parcel of the general validation of fear, as discussed in the previous chapter. For the opponents of nuclear power, scenarios of a future nuclear catastrophe turned fear into a new form of rationality. The philosopher Hans Jonas, a student of Martin Heidegger, described this "heuristic of fear" as a central element of the "principle of responsibility" in the technological age. According to Jonas, precisely the "foresight of the imagination and emotional sensitivity" would identify objects of fear in the distant future. He saw "the conscious effort to experience selfless fear" as a way to bring into view "the good that needs to be saved." Fear, he said, would "conserv[e] responsibility toward the future." Jonas shared the general validation of fear and conceived of it as an ethical position against the dangers of the technological age. To him, fear represented an indispensable warning sign against the dangers

---

[70] Ibid. 148–50.

[71] Rucht, *Von Wyhl nach Gorleben*, 89–136, Dieter Rucht, "Anti-Atomkraftbewegung," 245–66, Pettenkofer, *Die Entstehung der grünen Politik*, 210–60, Tompkins, *Better Active than Radioactive*, 149–94, Milder, *Greening Democracy*, 129–63, Augustine, *Taking on Technocracy*, 139–41.

[72] Milder, *Greening Democracy*, 163–237. On the founding history of the Greens, see Silke Mende, *"Nicht rechts, nicht links, sondern vorn." Eine Geschichte der Gründungsgrünen* (Munich: Oldenbourg, 2011).

[73] This opposition is emphasized in Hahn, Radkau, *Aufstieg und Fall der deutschen Atomwirtschaft*, 308–9, and Hahn, Radkau, "Mythos German Angst," 73–4.

threatening the existence of humanity. It was not fear itself that anyone should fear; avoiding "appropriate" fear was rather "a sign of timidity."[74]

The first comprehensive compendium regarding the risks of nuclear power was Holger Strohm's book, *Peaceful into the Catastrophe* (*Friedlich in die Katastrophe*), in 1973. The reprint edition from 1981 sold 130,000 copies. Strohm served as chairman of the German section of the American environmental group *Friends of the Earth*. His contacts in the American anti-nuclear movement provided him with a more advanced knowledge regarding the risks of nuclear power.[75] On more than 1,200 pages, he discussed the risks of nuclear energy, especially the harmful and carcinogenic effects of radioactive radiation, the risk of an accident or a planned attack on a nuclear power plant, and the issue of nuclear waste.

The nature of these fears of nuclear power differed fundamentally from previous national fears in at least three respects. First, detecting radioactive radiation required scientific instruments because human senses could not perceive it. Opponents of nuclear power repeatedly rejected the thesis of "safe" radiation levels and argued that any form of radioactive radiation was harmful to human health.[76] The increased fear of carcinogenic substances that had arisen in the 1960s had significantly contributed to the formation of the early anti-nuclear movement.[77] Second, before Chernobyl (1986), Harrisburg (1999), and Fukushima (2011), the fear of a nuclear accident was based on largely hypothetical or imaginary scenarios for the future. A scientific counter-expertise undermined the security pledge by supporters of nuclear power. The anti-nuclear movement popularized this counter-expertise and thus challenged the authority of pro-nuclear power scientists.[78] Third, the unresolved problem of nuclear waste also implied an irreversibility of the nuclear choice. Activists feared that nuclear power would burden future generations for centuries.[79] Invisibility, imagination, and irreversibility thus represented qualitatively new dimensions of the fear of nuclear power. This new and different nature of the threat also explains the mass mobilization and partial militancy of the anti-nuclear movement. Opponents saw

---

[74] Hans Jonas, *Das Prinzip Verantwortung. Versuch einer Ethik für die technologische Zivilisation* (Frankfurt a/M: Insel, 1979), 391–2. See also Albrecht Weisker, "Expertenvertrauen gegen Zukunftsangst. Zur Risikowahrnehmung der Kernenergie," in Ute Frevert, ed., *Vertrauen. Historische Annäherungen* (Göttingen: Vandenhoeck & Ruprecht, 2003), 412, and Richard Wolin, *Heidegger's Children. Hannah Arendt, Karl Löwith, Hans Jonas, and Herbert Marcuse* (Princeton: Princeton University Press, 2001), 113–20.

[75] On Strohm, see Uekötter, *The Greenest Nation?*, 96, Radkau, *Geschichte der Zukunft*, 164, Augustine, *Taking on Technocracy*, 82–3. For a similar emphasis on scientific warnings against the civilian use of nuclear energy, see Ewald Gaul, *Atomenergie oder, Ein Weg aus der Krise: Von der lebensbedrohlichen Leichtigkeit der Energieplaner* (Reinbek: Rowohlt, 1974).

[76] Holger Strohm, *Friedlich in die Katastrophe. Eine Dokumentation über Atomkraftwerke*, 2nd edn (Frankfurt a/M: Zweitausendeins, 1981), 69–348, Gaul, *Atomenergie*, 22–45.

[77] Radkau, "Mythos German Angst," 74. See also Wolfgang Barthel, *Der unsichtbare Tod. Die Angst des Bürgers vorm Atom* (Hamburg: Gruner und Jahr, 1979), 160–73.

[78] Augustin, *Taking on Technocracy*, 84–7.

[79] Strohm, *Friedlich in die Katastrophe*, 686–759, Gaul, *Atomenergie*, 85–8.

the introduction of nuclear power as an existential and irreversible choice. To them, the traditional mechanisms of parliamentary democracy appeared no longer appropriate to negotiate and discuss such existential issues. The demand for more direct forms of democracy in the anti-nuclear movement, and later also in the peace movement, illustrated the search for a new form of politics that would be appropriate to these existential threat scenarios.

Fear of nuclear power also entailed a gender dimension. It was often connoted as feminine in contrast to a male-defined optimistic belief in progress. Concern for the future of unborn or living children was women's purview. Organizations such as the Baden Women's Initiative against the Wyhl nuclear power plant, which was founded in October 1974, emphasized gender difference: the role of women activists as mothers and housewives not only underlined their special responsibility for unborn life, it also gave the protest a less ideological and more personal dimension. The alleged greater permeability of the female body to invisible and pathological substances, and their potentially catastrophic effects for unborn life, were at the center of the fear of radioactivity.[80] Anxiety about the harmful effects of radioactivity on women's health also united more traditional women with feminists. Eco-feminism later became influential in the Green Party. An allegedly specifically feminine connection to nature and emotionality appeared as the counterpart to an emotionally cold, male patriarchy. This also included a critique of the gender-specific nature of scientific knowledge: radioactivity was imagined as being particularly harmful to the female body and especially for female reproductive organs. The aim of female activism was not to "adjust to a male behavior" but to cultivate a specifically female identity as part of a future vision of an "androgynous society," a unity in difference.[81] Female activism in the anti-nuclear movement was thus also closely linked to new forms of emotionalized female subjectivity.

The specific threats of the civilian use of nuclear energy also became apparent in the industry's interaction with the insurance industry, which had grown significantly throughout the 1970s. This form of risk reduction and reduction of fear reached its limits in the case of nuclear power. Much like their US counterparts, a pool of private West German insurance companies limited the insurance sum for a nuclear accident to 60 million DM. The West German state offered a further liability guarantee of 500 million DM for each potential accident.[82] This meant not only that an accident would be a cost to taxpayers but also that state liability

---

[80] Jens Ivo Engels, "Gender Roles and German Anti-nuclear Protest," in Christoph Bernhardt, Geneviève Massard-Gilbaud, eds, *Le démon moderne. La pollution dans les sociétés urbaines et industrielles d'Europe/The Modern Demon. Pollution in Urban and Industrial European Societies* (Clermont-Ferrand: Presses Universitaires Blaise-Pascal, 2002), 407–24, Engels, *Naturpolitik in der Bundesrepublik*, 370. On similar arguments in the US context, see Zaretsky, *Radiation Nation*.

[81] Manon Andreas-Grisebach, *Philosophie der Grünen* (Munich: Olzog, 1982), 98, 103.

[82] Christoph Wehner, *Die Versicherung der Atomgefahr. Risikopolitik, Sicherheitsproduktion und Expertise in der Bundesrepublik Deutschland und den USA 1945–1986* (Göttingen: Wallstein, 2017).

would remain far below the projected costs of a nuclear accident.[83] For the critics of nuclear power, this limited liability was further proof of the dangerous nature of nuclear energy. The insurance industry's "anticipatory-pessimistic" style of thinking was compatible with the future fear scenarios as developed by the anti-nuclear movement. The limited liability for nuclear power plants on the basis of economic calculations enabled opponents of nuclear power to reject the accusation of an irrational fear.[84] In this sense, experts of the insurance industry became inadvertent key witnesses of the dangers of nuclear power plants and hence legitimized the apocalyptic fears of the anti-nuclear movement.

"Ecological Holocaust": The Dying Forest

While the protests against nuclear power remained largely limited to the left-wing alternative milieu, the debate over the "death of the German forest" (*Waldsterben*) that started in 1981 brought fears of environmental disaster to mainstream society. The alleged death of the forest was, as the writer Carl Amery stated, "the first massive ecological shock, which affected the entire nation."[85] At the height of the debate in June 1983, an Allensbach survey indicated that 99 per cent of West Germans had heard of the dying forest and 74 per cent supported measures against it.[86] From the late 1970s onward, individual foresters and botanists diagnosed more extensive damage to trees, which they began to interpret as an indication of a threatened ecological balance, as a threat to the entire forest. The forestry scientists Bernhard Ulrich from Göttingen and Peter Schütt from Munich played a key role in advancing the term "the dying forest" that became central to this debate. The dying forest became a new fear object. Indeed, in an interview with the magazine *Stern* in September 1981, Schütt stated that extensive forest damage had frightened him.[87] *Der Spiegel* ignited the national debate through a three-part series of articles on the subject in November 1981. The articles warned of a "ticking time bomb"—namely, a "large-scale dying of fir and spruce trees" due to growing air pollution from industrial emissions such as sulfur dioxide, which produced acid rain.[88] *Der Spiegel* described a threat to half all West German trees, including four-fifths of the Bavarian Forest. Peter Schütt described it as an

---

[83] Joachim Radkau, "Angstabwehr. Auch eine Geschichte der Atomtechnik," *Kursbuch* 85 (1986): 27–53.

[84] Wehner, *Die Versicherung der Atomgefahr*, 287–93. For an example of a contemporary critique, see Gaul, *Atomenergie*, 111–12.

[85] See Radkau, *Geschichte der Zukunft*, 326.

[86] Birgit Metzger, *"Erst stirbt der Wald, dann du!" Das Waldsterben als westdeutsches Politikum (1978–1986)* (Frankfurt a/M: Campus, 2015), 359.

[87] Cited in ibid. 188.

[88] *Der Spiegel* 35/47–9 (1981): 96–110, 188–200, 174–90. On the *Spiegel* series, see Metzger, *"Erst stirbt der Wald, dann du!"* 189–96.

"environmental disaster of unimaginable proportions," and Bernhard Ulrich said that forests would begin to die within five years.[89]

These predictions would turn out to be somewhat exaggerated if not wrong. Annual reports on the condition of the German forests, as they were compiled since 1982, revealed that the proportion of damaged forests oscillated between 23 per cent and 31 per cent between 1984 and 2014. A clear trend toward worsening conditions was not apparent.[90] Yet, much like at other moments in the history of fear in the Federal Republic, the fact that this fear scenario did not materialize should not lead us to ridicule or pathologize the contemporary feelings as a form of mental illness such as "hysteria" or "neuroticism."[91] Rather, the question arises as to how these fears were created and expressed in the first place, why contemporaries found them so plausible, and what political function they served.

The debate did not emerge in response to a new external reality but as a result of changed perceptions and sensitivities. In fact, discussions about damage to the forest as a result of sulfur dioxide and other air pollution dated back to the mid nineteenth century. The government of Sweden demanded compensation payments for damage to wildlife caused by sulfur exports from West Germany that went back decades into the 1970s.[92] While the Federal Republic rejected the demand, it could not cite any evidence that the damage had not occurred. Like the environmental movement in general, the public debate over the "dying of the forest" did not result from any new objective threat but rather from changed perceptions. The specific ways in which contemporaries articulated the fear of a dying forest reveals the multiple connections between this phenomenon and the more general culture of fear during the 1980s.

As in past moments of fear, the media played an important role in dramatizing the notion of a dying forest. The *Spiegel* series in 1981 directed attention to the phenomenon, and a broader public debate followed.[93] *Stern*, for example, published a headline in November 1983 stating that "Once upon a time there was a forest . . . " while, in March 1984, the Hamburg magazine advised its readers to "Look at it again . . . soon this forest will not exist anymore."[94] Direct observation of forest damage was central to the public resonance of the alleged death of the forest. While the senses could not observe air pollution or acid rain, the human eye could supposedly identify the damage to the trees. This visibility also distin-

[89]   *Der Spiegel* 35/47 (1981): 97, 99.

[90]   Kenneth Anders, Frank Uekötter, "Viel Lärm ums stille Sterben. Die Debatte über das Waldsterben in Deutschland," in Uekötter and Hohensee, eds, *Wird Kassandra heiser?*, 130, Radkau, *Geschichte der Zukunft*, 326, Metzger, *"Erst stirbt der Wald, dann du!"* 38.

[91]   This is the emphasis in Marcus Jauer, "Die Natur der Hysterie," *Frankfurter Allgemeine Zeitung*, October 18, 2013.

[92]   Anders and Uekötter, "Viel Lärm ums stille Sterben," 112–18.

[93]   Rudi Holzberger, *Das sogenannte Waldsterben. Zur Karriere eines Klischees: Das Thema Wald im journalistischen Diskurs* (Bergatreute: Wilfried Eppe, 1995).

[94]   Cited in ibid. 106.

guished the threat of the dying forest from the danger of radioactivity that stood at the center of the anti-nuclear movement. The newly established Advisory Council on the Environment thus also stated, in its special report on the dying of forests in June 1983, that the "feared ecological catastrophe had become unquestionably visible to us for the first time."[95] Environmental organizations organized field trips for interested parties and politicians to demonstrate the damage to the forests. Many media reports also contained graphic photographs of the dying forest, including an information sheet by Peter Schütt that was supposed to assist readers in identifying the damages to the forest that *Der Spiegel* published in 1983.[96] Yet, this information also demonstrated that laymen would have difficulty identifying damage to the forest. Even foresters sometimes needed specific training to detect damage. But this non-visibility of the damage then again served as indication of a more insidious threat—namely, an only superficial health of the forest that obscured the underlying pathologies.[97]

Yet, the notion of the dying of the forest was not simply a media product. The issue resonated with broader concerns and intersected with other anxieties of the time, especially body fears and shifts in West German commemorative culture. The condition of the forest, for example, was often cast in metaphors of "illness" and "death," which reflected the increased sensitivity to health issues during the 1970s. The soil scientist Bernhard Ulrich described the condition of the forest as "cancerous" in 1980, and journalists followed suit, using the language of cancer in describing the pathologies of the forest. In so doing, they linked concern for the forest to the increased body fears of the 1970s. Like cancer, they attributed the disease of the forest to invisible causes, and like cancer its consequence might be death.[98] This analogy of dying trees and human disease also anthropomorphized nature and assigned the forest its own agency. The dying of the forest appeared as a revenge of nature for unlimited economic growth, and even the trees participated in West German culture of fear by growing "branches driven by fear" (*Angstzweige*).[99]

The notion of a future ecological catastrophe was also articulated in the language of mass death and genocide, which had become increasingly present in public memory of the time. Several politicians described the dying of the forest as an "ecological Hiroshima," a phrase that *Der Spiegel* then picked up as well.[100] In 1982, the editor of a forestry magazine, *Allgemeine Forstzeitschrift*, Franz Bauer,

---

[95] "Waldschäden und Luftverunreinigungen. Sondergutachten März 1983 des Rates von Sachverständigen für Umweltfragen," Deutscher Bundestag, 10. Wahlperiode, Drucksache 10/113, 8. Juni 1983, 7, also cited in Metzger, *"Erst stirbt der Wald, dann du!"* 206.
[96] Peter Schütt, "Ein ganzer Strauß von Symptomen," *Der Spiegel* (1983): 89, also cited in ibid. 218.
[97] Metzger, *"Erst stirbt der Wald, dann du!"* 213–34.   [98] Ibid. 164, 378–9.
[99] Cited in ibid. 209.
[100] Ibid. 411. See also "Wir stehen vor einem ökologischen Hiroshima," *Der Spiegel* 38/7 (1983): 72–92.

saw the need to "ward off a Holocaust of the forest."[101] The weekly magazine *Die Zeit* invoked the "gassing" of the forest, while other environmentalists employed terms such as "gas chamber" or "gas attack" in order to describe the threats to the forest.[102] With the founding of *Die Grünen*, the rhetoric regarding the condition of the forest escalated as well. Supporters of the party compared the dying of the forest to a "war of annihilation against our own country," which would destroy the "foundations of human life."[103] This language underlines the increasing importance of Holocaust memory for the imaginations of the future in the 1980s. The notion of the German forest as a victim of this new war of annihilation also constituted a new version of the myth of Germans as victims, especially given the significance of the forest for German national identity. This also explains why the environmental commitment of the Kohl government was linked to the conservative project of redefining German national identity. The campaign to save the forest linked positive national traditions to a renewed emphasis on German suffering—the German forest as analogous to Holocaust victims. Its link to commemorative culture partly explains the broad popular and political resonance of the debate.

A new temporality of accelerated destruction also shaped the debate on the dying forest. Activists worried that time was running out and that little or no time was left to avert disaster. In a letter to the Committee on Internal Affairs (*Innenausschuss*) of the German parliament, the president of the German Forestry Council drew an alarming picture. The percentage of "severely ill firs" had increased from 20 per cent to 80 per cent between autumn 1981 and spring 1983, and that of "severely ill spruces" from 2 per cent to 70 per cent. He called on West German officials to prevent a "major environmental disaster."[104] Increasingly the message came across that it was already too late to save the forest. The Green Party in Hesse claimed in a brochure on "acid violence" in September 1983 that it was too late for a "large part of the forests in Hesse and in the Federal Republic." They predicted that the sites of forests would one day be "acid deserts where only a few grasses and shrubs can survive."[105] Images of dead trees illustrated this thesis of a "desertification" of the forest. This notion invoked the idea of a more general cultural decline, which would reduce Germany to the allegedly lower level of

---

[101] Metzger, *"Erst stirbt der Wald, dann Du!"*411.

[102] Cited in ibid. 409. Holzberger, *Das sogenannte Waldsterben*, 104–5.

[103] Flyer, Ökologischer Arbeitskreis der Grünen, Erlangen. "Waldsterben. Die Katastrophe nimmt unvorstellbare Ausmaße an," Archiv Grünes Gedächtnis (AGG), NL Wilhelm Knabe 23/2, "Vorschlag zur Initiierung eines breiten aktiven Widerstands gegen die Ursachen des Waldsterbens," AGG, BT II.1/1197, Herman Graf Hatzfeldt, 12 Thesen zum Waldsterben, February 17, 1983, AGG, NL Petra Kelly, Nr. 2780.

[104] Deutscher Forstwirtschaftsrat, Der Präsident to the Vorsitzenden des Innenausschusses des DBT, Axel Wenitz, Stellungnahme für die öffentliche Anhörung am October 24–5, 1983, AGG, BT II.1/5086.

[105] Brochure *Saure Gewalt*, ed. Die Grünen im Landtag, Wiesbaden, September 1983.

civilization of people of the desert or steppe. The death of the German forest implied the loss of German cultural superiority compared with eastern or southern peoples.[106] A *Stern* article from May 1984 then merged the apocalyptic crisis scenarios of desertification, environmental catastrophe, and nuclear war, and predicted that the death of the forest would turn Germany into a "Pershing-protected Dioxin steppe."[107]

As in the case of the anti-nuclear movement, scientific expertise was central to the notion of the dying forest. More than half the newspaper articles on the death of the forest were based on scientific studies, and the people sounding the warning, like Bernhard Ulrich and Peter Schütt, had scientific credentials.[108] The scientific counter-expertise, as it had emerged in the controversy over nuclear power, also shaped the debate on the death of the forest. The dramatization of the phenomenon often drew on a selective reception of scientific literature, which tended to confirm the alarming perception of a dying forest yet also largely ignored more critical or doubtful voices. A Special Report of the Council of Experts on Environmental Issues (*Sachverständigenrat für Umweltfragen*) that the federal government had appointed in 1972 attempted in June 1983 to arrive at a consensus regarding the death of the forest. The report concluded that "the dying of the forest" and "acid rain" had become "probably the biggest problems in environmental policy." It acknowledged a number of causes besides pollution for damage to the forest, such as a run of extremely dry summers and cold winters, forest mismanagement such as the planting of trees on inappropriate soil, and a resurgence of some tree-attacking pests. But the report also asserted that human-caused air pollution had created "a new kind of damage" to the forest.[109]

Proposed measures to combat the dying of the forest illustrated this sense of urgency. An "informed citizen" from Ravensburg suggested in September 1983 that the state should use the "new emergency law," which had been passed in 1968, in order to enforce environmental measures in power plants and industrial plants.[110] The Heidelberg branch of the Green Party proposed a "mass constitutional law suit" in July 1983, which millions of citizens would submit to the Constitutional Court.[111] In a similar way, a Coordinating Agency on the Dying Forest envisioned creating "democratic pressure" from "below" and "in the streets" in order to initiate necessary political changes.[112] Others, however, worried

---

[106] On "steppification," see Metzger, *"Erst stirbt der Wald, dann du!"* 393–7.
[107] Cited in ibid. 410.   [108] Holzberger, *Das sogenannte Waldsterben*, 146.
[109] "Waldschäden und Luftverunreinigungen. Sondergutachten März 1983 des Rates von Sachverständigen für Umweltfragen," Deutscher Bundestag, 10. Wahlperiode, Drucksache 10/113, June 8, 1983, 7, 64, 67, 79–83, 93–5.
[110] Erich Voigt, Ravensburg, Offener Brief eines informierten Bürgers an die deutschen Politiker, im September 1983, AGG, BT II.1/3986.
[111] Hanshorst Thorspecken, Kreisvorstand der Grünen, Heidelberg, July 22, 1983, AGG, BT II.1/3989.
[112] Arbeitsmappe "Den Wald Retten," ed. "Koordinationsbüro Waldsterben," Hagen mit organisatorischer Unterstützung der Grünen und des BBU, AGG, BT II.1/1174.

that the massive political mobilization of the West German peace movement, which will be analyzed later, had robbed demonstrations of their power. A proposal of the Green Party asked rhetorically: "What are rallies of 40,000 or 50,000 participants compared to those who managed to mobilize 300,000 or more?" Environmentalists compared their own situation to the military dictatorship in Communist Poland and advocated "civil disobedience" and "nonviolent actions" as practiced by Communist dissidents as a model.[113] Such ideas reflected declining trust in parliamentary democracy as being capable of containing seemingly existential threats. Yet, environmentalists also needed to define their own strategies vis-à-vis the dying forest because other political parties, including conservatives, acknowledged the danger of dying forests and presented themselves as "protectors of the German forest" in the media.[114] In fact, proponents of nuclear energy invoked the dying of the forest as an argument on behalf of nuclear power. Sulfur dioxide, the "satanic substance" (*Der Spiegel*) that caused acid rain, arose mainly from coal-fired power plants, which represented an alternative to nuclear energy.[115] In contrast, environmental activists tried to prove, although largely unsuccessfully, that the dying of the forest in the vicinity of nuclear power plants was particularly pronounced. In so doing, they sought to counteract the attempt to portray nuclear energy as the environmentally friendly alternative to coal.[116]

The broad and emotional public debate also led the new center-right government under Chancellor Helmut Kohl to combat the dying of the forest and to develop an unprecedented investment program to reduce air pollution.[117] Drawing on plans of the previous Social Democratic government, the federal government mandated elaborate desulphurization systems for coal power plants requiring private investments of 7–12 billion DM. In September 1983, it instituted an action program to "save the forest." The introduction of the catalyst for gas engines and of unleaded gas in 1985 served to reduce nitrogen oxides, which had also been identified as a cause of the dying forest. The plan also funded 850 research projects with a total budget of 465 million DM. Yet this intensified research did not lead to a deepening of the scientific consensus but rather to the opposite: a further proliferation of competing diagnoses and ostensible causes of the dying of the forest.[118] The sense of confusion and unpredictability this cre-

[113] "Vorschlag zur Initiierung eines breiten aktiven Widerstands gegen die Ursachen des Waldsterbens," AGG, BT II.1/1197.

[114] Wilhelm Knabe to Interessenten der Bundes AG Waldsterben, Landesvorstände und Landesparlamente, n.d., AGG, NL Wilhelm Knabe 23 (1).

[115] Radkau, *Geschichte der Zukunft*, 325.

[116] Informationen der sozialdemokratischen BT Fraktion, May 30, 1985, Ausgabe 1042, Abg. Michael Müller, AGG, BT II.1/1165. See also Metzger, *"Erst stirbt der Wald, dann du!"* 465–76.

[117] Uekötter and Hohensee, "Einleitung," in Uekötter and Hohensee, eds, *Wird Kassandra heiser?*, 20.

[118] Anders and Uekötter, "Viel Lärm ums stille Sterben," 124–5, Radkau, *Geschichte der Zukunft*, 326, Metzger, *"Erst stirbt der Wald, dann du!"* 443–50, 484–505.

ated became in itself anxiety-producing. Still, the measures taken appeared to have an effect: the emission of sulfur dioxide decreased by 70 per cent by 1988 and declined even further due to the de-industrialization of the German Democratic Republic (GDR) during the 1990s. As a result, the acidity of the rain decreased, and nitrogen emissions stabilized at the levels that prevailed in 1980.[119]

From the late 1980s onward, it became increasingly clear that the German forest was by no means dying. In certain areas, the forest was actually growing.[120] To this day, it remains unclear whether political intervention prevented ecological catastrophe or whether the alarm was unfounded.[121] The mere fact that even a series of scientific studies cannot fully answer this question points to the ambiguity of anxiety about the future. On the one hand, such anxiety creates an awareness of possible undesirable developments and thus helps to prevent the feared development from becoming reality. On the other hand, when foretold disaster does not occur, it may seem like fear was exaggerated or unjustified. It is clear that the rampant apocalyptic fears of the 1980s drove some of the predictions of a dying forest. The misdiagnosis resided in the fact that a "chronic process" was defined as an "imminent catastrophe."[122] At least some trees also adjusted better to increased levels of acidity than expected.[123] The forest would probably have survived without the debate about its dying and the related political measures. But without these measures, the forest would most likely be "worse off" today.[124]

The debate about the "dying forest" raises important issues for environmental activism today. How useful is the dramatizing of future dangers and the significance of fear for political mobilization? During the 1980s, the transformation of chronic processes into acute dangers or—to put it in the language of the history of emotions—the mobilization of ecological anxiety served as a decisive instrument to enforce political action. On the other hand, a dramatizing and often selective representation of future dangers in the media can lead to habituation, a kind of getting used to permanent alarm, which then can paralyze action. Fear thus acts as a motivation for action if it is not chronic or permanent. The current debate on climate change faces this difficulty as well, even if the ambiguity in scientific opinion that had still existed with respect to the dying forest has essentially evaporated regarding climate change.

---

[119] Ibid. 505–6.   [120] Ibid. 584.
[121] For the first position, see Wirsching, *Abschied vom Provisorium*, 435. On the history of eco-alarmism, see Uekötter and Hohensee, eds, *Wird Kassandra heiser?*
[122] Radkau, *Geschichte der Zukunft*, 327.
[123] Kerstin Vierung, "Was wurde aus dem Waldsterben?" *Spektrum.de*, March 11, 2016, https://www.spektrum.de/news/was-wurde-aus-dem-waldsterben/1402487 (last accessed March 5, 2020).
[124] Anders and Uekötter, "Viel Lärm ums stille Sterben," 138.

The Peace Movement

The peace movement was by far the largest protest movement in the history of the Federal Republic. At its height in the early 1980s, hundreds of thousands of West Germans protested in huge demonstrations against the deployment of new intermediate range missiles on the territory of the Federal Republic. Public expression of fear mobilized the peace movement more than in any other social movement in the Federal Republic. It was based on the revaluation of emotions, including fear, which, in the wake of the psychoboom, now attached themselves to new international tensions and to the external danger of nuclear war.[125] With the peace movement of the 1980s, the history of fear in the Federal Republic reached a culmination point.

The most important external occasion was the NATO double-track decision. As early as 1977, Federal Chancellor Helmut Schmidt was concerned about the superiority of the Soviet Union in the field of intermediate-range missiles. He worried about a decoupling of Western European security from the United States. If the Soviet Union were able to threaten Western Europe with intermediate range missiles, the US would be forced to retaliate with its intercontinental missiles and risk a global nuclear war to defend Western Europe. Schmidt's concern was less the likelihood of this scenario but rather the possibility that Western Europe might be subjected to Soviet political pressure and blackmailing.[126] This was the background for the double-track decision, which was adopted at the NATO meeting in December 1979. Negotiations with the Soviet Union were supposed to lead to the disarmament of Soviet SS-20 missiles in Eastern Europe. If this were not to happen, NATO would station 464 cruise missiles in Western Europe and the Federal Republic of Germany as well as 108 Pershing II intermediate-range missiles in the Federal Republic alone from 1983 onward. With the Soviet invasion of Afghanistan in December 1979 and the election of Ronald Reagan as US President, prospects of a negotiated settlement worsened. After the negotiations actually failed, the West German parliament approved the stationing of nuclear weapons in November 1983 and their deployment began shortly thereafter. At the same time, the US under Reagan was working to develop a Strategic Defense Initiative (SDI) in space, which was supposed to protect the American continent against Soviet intercontinental missiles. Critics feared that the US was seeking the capacity for a nuclear first-strike against the Soviet Union, which would overcome

---

[125] Benjamin Ziemann also emphasizes this link in "German Angst? Debating Cold War Anxieties in West Germany, 1945–1990," in Matthew Grant, Benjamin Ziemann, eds, *Understanding the Imaginary War: Culture, Thought and Nuclear Conflict, 1945–90* (Manchester: Manchester University Press, 2016), 131.

[126] For a review of recent literature on Schmidt and the double-track decision, see Noel D. Cary, "Helmut Schmidt, Euromissiles and the Peace Movement," *Central European History* 52/1 (2019): 148–71.

the previous logic of deterrence and make a nuclear war feasible and winnable.[127] The second Cold War reached its high point in the fall of 1983. An erroneous rocket alert in the Soviet Union in September 1983 and then the NATO exercise *Able Archer* two months later, which simulated a nuclear war in Western Europe, intensified international tensions. According to some observers, 1983 became the most dangerous year in the Cold War.[128]

Opposition to the NATO double-track decision began to form quickly. In November 1980, the former *Bundeswehr* General Gert Bastian and Josef Weber, a board member of the German Peace Union (DFU, which received financial support from the East German Communist Party), compiled the Krefeld appeal. It called on the federal government to "withdraw its consent for the deployment of Pershing II missiles and cruise missiles in Central Europe" as well as to avoid "a nuclear arms race which endangers especially the Europeans."[129] The Krefeld appeal garnered five million signatures by 1983.[130] It formulated the rejection of the NATO double-track decision as a minimum consensus of the peace movement. Yet the appeal also met with criticism from within the peace movement because it did not explicitly reject Soviet intermediate-range missiles. Although Green Party leader Petra Kelly was one of the co-initiators, the appeal became controversial even within the Green Party. Critics cited "omissions and one-sidedness" and pointed out "many contradictions" between Soviet reality and the position of the Green Party.[131] By contrast, other members of the Green Party saw the deployment of the American Pershing II as a one-sided attempt to gain an advantage over the Soviet Union and potentially as "preparation of an American war of aggression."[132] These conflicts also shaped the ensuing meetings of the Krefeld initiative in November 1981 in Dortmund and in September 1983 in Bad Godesberg. The discussion focused especially on the refusal of left-wing Social Democrats such as Peter Glotz and Erhard Eppler to sign the Krefeld appeal.[133]

The role of fear in the peace movement became codified in the slogan "Be afraid," an ironic spin on the official motto of the Protestant Church Congress

---

[127] This was a widely held view. See, for example, Ernst Tugendhat, "Vorwort," in Ernst Tugendhat, *Nachdenken über die Atomkriegsgefahr und warum man sie nicht sieht* (Berlin: Rotbuch, 1986), 15.

[128] Georg Schild, *1983. Das gefährlichste Jahr des Kalten Krieges* (Paderborn: Schöningh, 2013), 164–85.

[129] Krefelder Appell, October 15–16, 1980, https://www.1000dokumente.de/index.html?c=dokument_de&dokument=0023_kre&object=facsimile&l=de (last accessed March 5, 2020).

[130] Andres Buro, "Die Friedensbewegung," in Roland Roth, ed., *Die sozialen Bewegungen in Deutschland seit 1945*, 274–5.

[131] Ernst Hoplitschek, Klaus Wolschner, "Das 2. Krefelder Forum und der Breschnew-Besuch vor dem Beginn der offiziellen Rüstungsverhandlungen zwischen den USA und der UdSSR werden eine Nagelprobe für die Identität der Grünen in der Friedensbewegung sein," AGG, BI.1/630.

[132] Kreisverband Nürnberg to LV und BV der Grünen, November 15, 1981, AGG, BI.1/629.

[133] "Drittes Forum der Krefelder Initiative," September 17, 1983, Bonn–Bad Godesberg, "Dokumentation: Das atomare Inferno verhindern. Wehrt Euch!" Dieter Lattmann, ed., *Krefelder Initiative. Der Atomtod bedroht uns alle–Keine Atomraketen in Europa. Entstehung, Ziel, Wirkung* (Neuss, 1985) HIS, SBe 544, Box 4.

(*Kirchentag*) in 1981, "Do not be afraid!" Intellectuals and activists repeatedly emphasized the productive function of fear. It was, they said, perfectly reasonable given the reality of the threats.[134] By contrast, "neurotic absence of anxiety" was pathological. Activists emphasized that it was important to distinguish between a "false fear" that was directed at a bogeyman, such as Communism, and a "fearless" and "animating" fear of the "greater danger of the annihilation of all life."[135]

Theorists of fear repeatedly resorted to the theses of the philosopher Günther Anders, who had already criticized the pathological "apocalypse blindness" in the face of the nuclear threat in the 1950s.[136] The philosopher Ernst Tugendhat, for example, took up Anders's notion of the "antiquity of man" and identified an anachronism of emotional life in the atomic age. While "fear" constituted an important indicator for danger and was thus an emotion necessary for survival, nature and evolution had not equipped human beings to face the novel dangers of the nuclear age. In particular, the fact that the senses could not anticipate the nuclear danger made it difficult to overcome "cognitive inertia" and to transfer fear into action.[137] The psychoanalyst Horst-Eberhard Richter, who played a prominent role in the peace movement, explained what he saw as the pathological absence of fear as a consequence of a series of repressions that were responsible for outward aggressiveness and ultimately the philosophy of deterrence.[138] Recalling the metaphor that appealed to environmentalists, Richter wrote that the expression of feelings and of anxiety increased the resilience of cancer patients just as the open expression of anxiety constituted an appropriate and healthy response to the danger of nuclear war. Like cancer, the arms race was a "type of disease that originates to a considerable extent in people's interior life."[139]

The peace movement did not just replicate the philosophical and psychological validation of fear: it also cultivated the ability of individuals to experience and to articulate fear. A newly sensitized subjectivity was an important precondition for the articulation of fear in the peace movement. The sensual and subjective experience of fear or, as it was called in the language of the time, a sense of "personal concern" (*persönliche Betroffenheit*), was central for the productive processing of fear and its translation into action.[140] Psychotherapies often supported this process. Hanna, a 35-year-old high school teacher, described her mental state thus:

---

[134] Martin Schrenk, *Angst=Vernunft in unserer bedrohten Welt* (Neunkirchen, n.p., n.d.).

[135] Franz-Josef Ensel, *Richtige Angst und falsche Furcht. Psychologische Friedensvorbereitung und der Beitrag der Pädagogik* (Frankfurt a/M: Fischer, 1984), 57, 59–60. See also Judith Michel, "'Richtige' und 'falsche' Angst in der westdeutschen Debatte um den Nato-Doppelbeschluss," in Bormann et al., eds, *Angst in den internationalen Beziehungen*, 251–72.

[136] Günther Anders, *Die Antiquiertheit des Menschen, Band 1: Über die Seele im Zeitalter der zweiten industriellen Revolution*, 2nd edn (Munich: C.H.Beck, 2002), 235–308.

[137] Tugendhat, *Nachdenken über die Atomkriegsgefahr*, 86, 107–8.

[138] Horst-Eberhardt Richter, *Zur Psychologie des Friedens* (Reinbek: Rowohlt, 1984), 43–55.

[139] Ibid. 78–88.   [140] Ensel, *Richtige Angst und falsche Furcht*, 66.

Through therapy, I have learned to differentiate within this larger turmoil of fear. I have only now become aware of this fear of the end of the world, this fear for humanity and nature, and for everything that is vital, even for my own psychic well-being.... And I can do something about it too.[141]

The experience of fear, however, was not just directed outward, as a demonstration to others of one's own deeper insight and moral superiority, but also repeatedly articulated in private testimonies. Political communication with the outside world and inner emotional experience remained closely intertwined. In letters to the Green Party or to members of the West German parliament, activists articulated intense experiences of fear in the aftermath of the *Bundestag*'s decision to approve the stationing of American intermediate-range missiles in November 1983. A Reiner N. reported, for example, that he was "sickened" at the result of a "deep fear" that he had "always suspected" of having and that was now "there."[142] Others stated their apocalyptic fears even more openly. "We are a bit closer to the abyss, that's clear. Our life is a life on call," wrote one Marlis F.-R.[143] A third letter demanded the distribution of cyanide capsules in order to prevent "dying slowly or very slowly from radiation poisoning in the case of a nuclear war."[144] Activists also invoked the psychoanalytic arguments of Horst-Eberhard Richter and recognized an "irrational psychic dynamic" among the proponents of stationing the missiles, who allegedly sought to cope with their own inner uncertainties and fears by transforming them into hatred for, and aggression toward, the outside world. Here too, not being afraid was pathological and irrational.[145]

The anticipation of a hitherto unprecedented destructive power of a possible nuclear war was central for the notion of fear within the peace movement. Past experiences no longer provided any guide to future catastrophes. Activists argued that Second World War veterans who approved of the missile stationing erroneously projected their own wartime experience into the future, that they failed to understand the fundamental difference between a possible Third World War and the Second World War.[146] There appeared to be only one historical event that was relevant to the future nuclear war: the Holocaust. For peace activists, popular Holocaust memory and a future vision of a nuclear war converged.[147] Much like environmental activists, peace activists repeatedly invoked the notion of an "atomic" or "nuclear" Holocaust.[148] In 1981, the journalist Anton-Andreas Guha

---

[141] Cited in ibid. 68–9.   [142] Rainer N. to Hans Adolf, December 10, 1983, AGG, BII, 1/38.

[143] Marlis F.-R. to Die Grünen, November 22, 1983, AGG, BII, 1/38.

[144] Helmut F. to Die Ärztekammer Hamburg, AGG, BII, 1/38.

[145] Theo W. to Alois Mertes, CDU, November 23, 1983; Bianca Vowinckel, November 24, 1983, AGG, BII, 1/38.

[146] G.G. to Die Grünen, November 22, 1983, AGG, BII, 1/38.

[147] On such links, see Achim Landwehr, *Die anwesende Abwesenheit der Vergangenheit. Essay zur Geschichtstheorie* (Frankfurt a/M: S. Fischer, 2016), 149–65.

[148] See, for example, G.G. to Die Grünen, AGG, BII, 1/38.

published a book entitled *The NATO Stationing Decision: Europe's Holocaust.*[149] American military bases were often represented as concentration camps sealed off with barbed wire. During a demonstration in the Swabian town of Mutlangen, where the US planned to station Pershing II missiles, demonstrators appeared in costumes meant to invoke clothes of concentration camp inmates. Other demonstrators displayed a banner stating "Pershing makes you free," referencing the inscription "Work makes you free" at the entrance gate of the Auschwitz and other concentration and extermination camps. The theologian Dorothee Sölle called the Pershing II missiles "flying crematoria."[150]

Holocaust analogies also appeared in activists' private correspondence. An Inge M. compared the vote of the *Bundestag* in November 1983 approving the stationing of US intermediate range missiles with a "past history," in which "people consciously and knowingly almost managed to extinguish an entire people."[151] Another letter writer, Ingolf F., described his own experience of the impending stationing of nuclear missiles in West Germany thus: "Slowly I begin to understand," he wrote, "what people in Auschwitz, Majdanek, and Treblinka, etc., must have felt."[152] Such sentiments led the historian Dan Diner to speculate in the fall of 1983 whether fear in the peace movement really reflected a "hidden fear retaliation" for Nazi crimes, a "kind of archaic expectation for retribution as a form of collective annihilation."[153] This masked fear of retaliation, he argued, became more and more public over the course of the 1980s. At the same time, the invocation of Holocaust memory in this context also reflected a genuine effort to apply the lessons of the past to the present. Holocaust imagery thus also projected an image of the "good German" to the outside world, which had internalized the memory of the Nazi past.

Popular conceptions of fear and security often hinged on the perception of the US. A view of the US as the Federal Republic's most important ally had been crucial to West Germans' sense of security throughout the postwar period.[154] An increasing trust in the US had been an important factor in the gradual reduction of fears during the Cold War. Yet for the peace movement of the 1980s, the US again appeared as a source of anxiety. "I believe Reagan might do anything," one activist wrote forebodingly in December 1983 to another, describing the peace movement's critique as centered on the foreign policy of the

---

[149] Eckart Conze, "Missile Bases as Concentration Camps," in Conze, Klimke and Varon, eds, *Nuclear Threats, Nuclear Fear*, 79–97, quotation on 88.

[150] Ibid.   [151] Inge M. to Die Grünen, November 24, 1983, AGG, B II, 1/38.

[152] Ingolf F., November 23, 1983, B II, 1/38, AGG.

[153] Dan Diner, "Hier stimmt was nicht. Mutmaßungen über Angst in der Friedensbewegung," *Links* 15/162 (1983): 22.

[154] See Michael Geyer, "Amerika in Deutschland. Amerikanische Macht und die Sehnsucht nach Sicherheit," in Frank Trommler, Elliott Shore, eds, *Deutsch-amerikanische Begegnungen. Konflikt und Kooperation im 19. und 20. Jahrhundert* (Stuttgart: DVA, 2001), 155–87, and Chapter 3 in this book.

Figure 8.2. Poster of the Young Socialists (*Jusos*) on the occasion of the "anti-war" day, September 1, 1983.

The peace movement of the 1980s combined a newly popularized memory of the Holocaust with an apocalyptic vision of the future. This image combines a depiction of the entrance gate of the Auschwitz extermination camp in the foreground with a representation of a bombed city in the background. The caption reads "Never again war, never again fascism."

Source: 6/PLKA038398. The rights for this image could not be determined.

Reagan administration.[155] According to the critique of the double-track decision and rising Social Democratic Party (SPD) politician Oskar Lafontaine, there was ample cause to be "afraid of our friends."[156] An anonymous writer condemned the decision in favor of stationing new US rockets as a "blank check for adventurous occupying power" and called the day of the decision Germany's "blackest day in history."[157] Some activists described the Federal Republic as a US-occupied country with limited sovereignty, a launching pad for American nuclear weapons. This view gave rise to distinctly nationalist ideas.[158] Peace activists, such as the former *Bundeswehr* officer and political scientist Alfred Mechtersheimer, who joined the right-wing extremist scene in the late 1990s, seemed to confirm such affinities.[159] Writing on the cult of "subjective concern" (*Betroffenheitskult*), journalist Cora Stephan described the apocalyptic expressions of fear in the peace movement as a form of German megalomania, and activists as motivated by a desire "to be great, great in guilt, great in one's conversion, great as an imaginary victim of the apocalypse as form of repentance."[160] However, such nationalist ideas ultimately played only a minor role in the peace movement. Many activists were keenly interested in constructing analogies to the history of National Socialism and the Holocaust, which ran contrary to right-wing efforts to repress or relativize that past.[161] Moreover, the activism of the peace movement took place not only, or not even primarily, within the national framework. Instead, the local context was crucial for peace activism precisely because of the significance of the subjective-emotional dimension for activism.[162]

Indeed, the local anchoring was one of the main reasons for the successful mobilization of the peace movement. In early 1981, the magazine *Stern* published a map with the locations of American nuclear weapons in Germany.[163] According to the slogan, "missiles are magnets," these places now appeared as the potential first targets of a possible Soviet nuclear attack. The fear of a global nuclear war became tangible in the imagination of its local impact. Scenarios such as the one by a doctors' initiative in Ulm, which sought to describe in detail the potential local consequences of a nuclear war, were among the most important mobiliza-

[155] Rainer N. to Hans Adolf, December 10, 1983, AGG, B II, 1/38.

[156] Oskar Lafontaine, *Angst vor den Freunden. Die Atomwaffen-Strategie der Supermächte zerstört die Bündnisse* (Reinbek: Rowohlt, 1983). For a similar critique of the US, see Tugendhat, *Nachdenken über die Atomkriegsgefahr*, 15, 18.

[157] Anonymous, B II, AGG, 1/38.   [158] See Conze, "Missile Bases as Concentration Camps," 86.

[159] Alfred Mechtersheimer, "Rüstungsverweigerung statt Rüstungskontrolle. Wie die Friedensbewegung in das atomare Wettrüsten eingreifen kann," in Walter Jens, ed., *In letzter Stunde. Aufruf zum Frieden* (Munich: Kindler, 1982), 79–99.

[160] Cora Stephan, *Der Betroffenheitskult. Eine politische Sittengeschichte* (Berlin: Rowohlt, 1993), 181.

[161] See also Heinrich Albertz, "Von der Nation—und von Wichtigerem," in Jens, ed., *In letzter Stunde*, 135–42.

[162] Ensel, *Richtige Angst und falsche Furcht*, 75–98. See also Michel, " 'Richtige' und 'falsche' Angst."

[163] Susanne Schregel, *Der Atomkrieg vor der Wohnungstür. Eine Politikgeschichte der neuen Friedensbewegung in der Bundesrepublik 1970–1985* (Frankfurt a/M: Campus, 2011), 89.

tion strategies.[164] The brochure portrayed the catastrophic consequences of a nuclear war for the population of the city of Ulm and its surroundings in an especially vivid manner. The authors left no doubt that medicine would have little help for the civilian victims of a nuclear war. Even those who survived the initial blast would die a painful death as a result of burns and radiation sickness. This scenario underlined another slogan of the peace movement—namely, that the living would "envy the dead." These terrible local consequences stood in stark contrast to the possible reasons for a nuclear war. In most hypothetical scenarios, nuclear war resulted either from negative stereotypes about the Cold War enemy or from an accidental, technical error. Not genuinely political conflicts, but rather irrational psychic needs or the loss of control over technology appeared as the most likely causes of a nuclear war.[165]

The imagination of a local catastrophe that made the danger tangible was often the starting point for local peace activism. Many towns and municipalities began to declare themselves nuclear-weapon-free zones. The aim of these declarations was to anchor peace activism in the local sphere and in personal experience.[166] Even though the Federal Administrative Court ruled in 1990 that such declarations exceeded municipal powers, they nevertheless expressed a form of bottom-up protest.[167] They were exercises of a grassroots democracy that sought to contrast the majority position of the population with the position of parties and the federal government. In so doing, these protests illustrated severe doubts regarding the mechanisms of representative democracy in general; they questioned whether parliament would truly represent the will of the people.[168] Traditional mechanisms of parliamentary democracy seemed inadequate given the existential significance of the nuclear threat and activists sought new forms of political decision making. Because the stationing decision would produce a potentially irreversible nuclear destruction, activists argued that the majority will of the population needed to be heard directly. They tried to organize a referendum in June 1984 to reverse the stationing decision of the West German *Bundestag* from the previous November, which, however, ultimately did not materialize.[169]

---

[164] Ulmer Ärzteinitiative, *Tausend Grad Celcius. Das Ulm-Szenario für einen Atomkrieg* (Darmstadt: Luchterhand, 1983).

[165] Schregel, *Der Atomkrieg vor der Wohnungstür*, 156.

[166] Klaus Vack, "Hinweise, Tipps und Vorschläge für eine Kampagne 'atomwaffenfreie Zone von unten," in *Gruppe Friedens-Manifest. Schafft eine, zwei, drei, viele atomwaffenfreie Zonen! Handreichung für Friedensgruppen und Friedensstifter*, pamphlet (October 1982).

[167] See Schregel, *Der Atomkrieg vor der Wohnungstür*, 295–330.

[168] Vack, "Hinweise, Tipps und Vorschläge für eine Kampagne 'atomwaffenfreie Zone von unten," 36.

[169] Ja zum Frieden, Keine Pershing II und Cruise Missiles, Bibliothek für Zeitgeschichte, Stuttgart (BfZ).

Local events such as the Stuttgart "peace days" of the Protestant parish community Zuffenhausen in November 1981 offered an opportunity to communicate individual fears. The two-week-long event ended with a concluding discussion on the topic, "We hope against fear." Participants were asked to write down their fears on a sheet of paper in the form of a leaf and then pass it on to the next person, who then should write on the back "what helps to minimize this fear." This exercise yielded a cross-section of contemporary fears ranging from "nuclear warfare" to "the next math test" as well as numerous suggestions to overcome these fears through activism because "many of us feel the same way."[170] Similar events took place in the early 1980s throughout the Federal Republic, often under the guidance of church groups.[171] Many of these activities were located at the intersection of activism and group therapy, and hence built on the expressive emotional culture of the seventies. For example, the members of an Einbeck peace group, who had gotten to know each other in a group seminar on "self-awareness," reported how they learned to express their feelings in role-playing games and hence sought to reduce their own internal "enemy images."[172] Another important medium for expressing feelings was music. The hit song, "A Little Peace," with which the singer Nicole won the Eurovision Song Contest in 1982, marked the beginning of an entire series of other pop songs, which explicitly declared their support for the peace movement and asked for more than "a little" peace.[173] A song booklet for the "Peace Camp" in Schwäbisch Gmünd in August and September 1983, for example, included songs by politically committed songwriters such as Hannes Wader and Wolf Biermann, as well as an invitation to write a song "together with others."[174] Many of these local events sought to bridge the gap between the articulation of fears and overcoming them through activism. But not everyone agreed with the peace movement's celebration of fear as a new rationality. Adhering to a more traditional emotional regime, journalistic critics worried that the performative display of emotions would render activists incapable of rational discussion. They also revived the association of this excessive emotionality with National Socialism.[175] The conflict over the NATO dual-track

---

[170] Stuttgarter Friedenstage Zuffenhausen, "Frieden Schaffen," November 1–18, 1981, BfZ, D 04082.

[171] Ninety-three per cent of all "peace weeks" in 1983 took place with participation of the churches. Sebastian Kalden, Jan Ole Wiechmann, "Kirchen," in Christoph Becker-Schaum, Philipp Gassert, Martin Klimke, Wilfried Mausbach, Marianne Zepp, eds, *"Entrüstet Euch!" Nuklearkrise, NATO-Doppelbeschluss und Friedensbewegung* (Paderborn: Schöningh, 2012), 247–61.

[172] Die Einbecker Friedensgruppe, Herbst 1984, BfZ, D04366.

[173] Nicole later also distanced herself from the peace movement and communicated the conservative gender ideals of an innocent, vulnerable girl; see Philipp Gassert, "Die Vermarktung des Zeitgeistes. Nicoles 'Ein bißchen Frieden' als akustisches und visuelles Dokument," *Zeithistorische Forschungen/Studies in Contemporary History* 9/1 (2012): 168–74.

[174] "Gemeinsam gegen Atomraketen," Liederheft, SB 544, Box 6, HIS.

[175] On this critique, see Frederike Brühöfener, "Politics of Emotion. Journalistic Reflections on the Emotionality of the West German Peace Movement, 1979–1984," *German Politics and Society* 33/4 (2015): 97–111.

decision thus also became a contest between competing emotional regimes and over the role of emotions in democratic politics more generally.

The reliance on an emotional politics certainly contributed to the peace movement's success in mobilizing large segments of West German society. While there had been 2,800 protest events per year between 1975 and 1978, their numbers tripled to 9,327 demonstrations in 1983.[176] The peace movement's mobilizing force partly rested on its broad social and political basis. The emphasis on fear as a new form of rationality and the public performance of this emotion linked different strands of the movement, which ran the gamut from left-wing communists to church and conservative circles. More than 30 different groups were represented in a "coordination committee" of the peace movement.[177] While the German Communist Party played an important role, the movement was too heterogeneous ideologically for forces subservient to Moscow to control it, as some contemporaries and later historians have claimed.[178]

The movement combined at least three different major strands. First, it originated from the already existing environmental movement. The discussion about the neutron bomb in 1977 served as an important link between the environmental movement and the peace movement. This debate combined criticism of the civilian use of nuclear energy with criticism of nuclear weapons.[179] The opposition to the neutron bomb also marked a transition to an apocalyptic discourse. Critics feared that humanity only had "a grace period of a few years" left if the "antimilitarist movement" failed to create a broad "awareness of the danger" of nuclear weapons.[180] Much like counter-experts in the struggle over nuclear power, counter-experts of the peace movement emphasized the "degree of irrationality" inherent in the logic of deterrence.[181] The campaigns against the dying of the forests and against the NATO double-track decision also employed similar rhetoric and symbols.[182] Second, the peace movement enjoyed broad support within the left-green milieu, especially among the new party, *Die Grünen*.

---

[176] Michael Sturm, "Polizei und Friedensbewegung," in Becker-Schaum, et al., eds, *"Entrüstet Euch!", Nuklearkrise, NATODoppelbeschluss und Friedensbewegung, 278.*

[177] Zepp, "Ratio der Angst. Die intellektuellen Grundlagen der Friedensbewegung," in ibid. 135–50, Becker-Schaum, "Die institutionelle Organisation der Friedensbewegung," in ibid. 151–68.

[178] For example, Jeffrey Herf, *War by Other Means: Soviet Power, West German Resistance, and the Battle of the Euromissiles* (New York: The Free Press, 1991).

[179] Susanne Schregel, "Konjunktur der Angst. 'Politik der Subjektivität' und 'neue Friedensbewegung,'" in Greiner et al., eds, *Angst im Kalten Krieg* (Hamburg: Hamburger Edition, 2009), 53.

[180] Cited in Andreas Pettenkofer, "Erwartung der Katastrophe, Erinnerung der Katastrophe. Die apokalyptische Kosmologie der westdeutschen Umweltbewegung und die Besonderheiten des deutschen Risikodiskurses," in Lars Clausen, Elke M. Geenen, Elísio Macamo, eds, *Entsetzliche soziale Prozesse. Theorie und Empirie der Katastrophen* (Münster: Lit Verlag, 2003), 196.

[181] Erhard Eppler, "Friedensbewegung," in Jens, ed., *In letzter Stunde,* 143–66, quotations on 150, 154.

[182] Becker-Schaum, "Die institutionelle Organisation der Friedensbewegung," in Becker-Schaum et al., eds, *"Entrüstet Euch!,"* 151–68.

Yet perhaps even more important was the growing support for the peace movement within the Social Democratic Party (SPD). After the party lost power to a new center-right government under Helmut Kohl (CDU), the SPD increasingly distanced itself from the dual-track decision, even though its initiator had been the former SPD Chancellor Helmut Schmidt. Finally, the mobilizing force of the peace movement extended far into the middle classes of West German society. The Christian churches, in particular, were generally supportive of the movement. Thirteen out of 17 regional Protestant churches took part in actions of the peace movement. Church groups also participated in over 90 per cent of the so-called "peace weeks."[183] Sections of the Catholic church opened up to the peace movement as well. In the early 1980s, for example, a "peace truck" of Catholic rural youth movement toured through Germany and propagated the ideas of the peace movement in rural areas.[184]

Another important aspect of fear in the peace movement was the rejection of the state's promise of security, especially through civil defense. As described in Chapter 3, civil defense had been controversial since its reintroduction in the late 1950s. The limited acceptance of civil defense from the 1960s onward was a consequence of declining Cold War fears. By reviving earlier arguments, the peace movement of the 1980s renewed the criticism of civil defense. Peace activists bemoaned the inclusion of nuclear warfare in civil defense planning and stressed instead the impossibility of protection in the case of a nuclear war. They denounced civil defense as part of a militarization of society and drew explicit links to civil defense practices in the Third Reich.[185] One of the stated goals of civil defense—the propagation of cool rational behavior during a military crisis situation and the avoidance of popular panic—now appeared as a form of suppressing political dissent. For the peace movement, excessive fear, even panic, constituted an entirely normal, healthy reaction to the threat of nuclear war.[186] Criticism also targeted the construction of bunkers as a civil defense measure. Because of the high costs, the federal government had suspended the legal obligation to include bunkers in new construction projects as mandated by the Civil Defense Law from 1957. Peace activists not only criticized the inadequate supply of bunkers but—citing doctors and architects—also questioned whether bunkers could offer protection at all. Bunkers might not withstand the tremendous pressure wave of a nuclear blast and they would not offer a chance for the long-term survival of radioactive contamination. For the peace movement, bunkers signified a

---

[183] Sebastian Kalden and Jan Ole Wiechmann, "Kirchen," in ibid., 247–61, quotation on 249.

[184] Friedensmobil der Katholischen Landjugendbewegung Deutschlands, HIS, KLB, in Sbc 450.

[185] Martin Diebel, *Atomkrieg und andere Katastrophen. Zivil- und Katastrophenschutz in der Bundesrepublik und Großbritannien nach 1945* (Paderborn: Schöningh, 2017), 211–13.

[186] On changing conceptions of panic and military psychiatry in the 1980s, see my essay, "The Concept of Panic," in Biess and Gross, eds, *Science and Emotions after 1945*, 181–205, especially 199–200.

"paradoxical site of helplessness," which did not represent the "survivability" of war but rather the "nowhere of protection." As in the 1960s, activists criticized the government bunker in the Ahr valley, although not because it offered dispropor- tionate protection for political elites but because its sheer existence seemed to prove the federal government was planning for its political survival of a nuclear war.[187] As in the 1950s, the increasing fear of war called into question the state's promise of security.

The enormous mass peace demonstrations of the first half of the 1980s reflected the mobilizing force of fear. As many as 300,000 participants attended a demon- stration in Bonn on October 10, 1981, and 400,000 people demonstrated in Bonn on the occasion of the NATO summit on June 10, 1982. The peace movement reached its climax in the fall of 1983, which preceded the stationing decision of the West German parliament in November 1983, with up to 500,000 people dem- onstrating. The peace movement's most spectacular action was a human chain of up to 250,000 people extending over more than 100 kilometers between Stuttgart, the site of NATO headquarters in Europe, and the Wiley barracks in Neu-Ulm, a prospective site of US nuclear missiles.[188] To this day, these were by far the largest demonstrations in the history of the Federal Republic.

For the peace movement, this mass mobilization signified the "concerns and legitimate fears of men and women of this country." These attitudes stood in con- trast to the "deadly cynicism" of the West German federal government and the "despisers of human beings" (*Menschenverächter*) such as Ronald Reagan or US Secretary of Defense Caspar Weinberger.[189] This moral antagonism was typical of the peace movement. Many flyers of the movement entailed comics that reflected the movement's claim to humanity and to transcending Cold War ideologies. The most common one depicted a motley crowd of men and women, adults and chil- dren, who joined forces to topple a nuclear missile that state officials and police forces failed to hold up. Despite the huge crowds mobilized by the peace move- ment, these representations recognized demonstrators as individuals.

The goal of the demonstrations was not just to prevent the stationing of new nuclear weapons but to organize "peace." In fact, activists like Matthias Horx warned as early as 1981 against a fixation on the fear of nuclear weapons. Instead, a looming nuclear war needed to be understood as the logical consequence of an ideology of domination over nature and unlimited growth. Its rejection required not just the public performance of fear or mass demonstrations but also a "more comprehensive notion of peace," which would have to include a social and

[187] On the entire paragragh, see Schregel, *Der Atomkrieg vor der Wohnungstür*, 186–225, quotation on 225, and Claudia Kemper, "Zivilschutz," in Becker-Schaum et al., eds, *"Entrüstet Euch!"* 309–24.
[188] Figures in Michael Sturm, "Polizei und Friedensbewegung," in ibid. 277–93, here 279, Conze et al., "Introduction" in ibid. 1–25.
[189] "Ermutigung," BfZ, 2517.

Figure 8.3. Human chain on October 22, 1983, between Neu-Ulm and Stuttgart.

The peace movement was the largest protest movement in the history of the Federal Republic—250,000 people participated in this human chain. The movement was based on the public display of fear, which assumed the character of a higher form of rationality. The author and his future wife were both there at different locations.

Source: dpa Picture-Alliance, No. 13694531.

ecological dimension as well.[190] Still, this vision of peace as an alternative social order remained rather vague. It included not just the absence of war but also the reduction and elimination of material hardship, the end of any form of oppression, and the protection of human rights and of the environment.[191] The 68ers had already combined utopia and paranoia in a peculiar fashion, as we have seen in Chapter 6. While the fears of the peace movement went much further than those of the "68ers" and assumed truly apocalyptic dimensions, their utopian vision of peace was more limited. It did not entail grandiose visions of revolution and a new human being but a more defensive vision of the good life, one that was more rooted in local activism, interpersonal relations, and the politics of daily life.

In the end, traditional diplomacy, not activism, solved the nuclear crisis of the 1980s. Mikhail Gorbachev, who was appointed as secretary-general of the Soviet Communist Party in March 1985, pursued a reform policy that also entailed a foreign policy dimension. It ultimately entailed the withdrawal of all

---

[190] Paul Planet, Matthias Horx, "Nachrichten vom großen Ende, Teil 1," *Pflasterstrand* 105 (1981), 18–22.

[191] Pershing, Cruise Missiles, Nein—Leistet Widerstand! BfZ, 1820.

intermediate-range land-based missiles from Europe, which had been the goal of the peace movement all along. After some hesitation, US President Ronald Reagan eventually accepted Gorbachev's disarmament proposals and at least partially refuted the peace movement's image of him as a warmonger. In December 1987, both leaders signed the Intermediate-Range Nuclear Forces (INF) Treaty, which stipulated a "zero solution"—that is, the withdrawal of all land-based intermediate-range missiles from the European continent.[192] As a result of this relaxation of foreign policy, which was hardly foreseeable at the beginning of the decade, the wave of fear abated and a new optimism emerged among West German citizens in the second half of the1980s. For example, in 1985, almost twice as many Germans (61 per cent) stated that they looked to the future with optimism as in 1981 (when it was 32 per cent).[193] These numbers speak to the transient quality of political mobilization based on fear. The focus on a specific anxiety-inducing event, such as the planned missile deployment in the fall of 1983, was well suited for a temporary mass mobilization but not for the creation of a sustainable movement, even though political parties such as the SPD and the Greens took up the arguments of the peace movement. The peace movement also declined in response to its short-term political failure—that is, the impossibility of preventing the decision of the *Bundestag* approving the stationing of US nuclear missiles on West German territory. The general "climate" of worry and fear that the peace movement sought to create in light of the nuclear danger also dissipated rather quickly again, in part because the fearful futures culminating in an apocalyptic nuclear war, which the movement so vividly imagined, did not materialize.

That said, Chernobyl to some extent realized the peace movement's fears when an explosion occurred in the Ukrainian nuclear power plant in Chernobyl the night of April 25, 1986. The melting of the nuclear core and the release of radioactive substances was a nuclear catastrophe. A radioactive cloud moved to Central Europe and led, in early May, to increased radioactivity readings in Germany as well.[194] The invisibility of the threat—that is, the impossibility to detect radioactivity with the senses—prompted significant popular fear at the time.[195] However, there was no mass mobilization of West Germans in response to the accident at Chernobyl at this time. The political instrument of mass demonstrations, it seems, had been exhausted.

---

[192] Florian Pressler, "Ein Sieg für die Rüstungskontrolle. Die 1980er Jahre und das internationale politische System," in Becker-Schaum et al., eds, *"Entrüstet Euch!"* 339–53.

[193] Wirsching, *Abschied vom Provisorium*, 434.

[194] See Melanie Arndt, *Tschernobyl. Auswirkungen des Reaktorunfalls auf die Bundesrepublik Deutschland und die DDR* (Erfurt: Landeszentrale für politische Bildung, 2012) (Kindle edn), 364–82, Brüggemeier, *Tschernobyl, 26. April 1986*.

[195] Augustine, *Taking on Technocracy*, 161–6.

The imagined catastrophe that the peace and environmental movements envisioned appears to have shaped the ability to respond to an actually occurring catastrophe. For many activists, Chernobyl simply confirmed their long-held fears, including their long-held impression that the state was simply not prepared to deal with a nuclear accident. As much as the increased radioactivity measurements, the inconsistent and, at times, chaotic reaction of state officials provoked fear and distrust among the population. Federal, state, and local authorities responded very differently to increased radioactivity. While the conservative Federal Interior Minister Friedrich Zimmermann (CSU) sought to calm the population and denied that there was any radioactive danger, the Red–Green coalition in the state of Hesse shut down sports and leisure facilities. The federal government defined the maximum level of radioactivity in milk to be 500 becquerels per liter, while the maximum value in Hesse was 20 becquerels. The assessment of danger thus differed widely between the CDU/CSU-led federal government and the red-green state government with Environment Minister Joschka Fischer in Hesse.[196] Science, too, offered no consolations. Scientists' assessments of the danger related to exposure to radioactivity differed widely. "Two experts, three opinions," a greengrocer from Hanover concluded, speaking to a *Der Spiegel* reporter.[197] This persistent uncertainty about the actual extent of the threat may also have prevented a collective response similar to the peace movement. Still, the catastrophe in Chernobyl produced a significant change in the attitude of West Germans toward nuclear power. While 53 per cent of Germans were in favor of building new nuclear power plants in March 1982, only 29 per cent favored it in May 1986. Two-thirds of Germans favored the decommissioning of all nuclear power plants either immediately or after a transitional period.[198]

The Chernobyl catastrophe lent immediate plausibility to contemporary social science diagnoses such as sociologist Ulrich Beck's description of a "risk society," which he published shortly before the nuclear accident in 1986. In the risk society, social inequality not only resulted from traditional class stratification but rather from the unequal distribution of risks that crossed class boundaries. Individuals, however, cannot perceive these risks directly but rely on scientific expertise in order to do so. Commenting on the aftermath of Chernobyl, Beck said that the notion of an "(industrial) risk society" entailed a "bitter aftertaste of truth" and read like a "flat description of the present."[199] Beck had developed the theory of risk society as a new stage in the process of "self-reflective

---

[196] Arndt, *Tschernobyl in Deutschland* (Kindle edn), 688–850, Augustine, *Taking on Technocracy*, 169–70. The lack of coordination was one reason for the establishment of a Federal Environmental Ministry one week later.

[197] "Die Sache hat uns kalt erwischt," *Der Spiegel* 40/20 (1986): 24.

[198] "Neue Mehrheit für den Ausstieg," *Der Spiegel* 40/20 (1986): 28–32, Arndt, *Tschernobyl in Deutschland*, 893–4 (Kindle edn).

[199] Ulrich Beck, *Risikogesellschaft. Auf dem Weg in eine andere Moderne* (Frankfurt a/M: Suhrkamp, 1986), 10.

modernization." Precisely because risks become part of the self-description of modern societies, they signify, according to Beck, a new form of modernity, a reflexive modernity. This modernity always entails a catastrophic dimension, because it relates significantly to future risks that need to be avoided at all costs.

The similarity of Beck's social theory and the history of fear in the Federal Republic is not accidental. Beck identified the development from the "community of scarcity" in class society to a "community of fear" in the risk society as an essential aspect of this new form of modernity, even though he remained unclear about the political implications of a politics of fear.[200] As we have seen, a fearful anticipation of the future constituted a constant and important element in the history of the Federal Republic. The uncertainties that defined West German postwar history thus also shaped Beck's sociological diagnosis. The "risk society" was not only a general theory of modernity but also a product of particular historical and national contexts—that is, the history of fear in the Federal Republic and especially the apocalyptic fears of the 1980s.[201] This historical context makes it possible to historicize supposedly general sociological theories such as the "risk society."[202]

The completely surprising fall of the Berlin Wall in November 1989 and ensuing German reunification stood in stark contrast to the apocalyptic predictions of the 1980s. Many activists of the peace and environmental movements, including the author of this book, needed to realize that their fearful future scenarios had not materialized. Yet, as with other cycles of fear discussed in this book, it would be wrong to dismiss the peace and environmental movements as ineffective, irrational, and irrelevant. The mobilization of millions of people in the peace movement created an awareness of the imminent danger of nuclear war and put the topic of disarmament on the agenda of international politics. Likewise, the peace movement worked across the Iron Curtain. It undermined the Eastern image of an aggressive and militant West and inspired a similar protest movement in the East that then also turned against Soviet missiles in the GDR and in other Eastern Bloc countries. The fact that Western politicians, including the hated Reagan, took up and responded to Gorbachev's disarmament initiatives was an indirect result of massive pressure from below on democratically elected politicians, who needed to respond to popular moods. The mobilization of fear in the peace movement thus also affected those politicians, who repeatedly rejected this fear for themselves. The same applies to the environmental movement. Given the still-unresolved question of the disposal of nuclear waste and the nuclear catastrophe in Fukushima in March 2011, the anti-nuclear movement's criticism of nuclear

---

[200] Ibid. 66.

[201] On this argument, see Pettenkofer, "Erwartung der Katastrophe, Erinnerung der Katastrophe."

[202] On this aspect of contemporary history, see Rüdiger Graf, Kim Christian Priemel, "Zeitgeschichte in der Welt der Sozialwissenschaften. Legitimität und Originalität einer Disziplin," *Vierteljahreshefte für Zeitgeschichte* 59/4 (2011): 479-508.

energy from the seventies onward actually appears quite forward-looking.[203] Moreover, the rupture of 1989–90 was not absolute. Instead, the culture of fear from the 1980s continued into the Berlin Republic. As Chapter 9 will show, it shaped the popular protests against the Iraq wars in 1991 and 2003. In addition, the final abolition of nuclear power in the aftermath of the Fukushima accident in 2011 marked a line of continuity that extended from the 1970s to the Berlin Republic.

As this book has sought to demonstrate, the history of the "old" Federal Republic is also the history of its fears. For West Germans, postwar history did not just consist of a steady upward trend and progressive democratization. It was also a history of episodes of fear, which occasionally turned into panic, horror scenarios, and apocalyptic visions. These cycles of fear shaped the process of democratization at every turn. Fear was an essential, perhaps even a decisive, aspect of post-1945 German political culture. But is this still the case in contemporary Germany? To what extent did the culture of fear of the old Federal Republic live on in the post-1990 Berlin Republic? And how does that culture shape, if at all, contemporary fears? The following chapter analyzes the Federal Republic's history of fear from German unification up to our present time.

---

[203] This example also illustrates the transient and historically specific nature of conceptions of rationality. Hans-Ulrich Wehler, *Deutsche Gesellschaftsgeschichte. Fünfter Band: Bundesrepublik und DDR, 1949–1990* (Munich: C.H.Beck, 2008), 61, characterizes opponents of nuclear energy as "not open to rational arguments."

9

German *Angst*

In September 2018, the annual poll by the R&V insurance company on the fears of the Germans yielded a surprising result. The greatest fear of the Germans in 2018 did not consist of terrorism, climate change, or economic decline, but rather in the threat of a more dangerous world as a result of the policies of US President Donald Trump. This finding immediately brought back the notion of a specific "German angst," this time prompted by the erratic policy of the United States.[1] The fact that US policies topped the list of German fears illustrates that many of the parameters that have defined the history of the Federal Republic until recently have collapsed. Many postwar Germans had imagined the United States as the embodiment of a "normal" Western liberal democratic order, to which the Federal Republic would gravitate. And historians liked to tell the Federal Republic's history as one of "Westernization" or "Americanization." But the rise of new authoritarianism and right-wing populism in the US and other Western countries increasingly called into question the basic assumptions of this postwar liberal order. Whereas the anxiety that "Bonn" could become "Weimar" constituted a hallmark of the culture of fear in the Federal Republic, critical voices within the US now began to invoke "Trump's Weimar America."[2] While West Germans' trust in the US security guarantees had contained, at least temporarily, German fears throughout the Cold War, the US was again perceived, as in the peace movement of the 1980s, as a major threat to world peace. More than at any other moment in the postwar period, the rise of right-wing populism in the US and elsewhere undermined the certainties of the post-war order. This development reminds us that the future of liberal democracy is by no means certain. A gradual (or sudden) descent into authoritarianism has again emerged as a distinct possibility. This contemporary predicament brings our present closer to the fears of the old Federal Republic, making them again more comprehensible and perhaps more pertinent.

---

[1] "Trump stachelt die 'German angst' an," September 6, 2018, https://www.dw.com/de/trump-stachelt-die-german-angst-an/a-45381871 (last accessed March 5, 2020). The R&V study is based on 2,335 people aged 14 years and older (https://www.ruv.de/presse/aengste-der-deutschen, last accessed March 5, 2020). The 2019 version of the study registered a decline in the overall level of fear and listed the fear of refugees as the most important fear, slightly ahead of the fear of the consequences of Trump's policies.

[2] See, for example, Roger Cohen, "Trump's Weimar America," *New York Times*, December 14, 2016.

German Angst: Fear and Democracy in the Federal Republic of Germany. Frank Biess, Oxford University Press (2020).
© Frank Biess.
DOI: 10.1093/oso/9780198714187.001.0001

German angst and Its Historical Context

The notion of a German angst was an invention of the 1980s and 1990s. As this book has demonstrated, the perception of a specifically German inclination to fear and anxiety has been part of West German self-observation since 1945. It resulted from a specific uncertainty regarding the future, an interplay of memories of the past and anticipations of the future. The idea of a national collective pathology, a German angst, however, is of more recent origins. It emerged in the 1980s in the context of ecological fears and the peace movement, as discussed in the previous chapter, and it was part and parcel of the culture of fear of the 1980s. Contemporary perceptions in Germany and abroad at the time condensed environmental fears, such as those of the death of the forest or the mass mobilization in the peace movement, into the idea of a special German angst.

German angst featured especially prominently in public debates surrounding the first Gulf War in 1991. The Federal Republic provided financial and logistical, but not military support, to this American-led campaign. The Gulf War reactivated the apocalyptic fears of the 1980s peace movement. These fears featured prominently, for example, in the diary of 19-year-old Christiane M. In December 1990, shortly before the US ultimatum to Iraq to withdraw from Kuwait expired, she described the impending US war as "a global decision." A few days later, she feared nothing less than "World War III with nuclear bombs, environmental disasters triggered by burning oil fields, a climate catastrophe." In short, an "end of the world *would be* possible" (emphasis in original).[3] The protests against the Gulf War in 1991 perpetuated the apocalyptic expressions of fear from the 1980s.[4] On January 26, 1991, for example, almost 200,000 people demonstrated in Bonn against the Gulf War. Two-thirds of Germans said they were "afraid" because of the Gulf War, even though a majority (three-quarters in January 1991, which slipped to two-thirds in February) supported the military intervention.[5] The disturbing aspect of this feeling of fear lay in the fact that it derived from a war that a majority of Germans appear to have supported.

This mobilization of the culture of fear of the 1980s by a new peace movement led to the perception of Germans as particularly anxiety-ridden even outside their country. After traveling in the south-western US in January 1991, the German tourist Ursula P. reported: "The German 'angst' (this noun in small letters) has become a technical term in American language. Political scientists and psychologists alike use it in their commentaries. It denotes a certain desire for fear, the cult of fear so to speak."[6] Thus the notion of a German angst essentially served as a

---

[3] Diary, Christiane M., entry December 25, 1990, January 3, 1991, DTA, Nr. 936, I,7.
[4] Jennifer Allen, "Against the 1989/90 Ending Myth," *Central European History* 52/1 (2019): 125–47.
[5] Harald Schoen, "Beeinflusst Angst politische Einstellungen? Eine Analyse der öffentlichen Meinung während des Golfkriegs 1991," *Politische Vierteljahresschrift* 47/3 (2006): 449.
[6] Ursula P., "Erlebnisse und Wahrnehmungen in einem kriegführenden Land," DTA, Nr. 1759, 7.

Figure 9.1. Demonstration against the Gulf War in Frankfurt, January 1991.

The protests against the Gulf War in 1991 continued the culture of fear from the peace movement of the 1980s. The protests fueled the notion of a "German angst" that conservative critics used to denounce the peace movement.

Source: Bpk-Bildagentur, No. 30014147.

critique of German non-participation in the Iraq War in Germany as well as abroad.[7] The Google Ngram viewer, which measures the frequency of specific terms in German-language publications, also confirms this thesis. The use of the concept of German angst appears for the first time in the late 1970s, becomes more frequent during the 1980s, but increases sharply during the early 1990s.

In the ensuing years, German angst became mostly a tool for conservative critiques of left-wing pacifism and alleged skepticism toward technological progress. For example, on the occasion of a new building for the Max Planck Society in Munich, Bavarian Prime Minister Edmund Stoiber criticized an ostensible "hostility toward technology," "bureaucracy," and "encrusted structures at the universities" as evidence of an "internationally recognized 'German angst'."[8] The historian and former adviser of Chancellor Helmut Kohl, Michael Stürmer, repeatedly criticized a supposedly typical German despondency and fear that stood in the way of a

---

[7] Daniel Bax, "Generation Golfkrieg," *die tageszeitung*, August 24, 2001, on the debate about the first Gulf War, see Ulrich Herbert, *Geschichte Deutschlands im 20. Jahrhundert* (Munich: C.H.Beck, 2014), 1159–64.

[8] "Lob für Max-Planck-Gesellschaft. Forschung statt 'German angst'. Stoiber wettert gegen hemmende Technikfeindlichkeit—Neuer Bau," *Nürnberger Nachrichten*, March 14, 1996.

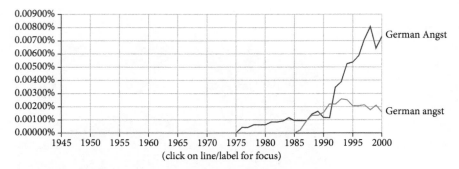

Figure 9.2. Google Ngram viewer "German Angst" and "German angst."

Source: https://books.google.com/ngrams/graph?content=German+Angst%2C+German+angst
&year_start=1800&year_end=2000&corpus=20&smoothing=3&share=&direct_
url=t1%3B%2CGerman%20Angst%3B%2Cc0%3B.t1%3B%2CGerman%20angst%3B%2Cc0 (last
accessed March 11, 2020).

more extensive military and foreign policy commitment of the Federal Republic.[9] As late as 2017, the campaign platform of the Free Democratic Party operated with the slogan, "German courage instead of German angst."[10] In these perceptions, the notion of German angst served as a way to discredit West German pacificism and environmental consciousness as nothing less than a collective pathology. Conservatives thus sought to counter the West German culture of fear of the 1980s by (re)pathologizing fear and turning it into a kind of national disease. In so doing, they were able to count on the support of transnational allies in the US and other Western countries, who denounced German military reticence as indication of a pathological fear of all things military. This rhetorical strategy made it possible for West German conservatives to denounce the environmental and peace movements as psychopathological disorders. It also enabled them to reject the mobilization of Holocaust memory for the sake of pacifism, and allowed them to assert a German identity that was very much predicated on overcoming rather than remembering the past. If German angst was linked to a traumatic persistence of the German past into the present, then overcoming German angst implied moving out of the shadow of the past and arriving at a less complicated national identity, which would then also enable a more active military role for the newly unified Federal Republic.

To this day, the thesis of a specific German angst serves to discredit German pacifism and alleged hostility toward scientific and technical progress. *Spiegel*

---

[9] Michael Stürmer, "'German Angst': Deutschland, die Hochburg der Skepsis," *Welt Online*, January 13, 2013, Michael Stürmer, "Dem Zeitgeist nicht zu schmeicheln muss gestattet sein," *Welt am Sonntag*, April 9, 2000.

[10] Richard Herzinger, "Die Liberalen machen sich locker; Weg mit der 'German angst'," *Die Welt*, May 18, 2015, "FDP will für 'German Mut' statt 'German Angst' werben. Liberale stellen Entwurf für Wahlprogramm vor," *Agence France Presse—German*, March 31, 2017.

journalist Jan Fleischhauer argued, for example, that the "lust for anxiety" made the "Left-Green milieu great."[11] As we have seen, the left-alternative milieu was indeed a source of expressive emotional culture and of a more positive evaluation of anxiety. But, as this book has shown, fear has never been the exclusive purview of the Left. A conservative mobilization of fears had a long tradition in the Federal Republic—for example, in the anti-Communism of the 1950s and the reaction to the student movement and to Red Army Faction (RAF) terrorism in the 1970s. Political fears in the Federal Republic were always part of a dialectic, in which the fears of one side mobilized those of the other and vice versa. Fear was therefore never the privilege—nor the pathology—of just one political camp but rather an integral part of both sides of the Left/Right divide. Within this dialectic of reciprocal expressions of anxiety and apprehension, the reference to German angst served (and continues to serve) a very specific political function: that of criticizing a supposedly left-wing culture of fear. It was only very recently that conservatives claimed the concept of German angst for themselves—namely, in response to the "refugee crisis" of 2015–16. In an interesting reversal, *Welt* journalist Dirk Schümer conceded that past left-wing fears of environmental damage or war had been rather justified—for example, with respect to the Iraq War. He also praised neurobiologists and psychologists who had "long rehabilitated" the emotion of fear. At the same time, he propagated a right-wing version of German angst that centered on fears of migration. This fear, he argued, was equally justified when "housing facilities for refugees and migrants are established in every town and village."[12]

The concept of German angst also gained currency after reunification because it formed the counterpart to the Berlin Republic's longing for "normalcy." Contemporaries as well as later historians described the aftermath of unification as a period of a new, finally attained normalcy. After all the special paths and catastrophes of the recent past, the self-description of being neither a "particularly exemplary model" nor featuring an "alarming political backwardness" was deeply reassuring.[13] The Berlin Republic thus radiated a "competent normalcy": it was simply "normal and perhaps a bit boring."[14] The alleged end of German angst constituted an essential element of this newly diagnosed normalcy. In 2009, the *Zeit* journalist Ulrich Greiner, as well as the *New York Times* correspondent Roger Cohen, interpreted Germans' relatively calm reaction to the international financial crisis as an indication of the end of German angst. For Greiner, Chancellor Merkel's "sober charm" and "embodied measurement" (*wandelnde[s] Augenmaß*)

[11] Jan Fleischhauer, "Merkels Mediengroupies: Gute Ängste, schlechte Ängste," *Der Spiegel*, July 5, 2018.

[12] Dirk Schümer, "Deutsche Seele. Warum die 'German Angst' berechtigt und klug ist," *Welt Online*, December 21, 2015.

[13] Edgar Wolfrum, *Die geglückte Demokratie. Geschichte der Bundesrepublik Deutschland von ihren Anfängen bis zur Gegenwart* (Stuttgart: Klett-Cotta, 2006), 16.

[14] Konrad H. Jarausch, "The Federal Republic at Sixty. Popular Myths, Actual Accomplishments, and Competing Interpretations," *German Politics and Society* 28/94 (2010): 25.

constituted the best proof of a long-desired "normalization."[15] The perception of a new normalcy thus went along with a sense that a particular German inclination toward fear and anxiety had come to an end at last.

The recurring assertion of German normalcy, however, raised the question: how normal is a normalcy that needs to be publicly asserted time and again?[16] It was also not clear how this supposed normalcy was actually defined. If it denoted the longed-for convergence of the Federal Republic with "the West," then this normative model was undergoing dramatic changes. In this sense, achieving a supposed normalcy entailed adapting to a normative framework that appeared to be falling apart. On the other hand, as the historian Norbert Frei recently noted, the Federal Republic has become "normal in ways that no democrat could wish for" in that a right-wing populist movement similar to those in other European countries and the US has emerged.[17] Instead of seeing the history of the Federal Republic as converging with a vaguely defined and increasingly questionable Western "normalcy," it seems methodologically more innovative and productive to accept the openness of the future.[18]

The history of fear and anxiety may not be over either. Contrary to what contemporaries stated at the time, the history of fear did not end with the alleged "normalcy" of the Berlin Republic. But, since 2011, according to the R&V study, fears and anxiety increasingly diverged from national frames of reference and assumed international and transnational dimensions. Before Donald Trump, the European Union (EU) debt crisis took the top spot from 2011 to 2015, and terrorism was the top concern in 2016 and 2017. After the 1960s, fears and anxiety in the Federal Republic were defined by their increasingly abstract and invisible nature. Future scenarios, such as automation or radioactive poisoning, could no longer be perceived directly but needed to rely on experts to assess. In a time of rapidly accelerating global connections, it is now, above all, the spatial uncertainty, the difficulty to locate fears at a particular place, that seems particularly disturbing. The traditional instruments of the nation state were no longer capable of containing these fears. Their disturbing quality derived from the feeling of individual and national loss of control, a sense of powerlessness that then fueled anxieties and fears. No wonder, then, that one reaction to such globalized fears lay in the creation of new internal or external boundaries, such as the defense of territoriality through border fortifications and walls, or the search for a new national or ethnic collective. This chapter analyzes the ways in which new kinds

---

[15] Ulrich Greiner, "Was ist aus der German Angst geworden?" *Die Zeit*, May 14, 2009, Roger Cohen, "German Angst," *Süddeutsche Zeitung*, March 19, 2009.

[16] For a similar argument with respect to the end of the "postwar," see Klaus Naumann, "Die Frage nach dem Ende. Von der unbestimmten Dauer der Nachkriegszeit," *Mittelweg 36*, 8/1 (1999): 21–32.

[17] Norbert Frei, "Die blinden Flecken der Historiker," *Süddeutsche Zeitung*, September 16, 2018.

[18] On this problem, Rüdiger Graf, "Die Unkenntnis der Zukunft und der Zukunftsbezug der Zeitgeschichte," in Lucian Hölscher, ed., *Die Zukunft des 20. Jahrhunderts. Dimensionen einer historischen Zukunftsforschung (Frankfurt: Campus). Dimensionen einer historischen Zukunftsforschung* (Frankfurt a/M: Campus, 2017), 303–19.

of fear have shaken the Berlin Republic since reunification. The new German fears resulted from the problem of defining the newly reunified Germany's role in the world as well as from the increasing presence of "the world" in Germany— namely, through immigrants and refugees. The chapter then analyzes the rise of the populist Right as a movement of fear. It also compares and contrasts right-wing fears of refugees and immigration with another contemporary fear—that of climate change. The chapter concludes with some speculations about the possibilities of a democratic politics of emotions in the present.

Deterritorialized Fears

In the 1990s, the contrast between external and internal fears, which had been central to the history of fear in the old Federal Republic, gradually dissolved. As we have seen, in the 1940s and 1950s, fears resulted mainly from the uncertain external situation of the Federal Republic as a result of defeat, occupation, and the onset of the Cold War. From the 1960s onward, however, "inner" fears that emanated from within society or even from within individual subjects came increasingly into view. By the 1980s, this distinction began to dissolve. Internal ecological fears, for example, derived from external hazards such as "acid rain" or the radioactive cloud after Chernobyl. A similar process—that is, the perception of external dangers such as toxic substances in the air or the food that caused "inner" damage—occurred with respect to contemporary body fears, which, like cancer, played an important role in defining fears. Cross-border infectious diseases rather than cancer, moreover, now became the focus of media attention, starting with AIDS in the 1980s, then BSE, Avian Influenza, SARS, Ebola, and, most recently, as this book goes to press, the global Coronavirus pandemic. Cultural responses to such diseases provided the metaphors of containment, fortification, and quarantine, which then were deployed not just against biological pathogens but also against migrants and refugees. Such concerns became the elements of what the sociologist Ulrich Bröckling characterized as a "regime of immunization" as one characteristic way of anticipating future dangers.[19] By the 1990s, the concept of "globalization" increasingly provided the conceptual framework to understand a new interrelationship between "outside" and "inside."[20]

The deterritorialization of threats also manifested itself in new forms of terrorism. A series of terrorist attacks occurred since 2015 and many, although not all of them, were committed by Islamic extremists. The list of attacks constitutes a chronicle of a new kind of horror in European metropolises: the attack on the

---

[19] Bröckling, cited in Eva Horn, *Zukunft als Katastrophe* (Frankfurt a/M: S. Fischer, 2014), 302–4.
[20] Jan Eckel, "'Alles hängt mit allem zusammen.' Zur Historisierung des Globalisierungsdiskurses der 1990er und 2000er Jahre," *Historische Zeitschrift* 307/1 (2018): 42–78.

satirical magazine *Charlie Hebdo*, in Paris in January 2015 (12 deaths); a series of coordinated attacks in Paris on November 13, 2005 (a total of 130 deaths and hundreds injured); an attack with a lorry in Nice, France, on July 14, 2016 (86 deaths, 434 injured); suicide bomber attacks in Brussels on March 22, 2016 (35 deaths, including 3 suicide bombers, and 340 people injured); an attack in Manchester on May 22, 2017 (30 deaths, including 1 suicide bomber, and 59 injured); another lorry attack in Barcelona on August 17, 2017 (13 deaths, 130 injured).[21] Germany did not remain immune from such attacks. After a series of smaller terror attacks in the summer of 2016, an attack on the Christmas market in Berlin on December 19 of the same year killed a total of 12 people and injured 56. While the total number of victims of terrorism actually declined in the twenty-first century, it became more unpredictable and was no longer confined to regional acts of terror such as those committed by ETA in Spain or the IRA in the United Kingdom.[22] More than ever, the autotelic nature of terrorist violence became apparent: its sole purpose consisted of inciting fear among civilian populations who could become victims of terror at any time and in any place. A profound and visceral sense of physical insecurity thus accompanied a broader sense of insecurity as a result of accelerated globalization. While these incidents clearly fueled right-wing populists' efforts to mobilize fear of migration from Islamic countries in general, too-overt attempts at exploiting these tragedies also failed. In Germany, for example, the statement by the North Rhine-Westphalian leader of the AfD (Alternative for Germany) that the deaths at the Berlin Christmas market were "Merkel's deaths" was widely condemned. In fact, media reports categorized the popular reactions to terror attacks in Germany as "remarkably calm" and as exhibiting an "astonishing resistance to fear."[23] As in the case of previous catastrophes, such as the nuclear accident in Chernobyl in 1986, Germans' anxieties about imagined catastrophes in the future appeared to be more intense than their reaction to actual incidents of catastrophic violence. Perhaps the habituation to fearful and often apocalyptic scenarios for the future enabled many postwar Germans to face actually occurring crises more calmly and with more equanimity.

These terror attacks went along with an expansion of state control and enhanced global surveillance mechanisms in the so-called "war on terror."[24] The revelations of Edward Snowden, a former intelligence officer in the US National Security Agency, in the spring and summer of 2013 revealed the extent of this global surveillance of international telephone and email communications. Both

---

[21] Ian Kershaw, *Rollercoaster: Europe, 1950–2017* (London: Allen Lane, 2018), 519–23.

[22] Lenz Jacobsen, "Terror in Zahlen," *Die Zeit*, March 23, 2016.

[23] First quotation: "Pure Reason. How Germans Handle Terror," *The Economist*, July 30, 2016, Peter Dausend, "Erstaunliche Angstresistenz," *Die Zeit*, December 21, 2016, "Maximal unbeeindruckt," *Der Spiegel*, December 21, 2016.

[24] Herfried Münkler, *Kriegssplitter. Die Evolution der Gewalt im 20. und 21. Jahrhundert* (Berlin: Rowohlt, 2015), 276.

the threat of terrorism, which could no longer be localized, *and* the state's response to it, especially the unprecedented extension of surveillance, induced fear and anxiety. Much like in the 1970s, the state's response to terrorism in the 2000s became a source of new fears, exacerbated by the expanded technological possibilities of the internet age.

New German *Angst* 1: Germany in the World

The issue of unified Germany's new role in the world was on the agenda of German politics especially with respect to military action abroad. During the Cold War, the impact of world politics on Germany as an object produced fear and anxiety. Now fear largely centered on the question of the Federal Republic's new role as an active subject of world politics. The participation of the German air force in the war against Serbia in March 1999 marked a key turning point. For the first time since the Second World War, the German military was engaged in war. Holocaust memory, as it had been firmly established in political culture, served as an important frame of reference for the redefinition of the Federal Republic's role in the world. Referencing Serbian action against the Albanian population in Kosovo and, less directly, the Serbian massacre of Bosnian Muslims in Srebrenica in 1995, the Green Foreign Minister Joschka Fischer privileged the command "Never again Auschwitz" over the pacifist commitment "Never again war."[25] Since Russia and China had blocked a corresponding resolution in the UN Security Council, NATO intervened in Serbia without a UN mandate. This conflict too provoked fear among 58 per cent of West Germans and 70 per cent of East Germans in May. While 70 per cent of East Germans opposed NATO air strikes against Serbia, 60 per cent of West Germans supported them.[26] Unlike during the Gulf War in 1991, however, this public sentiment did not lead to a political mobilization. There were no large-scale demonstrations against the war in Serbia. Instead, a majority of Germans, at least in the West, appear to have supported the federal government's argument that Holocaust memory justified the military intervention in Serbia, even if this attitude provoked fears as well.[27]

The second Iraq War in 2003, by contrast, activated a very different relationship between memories of the past and fears of the future. The refusal of the federal government under Chancellor Gerhard Schröder (Social Democratic Party, SPD) to participate in war against Iraq was a decisive reason for the narrow election victory of the Red–Green coalition in the 2002 federal elections. It was also

[25] On the Kosovo conflict, see Herbert, *Deutsche Geschichte*, 1220–31, Edgar Wolfrum, *Rot-Grün an der Macht. Deutschland 1998–2005* (Munich: C.H.Beck, 2013), 64–109.
[26] Schoen, "Beeinflusst Angst politische Einstellungen?" 184.
[27] Wolfrum, *Rot-Grün an der Macht*, 64–109.

testimony to the Federal Republic's more independent role in world politics, especially vis-à-vis the US. On February 15, 2003, massive protests against the looming Iraq War took place worldwide. They constituted, according to social scientists, the largest protest movement in human history.[28] Yet the motivations to participate in these demonstrations varied widely. In Germany, "moral-affective reasons"—that is, fear and other emotions—dominated in comparison to other countries.[29] One reason for this emotional dimension was the link to a newly activated discourse on Germans as victims, which focused especially on Allied bombing in the Second World War. Commentators argued that contemporary fears of war converged with anxious memories of being exposed to bombing in the Second World War. Popular books such as *The Fire* by the historian Jörg Friedrich brought this historical reality to life again.[30] The opposition to the American war in Iraq coincided with a shift in German commemorative culture, which, much as it had in the 1950s, tended to emphasize again the role of Germans as victims.[31]

Unlike during the early Federal Republic, however, the category of the "traumatized victim" had undergone a dramatic expansion as a result of the "psychoboom" of the seventies. The notion that a set of very different experiences, running the gamut from divorce to torture to wartime violence, can cause prolonged psychological damage or trauma became increasingly popular since the 1990s.[32] This is why it now seemed plausible that German trauma originating from the Second World War could produce massive fears during the Iraq War 60 years later. A large-scale study of 89 German cities from 2017 actually failed to document an empirical link between higher incidences of psychiatric illness and depression as indicators of German angst, on the one hand, and extensive bombing in the Second World War, on the other.[33] Notwithstanding the methodological difficulties of empirically proving such links over more than half a century, the assertion of such a connection between memories of the past and renewed fears of war served an important function within a new commemorative culture of the early twenty-first century. The debate on the war in Iraq also converged with a new attention to so-called "war children" (*Kriegskinder*), which also arose

---

[28] Stefaan Walgrave, Dieter Rucht, "Introduction," in Stefaan Walgrave, Dieter Rucht, eds, *The World Says No to War. Demonstrations against the War on Iraq* (Minneapolis: University of Minnesota Press, 2010), xiii.

[29] Dieter Rucht, Joris Verhulst, "The Framing of Opposition to the War on Iraq," in ibid. 245.

[30] Jörg Friedrich, *Der Band. Deutschland im Bombenkrieg, 1940–1945* (Berlin: Propyläen, 2002).

[31] There is an extensive literature on this topic. For an introduction, see Robert G. Moeller, "Germans as Victims? Thoughts on a Post-Cold War History of the Second World War's Legacies," *History and Memory* 17/1–2 (2005): 147–94.

[32] Svenja Goltermann, *Opfer. Die Wahrnehmung von Krieg und Gewalt in der Moderne* (Frankfurt a/M: S. Fischer, 2017), 213–19.

[33] Martin Obschonka et al., "Did Strategic Bombing in the Second World War lead to 'German Angst'? A Large-Scale Empirical Test Across 89 German Cities," *European Journal of Personality* 31/3 (2017): 234–57.

at that time. The notion of "war children" operated with this idea of a psychic trauma as well, yet also further expanded the concept in two different ways. First, trauma, which constitutes a category of individual psychology, was now ascribed to a whole collective—namely, those born between 1928 and 1945. Second, the debate introduced the notion of an intergenerational transmission of the trauma. This then also produced another explanation of the alleged German angst. As the journalist Sabine Bode argued in her bestselling book on German angst, the war generation had passed on their "unconscious fears to their descendants," creating "collective peculiarities" among Germans.[34] In this case, German angst was not so much part of the conservative critique of left-green pacifism and skepticism toward technological progress but rather an aspect of a renewed emphasis on German suffering in the past. Not accidentally, the claim of an intergenerational transmission of suffering and trauma was modeled on the example of Holocaust victims. Independently of its potentially apologetic dimension, the idea of German angst resulted from a specific discursive and historical context of the post-unification period. German angst was a historical construct that served very specific functions in public discourse—in this case, buttressing the German claim for victimhood.

New German *Angst* 2: The World in Germany

Even more than the new role of Germany in the world, the presence of the world in Germany became an object of fear during the post-unification period. A non-European and often Muslim minority, which was increasingly perceived as the non-assimilable, incompatible "other" of European societies, advanced to be a fear object of the first order. The "refugee crisis," which began in the fall of 2015, therefore did not constitute a historical novelty. Instead, immigration had been a central feature of the Federal Republic's history, which entailed a series of "refugee crises" even before reunification. Likewise, the practice of exclusion and discrimination against strangers is deeply rooted in the history of the Federal Republic. For example, the term "economic refugee" was first applied to asylum seekers from socialist Yugoslavia in the late fifties and early sixties.[35] Then the economic crisis of the seventies prompted both the Social Democratic and Christian Democrat-led federal governments to seek to limit the influx of "guest workers" and especially of their family members, who, since 1974, have been denied work permits in Germany. This

---

[34] Sabine Bode, *Die deutsche Krankheit—German Angst* (Stuttgart: Klett-Cotta, 2006), 32–3.

[35] Lauren Stokes, "The Permanent Refugee Crisis in the Federal Republic of Germany, 1949," *Central European History* 52/1 (2019): 19–44. On the history of migration in Germany and Europe, see also Philipp Ther, *Die Außenseiter. Flucht, Flüchtlinge und Integration im modernen Europa* (Berlin: Suhrkamp, 2017) and Jan Plamper, *Das neue Wir. Warum Migration dazugehört. Eine andere Geschichte der Deutschen* (Frankfurt a/M: S. Fischer, 2019).

meant that many Turkish women especially were barred from integrating in the labor market. The center-right government under Chancellor Helmut Kohl went one step further and attempted, in 1982, to create incentives for the repatriation of up to half the Turkish population. Public policy now shifted to what historian Philipp Ther calls "deintegration." In so doing, the federal government responded to a fundamental change in the public perception of foreigners, but also contributed significantly to this more critical view of them. While only 39 per cent of Germans favored the return of guest workers to their country of origin in 1978, 80 per cent of the population held the same view in 1983.[36] This was also the time when politicians repeatedly reiterated the self-definition of the Federal Republic as "not being an immigration country."[37] However, this self-perception increasingly ran counter to the lived reality in the Federal Republic at the time: the number of foreigners in the Federal Republic had increased from 2.7 million in 1970 to 5.6 million, or 8.9 per cent of the total population in the year of reunification in 1990, largely because former guest workers now also brought their families to West Germany. As a result, foreign migrants were no longer just part of the workforce but had become a permanent factor of daily life. In 2018, over 10 million foreigners lived in the Federal Republic, most of them EU citizens (4.2 million) or from other parts of Europe (2,794 million). Approximately 1.5 million Turkish nationals made up the largest group of foreigners, and almost that number of German citizens of Turkish descent currently live in Germany as well.[38]

Especially with respect to this Turkish minority, a new perception emerged in the 1980s that defined an alleged incompatibility with Western society that was not primarily biological but cultural. Yet, the line between such cultural essentialism and biological racism remained always porous. This convergence became apparent, for example, in the Heidelberg Manifesto of a group of university professors in June 1981, which bemoaned "foreign infiltration of our language, our culture, and our nationality" and spoke out against a "multiracial society."[39] However, both forms of demarcation—cultural and racial—were intended to have the same effect and aimed at excluding, in particular, the Turkish minority.[40] Turks were increasingly subjected to an intensified form of popular racism, which occasionally also turned violent.[41] In this sense, the Muslim Turk assumed, from the 1980s onward, the position of a prominent object of fear and thus stood in the

[36] Herbert, *Geschichte Deutschlands*, 990–1, Ther, *Die Außenseiter*, 318–28, quotation on 326.
[37] Ulrich Herbert, *Geschichte der Ausländerpolitik in Deutschland. Saisonarbeiter, Zwangsarbeiter, Gastarbeiter, Flüchtlinge* (Munich: C.H.Beck, 2001), 249–62.
[38] http://www.bpb.de/nachschlagen/zahlen-und-fakten/soziale-situation-in-deutschland/61631/staatsangehoerigkeit (last accessed March 6, 2020).
[39] "Heidelberger Manifest," *Die Zeit*, February 5, 1982.
[40] Rita Chin, *The Guest Worker Question in Postwar Germany* (New York: Cambridge University Press, 2009), 141–90.
[41] Norbert Frei, Franka Maubach, Christina Morina, Maik Tändler, *Zur rechten Zeit. Wider die Rückkehr des Nationalismus* (Berlin: Ullstein, 2019), 103–6.

tradition of a long list of figures embodying contemporary fears, including displaced persons in the immediate postwar period, the recruiter to the Foreign Legion, the subversive Communist, and the terrorism sympathizer. This situation has not significantly changed since, except that Muslims regarded as suspicious now also include asylum seekers and refugees from Syria, Iraq, and Afghanistan.

The popular mobilization of fears against foreigners and refugees buildt on a long tradition in the history of the Federal Republic. After reunification, however, such sentiments turned into open racist violence in many places. The circle of migrants now expanded beyond former guest workers and also included rapidly increasing numbers of asylum seekers and immigrants. The largest group consisted of ethnic Germans from the Soviet Union and Eastern Europe (especially Poland and Romania), who now used their claims to German citizenship to move back to Germany. In total, the influx from this group amounted to fewer than one million in the 1980s, just over two million in the 1990s, and just over 500,000 in the 2000s.[42] Public attention, however, focused on the also rapidly increasing (though much smaller) group of asylum seekers, which peaked during the wars in Yugoslavia (1991–5) and amounted to 438,000 people.[43] The violent excesses in the early 1990s did not target the numerically larger group of ethnic German migrants but rather mostly non-white asylum seekers, Turks, and other foreigners. Public responses to migrants thus demonstrated the persistence of ideas of racial and ethnic homogeneity across the 1989–90 divide. A new nationalism, which unification had further fueled, showed its ugly face with a series of post-unification pogroms. Neo-Nazis from the West joined with segments of the local population to orchestrate violent attacks on asylum seekers and Vietnamese foreign workers in the East German towns of Hoyerswerda and Rostock-Lichtenhagen in September 1991 and August 1992.[44] Local police forces were outnumbered and failed to contain increasingly aggressive crowds. In the aftermath of the incident in Rostock, hundreds of attacks on residences of asylum seekers occurred each month in East and West Germany.[45] Lethal arson attacks on houses inhabited by Turks in the northern German town of Mölln in November 1992 and in Solingen in May 1993 refuted attempts to attribute such incidents of racist violence exclusively to East Germans. In total, eight people were killed and many more were injured during these attacks. Between 1990 and 1993, a total

---

[42] Figures based on Bundeszentrale für politische Bildung, "Zuzug von (Spät-)Aussiedlern und ihren Familienangehörigen," 1.4.2018, http://www.bpb.de/nachschlagen/zahlen-und-fakten/soziale-situation-in-deutschland/61643/spaet-aussiedler (last accessed March 11, 2020). See also Ther, *Die Außenseiter*, 267–72.

[43] Bundeszentrale für politische Bildung, "Asylbewerber und Entscheidungen über Asylanträge in abs. Zahlen, Gesamtschutzquote in Prozent, 1975 bis 2017," April 1, 2018. http://www.bpb.de/nach-schlagen/zahlen-und-fakten/soziale-situation-in-deutschland/61634/asyl (last accessed March 10, 2020).

[44] Frei et al., *Zur rechten Zeit*, 161–5.

[45] See the numbers of racist attacks in 1992 cited in ibid. 172: July, 126; August, 235; September, 535; October, 384; November, 344; December 283.

of 49 people were killed as a result of right-wing extremist violence.[46] Importantly, the outbreak of racist violence also provoked a strong backlash in German society, with large demonstrations and vigils in many German cities. For example, 400,000 people demonstrated in Munich in December 1992. The dialectic of fear in which right- and left-wing fears had constantly reinforced each other now shaped the increasing polarization of civil society around the issue of migration: racist violence on the one hand, anti-racist mobilization on the other.[47]

The asylum compromise of 1993 both anticipated and defined the more recent refugee crisis of the fall of 2015. It stipulated that refugees could only gain asylum if they were not entering the Federal Republic of Germany via a safe third country. The Dublin agreement of 1997 applied this restriction to the entire territory of the EU. On the one hand, the reform of the asylum law illustrated the state's capacity to reduce the influx of asylum seekers. On the other hand, the asylum compromise also retroactively validated the violent excesses against foreigners of 1991–3 as motivated by realistic fears. While condemning attacks on foreigners, Chancellor Kohl (Christian Democratic Union, CDU), for example, also criticized the "misuse of the asylum law" in the same statement.[48] Since Germany is surrounded only by countries considered "safe," the Dublin agreement transferred control of the borders to the border states of the EU, above all Italy and Greece. This proved untenable in the summer of 2015 after millions of refugees, mostly from Syria and Afghanistan, entered the territory of the EU. The numbers of asylum seekers in Germany had been 20,000 at its low point in 2007; in 2015, it was 441,899; and in 2016, 722,370.[49]

The popular receptivity to fears of refugees and migrants increased after 1990 as a result of two more developments. One was the unification crisis, which led to extensive deindustrialization and exploding unemployment in East Germany. By 1993, the number of employed persons in the former East Germany had fallen by a third from 9.7 million to 6.2 million.[50] A survey of East Germans in 2009 found that half felt like second-class citizens.[51] Fear and insecurity among East Germans

---

[46] Herbert, *Geschichte Deutschlands*, 1177.

[47] On the significance of these events, see Ulrich Herbert, "Ausländer-Asyl-Pogrome. Das hässliche Gesicht des neuen Deutschlands," in Frank Bajohr, Anselm Doering-Manteuffel, Claudia Kemper, Detlef Siegfried, eds, *Mehr als eine Erzählung. Zeitgeschichtliche Perspektiven auf die Bundesrepublik* (Göttingen: Wallstein, 2016) 145–55. See also Frank Biess, Astrid M. Eckert, "Introduction: Why Do We Need New Narratives for the History of the Federal Republic," *Central European History* 52/1 (2019).

[48] Oliver Decker, Elmar Brähler, "Autoritäre Dynamiken: Ergebnisse der bisherigen 'Mitte' Studien und Fragestellung," in Oliver Decker, Johannes Kiess, Elmar Brähler, eds, *Die enthemmte Mitte. Autoritäre und rechtsextreme Einstellungen in Deutschland* (Gießen: Psychosozial-Verlag, 2016), 15, Frei et al., *Zur rechten Zeit*, 166–88, quotation on 166.

[49] http://www.bpb.de/nachschlagen/zahlen-und-fakten/soziale-situation-in-deutschland/61634/asyl (last accessed March 6, 2020).

[50] Herbert, *Geschichte Deutschlands*, 1147. Draghi statement, "Speech by Mario Draghi, President of the European Central Bank at the Global Investment Conference in London," July 26, 2012, https://www.ecb.europa.eu/press/key/date/2012/html/sp120726.en.html (last accessed April 2, 2020).

[51] See also Thomas Großbölting, Christoph Lorke, "Vereinigungsgesellschaft: Deutschland seit 1990," in Thomas Großbölting, Christoph Lorke, eds, *Deutschland seit 1990. Wege in die Vereinigungsgesellschaft* (Stuttgart: Franz Steiner Verlag, 2017), 12.

did not only arise from social disadvantage but also a sense of degradation of previous lives under the East German dictatorship, especially among men. The current popular dissatisfaction in the former East Germany is not so much the product of some ingrained authoritarianism dating back to East German times but rather results from the distinct experience of unification and its aftermath.[52]

The second problem was the intensification of European integration, in particular through the Maastricht Treaty in 1991 and the subsequent introduction of the euro in 2002. Such measures were supposed to curb fears of a new and enlarged Germany in the middle of Europe and, according to Chancellor Kohl, to make a "return to the earlier nationalist thinking and its dire consequences impossible."[53] Increased European integration was also necessary in order to maintain the capacity for politics within an increasingly globalized economy. At the same time, the EU also suffered from a long-standing democratic deficit. European citizens found it difficult to identify with the EU and criticized unelected Brussels bureaucrats. Public approval of EU membership dropped Europe-wide from 70 per cent in the 1990s to 50 per cent in 2006.[54]

With the onset of the financial crisis, the EU itself became the subject of fear. The financial crisis originated in the US real estate market and began in September 2008, when the investment bank Lehman Brothers collapsed. In the ensuing weeks, German politicians needed to reassure citizens that the crisis would remain confined to the US. When the German bank Hypo Real Estate came under pressure shortly thereafter, a title story in *Der Spiegel* warned of the "fear of fear"—that is, that German citizens would begin to withdraw their savings from banks and thus reduce the liquidity of the banks even further. This is why Chancellor Merkel and Finance Minister Steinbrück publicly declared, on October 5, 2008, that German citizens do "not have to fear that they will lose one euro of their savings."[55] Here political elites again portrayed themselves as rational actors who sought to forestall potential irrational fears of the populace, which would have threatened to destabilize the entire financial system.

By 2010, the crisis began to affect the entire EU. Some southern European countries had built up enormous debt as a result of the progressive liberalization of the credit markets. Germany and France had already exceeded the limit of 3 per cent of gross domestic product allowed in the Maastricht Treaty and thus weakened the European Stability Pact in the early 2000s. At the end of 2009, Greece was no longer able to cover its growing budget deficit on the capital market. In the spring of 2010,

[52] See now Ilko-Sascha Kowalczuk, *Die Übernahme. Wie Ostdeutschland Teil der Bundesrepublik wurde* (Munich: C.H.Beck, 2019).

[53] Quoted in Herbert, *Geschichte Deutschlands*, 1182.

[54] Stefan Collignon, "Europa reformieren—Demokratie wagen. Internationale Politikanalyse Europäische Politik," April 2006 (Friedrich Ebert Stiftung), "Ohne Demokratie keine Europa," *Die Zeit*, January 6, 2016.

[55] Quoted in *Der Spiegel* 52/41 (2008).

the EU decided to give Greece €60 billion in grants, along with loan default guarantees of up to €440 billion. Overall, the European bailout for Greece, Ireland, Portugal, Spain, Cyprus, and Slovenia constituted € 700 billion (including the funds from the International Monetary Fund), of which just under 90 per cent were guarantees. More than €500 billion had been disbursed by 2013. For comparison, the total German federal budget for 2018 amounted to € 343.6 billion.[56] Strict austerity measures accompanied the bailouts, which eventually led to an unemployment rate of 27 per cent in Greece in the summer of 2013, 20 per cent in Spain, and affected about 40 per cent of young people in both countries. Greek pensions had been cut by 40 per cent since 2011 with further cuts scheduled for 2019.[57] People in the southern European countries thus ultimately bore the burden of the euro crisis through spending cuts and tax increases. Against the resistance of the German government under Chancellor Merkel and Finance Minister Schäuble, the European Central Bank (ECB) intervened in 2011–12 and bought government bonds of affected countries to the amount of billions. ECB President Mario Draghi subsequently declared in July 2012 that the bank would do whatever it took to preserve the euro. This rescue operation proved to be at least temporarily successful and stabilized the euro zone.[58] Yet, it also produced increased fears among German citizens that they would be held liable for financial assistance to Greece and other countries. The EU debt crisis thus became a privileged fear object for Germans. In the annual R&V survey, the fear of increased "cost to taxpayers because of the EU crisis" became Germans' greatest fear from 2011 to 2015. In 2012, 73 per cent of Germans articulated this fear, which was the second highest value ever since the data was collected in 1992.[59] Commentators and experts explained these fears as a result of the German historic trauma of hyperinflation in the 1920s, which, they argued, had significantly contributed to Hitler's rise to power. In so doing, they again invoked memories of Weimar in order to justify a politics of austerity in the present. However, they reversed the historical causality in the interest of contemporary politics. For it was not inflation but rather its opposite, austerity politics and the policy of deflation under Chancellor Heinrich Brüning in the early 1930s, that

[56] https://www.bundesfinanzministerium.de/Monatsberichte/2018/08/Inhalte/Kapitel-3-Analysen/3-1-Sollbericht-2018-Ausgaben-Einnahmen-Bundeshaushalt.html (last accessed March 6, 2020).

[57] Kershaw, *Rollercoaster*, 511.

[58] This is a very brief summary of a complex development. I mainly follow the analysis in Adam Tooze, *Crashed. Wie zehn Jahre Finanzkrise die Welt verändert haben* (Berlin: Siedler, 2018), 373–571, 591–623. Figures and quotation according to Andreas Rödder, *21.0. Eine kurze Geschichte der Gegenwart* (Munich: C.H.Beck, 2016), 330, and Kershaw, *Rollercoaster*, 496.

[59] https://www.ruv.de/static-files/ruvde/downloads/presse/aengste-der-deutschen/langzeit-grafiken/StaticFiles_Auto/ruv-aengste-langzeitgrafik-platz1-seit2004.jpg (last accessed March 5, 2020).

had arguably worsened the effects of the Depression in Germany and hence facilitated the electoral gains of the Nazi Party.[60]

The convergence of the financial and the euro crises fueled more long-standing anxieties about socio-economic decline, especially in the middle class. The increase of flexible and temporary jobs, and the decreasing likelihood of securing permanent and lifelong employment, threatened with social decline even those social strata that were initially not affected by these transformations. Declining or only slowly increasing real wages, the prospect of job loss, and growing uncertainty about necessary educational qualifications combined to create a new, more general uncertainty about the future, which only increased further in the 2000s.[61] This difficulty of predicting future job profiles and educational requirements was rather similar to the "modern fears" during the accelerated modernization process since the late 1950s. But, while strong economic growth and the expansion of the welfare state compensated for these fears in the 1950s and 1960s, the 2000s stood under the sign of the "Agenda 2010"—that is, the reform (or curtailment) of the welfare state under the Red–Green coalition of Chancellor Gerhard Schröder. The restriction of unemployment benefits to only one year (and two years for older workers) and subsequent relegation to the much less generous "Hartz IV" rate, regardless of the length of the previous contribution to unemployment insurance, provoked particularly strong criticism, as did the failure to place some of the burden on higher incomes through tax increases.[62] While large segments of East Germans had experienced social decline as a result of post-unification deindustrialization, the increasing restrictions of the welfare state through the Schröder reforms increased social inequality and uncertainty about the future in the West as well. A combination of stagnating incomes and rising costs of living, especially for housing, further fueled middle-class anxiety, particularly among skilled workers and non-academic professionals. During the period of the financial and euro crises since 2008, this predicament overlapped with the perception of a loss of control by the nation state, which seemed increasingly powerless vis-à-vis the dynamics of global financial markets. For many Germans, the billions spent on rescuing private banks and southern European countries stood in stark contrast to the real and perceived curtailments of a social safety net and to their own growing individual insecurity. This, as well as real experiences of social decline, constituted one of the central structural prerequisites for the rise of a new

---

[60] On this context, see Mark Schieritz, *Die Inflationslüge. Wie uns die Angst ums Geld ruiniert und wer daran verdient* (Munich: Knaur, 2013). Tooze, *Crashed*, is also very critical of German policy in the euro crisis.

[61] Holger Lengfeld, Jochen Hirschle, "Die Angst der Mittelschicht vor dem sozialen Abstieg. Eine Längsschnittanalyse 1984–2007," *Zeitschrift für Soziologie* 38/5 (2009): 379–98, Heinz Bude, *Gesellschaft der Angst* (Hamburg: Hamburger Edition, 2014), 60–82.

[62] Wolfrum, *Rot-Grün an der Macht*, 528–83. See also Alexander Hagelüken, "Die Angst der Mittelschicht vor dem Abstieg droht die Republik zu zerreißen," *Süddeutsche Zeitung*, January 27, 2018.

right-wing populism in many Western countries. In Germany, it manifested itself in the founding of a new political party, the Alternative for Germany (AfD).[63]

Right-Wing Fears

Similar to Trump's presidency and Great Britain's decision to leave the EU ("Brexit"), the AfD and its German version of right-wing populism is primarily a movement based on fear.[64] A catastrophic horizon of expectation was foundational for the party. When it was founded in April 2013 under its first chairman, the economics professor Bernd Lucke, it focused, above all, on the euro crisis. The party campaigned on the basis of fear for the decline of the currency. It called for an exit from the euro zone and rejected the burden German taxpayers were bearing from the rescue packages for Greece and other southern European countries. From the outset, however, the party also encompassed a national-conservative and racist wing, which cultivated the horror scenario of an endangered "Christian" and "German" culture.[65] In the 2013 federal election, the AfD narrowly missed the threshold to enter parliament with 4.7 per cent. But Luckes's attempt to establish the AfD as a liberal-conservative alternative to the Christian Democrats and to delimit the party from right-wing extremism failed. Since its Essen party conference in July 2015, when Lucke was voted out of office and subsequently left the party, the AfD has radicalized into a nationalist, Islamophobic, and, at least in parts, racist and right-wing extremist party. Still, the party was increasingly successful in elections and achieved double-digit results, especially in Western Germany, with 15.1 per cent in the state elections in Baden-Württemberg and 12.6 per cent in state elections in the Rhineland-Palatinate. In the East, the AfD was even more successful, advancing to the second largest party after the CDU in Saxony-Anhalt in 2016, with 24.3 per cent of the vote. In the 2017 federal election, it reached 12.6 per cent and represented, after the formation

---

[63] Tooze, *Crashed*, 624–91. On the origins of right-wing populism in Germany and Europe, see Jan-Werner Müller, *Was ist Populismus? Ein Essay* (Berlin: Suhrkamp, 2016), Volker Weiß, *Die autoritäre Revolte. Die Neue Rechte und der Untergang des Abendlandes* (Stuttgart: Klett-Cotta, 2016), Karl-Siegbert Rehberg, Franziska Kunz, Tino Schlinzig, eds, *PEGIDA-Rechtspopulismus zwischen Fremdenangst und "Wende"-Enttäuschung? Analysen im Überblick* (Bielefeld: transcript, 2016), Melanie Amann, *Angst für Deutschland. Die Wahrheit über die AfD, wo sie herkommt, wer sie führt, wohin sie steuert* (Munich: Droemer, 2017), Uffa Jensen, *Zornpolitik* (Berlin: Suhrkamp, 2017), Thomas Wagner, *Die Angstmacher. 1968 und die Neuen Rechten* (Berlin: Aufbau, 2017), Everhard Holtmann, *Völkische Feindbilder. Ursprünge und Erscheinungsformen des Rechtspopulismus in Deutschland* (Bonn: Bundeszentrale für politische Bildung, 2018), Wilhelm Heitmeyer, *Autoritäre Versuchungen. Signaturen der Bedrohung 1* (Berlin: Suhrkamp, 2018), 231-76, "Heitmeyer prefers the term authoritarian nationalist radicalism," Frei et al., *Zur rechten Zeit*.
[64] Tooze, *Crashed*, 624–50.   [65] Holtmann, *Völkische Feindbilder*, 80–1.

of another Grand Coalition of CDU/CSU and SPD, the largest opposition party.[66]

Although the structural conditions for the rise of the AfD to its current strength
were already in place, the party's electoral successes were closely related to the dramatic increase in refugee numbers in 2015–16.[67] Facing hundreds of thousands of
refugees who had entered the EU via Greece and Turkey, the federal government
under Chancellor Angela Merkel decided to suspend the Dublin agreement in the
fall of 2015. Merkel did not open the borders but rather decided against closing
the border with Austria, possibly with military means. The surge to almost
three-quarters of a million asylum seekers in 2016 was the result. Following the
EU's agreement with Turkey, in which Turkey pledged to prevent the refugees from
entering Greece, the number of asylum seekers again fell to 198,317 in 2017.[68] Yet,
in spite of declining numbers of refugees, the AfD's share of the vote continued to
rise. Because the anxiety about the stability of the euro had been exhausted at the
time and the party's poll numbers were declining, the refugee crisis provided a
political opportunity for the AfD. From October 2015 onward, it increasingly
radicalized and evolved into a racist and Islamophobic party.

The link between the rise of the AfD and migration demonstrated that support
for the AfD is not primarily based on fears of social decline. Opinion polls show
that only 28 per cent of AfD voters feel socially or economically disadvantaged
while 58 per cent describe their economic situation as "good."[69] Yet AfD supporters articulated a strong pessimism for the future: one-third of AfD voters
anticipated a worse economic situation for themselves in the future, and two-
thirds expected the general economic situation to be worse. What distinguishes
AfD followers was therefore not so much their social situation but their pessimistic worldview. The party drew on and benefited substantially from fears of the
future. However, these fears referred not only to economic decline but also to a
more general cultural and national decay. According to the sociologist Wilhelm
Heitmeyer, the strategy of the AfD consisted of the "culturalization of the
social"—that is, the shifting of fears of social and economic decline to a future
scenario of cultural decline. In the context of the increasing migration to Germany
in 2015–16, the program of the AfD read like a "never-ending call for thwarting
dangers."[70] The AfD presented itself as the sole defender of a "German culture,"

---

[66] https://www.welt.de/politik/deutschland/article181547734/Emnid-Umfrage-Union-und-SPD-
legen-deutschlandweit-zu-AfD-im-Osten-staerkste-Kraft.html?wtrid=amp.article.free;
https://www.infratest-dimap.de/umfragen-analysen/bundesweit/sonntagsfrage (both last accessed
March 6, 2020).

[67] See Holtmann, *Völkische Feindbilder*, 83. This also means that a reduction in the number of refugees will not automatically lead to a reduction in the electoral strength of the AfD, see Heitmeyer,
Autoritäre Versuchungen, 344–9.

[68] http://www.bpb.de/nachschlagen/zahlen-und-fakten/soziale-situation-in-deutschland/61634/
asyl (last accessed March 6, 2020).

[69] Holtmann, *Völkische Feindbilder*, 72.

[70] Ibid. 88. See also Heitmeyer, *Autoritäre Versuchungen*, 226, 352.

which it portrayed as being under threat as a result of migration. At the same time, the party reactivated a folkish idea that demanded, at the least, an unconditional adaptation to a German dominant culture (*Leitkultur*) but more often propagated the separation of everything "foreign" from a homogenous German identity that was either culturally or ethnically defined. In this project, fear and hatred of Islam acted as the key integrating force of the party's supporters.[71] Not only did the AfD, as the first and only party, apodictically declare that "Islam does not belong to Germany," it also described the "presence of more than 5 million Muslims, whose numbers were constantly growing" as a "great danger to our state, our society, and our value system."[72]

Of course, the AfD did not invent Islamophobia or racism. The party built on some important antecedents without which its electoral success would not have been possible. Among these were the publications of Thilo Sarrazin, an SPD politician, former finance senator of the city of Berlin, and former member of the executive board of the federal bank (*Bundesbank*), especially his 2010 book, *Germany Abolishes Itself* (*Deutschland schafft sich ab*). Mixing biological and culturalist arguments, Sarrazin painted a horror scenario of a declining German people due to the higher reproductive rate of what he considered to be less intelligent ethno-cultural minorities, especially Muslims and Turks. Against what he saw as gradually dissolving borders, Sarrazin emphasized the importance of a closed territory and "group membership" as a source of individual and collective identity as well as human cultural achievement.[73] The book mobilized resentments against immigrants and Muslims prevalent in society since the 1970s and turned them into a kind of national anxiety scenario. In so doing, Sarrazin significantly widened what could be said in public and introduced ideas from the extreme Right into mainstream discourse.[74] The book ends with the future scenario of a completely Islamized Germany in the late twenty-first century when Christian buildings such as the Cologne or Ulm cathedrals are handed over to Islam and converted, based on the model of the Hagia Sophia in Istanbul, into mosques.[75] With 1.3 million copies sold, the book became the bestselling book of the year in Germany in 2010. While Sarrazin assiduously avoided using the term "race," his argument built on the racist notion of a hierarchy of higher and inferior peoples and strata. The book provoked significant criticism but also attracted notable defenders. The then chairman of the SPD, Sigmar Gabriel, the editor of

---

[71] Holtmann, *Völkische Feindbilder*, 74, 85, 101.

[72] AfD, "Wahlprogramm zur Bundestagswahl 2017," 34, https://www.afd.de/wp-content/uploads/sites/111/2017/06/2017-06-01_AfD-Bundestagswahlprogramm_Onlinefassung.pdf (last accessed March 6, 2020).

[73] Thilo Sarrazin, *Deutschland schafft sich ab. Wie wir unser Land aufs Spiel setzen* (Munich: DVA, 2010), 255–6. This mixture of cultural and biological arguments has a long tradition in the history of racism. Hitler made use of it as well: see Jürgen Brokoff, *Die Apokalypse in der Weimarer Republik* (Munich: Wilhelm Fink, 2001), 127–59.

[74] Weiß, *Die autoritäre Revolte*, 10.   [75] Sarrazin, *Deutschland schafft sich ab*, 402.

Figure 9.3. Election ad of the "Alternative for Germany" (AfD), Berlin-Kreuzberg, September 2017.

The AfD increasingly became an Islamophobic and right-wing extremist party. It sought to mobilize popular fears of foreign, especially Islamic, influences. This ad demands "Stop Islamization."

Source: dpa Picture-Alliance, No. 94994278.

the *Frankfurter Allgemeine Zeitung*, Frank Schirrmacher, and the feminist Alice Schwarzer shielded Sarrazin against accusations of racism. An attempt to exclude Sarrazin from the party reduced the initial charge of "racism" to "social Darwinism." The effort stalled for a long time and was not revived until January 2020.[76] Public discussion portrayed Sarrazin's argument as focusing mainly on the issue of an allegedly failed integration of Turks into German mainstream society. The reception of the book thus revealed a recurrent difficulty in explicitly naming racism in German public discourse.[77]

The rise of the AfD also followed the emergence of a grassroots movement, "Patriotic Europeans Against the Islamization of the West" (*Patriotische Europäer gegen die Islamisierung des Abendlandes*, Pegida). Beginning in the autumn of 2014, Pegida organized xenophobic and racist demonstrations. Some of these demonstrations turned violent, and several leading Pegida members were charged with right-wing extremist hate crimes. The AfD repeatedly debated its relationship to Pegida, yet also organized joint demonstrations.[78] Pegida agitated against "Merkel sympathizers" and "supporters of the system" (*Systemlinge*), describing the AfD as the only party that advocated for "the rights and freedoms of citizens and clearly identified the problems in this country."[79] Pegida's political rhetoric echoed the National Socialist critique of the Weimar Republic during the 1930s. It combined an Islamophobic fear scenario with a fundamental opposition to the "system" of the Federal Republic. Pegida had often been characterized as a specifically East German or regional Saxon phenomenon, and this was indeed where the movement was particularly active. The movement thus also illustrated the lack of experience with representative democracy and multiculturalism in at least parts of East German society.[80] Yet the particular strength of right-wing populism in East Germany was also the result of the confluence of right-wing politicians from the West with popular attitudes in the East. Western activists managed to stimulate the already existing popular dissatisfaction in the East and mobilize into a rebellion against foreigners and the larger idea of a multicultural Germany. The use of the slogan "We are the people," which had inspired the East German revolution against the Communist regime in 1989 now assumed a distinctly ethnic-fundamentalist bent.[81] In the same vein, the AfD now portrayed itself as

---

[76] More recently, the SPD revived the effort to exclude Sarrazin from the party.

[77] This argument follows Michael Meng, "Silences about Sarrazin's Racism in Contemporary Germany," *Journal of Modern History* 87/1 (2015): 102–35, quotations on 116–17.

[78] On the use of Pegida by the AfD, see Olaf Sundermeyer, *Gauland. Die Rache des alten Mannes* (Munich: C.H.Beck, 2018), 63–71.

[79] https://www.pegida.de (last accessed March 7, 2020).

[80] Michael Bittner, "Dresden zeigt, wie's geht? Ein Versuch über Pegida und die 'sächsichen Verhältnisse'," in Rehberg et al., eds, *PEGIDA-Rechtspopulismus*, 339–45.

[81] The emphasis on East–West cooperation in explaining the strength of right-wing populism in the East is the key insight in Frei et al., *Zur rechten Zeit*, 183–206. The authors cite especially the party chairman of the AfD, Alexander Gauland, the regional AfD party chairman, Bjorn Höcke, and the right-wing publisher, Götz Kubitschek, as such right-wing activists from the West; see ibid. 202.

the party that would "complete" the legacy of the East German revolution of 1989. While former activists had rejected this appropriation of the East German revolution by the Right, the AfD's claim to "1989" was not completely spurious. It brought into view some of the authoritarian and illiberal elements of the 1989 revolutions. As historian Paul Betts has shown, these events entailed Christian, nationalist, and populist elements that fueled contemporary illiberal authoritarianism in the former Eastern Europe more broadly.[82]

In this construction of an ethnic German identity, Islam assumed the role of the necessary "other." Islamophobia served a similar function to that of antisemitism before 1945. This was one reason why the occasional right-wing appeal to a "Christian–Jewish identity" in opposition to Islam was particularly problematic. The fear of a supposed "Islamization" of Europe exhibited structural similarities to the fear of "Jewification" in the late nineteenth and early twentieth centuries. Some commentators even identified Thilo Sarrazin as the "Treitschke of the early 21st century," who made Islamophobia respectable, in much the same way as the eminent historian Heinrich von Treitschke did with respect to antisemitism in the late nineteenth century.[83] As we have seen, antisemitism formed a kind of dispositive for the "other" in the history of fear in the Federal Republic. Other objects of fear were repeatedly inscribed into it and continued to inhabit some of the characteristics of "the Jew" as an enemy image, in particular the idea of an invisible force that subverted the existing order from within. Much like in classical antisemitism, Islamophobia identified religion as an integrating force that bound "otherwise disparate members of a group into a supposedly steel-like structure."[84] The collective "other" arising from the "ethnicization of Islam" then not only stood in incompatible contrast to German majority society but also appeared as homogenous, static, doctrinaire, and immune to any change.[85] The critique of Islamophobia and analysis of its function within the Right does not necessarily imply an uncritical acceptance of, or silence toward, repressive features within Islamic communities.[86] Instead, the New Right's racism consists precisely in denying to another group what we all claim for ourselves: individualism, complexity, the ability to learn and to change. Islamophobia denies the possibility of acculturation and integration to individual Muslims as well as to Islamic communities.

Unlike Jews as an object of fear, Muslims do not appear exclusively as a force of inner subversion. Islamophobia rather links the ostensible danger emanating from the "inside" and from the "outside." This fear scenario sees German society

---

[82] See Paul Betts, "1989 at Thirty. A Recast Legacy," *Past and Present* 244/1 (2019): 271–305.

[83] Micha Brumlik, "Ist die Islamophobie der neue Antisemitismus?" *Frankfurter Rundschau*, December 15, 2010. See also Matti Bunzl, *Antisemitism and Islamophobia. Hatreds Old and New in Europe* (Chicago: Prickly Paradigm Press, 2007).

[84] Jensen, *Zornpolitik*, 109.

[85] This is the term of Naime Çakir, cited in Michael Wildt, *Volk, Volksgemeinschschaft, AfD* (Hamburg: Hamburger Edition, 2017), 111.

[86] Here I disagree with Weiß, *Die autoritäre Revolte*, 243–7.

as overwhelmed by Islamic immigration from outside, which then, however, continues to subvert German norms and culture from the inside.[87] This fear fantasy is based on the visible otherness of Islam—headscarf and burka—as well as on the invisible threat of a hidden Islamist terror. Right-wing populists also mobilize accusations of antisemitism among Muslims in order to justify their exclusion. The AfD portrays itself, according to AfD executive committee member Beatrix von Storch, as "one of the few political guarantors of Jewish life even in times of illegal antisemitic migration."[88] The party participates in an increasingly common equation of criticism of Israeli state policies with antisemitism but also distracts from the real antisemitism on the political Right.[89] Open antisemitism is still not acceptable to moderate voters and is rightly considered a sign of right-wing extremist attitudes in Germany. Islamophobia, by contrast, has moved far beyond the circles of right-wing populism and has almost become a basic consensus among Western societies. In 2006, before the last influx of refugees in 2015–16, 91 per cent of respondents in Germany associated Islam with "discrimination against women," 83 per cent with "fanaticism," and 71 per cent with "intolerance," while 60 per cent considered it "undemocratic."[90]

As this book has demonstrated, political fears were always closely related to a changing commemorative culture. This has also been true of the rise of right-wing populism, and in two different ways. First, right-wing populism was part and parcel of the decline of a post-war antifascist consensus in all Europe.[91] With increasing temporal distance, the memory of fascism and the Second World War lost its normative force for the present, as it had still existed on both sides of the Iron Curtain for much of the postwar period. The deliberate attack of leading AfD politicians on the Federal Republic's established commemorative culture is part of a comprehensive historical revisionism, which aims to relativize the period of National Socialism—what AfD leader Alexander Gauland dismissed as nothing but "bird shit in over 1,000 years of successful German history," in June 2018 in a speech before the AfD youth in Thuringia.[92] A gradual expansion of what can be said in public discourse thus reflects a transformed commemorative culture. Right-wing populists break taboos through deliberate provocations, which they then partly take back or relativize shortly thereafter. But in so doing, they signal to possible supporters in the far-right camp that the AfD rejects Holocaust memory as an essential part of the political culture of the Federal Republic.

---

[87] Jensen, *Zornpolitik*, 110.
[88] Quoted in Roman Steinke, "Ein Feigenblatt," *Süddeutsche Zeitung*, September 30, 2018.
[89] Moshe Zimmermann, "Postscript," in Christian Heilbronn, Doron Rabinovici, Natan Sznaider, eds, *Neuer Antisemitismus? Fortsetzung einer globalen Debatte* (Berlin: Suhrkamp, 2019), 451–6.
[90] Cited in Wildt, *Volk, Volksgemeinschaft, AfD*, 111.
[91] Dan Stone, *Goodbye to All That? The Story of Europe since 1945* (New York: Oxford University Press, 2014), 294.
[92] https://www.welt.de/politik/deutschland/article176912600/AfD-Chef-Gauland-bezeichnet-NS-Zeit-als-Vogelschiss-in-der-Geschichte.html (last accessed March 7, 2020).

The second connection between right-wing populism and postwar commemorative culture was less obvious. The rise of right-wing populism did not only happen against an increasingly established Holocaust memory but also in conjunction with the emergence of this commemorative culture. Of course, this did not mean that Holocaust memory was somehow responsible for right-wing populism. But the increasing centrality of Holocaust memory in West German political culture since the 1980s clearly raised the question as to why its increasing presence did not constitute a stronger defense against everyday racism and Islamophobia? Here, the redemptive power of Holocaust memory also entailed an ambivalent, even paradoxical effect. An increasingly extensive Holocaust memory appeared to indicate that postwar Germans had finally overcome the problem of racism. But because racism was often equated with antisemitism, Holocaust memory might have made it more difficult to remain sensitive to other forms of racism. Racism was primarily equated with the National Socialist, biological, and ultimately genocidal version, not with more everyday forms of racist exclusion. And because only outspoken neo-Nazi groups advocated this form of biologically based antisemitism, the problem of racism appeared as a past problem that postwar society had finally overcome, not as a still-living phenomenon of German society.[93] The rejection of antisemitism served as a cover to disavow and render invisible other forms of racism within West German society. Increasingly, the Holocaust was also not understood as a universal phenomenon pertinent to any form of racism, but as a specifically German–Jewish event. The so-called "Historians' Debate" of the 1980s confirmed the notion of the "singularity" of the Holocaust and cemented the alleged incomparability of antisemitism and other forms of racism.[94] Paradoxically, this argument rendered it more difficult to draw a link between past and present forms of racism. Thus Holocaust memory might even have had an exclusionary effect within an increasingly multicultural society. After all, it presupposed what was often imagined as a homogenous German collective subject, which was then supposed to face up to its own history. An increasingly extensive Holocaust memory might have fostered concepts of "Germanness" that tended to marginalize Muslims and migrants.[95] How this collective memory could be made accessible to Turkish guest workers or refugees from Syria and Afghanistan remains an open question to this day.[96]

The rise of right-wing populism as a movement based on fear also promoted an existent transformation of West German emotional culture. As we have seen in

---

[93] Meng, "Silences about Sarrazin's Racism in Contemporary Germany."
[94] Michael Rothberg, Yasemin Yildiz, "Memory Citizenship: Migrant Archives of Holocaust Remembrance in Contemporary Germany," *Parallax* 17/4 (2011): 38.
[95] Chin, *The Guest Worker Question.*
[96] On this question, see Viola B. Georgi and Rainer Ohliger, eds, *Crossover Geschichte. Historisches Bewusstsein Jugendlicher in der Einwanderungsgesellschaft* (Hamburg: Edition Körber, 2009), Damani J. Partridge, "Holocaust Mahnmal (Memorial). Monumental Memory amidst Contemporary Race," *Comparative Studies in Society and History* 52/4 (2010): 820–50.

Chapter 7, a new expressive emotional culture emerged in the left-wing alternative milieu of the 1970s and became influential in social movements, especially in the environmental and peace movements. Although conservatives mobilized fear time and again in the history of the Federal Republic, the political use of public confessions of fear constituted more of a political instrument of the Left. This political valence of fear changed with the rise of right-wing populism. The AfD claims to name and represent citizens' fears of the future. Right-wing populism operates within an expressive emotional regime that has emerged since the seventies, yet also transforms this emotional regime and directs it toward new fear objects: Muslims, migrants, and occasionally even the political system as such. In its self-description as an "Alternative for Germany," the AfD's surprising affinity with left-alternative is still apparent.[97] The party propagates the kind of apocalyptic scenarios similar to those of the environmental and peace movements. According to one survey, 74 per cent of AfD supporters assume that "Germany is headed toward a catastrophe" if "politics does not change."[98] The exclusive fixation on migration and Islam also gives the AfD a unique selling point that distinguishes it from other parties.[99]

These new right-wing fears differ from traditionally conservative fears because they mainly aim at the state and political elites. Conservatives traditionally feared declining state authority as a result of the activities of left-wing and potentially revolutionary forces. Conservative fears were more defensive and state-oriented than left-wing fears. They tended to bring into view the dangers to state authority emerging from society. By contrast, left-wing fears identified the state as a massive source of danger. This dialectic of Left and Right fears has virtually been reversed. Now there are right-wing populist movements that blame state policy, especially immigration, for their fears, while a Grand Coalition from the left to the bourgeois camp identifies with the state and looks at right-wing populism as a threat. In this respect, right-wing populism also marks a break with traditional conservative fears. It is less concerned with defending the authority of the state but, like its left-wing predecessors, questions state authority per se. The AfD both builds on and stimulates a far-reaching loss of trust in politicians and state elites. For example, 61 per cent of Germans fear that politicians are "not capable" (*überfordert*) of addressing and containing contemporary fears.[100] Current fears exhibit similarities to fears of the early days of the Federal Republic, which were founded on the perception of a weak and not fully sovereign state. As we saw in Chapters 1–3, the fears of the 1940s and 1950s built on the notion that the West German state would not be capable of offering sufficient protection—for example, against

---

[97]   Amann, *Angst für Deutschland*, 243.   [98]   Cited in ibid. 221.

[99]   Sundermeyer, *Gauland*, 143, with comparison to a similar function of ecology for the formation of the Green Party.

[100]   https://www.ruv.de/static-files/ruvde/downloads/presse/aengste-der-deutschen/grafiken/StaticFiles_Auto/ruv-aengste2018-grafik-trump-top7.jpg (last accessed March 7, 2020).

the policies of the occupying powers or the dangers of the Cold War. While these fears originated from a lost war and postwar occupation, today's similar fears are the product of an increasing global interconnectedness that limits the sovereignty of the nation state. And, while increasing trust in the US contained German fears during the Cold War, the current US President elected in 2016 arguably stands at the helm of a populist attack on the institutions of postwar liberal democracy.

Given their strategy of deliberately provoking authority, right-wing populist movements were also continuous with left-wing protest movements. This continuity exceeded the political conversions of some "68ers" from the Left to the Right (for example, Frank Böckelmann, Bernd Rabehl, Horst Mahler).[101] Rightwing populist movements not only adopted the strategies of the "68ers" but also their anti-state thrust, as it was articulated, for example, in the writings of Johannes Agnoli and Peter Brückner on the transformation of democracy (see Chapter 6). Similarly, to the student movement, the AfD positioned itself as an extra-parliamentary protest movement against a Grand Coalition. And like the New Left at that time, the AfD's fundamentalist opposition occupied a radical political space that the move of a large party to the political center made possible: the Godesberg-SPD in the 1960s, the Merkel-CDU since 2005.[102] Outraged citizens or the protagonists of what Uffa Jensen called the "politics of anger" thus perpetuated the expressive emotional culture of the post-1968 period, which enabled the public performance of emotion. Historical continuity, however, did not imply causality. The "68ers" did not of course produce right-wing populism, nor can this phenomenon be traced back to the student movement. Still, rightwing populism embraced the new role of emotions in politics that had been established from the 1960s onward, and it exploited these public emotions for its own purposes. The AfD operated on the basis of an "outspoken emotionality" and "extremely condensed feelings." Marc Jongen, a member of the AfD faction in the *Bundestag*, followed his former teacher, the philosopher Peter Sloterdijk, by calling for the revival of Germans' "thymotic energies"—that is, the conscious cultivation of anger, pride, and outrage. This was to serve the German self-assertion in what he conceived of as a "fight" (*Kampf*) against a vital and young Islam. It goes without saying that this self-assertion also entailed a stabilization of threatened masculinity.[103] Much like for the "68ers," the open cultivation of emotions was part of a new subjectivity and male self-stabilization. However, unlike in the leftist and alternative milieu, this did not entail a new male sensibility that would be

---

[101] On the less well-known case of Frank Böckelmann, see Wagner, *Die Angstmacher*, 180–9.

[102] On this link, see Wildt, *Volk, Volksgemeinschaft, AfD*, 102–4, and David Bebnowski, "Fundamentalopposition: Die ambivalente Anlehnung der AfD an '68," *Zeitgeschichte Online*, September 5, 2016. (https://zeitgeschichte-online.de/kommentar/aus-aktuellem-anlass)

[103] On emotionality, see Heitmeyer, *Autoritäre Versuchungen*, 264. On the continuity with "68," see Wagner, *Die Angstmacher*, 235–6. The argument is based on Peter Sloterdijk, *Zorn und Zeit. Politisch-Psychologischer Versuch* (Frankfurt a/M: Suhrkamp, 2006).

expressed in recurrent expressions of anxiety but rather the exact opposite: an entitlement to anger, outrage, and male self-assertion. In this sense, the AfD turned expressive emotion against a "left-red-green contaminated 68er Germany," as the AfD spokesperson Jörg Meuthen declared at the Stuttgart party congress in 2016.[104]

In the emotional economy of right-wing populism, the consequences of 1968 were present in another form as well, as a consequence of the sexual revolution. As we saw in Chapter 6, the notion of sexual liberation as a form of political liberation was one of the central features of a newly expressive subjectivity. In the present Islamophobic discourse, the realm of gender and sexuality is constructed as a central piece of evidence for the incompatibility of Islam with Western societies. During the 2000s, secular Islamic women such as the pedagogue Necla Kelek or the lawyer Seyran Ateş established themselves as prominent critics of the oppression of women in Islam.[105] Their writings on arranged or coerced marriage and the need for a sexual revolution in Islam were supposed to highlight the categorial incompatibility of Islam with liberal democracy. The critique of gender relations in Muslim communities thus serves to exclude *all* Muslims, no matter what their sexual attitudes might be, from majority society. Of course, this does not mean to justify the patriarchal suppression of women within Islamic (or, for that matter, other religious) communities in the name of cultural difference. But it is important to bestow on Islamic communities the same heterogeneity and multifaceted nature that is routinely granted to other (Christian, Jewish) religious communities. Moreover, the realm of sexual politics also complicates the New Right's relationship to Islam. For the assertion of strict gender differences in conservative Islam is quite compatible with the New Right's struggle against the diffusion of gender boundaries and sexual tolerance in Western-style modernity. In other words: the Right supports the assertion of gender boundaries and traditional roles for women as long as it is not part of Islam. Based on their ethno-fundamentalist view of the world, right-wing populists thus do not object to Islam per se but rather to its presence within Germany and Europe.

Emotional and historical continuities between right- and left-wing fears notwithstanding, these versions of fear also differ significantly. Fear is a tremendously versatile feeling that can attach itself to a variety of objects. But the nature of the object of fear also defines fear's functions and effects. Fears that center on specific persons or groups give rise to the desire to remove the object of fear. Such personalized fears have a potential to evolve into hatred and violence. Left-wing fears tended to be more abstract and did not become violent until the terrorist RAF

---

[104] Jörg Meuthen, Speech on the Stuttgart Party Congress, April 30, 2016, https://www.youtube.com/watch?v=WcU2eLwVNsc&feature=youtu.be&t=458 (last accessed March 7, 2020).

[105] Seyran Ateş, *Der Islam braucht eine sexuelle Revolution* (Berlin: Ullstein, 2009), Necla Kelek, *Die fremde Braut. Ein Bericht aus dem Inneren des türkischen Lebens in Deutschland* (Munich: Wilhelm Goldmann Verlag, 2006).

defined individual persons as representatives of the supposedly fascist Federal Republic. The Right's Islamophobia and fear of foreigners, by contrast, is represented by and manifests itself in human beings living within our midst. For right-wing fears, every single Muslim person (or refugee) serves as a representative of a collective "otherness." Because they personalize their objects of fear, right-wing fears have the potential to turn into hatred and practices of violent exclusion. Fear is a rather passive feeling that often grows out of helplessness. Hatred, by contrast, animates action and ultimately engenders violence. Right-wing violence has its origin there. In comparison to the left-wing violence, right-wing violence in the Federal Republic has not yet been sufficiently researched, even though it has been much more lethal and the number of victims many times higher. Between 1990 and 2000 alone, right-wing violence claimed more than a hundred casualties. According to the statistic of the *Amadeu Antonio Stiftung*, there were 208 deaths as a result of right-wing violence after 1990.[106] By comparison, the RAF was responsible for 34 murders between 1970 and 1998. Right-wing violence continued after 2000; the most prominent was a series of murders by the National Socialist Underground between 2000 and 2006, in which they killed nine people of Turkish descent and one Greek man. For years, police forces suspected the perpetrators to be Turkish drug dealers and exhibited a "structural incapacity" to recognize racism as a motivating force. It was only the suicide of two perpetrators in 2011 and the ensuing trial of a third, Beate Zschäpe, that brought the true nature of these crimes as right-wing terrorism to light.[107] With the growing fear of migration and refugees after 2015, the number of right-wing, extremist acts of violence rose by 50 per cent, from below 1,000 in the years before 2015 to 1,600 in 2016. This trend culminated in the murders of the CDU politician Walter Lübcke, who had supported a humane treatment of refugees, by a known neo-Nazi on June 2, 2019, and of two people during an attack on a synagogue in Halle on October 9, 2019.[108] Finally, on February 19, 2020, 10 people were killed by a racially motivated attack in Hanau.

Historically, violence always serves as a compensation for a damaged male subject.[109] In fact, such new fears are directed not only to an outside object like refugees or Islam but also projected inward at the self. They produce a "fragile ego" (Heinz Bude), which is afraid of being left behind in an increasingly complex world. Fear of strangers, of Muslims and migrants, provides an object for a more diffuse anxiety, which political movements like the AfD activate and confirm.

---

[106] On the various figures, see Herbert, *Geschichte Deutschlands*, 1177, Frei at al., *Zur rechten Zeit*, 174, and https://www.amadeu-antonio-stiftung.de/rassismus/todesopfer-rechter-gewalt (last accessed March 7, 2020).

[107] Ibid. 178–81. Zschäpe was sentenced to life in prison in July 2018.

[108] Figures according to Bundeszentrale für politische Bildung, "Straf- und Gewalttaten von rechts: Was sagen die offiziellen Statistiken?" February 6, 2018, http://www.bpb.de/politik/extremismus/rechtsextremismus/264178/pmk-statistiken (last accessed March 7, 2020).

[109] See Klaus Theweleit, *Männerphantasien*, 2 vols. (Frankfurt a/M: Fischer, 1977).

According to populists, foreigners are to blame for everything—they serve as the well-known scapegoat.[110] As shown in Chapter 7, the self increasingly became the object of fear in the 1970s. With the psychoboom, individuals searched for inner pathologies but also placed growing demands on the realization of an authentic, singular self. The increased importance of signifying a successful individuality— good food, slim body, nice apartment, interesting travel—made the self also more vulnerable and produced an increased potential for social decline, especially within the middle class.[111] Even more than such fears of social decline, AfD supporters appear to be driven by the search for a new community, the desire for a collective that offers familiarity and security. They try to stabilize an increasingly precarious self in another particular entity, the national or even folkish collective that defines itself in opposition to a foreign, mostly Islamic "other." Especially in the former East Germany, a post-reunification experience appears to be repeated here: the disappointment about the false promises of reunification created a "half-distance" to the state from which the agitation of the AfD and Pegida against the "system politicians" now benefits. The susceptibility of East Germans to authoritarian ideas is therefore not a consequence of the era of the German Democratic Republic but of the post-unification period.[112] The emotional community of a "homogenous people" is supposed to compensate for individual failure. This is where one gets recognition as well as the sense of being part of a superior collective that one misses in ordinary life. In this context, it helps that AfD politicians such as Björn Höcke also propagate a new "resilient masculinity."[113] Similar to Trumpism in the US, right-wing populism in Germany serves as a movement to stabilize a fragile white masculinity. More than a fifth of East Germans, 21.5 per cent, voted for the AfD in the federal elections of 2017, more than a quarter of East German men. By the autumn of 2019, the AfD's share of the vote had risen to 26 per cent in East Germany. This means that almost one in three men in East Germany supports an Islamophobic and racist party, which is committed to the founding of a very different republic.

The emergence of right-wing populism in Germany and elsewhere thus poses a threat to the kind of liberal democracy that has emerged in the Federal Republic since 1945. This is also why current trends in German contemporary public and academic discourse to parallelize or equate right-wing fears of migration with left-wing fears of climate change are problematic and not wholly convincing. While individuals of course experience both fears as equally real, these fears are also

---

[110] Jensen, *Zornpolitik*, 98–100, quotation in Bude, *Gesellschaft der Angst*, 96.

[111] Andreas Reckwitz, *Die Gesellschaft der Singularitäten. Zum Strukturwandel der Moderne* (Berlin: Suhrkamp, 2017).

[112] Karl-Siegbert Rehberg, "Dresden Szenen: Eine einleitende Situationsbeschreibung," in Rehberg et al., eds, *PEGIDA-Rechtspopulismus*, 15–50; Wolfgang Engler, Jana Hensel, *Wer wir sind. Die Erfahrung, ostdeutsch zu sein* (Berlin: Aufbau Verlag, 2018).

[113] Oliver Nachtwey, "PEGIDA, politische Gelegenheitsstrukturen und der neue Autoritarismus," in Rehberg et al., eds, *PEGIDA-Rechtspopulismus*, 308, Rehberg, "Dresden Szenen," 20.

categorically different. When the climate activists Greta Thunberg called on the participants of the World Economic Forum in Davos in 2018 "to feel the fear I fear" and "to panic," she inadvertently placed herself in the continuity of apocalyptic fears of environmental destruction or of nuclear war in the 1970s and 1980s.[114] As in these cases, threats are imagined as abstract and are difficult or— in the case of radioactivity—impossible to perceive with the senses. More than ever, these fears also transcend national boundaries: they can no longer be localized in a particular place. Precisely because the threats of climate change are difficult to localize or to experience, it is hard to fight them with violence. The fear of climate change that animates the "Fridays for Future" movement also differs fundamentally from fears of a nuclear catastrophe or of nuclear war during the 1980s. While these fears had centered on the anticipation of one cataclysmic event, climate change, by contrast, is very much, according to the literary critic Eva Horn, a "catastrophe without event." The fear scenario originates from the ordinariness of daily life, that is billions of individual acts resulting in CO_2 emissions.[115] Only extreme weather events, such as hot summers or hurricanes, or melting icebergs, make it possible to make climate change accessible to the senses.

The political implications of right- and left-wing fears also diverge significantly: whereas the fear of migrants aims to restrict solidarity to an ethnic core, the struggle against climate change is predicated on an extension of solidarity and depends on global coordination. Right-wing fears are also not simply the flip side of left-wing fears *of* the Right. As this book has sought to demonstrate, such democratic fears of a potential authoritarian transformation exerted a powerful stabilizing effect and contributed much to the democratization of postwar society. Their political function is very different from populist right-wing fears that have coarsened public discourse and tend to attack and belittle democratic institutions such as the free press or parliamentary government. Finally, whereas right-wing fears of migrants are based on the false and demagogic theory that immigration lies at the heart of all contemporary social and political problems, left-wing fears of climate change are supported by a virtually unanimous scientific consensus. In fact, it is precisely the anti-elitist impulse of populist movements that likes to cast doubt on fears that are often mediated and communicated by academic and scientific elites. By contrast, the visible "otherness" of the headscarf or the burka in public provides a more concrete and tangible fear object than the latest scientific study of climate change. This fear perception runs counter to the fact that the overwhelming majority of migrants do not pose a threat to majority society but are rather likely to make the host societies more productive, as immigration has

[114] "Our House Is on Fire," speech at the World Economic Forum, Davos, January 25, 2019, https://www.fridaysforfuture.org/greta-speeches#greta_speech_jan25_2019 (last accessed March 7, 2020).
[115] Horn, *Zukunft als Katastrophe*, 111, 379.

Figure 9.4. "Fridays-for-Future" demonstration at the Brandenburg Gate in Berlin, September 20, 2019.

Inspired by the Swedish schoolgirl Greta Thunberg, young people all over the world began to demonstrate for an effective policy against climate change. This movement was also based on a public display of fear. But these fears were very different than the parallel fears of migration and Islam propagated by right-wing populism.

Source: dpa Picture-Alliance, No. 124584505.

historically done.[116] By contrast, there is much evidence that the gradual warming of the planet puts the future of humanity at risk.

A Democratic Politics of Emotion

How might we counteract the politics of fear as represented and propagated by right-wing populism? During the refugee crisis in the fall of 2015, political scientist Herfried Münkler argued that politics had to transform a diffuse anxiety and uncertainty into a specific fear that could then be negotiated and politically contained.[117] Yet, as has been argued above, the distinction between fear and anxiety is difficult to maintain. For right-wing populism, the objects of fear are also quite concrete. It's just that the causal link between refugees and Islam, on the one

---

[116] See Ther, *Die Außenseiter.*
[117] Herfried Münkler, "Gefährliche Angst in der Mitte der Gesellschaft," *Süddeutsche Zeitung,* August 30, 2015.

hand, and social decline or threatened masculinity, on the other hand, is simply wrong. Yet, the pure gesture of rational enlightenment alone is probably not sufficient here. The fault lines and internal contradictions of right-wing populism should of course be highlighted, and false facts that are supposed to incite fear should be named.[118] But the discrediting of right-wing fears as simply irrational appears to be counterproductive because they are subjectively always experienced as true. To be diagnosed as being sick or insane by liberal elites hardly constitutes a promising means of persuasion.[119]

Instead, the question is what a democratic politics of emotion might actually look like? Right-wing fears stand in the continuity of a broader culture of emotional expressiveness that was dominant in the Federal Republic from the 1960s onward—first among the intellectual elites (Chapter 5), then in social movements (Chapter 6), and finally in society as a whole (Chapter 7). The struggle against right-wing populism cannot undo this culture of emotional expressiveness and simply assume an attitude of rational enlightenment, especially since the contrast between emotion and reason is fictitious to begin with. Precisely because right-wing populism draws on emotions—fear, but also anger and hatred—it is important to address it at the emotional level as well. But not all emotions are equally legitimate. It is possible to take fears seriously while, at the same time, seeking to prevent their transformation into resentment and hatred because these emotions are no longer susceptible to political negotiation and lead to violence and civil war.

Paradoxically, one way to cultivate democratic emotions might be the mobilization of democratic fears. As the history of fear in the Federal Republic demonstrates, it was precisely the permanent anxiety of succumbing to a new authoritarianism that constituted one of the basic aspects of postwar democratization. As I have tried to demonstrate, fear can and has served very different political goals and by no means always stands in opposition to democracy. Given the rise of right-wing populism, the present task would have to be to mobilize anxiety about the loss of liberal democracy and pluralistic society. As discussed in Chapter 3, the first Federal Chancellor Adenauer already realized that the mobilization of competing fears (the fear of Communism) can also serve to contain other fears (the fear of war). Democratic fears therefore play an important role in the defense of democracy. They encapsulate a fundamental "lesson" of the old Federal Republic—namely, the realization that the success and future existence of democracy is by no means self-evident. Democratic fears thus also reflect an emotional investment in liberal democracy as well as in some of the progressive accomplishments of the Federal Republic, such as a critical view of the national past, an at least tenuous acceptance of the reality of a multicultural society, and a theoretical (if not always realized) commitment to the equality of the sexes. An emotional defense of liberal

---

[118] Amann, *Angst für Deutschland*, 263–76.   [119] Jensen, *Zornpolitik*, 99–100.

democracy does not need to degenerate into a misguided and pathological "tyrannophobia," as historians Samuel Moyn and David Priestland characterized it.[120] It also does not mean an endless recycling of the specter of a new fascism. Democratic fears can rather reflect a historically grown attachment to liberal democracy and an open society. An emotional commitment to what we might have to lose thus might serve as an antidote to the politics of fear from the Right. This intensified concern for democracy also does not preclude the recognition that growing social inequality is incompatible with liberal democracy. Instead, the defense of democratic institutions must go hand in hand with creating economic prospects and a basic social safety net.[121]

As this book has demonstrated as well, fearful futures were always closely intertwined with a shifting commemorative culture. What memory would therefore be productive for the mobilization of democratic fears? An ossified Holocaust remembrance that expresses itself in increasingly empty rituals or monumental memorials does not seem particularly useful here, especially if it insists too much on historical singularity and national specificity. Instead, it would be more important to reconnect the Holocaust memory with more everyday forms of racism. Holocaust memory might focus less exclusively on the truly "singular" historical endpoint of the Holocaust in Auschwitz and Treblinka, and also on everyday forms of discrimination and racial exclusion during the 1930s. The Holocaust memorial in the Bavarian quarter in Berlin is a good example of this approach. On 80 signs placed throughout the neighborhood, they depict racist restrictions on Jewish life in Nazi Germany. The monument was established in May 1993 only one week after the racist arson attack on a Turkish family in Solingen that killed five people and injured 14 more. City officials did not hesitate to draw the connection between commemorating past racist exclusions and present racist violence, and the creators of the monument—the artists Renata Stih und Frieder Schnock—continue to emphasize its relevance for the present.[122] Such a lively commemorative culture might also serve as the basis for a German identity that respects ethnic and cultural differences precisely because it demonstrates the possible, yet not inevitable, consequences of rejecting difference and the concomitant longing for ethnic homogeneity.

Equally important is a heightened awareness of the longer history of racism and exclusion, which predates the rise of National Socialism and also includes the German colonial past. A broader public discussion of colonial racism in the late

---

[120] Samuel Moyn, David Priestland, "Trump Isn't a Threat to our Democracy, Hysteria Is," *New York Times*, August 11, 2018.

[121] This insight already existed in Weimar: see Tim B. Müller, *Nach dem Ersten Weltkrieg. Lebensversuche moderner Demokratien* (Hamburg: Hamburger Edition, 2014).

[122] On this monument and its relevance for contemporary commemorative culture, see Frank Biess, "Vom Hinsehen und Wegsehen: Das Denkmal im bayrischen Viertel und die Holocaust-Erinnerung heute," in Harald Roth, ed., *Nie Wegsehen* (Bonn: Dietz, forthcoming, 2020).

nineteenth and early twentieth centuries, which was based on notions of civiliza-
tional superiority and the assumption of a fundamental otherness of non-white
people, might sharpen the sensitivity to such attitudes in the present. For example,
the critique of traditional gender ideologies in Islam adopts an argument that has
historically served the justification of Western colonialism. The liberation of
women in Asia and Africa from their traditional shackles then served to legitimize a Western civilizing mission. This justification of racism in the colonial past
provides the historical ground for similar forms of racism toward ethnic minorities in the present. The AfD is very much aware of this link. This is one reason
why the party rejects a postcolonial confrontation with the past—for example, in
the debate about stolen colonial artifacts on display in Berlin museums.[123]

Besides mobilizing democratic fears, a democratic politics of emotions might
also mobilize countervailing emotions that act to contain fear. Specific emotions
never exist in isolation. They are always relational—that is, they correspond with
each other and occasionally converge. For example, right-wing fears can easily
turn into anger or hatred and thus justify not just the discursive but also the
actual and potentially violent exclusion of others. At the same time, other emotions such as trust or even love can reduce fear. Unfortunately, recent polls suggest that trust in politics and in political elites to solve the pressing problems of
the day is rapidly declining in Germany. Ironically, it is precisely right-wing
populism that promotes more direct democracy and participation of the "people,"
albeit always conceived of as ethnically homogenous. By contrast, established
political parties tend to promote trust in the representative institutions of the
state and, above all, in their own significance in educating and shaping popular
attitudes.[124] Trust, or, as historian Ute Frevert argues, a more passive and less
morally charged confidence in the problem-solving capacity of the political system, is indispensable for representative democracy.[125] A renewed confidence in
democratic processes and institutions may also be a product of democratic fears.
For example, Donald Trump's electoral victory in 2016 motivated the *Indivisible*
movement, which seeks to increase democratic participation at the local level and
motivated a record number of candidates without previous experience to run for
office. In this case, the fear of losing democratic freedoms led to a new political
mobilization of citizens, especially at the local level.[126] Political participation in
local communities has the potential to produce visible and perceptible results,
such as the election of a member of Congress, or even just a representative on the

---

[123] Jörg Häntzschel, "So raffiniert wie zwielichtig," *Süddeutsche Zeitung*, July 26, 2018. See also
Deutscher Bundestag, 19. Wahlperiode, Große Anfrage der AfD-Fraktion, "Aufarbeiten der
Provinzienzen von Kulturgut aus kolonialem Erbe in Museen und Sammlungen," Drucksache 19/3264.
On this link, see also Rita Chin, *The Crisis of Multiculturalism in Europe. A History* (Princeton:
Princeton University Press, 2017), 192–236.
[124] Wildt, *Volk, Volksgemeinschaft, AfD*, 97–104.
[125] Ute Frevert, *Vertrauensfragen. Eine Obsession der Moderne* (Munich: C.H.Beck, 2013), 209–11.
[126] https://www.indivisible.org (last accessed March 7, 2020).

state parliament or city council. Such practices might help to reduce the feeling of powerlessness, which is a basic condition of fear.

Besides trust, empathy is an emotional resource to contain right-wing populism. Empathy has gained increasing popularity in modernity. It now appears as an emotional antipode to the violent excesses of the first half of the twentieth century, which the denial of empathy for those who were not part of one's own community (as defined either by racial or class boundaries) made possible. Yet, as we have seen, memories of the past can be mobilized for envisioning many different futures. Germans' own experience of mass displacement in the aftermath of the Second World War thus might also enhance empathy with today's refugees who experience a similar fate. Indeed, there is evidence that precisely this psychic operation of projecting one's own experience of suffering onto other groups formed the starting point of the West German human rights movement. Of course, empathy is an ambivalent emotion, as Friedrich Nietzsche has already pointed out. The emotion creates a hierarchy between the empathic person and the person who represents the object of empathy.[127] Empathy can also exacerbate existing cleavages and fuel polarization in a society if it is directed primarily at the members of one's own political, ethnic, or religious community.[128] This is why a third collective is necessary, a different and new "we" in which both sides can participate. This is the basis for what sociologist Heinz Bude sees as a new form of solidarity.[129] Still, as a perquisite for such solidarity, empathy can help to dissolve the abstract notion of a collective other which easily functions as an object of fear.

Empathy also means relating to the emotions of others. Whose emotions are being heard is ultimately a question of political and cultural power. In contemporary discourse, much attention has been given to the fears that are articulated by majority society. In so doing, one runs the risk of engaging in what the critic Max Czollek has called a "rhetorics of tenderness" toward the Right that pays disproportionate attention to fears of foreigners.[130] What then gets lost in this perspective are the fears of the "others"—that is, members of cultural or ethnic minorities who are the target of hatred and, increasingly, of violence as well. A more complete history of fear in the Federal Republic would thus have to expand the focus beyond majority society and give a voice to the fears of these actual and potential victims of racist violence. A democratic politics of emotion would apply Judith Shklar's notion of a "liberalism of fear" to the situation of minorities and define the protection of such minorities as one of the most prominent tasks of the liberal-democratic state.

---

[127] On the history of empathy, see Ute Frevert, *Vergängliche Gefühle* (Göttingen: Wallstein, 2013), 44–8, 72–81.

[128] See Elizabeth N. Simas, Scott Clifford, Justin H. Kirkland, "How Emphatic Concern Fuels Political Polarization," *American Political Science Review* 114/1 (2020): 258–69.

[129] Heinz Bude, *Solidarität. Die Zukunft einer großen Idee* (Berlin: Hanser, 2019), 103–14.

[130] Max Czollek, *Desintegriert Euch!* (Munich: btb, 2020), 117.

The emotional sensibilities of majority society thus would have to extend to the feelings of minorities.[131] Perhaps big problems need to be tackled by seemingly small solutions that are nevertheless woven into the fabric of daily life.[132] Sociologist Zygmunt Bauman reminds us, for example, that conversation is the best means of overcoming fear. For it is precisely personal contact that promotes empathy and reduces fears of an abstract "other." It is therefore not surprising that the AfD is most successful in those areas with the fewest foreigners—in the states of Saxony and Saxony-Anhalt, foreigners make up 3.9 per cent of the population, but the national average is 10.5 per cent.[133] Fear is mainly a fantasy product that does not result from intensive contact with the world but rather from the opposite: a sense of isolation. In this context, sociologist Hartmut Rosa's proposal to combine the struggle against xenophobia and racism with new infrastructure appears productive as well. A better connection of rural areas to urban centers as well as the strengthening of local infrastructure might counteract feelings of isolation, abandonment, and backwardness. It is precisely this "exclusion of the world" that, according to Rosa, leads to a "petrifaction of the self" and hence makes individuals susceptible to anxiety but incapable of empathy and solidarity.[134]

---

[131] This perspective in Jan-Werner Müller, *Furcht und Freiheit. Für einen anderen Liberalismus* (Berlin: Suhrkamp, 2019).

[132] See, for example, the initiative of the German Society, https://www.deutsche-gesellschaft-ev.de/veranstaltungen/bildungsangebote/185-2016-18-buergergespraeche-meine-neue-heimat.html (last accessed March 7, 2020).

[133] https://www.laenderdaten.de/europa/deutschland/bundeslaender/auslaenderanteil.aspx (last accessed March 7, 2020).

[134] Hartmut Rosa, "Der Versuch einer sklerotischen Gesellschaft, sich die Welt vom Leibe zu halten—und ein Vorschlag zum Neuanfang," in Rehberg et al., eds, *PEGIDA-Rechtspopulismus*, 289–96.

Conclusion

How "German" were postwar German fears? This book has provided three answers to this question. First, a specific German inclination toward fear after 1945 resulted from an intersection of memories of the past and expectations for the future. The nationally specific catastrophe of war, fascism, and the Holocaust formed a space of experience that was then projected into the future and hence led contemporaries to doubt the eventual success of West German democracy. The history of these West German fears confirms the observation that defeated societies might be better capable of learning from past experiences than victorious ones. Their historical awareness entails a deeply engrained knowledge of negative contingencies, of unintended outcomes, of plans gone awry. These were indeed national historical specificities, which, however, did not manifest themselves as collective pathologies but rather as different configurations linking past and future. While many of the fears discussed here—fears of war, of automation, of environmental destruction—also existed in other countries, the specifically German nature of these fear cycles resulted from the distinct context of Germany's catastrophic past.[1] This was, in other words, a "German" German *Angst,* that emerged out of the self-observation of postwar society.

The precise contours of West German democracy were not predetermined at the Federal Republic's founding, partly because the West German state emerged out of total defeat and postwar occupation. The institutional framework of the Basic Law needed to be filled with life, and how "democracy as a way of life" was supposed to look was a matter of heated and controversial debates.[2] Political fears in the Federal Republic emerged because competing political camps continued to harbor suspicions that the other side was seeking to transform the Federal Republic in an authoritarian direction. This dialectic of fears between a center-left and a center-right fueled heated political debates into the 1980s. What were at stake here were not just competing policy proposals but the very nature of the Bonn democracy. Here too, memories of the past fueled a keen awareness on the Left and on the Right that democracy can indeed fail. The emotional intensity of postwar politics owed much to this basic uncertainty and catastrophic imagination.

---

[1] Reinhart Koselleck, "Erfahrungswandel und Methodenwechsel," in Reinhart Koselleck, *Zeitschichten. Studien zur Historik* (Frankfurt a/M: Suhrkamp, 2003), 27–77, here 68–9, 77.

[2] Till van Rahden, *Demokratie. Eine gefährdete Lebensform* (Frankfurt a/M: Campus, 2019).

German Angst: *Fear and Democracy in the Federal Republic of Germany.* Frank Biess, Oxford University Press (2020).
© Frank Biess.
DOI: 10.1093/oso/9780198714187.001.0001

Postwar fears were also based on the creation of an "emotional community" that defined itself against internal enemies.[3] The changing images of the "other" after 1945 (displaced persons, recruiters, Communists, terrorist sympathizers, asylum seekers, Muslims) also integrated elements of "the Jew" as the traditional internal enemy before 1945. In this respect, the history of postwar fears continued a "dramatization of politics" that extended back into the interwar period.[4] Yet the specific forms and especially the consequences of this marginalization of "others" differed in the Federal Republic and in the Third Reich. So did the forms of this emotional dramatization: from an activist emphasis on struggle, hatred, and violence after the First World War to a more passive cultivation of suffering and victimhood after 1945. The German self-victimization after 1945, however, worked both retrospectively and prospectively. It projected the status of German victimhood into the future and conjured up threatening future scenarios of foreign enslavement and nuclear destruction, totalitarian dictatorship and ecological disaster."

A second answer to the question posed at the outset can be found in the discursive history and political uses of the notion of "German angst." What is often cast as a German national pathology was actually a rhetorical figure that was mobilized, above all, in the political debates of the 1980s and 1990s. It was projected from the outside onto Germans, but then also adopted by commentators within Germany. Th notion of a "German angst" served as a conservative argument within a broader critique of pacifist positions or of those critical of unhindered technological progress. During the 2000s, "German angst" also came to serve as an expression of a long-lasting traumatization in the Second World War, inherited by both "war children" and "war grandchildren." The historical specificity of the idea of German angst means that it cannot be described as a collective national pathology. It was rather an idea that emerged in a specific historical and political context, and that served primarily conservative political interests and commemorative goals.

Third, this book has shown that, although the culture of fear that underlies current right-wing populism stood in the continuity of specifically German fears, the rise of the Right was reflective of a broader transnational phenomenon. German right-wing populism benefited from a changed emotional regime that enabled and promoted the public expression of emotions. At the same time, right-wing populists also transformed this emotional culture and propagated an emotional politics that resembled that of the interwar period, especially through the cultivation of resentment and hatred toward alleged internal enemies. German right-wing populism's ambivalent relationship to established commemorative

---

[3] Barbara H. Rosenwein, "Worrying about Emotions in History," *American Historical Review* 107/3 (2002): 821–45.

[4] Bernd Weisbrod, "Die Politik der Repräsentation. Das Erbe des Ersten Weltkrieges und der Formwandel der Politik in Europa," in Hans Mommsen, ed., *Der Erste Weltkrieg und die europäische Nachkriegsordnung. Sozialer Wandel und Formveränderung der Politik* (Cologne: Böhlau, 2001), 13–41.

culture—it questioned established Holocaust memory yet also emerged within it—marked it as specifically German. But German right-wing populism shared with similar movements in Europe and in the United States the political focus on immigration as well as forms of action such as the strategy of deliberate provocation. In this respect, it was a German version of a transnational phenomenon.

Fear had a long and complex history in the Federal Republic. Historical fears were subject to constant change throughout the postwar period. The objects of fear constantly shifted, and intensive periods of fear emerged but then also dissipated again in the history of the Federal Republic. Its causes, functions and protagonists varied widely across time. Fear, as this book has demonstrated, is an eminently historical category without a stable meaning. What factors explain the rise and fall of German fears after 1945? And what conclusions can we draw from this for the role of fear in our present?

Changing international and global contexts constituted one factor in the emergence and the ensuing decline of specific fears. Fears of war, for example, weakened significantly after the mid 1960s with the onset of détente in the Cold War. Such larger contexts for the formation of political emotions are beyond the control of individuals or even nation states. As this book has repeatedly shown, however, fears and emotions in general were not just epiphenomenal—that is, a secondary product of changing larger contexts. These emotions were never just the quasi-natural expression of certain objective conditions but rather resulted from new sensibilities and changed subjective perceptions. Fears resided in the realm of the imaginary; they constituted fantasies of an undesirable future. This is why the containment of fears cannot be achieved solely by changing external realities but must begin at the level of subjective perception. The containment of fear in the present thus requires the stabilization of fragile, especially male, subjectivities—but not through the misguided and dangerous mobilization of fear and hatred of ethnic or religious "others," rather the developing and securing of positive social and economic perspectives for the future. The emotional broadening of subjectivities in terms of compassion, understanding, and empathy is equally important.

Fears also declined because their inner contradictions and lack of plausibility became apparent, as in the case of the Foreign Legion. This example demonstrates the significance of education and a pursuit of factual truth in at least some situations. Even if fears cannot be overcome simply by proving that they are unjustified, public evidence of the erroneous assumptions on which contemporary fears are based constitutes one means of containing them. Insisting on facts, plausibility, and truth can indeed reduce fears, especially because they are often based on a deliberate denial, or manipulation, of facts.

This insight also points to the role and responsibility of the media. Media attention played an important, indeed crucial, role in the history of fear in the Federal Republic after 1945. Which objects of fear came into public focus was always also a question of their thematization in the media. In fact, the deliberate use of emotions like fear often constituted a means of attracting public attention. The media co-produced, for example, the fear of recruiters for the Foreign Legion or of sympathizers of terrorism. The same mechanisms also applied to left-wing fears—for example, in the 1980s debate over whether Germany's forests were dying. That is not to say that the media can arbitrarily and single-handedly mobilize specific fears. Crises of fear only occur when the stimulation of fears in the media meets broader social and cultural uncertainties. This was the precondition for the signification spirals that ensured the social and cultural resonance of threat scenarios as propagated in the mass media. When these broader uncertainties declined—for example, regarding Allied retribution after the Second World War or fears of a nuclear war in the Cold War—specific fears declined and shifted to other objects, which then also gained new media attention. When and under what conditions predispositions to fear and anxiety were activated is a historical question that requires the analysis of special political contexts. Right-wing populist movements currently benefit from the very real uncertainties and fears associated with deep structural and transnational transformations. Yet, political actors such as the Alternative for Germany (AfD) and other right-wing parties also dramatize and intensify these fears, and they transform them into resentment toward, and hatred of, minorities.

The last example drives home the point that fears to this day have been, and are, consciously produced and mobilized by a specific politics of fear. In some cases, social movements mobilized fears and emotions, be it the environmental and peace movements of the seventies and eighties or right-wing populism today. The state functioned (and continues to function) more as a force of restraint on fear. Yet, in other cases, the state also engaged in a politics of fear that produced (and still produces) fear "from above," such as in state-sponsored anti-Communism after 1945 or the deliberate agitation against immigrants in Trump's America. These examples underline the power of the modern bureaucratic state to pursue a specific politics of emotions that aims either at their stimulation or at their containment. This also means that the role of emotions in politics must become part of the political debate. A greater awareness and knowledge of what emotions are and how they function in politics might thus assist in engaging with emotions more consciously for the defense of democracy. Democratic counter-strategies need to expose and criticize a politics of fear that seeks to exclude and ostracize "others," no matter whether it emanates from the state or from political movements. As a result, the deliberate mobilization of existing fears through authoritarian nationalism could lose some of its plausibility. It could be unmasked for what it is—a conscious politics of emotions to foster hatred and resentment, mostly for authoritarian political purposes.

This history of fear in the Federal Republic repeatedly also demonstrated the close link between history of knowledge and history of emotions. Academic disciplines—first, the social sciences, then, from the sixties onward, the psychosocial sciences—took on a normative role in the diagnosis and evaluation of fears. The rise of the psychological sciences brought into focus new fears that were anchored in society and in the self. During the 1980s, an emerging scientific counter-expertise elevated fear to a central emotion in the environmental and peace movements. Fear and science were never antithetical but always remained deeply interwoven. Scientific authority has become ever more central to the ways in which fears are debated and articulated—for example, in the discussion about climate change. In modern "risk society," to use Ulrich Beck's concept, fears do not attain an independent, quasi-objective existence.[5] On the contrary, scientific expertise is often necessary to make visible the underlying dangers that give rise to fears and hence make them socially negotiable.

Yet, many of the fears of migrants or Islam currently articulated by right-wing populists are not based on scientifically verifiable experiences or facts. Instead, these fears perhaps also indicate a longing for a more immediate emotional expression that is not submitted to the scrutiny of scientific authorities. In fact, experts and scientific authorities often question the alleged facts underlying these fears, such as the causal connection between downward mobility and immigration. An anti-elitist impulse turns against scientific authority and asserts a right to an immediate and supposedly authentic form of emotional expression by "the people." In this respect too, right-wing fears build on an expressive emotional regime as it has emerged since the 1960s.

As this book has demonstrated, emotions do not have an independent or fixed political meaning. Their function and significance always depend on their specific contexts. This is also why the case studies assembled in this book do not lend themselves to a general theory of the relationship between fear and democracy. The mobilization of fear can undermine democracy by justifying discrimination and reprisals against minorities. A perceived internal or external threat can justify the use of state power to restrict democratic control, civil liberties, or pluralism. On the other hand, this book has also underlined the ways in which fear strengthened democratic sensibilities and thus promoted the democratization of the Federal Republic.

The analysis of the role of fear, and of emotions in general, in the history of the Federal Republic also reveals that fears have often evaded deliberate manipulation—with respect to both their mobilization and containment. There is something resistant, willful, about emotions. As we all know from our own experience, they cannot always be controlled or subjected to conscious manipulation. We have to live with them without letting them completely guide our actions. Contrary to the expectations of contemporaries in the Federal Republic, things often turned out better than anticipated. And when actual crises occurred—Chernobyl, 9/11, the

[5] Ulrich Beck, *Risikogesellschaft. Auf dem Weg in eine andere Moderne* (Frankfurt a/M: Suhrkamp, 1986), 10.

financial crisis, a string of terrorist attacks—Germans tended to react, according to the general perception, more calmly than expected. They might have confirmed the observation of the Danish philosopher Søren Kierkegaard, according to which the hypochondriac, who is "anxious about every insignificant thing" begins "to breathe more easily" when "the significant appears." Because this "significant actuality" turns out to be "not so terrible as the possibility he himself had fashioned, and which he used his strength to fashion, whereas he can now use all his strength against actuality."[6]

If post-1945 German society indeed had something hypochondriac, then, this dramatization of the future would be, according to Kierkegaard, one of the preconditions for overcoming actual crises. This experience of fears that did not come true, however, was not just an expression of an existential human condition. It was also a specific historical feature of the period after 1945. Many of the fears that were derived from the catastrophic first half of the twentieth century did not come true in post-1945 Europe. This discrepancy between the experience of fear and actually lived reality, between imagined futures and historical experience, constituted itself a hallmark of the period of Cold War reconstruction. The persistent yet constantly changing presence of a catastrophic and violent past shaped contemporaries' anticipation of the future throughout the postwar era. In fact, this intersection of the past and of the future was one of the factors that defined the post-1945 period as "postwar."

In light of the very different historical circumstances of the early twenty-first century, this historically specific experience of fears that did not come true has itself become history, a history that this book has attempted to tell. This analysis might provide clues for today's confrontation with political fears. Yet, ostensible historical lessons can also be misleading. It would be wrong, for example, to derive from the post-1945 experience an emotional indifference that simply assumes that everything will turn out well. Contemporary problems such as climate change or globalization differ from the objects of past fears too much to justify such a "wait and see" attitude. At the same time, fading memories of the past that had been so present after 1945 also enable the return of past dangers, such as a new authoritarianism from the Right. Fear and democracy remained connected in multiple ways in the Federal Republic after 1945. Yet, the historical experience of catastrophe that did not happen can no longer serve as a guide to action today. We should better think very carefully what exactly we want to be afraid of. Because these fears could indeed prevent the future that they imagine.

---

[6] Søren Kierkegaard, *The Concept of Anxiety. A Simple Psychologically Orienting Deliberation on the Dogmatic Issue of Hereditary Sin* (Princeton: Princeton University Press, 2013 [1844]), 162.

Primary Sources

Akademie der schönen Künste, Berlin, Kempowski Archiv (KA)

Nr. 40, Nr. 1676, Nr. 3237, Nr. 3675, Nr. 3715

Archiv der Rheinischen Kliniken

Patientenakte Hans-Georg G.

Archiv der Sozialen Demokratie, Friedrich Ebert-Stiftung, Bonn (ASD)

IGMA *IG Metall Archiv*
NL Fritz Erler
PLKA
ZASS2, DW 2-9e3, Zeitungsausschnittssammlung

Archiv Grünes Gedächtnis (AGG)

BI.1 Die Grünen (1980–93)
BII.1 Die Grünen, Bundestagsfraktion (1983–90)

Archiv für Christlich-Demokratische Politik, Sankt Augustin (ACDP)

Plakatsammlung

Bayerisches Hauptstaatsarchiv München (BHStA)

LFlüV Landesflüchtlingsverwaltung
MSo Ministerium für Sonderaufgaben, Ministerium für Politische Befreiung
Stk Staatskanzlei

Bibliothek für Zeitgeschichte, Stuttgart (BfZ)

Neue soziale Bewegungen
Zeit der Weltkriege

Bundesarchiv Koblenz (BArch)

B106 Ministerium des Inneren
B134 Ministerium der Arbeit
B141 Ministerium der Justiz
NL Fraenkel

Deutscher Bundestag, Pressearchiv (DB-PA)

060
911

Deutsches Film Museum (DFM)

Filmrezensionen

Deutsches Tagebucharchiv, Emmendingen (DTA)

Nr. 185, Nr. 389, Nr. 528, Nr. 1495, Nr. 2683, A 789

Hamburger Institut für Sozialforschung (HIS)

HBA Hochschule Bayern
HHE Hochschule Hessen
SAK Sozialistisches Anwaltskollektiv, Kommune 1
SBe Protestbewegungen, Neue Soziale Bewegungen

Hauptstaatsarchiv Baden-Württemberg (HStABaWü)

EA 2 Innenministerium

Historisches Archiv des Westdeutschen Rundfunks (WDR Archive)

Quellen zur Fernsehserie *Holocaust*

Hoover Institution, Palo Alto (HI)

Bund Freiheit der Wissenschaft
Office Military Government, Berlin (OMGB)

Landeshauptarchiv Koblenz (LHAK)

Nr. 880, Ministerium des Innern und für Sport

National Archives, College Park, Md (NA)

RG 260 Records of US Occupation Headquarters, Second World War

Nordrhein-Westfälisches Hauptstaatsarchiv (NRWHStA)

NW 34 Innenministerium NRW
NW 36 Arbeits- und Sozialministerium NRW
NW 59 Innenministerium NRW
NW 061 Arbeits- und Sozialministerium NRW
NW112 Innenministerium NRW
NW 377 Justizministerium NRW
NW 648 Ministerium für Arbeit, Gesundheit und Soziales

Politisches Archiv des Auswärtigen Amtes (PAA)

B 10 Politische Abteilung

Rheinisch-Westfälisches Wirtschaftsarchiv (RWWA)

Abt. 3 Industrie- und Handelskammer Koblenz
Abt. 122 Johan Wülling und Sohn
Abt. 130 Gutehoffnungshütte

Staatsarchiv Freiburg (StA Freiburg)

B 719/2 Landratsamt Lörrach
F30/1 Regierungspräsidium Freiburg
S60/1 Landkreistag Baden-Württemberg

Stadtarchiv München (StaMü)

Bürgermeister und Rat

Zentralarchiv für Empirische Sozialforschung, Köln (ZAK)

Allensbacher Berichte
Emnid Informationen

Newspapers and Magazines

Aachener Nachrichten
Allgemeine Zeitung, Mainz

Bundesgesetzblatt
Christ und Welt
Coburger Neue Presse
Düsseldorfer Nachrichten
Echo der Woche
Der Fortschritt
Frankfurter Allgemeine Zeitung
Frankfurter Neue Presse
Frankfurter Rundschau
Generalanzeiger
Hamburger Echo
Industrie-Kurier
Kölnische Rundschau
Der Mittag
Münchner Abendzeitung
Neue Tagespost Osnabrück
Die Neue Zeitung
New York Times
Nürnberger Nachrichten
Psychologie Heute
Recklinghäuser Zeitung
Revue
Rheinische Post
Rhein-Neckar Zeitung
Rhein Zeitung Koblenz
Ruhr Nachrichten Dortmund

Saarbrücker Landeszeitung
Schwäbische Tageszeitung

Spektrum
Der Spiegel
Stenographische Berichte, Deutscher Bundestag
Stern
Stuttgarter Zeitung

Süddeutsche Zeitung
Der Tagesspiegel
Taz

Vorwärts
Die Welt
Weser Kurier
Westdeutsche Allgemeine
Westfalenpost Hagen
Die Zeit
Ziviler Luftschutz

Index

Note: Figures are indicated by an italic "*f*" following the paragraph number. Footnotes are indicated by the letter "n" after the page number.

For the benefit of digital users, indexed terms that span two pages (e.g., 52–53) may, on occasion, appear on only one of those pages

Aachen, Technical University 136–7
abduction narrative
    decline of 84–94
    see also Foreign Legion
Abendroth, Wolfgang 191
academics, and emergency laws 185
accessory justice 176, 178–9
acid rain 309, 311–13, 337
"acid violence," 310–11
Adenauer, Konrad 21–2, 74–5, 77, 84, 97–9,
        163–8, 363–4
    and anti-Communism 106–7
    and brochure "Everybody Has a
        Chance," 119–21
    on fear of nuclear war 106–7
    gender politics of 118–19
    policy of rearmament 104–5
    policy of Western integration 101–2,
        104–5, 111–12
    as role model for students 206
    on *Rückversicherer* 104–5
Adorno, Theodor 136–7, 150, 191, 234
    "Education after Auschwitz," 174
    "What is the Meaning of Coming to Terms
        with the Past?" 173–4
Advisory Council on the Environment 308–9
AfD (Alternative for Germany) 143–5, 337–8,
        347–59, 367
    and apocalyptic scenarios 355–6
    election ad 351*f*
    and emotionality 357–8, 370–1
    link with migration 349–50
    and loss of trust in authority 356–7
Afghanistan,
    invasion by Soviet Union 291–2, 314–15
    refugees from 342–4, 355
Africa 165–6
    French colonies in 71
African Americans, as soldiers 13–14, 24
Africans, colonial 78–9

Agenda 2010 347–8
aggression 207–8, 219–21, 229–30,
        247–8, 265–6
Agnoli, Johannes 357–8
    Transformation of Democracy, The 201
Ahr valley, government bunker 324–5
AIDS 337
air defense measures 107–8
air raid shelters 121
Albanians, in Kosovo 339
Albertz, Heinrich 196
Albrecht, Ernst 303–4
alcoholism 51–2
alexithymia 245–6
Algeria 67, 70–1, 76, 93
alienation 148–9, 203–4, 247, 266–7
Allemann, Fritz René 161–2
    Bonn is not Weimar 159–60
Allensbach Institute for Demoscopy 108,
        110–11, 125–6, 206, 284–5, 291–2, 307–8
Allgemeine Forstzeitschrift 309–10
Alliance, Western 97–8
    occupation authorities 107–8
Allied Control Council 84
    Law No. 11 70–1
Allied forces 4–5
    bombing by 28, 31–3, 54–6, 108–10, 116–18,
        123, 339–40
    fears of revenge by 27–8
    liberation of death and concentration
        camps 26–7
    Normandy landing 40–1
    occupation by 18, 27–8
Allied High Commission 73–5, 107–8
Allies,
    denazification policies 170
    emergency rights 184
    and fears of retribution 370–1
    internment camps 60–1
Alsace 300

Altmann, Rüdiger 164–5
Altmeier, Peter 74–5
Aly, Götz 198–9
Amadeu Antonio Stiftung 358–9
Amberg 51–2
Americanization 2–3, 333–4
Amery, Carl 167, 307–8
amnesty campaigns (for Nazi crimes) 101–2
Amsterdam 222
Anders, Günther 276–7, 316
  "Us, Sons of Eichmann," 178
anger 20, 363, 365–6
  at government officials 123–4
  politics of 357–8
angst, German,
  and Cold War 21–2, 95–129
  as concept 1–2, 332–7, 369
  democratic 22
  as historical construct 340–1
  modern 22
  moral 21
  post-unification 23
  postwar 21, 63–5
  proliferating 23
  revolutionary 22
  and US policies 331
animal films 296
animals, environmental threats to 296
Ansbach 41–2
anthropology, philosophical 140–1
antibiotics 295–6
anti-Bolshevism 98, 101–2, 165–6
anti-colonialism 211–13
anti-Communism 97–107, 128–9, 197, 334–5
  legislation for 103–4
  state-sponsored 371
anti-elitism 372
anti-emotionality 116–18
antifascism 102–3, 213, 226, 231–2
  consensus on 354
anti-imperialism 210–11, 213
anti-intellectualism 151–2
anti-nuclear movement 287–8, 298–307
  democracy in 305–6
  scientific counter-expertise 302–6, 311
antisemitism 25, 31–2, 37–8, 183–4,
    196, 208–11
  and anti-Bolshevism 101–2
  and anti-democracy 173–4
  contrasted with Islamophobia 353–4
  and democracy 173–4
  and fear of blood pollution 83–4
  graffiti 170, 173
  incidents of late 1950s/early 1960s 172–5

in New Left 210–11
and "other," 353
perceived, among Muslims 353–4
propaganda 102–3
"secondary," 37–8
"anti-war" day (1983) 319f
anti-war movement 211–13
anti-Zionism 209–11
anxiety,
  existential 64–5
  and fear 253–4
  internalization of 19, 37–8
  "neurotic absence of," 315–16
  normal and abnormal 253
  over automation 135
  preventive basic 266–7
  in schools 254
"apocalypse blindness," 316
apocalyptic fear 284–5, 289, 312–13, 317, 329,
    332, 360–1
  and insurance companies 306–7
apocalyptic visions 244, 278, 319f
  AfD and 355–6
Apollo space program 293–4
Arbeitsgeber, Der 148–9
Arendt, Hannah 177–8, 181–2
  "Report from Germany," 63–4
Asia 165–6
  French colonies in 71
assassinations 213–14
  targeted 287–8
astronauts 134–5
asylum seekers 3, 20, 341–5
  attacks on 343–4
  legislation on 344
  numbers in Germany 344, 349
  as "others," 369
Ateş, Seyran 358
Atlantic Charter 4–5
Auflockerung (partial evacuation) 114
Augsburg 36
Augstein, Rudolf 186–7
Augustine of Hippo 6
Ausch, Karl 141–2
Auschwitz concentration camp 34–5, 37–8,
    57–9, 177, 180f, 211–13, 278, 317–18,
    319f, 339, 364
  trial 128–9, 170, 174–6, 179–82, 180f, 272–3
austerity politics 345–7
Austria 165–6
  border with Germany 349
authenticity, emotional 22
authoritarianism 3, 6, 18–19, 22, 129, 132–3,
    137, 139, 162–3, 165–9, 368

Agnoli on 201
and childhood sexuality 230
and child-rearing 213–14, 231–2
and concerted action 200–1
and democracy 182, 184, 192, 200–1, 331
descent into 193–4, 201
in East Germany/Eastern Europe 345, 352–3
and education 231–2
and emergency laws 185
in families 229–30
and fascism 229–30, 265
fear of 168–9, 174, 188, 202, 233–4, 265,
    286–9, 302–3, 331, 361–4
Jaspers on 189–90
and mobilization of fears 371
new 288–9, 331, 363–4, 373
rise of 331
skepticism regarding 302–3
temptations of 183–4
automation 22, 133
cultural consequences 143–5
debate on 134–58, 168, 170–3, 178
    at Tutzing conference 141–2
and deskilling of workers 143–5, 147
"Detroit," 135
and economic recession 156–7
and education 152–3
emotional dimension 138, 143–5
and employment 137, 143–5, 144f, 147–8
fears of 336–7, 368
and moderate Left 145–6
positive aspects of 150–1, 156–7
potential consequences 135, 156–7
public reaction to 141–2
and religion 150
Schelsky's analysis 138
and state planning 145–6
as threat to individuality 150
automatisms 140–1
autonomy, anxiety regarding 78–9
avian influenza (bird flu) 337
avoidance, discourse of 178–9

Baader, Andreas 221–2, 227, 279, 286–7
suicide of 280
"Baader–Meinhof Gang," 283–4, 286–7
Bachmann, Josef 208
Bad Canstatt, Protestant Church 286–7
Baden-Baden 76
Baden-Württemberg 77, 104, 286–7, 301
state elections 348–9
Bad Godesberg 315
Bad Nauheim, Hesse, protest march against
    housing requisitions 58f

Bad Reichenhall 53–4
Bad Tölz, Bavaria 25
Baeyer-Katte, Wanda von 252–3
Baeyer, Walter von 252–3
Baldner, Max 55–6
Baltic states 40
Bangkok, German embassy 88
Barcelona, terrorist attack in 337–8
Bargatsky, Walter 95–6
Bartov, Hanoch, The Brigade 33–4
Bastian, Gert 315
Bataillon des Teufels, Das 92
Bauer, Franz 309–10
Bauer, Fritz 176
Bauman, Zygmunt 4–5, 367
Bavaria 42–3, 45–6, 55–6, 104, 237, 307–8
"Be afraid" slogan 315–16
Beck, Ulrich 328–9, 371–2
Beer Hall Putsch 36
Belgrade 28–9
Berlin 57–9, 72–3, 95–6, 99–101, 127–8
    "Battle on the Tegeler Weg," 216, 218
    Charlottenburg, Kinderläden 229–30
    City hall 195–6
    crisis (1961) 127–8, 170–1
    Free University 195–6, 218, 223, 239
        Otto Suhr Institute for Political
            Science 235–6
        Political Science Department 238–9
        Romance Language Department 235–6
    "Fridays for Future" demonstration 362f
    Gedächtniskirche 220–1
    Holocaust memorial 364
    Jewish Community Center failed bombing
        attack 210–11
    Kurfürstendamm 217–20
    Opera 196
    squatters 270–1
    student demonstrations in 82–3, 217–21
    terrorist attack on Christmas market 337–8
    Tunix (Do Nothing) Congress (1978) 270–1
    visit by Hubert H. Humphrey 222
    visit of Shah 195–7
Berliner Morgenpost 235–6
Berlin Republic (post-1990) 1–2, 23, 293,
    329–30, 335–7
Berlin Wall,
    building of 72–3, 95–6, 128–9, 168–9
    fall of 1–2, 329–30
Berlin (West) 203–4
    Technical University, Vietnam Congress
        (1968) 202–5, 213, 220–1, 230
Bertoldsheim, Bavaria 298–9
Betts, Paul 352–3

Bewegung 2. Juni 279–80
BFW, *see* League for the Freedom of Science
Bhagwan Shree Rajneesh 245–6
Biermann, Wolf 322–3
Bild 207–8, 231
black market 25, 34–5, 50, 56–7
Blank, Theodor 108
Bloch, Ernst 191
blood pollution, fear of 83–4
Böckelmann, Frank 357–8
  Liberation in Daily Life 232–3
Boger, Wilhelm 179–81
Böll, Heinrich 281–2
Bolshevism 27–8, 101–2, 150
Bonn 86–7, 123–4, 195–6
  demonstrations against first Gulf War 332
  founding congress of BFW 237
  peace demonstrations (1981–2) 325
  University of 185–6
Bonn Republic 132, 159–60
bourgeois society/ideology 221–2, 226–32
  education 227
  environment 225–6
  experience of 64–5, 82, 179–81
  and National Socialism 209–10
  and New Left 236–7
  press 231–2
Bourke, Joanna, *Fear: A Cultural History* 16–17
Bracher, Karl Dietrich 165–6, 185–6, 188–9,
    191–3, 199, 233–4, 275–6
Bradley, General Omar 50–1
Brändle, Reinhold 279–80
Brandt, Leo 142
Brandt, Willy 167, 271, 297
breast cancer 248–50
Brenner, Otto 153, 191–2
Brentano, Heinrich von 108
Britain,
  and automation 135, 142–3
  and civil defense 95
  decision to leave EU ("Brexit") 348–9
  8th Army 33–4
  IRA terrorist attacks in 337–8
  state planning 145–6
Bröckling, Ulrich 275–6
Brokdorf, Schleswig-Holstein, nuclear power
    plant 301, 302*f*, 303–4
Broszat, Martin 177, 275–6
Brückner, Peter 281–2, 357–8
Brüning, Heinrich 345–7
Bruns, Ingeborg, *Das wiedergeschenkte Leben.*
    Tagebuch einer Leukämieerkrankung
    eines Kindes 268–9

Brussels,
  department store fire 222
  terrorist attacks in 337–8
BSE (bovine spongiform encephalopathy) 337
Buback, Siegfried 279–82
Buchenwald concentration camp
    172–3, 211–13
Bude, Heinz 358–9, 366
Buhmann, Inga 205, 219–21, 227
Bund Freiheit der Wissenschaft (BFdW)
    281–2
bunkers 95, 107–10, 113, 115, 121
  government 123–4, 324–5
bureaucracy, European 345
businesses, and automation 142–3
Büttner, Günter 251–2
Butzbach, Hesse 54–5

Cambodia 278
cancer 337
  as analogy for arms race 316
  as analogy for death of forest 309
  autobiographies on 268–9
  etiology of 247–51, 268–9
  and food 269–70
  pollution and 295–6
  psychosomatic explanations of 268–9
  "cancer personality," 248–51, 249*f*, 295–6
  misogynist assumptions regarding 250–1
capital, concentration of 137–8
capitalism,
  contradictions of 200–1
  crisis of 202–3
  dehumanizing effect of 266–7
  fear generated by 254–5
  late 200–1, 238
Caritas 89–90
Carson, Rachel, *Silent Spring* 293–4
case studies 20
catastrophe,
  environmental 310–11
  fear of 6–7, 22, 26–7, 63–4, 132, 159, 166–7,
    244, 278, 304–5, 337–8, 368, 373
catharsis 214–15, 274–7
Catholic Church 30–2, 42–5, 54–5, 80, 97–8
  and peace movement 323–4
  youth organizations 89–90
CDU/CSU (governing faction) 98–9, 105–6,
    108–9, 119–21, 165–6, 192–3
  coalition with FDP 124–5
Central Agency for the Prosecution of Nazi
    Crimes 174–5
Central Council of Socialist *Kinderläden* 229–30

Charlie Hebdo, attack on 337–8
Chernobyl nuclear power plant, Ukraine,
      disaster 305–6, 326–9, 337–8, 372–3
child-rearing 229–32, 256
children,
   emotions of 230
   and *Holocaust* (television series) 275
   sexuality of 230
China 72–3, 339
Christian Democratic Union (CDU) 77, 82–3,
      98–101, 105–8, 119–21, 166–7, 271
   and asylum seekers 344
   election campaigns 98–9, 100*f*
   and guest workers 341–2
   and terrorism 283–4, 286
   under Angela Merkel 357–8
   see also Grand Coalition
Christianity 30–1, 60–1, 130–1, 165–6,
      191–2, 348–9
   and AfD 350–2
   and East Germany 352–3
   and peace movement 323–4
Christian Social Union (CSU) 98–9, 105–6, 108,
      119–21, 237, 283–4, 287–8
   and AfD 348–9
   and death penalty 284–5
Christ und Welt 151–2
civil defense 48–9, 96–7, 105–8
   advertising campaign on behalf of 116–18
   brochures 95–6, 115–27, 120*f*, 122*f*
   and Cold War fears 324–5
   early warning systems 113
   evacuation scenarios 113–14
   and peace movement 324–5
   public reaction to 125–7, 154–5
   re-establishing 107–16
Civil Defense Law 324–5
civil disobedience 311–12
civil liberties 30
Clay, General Lucius D. 55–6
clericalism 167
climate change 313, 373
   fear of 336–7, 360–2
Club of Rome, *The Limits of Growth* 294–5
Coburg 41–2
"cognitive inertia," 316
Cohen, Roger 335–6
Cohen, Stanley 76
Cold War 4–5, 18–22, 50, 59, 64–5, 93–4, 320–1
   and anti-Communism 104–5, 161–2, 240
   and civil defense 115
   Communists and 283
   decline of 128–9, 170–1

détente in 128–9, 370
   end of 23
   fear of victimization during 123
   liberalism 130–1
   and nuclear weapons 110–13, 127–8, 325–6
   reconstruction 373
   second 314–15
   student activists and 203–4
   "technology gap," 135
   tensions of 189, 289, 337, 339, 356–7
   and trust in US 318–20, 331
   and US protections 220–1
collective bargaining agreements 155–7
collective delusion 78
Cologne 108, 116–18
   Cathedral 350–2
   synagogue 173
   University of "Hillgruber Committee," 238–9
colonialism,
   French 66–7, 71–2, 78–80, 93
   German 364–5
colonization, reverse 21
commemorative culture, West German 8–9,
      14–15, 128–9, 132, 170–1, 244, 270–4,
      278, 309, 339–40, 354, 364
   emotionalization of 273–4
communes (*Wohngemeinschaften*, WGs),
      communal living 227–30, 232–3,
      258–61, 260*f*
   emotional communities within 259
   high turnover in 259–61
communications 202–3
Communism 3, 6–7, 21–2, 78, 93–4, 163–4, 179,
      196, 283
   and antisemitic incidents 173–4
   in Cold War 161–2
   and emergency laws 191–2
   fear of 96–107, 315–16, 363–4
   in Poland 311–12
   propaganda for 104–5, 171
   Shah of Persia and 195
   in Weimar Republic 217–18
"Communism Unmasked," 102–3
Communist Party (East Germany) 315
Communist Party of Germany (KPD) 101–5
   outlawing of 103–5
Communists 342–3
   dehumanization of 102–3
   as "others," 369
community, sense of 29–31
computers 200–1, 286, 294–5
concerted action 200–1
concrete interaction (*Vermittlung*) 211–13

"Confessing Church," 101–2
Congo, Democratic Republic of the 211–13
consciousness-raising through activism 213–16
conservatism 130–1, 159, 161–4, 168, 209–10
   in AfD 348–9
   and emergency laws 191–2
   and environmental and peace
      movements 333–4
   and response to terrorism 281–4
   traditional fears of 356–7
   see also liberal-conservatism
conspiracy theories 25
constitutional law 163–4
consumerism 182
consumption, consumer 254–5
   and automation 149–50
contingency,
   negative 3–4
   sense of 4, 24
contraception 226–7
conversation, and overcoming of fear 367
Conze, Werner 238–9
cooperation, principle of 297
"coordinated society" (formierte
      Gesellschaft) 164–5, 200–1
Coordinating Agency on the Dying
      Forest 311–12
Coronavirus pandemic (COVID-19) 337
Council of Experts on Environmental Issues
      (Sachverständigenrat für Umweltfragen),
      Special Report 311
counter-violence 215–16, 215f, 218
Cramer, Heinz von 167
Cremerius, Johannes 245–6
crime rates 44–6
"crimes against humanity," 73
Cuba, missile crisis 127–8, 170–1
cultural pessimism 134, 136–7, 139, 149–50
cultural shift 18–19, 23
cybernetics 135
Cyprian, Gudrun 258
Cyprus 345–7
Czollek, Max 366

Dahrendorf, Ralf 168, 191
Daimler-Benz 146–7
Dakar, University of 216–17
Dancyger, Szmul 42–3
Darmstadt conversations 179
Darwinism, social 350–2
Davos, World Economic Forum, (2018) 360–1
Day After, The 290–1
DDT 293–4
death penalty 285–6
   support for 284–5

decentralization 161–2
decolonization 165–6
defeat 21–2, 25–7, 29–30, 48, 65, 337
   total 2, 18, 28, 69, 78, 368
deflation 345–7
De Gaulle, Charles 22, 161–3, 165–6, 194
Degree on Radicals in Public Service 266–7
deindustrialization 344–5
deintegration 341–2
Delumeau, Jean 16–17
demilitarization 107–8
Demmerle, Jakob 82–3
democracy 22, 44–5
   Adorno on 173–4
   as challenge to authority of state 159,
      161–4
   crisis of 158–9
   and critique of politics of fear 371
   debate on nature of 191–2, 368
   and dictatorship 159–60
   fears concerning 128–9, 156–7, 183–5,
      189–90, 193, 199–200, 202, 281,
      286–9, 363–4
   fragility of 165–6, 186, 191–2
   ideals of 172–3
   Jaspers on 191
   parliamentary 236–7, 321
      declining trust in 311–12
   and politics of emotion 363–7
   postwar 18–19
   potential failure of 368
   prospects of 4
   representative 352–3
   threat to 179, 182
   transformation of 357–8
   and trust in political system 365–6
democratization 2–6, 16–18, 22, 159, 169, 188,
      191–2, 284–5
   and authority of state 162–3
   emotional dimension of 6–7
   inner or internalized 159–60, 163–4,
      185–6
   liberals and 193–4
   strengthened by fear 372
   of universities 239–40
denazification 49, 59–63, 170
   courts (Spruchkammern) 62–3
Denmark 95
depoliticization 168
depression 340–1
Depression (in Germany) 345–7
desertification 310–11
Desert Legion 91–2
"desk perpetrators," 176–7
deterritorialization of fears 337–9

Deutsche Gewerkschaftsbund (DGB),
    working conferences on automation
        152–3, 156–7
    yearly congresses 156–7
Deutsche Industrieinstitut, "Reports on Social
        Policy," "The American Auto Unions and
        Automation," 142–3
diary writers 28–30, 32, 35–6, 46–8, 53–6,
        270–1, 287–8, 332
dictatorship 4–5, 159–60
    East German 168–9
    militaristic 189–90
    Nazi 164, 167
    totalitarian 369
Dien Bien Phu, Battle of 75–6
digitalization 133
Diner, Dan 318
diplomacy, international 127–8
direct action 213–15, 223, 234, 236–7
disarmament initiatives 329–30
discrimination 364
disease,
    causes of 268–9
    fear of 267–8, 337
    metaphors derived from 337
dislocation, experience of 64–5, 300
disorientation, experience of 64–5
displaced persons (DPs) 20, 28, 39*f*, 366
    accusations of criminality 44–5
    camps 42–3
    demonstration in Frankfurt 38*f*
    from Eastern Europe 21, 25–6, 39–42
    and housing requisitions 56–9
    Jewish 34–7, 42–3, 79–80
    memories of 300
    non-Jewish 39–40
    as "others," 369
    Polish 40–4
    repatriation of 34–5, 40
    Russian 39–42
    Ukrainian 41–2
    violence and 39–46
distancing mechanism 178–9
Dohnanyi, Klaus von 239
Dölker-Rehder, Grete 30
Dollfuss, Engelbert 165–6
Dollinger, Friederike 196
Dorland (PR agency) 116–19
Dortmund 315
Draghi, Mario 345–7
Drenkmann, Günter von 279–80, 283–5
drugs, use of 269
Dublin Agreement (1993) 344, 349
Dubos, René, *The Unencumbered Progress* 293–4
Duensing, Erich 196

Duhm, Dieter, *Fear in Capitalism* 254–5
Düsseldorf 86, 116–18
    Majdanek trial 272–3
    synagogue 172–3
Dutschke, Martin 72–3
Dutschke, Rudi 199–209, 211–14, 217–20
    assassination attempt on 208, 215–16, 220–2,
        224–5, 234
    attacked by former Nazi 220–1
    and counter-demonstrations 220–1
    on education 229–30
    and Habermas 214–15
"dynamic pension," 130–1

earth, view from space 134–5
Eastern Europe 134–5
Eastern Europeans 21, 25–6, 39–42, 64
    characterized as criminals 44–5
"Easter riots" (1968) 208, 220–1, 224–5, 234
East Germany, *see* German Democratic
        Republic (GDR)
East Germany (post-reunification),
    and authoritarianism 358–9
    right-wing populism in 352–3
    unemployment in 344–5
East Prussia 30
East–West contrast 166–7
Ebert, Friedrich 77
Ebola virus 337
eco-feminism 306
ecological balance 295, 307–8
ecological group (*Ökogruppe*) 270–1
ecological society 302–3
Ecologist, The 293–4
ecology,
    fears about 270–1, 317, 337, 369
    see also environmental movement
economic crisis 23, 129, 242–3, 298, 349–50
    fear of 199–200
economic growth 106–7, 130–1, 156,
        200–1, 347–8
    ideology of 301–2
    quantitative and qualitative 298
    slowed-down 186
"economic miracle," 135–6, 293
economic planning 146
economic power, misuse of 156
economic recession 130–1, 156–7, 200–1
economic reconstruction 182
economic stability 132
education 22, 147–8, 150–1, 172–3, 370
    Adorno on 174
    and authoritarianism 231–2
    and communal living 229–32
    debate on 151–2

education (*cont.*)
  and discussion on fear 254
  requirements for employment 347–8
  sexual 232–3
  technical 139
Eggebrecht, Axel 166–7
Ehrlich, Paul, *The Population Bomb* 293–4
Eichler, Willi 165–6
Eichmann, Adolf 128–9, 178–9
  characterization by Anders 178
  trial 174–5, 177–9, 181–2, 272–3
Einbeck, Lower Saxony, peace group 322–3
Eisele, Hanns 172–3
Eisenhower, General Dwight D. 48–9
elites, political, military, and scientific 127
emergency laws 114, 138, 161–4, 184–94,
      201, 223
  on environmental measures 311–12
  final version of proposals 193
  Jaspers on 190–1
  opposition to 185–6, 187*f*, 191–2,
      202, 234
  powers to declare 189
  protests against 191–3
  secrecy over agreements on 186–8
  and Shah's visit to Federal Republic 195–6
  softening of proposals for 185–6
  and student demonstrations 218
  support for 206
emergency situation, definitions 192–3
emigration 235–6
  return from 191
Emnid Institute 267–8
emotions,
  absence of 177, 182–4, 262–3
  alienation from 247, 281
  articulation of 259, 285–6
  blocked 223–4, 247–8, 257–8
  containment of 183–4, 190–1, 198, 233–4
  democratization of 6–7
  emotional catharsis 214–15, 274–7
  emotional change 126–7, 138
  emotional community 17, 32–3, 197–8, 369
  emotional culture 23, 223–4, 295, 355–6
    and feminism 261
  emotional distancing 272, 278
  emotional expressivity 243–4, 247–8, 256,
      259–61, 289, 357–8, 363, 372
    as new cultural norm 232–3, 244, 251,
      255–6, 258–9, 262, 276, 295, 301
  emotional intensity 192–3, 199, 223, 239
  emotional management 111–12,
      116–18, 285–6
  emotional politics 191, 197–8, 369–70
emotional regimes 6–7, 17–18, 63–4, 123, 125,
      159–61, 167–8, 183–4, 198, 243–6, 271,
      277, 322–3, 369–70
emotional rigidity 268–9
  history of 20
  of males 261–3
  politics of 23, 297, 371
  repression of 246–50
  restraint of 285–6
  revalidation of 245–7
empathy 366–7, 370
  lack of 182–4
employers, and automation 139, 143–5
employment, changes in 347–8
Emrich, Louis 142–3
Enabling Act (1933) 190–1
"enemies of the state," proposed internment
      of 187–8
energy gap 295
engineers 142–3
Enke, Helmut 244–5
enlightenment 304–5, 363
Enlightenment (historical period) 4–6, 17–18,
      130, 251–2
enslavement, fear of 369
Ensslin, Gudrun 222, 265–6, 279, 286–7
  suicide 280
environment,
  crisis of 293–5
  and culture of fear 332
  hazards of 295
  sensitization to 295–6
  threats to 3, 23
  threats to animals 296
  see also forest, dying of
environmental destruction, fear of 368
environmental movement 19, 23, 244, 270–1,
      278, 287–9, 292–8, 303–4, 360–1
  effects and influence of 329–30, 371
  links with peace movement 323–4, 328
environmental protection (*Umweltschutz*) 297
  legislation on 297
Enzensberger, Hans Magnus 194, 203–4, 300
Enzensberger, Ulrich 227
Eppler, Erhard 191, 315
Erdmann, Karl Dietrich 130
Erhard, Ludwig 164–5, 200–1
Erler, Fritz 77, 143–6
Eschenburg, Theodor 164
Essen,
  AfD conference (2015) 348–9
  alleged recruiter for Foreign Legion 83*f*
  SDS anti-Vietnam War demonstration 212*f*
ETA (separatist group) 337–8

euro,
  introduction of 345
  stability of 349
Europe, integration in 345
European Central Bank 345–7
European Convention on Human Rights 80
European Defense Community (planned) 77
European Stability Pact 345–7
European Union (EU) 341–2, 345
  border states 344
  debt crisis 336–7, 345–9
  grants to Greece 345–9
  as subject of fear 345
  UK decision to leave ("Brexit") 348–9
Eurovision Song Contest 322–3
euro zone 345–9
"Everybody Has a Chance" 95–6, 115–26,
  120f, 122f
"Everybody Should Live Better," 134–5
existential anxiety or uncertainty 2–3, 23,
  28, 190–1
Extraparliamentary Opposition (APO) 191–2,
  216, 218

factory farming 295–6
Fanon, Frantz 218
Farah Pahlavi, Empress of Iran 195–6
fascism 2, 6–7, 22, 33, 165–9, 188, 194,
  197, 199
  attitudes within West German
    democracy 174–5
  and authoritarianism 229–30
  counter-accusations of 235–6
  discussion of sources of 265
  and emotions 183–4
  fear of 233–4, 248–50, 368
  and irrationalism 159, 183–4
  Marxist concept of 208–9
  memory of 354
  New Left and 208–11, 214–15, 234–6
  and "others," 272
  and sexuality 225, 230
  state, perception by student activists 216–17
  threat of 201–3
Faulhaber, Cardinal Michael von 54–5
"fear of fear," 154–5
fear psychosis 108
fear(s),
  Adorno on 174
  and anxiety 253–4, 362–3
  attempted manipulation of 372–3
  containment of 19–20, 370
  cycles of 1–2, 329–30
  as defense mechanism 63–4

  and democracy, see democracy, fears
    concerning
  denial of 221–2
  deterritorialized 337–9
  dialectic of 3, 22, 185, 192–3, 233–4, 244, 279,
    281, 292–3, 334–5, 343–4, 356–7, 368
  discrepancy with reality 373
  of domination 242
  external and internal 337
  as fantasy 370
  "feminization" of 19–20
  as form of rationality 190–1, 323–5
  freedom from 4–5
  of future 242
  gender connotations of 19–20
  German nature of 368–70
  historical context 329
  histories of 3, 6, 368–70
  Jaspers on 190–1
  mobilization of 371–2
  modern 133–4, 156–7
  narrativization of 251–2
  overcoming 367
  pathologization of 6
  personalized 358–9
  politics of 23, 329, 371
  of pollution 242
  polyvalence of 6
  as positive emotion 251–2, 315–16, 334–5
  and principle of responsibility 304–5
  proliferating 242–4, 243f
  reevaluation of 295, 314
  regarding automation 143–5
  rehabilitation of 251–5
  related to EU debt crisis 256, 345–7
  of retribution 21
  revolutionary 199
  right-wing 348–62
  rise and fall of 370
  servile and filial 6
  shifting objects of 18–19, 22
  of social decline 242, 347–8
  social and political functions of 19–20
  by student activists 198–9
  theorists of 316
  unfulfilled 373
  validation of 243–4, 255–6, 303–5
Federal Administrative Court 321
Federal Agency for Civic Education 173
Federal Border Police 218
Federal Bureau for the Protection of the
  Constitution 282–4
Federal Civilian Air Defense League
  (*Bundesluftschutzverband*) 107–8, 118

Federal Criminal Police 286–7
federalism 163–4
Federal Office for Civilian Air Defense (later
    Federal Agency for Civil
    Defense) 107–10
Federal Office for the Protection of the
    Constitution
    (*Bundesverfassungsschutz*) 302–3
Federal Republic of Germany,
  air force 339
  alleged continuities from Third
    Reich 173, 191
  anti-Communism in 97–107
  anti-terrorist legislation 282–3
  and authoritarianism 188–9
  Basic Law (constitution) 162–4, 368
  budget for 2018 345–7
  Bundesbank 350–2
  Bundestag 67, 74–5, 77–8, 80, 88, 103–4, 108,
    141–2, 172–3, 184–6, 192–4,
    303–4, 357–8
    Committee on Internal Affairs 310–11
    Common Committee 193
    limitation of rights of 186
    and US missiles 317–21, 326–7
  Bundeswehr 93, 96–7, 106–7, 130–1, 193, 298,
    315, 318–20
    School for Psychological Defense 253
  Civil Defense Law 113
  civil defense program 111–27
  civil service 266–7
  Constitutional Court 311–12
  criminal code 84–6
  criminal law 176, 179
  democratization of 174
  education system 151–2
  elections
    1957 165–6
    1961 119–21, 166–7
    2013 348–9
    2017 348–9, 358–9
  emotional acceptance of 288–9
  emotional attachment to US 127–8
  environmental action program 297
  fascism in 199
  Finance Ministry 115
    expenditure on civil defense 115
  Foreign Office 73, 191
  founding of 59, 69, 368
  future of 130–2, 191
  and Gulf Wars 332
  "Hispanicization" of 168–9
  housing crisis 115
  Housing Ministry 115
    as industrial society 141
    intelligence services 103–4
    Interior Ministry 66–7, 95–6, 107–10, 114,
      116–21, 185–8, 193, 297
      department of environmental protection
        (*Umweltschutz*) 297
    liberalization 198–9
    as "militant democracy," 104–5
    militarization of civilians 115–16, 189
    military and foreign policy 333–4
    Ministry of All German Affairs 101–3, 128–9
    Ministry of Economics 154–5
    Ministry of Justice 85–6
    modernization 136–7
    and national identity 309–10, 352–3
    new role after reunification 339
    nuclearization of armed forces 112–13
    nuclear program 298
    numbers of foreigners in 341–2
    oppression of women in 265
    parliament, *see Bundestag*
    polarization of political culture 233–4
    post-boom period 158
    as quasi-fascist state 202
    rearmament 96–7, 111–12
    Red–Green coalition 328, 339–40, 347–8
    relationship with US 127–8, 318–20
    reunification with East Germany 69, 339
    self-description 131–4, 141
    sense of victimhood among Germans 339–41
    sovereignty 184
    stability of 165–6
    stabilization 93–4, 129–31, 168
    Strafrechtsänderungsgesetz 103–4
    and Treaty of Warsaw 271
    and unification 333–4
    Verfassungsschutz 103–4
    in war on Serbia (Kosovo) 165–6
  feminism 250–1, 261–2
    and fear of nuclear power 306
    and women's groups 262–3
  feminization 19–20
  Feuchtwangen 51
  Fichter, Tillman 208–9, 211–13
  Fighting Group Against Inhumanity
      (*Kampfgruppe gegen Unmenschlichkeit*,
      KgU) 101–2, 128–9
  Fighting League Against Nuclear Damage
      (*Kampfbund gegen Atomschäden*) 298–9
  Filbinger, Hans 301
  "final solution," 31
  financial crisis 1–2, 345–8, 372–3
  Finland 95
  Fischer, Joschka 198–9, 328, 339

Fleischhauer, Jan 334–5
Flohr, Heiner 251–2
Föhrenwalde DP camp 35–7
"folk devils," 76–7, 82–4, 283
food 23, 269–70
"Fordism," 135–6, 143–5, 156–7
Foreign Legion, French,
   and alleged abduction of young Germans 3,
      21, 65–88, 133–4, 280–1
   decline of fear of 370
   recruiters for 66–70, 76–7, 81–90, 83f, 93–4,
      102–5, 179, 184, 283, 342–3, 369–71
   recruitment bureaus in Germany 76
   scandals concerning 71–5
   voluntary entry by young Germans 86–94
forest, death of (*Waldsterben*) 23, 291–2,
     307–13, 370–1
   as acute danger or chronic process 313
   and German angst 332
   and health-related analogies 309
   and language of mass destruction 309–10
   and peace movement 323–4
   scientific expertise and counter-expertise 311
Forsthoff, Ernst, *The Total State* 162–3
Fortschritt, Der 75–6
"45ers," 136–7, 170–1
Foucault, Michel, *The History of Sexuality: The
    Will to Knowledge* 264–5
Fraenkel, Ernst 235–6
"fragile ego," 358–9
France 165–6
   and civil defense 95
   and colonial Africans 78–9
   colonialism 79–80
   conservatism in 162–3
   and decolonization 70–1
   defeat at Dien Bien Phu 75–6
   Fifth Republic 161–2
   Franco–German reconciliation 67–9
   and Senegal 216–17
   student demonstrations
     (May 1968) 191–2, 194
   terrorist attacks in 337–8
   see also Foreign Legion
Franco, Francisco 22, 162–3, 165–6, 188
Franconia 172–3
Franco–Prussian War 70–1
Fränkel, Wolfgang 171
Frankfurt 31–2, 153, 261–2
   alternative scene 270–1
   Auschwitz trial 128–9, 170, 174–5,
     178–9, 272–3
   Book Fair (1968) 216–17
   department store fires 222

Kinderläden in 229–30
   protest against Gulf War (1991) 333f
   SDS conference (September 1967) 213–14
   squatter movement 256
   University of 237
Frankfurter Allgemeine Zeitung 74, 76–7,
    271, 350–2
Frankfurter Hefte 25
Frankfurter Neue Presse 114, 172–3
Frankfurter Rundschau 172–3
Frankfurt Institute for Social Research 136–7,
    169, 173–4, 182
Frankfurt School 136–7, 174, 181
fraternization (of US soldiers with German
    civilians) 48–9, 78–9
Frauenraub in Marokko (*Ten Tall Men*) 91–2
Free Corps 265
Free Democratic Party (FDP) 80, 119–21,
    124–5, 233
   and environmental protection 297
   and German angst 333–4
   law on civil service appointments 240
free press and free speech 186, 201
Freiburg 66, 76, 299–300
   University of 234
Frei, Norbert 336
French Revolution 201
Frevert, Ute 365–6
Freyer, Hans, *Theory of Contemporary
    Society* 150
"Fridays for Future" movement 360–1
   demonstration in Berlin 362f
Friedberg, Hesse 36
Friedeburg, Ludwig von 240
Friedländer, Ernst 159–60
Friedrich, Günter 154–5
Friedrich, Jörg, *The Fire* 339–40
Frings, Klaus 208
Fronius, Sigrid 226
Führer principle 162–3
Fukushima Daiichi nuclear power plant,
    Japan 305–6, 329–30
Fürstenfeldbruck 44–5
Fürth 31–2
FU Spiegel 235–6
futures,
   individual and collective 29–30
   uncertainty about 138, 244, 349–50
   see also utopianism

Gablentz, Otto Heinrich von 163–4
Gabriel, Sigmar 350–2
gas chambers 275–6, 302–3, 309–10
gas engines 312–13

Gauland, Alexander 354
Gaus, Günter 202–3
Gehlen, Arnold 136–7, 139–41, 150
　Soul in the Age of Technology, The 139–40
Geiss, Immanuel 165–6
Geißler, Heiner 283–4
Geist und Tat 165–6
gender 19–20
　norms of 69–70
　politics of 118–19
generations 17
genocide 2, 33–5, 123, 176, 178–9, 278, 309–10
Genscher, Hans-Dietrich 297
German Autumn (1977) 244
German Book Trade, peace prize 216–17
German Committee for Protection (Deutsche
　　Schutzkommission) 107–8
German Communist Party (DKP)
　　(re-founded) 103–4, 240, 323
"German culture," as concept 348–50
German Democratic Republic (GDR) 95–6
　and authoritarianism 358–9
　and Communism 352–3
　and criticism of West German
　　democracy 168–9
　de-industrialization 312–13
　living conditions 268–9
　propaganda attacks on Federal Republic 171
　revolution (1989) 352–3
　secret police 173
　Soviet missiles in 329–30
　Stasi (secret police) 196
　uprising (1953) 98–9
German Forestry Council 310–11
German/French border 74–5
German Peace Union (DFU) 315
German Research Foundation 107–8
Germans, ethnic, expulsion from former Eastern
　　territories 26–7, 54–5, 343–4
"Germans in the Foreign Legion" 71–2
Geyer, Michael 123–4
GIs, see United States of America, soldiers
globalization 337, 373
Globke, Hans 98
Glotz, Peter 315
Göbel, Wolfgang 279–80
Goebbels, Joseph 31, 101–2, 116–18, 202
Gollwitzer, Helmut 172–3
Google, Ngram graph, on fear 242, 243f,
　　332–3, 334f
Gorbachev, Mikhail 326–7, 329–30
Gorleben, Lower Saxony, proposed nuclear waste
　　depot 303–4
Göttingen 281–2, 307–8
Göttingen Eighteen 106–7, 112–13, 298

Grand Coalition (CDU/CSU/SPD) 127, 165,
　　184, 191–2, 200–1, 348–9, 357–8
Greece 344
　EU grants to 345–9
　military coup in 188, 193–4, 202
　refugees entering EU 349, 358–9
　unemployment rate 345–7
Green Party (Die Grünen) 150, 292, 303–4, 306,
　　309–12, 315, 317, 339
　and peace movement 323–4
Greiner, Ulrich 335–6
Grohnde, Lower Saxony, nuclear power
　　plant 301–2
group therapy 322–3
Grzimek, Bernhard 296
guerrilla fighters 213–14
guest workers 48,
　Turkish 27–8, 355
Guevara, Ernesto "Che," 213–14
Guha, Anton Andreas,
　ENDE: Diary from the Third World
　　War 290–1
　NATO Stationing Decision, The: Europe's
　　Holocaust 317–18
guilt 48, 63–4, 182, 253
　and responsibility 57–9, 64–5
Gulf War (1991) 329–30, 332, 334–5, 339
　protests against 333f
　see also Iraq, wars
Gundremmingen, Bavaria, nuclear power
　　plant 298–9
Guttenberg, Karl, Freiherr von und zu 191–2

Habermas, Jürgen 141, 166, 168–9, 191, 205–7,
　　214–15, 240
　on Kohl government 292–3
　and terrorism 287–8
Hacke, Jens 160–1
Hagana 33–4
Halle, Saxony-Anhalt, attack on
　　synagogue 358–9
Hamburg 59–60, 150, 186–7
　squatters 270–1
Hampe, Erich 109–10, 115–16
Hanau, Hesse, racist attack 358–9
Hanover, SDS congress (June 1967)
　　202–3, 214–15
Harpprecht, Klaus 172–3, 175
Harrisson, Earl 34–5
Hartmann (PR agency) 124–5
Hartung, Klaus 204–5
Hartz IV (plan for labor market) 150
hatred 365–6, 370–1
　contrasted with fear 358–9, 363
Hattingberg, Immo von 251–2

Hauser, Siegfried 279–80
Häußler, Erwin 77
heart disease 295–6
Heck, Bruno 271
Heidegger, Martin 64–5, 178, 190–1, 304–5
Heidelberg 47, 54–5, 238–9, 311–12
    psychiatric-neurological clinic 252–3
Heidelberg Manifesto 342–3
Heimat, concept of 300
Heimbuchtal 41–2
Heinemann, Karl Heinz 231–2
Heitmeyer, Wilhelm 349–50
helplessness, sense of 123–4
Hennis, Wilhelm 234
Herder Correspondence 242
Herold, Horst 286
Hertel, Eugen 78–9
Herzog, Dagmar 81
Hesse 44–5, 98–9, 172–3, 240, 310–11
    Red–Green coalition 328
Hesse, Count of 78–9
heterosexuality,
    fragility of 81
    (re)assertion of 81
Heuss, Theodor 73–4
Heydrich, Reinhard 176
Hilberg, Raul, *The Destruction of European
    Jews* 278
Hildebrandt, Klaus 101–2
Hillegaart, Heinz 279–80
Hillgruber, Andreas 238–9
Himmler, Heinrich, and Nazi trials 176
Hiroshima 95, 110–11, 278
    as analogy for death of forest 309–10
historians,
    at Nazi trials 175–6
    and *Holocaust* television series 275–6
"Historians' Debate," 278, 355
historiography 8–9, 16–17, 25–6, 44–5, 48–9,
    133–4, 231–2, 242–3, 275–6, 292–3
Hitler, Adolf 164, 167
    as dictator 190–1
    emotional responses to loss of 182
    exploitation of emotion by 276–7
    "Hitler in me," 265–6, 301–2
    "Hitler within us" slogan 173
    and Nazi trials 176
    promise to build bunkers 109–10
    putsch of 1923 36
    rise to power 143–5, 345–7
    seizure of power 189–90
Hitler salute 35–6
Höcherl, Hermann 121–5
Höcke, Björn 358–9
Hof 41–2

Hofmeyer, Hans 175–6
Hofstätter, Peter 150
Hollywood movies 91–2
Holocaust 33–4, 317–18
    AfD and 354
    analogies with nuclear threat 317–20
    deaths in 26–7
    and discourse on environmental
        damage 296, 309–10
    equated with Vietnam War 211–13
    imagery of 318
    Jewish victims of 211–13
    memory of 23, 165–6, 208–9, 309–10, 333–4,
        354–5, 364, 368–70
    nuclear 317–18
    perceived passivity of victims 218–20
    proposed exhibition on 208–9
    research into 278
    sanitized image of 178–9
    "singularity" of 355, 364
    structural-functional explanation of 178–9
    survivors of 20–1, 25–6, 32–5, 43–5, 56–7,
        175–6, 235–6
Holocaust (television series) 244, 273–8
    "emotionalization" of subject 275–6
    leftist critique of 276–7
    public response to 274–6, 278
Holsten, Jack 72–4
Holsten, Rita 73
homophobia 81–3, 263
homosexuality,
    criminalization under Nazi regime 86
    female 261
    language of 78, 81–4
    men's groups and 263
    and seduction 21, 80–4, 86
hope 20
Horkheimer, Max 136–7, 150
Horn, Eva 360–1
Horx, Matthias 325–6
Höß, Rudolf 177–9
hostage taking 284–5
housing 347–8
housing requisitions 49, 54–9, 58*f*
Hoyerswerda 343–4
Hülbrock, Klaus ("Mescalero") 281–2
human rights,
    language of 80
    movement 224, 366
humor and parody 222
Humphrey, Hubert H. 222
Hünemörder, Kai 293–4
Hungary 98–9
hunger, world 295
Huyssen, Andreas 276–7

hyperinflation 345–7
Hypo Real Estate (German bank) 345
"hysteria," 280–1

identity"Christian–Jewish" 353
Ifo-Institute for Economic Research 154–5
IG Metall (metalworkers' union) 136, 156–7
　automation committee 153–7
　and civil defense measures 189
　and emergency laws 191–2
　training program 156–7
illness, fear of 291–2
immigration 1–2, 23, 341–52, 369–70
　fear of 336–7, 341–5, 356–62, 371
income, guaranteed 145–6
India 269
individuality 150
Indivisible movement 365–6
Indochina 66–7, 71–3, 76, 87–8, 93
industrialization 130–1
Industrial Revolution 146
"injured citizenship," sense of 123–4
insecurity 25–6, 44–6, 54, 337–8
insurance industry 306–7
intellectuals,
　concerns of 160–1, 166–71
　and democracy 287–8
　and emergency laws 185, 191–2
　Jewish 191
　left-wing, marginalization of 168–9
　and New Left 233
　and rejection of violence 287–8
interests, rule of special 164
Intermediate-Range Nuclear Forces (INF)
　　Treaty 326–7
International Court of Justice 78
International Monetary Fund 345–7
involution 201
IRA (Irish Republican Army) 337–8
Iran 195–6
Iraq,
　invasion of Kuwait 332
　refugees from 342–3
　wars 329–30, 332, 334–5, 339–41
Ireland 345–7
Iron Curtain 168–9, 329–30, 354
irrationalism 300
　fascist 159
Islam,
　extremists, terrorist attacks by 337–8
　oppression of women 358
　and sexuality 358
　see also Muslims
"Islamization" of Europe 353
Islamophobia 350–5, 358–9

　in AfD 348–50, 351*f*, 355–6
　contrasted with antisemitism 353–4
Israel 209–10
　and Munich Olympics attack 280
　travel to 269
Istanbul, Hagia Sophia mosque 350–2
Italians, as recruiters for Foreign Legion 66–7
Italy 33–4, 344

Jacobmeyer, Wolfgang 44–5
Jacobson, Hans 275–6
Jacobson, Walter 173
Japan 95
Jaspers, Karl, "Where is the Federal Republic
　　Drifting?" 189–91
Jensen, Uffa 357–8
Jerusalem, Eichmann trial 174–5, 272–3
"Jewification," fear of 353
Jewish Brigade 33–4
Jewish revenge,
　alleged acts of 31–8
　fears of 21, 25–8, 31
"Jewish war," fear of 21, 31–2
Jews,
　accusations of ritual murder and
　　sacrifice 37, 172–3
　alleged special privileges of 34–6
　alleged worldwide conspiracy of 25, 283
　associated with terrorism 283
　deportation and murder of 32–3
　as displaced persons 34–7, 42–3, 79–80
　emigration to Palestine 33–4
　as Holocaust survivors 21, 25–6, 32–3
　and housing requisitions 55–6
　as intellectuals 191
　and Nazi ideology 125
　and Neunburg incident 61–2
　as objects of fear 353–4
　as "others," 369
　perceived as passive victims 218–20
　persecution of 31–2, 54–7, 64, 79–80,
　　176–7, 272–3
　and racial stereotyping 102–3
　and racism in Nazi Germany 364
　resistance during war 25–6
　as returned emigrants 235–6
　as witnesses at Nazi trials 175–6
　see also antisemitism; Holocaust
jobs and professions 147–8
Johnson, Edgar 50–1, 55–6
Johnson, Lyndon B. 217–18
Jonas, Hans 304–5
Jongen, Marc 357–8
judges, and Nazi crimes 170–3
Junge Kirche 150

Jünger, Ernst 32
Jungk, Robert 302–3

Kahl, Franconia, nuclear reactor 298
Kahl, Werner 281–2
Kalisch, Christel 205, 229
Kalkar, North Rhine-Westphalia, nuclear
        reactor 303–4
Kaltherberge settlement 56–7
Kapp putsch 189
Karlsruhe 171
Kehl 89
Kelek, Necla 358
Kelly, Petra 315
Kennedy, John F. 127–8, 195
Keynes, John Maynard 136, 200–1
Kierkegaard, Søren 64–5, 373
Kiesinger, Kurt Georg 191
Kinderläden (day care sites) 229–32
Kleining, Gerhard 251–2
Klüger, Ruth 34–5
Koblenz 85–6, 92
Kohl, Helmut 292–3, 309–10, 312–13,
        323–4, 333–4
    and asylum law 344
    on European integration 345
    and Turkish immigrants 341–2
Kommune 1 217–18, 222, 227–8, 258
Kommune 2 218, 228–9, 231–2, 258
Königsberg, University of 136–7
Korean War 103–4, 161–2
Kosovo War 165–6
Kössler, Till 104
Krahl, Hans-Jürgen 202–3, 213–14, 219–20
Kraushaar, Wolfgang 210–11
Krefeld Initiative 315
Kristallnacht 172–3
Kröger, Ulrike 196
Krüger, Anne 55–6
Kuby, Erich 167
Küchling-Marsden, Evamaria 54–5
Kühnl, Reinhard 208–9
Kunzelmann, Dieter 209–13, 217–18, 222, 227
Kuratorium "Notstand der Demokratie,"
        185–6
Kurras, Karl-Heinz 196
Kursbuch 202–4
Kuwait 332

labor,
    forced 40–1
    human and automated 135
    unions 104
labor movement 191–2
Ladd, Alan 91–2

Lafontaine, Oskar 318–20
Lancaster, Burt 91–2
Landau 72–3, 76, 85–6, 90–1
Landsberg 36–7
Landshut 55–6
Langhans, Rainer 211–13, 221–2, 227
Latin America 211–14, 278
law, rule of 288–9
law and human rights, language of 80
Law for the Liberation from National Socialism
        and Militarism 62–3
lay-offs, mass 155–6
Lazarus, Richard S. 252–3
League for the Freedom of Science (Bund
        Freiheit der Wissenschaft, BFW) 237–41
    activities of 237
    founding document 238
    perceived threats to 238–9
Lefebvre, George, Great Fear, The 16–17
Lefèvre, Wolfgang 205, 220–1
left-alternative milieu (1970s) 18, 255–8, 265–6
    communication within 259–61
    distrust of state 286–7
    and Duhm's study on fear 255
    and emotions 262, 334–5, 355–6
    new sensibility in 267–8, 287–8
    and sexuality 263–5
left-liberal alliance 128–9, 159, 183–4,
        193–4, 240
left wing, leftists 3, 22, 159, 165–6, 184, 199–200
    and emergency laws 192–3
    and fascist impulse 272
    fears of 286–7
    hedonistic 232–3
    marginalization of 168–9
    response to terrorism 281
    and totalitarianism 162–3
    see also New Left; student activists
Legionär, Der 67
Lehman Brothers 345
Leinemann, Jürgen 291–2
Leipzig 47
Leitkultur (dominant culture) 349–50
liberal-conservatism 348–9
    and New Left 233–41
liberal democracy 22, 131, 136–7, 159, 168, 201,
        236–7, 331, 356–7
    Adenauer and 97–8
    AfD as threat to 360–1
    and authoritarianism 201
    crisis of 4
    loss of 363–4
    and totalitarianism 4–5
liberalism 21–2, 130–1, 159, 165–6, 184,
        191–2, 199–200

"liberalism of fear," 366
liberalization 2–6, 16–18, 130–1, 198–9
Linke, Georg 279
Lohmar, Ulrich 172–3
Lorenz, Peter 279–80, 284–5
Lost Sons 67
Löwenthal, Richard 233, 235–7
Lower Saxony 303–4
Lübbe, Hermann 168, 233, 237
Lübcke, Walter 358–9
Lübke, Heinrich 196, 223
Lucke, Bernd 348–9
Ludwigsburg 174–5
Lufthansa, hijacking of airplane 280
Lutz, Burkart 147–8

Maastricht Treaty 345–7
machinelikeness (*Maschinenhaftigkeit*) 178
machines, "dictatorship" of 137
Madeleine und der Legionär 67, 93
Mahler, Horst 210–11, 216, 357–8
Maier, Hans 237
Maihofer, Werner 186–7
Majdanek concentration camp 318
    trial (Düsseldorf) 272–3
Malthus, T. R. 134–5
Malville, France 303–4
Manchester, terrorist attack in 337–8
Mängelwesen (deficient human being) 140–1
manipulation, by state 206–7
Mann, Golo 275–6, 283
Manstein, Bodo, *In the Chokehold of Progress*
    (*Im Würgegriff des Fortschritts*) 298–9
Mantell, David 272
Maoism 300
Marburg 50–2
Marcisz, Heinz 279–80
Marcuse, Herbert 211–13, 218, 226–7, 263–4
Marion (student activist) 218
Marktheidenfeld 37–8
Marplan (media research company) 274–5
Marseilles 76
Märtesheimer, Peter 273–4, 276
Martini, Winfried, *Freedom at Call: The Life*
    Expectancy of the Federal Republic 161–3
Marxism 98–9, 146, 202–3, 205, 207–9,
    216–17, 223–4
    among university professors 240
    discussion of theory 218
    failure to deal with emotions 229
    and human psyche 254–5
    late 240, 261
    and political economy 137–8
    theories of fascism 265
Marx, Karl 203–4

masculinity,
    changed ideas of 262–3
    and civil defense 116–18
    and emotions 357–8
    feminized 47, 91
    homosexuals as threat to 83–4
    and moral fragility 48, 81, 370
    norms of 263
    "resilient," 358–9
    threatened 357–8, 362–3
Masai people 296
mass culture 91–2
mass destruction, language of 296, 309–10
mass hysteria 78
mass production 130–1
Matthöfer, Hans 143–6
Max Planck Institute for Biophysics 298–9
"May Offensive" (1972) 279
Mechtersheimer, Alfred 318–20
media, role and responsibility of 370–1
medicine, psychosomatic 246–7
Mehring, Altötttingen 43–4
Meinhof, Ulrike 195–6, 209–10, 221–2, 279
    suicide 279
Meins, Holger 279–80, 284–5
memory, politics of 170
Mende, Erich 80
Mende, Lutz Dieter 220–1
Menke-Glückert, Peter 297
men's groups 262–5
    and articulation of fears 263
mental illness 245, 340–1
Merkel, Angela 335–8, 345–7, 349,
    352–3, 357–8
Meuthen, Jörg 357–8
middle class, male 64–5
middle-class men 62–3
migration 334–5, 337–8
    AfD and 349–50
    fear of 358–62
    see also immigration
Milgram, Stanley, experiment 272
militarization of civilians 115–16
military strategy 127–8
Miller, Alice 276–7
minorities, feelings of 367
Minow, Hans-Rüdiger 196
Mirbach, Andreas von 279–80
misogyny, in communes 227
missiles, Soviet 329–30
missiles, US,
    cruise 314–15
    intermediate range, stationing in West
        Germany 314–15, 317–21, 325
    Pershing II 314–15, 317–18

SS-20 314–15
  withdrawal of 326–7
Mitscherlich, Alexander 189, 229–30, 246–50
Mitscherlich, Alexander and Margarete, *The Inability to Mourn* 182–4, 244–5, 248–50
modernity 40, 50, 89, 134
  reflexive 328–9
modernization 46, 50, 132–3
  accelerated 178
  fear of 147–8
  potential negative consequences 178
  socio-economic 134–6
Mohammed Reza Pahlavi, Shah of Persia 195–7, 218
Mohnhaupt 279
Möller, Irmgard 279–80
Mölln 343–4
Montesquieu, Charles-Louis de 251–2
  Spirit of the Laws, The 29–30
moon landing 293–4
moral integrity, anxiety regarding 82–3
moral panic 75–6, 78, 82–4, 283
Mossadeq, Mohammed 195
Moβmann, Walter 287–8
mourning 182
MSB Spartacus 240
Müller, Heinz 72–3
Müller-Meiningen, Ernst 174–5
multiculturalism 352–3
Munich 28, 54–7, 59–60, 195–6, 307–8
  Bogenhausen 56–7
  Institute for Contemporary History 275–6, 278
  Max Planck Society 333–4
  Olympics (1972), terrorist attack 280, 286–7
  police department 218
  Ramersdorf 56
  visit of Shah 195–6, 218
Münkler, Herfried 362–3
Münster 168
Münster, University of 86–7
murder 41–6, 50
  of Jews 27–8, 31–3
  ritual 37
Murderers Among Us, The 174–5
Muslims 3
  Bosnian, in Srebrenica 165–6
  as minority in Germany 341–2, 349–52
  as "others," 369
  Turks as 342–3
  see also Islam
Mussolini, Benito 287–8
Mutlangen, Swabia 317–18
mysticism, Far Eastern 269

Nakam 33–4
Nannen, Henri 171, 278
Napoleonic wars 46–7, 54–5
National Association for Citizens' Initiatives for Environmental Protection (*Bürgerinitiative Umweltschutz*, BBU) 298
National Democratic Party (NPD) 186, 200–1
national identity 309–10
nationalism 29–30, 64, 318–20, 343–4, 348–9, 352–3
  Arab and Palestinian 209–10
national liberation movements 209–10
National Socialism 4–5, 28–9, 162–3
  alleged emotional excesses of 118–19
  amnesty campaigns for crimes of 101–2
  and antisemitism 83–4, 173–4
  and authoritarianism 167
  and civil defense 109–10
  and collapse of Germany 26–7
  collapse of 64, 136–7
  critique of Weimar Republic 352–3
  death and concentration camps 26–7, 31–2, 40–2, 57–62, 102–3, 202, 286–7
  and "death marches," 26–7, 34–5, 40
  and decline of state authority 162–3
  and denazification 60–1
  and discourse on environmental damage 296
  and education 151–2
  excessive emotionality associated with 322–3
  Forsthoff and 162–3
  and homosexuality 81, 86
  ideology 125, 265–6
  legacies of 18–19, 22
  New Left view of 208–9
  People's Court (*Volksgerichtshof*) 101–2
  Pollock and 136–7
  propaganda 21, 27–33, 40–1, 98, 101–2, 116–18
  racist ideology 125
  Reichsjustizministerium (Ministry of Justice) 171
  and service in French Foreign Legion 70–1
  statute of limitation for crimes of 170
  trials 272–3
    see also Auschwitz, trial
  victims of 253
  Volksgemeinschaft 20, 109–10, 131, 197
    see also Third Reich
National Socialist Underground 358–9
NATO (North Atlantic Treaty Organization) 88–9, 106–7, 202
  Able Archer exercise 314–15
  "Carte Blanche" maneuver 110–11
  double-track decision 314–15, 318–20, 322–4
  integration of West Germany into 130–1

NATO (North Atlantic Treaty Organization) (*cont.*)
  intervention in Serbia 339
  military strategy 110–11
  reliance on nuclear weapons 110–13
  "stay at home" policy 114
  summit (1982) 325
Nazi crimes 2, 63–4, 73–4, 178, 206, 224
  amnesty for 101–2
  and "cancer personality," 248–50
  and fear of retaliation for 318
  judges and 170
  and New Left 208–9
  and peace movement 318
  prosecution of 174–5
  shock of 209–10, 224
  statute of limitations for 170, 189–90
  see also Nazi trials
"Nazi justice" exhibition 171
Nazi Party (NSDAP, National Socialist
    German Workers' Party), regime of
    60–3, 191
  and civil defense 109–10
  electoral gains of 345–7
  Gestapo 286–7
  Security Service (SD) 31–4, 45–6, 56–7, 71
  Stormtroopers (SA, *Sturmabteilung*) 63,
    191, 235–6
  Waffen SS 85–6
  Wehrmacht 28, 93, 252–3
Nazi past,
  associated with nuclear power 302–3, 318–20
  continuities with 199, 210–11, 286–7
  dissociation from 272–3
  emotional dimension of 277–8
  Holocaust (television series) and 275, 277
  memories of 22, 93, 128–9, 138, 159, 167,
    186, 192–3, 202, 235–6, 248–50
  opinions regarding 244
  return of 170–84, 211–13
Nazis, former,
  and denazification 59, 63
  and housing requisitions 55–7
  Jaspers on 189–90
  in KgU 101–2
  and recruitment to French Foreign Legion 71
  rehired to leadership positions 59, 170, 191
Nazi trials 128–9, 174–82, 180*f*, 185,
    210–11, 286–7
  effect on democratic fears 182
  emotional impact of 175–7
  and image of perpetrators 178–9
  and individual agency 176
Negt, Oskar 207–8, 211–13, 218
Neill, A.S., *Summerhill* 256

neo-colonialism 296
neo-liberalism 149–50, 165, 269–70
neo-Marxism 141, 197–8, 232–3, 238
neo-Nazism 167, 172–3, 186, 189–90, 216, 283,
    343–4, 355, 358–9
Nervenarzt, Der 252–3
Neues Beginnen 149–50
Neue Zeitung, Die 50–1
Neumann, Franz 4–5
Neunburg vorm Wald 61–2
neutron bomb 323–4
Neu-Ulm 326*f*
  Wiley barracks 325
New Left 193–7, 199–200, 202–5
  anti-imperialism 209–10
  antisemitism in 210–11
  anti-Zionism in 209–11
  associated with fascism 234–6
  backlash against 220–1
  clash between personal and political
    concerns 225, 236–7
  counter-demonstrations against 220–1, 221*f*
  criticism by men's groups 263
  critics of 236–7
  and ecology movement 300
  emotions and 255–63
  and expression of emotions 245–6, 272
  gendered culture of 205
  initial support for Israel 209–10
  and liberal-conservatism 233–9
  and liberal values 236–7
  male dominance of 204–5, 261
  and membership of SDS 206
  and Nazi past 208–9
  perceived irrationalism and
    emotionality 233–5
  publications 216–17
  and Red Army Faction 279
  revolutionary future 290–1
  and sexuality 226
  splintering of 234
  and terrorism 241
  totalitarian leanings 236–7
  and US involvement in Vietnam 220–1
  and violence 213–14
  see also direct action; student activists
New Right,
  racism of 353
  and role of women 358
newspaper and magazine market 207–8
New Ulm 66
New York Times 335–6
Nicole (singer), "A Little Peace," 322–3
Nieder, Heinrich 90–1

Niemöller, Martin 101–2
Nietzsche, Friedrich 366
9/11 terrorism attacks 4, 372–3
"1968," 197–9
Nipperdey, Thomas 233, 237
Nirumand, Bahman 195–6, 202, 205
nitrogen oxides 312–13
Nitschke, August 251–2
Nobel Peace Prize 271
Nollau, Günter 283–4
Nolte, Ernst 238
Nolte, Paul 132–4
normalcy 335–7
Normandy landing 40–1
North Africa 66–7, 71–3, 88
North Rhine-Westphalia 66–7, 91–2, 142,
    233, 337–8
nuclear accidents 303–6, 320–1, 327–30, 337–8
    and insurance companies 306–7
    and state liability 306–7
nuclear attack,
    fear of 95–6, 320–1
    preparation for 190–1
nuclear energy 298
    civilian use of 142, 306–7
    and insurance industry 306–7
nuclear fallout 113
nuclear family, image of 118–19, 258
nuclearization 112–13
nuclear power,
    abolition of 329–30
    and carcinogenic substances 305
    and dying of forest 311–12
    fear of 300
        gender dimension 306
    protests against 299–301, 303–4, 323
    risks of 304–5, 316
nuclear power plants 298–302
    analogies with Nazi state 301–2
    breeder reactor 302–3
    decommissioning of 328
    symbolism of 301–2
"nuclear state," 302–3
nuclear war 93–4, 184, 369
    advice on preparation for 95–6, 121, 123–6,
        320–1, 324–5
    decline of fear of 126–9
    fear of 3, 21–2, 104–7, 110–11, 118, 123–4,
        128–9, 133–4, 199–200, 253, 284–5,
        290–3, 310–11, 320–1, 360–1
    and Holocaust memory 278, 317–18
    prospect of 314–15, 329–30
    see also civil defense
nuclear waste 304–6, 329–30

nuclear weapons,
    in Central Europe 127–8
    demonstrations against 23
    NATO and 110–11
Nuremberg 298–9
    attack on zoo 41–2
    poisoning plot in 33–4
    trials 73, 80
Nussbaum, Martha 4–5, 11, 31

Oberländer, Theodor 98
occupation, postwar 18, 21–2, 29–30, 65, 78,
        184, 356–7, 368
    alleged alliance between US officials and
        Jewish DPs 36–7
    French 66–7
        recruitment bureaus for Foreign Legion
        75–6, 93
    negative feelings by Germans about 48–50, 337
    shock of 46–59
    Soviet 21, 44–5, 99–101
    US 21, 25–30, 36–7, 41–2, 44–5, 47–9, 59–60
    and reconstruction 64–5
    zones 26–7, 34–5, 41–2, 54–5, 66–7
Oder–Neisse line 271
Offenburg 76, 172–3
Ohnesorg, Benno 196–7, 202–4, 214–15, 220–1,
        223, 286
oil crisis (1973) 298
Olle & Wolter (publishers) 278
opinion polls 13, 21–2, 54, 95–6, 105–6, 108–11,
        125–6, 173–4, 181–3, 206, 242–3, 267–8,
        291–2, 349–50
optimism,
    on antisemitism 172–3
    about automation 135–7, 142–3, 150–1
    in Federal Republic 50
    of former Nazi victims 39f
    loss of 158
    as male belief 306
    of New Left 206
    of 1960s 242–3
    of 1980s 326–7
    post-INF Treaty 326–7
    of student movement 198–9, 242
    by students 50–1, 198–9
    about technological change 133–4,
        149–50, 156–7
    in Weimar Republic 4
Oran, North Africa 72–3
Organization for European Economic
        Cooperation (OEEC) 142–3
orgasm, fixation on 211–13, 261, 263–4
Orwell, George 286–7

Ostpolitik 271
"other(s)," 3, 6, 17–18, 272, 283, 353, 358–9
   changing images of 369
   ethnic and religious 370
   fear of 361–2, 366
   marginalization of 369
   overcoming the past 182–3, 333–4

Pabst, Walter 235–6
pacifism, pacificism 124–5, 333–5
   critique of 369
Paderborn 66–7
Palestine 33–4, 209–10
   terrorist groups in 280
panic, languages of 67–9
paranoia 185, 199–203, 209–10, 325–6
paranoid schizophrenic disorders 63
Paris,
   student demonstrations (May 1968) 191–2,
      194, 208
   terrorist attacks in 337–8
parliamentary system 362*f*
passivity 218–20, 277
Patel, Kiran Klaus 69
pathogens 23, 337
pathos 6–7
patriarchy 233, 261, 306
Paul, Gerhard 179–81
Pausewang, Gudrun, *The Last Children of*
     Schewenborn 290–1
peace movement (1980s) 18–19, 23, 125–6, 244,
     270–1, 278, 289, 293, 313–30
   activists 317–18, 324–5
   and analogies with National Socialism and
     Holocaust 318–20
   coordination committee 323
   declarations of nuclear-weapon-free
     zones 321
   democracy in 305–6
   effects and influence of 329–30, 371
   and German angst 332–3, 333*f*
   human chain 325, 326*f*
   and INF Treaty 326–7
   links with environmental movement 323–4
   mass demonstrations 325–7
   mobilization by 323–6, 329–30, 332
   political mobilization 311–12
   and relations with US 318–20
   US and 331
   utopian visions of 325–6
Pegida (Patriotic Europeans Against the
     Islamization of the West, *Patriotische*
     Europäer gegen die Islamisierung des
     Abendlandes) 352–3

Pendorf, Robert 177
pensions 130–1, 345–7
People's Association for Peace and Freedom
     (*Volksbund für Frieden und Freiheit*,
     VVF) 101–3
Persia 269
personal concern (*persönliche Betroffenheit*) 316
personal and political life 225, 236–7, 257
pessimism, cultural 64–5, 183–4, 198–201,
     296, 349–50
   among AfD supporters 349–50
pesticides 293–4
Peterson, Val 112–13
Pettenkofer, Andreas 301–2
Pflasterstrand 261–2, 267
philosemitism 34–5
philosophy 139–41
Picht, Georg, *The German Educational*
     Catastrophe 151–2
Pieler, Roland 279–80
pill, contraceptive 226–7
pluralism 164, 363–4
Pocket Guide to Germany 48–9
pogroms,
   (1938) 31–2, 36
   post-unification 343–4
Poland,
   dictatorship 311–12
   former Eastern German territories
     in 271, 343–4
   martial law in 291–2
Poles 25, 37–8, 40–4, 46, 56–7
   Catholic priests 44–5
   Jewish 34–5
   and Neunburg incident 61–2
   as slave laborers 42–3
police,
   secret 2–5, 7, 81–2, 173
   violence by 196–7, 215–17, 286, 301–2
political context 19–20, 52–3, 64–5, 126–7
   and personal 317
political cultures, democratic 160–1
political fears 280–1, 288–9
   escalation of 279, 283–4
politics of emotion, democratic 363–7
Pollock, Friedrich 136–9, 143–5, 153–4
polluter principle 297
pollution 311
   blood 83–4
   environmental 242, 295–7, 301–2, 307–9
Ponto, Jürgen 279–80
popular culture 254–5
Popular Front for the Liberation
     of Palestine 280

population growth 134–5, 293–4
population movement 114
populism, right-wing 23, 331, 336–7, 347–9,
    352–9, 362–6
    and commemorative culture 355
    and emotions 363, 369–71
    objects of fear 362–3
pornography, soft 207–8
Portugal 162–3, 165–6, 188, 345–7
postcolonialism 364–5
postmodernism 134
power plants,
    coal-fired 311–12
        desulphurization systems 312–13
    see also nuclear power plants
POWs, see prisoners of war
PR agencies 116–19, 124–5
pragmatic decisionism 168
pragmatism 31
precautionary principle 297
press,
    freedom of 186, 201, 361–2
    influence of 207–8
    left-alternative 266–7
        contact ads in 267
    perceived bias of 239
primal scream therapy 245–6
prisoners of war (POWs) 28–9
    camps 71–2
    German 28–9, 54–5, 69–71, 130–1, 170–1,
        246–7, 253
    Russian 39–41
proletariat, student activists and 232
proliferation of fear and anxiety 51
Proll, Astrid 286–7
prosperity, postwar 130–1
prostitution 82–3
Protestant Aid Society 89–90
Protestant Church Congress 315–16
Protestantism 150, 322–3
protest movements 185–6, 189, 192–4
    against Iraq War 339–40
provos 222
Pryztulla, Dagmar 205, 227
psychiatry 22, 116–18
    anthropological 252–3
psychoanalysis 170–1, 317
"psychoboom," 244–6, 314, 340–1,
    358–9
psychological analysis 182
psychological rationalization 148–9
psychological sciences 371–2
Psychologie Heute 244–6
Psychologische Beiträge 251–2

psychology 49
    developmental 251–2
    industrial 148–9
psychopathology 28, 280–1
psychosomatic medicine and theories
    246–8, 250–1
psychotherapy 244–5, 255–7, 269, 316
Pullach 43–4

Quick 123–4
Quinn, Freddy 67

R&V insurance company, annual poll on fears of
    Germans 331, 336–7, 345–7
Rabehl, Bernd 203–4, 210–11, 221–2, 357–8
race, racial norms 69–70
race pollution, fear of 83–4
racism 46, 79–80, 102–3, 125, 208–9, 350–2
    in AfD 348–52
    demonstrations 352–3
    equated with National Socialism 355
    and immigration 342–4
    longer history 364–5
radiation 302–3
    effects of 113
    radioactive 298–300, 305
radicalization 244
radioactivity 304–5, 327, 336–7, 360–1
    and women's health 306
Radkau, Joachim 135–6
RAF, see Red Army Faction
rape 41–2, 50–3, 78–9, 261–2
    mass 98–9, 100f
Raspe, Jan Carl 279–80
Rationalisierungs Kuratorium der deutschen
    Wirtschaft ("rationalization committee
    of German business") 134–5
rationalism, rationality 30–1, 43–4, 48–9, 63–4,
    116–19, 192–3, 198, 223, 233–4, 262–3,
    281, 304–5, 345, 363
rationalization 133–5, 149–50
rationalization committee (RKW,
    Rationalisierungskomitee der deutschen
    Wirtschaft) 154–5
rational planning 135–6
Ravensburg 311–12
Reagan, Ronald 291–2, 314–15, 318–20,
    325, 329–30
realism 31
rearmament 88–9, 104–5, 111–12
Recklinghausen 104–5
reconstruction 6–7, 9, 64–5
Red Army Faction (RAF) 195–6, 244, 265–6,
    279–88, 303–4, 334–5

Red Army Faction (RAF) (*cont.*)
  arrest of founding members 279–80
  hunger strikes 279, 284–5
  murders by 358–9
  and personalized fears 358–9
  role of women in 283–4
  supporters and sympathizers 281–4, 302–3
  surveillance of interned members 286–7
Reddy, William 259
refugees 48
  crisis of (2015–16) 334–5, 349
  and demand for housing 54–5
  economic 341–2
  empathy with 366
  fear of 336–7, 358–9
  increase and decline in numbers 349
  Muslim 27–8, 362–3
  "refugee crisis," 341–4
  status as 34–5
Regehr, Elke 205
Reich, Wilhelm 216–17, 225–7, 261
Reichardt, Sven 267
Reiche, Reimut 224–7
Reichskristallnacht 31–2, 210–11, 272–3
Reichskuratorium für Wirtschaftlichkeit
    (rationalization committee) 134–5
Reichsluftschutzverband 107–8
Reinhold, Johannes 149–50
religion, religious beliefs 30, 150
repatriation 34–5, 40
repetition structures 27–8
repression, of emotions 246–50
repressive de-sublimation 263–4
responsibility 64–5
retaliation, fear of 318
retirement limit 145–6
retraining 145–6
retribution, fears of 25–8, 36, 39–40, 46, 48,
    59–60, 63–5, 69, 93–4, 133–4, 370–1
reunification 69, 159–60, 329–30, 335–6, 341–2
  crisis of 344–5
Reuther, Walter 143–5
revolution,
  fear of 50–1, 194, 210–11, 233–4, 238–9,
    244, 281
  as male vision 204–5
  New Left and 202–3, 232
  visions of 203–8
Revue 74
"rhetorics of tenderness," 366
Rhineland-Palatinate 66–7, 74–5, 78–9,
    82–3, 86, 88
  state elections 348–9
Richter, Emma 73

Richter, Hans Werner 167–8
Richter, Horst-Eberhard 177, 245, 316–17
Richter, Siegfried 72–3
Richter, Willi 152–3
Ridder, Helmut 185, 188
Riesman, David, *The Lonely Crowd* 140–1, 150
right wing 27–8, 337–8
risk reduction 306–7
"risk society," 112–13, 328–9, 371–2
Ritter, Gerhard A. 236–7
Ritter, Joachim 168
ritual murder fantasies 83–4
"robot, age of," 152
Romania, ethnic Germans from 343–4
Roosevelt, Franklin D. 29–30
Roper, Lyndal 78
Röpke, Wilhelm 149–50
Rosa, Hartmut 367
Roseman, Mark 33–4
Rosen für den Staatsanwalt 171
Rosenwein, Barbara 42–3
Rostock-Lichtenhagen 343–4
Rückversicherer 104–5
Ruegg, Walter 237
Ruhr area 104
Russia 29–30
  see also Soviet Union
Russians 34–5, 41–2, 45–6

Salazar, Antonio 162–3, 188
Salomon, Ernst von, *Questionnaire, The* 62–3
Sarrazin, Thilo 353
  Germany Abolishes Itself (*Deutschland schafft
    sich ab*) 350–2
SARS (severe acute respiratory syndrome) 337
Sattelzeit 132
Sattler, Dieter 25
Saxony 46–7, 367
Saxony-Anhalt 348–9, 367
Schachtschabel, Hans Georg 141–2
Schäffer, Fritz 174–5
Schallück, Paul 167
Scharnagl, Karl 54–5
Schäuble, Wolfgang 345–7
Schelsky, Helmut 136–40, 146, 169, 236–7
Scheuch, Erwin K. 233–5, 240
Schibrowski, B. 225–6
Schirrmacher, Frank 350–2
Schleyer, Hanns-Martin 279–80, 284–6
Schmidt, Helmut 127, 143–5, 242–3, 280, 283–6,
    314–15, 323–4
Schmitt, Carl 162–5, 168, 189, 236–7
Schneider, Michael 255–6
Schneider, Peter 195–6, 198–9, 218, 223–4, 262

Schnock, Frieder 364
Schnurre, Wolfdietrich 166–8
Schoenberger, Gerhard 166–7
Schongau 41–3
schools,
    and discussion on fear 254
    numerus clausus 254
school system, "double track," 152
Schreck, Rüdiger 208
Schröder, Gerhard 88, 108, 191, 339–40, 347–8
Schulze, Fred 83*f*
Schumacher, E.F. 298
Schumacher, Kurt 99–101
Schumann, Jürgen 280
Schümer, Dirk 334–5
Schunter-Kleemann, Susanne 213
Schütt, Peter 307–9, 311
Schwäbisch Gmünd,
        Baden-Württemberg 322–3
Schwarzenau, Annette 205
Schwarzer, Alice 350–2
    Der kleine Unterschied 261
Schwarz, Hans-Peter 6–7
Schweigen, scandal caused by event at 74–6
Schweinfurt 54
Schweitzer, Albert 106–7
science,
    expertise and counter-expertise 302–6,
        311, 371–2
    role of 112–13, 371–2
scientists, nuclear 112–13
Second World War 4–5, 70–1, 252–3
    aftermath 78, 99–101
    civil defense during 109–10, 113,
        121–3, 125–6
    conduct of soldiers in 93
    demographic losses 134–5
    disregard for human beings during and
        after 79–80
    end of 27–8
    and fear of nuclear war 123–4
    flight and expulsion during 114
    hostage taking in 284–5
    as "Jewish war," 31–3
    memory of 123–4, 128–9, 277, 354
    onset of 161–2
    and possible Third World War 317–18
    trauma derived from 339–41, 369
    veterans of 317–18
security 6–7, 18
    promise of 107, 331
Seeber, David A. 242
Seifert, Monika 229–30
Seipp, Adam 42–3

self,
    and community 257–61
    empowerment of 255
    petrifaction of 367
    psycho-knowledge of 255–7
    psychotherapy and 244–5
    sensitization of 23, 267, 269–71, 296, 316
    as source and site of fear 197–8, 358–9
self-alienation 150
self-description 2, 328–9
self-determination 46–7
self-fashioning 203–4
self-justification 63
self-reflection 63–4
self-victimization 369
Semler, Christian 200–1, 218
Senegal 216–17
Senghor, Léopold 216–17
Serbia (Kosovo), German action against 165–6
Serengeti 296
sexuality,
    childhood 230
    discussed in men's groups 264–5
    and emotions 262–4
    male 264–5
    and political liberation 225, 232–3, 262
    repressive 225
    sexual liberation 225–8, 256, 261–4, 358
    sexual politics 225
    sexual revolution 358
    sex-wave 254–5
    sublimation of 226–7, 230
sexual offences 41–2, 47, 50–4
sexual politics 358
shame 20–1, 62–3, 182
Shell (Germany), youth department 292
Shklar, Judith 4–5, 366
Sidi-Bel-Abbès, Algeria 76
Siegen 66–7
Sielmann, Heinz 296
Silesia 46–7
Sinus Institute 292
Six-Day War 209–10
    68-ers 197–200, 204–5, 208–9, 224–5,
        232–3, 235–6, 325–6
    political conversions of 357–8
slave labor 25–6, 41, 43–4
    Polish 42–3
slavery 46–7
    fears of 133–4
    language of 78–81, 83–4
    "white," 93–4
Slavs, dehumanization of 102–3
Sloterdijk, Peter 357–8

Slovenia 345–7
Snowden, Edward 338–9
sobriety 6–7, 17–18, 63–4, 159, 175–7,
    192–3, 285–6
  admonitions to 239
  ethics of 190–1
social analysis, psychologization of 148–9
social decline 242, 347–8, 362–3
Social Democratic Party (SPD) 33, 66–7, 68f,
    77–9, 84, 98–101, 124–5, 127, 239,
    350–2
  and automation debate 141–5
  and BFW 237
  and civil defense program 112–13
  conference (Frankfurt, 1967) 213–14
  and death of forest 312–13
  demonstration equating Vietnam War with
    Holocaust 212f
  and education debate 151–2
  Eichler and 165–6
  election slogan 99–101
  and emergency laws 192–3
  and fears of nuclear war 106–7, 318–20
  and fears of unemployment 143–5
  Godesberg Program 357–8
  and guest workers 341–2
  and Krefeld Initiative 315
  law on civil service appointments 240
  and liberal-conservatism 233
  membership numbers 206
  and NATO double-track decision 323–4
  party congress (1956) 142
  and peace movement 323–4
  policies inherited by successors 292–3
  and terrorism 283–4, 286–7
  see also Grand Coalition
social diagnosis, shift in 181–2
Socialist German Student Association
    (SDS) 171, 194–5, 197, 219, 224–5
  conferences and congresses 202–3, 213–15
  dissolution of 234
  and humor 222
  and left-wing activists 237
  report on police violence 216–17
  theoretical discussions 222
Socialist Patient Collective 281–2
Socialist Unity Party (SED) 99–103
social movements 150
social policy benefits 98–9
social sciences 371–2
social stability 132
socio-economic decline, fear of 347–8
solidarity 366–7
Solingen, North Rhine-Westphalia, attack on
    Turkish family 343–4, 364

Sölle, Dorothee 317–18
Sonderweg thesis 4
Sontag, Susan, Illness as Metaphor 250–1
Sontheimer, Kurt 166, 191, 234–5,
    281–2, 288–9
Sorel, Georges 243–4
South Africa 223–4
sovereignty 184, 235–6
  anxiety regarding 78–9, 82–3, 160–1
  regaining of 130–1, 158–9
Soviet Union,
  Adenauer and 97–8
  atrocities 31–2, 48
  and automation 135, 142–3
  Communist Party 326–7
  conventional weapons 110–11
  education in 151–2
  ethnic Germans from 26–7, 54–5, 343–4
  expansionism 195
  fears of invasion by 112–13
  fears of nuclear attack by 320–1
  fears of victory and revenge by 47–8
  and German prisoners of war 28–9, 54–5,
    69–70, 130–1, 246–7, 253
  and Hungarian uprising 98–9
  and INF Treaty 326–7
  and intermediate range missiles 314–15
  invasion of Afghanistan 291–2, 314–15
  and Kosovo War 339
  legionnaires in 72–3
  Niemöller and 101–2
  nuclear testing 95–6
  and nuclear weapons 110–11
  occupation zone 21
  and peace movement 323
  propaganda against 102–3
  Red Army 27–8, 32–5, 44–5, 47–8, 98
  relations with US 314–15
  and Sputnik launch 135
  state planning 145–6
Spain 22, 162–3, 165–6, 188, 337–8, 345–7
specialists, control of work process by 137
Speyer, University for Civil Service
    (Verwaltungswissenschaft) 136–7
Spiegel, Der 82–3, 135, 183–4, 186, 199–200,
    242–3, 267–8, 271, 279, 307–9,
    328, 334–5
  on apocalyptic fear among Germans 291–2
  on automation 146–7
  "Automation in Germany," 142–3, 144f
  "Cancer—Disease of the Soul"
    247–8, 249f
  on death of forest 307–12
  on environmental crisis 295–6
  on financial crisis 345

imprisonment of journalists for treason
    123–4, 186–7
and Klaus Traube 302–3
opinion poll on fear 292
on RAF sympathizers 281–2
spirit of the age 6–7
Springer, Axel (publishing house) 197, 207–10,
    235–6, 239
demonstrations against 216
squatter movement 256, 270–1
Srebrenica 339
Sroka, Knut 247
stability, stabilization 6–7, 18–19, 22,
    158–9, 168–9
historiography of 292–3
psychic 224–5
Stalingrad, Battle of 27–8
Stammheim, Stuttgart, prison 280
Stargardt, Nicholas 31
state,
    "deficient" and "excessive," 164
    fear of and for 244
state authority, Left and Right fears of 356–7
state planning 145–6, 155–6
Staudte, Wolfgang 67, 174–5
Stearns, Peter 16–17
Stefan, Verena, *Häutungen* 261–3
Stehle, Hansjakob 271
Steinbrück, Peer 345
Stephan, Cora 318–20
Stephans, Lydia, *Du hättest gerne noch ein
    bisschen gelebt* 268–9
stereotypes, cultural,
    of Communists 102–3
    racist 46, 102–3
    sexual 81–4
Stern 67, 71–4, 83f, 93, 147–8, 171, 220–1, 231,
    278, 307–11, 320–1
Stern, Horst 296
Stih, Renata 364
Stockholm, West German embassy 279–80
Stoiber, Edmund 333–4
Storch, Beatrix von 353–4
Strasbourg 76, 89
Strategic Defense Initiative (SDI) 314–15
Strauß, Franz Josef 119–21, 167–8, 186–7,
    283–4, 287–8
streetcars, and antisemitic incidents 37–8
strikes,
    restrictions on 186
    right to strike 193
    wildcat 156–7
Strohm, Holger, *Peaceful into the Catastrophe
    (Friedlich in die Katastrophe)* 305
Struck, Karin, *Klassenliebe* 261, 269–70

student activists 196–241
    compared to Nazi stormtroopers 235–6
    demonstrations and protests by 206–8, 215f,
        216–18, 234–5
    paternalistic attitude 206–7
    perception of reality 224–5
    and proletariat 232
    self-description as "new Jews," 199, 224
    sexual lives of 225–8
    and Springer tribunal 207–8
    and suffering of others 224
    see also New Left
student movement (mid 1960s–1970s) 18, 22,
    169, 185, 191–2, 357–8
    and emotions 255–6, 334–5
    and psychotherapy 244–5
    radicalization of 162–3, 191–2, 233
    state reactions to 301
    utopianism in 266–7
    and visit of Shah to Federal
        Republic 195–7
    in West Germany 199–241
students,
    and emergency laws 185, 206
    study of political attitudes 169
Stürmer, Michael 333–4
Stuttgart 42–3, 146–7, 326f
    NATO headquarters 325
    Zuffenhausen "peace days," 322–3
"subjective concern," cult of
    (*Betroffenheitskult*) 318–20
subjectivities 25–6, 29–30, 33–4, 210–11,
    232–3
    healthy 22
    male and female 19–20, 261–2
    neo-liberal 269–70
    new 19, 23, 255–6, 289, 295, 357–8, 370
    other-directed 140–1
    political 22
    revolutionary 213–14
    sensitized 23, 316
Suez Canal 88
suffering,
    concern for 224
    cultivation of 369
suicide 30–1, 198–9, 279–80
sulfur dioxide 308, 311–13
Summerhill School, Suffolk, UK 256
surveillance, global, as response to
    terrorism 338–9
swastika 32
Sycyesny, Gerhard 183–4
"sympathizers," 3, 239, 241, 281–4, 287–8,
    302–3, 342–3, 370–1
Syria, refugees from 342–4, 355

Taubert, Eberhard 101–2
"Open Your Eyes. Communism Through the
Backdoor" 102–3
Taylor, Gordon Rattray,
The Biological Time Bomb 293–4
Das Selbstmordprogramm (*The Suicide
Program*) 293–4
"Taylorism," 135–6, 143–5
technological change 133–4, 369
and jobs and professions 147–8
technologization 139
technology 22
Gehlen's concept of 140–1
pessimistic view of 140–1, 178, 200–1
role of 133–4, 139–40
see also automation
teleology 2–4
television 202–3, 207–8
programs on Nazi period 272–8
proposed privatization 239
terrorism 1–3, 23, 278
attacks by Islamic extremists 337–8, 372–3
escalation of violence 287–8
fear of 241, 244, 281–2, 284–5
international 280
leftist 244, 279–89
state reactions to 301
legislation against 282–3, 286
penalties proposed for 284–6
public response to 281–3
sympathy for 283, 342–3, 369–71
Teufel, Fritz 222, 227
textile industry 155–6
"therapeutic left," 255–6
Ther, Philipp 341–2
Theweleit, Klaus, *Male Fantasies* 265–6
Third Reich 40–1, 63–4, 102–3
alleged continuities to Federal Republic 191,
202, 239
anti-democratic ideals 172–3
anti-intellectualism of 151–2
civil defense in 107–10, 324–5
collapse of 32–3, 131, 182
East Germany on 171
persecution of leftists 168–9
persecution of minorities 239
social and racial order of 35–6
totalitarianism of 178
Third World 209–13
suffering in 224
Third World War, fears of 317–18, 332
Thompson, E.P. 28–9
Three Mile Island nuclear reactor, Harrisburg,
USA 303–6
Thunberg, Greta 360–1, 362*f*

Thuringia 354
"thymotic energies," 357–8
Tillich, Ernst 101–2
Time Magazine 291–2
Toffler, Alvin, *Future Shock* 293–4
totalitarianism 29–30, 43–4, 139, 143–5, 162–3,
166–8, 369
machinelike 178
technocratic and political 178
toxins 295–6
trade unions 135–6, 139
and automation 142–5, 147, 152–7
and emergency laws 185, 189, 191–2
general strike (1920) 189
seniority principle 155–6
in US 155–6
Traube, Klaus 302–3
trauma, psychic 340–1, 369
travel, in search for identity 269
Treblinka death camp 318, 364
Treitschke, Heinrich von 353
Trump, Donald 331, 336–7, 348–9, 356–9,
365–6, 371
trust 20, 365–6
Tshombe, Moise 211–13
Tübingen 164, 286–7
Tu BiShvat (Jewish holiday),
parade 36–7
Tugendhat, Ernst 316
Tunix (Do Nothing) Congress (Berlin,
1978) 270–1
Turks,
as guest workers 3, 355
as immigrants 341–4, 350–2
murders of 358–9
as refugees entering EU 349
Solingen attack on 343–4, 364
Tutzing, Protestant Academy 141–2

Ukrainians 40
Ulbricht, Walter 168–9, 217–18
Ulich, Eberhard 148–9
Ulm 320–1
Cathedral 350–2
Einsatzgruppen trial 174–5, 181–2
Ulmer, Herbert 279–80
Ulrich, Bernhard 307–9, 311
uncertainty, sense of 28–9, 53–4, 138, 332,
336–7, 347–8, 368
unemployment 50, 90–1
fear of 143–5, 147
female 147–8
in Greece and Spain 345–7
insurance against 145–6
mass 137, 143–5, 144*f*, 147, 344–5

restriction of benefits 347–8
technological 152–6
United Auto Workers (UAW) (US) 143–5
United Kingdom, *see* Britain
United Nations 78, 80
   Relief and Rehabilitation Administration
      (UNRRA) 40
   Security Council 339
United States of America 29–30
   associated with "Jewish interests" 25, 34–5
   and automation 135, 142–5
   cancer research in 248–50
   Central Intelligence Agency (CA) 101–2, 195
   civil defense 95
      advertising 118
      "Operation Alert" exercise 114
   Congress 29–30, 365–6
   Federal Civil Defense Administration 112–13
   and German–Americans 32
   and immigration 369–71
   and insurance against nuclear
      accidents 306–7
   intelligence reports 36
   Joint Chiefs of Staff 48–9
   militarization of civilians 115–16
   military bases 317–18
   military police 41
   napalm bombing by 211–13
   National Security Agency 338–9
   nuclear weapons 51–2, 110–13, 127–8, 325
   Office of Military Government 54
   and peace movement 331
   policies under Donald Trump 331
   popular culture 51–2, 69–70
   postwar occupation of Germany 25–6, 29–30,
      33–4, 41–2, 44–5, 48, 59–60, 161–2
   and reconstruction 64–5
   "race fears" and "evangelical fears" in 41–2
   real estate market 345
   relationship with West Germany 127–8,
      318–20, 331
   relations with Soviet Union 314–15
   "rollback" policy 101–2
   security guarantees 331
   soldiers (GIs) 48
      African–American 53–4, 79–80
      demobilization 50
      fraternization with German civilians 48–9
      and housing requisitions 54–5
      negative feelings towards German
         civilians 48–50
      violence towards German civilians 49–54
   Strategic Bombing Survey 32–3
   trade unions in 155–6
   travel to 269

and Vietnam War 209–13, 220–1, 286–7
and Westernization in Federal Republic 331
universities,
   demand for reform of 238–40
   democratization of 239–40
   and League for the Freedom of
      Science 237–41
   and left-wing students 237–41
   student parliaments 240
   and sympathy for terrorists 283
urban guerrilla 213–14
utopianism 198–204, 206, 251, 266–7
   and antisemitism 209–10
   and communal living 229
   and peace movement 325–6

van Rahden, Till 231
Velmer, Günter 66
Vesper, Bernward, *Die Reise* 265–7
Vesper, Will 265–6
victim identity 64, 369
victimization, German, perceived 8–9, 21–2,
   44–5, 64, 75–6, 78–9, 123, 128–9
Vienna 48
Vietcong 211–13
Viet Minh 72–3
Vietnam, immigrants from 343–4
Vietnamese 93
Vietnam War 195, 209–13, 223–4, 234,
   286–7, 301
   Berlin congress on 202–5, 213, 220–1
   demonstrations against 220–1
   equated with Holocaust 211–13
   US and 220–1
Villingen 76
violence 8–9, 21
   and acts of revenge 25–6, 33
   alleged, between Jewish DPs and German
      civilians 36–7
   among New Left activists 199, 213–22
   by DPs 39–46
   during Soviet occupation 98
   and extra-parliamentary opposition 201
   face-to-face 178–9
   imperialist 22
   by police 215–20, 301–2
   racist 343–4, 352–3, 366
   right- and left-wing 358–9
   in Second World War 93–4, 123
   sexual 41–2, 47, 50–4
   and sexuality 216–17
   state 213–15, 218
   terrorist 280–1
   towards "others," 366
Vogel, Bernhard 283–4

Vogel, Hans-Jochen 283–7
Volk, concept of 131–2
Volkswagen factory, Wolfsburg 155–6
voluntarism,
  among New Left 194, 199, 202–3, 214–15
  and Foreign Legion 88–9, 93–4
  ideology of 214–15

Wachau, Friedrich Wilhelm Reinhard 220–1
Wader, Hannes 322–3
Walser, Martin 167–8, 179
  (ed.), *Do We Need a New Government?* 166–7
war,
  fear of 23, 105–6, 267–8, 270–1, 291–3,
    368, 370
  total 2, 18, 78, 115–16
"war children," 32, 340–1, 369
war crimes, *see* Nazi crimes
war criminals 71
"war grandchildren," 369
Warsaw,
  Jewish ghetto 271
  Treaty of (1970) 271
"war on terror," 338–9
water-cannons, use against student protesters 215f
Weber, Josef 315
Weber, Werner 163–4
Wehler, Hans-Ulrich 277
Weimar Republic 4, 22, 104–5, 116–18,
    132–4, 161–2
  academic milieu 164
  analogy with US under Donald Trump 331
  austerity in 345–7
  constitution 188
  fall of 168–9, 186
  fascism in 265
  left-wing paramilitary formations in 217–18
  Nazi critique of 352–3
  rationalization movement 134–5
  relationship to Federal Republic 159–60,
    165–6, 168–9, 286–7
  and student movement 199
  and unemployment 143–5
Weinberger, Caspar 325
Weisbrod, Bernd 17
Weizsäcker, Carl Friedrich von 127, 206
Weizsäcker, Viktor von 246–7
welfare state 136, 162–3, 347–8
Welt, Die 334–5
Welt am Sonntag, Die 235–6
Wessel, Ulrich 279–80
Westag (PR agency) 116–19
Westdeutsche Allgemeine 80
Westernization 2–4, 142–3

West German Broadcasting Station
  (WDR) 273–5
West German Historical Association,
  Historikertag 130
West Germany, *see* Federal Republic of Germany
"white slavery," 21
Widener, Don, *No Place for Human
  Beings* 293–4
Wiegand, Hans-Gerd 301
Wildflecken 42–3
wildlife, damage to 308
Wirsching, Andreas 292–3
Wirsing, Giselher 151–2
Wolf, Christa, *Nachdenken über
  Christa T.* 268–9
Wolfratshausen 35–6
women,
  as activists against nuclear power 306
  and communes 227–8
  and effect of radioactivity on health 306
  and emotionality 306
  as employees 155
  mass rape of 98–9, 100f
  Muslim 358
  oppression of 265, 358
  police violence against 216–17
  and Red Army Faction 283–4
  and resistance to civil defense 116–18
  role of 29–30
  sidelined in New Left movement 205
  Turkish 341–2
  unemployment among 147–8
  see also feminism
women's movement 261, 283–4
workers,
  blue- and white-collar 147, 155
  deskilling of 143–5, 147, 150–3, 155
  psychological problems of 148–9
  wage structures 155–6
work hours 145–6, 150–1, 156
Wulf, Joseph 275–6
Wuppertal 85–6
Wurm, Bishop Theophil 60–1
Wurster, Georg 279–80
Würzburg 31–2, 54–5, 60–1
Wyhl, Baden-Württemberg, proposed nuclear
  power plant 299–302
  Baden Women's Initiative against 306

xenophobia 352–3, 367

Yalta agreement 40
Young Socialists (*Jusos*) 66–7, 68f, 75–6,
  79–80, 319f

youth, German,
  concern about 69–70, 78
  male
    and fears of homosexual seduction 80–3
    fragility of 88–94
    homes for Foreign Legion
      volunteers 89–90

Yugoslavia, asylum seekers from 341–2

Zeit, Die 177, 309–10, 335–6
Zimmermann, Friedrich 328
Zivilschutzfibel ("primer for civil defense") 125
Zorn, Fritz, *Mars* 268–9
Zschäpe, Beate 358–9